Disclaimer

The publisher of this book is by no way associated with the National Institute of Standards and Technology (NIST). The NIST did not publish this book. It was published by 50 page publications under the public domain license.

50 Page Publications.

Book Title: Committee Report of the 92nd National Conference on Weights and Measures, July 8 - 12, 2007, Salt Lake City, Utah

Book Author: Linda D. Crown; L T. Sebring

Book Abstract: The 92nd Annual Meeting of the National Conference on Weights and Measures was held in Salt Lake City, Utah, July 8 - 13, 2007. The theme of the conference was United by common purpose we can and shall prevail in all that we do.The NCWM develops and recommends laws and regulations, technical codes for weighing and measuring devices used in commerce, tests, methods, enforcement procedures, and administrative guidelines for adoption by regulatory agencies in the interest of promoting uniformity of requirements and methods in state and local jurisdictions.The annual meeting brings together government officials and representatives of business, Industry, trade associations, and consumer organizations for the purpose of hearing and discussing subjects that relate to the field of weights and measures technology.

Citation: NIST SP - 1070

Keyword: legal metrology;mass0flow meters;motor-fuel dispensers;scales;specifications & tolerances;weights and measures

Report of the 92nd National Conference on Weights and Measures

Salt Lake City, Utah – July 8 through 12, 2007
as adopted by the 92nd National Conference on Weights and Measures 2007

Editors:
 Linda Crown
 Lynn Sebring
 Technical Advisors to the Standing Committees

 Carol Hockert, Chief
 Weights and Measures Division

 National Institute of Standards and Technology
 Weights and Measures Division
 Gaithersburg, MD 20899-2600

U.S. Department of Commerce
Carlos M. Gutierrez, Secretary

National Institute of Standards and Technology
James Turner, Acting Director

NIST Special Publication **1070**

November 2007

The National Conference on Weights and Measures is supported by the National Institute of Standards and Technology and is attended by officials from various states, counties, and cities, as well as representatives from the U.S. Government, other nations, industry, and consumer organizations.

Abstract

The 92nd Annual Meeting of the National Conference on Weights and Measures (NCWM) was held July 8 - 12, 2007, at the Snowbird Resort, Salt Lake City, Utah. The theme of the meeting was "United by common purpose we can and shall prevail in all that we do."

Reports by the NCWM Board of Directors, Standing Committees, and Special Purpose Committees constitute the major portion of this publication, along with the addresses delivered by Conference officials and other authorities from government and industry.

Special meetings included those of the Scale Manufacturers Association, Meter Manufacturers Association, Gasoline Pump Manufacturers Association, American Petroleum Institute, National Association of State Departments of Agriculture, the Industry Committee on Packaging and Labeling, and Associate Membership Committee.

Key words: laws and regulations; legal metrology; meters; scales; specifications and tolerances; training; type evaluation; uniform laws; weights and measures.

Note: The policy of the National Institute of Standards and Technology is to use metric units of measurement in all of its publications. In this publication, however, recommendations received by the NCWM technical committees have been printed as they were submitted and, therefore, may contain references to inch-pound units where such units are commonly used in industry practice. Opinions expressed in non-NIST papers are those of the authors and not necessarily those of the National Institute of Standards and Technology. Non-NIST speakers are solely responsible for the content and quality of their material.

Natl. Inst. Stand. Technol. Spec. Pub. 1070, 389 Pages (November 2007)

WASHINGTON: 2007

Table of Contents

	Page
Abstract	ii
Past Chairmen of the Conference	iv
Organization Chart	v

General Session

President's Address – Dr. Belinda Collins, NIST, Technology Services Director	GS - 1
New Chairman's Address – Judy Cardin, Wisconsin Department of Agriculture & Consumer Protection	GS - 21
2007 Annual Meeting Honor Award Recipients	GS - 23

Standing Committee Reports

Report of the Board of Directors (BOD)...BOD - 1
    Appendix A. NCWM National Survey...BOD - A1
    Appendix B. National Random Market Survey 2006..BOD - B1
    Appendix C. Auditor's Report for 2006...BOD - C1
    Appendix D. Report on the Activities of the International Organization of Legal Metrology (OIML)
        and Regional Legal Metrology Organizations..BOD - D1
    Appendix E. Final Report of the NCWM Associate Membership Committee (AMC).....................BOD - E1

Report of the Committee on Laws and Regulations (L&R)..L&R - 1
    Appendix A. L&R Committee Work Group on Moisture Loss...L&R - A1

Report of the Committee on Specifications and Tolerances (S&T)...S&T - 1
    Appendix A. Item 360-2: Developing Items..S&T - A1
        Part 1, Item 1, Scales: S.1.4.6. Height and Definition of Minimum Reading Distance, UR.2.10.
            Primary Indicating Elements Provided by the User, UR.2.11. Minimum Reading Distance,
            and Definitions of Minimum Reading Distance and Primary Indications..............................S&T - A1
        Part 2, Item 1, Belt-Conveyor Scale Systems: UR.3.2.(c) Maintenance; Zero Load Tests..............S&T - A4
        Part 3, Item 1, Liquid-Measuring Devices: T.5. Predominance – Retail Motor-Fuel Devices........S&T - A5
        Part 3, Item 2, Liquid-Measuring Devices: Price Posting and Computing Capability and
            Requirements for a Retail Motor-Fuel Dispenser (RMFD)..S&T - A6
        Part 4, Item 1, Water Meters: UR.2.1. Accessibility for Reading...S&T - A8

Report of the Professional Development Committee (PDC)..PDC - 1
    Appendix A. Strategic Direction for the Professional Development Committee................................PDC - A1
    Appendix B. Curriculum Package (Guideline for Creating a Basic Inspector Curriculum)..................PDC - B1
    Appendix C. National Training Curriculum Outline..PDC - C1
    Appendix D. NCWM Curriculum Work Plan..PDC - D1

Report of the National Type Evaluation Program (NTEP) Committee...NTEP - 1
    Appendix A. NTEP Certification Mark License..NTEP - A1
    Appendix B. NTETC Grain Analyzer Sector Meeting Summary..NTEP - B1
    Appendix C. NTETC Measuring Sector Meeting Summary...NTEP - C1
    Appendix D. NTETC Weighing Sector Meeting Summary..NTEP - D1
    Appendix E. NTETC Software Sector Meeting Summary...NTEP - E1

2007 Annual Meeting Attendees...ATTEND - 1

Past Chairmen of the Conference

Conference Year Chairman

Conference	Year	Chairman
43rd	1958	J. P. McBride, MA
44th	1959	C. M. Fuller, CA
45th	1960	H. E. Crawford, FL
46th	1961	R. E. Meek, IN
47th	1962	Robert Williams, NY
48th	1963	C. H. Stender, SC
49th	1964	D. M. Turnbull, WA
50th	1965	V. D. Campbell, OH
51st	1966	J. F. True, KS
52nd	1967	J. E. Bowen, MA
53rd	1968	C. C. Morgan, IN
54th	1969	S. H. Christie, NJ
55th	1970	R. W. Searles, OH
56th	1971	M. Jennings, TN
57th	1972	E. H. Black, CA
58th	1973	George L. Johnson, KY
59th	1974	John H. Lewis, WA
60th	1975	Sydney D. Andrews, FL
61st	1976	Richard L. Thompson, MD
62nd	1977	Earl Prideaux, CO
63rd	1978	James F. Lyles, VA
64th	1979	Kendrick J. Simila, OR
65th	1980	Charles H. Vincent, TX
66th	1981	Edward H. Stadolnik, MA
67th	1982	Edward C. Heffron, MI
68th	1983	Charles H. Greene, NM
69th	1984	Sam F. Hindsman, AR
70th	1985	Ezio F. Delfino, CA
71st	1986	George E. Mattimoe, HI
72nd	1987	Frank C. Nagele, MI
73rd	1988	Darrell A. Guensler, CA
74th	1989	John J. Bartfai, NY
75th	1990	Fred A. Gerk, NM
76th	1991	N. David Smith, NC
77th	1992	Sidney A. Colbrook, IL
78th	1993	Allan M. Nelson, CT
79th	1994	Thomas F. Geiler, MA
80th	1995	James C. Truex, OH
81st	1996	Charles A. Gardner, NY
82nd	1997	Barbara J. Bloch, CA
83rd	1998	Steven A. Malone, NE
84th	1999	Aves D. Thompson, AK
85th	2000	G. Wes Diggs, VA
86th	2001	L. Straub, MD
87th	2002	Ron Murdock, NC
88th	2003	Ross J. Andersen, NY
89th	2004	Dennis Ehrhart, AZ
90th	2005	G. Weston Diggs, VA
91st	2006	Don Onwiler, NE

National Conference on Weights and Measures, Inc.
Organization Chart
2006/2007

Board of Directors

Office Representation	Name/Affiliation	Term Expires
Chairman:	Michael Cleary, CA*	2007
Chairman-Elect:	Judy Cardin, WI*	2007
NTEP Committee Chair:	Don Onwiler, NE*	2007
Treasurer:	Will Wotthlie, MD	2007
Active Membership/Northeastern:	Charles Carroll, MA*	2009
Active Membership/Central:	Steven Malone, NE	2010
Active Membership/Southern:	Randy Jennings, TN*	2008
Active Membership/Western:	Joe Gomez, NM	2007
At-Large:	Christopher Guay, Procter & Gamble	2008
At-Large:	Jack Kane, MT	2011
Associate Membership:	Darrell Flocken, Mettler-Toledo	2007

*National Type Evaluation Program (NTEP) Committee Member

Honorary NCWM President:	Dr. William A. Jeffrey, NIST Director
NCWM Executive Secretary:	Carol Hockert, Chief, NIST W&M Division
NCWM Executive Director:	Beth Palys, CAE, NCWM Headquarters
BOD Advisor:	Gilles Vinet, Measurement Canada
NTEP Director:	Stephen Patoray, NCWM Headquarters
NTEP Committee Technical Advisor:	Steven Cook, NIST W&M Division

Committees

Laws & Regulations Committee		Specifications & Tolerances Committee	
Position	Name/Affiliation (Term Ends)	Position	Name/Affiliation (Term Ends)
Chair:	James Cassidy, Cambridge, MA (2007)	Chair:	Michael Sikula, NY (2007)
Members:	Vicky Dempsey, Montgomery Co., OH (2008)	Members:	Carol Fulmer, SC (2008)
	Roger Macey, CA (2009)		Todd Lucas, OH (2009)
	Stephen Benjamin, NC (2010)		Brett Saum, San Luis Obispo, CA (2010)
	Joe Benavides, TX (2011)		Kristin Macey, CO (2011)
Associate Member Rep:	O.R. "Pete" O'Bryan, Foster Farms		
Canadian Tech Advisors:	Doug Hutchinson	Canadian Tech Advisor:	Ted Kingsbury
NIST Tech. Advisors:	Thomas Coleman	NIST Tech. Advisors:	Richard Suiter Steven Cook

Org Chart

Professional Development Committee		Metrology Committee	
Position	**Name/Affiliation (Term Ends)**	**Position**	**Name/Affiliation (Term Ends)**
Chair:	Agatha Shields, Franklin Co., OH (2007)	Chair:	TBD
Members:	Kenneth Deitzler, PA (2007)	Co-Chair:	TBD
	Ross Andersen, NY (2007)	Members:	
	John Sullivan, MS (2011)		
	Stacy Carlsen, Marin Co., CA (2011)		
	Tina Butcher, NIST/W&M Division (2011)		
Safety Liaison:	Charles Gardner, Suffolk Co., NY		
Staff Liaison:	Linda Bernetich, NCWM		
Associate Member Rep:	TBD		
NIST Tech Advisor:	Tina Butcher	NIST Tech Advisor:	Val Miller
Nominating Committee		**Legislative Liaison**	
Chair:	Don Onwiler, NE	Chair:	TBD
Members:	Dennis Ehrhart, AZ	Members:	TBD
	Ross Andersen, NY		
	Maxwell Gray, FL		
	Thomas Geiler, Barnstable, MA		
	Steven Malone, NE		
	James Truex, OH		
Credentials Committee		**Appointed Officers**	
Chair:	Mark Buccelli, MN (2008)	Parliamentarian:	Lou Straub, Fairbanks Scales
Members:	Jeff Humphreys, CA (2007)	Chaplain:	F. Michael Belue, Belue Associates
	Raymond Johnson, NM (2011)		
Coordinator:	Linda Bernetich, NCWM Staff	Sergeants-at-Arms:	Mitzi Hansen, UT
			Bill Rigby, UT
		Presiding Officers:	Kirk Robinson, WA
			Manuel Villicana, Kern Co., CA
			Brett Gurney, UT
			Tim Chesser, AR
Associate Membership Committee			
Chair:		Stephen Langford, Cardinal Scale (2007)	
Vice Chair:		Christopher Guay, Procter and Gamble (2008)	
Secretary/Treasurer:		Paul Lewis, Rice Lake Weighing Systems (2009)	
Members:		William Sveum, Kraft Foods (2007)	
		Darrell Flocken, Mettler-Toledo (2008)	
		Cary Frye, International Dairy Foods Assoc. (2008)	
		Michael Gaspers, Farmland Foods, Inc. (2009)	
		Thomas Herrington, Nestlé USA (2010)	

National Type Evaluation Technical Committees (NTETC)			
Weighing Sector		**Measuring Sector**	
Chair:	Darrell Flocken, Mettler-Toledo	Chair:	Michael Keilty, Endress & Hauser Flowtec AG
Technical Advisor:	Steven Cook, NIST/W&M Division	Technical Advisor:	Richard Suiter, NIST/W&M Division
Public Sector Members:	Cary Ainsworth, GIPSA Ross Andersen, NY William Bates, GIPSA Andrea Buie, MD Luciano Burtini, Measurement Canada Tina Butcher, NIST/W&M Division Gary Castro, CA Terry Davis, KS Ken Jones, CA Jack Kane, MT Don Onwiler, NE James Truex, OH Juana Williams, NIST/W&M Division Russ Wyckoff, OR	Public Sector Members:	Ross Andersen, NY Tina Butcher, NIST/W&M Division Jerry Butler, NC Gary Castro, CA Steve Hadder, FL Ted Kingsbury, Measurement Canada John Makin, Measurement Canada Steven Malone, NE Don Onwiler, NE Dan Reiswig, CA Richard Wotthlie, MD
Private Sector Members:	Steven Beitzel, Systems Associates, Inc. Doug Biette, Sartorius North America John Elengo, Contractor Robert Feezor, Norfolk Southern Corp. William GeMeiner, Union Pacific Railroad David Hawkins, Thurman Scale Co. Scott Henry, NCR Rafael Jimenez, Association of American Railroads Gary Lameris, Lameris Consulting Stephen Langford, Cardinal Scale Mfg. Paul Lewis, Rice Lake Weighing Systems L. Edward Luthy, Brechbuhler Scales, Inc. Nigel Mills, Hobart Corporation Naresh Puri, NMB Technologies, Inc. David Quinn, Weighing Consultants, Inc. Louis Straub, Fairbanks Scales, Inc. Jerry Wang, A&D Engineering, Inc. Otto Warnlof, Consultant William West, Consultant Nathaniel Wieselquist, Sick, Inc. Walter Young, Emery Winslow Scale	Private Sector Members:	F. Michael Belue, Belue Associates Marc Buttler, Emerson Process Management - Micro Motion Joe Buxton, Daniel Measurement & Control Rodney Cooper, Actaris Neptune Maurice Forkert, Tuthill Transfer Systems Mike Gallo, Clean Fueling Technologies Paul Glowacki, Murray Equipment Alex Gutierrez, MEGGITT Fueling Products, Whittaker Controls Gordon Johnson, Gilbarco, Inc. Yefim Katselnik, Dresser Wayne, Inc. Douglas Long, RDM Industrial Electronics Wade Mattar, Invensys/Foxboro Daniel Maslowski, LTS Scales Richard Miller, FMC Measurement Solution Robert Murnane, Jr., Seraphin Test Measure Andre Noel, Neptune Technology Charlene Numrych, Liquid Controls, LLC Johnny Parrish, Brodie Meter Company, LLC David Rajala, Veeder-Root Company Otto Warnlof, Consultant

National Type Evaluation Technical Committees (NTETC) (continued)	
Software Sector	

Chair:	Jim Truex, OH	Chair:	Cassie Eigenmann, DICKEY-john Corp.
Technical Advisor:	Stephen Patoray, NCWM	Technical Advisors:	G. Diane. Lee, NIST/W&M Division John Barber, J. B. Associates
Public Sector Members:	Dennis Beattie, MC Andrea Buie, MD Bill Fishman, NY Mike Frailer, MD Norman Ingram, CA Todd Lucas, OH Don Onwiler, NE John Roach, CA Wayne Stiefel, NIST	Public Sector Members:	Randy Burns, AR Tina Butcher, NIST/W&M Division Don Onwiler, NE Richard Pierce, GIPSA Edward Szesnat, Jr., NY Cheryl Tew, NC Robert Wittenberger, MO
Private Sector Members:	Doug Bliss, Mettler-Toledo George Brazis, Avery Weigh-Tronix André Elle, Endress & Hauser Flowtec AG Travis Gibson, Rice Lake Weighing Systems Teri Gulke, Liquid Controls LLC Keith Harper, Gencor Industries, Inc. Bryan Haynes, Liquid Controls Tony Herrin, Cardinal Scale Mfgr. Co. Robert Hoblit, IBM Gordon Johnson, Gilbarco, Inc. Gary Lameris, Lameris Consulting Paul Lewis, Rice Lake Weighing Systems Mike McGhee, Actaris US Liquid Measurement Richard Miller, FMC Measurement Solutions Tim Morrison, KJM Software Charlene Numrych, Liquid Controls, LLC Michael Parks, Vulcan Materials Co. Jim Pettinato, FMC Measurement Solutions Mike Roach, Verifone Robin Sax, CompuWeigh Corp. Jim Sexton, Rice Lake Weighing Systems Chris Scott, Gilbarco, Inc. David Vande Berg, Vande Berg Scales Roland Wagner, Flow Measurements & Engineering GmbH Kevin Williams, Gilbarco, Inc. Nathaniel Wieselquist, Sick, Inc.	Private Sector Members:	James Bair, NA Miller's Association Martin Clements, The Steinlite Corp. Victor Gates, Shore Sales Company Andrew Gell, Foss North America Charles Hurburgh, Jr., Iowa State University David Krejci, Grain Elevator & Processing Society John Kennedy, Perten Instruments Thomas Runyon, Seedboro Equipment

Belt Conveyor Sector	
Chair:	TBD
Technical Advisor:	Steven Cook, NIST/W&M Division
Public Sector Members:	Andrea Buie, MD
Private Sector Members:	Rafael Jimenez, Association of American Railroads Lars Marmsater, Merrick Industries Bill Ripka, Thermo Electron Peter Sirrico, Thayer Scale - Hyer Industries, Inc. Thomas Vormittag, Sr., SGS Minerals Services Otto Warnlof, Consultant

Regional Weights and Measures Associations	
Regional Weights and Measures Contacts	
Northeastern Weights and Measures Assn. (NEWMA): Annual Meeting 2007: May 14 - 17 Springfield Marriott Springfield, Massachusetts	Bill Timmons City of Medford (781) 393-2463 mwtimmons@medford.org
Southern Weights and Measures Assn. (SWMA): Annual Meeting 2007: October 21 - 24 Doubletree Hotel Little Rock Little Rock, Arkansas	Tim Chesser Arkansas Bureau of Standards (501) 570-1159 tim.chesser@aspb.ar.gov
Central Weights and Measures Assn. (CWMA): Annual Meeting 2007: April 29 - May 2 Crown Plaza North Minneapolis, Minnesota	Julie Quinn Minnesota Department of Commerce (615) 215-5823 julie.quinn@state.mn.us
Western Weights and Measures Assn. (WWMA): Annual Meeting 2007: September 9 - 13 Harveys Lake Tahoe Lake Tahoe, Nevada	Steven Grabski Nevada Division of Measurement Standards (775) 688-1166 sgrabski@agri.state.nv.us

Org Chart

THIS PAGE INTENTIONALLY LEFT BLANK.

President's Address
National Conference on Weights and Measures
Salt Lake City, Utah
July 12, 2007

Dr. Belinda Collins
NIST, Technology Services Director

Dr. Belinda Collins addressed the National Conference on Weights and Measures Annual Meeting attendees in Salt Lake City, Utah, on July 12, 2007. Dr. Collins presented the National Institute of Standards and Technology (NIST) mission to promote U.S. innovation and industrial competitiveness by advancing measurement sciences, standards, and technology in ways that enhance economic security and improve the quality of life.

The presentation gave an overview of NIST and its pivotal role in the U.S. economy, covering key points such as the American Competitiveness Initiative, details of planned research, the U.S. measurement system, and NIST's partnership with the National Conference on Weights and Measures (NCWM) in standards development and the newest area of enabling a hydrogen economy. The slides presented here cover some of the broad areas of research and contributions made by NIST and give an idea of the impact the agency has in domestic and worldwide arenas.

This presentation ended on a note of cooperation for a continued successful collaboration between NIST Weights and Measures and the NCWM.

THIS PAGE INTENTIONALLY LEFT BLANK

NIST and the Future: Supporting Innovation and Competitiveness

NCWM Annual Meeting

Belinda L. Collins, Ph.D.
Director, Technology Services, NIST

July 10, 2007

NIST
National Institute of Standards and Technology
Technology Administration
U.S. Department of Commerce

Outline

- NIST – Overview
- American Competitiveness Initiative
    - Details of planned research
- The U.S. Measurement System
- Partnering with NCWM
    - Standards Development
    - Enabling the Hydrogen Economy

NIST Mission

To promote U.S. innovation and industrial competitiveness by advancing

> measurement science,
> standards, and
> technology

in ways that enhance economic security and improve our quality of life

NIST's Pivotal Role in U.S. Economy

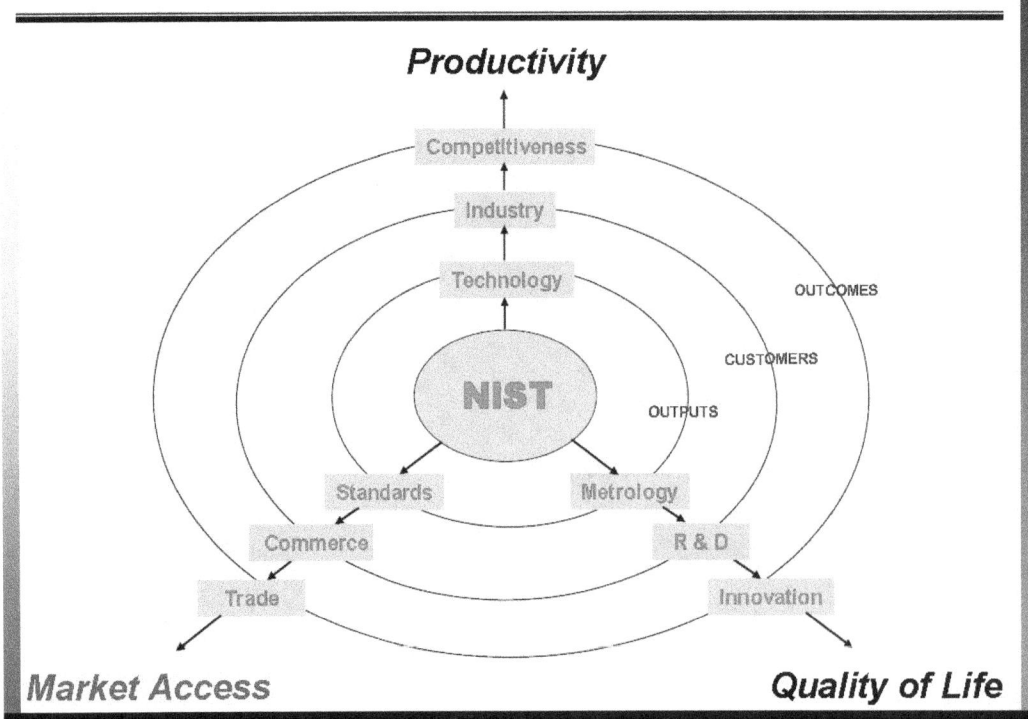

NIST at a Glance - 2006

2,448 Full time employees
- Gaithersburg, Maryland
- Boulder, Colorado
- Charleston, South Carolina

- 3 Nobel Laureates (Physics)
- 1 National Medal of Science (Materials)
- 1 MacArthur Fellowship
- 14 National Academy Members

1,800 guest researchers
850 users of facilities

NIST Laboratories
Advanced Technology Program
Manufacturing Extension Partnership
Baldrige National Quality Program

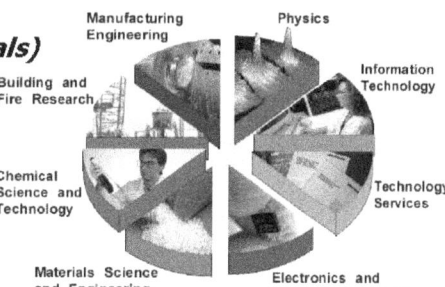

Manufacturing Engineering, Physics, Information Technology, Building and Fire Research, Chemical Science and Technology, Technology Services, Materials Science and Engineering, Electronics and Electrical Engineering

American Competitiveness Initiative
... announced in 2006 State of the Union Address

$50B to be invested over the next 10 years in:
- NIST core (laboratory and infrastructure)
- National Science Foundation
- DOE Office of Science

The role of government is not to create wealth. The role of our government is to create an environment in which the entrepreneur can flourish, in which minds can expand, in which technologies can reach new frontiers.

American Competitiveness Initiative (ACI)
- Proposed in FY 2007 and continued in FY 2008 budget request
- Doubles, over 10 years, investment in:
  - NIST core (laboratory and infrastructure)
  - National Science Foundation
  - DOE Office of Science

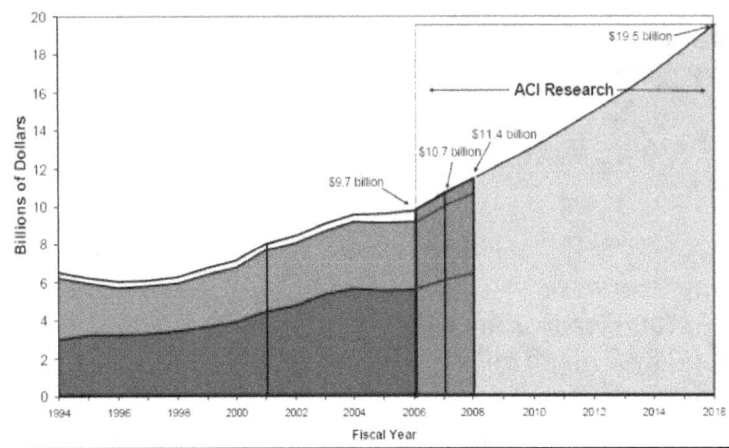

American Competitiveness Initiative
New NIST Programs for FY07

Rapidly developing technologies
- **Nanotechnology from Discovery to Manufacture**
- **Quantum Information Science**
- Enabling the Hydrogen Economy
- **Innovations in Measurement Science**
- **Cyber Security**

Critical national assets
NIST Center for Neutron Research
Synchrotron Measurement

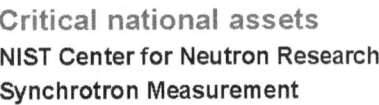

Immediate measurement needs
Innovation through Supply Chain Integration
Structural Safety
International Standards and Innovation
Bioimaging, Biometrics

Center for Nanoscale Science and Technology (CNST)

- New multidisciplinary center aimed at converting nanotechnology discoveries to products

- Mission: develop the necessary measurement science and instrumentation to meet emerging needs

- Establish the materials and process characterization to enable scaled-up, reliable, cost effective manufacturing of nanoscale materials, structures, devices, and systems

- Partner with industry, academia, and government to turn the potential of nanotechnology into reality

NIST Center for Neutron Research

National resource for neutron- based measurements
- "See" structure at the nanoscale
- Uniquely sensitive to hydrogen
- Probe magnetic structure
- Non-destructive probe

Preservation of pharmaceuticals

Magnetic data storage

Chemistry of cement

Petrochemicals

Fuel cells
H_2 storage materials

Enabling the Hydrogen Economy

Hydrogen Fuels Benefits
- Reduced dependence on foreign energy sources
- Lower environmental impact

NIST Brings:
- More than 50 years of technical expertise in fuels
- Congressional mandates for weights and measures, pipeline safety

NIST will:
- Improve efficiency, durability, manufacture of hydrogen fuel cells
- Develop standards for pipeline safety and reliability
- Develop standards, calibrations for equitable trade of hydrogen

International Standards and Innovation

Standards-related barriers to trade constrain innovation, entrench inferior technologies, raise transaction costs, and hinder interoperability

NIST works to open markets for American workers and exporters

NIST will:
- Provide technical leadership to ensure standards are not a barrier to U.S. exports
- Provide information and effective U.S. coordination with international standards organizations

NIST FY 2008 Budget Request
(In millions of dollars)

	FY 2006 Enacted	FY 2007 JR Cont'g Res.	FY 2008 Request
STRS (w/o directed grants)	$382.9	$432.8	$500.5
CRF (w/o directed grants)	48.2	58.7	93.9
NIST Core Total:	$431.1	$491.5	$594.4
NIST Core Increase = +$102.9 (21%)			
ITS	$183.6 (MEP+ATP)	$183.6 (MEP+ATP)	$46.3 (MEP)
Directed Grants	$137.3	N/A	N/A
Total NIST	$752.0	$675.1	$640.7

Enabling Nanotechnology from Discovery to Manufacture

- Manufacturing with nanoscale components expected to be a dominant factor in the 21st century economy
- Exploiting nanoscale behaviors and properties requires new tools and methods
    - NIST is the NNI lead agency on "*Nanoscale measurement science, instrument calibration, standard reference materials, and nanoscale physical and chemical properties standard reference data.*"
- Initiative continues the creation of the Center for Nanoscale Science and Technology (CNST)
    - Partner with industry, universities, and other agencies to bridge the gap between science and production
    - Over 300 new researchers from industry and academia
- Expands research to support industry through nanoscale measurement science and standards
    - Develop new atomic-scale measurement capabilities
    - Support standards for environment, health, and safety

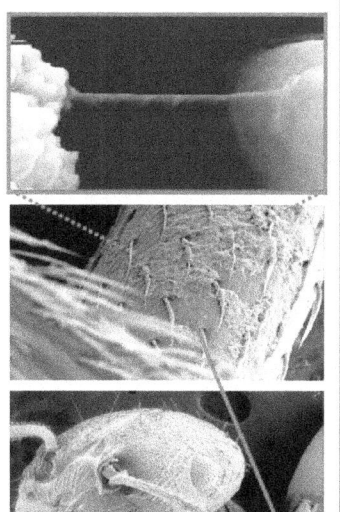

Carbon nanotube on the hair of an ant's leg

Quantum Science:
Infrastructure for 21st Century Innovation

- The laws of physics are fundamentally different in the quantum world of atoms, electrons, and light particles. This enables revolutionary potential for:
  - Measurement capabilities otherwise impossible "classically"
  - "Unbreakable" codes (i.e. to protect financial transactions)
  - Powerful computers capable of solving problems impractical to solve today
- NIST is a recognized world leader in the field
- This initiative will
  - Accelerate the economic potential for exploiting the unique properties of the quantum world
  - Advance research on quantum information
  - Develop fundamentally new and unique measurement tools and methods
  - Further leverage the partnership with the Joint Quantum Institute (NIST, Univ. of MD, and NSA)

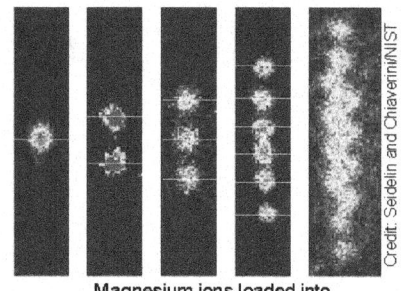

Magnesium ions loaded into NIST's new planar ion trap.

Measurements and Standards for the Climate Change Science Program

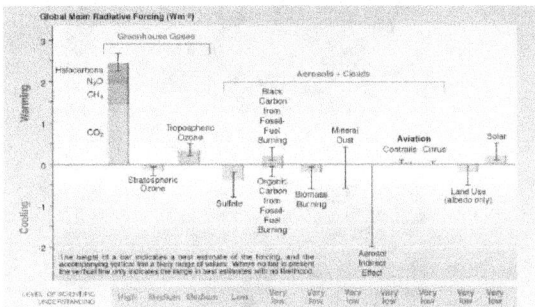

- Critical measurement uncertainties in solar output and effects of aerosols limit Nation's ability to model global climate change
- Initiative addresses 2 critical gaps identified in Interagency Strategic Plan
  - Resolves discrepancies in satellite-based measurements of solar intensity
  - Provides quantitative understanding of effects of atmospheric aerosols on sunlight

- Results will help modelers to create an accurate picture of Earth's climate through calibrations traceable to international standards
  - Standardized instrument calibration for satellites for accurate international inter-comparisons and lower uncertainties
  - New measurement methods for aerosols
  - Database of aerosol properties

Total Solar Irradiance Database

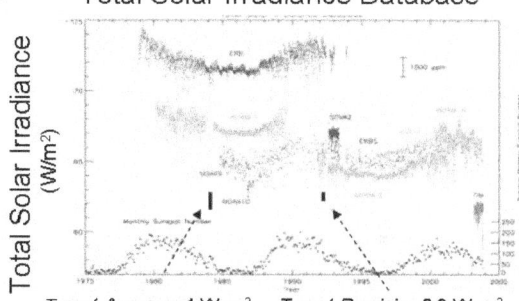

Target Accuracy 1 W m^{-2} Target Precision 0.3 W m^{-2}

Disaster-Resilient Structures and Communities

- Risk to lives, property, and major disruption of commerce increases as communities encroach on hurricane-prone coasts and fire-prone wildland-urban interface regions
- Single major event (e.g., hurricane) can cost $80B-$200B
- Need to assess community and regional scale risks
- This initiative will develop predictive tools that enable:
  - Local officials to evaluate and mitigate risks via land-use planning and practices;
  - Development of risk-based hazard maps at the community-scale; and
  - Development of risk-consistent and cost-effective mitigation solutions incorporated into next-generation building codes and standards.

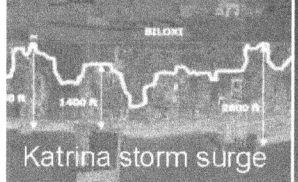
Katrina storm surge

NOAA Fire Weather **8 km** ← New link **1 km** NIST Fire Behavior (WFDS)

Regional   Community   Residence   Components

Predict fire behavior for communities based on fuel maps, local topography, cultural features, and micro wind patterns for real-time firefighting as well as improved building codes and community planning.

National Earthquake Hazards Reduction Program (NEHRP)

- Earthquakes strike without warning – and a single major event can cost $100B - $200B
- 75 million Americans and $8.6 trillion worth of structures in the U.S. in moderate to high-risk areas
- NIST tasked with conducting research to bridge the gap from construction theory to practice and to promote its adoption
- This initiative will enhance the safety of:

1994 Northridge Earthquake, Los Angeles (NIST)

  - **New structures** by establishing and promoting performance-based standards for entire building designs and by accelerating the adoption of basic research into the model building codes, standards, and practices
  - **Existing structures** through research on actual building performance in earthquakes; developing structural performance models and tools; and establishing cost-effective retrofit techniques for existing buildings

NIST Center for Neutron Research (NCNR) Expansion and Reliability Improvements

- Neutron-based measurements are critical for 21st century innovation – for example:
    - Design of new medications by determining protein structure & function
    - Development of practical alternative energy sources, including Hydrogen
    - Determining the structure of materials and devices at the nanometer scale
    - Discover advanced new materials for technologies beyond semiconductors
- Due to tremendous scientific value – demand for access by industry and academia far exceeds capacity
- NCNR serves more customers than all other U.S. neutron facilities combined – and this initiative will:
    - Further increase capacity by 30% to serve 500 additional researchers each year
    - Add additional cold source and new guide hall
        - New cold source is 2x brighter; Guide system is up to 4x more efficient
    - Provide new generation of world-class instruments
        - Critical new instruments either not available in U.S. or 100x improvement

Boulder Laboratories: Building 1 Extension

Nanofabrication Capabilities

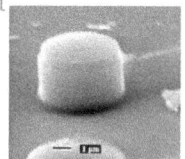 

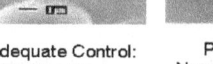

Adequate Control: Working Device   Poor Control: Non-working device

Extension

- Modern measurement science requires extremely advanced capabilities such as manipulating objects at the atomic scale
- The 1950s infrastructure in Boulder is insufficient to meet the Nation's needs for increasingly accurate measurements
    - High speed/high frequency measurements required for advanced electronics, defense, and homeland security;
    - Measurements and tests at the single atom level;
    - Measure forces below 1 billionth of a penny's weight: forces between cells, nanoscale systems, etc;
    - Measure time to 1 second in 30 billion years enabling new science and vastly improved navigation/positioning systems
- Create a 21st-century measurement capability for the Nation
    - Construct a high-performance laboratory extension to existing Building 1 with stringent control of temperature, vibration, humidity, and air cleanliness.
    - Deliver higher performance laboratory space sooner and at lower cost than previous plans

Budget Summary

- The proposed FY 2008 budget is an excellent budget
    - Enhances NIST's ability for world-class research on measurement problems that impact our Nation's economic security and quality of life;
    - Provides the facility capabilities necessary to carry out our mission well into the future; and
    - Shows continued strong support for our Nation's science and technology
- Keeps NIST on the path to support the American Competitiveness Initiative

---

Measuring Up To the Nation's Innovation Challenge
The U.S. Measurement System

A Matter of Competitiveness: Addressing Measurement Barriers to Accelerate Innovation

"America's economic strength and global leadership depend in large measure on our nation's ability to generate and harness the latest in scientific and technological developments and to apply these developments to real world applications."
--*President's American Competitiveness Initiative*

Measurements are fundamental to the nation's capacity to innovate

What is the U.S. Measurement System?

What is the U.S. Measurement System?

The National Measurement System, which includes the national measurement institute (NIST, in the United States), calibration laboratories, accreditation services, weights and measures regulations, and other elements, is situated within—and operates in support of—the broader USMS.

The U.S. Measurement System (USMS) is a complex set of entities that develop, supply, use, or ensure the validity of measurements. It is a broad and autonomous system which encompasses:
- Measurement research and development
- Measurement technology suppliers and users – in both the public and private sectors

The USMS relies on, but also contributes to, the scientific research enterprise

A Sense of Urgency, An Economic Imperative

Assessing the U.S. Measurement System

- **Why?** Ensure that capabilities required by science and industry to accelerate innovation are available, under development, or planned
    - Identify measurement infrastructure needs
    - Identify system gaps and weaknesses
    - Engage stakeholders in search for solutions
- **What's the Risk?** Without an advanced measurement system, U.S. risks serious declines in competitiveness and quality of life
    - Other nations view measurement capabilities as source of potential advantage

The USMS Assessment

NIST Conducted a Fact-Based Assessment . . .

- Reviewed 164 Industry Technology Roadmaps
- Conducted 15 NIST-Industry Workshops
- Interviewed Industry Representatives
- Solicited Input from Businesses and Trade Associations
- Hundreds of Participants from Industry, Universities, and Government

. . . Obtained 723 Measurement Needs in 11 Industry Sectors and Technology Areas

- Representative Sample of Barriers to Innovation

Measurement Needs Cross Both Sectors, Technologies

Needs Across 11 Sector/Technology Areas for...

- Increased Accuracy, Resolution
- Fundamentally New Measurement Methods
  - Some Existing Capabilities Pressed to Their Limits
  - Advances in Science & Technology, Changes in Society Require Novel Responses
- Affordable, Accurate Sensors for Real-Time Process Monitoring and Control
- Standards and Metrics for Evaluating System-Level Performance
- Practical, Cost-Effective Methods to Demonstrate Regulatory Compliance

The USMS - NIST and the Future

NIST will continue to provide measurement solutions through cutting edge research, calibrations, standard reference materials, standard reference data, laboratory accreditation, and technology transfer

NIST will continue to provide leadership for the USMS

- Collect new Measurement Needs
- Work with external stakeholders to identify needs
- Collaborate with solution providers, internal and external, to NIST to develop solutions needed for priority Measurement Needs
- Regularly report on state of USMS

Historically Close Relationship Between NIST and NCWM

NCWM
- Formed in 1905, shortly after creation of NBS (1901)
- NIST/WMD staff are members of NCWM
- Maturing into a productive partnership

NIST and NCWM share the common objective of enhancing the uniformity and strength of the U.S. weights and measures infrastructure

To evaluate and monitor the weights and measures infrastructure, NCWM and NIST partner in developing measures such as inspector certification, lab and field proficiency and marketplace surveys

---

NIST – Partnership and Support for NCWM

NCWM mission: To advance a healthy business and consumer climate through fair and equitable weights and measures standards

NIST support focuses on:
- Standards development
- Training of personnel
- Laboratory support

NIST and NCWM – Long History of Collaboration

Specific Examples of recent or current collaborative efforts:
- Marketplace Survey last year – plan on continuing support for additional surveys
- Professional Development Committee (PDC) and Certification of Inspectors – long term joint goal
- Mutual Acceptance Arrangement – joint efforts led to signing last year
- Standards development and improvement (ongoing)
- Potential adoption of common device definitions for use in national surveys – next step will be data collection and analysis

New NIST Activities in Legal Metrology Support for the Hydrogen Economy

NIST received funding through the American Competitiveness Initiative to support the U.S. transition to a hydrogen economy

The Weights and Measures Division received a small portion of this funding to develop hydrogen standards for weights and measures
- Prior funding dedicated to H_2 =10% of one FTE
- Current funding = 1 FTE + funding for Nat'l Working Group

Over the past year WMD has developed a draft Hydrogen Gas Meters Code and distributed copies to interested parties (weights and measures officials, equipment manufacturers, hydrogen SDOs working in related areas of the hydrogen infrastructure, etc.)

Regular updates to the S&T Committee have taken place to keep them apprised of code and standards work

NIST Hydrogen Initiative

Draft long range plan through 2011 for WMD to support the development of an H_2 infrastructure

- The long range plan encompasses key components such as:
  (1) Establishing a Work Group
  (2) Developing standards to address gaseous, liquid, and other blends of hydrogen,
  (3) Developing Method of Sale Regulations, sampling and test procedures, and test equipment, and,
  (4) Participating in the development of related international standards

NIST Hydrogen Initiative and NCWM, Cont'd

An important component will be to partner with the NCWM at every opportunity in the development of the hydrogen code and for subsequent field trials of test procedures and to coordinate educational and other training events

- WMD will continue to brief the S&T Committee and the NCWM Board of Directors as time becomes available on their agendas
- Juana Williams of WMD is at this meeting and wants to get your ideas!

The first draft of the Hydrogen Gas Meters Code is currently posted at

Conclusions

NIST looks forward to working with NCWM and its members as we face the new challenges in measurements and standards contained in the American Competitiveness Initiative, including the standards and training needed to support the Hydrogen Economy

NIST also looks to NCWM as a solution provider for many of the measurement needs identified in the USMS

- Would welcome opportunity to discuss specific opportunities and ideas

NIST values its long-standing partnership with NCWM!

New Chairman's Address
92nd National Conference on Weights and Measures
Salt Lake City, Utah
July 12, 2007

Judy Cardin
Wisconsin Department of Agriculture & Consumer Protection

Good morning, everyone, and thank you all for being here. I am honored to accept the responsibilities of Chair and the trust you have placed in me to lead the National Conference. What a great organization this is! As difficult as some of our work was this week, we'll leave here friends, ready to continue the work of the Conference.

Thanks to the standing committees for the long hours and fortitude you displayed this week. With your continuing involvement and determination, we'll handle the challenges before us as we always do—seeking balance to provide equity and making the correct technical decisions.

My theme this year is "Seeking Balance." All issues and proposals we consider require us to seek balance. We determine the best science and measurement available, at a cost the market and consumers can bear. Temperature compensation is a tremendous challenge and opportunity that will require a focus on seeking balance during the next year and beyond. Together we will find that balance.

My other goals for the year include:

1. continuing to build our partnerships with NIST and Canada, and our work on OIML agreements;
2. involving and supporting our standing committees and the membership in continued improvement of standards development;
3. improving the efficiency and cost effectiveness of NCWM;
4. improving and communicating the value of NCWM; and
5. retaining and increasing membership.

Please let me know what is important to you. Feel free to call, email, or tap me on the shoulder when you see me. I want to hear from you, and I'll need your help to improve and grow the Conference.

At this time I would like to make the following appointments:

To the Board of Directors, to fill the vacancy caused by Jack Kane's advancement to Chair-elect: Tim Tyson, Kansas.

To the NTEP Committee: Don Onwiler, Nebraska, as Chair.

To the Laws and Regulations Committee: John Gaccione, Westchester County, New York.

To the Specifications and Tolerances Committee: Rick Fogal, Pennsylvania

To the Professional Development Committee (PDC): Ken Deitzler, Pennsylvania

In addition, I am announcing some corrections and changes to the term expirations of the members of the PDC.

Agatha Shields' term expiration was listed incorrectly in Publication 16. Agatha's term will expire in 2008. Ken Deitzler will serve until 2009; Ross Anderson, 2010; John Sullivan, 2011; and Stacy Carlsen, 2012.

Nominating Committee:
Don Onwiler, Chair, Nebraska
Thomas Geiler, Massachusetts
Ross Andersen, New York
Steven Malone, Nebraska
Dennis Ehrhart, Arizona
Maxwell Gray, Florida
Jim Truex, Ohio

Chaplain:
F. Michael Belue, Belue Associates

Parliamentarian:
Lou Straub, Fairbanks Scales, Inc.

Credentials Committee:
David Pfahler, South Dakota

Presiding Officers:
Jerry Butler, North Carolina
Kurt Floren, Los Angeles, California
Tim Chesser, Arkansas
Mike Sikula, New York

Sergeants-at-Arms will be Vermont officials.

Thank you again for your trust. I also appreciate the support and friendship so many of you have offered. I'll do my best to fulfill your expectations and leave NCWM an even stronger organization at the end of my term.

NCWM 2007 Annual Meeting Honor Award Recipients

Full Name	Organization	State	No. of Years
Stacy Carlsen	Marin County Weights & Measures	CA	10
Kurt Floren	Los Angeles County Weights & Measures	CA	10
Joe Gomez	New Mexico Department of Agriculture	NM	10
Bob Murnane	Seraphin Test Measure/Pemberton	NJ	10
Bill Ripka	Thermo Electron	MN	10
Lawrence Stump	Indiana Weights & Measures	IN	10
Norman Brucker	Precision Measurement Standards, Inc.	MN	15
Tina Butcher	NIST, Weights & Measures Division	MD	15
Michael Keilty	Endress & Hauser Flowtec AG	IN	15
Don Onwiler	Nebraska Division of Weights & Measures	NE	15
Robert Reynolds	Downstream Alternatives Inc.	IN	15
Will Wotthlie	Maryland Department of Agriculture	MD	15
Carol Fulmer	South Carolina Department of Agriculture	SC	20
Louis Straub	Fairbanks Scales Inc.	NC	20
F. Michael Belue	Belue Associates	AL	30

THIS PAGE INTENTIONALLY LEFT BLANK

BOD 2007 Final Report

Report of the Board of Directors

Michael Cleary
Special Assistant Law Enforcement Coordinator
California Department of Food and Agriculture

Reference
Key Number

100 INTRODUCTION

The Board held its quarterly Board of Directors (BOD) meeting on Saturday, July 7, 2007, and continued that meeting during work sessions throughout the remainder of the Annual Meeting. The Board of Directors and the NTEP Committee invited members to dialogue with the BOD on the following issues: Conformity Assessment, Improving Standards Development, Marketplace Surveys, Membership Marketing, Mutual Acceptance Arrangements, Increasing the Value and Attendance at Meetings, and participation internationally, i.e., OIML, CFTM, APLMF, and USNWG.

Table A
Table of Contents

Subject	Page
100 INTRODUCTION	1
1. Improving Standards Development	2
2. Marketplace Surveys	2
3. Meetings	2
4. Membership Marketing	2
5. NCWM Website – www.ncwm.net	3
6. Participation in International Standard Setting	3
7. Increasing the Value and Attendance at Meetings	3
8. Treasurer's Report	4

Table B
Appendices

Appendix	Title	Page
A	NCWM National Survey of Prepackaged Meats and Poultry	A1
B	National Random Market Survey 2006	B1
C	Auditor's Report for 2006	C1
D	Report on the Activities of the International Organization of Legal Metrology (OIML) and Regional Legal Metrology Organizations	D1
E	Final Report of the NCWM Associate Membership Committee (AMC)	E1

**Details of all Items
(In order by Reference Key Number)**

1. Improving Standards Development

Judy Cardin continued her efforts with instructing members on the use of Form 15 and made presentations to the remaining regional associations. The Board reviewed this item in an effort to ensure that the process is simple, clear, and transparent. The next step in the process is to incorporate the feedback received from the regional associations into a "How To" submit a Form 15. The intent is also to develop an online form for submittal.

In addition, the Board is recommending to the standing committees that they encourage members to submit written comments to the appropriate standing committee chair. The standing committee chair, if appropriate, will read the comments during the open hearing. This would include comments from members who are uncomfortable speaking at the microphone.

Since the Interim Meeting, the online overview and how to submit a proposal has been completed. In addition, the online form to submit a proposal has been completed. These items have been posted on the NCWM website under "Submit a Proposal" under the "About NCWM" topic. Editorial changes will also be made to the introduction sections of NIST Handbooks 44 and 130.

2. Marketplace Surveys

At the Interim Meeting, Roger Macey, Branch Chief, California Division of Measurement Standards, gave a PowerPoint presentation of the basic initial data from the recent national marketplace survey. Additional in-depth data will be presented at a later time. The Board welcomes any input from the general membership on the use of the data. The PowerPoint presentation and survey results are contained in Appendices A and B of the Board report. Once the work on this survey is completed, the Board will consider future surveys.

The information from the recent marketplace survey will be put on the website as well as an explanation of the methodology used and the findings. Future survey topics will be selected by the NCWM chairman.

3. Meetings

Interim Meetings
January 27 - 30, 2008   Hyatt Regency Albuquerque, Albuquerque, New Mexico
January 11 - 14, 2009   Hilton Daytona Beach Hotel, Daytona Beach, Florida

Annual Meetings
July 13 - 17, 2008   Sheraton Burlington Hotel & Conference Center, Burlington, Vermont
July 12 - 16, 2009   Marriott Plaza Hotel, San Antonio, Texas
July 11 - 15, 2010   Crowne Plaza St. Paul Hotel, St. Paul, Minnesota

4. Membership Marketing

The outreach efforts have begun to pay dividends. Membership is at its highest point in over four years. The Board has been involved in the following activities:

- Lapsed member letter sent by Mike Cleary
- E-mail   campaign
- New membership application has been developed. It is available on the NCWM website as a downloadable PDF or in hard copy from the NCWM office.
- First-timer mentoring by Board at 2006 and 2007 Annual Meeting
- Redesigned presentation for first-timer's orientation at the Annual Meeting was developed and presented in Salt Lake.

- Online membership applications and renewals
- The Board developed a first-timer's information packet and at-a-glance guide to the conference.
- Dreaded first-timer ribbons have been banished.

Mike Cleary reported that his goal for the past year was membership recruitment, retention and awareness of the significance of the Conference. Chairman Cleary indicated that membership is the highest that it has been since 2003.

5. NCWM Website – www.ncwm.net

The following website enhancements have been completed:

- Online meeting registration
- Online membership application and renewal

The Board would like to thank the AMC for a generous financial donation to help defray the cost of the website enhancements.

New enhancement suggestions include:

- Photo library
- Online NTEP applications
- Posting presentations from the Interim and Annual Meetings.

Chairman Cleary reviewed the enhancements made to the website. In addition to the items mentioned in the report, the information on how to submit a proposal has been developed and posted as has the information on the Annual Meeting process. The Board would like to see Annual and Interim Meeting presentations archived on the website. The Board has formed a committee to continually assess and make recommendations to enhance the usability of the website and newsletter.

6. Participation in International Standard Setting

Chuck Ehrlich briefed the Board on key activities of OIML and regional legal metrology organizations (see Appendix D).

7. Increasing the Value and Attendance at Meetings

Continued Use of Training Sessions: The Board recognized the value training sessions bring to the Annual Meeting and would like to continue to facilitate these during any available time. To accomplish this, the process will be that the PDC make recommendations to the chairman for topics. The chairman will select the presenters.

The use of Roundtables: The Board recognizes the value of a roundtable discussion format and will try to incorporate it into the first-timers' orientation session at the Annual Meeting.

Specifications & Tolerances Committee (S&T) – The S&T Committee will go first during the open hearings. Their addendum sheet will not be due until 6:00 p.m. on Tuesday.

The Board has recognized the value of posting electronic versions of the presentations made at the Interim and Annual Meetings on the NCWM website. These presentations will be posted on the Conferences page.

Chairman Cleary reviewed the information contained in the Interim Report under this section. There was discussion on whether Thursday's agenda should be moved to Wednesday if the voting moves more quickly. It was decided to follow the schedule as published in the conference agenda. The Board will work in the coming year to make the Annual Meeting schedule more efficient and effective.

BOD 2007 Final Report

8. Treasurer's Report

A brief treasurer's report will be included in the Board's agenda during the Annual Meeting. The 2006 Audit Report is included in Appendix C of this report.

Treasurer's Report

Income   (percentage of total income)

Dues 22	%
NTEP 62	%
Conferences 11	%
Publications 3	%

Direct Expense   (percentage of direct expenses)

Membership 2	%
NTEP 72	%
Publications 2	%
Conferences 24	%

Overhead Expenses   (percentage of overhead expenses)

Staff 43	%
BOD 24	%
Website 9	%
Charge Card Fees	8 %
Other 16	%

Reserves

NCWM currently has $612,000 in Certificates of Deposit.

Michael Cleary, California, NCWM Chairman
Judy Cardin, Wisconsin, NCWM Chairman-Elect
Don Onwiler, Nebraska, NTEP Chair
Charles Carroll, Massachusetts
Joe Gomez, New Mexico
Jack Kane, Montana
Randy Jennings, Tennessee
Steven Malone, Nebraska
Richard Wotthlie, Maryland
Christopher B. Guay, Procter & Gamble Co.
Darrell Flocken, Mettler-Toledo, Inc.
NCWM Staff: Beth Palys, CAE
NIST: Carol Hockert, Chief, Weights and Measures Division

Board of Directors

Appendix A

NCWM National Survey
Survey of Prepackaged Meat and Poultry

National Conference on Weights and Measures

National Survey

Presented by Roger Macey, California

Survey Coordinator

National Conference on Weights and Measures

15 Jurisdictions Participated

Alaska, California, Colorado, Illinois, Iowa, Kansas, Massachusetts, Nevada, New Mexico, New York (two jurisdictions), North Carolina, Ohio, South Dakota, Texas

National Conference on Weights and Measures

Protocol

- Check 10 lots each of meat and poultry
- Each lot to be 250 packages or less
- Sample of 12 from each lot
- Unused dry tare to determine net weight

National Conference on Weights and Measures

10 lots X 15 jurisdictions
= Minimum of 150 meat lots
and 150 poultry lots

12 samples/lot
= min of 1800 meat packages
= min of 1800 poultry packages

National Conference on Weights and Measures

Results

	Meat	Poultry
Lots Tested	204	117
Lots Failed	12	16
Compliance	94%	86%

National Conference on Weights and Measures

Reason for Lot Failure

	Meat	Poultry
MAV	4	3
-Avg Error	8	13

National Conference on Weights and Measures

Minimum of 3600 packages

Actual packages tested

Meat	2448
Poultry	1405
Total	3853 packages

National Conference on Weights and Measures

Average % Error for all Meat Packages was 0.69 %

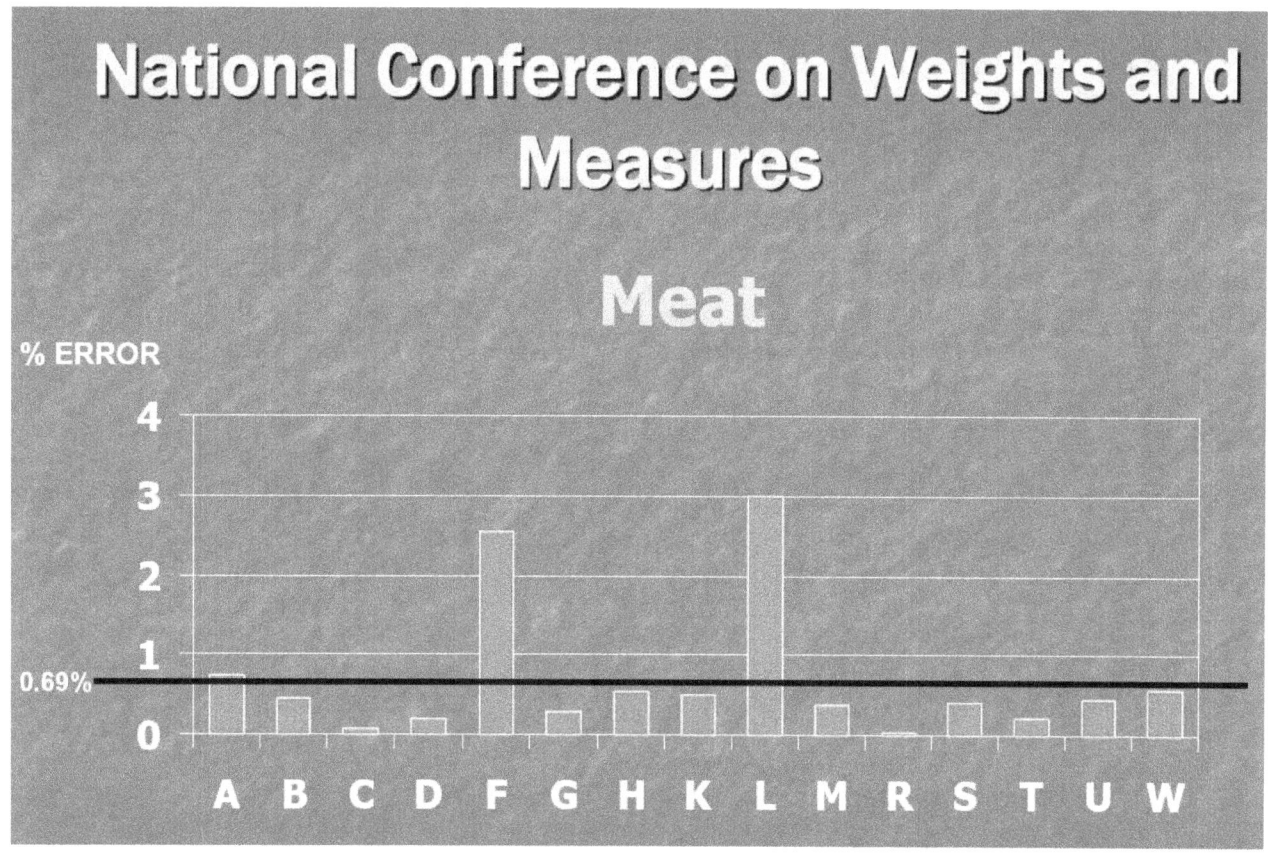

BOD 2007 Final Report
Appendix A – NCWM National Survey – Prepackaged Meat and Poultry

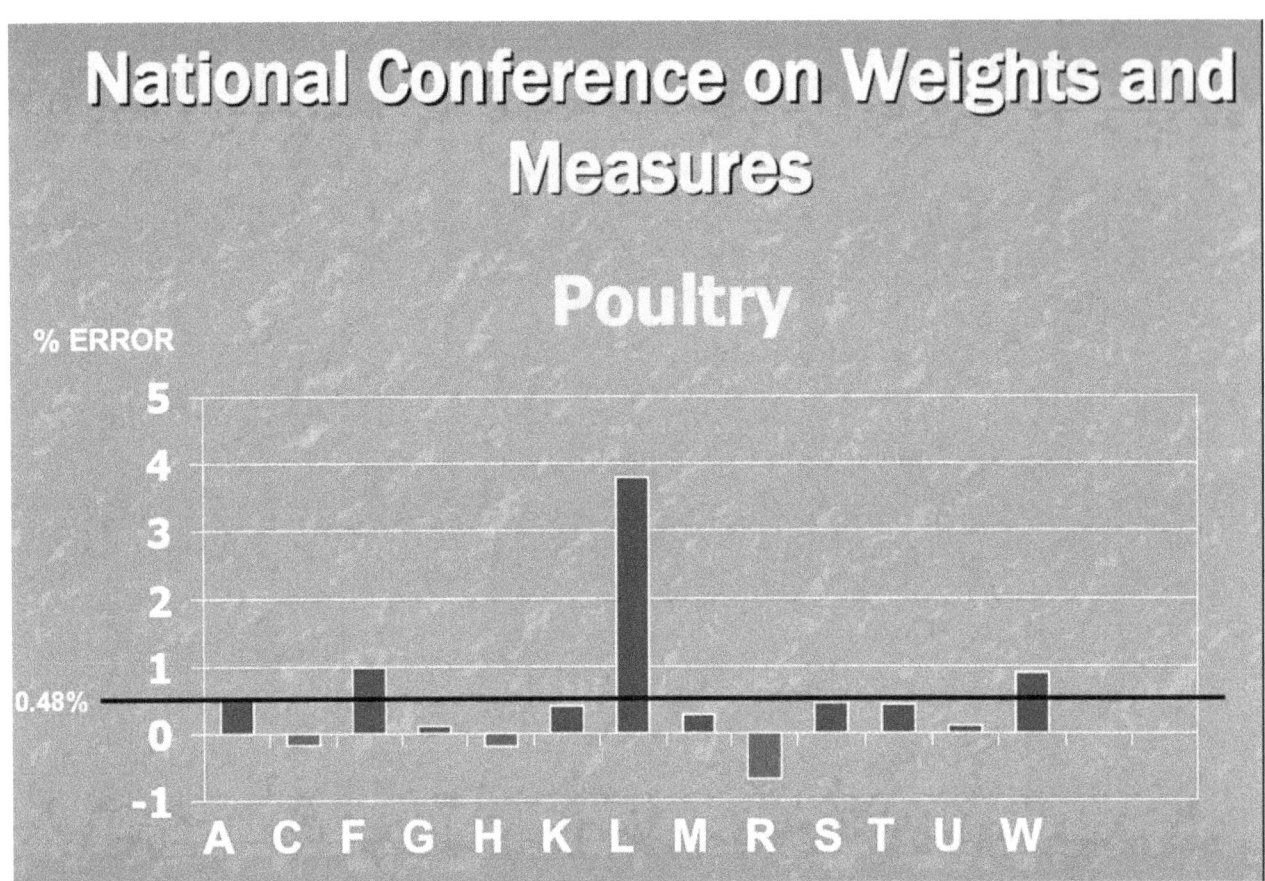

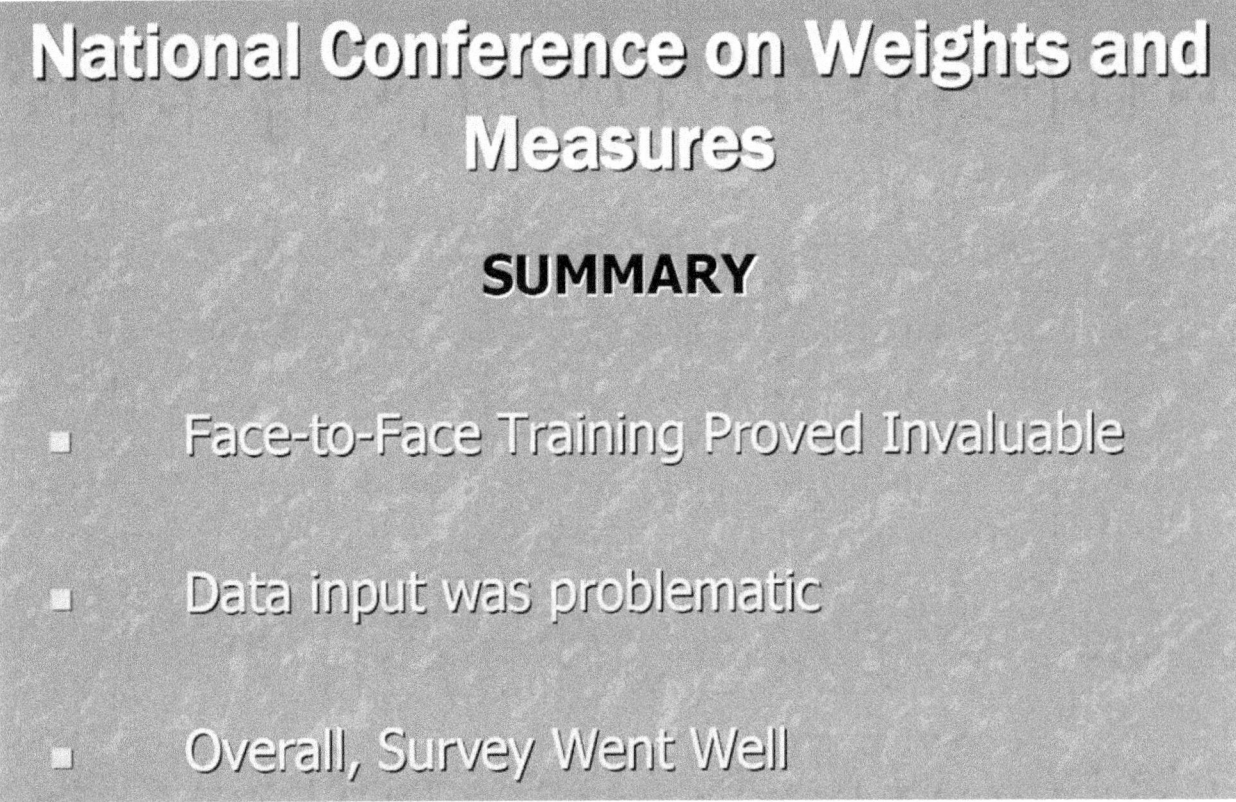

National Conference on Weights and Measures

National Survey

Presented by Roger Macey

California Division of Measurement Standards

THIS PAGE INTENTIONALLY LEFT BLANK

Appendix B

National Random Market Survey 2006

Jurisdictions	Sample Number	Program Activity Level	% Average Package Error	Average Price / lb	Lots Tested	Lots Passed	% Lots Passed	Lots Failed	= Lots Rejected For Avg Err Minus	= MAV
Meats										
A	120	High	0.73	$4.07	10	10	100	0	0	0
B	119	High	0.44	$4.16	10	10	100	0	0	0
C	119	None	0.07	$3.54	10	6	60	4	3	1
D	119	Med	0.19	$4.73	10	10	100	0	0	0
F	180	Med	2.54	$4.09	16	15	94	1	0	1
G	143	High	0.28	$4.76	12	12	100	0	0	0
H	119	High	0.54	$4.80	10	10	100	0	0	0
K	419	High	0.50	$3.99	35	35	100	0	0	0
L	117	High	3.00	$3.99	10	10	100	0	0	0
M	120	Med	0.38	$5.47	10	10	100	0	0	0
R	118	Low	0.04	$4.39	10	8	80	2	1	1
S	116	Low	0.42	$3.67	10	9	90	1	0	1
T	114	None	0.21	$4.42	10	9	90	1	1	0
U	274	None	0.44	$4.17	23	22	96	1	1	0
W	215	Med	0.58	$4.38	18	16	89	2	2	0
15	2412		0.69	$4.26	204	192	94	12	8	4
Poultry										
A	119	High	0.49	$1.58	10	10	100	0	0	0
C	82	None	-0.17	$2.22	7	4	57	3	2	1
F	47	Med	0.97	$1.76	4	4	100	0	0	0
G	144	High	0.10	$1.85	12	12	100	0	0	0
H	103	High	-0.20	$3.51	9	7	78	2	1	1
K	168	High	0.39	$2.42	14	13	93	1	1	0
L	104	High	3.79	$2.21	10	10	100	0	0	0
M	120	Med	0.28	$2.79	10	10	100	0	0	0
R	118	Low	-0.68	$2.20	10	3	30	7	6	1
S	65	Low	0.45	$2.69	6	5	83	1	1	0
T	24	None	0.43	$1.57	2	2	100	0	0	0
U	156	None	0.10	$2.40	13	11	85	2	2	0
W	119	Med	0.89	$1.83	10	10	100	0	0	0
13	1369		0.48	$2.28	117	101	86	16	13	3

Wednesday, January 17, 2007

THIS PAGE INTENTIONALLY LEFT BLANK

Appendix C

Auditor's Report for 2006

The Board reviewed the Auditor's report from the 2006 audit year ended September 30, 2006.

Statement of Activities Ending September 30, 2006

	2006 Actual	AMC Fund	2006 Budget
Revenue & Support			
Government Dues	$102,450 $102,210		
Associate Dues	$ 67,740 $		66,215
National Type Evaluation Program	$458,100 $462,750		
Interim Meeting Fees	$ 18,374 $		21,250
Annual Meeting Fees	$ 64,783 $		69,600
Publications	$ 22,428 $		24,200
Advertising	$ 750		$ 850
Investment Return	$ 28,094		$ 7,500
Associate Member Fund		$ 13,440	
Total Revenue & Support	$762,719	$ 13,440	$754,575
Expenses			
Programs			
Membership	$ 13,091 $		12,101
National Type Evaluation Program	$443,826 $455,739		
Interim Meeting	$ 45,324 $		50,488
Annual Meeting	$ 85,800 $		90,556
Publications	$ 11,847 $		16,140
Newsletter	$ 14,927 $		15,107
Refunds	$ 625		
Total Programs	$615,440 $640,131		
Management & General			
Management Fees	$ 51,267 $		51,267
Board of Directors	$ 24,121 $		29,700
Bank Fees	$ 10,897 $		10,200
Website	$ 12,350 $		10,679
Legal & Accounting	$ 5,861		$ 6,525
Committee Contingency Fund	$ 4,227		$ 5,500
Committee Travel	$ 1,691		$ 0
Insurance	$ 2,057		$ 2,500
Office Supplies	$ 2,455		$ 1,800
Telephone	$ 576		$ 1,200
Technology Fee	$ 1,960		$ 0
Printing & Duplicating	$ 1,443		$ 650
Marketing	$ 311		$ 0
Miscellaneous	$ 600		$ 0
Postage	$ 87		$ 50
Broadcast e-mail	$ 33		$ 0
Associate Member Fund		$ 13,991	
Total Management & General	$119,936	$120,071	
Total Expenses	$735,376 $	13,991	$760,202
Change in net assets	$ 27,343		(551)

BOD 2007 Final Report
Appendix C – Auditor's Report for 2006

	2006 Actual	AMC Fund	2006 Budget
Net Assets, beginning of year	$604,928	$5,425	
Net Assets, end of year	$632,271	$4,874	

Assets

Current Assets
Cash & Cash Equivalents	$210,511
Certificates of Deposit	$584,992
Accounts Receivable	$ 736
Prepaid Expenses	$ 2,165
Interest Receivable	$ 3,997

Total Assets $802,401

Liabilities & Net Assets
Accounts Payable	$ 8,271
Deferred Dues Revenue	$156,985

Total Liabilities $165,256

Net Assets
Unrestricted $637,145

Total Liabilities and Net Assets $802,401

Michael Cleary, California, NCWM Chairman
Judy Cardin, Wisconsin, NCWM Chairman-Elect
Don Onwiler, Nebraska, NTEP Chair
Charles Carroll, Massachusetts
Joe Gomez, New Mexico
Jack Kane, Montana
Randy Jennings, Tennessee
Steven Malone, Nebraska
Richard Wotthlie, Maryland
Christopher B. Guay, Procter & Gamble Co.
Darrell Flocken, Mettler-Toledo, Inc.
NCWM Staff: Beth Palys, CAE
NIST: Carol Hockert, Chief, Weights and Measures Division

Board of Directors

Appendix D

Report on the Activities of the
International Organization of Legal Metrology (OIML)
and Regional Legal Metrology Organizations

Weights and Measures Division, NIST

The Weights and Measures Division (WMD) of the National Institute of Standards and Technology (NIST) is responsible for coordinating U.S. participation in OIML and other international legal metrology organizations. Learn more about OIML at the OIML website at http://www.oiml.org and the WMD website at http://www.nist.gov/owm on the Internet. Dr. Charles Ehrlich, Group Leader of the International Legal Metrology Group (ILMG), can be contacted at charles.ehrlich@nist.gov or at (301) 975-4834 or by fax at (301) 975-8091.

Please note: OIML publications are available without cost at http://www.oiml.org.

Table A
Table of Contents

Subject	Page
I. Report on the Activities of the OIML Technical Committees	D2
II. Report on the 41st CIML Meeting in Cape Town, South Africa, October 18 - 20, 2006	D4
III. Future CIML Meetings	D6
IV. Regional Legal Metrology Organizations	D6

Table B
Glossary of Acronyms

BIML	International Bureau of Legal Metrology	IR	International Recommendation
CD	Committee Draft[1]	MAA	Mutual Acceptance Arrangement
CIML	International Committee of Legal Metrology	OIML	International Organization of Legal Metrology
CPR	Committee on Participation Review	PTB	Physikalisch-Technischen Bundsanstalt
DD	Draft Document[2]	R	Recommendation
DR	Draft Recommendation[2]	SC	Technical Subcommittee
DV	Draft Vocabulary[2]	TC	Technical Committee
DoMC	Declaration of Mutual Confidence	WD	Working Draft[3]

[1] CD: a draft at the stage of development within a technical committee or subcommittee; in this document, successive drafts are numbered 1 CD, 2 CD, etc.

[2] DD and DR: draft documents approved at the level of the technical committee or subcommittee concerned and sent to BIML for approval by CIML.

[3] WD: precedes the development of a CD; in this document, successive drafts are number 1 WD, 2 WD, etc.

BOD 2007 Final Report
Appendix D – Report on the Activities of the OIML

**Details of All Items
(In Order by Reference Key Number)**

I. Report on the Activities of the OIML Technical Committees

This section reports on recent activities and the status of work in OIML Technical Committees (TCs) and Technical Subcommittees (SCs) of specific interest to members of NCWM. Also included are schedules of future activities of the Secretariats, the U.S. National Work Groups (USNWGs), and the International Work Groups (IWGs) of the Committees and Subcommittees.

TC 3/SC 1 "Pattern Approval and Evaluation" (United States)
The subcommittee approved the U.S. proposal for a combined revision of OIML D 19 "Pattern evaluation and pattern approval" and D 20 "Initial and subsequent verification of measuring instruments and processes" into a single document entitled "Principles of metrological control of measuring instruments: type approval and verification." Key elements of OIML D 3 "Legal Qualification of Measuring Instruments," R 34 "Accuracy Classes of Measuring Instruments," and R 42 "Metal Stamps for Verification Officers" will also be incorporated into the combined revision of OIML D 19 and D 20. The revised documents will incorporate recent developments such as the OIML certificate system, D 27 "Initial verification of measuring instruments utilizing the manufacturer's quality management system," and the "Framework for a mutual acceptance arrangement (MAA) on OIML type evaluations." Consideration will be given to the appropriate conformity assessment options developed by the ISO Council Committee on Conformity Assessment (ISO CASCO), including quality systems, product certification, and accreditation. Consideration will be given also to information technology and statistical methods to increase or decrease verification intervals based upon proven instrument performance. For more information on this activity, contact Dr. Ambler Thompson at (301) 975-2333 or at ambler@nist.gov.

TC 5/SC 2 Software (Germany and BIML)
All OIML Documents and Recommendations published since 1990 have been reviewed for terms and requirements related to software. The ILMG submitted U.S. comments on a working draft of the document "Software in Legal Metrology" in June 2006. When complete, this document will serve as guidance for OIML technical committees addressing software requirements in Recommendations for software-controlled instruments. The ILMG participated in meetings of the NCWM Software Sector in Annapolis, Maryland, in October 2006. Most recently, the co-secretariat distributed the 1 CD of this document for subcommittee comment in June 2007. Please contact Dr. Ambler Thompson at (301) 975-2333 or at ambler@nist.gov if you would like a copy of the OIML CD or to participate in this project.

TC 8/SC 1 "Static Volume and Mass Measurement" (Austria and Germany)
The Secretariat submitted 2 CD revisions in January 2006 for OIML R 71 "Fixed Storage Tanks," R 80 "Road and Rail Tankers," and R 85 "Automatic Level Gages for Measuring the Level of Liquid in Fixed Storage Tanks." U.S. comments, including those of the American Petroleum Institute, on all three of these documents were sent in April 2006. The Secretariat held a subcommittee meeting in May 2006 in Hamburg, Germany. The United States provided a "no" vote with comments on the 2 CD for R 71 and comments on the 2 CDs of R 80 and R 85. The Secretariat circulated a 3 CD for R 80 in November 2006 and a 3 CD of R 85 in December 2006. U.S. vote and comments on R 80 and R 85 were returned in February 2007, and a subcommittee meeting was held in March 2007 in Vienna, Austria. All three documents were discussed in Vienna. A 3 CD of R 71 was received in July 2007. The next drafts of R 80 and R 85 are expected later in 2007. Please contact Ralph Richter at (301) 975-3997 or at ralph.richter@nist.gov if you would like copies of the documents or to participate in these projects.

TC 8/SC 3 "Dynamic Volume and Mass Measurement for Liquids other than Water" (United States and Germany)
OIML R 117 "Measuring Instruments for Liquids other than Water" has undergone an extensive revision, incorporating new instrument technologies and merging the document with OIML Recommendations R 86 "Drum Meters" and R 105 "Mass Flowmeters." This is a high priority project for OIML. ILMG is working with the USNWG on flowmeters, Germany, and the Netherlands on this effort. Meetings of the USNWG on flowmeters were held during the NCWM Interim Meeting in January 2007 in Jacksonville, Florida, and the NCWM Annual Meeting in July 2007 in Utah. Measurement Canada has been a strong contributor to this effort. A 2 CD of R 117

was circulated to the two international subcommittees and received over 90 % international "yes" votes. In October 2006, the CIML approved the merger of TC 8/SC 3 and TC 8/SC 4; the United States and Germany are now the co-secretariats of the combined TC 8/SC 3. Following the merger, the old subcommittee TC 8/SC 4 was disbanded. Work on R 117-2 "Test Methods" and R 117-3 "Test Report Format" has begun.

OIML member nations have voted on the DR of R 117-1 by postal ballot with over 90 % approval of the 34 nations that voted. Full CIML approval on R 117-1 is expected at the CIML meeting in October 2007. If you have any questions, would like a copy of the R 117-1 DR, or would like to participate in the next phases of this project, please contact Ralph Richter at (301) 975-3997 or ralph.richter@nist.gov.

TC 8/SC 7 "Gas Metering" (Belgium and France)
In April 2007, the Secretariat circulated a DR of the Recommendation "Measuring Systems for Compressed Natural Gas (CNG) for Vehicles" and annexes covering performance tests for electronic devices and basic test procedures. The postal ballot on this recommendation failed, but it is anticipated that recommendation will be approved by the CIML in October 2007.

Also in April 2007, a postal ballot was circulated on the DR "Measuring Systems for Gaseous Fuel" and U.S. comments were submitted in June 2007. This Recommendation is intended for large pipelines with large flowrates and high operating pressures, or systems not fitted with diaphragm gas meters. Different types of measuring systems are covered by the Recommendation: measuring systems providing indications of volume at base conditions or mass converted from a volume of gas determined at metering conditions, measuring systems providing directly the mass of gas, and measuring systems providing indication of energy corresponding to a volume at base conditions or a mass of gas. The postal ballot on this recommendation failed, but it is anticipated that recommendation will be approved by the CIML in October 2007. Please contact Ralph Richter at (301) 975-3997 or ralph.richter@nist.gov if you would like to obtain a copy of these documents or if you would like to participate in future work involving gas measurement systems.

TC 8/SC 8 "Gas Meters" (Netherlands)
Three recommendations in this subcommittee: R 6 "General provisions for gas volume meters," R 31 "Diaphragm Gas Meters," and R 32 "Rotary Piston Gas Meters and Turbine Gas Meters" have been combined into a single revised Recommendation. The United States voted "yes" with comments on the 3 CD of this document in January 2006. The final DR was approved by the CIML at their October 2006 meeting in Cape Town, South Africa, and will be published with the new designation of R 137-1 "Gas Meters." Development of R 137-2 "Test Methods" is now underway. Please contact Ralph Richter at (301) 975-3997 or ralph.richter@nist.gov if you would like to participate in the R 137-2 project.

TC 9 "Instruments for Measuring Mass" (United States)
Now that the revision of R 76 "Non-automatic Weighing Instruments" is complete, the United States will send an inquiry in 2007 to TC 9 members about revising R 60 "Load Cells." If you would like to participate in the revision of R 60, please contact Steve Cook at (301) 975-4003 or steven.cook@nist.gov.

TC 9/SC 1 "Nonautomatic Weighing Instruments" (Germany and France)
The revision of R 76 "Non-automatic Weighing Instruments" is of major importance to U.S. interests because the Recommendation serves as the foundation for a majority of the laws and regulations that govern weighing instruments around the world. The revision includes new language addressing metrological controls for type evaluations, conformity, initial and subsequent inspections, suitability of separable components and requirements for metrological software. The USNWG is being consulted concerning proposals to harmonize Handbook 44 and R 76. The DR of R 76-1 was approved by the CIML in October 2006. Most recently, the United States voted "yes" on the DR of R 76-2 "Test Report Format." For more information on these efforts, please contact Steve Cook at (301) 975-4003 or steven.cook@nist.gov.

TC 9/SC 2 "Automatic Weighing Instruments" (United Kingdom)
The Recommendation R 134-1 "Automatic Instruments for Weighing Road Vehicles in Motion – Total Load and Axle Weighing" was approved by CIML in October 2006 with the agreement that U.S. comments concerning terminology and document scope were to be incorporated before publication. The test report format of this document, R 134-2, has been approved by the subcommittee and is going through a final editorial process at the

BIML. Two other documents in this subcommittee are now under revision. The United States returned comments on the 2 CD of R 106 "Automatic Rail-weighbridges" in November 2006. The subcommittee approved a revision of R 107 "Discontinuous Totalizing Automatic Weighing Instruments (Totalizing Hopper Weighers)," and votes and comments on the DR are due in September 2007. If you would like to receive copies of these documents or work on these projects, Richard Harshman is the contact at (301) 975-8107 or at harshman@nist.gov.

TC 17/SC 1 "Humidity" (China)
The Secretariat (China) is working closely with the United States and a small IWG to revise OIML R 59 "Moisture Meters for Cereal Grains and Oilseeds." All drafts have been distributed to the USNWG, which for the most part is a subset of the NTEP Grain Sector. In October 2003, China hosted a meeting of the TC 17/SC 1 subcommittee in Beijing, China, to review and discuss this revised document. A 2 CD that incorporated U.S. comments was circulated in May 2004 by the Secretariat. A meeting of the IWG was held in Paris, France, in September 2004 to resolve conflicts on the document. U.S. comments on the 3 CD of R 59 were returned to the Secretariat in August 2005. A 4 CD was circulated to the IWG in August 2006. U.S. comments on the 4 CD were returned to the Secretariat in November 2006. A TC 17/SC 1 meeting is being hosted by NIST in September 2007 to discuss the 5 CD. Please contact Diane Lee at (301) 975-4405 or at diane.lee@nist.gov if you would like to participate in this work group.

TC 17/SC 8 "Quality Analysis of Agricultural Products" (Australia)
A new subcommittee has been formed to study the issues and write a working draft document "Measuring Instruments for Protein Determination in Grains." Australia is the Secretariat for this new subcommittee. A work group meeting was held in May 2004 in Sydney, Australia. A 2 WD of this document was received in August 2004, and a 3 WD was received in May 2005. A work group meeting was held in June 2005 in Berlin, Germany, to discuss the latest round of comments on the 3 WD. A 1 CD was circulated to the IWG in May 2006. U.S. comments on the 1 CD were returned to the Secretariat in August 2006. A work group meeting was held in September 2006 in Ottawa, Canada, to discuss comments on the 1 CD. A TC 17/SC 8 meeting is being hosted by NIST in September 2007 to discuss the 2 CD. Please contact Diane Lee at (301) 975-4405 or at diane.lee@nist.gov if you would like to participate in this work group.

OIML Mutual Acceptance Arrangement (MAA)
Note: The report on the OIML Mutual Acceptance Arrangement (MAA) has moved; it can now be found in Item 1. Test Data Exchange Agreements of the NTEP Section of the NCWM Annual Report. For further information on the MAA and its implementation, please contact Dr. Charles Ehrlich at charles.ehrlich@nist.gov or at (301) 975-4834 or by fax at (301) 975-8091.

II. Report on the 41st CIML Meeting in Cape Town, South Africa, October 18 - 20, 2006

The CIML gave final approval to the following Recommendations in South Africa:

- R 39 Rockwell hardness machines;
- R 49-1 Water meters intended for the metering of cold, potable water and hot water:
  - Part 1: Metrological and technical requirements;
- R 49-2 Water meters intended for the metering of cold potable water and hot water:
  - Part 2: Test methods;
- R 51-1 Automatic catchweighing instruments:
  - Part 1: Metrological and technical requirements – Tests;
- R 65 Force measuring system of uniaxial material testing machines;
- R 76-1 Non-automatic weighing instruments:
  - Part 1: Metrological and technical requirements – Tests;
- R 82 Gas chromatographic systems for the measuring pollution from pesticides and other toxic substances;
- R 83 Gas chromatograph/mass spectrometer systems for the analysis of organic pollutants in water;
- R 116 Inductively coupled plasma atomic emission spectrometers for the measurement of metal pollutants in water;
- R 134-1 Automatic instruments for weighing road vehicles in motion and axle-load measuring:
  - Part 1: Metrological and technical requirements – Tests;

- R 137-1 Gas Meters:
  - Part 1: Requirements (new Recommendation).

The Committee also approved the withdrawal of R 74 *Electronic weighing instruments.*

The CIML approved the following new work projects:
- New projects of TC 3/SC 5:
  - Revision of B 3 OIML Certificate System for Measuring Instruments;
  - Revision of B 10-1 Framework for a Mutual Acceptance Arrangement on OIML Type Evaluations (MAA);
  - Revision of B 10-2 Checklists for Issuing Authorities and Testing Laboratories Carrying Out OIML Type Evaluations;
- New projects to be allocated by the CIML President to the appropriate TC or SC, based on BIML proposals:
  - Guide for the application of ISO/IEC Guide 62 to the assessment of quality system certification bodies in the field of legal metrology;
  - Guide for the application of ISO 9001 to legal metrology controls;
- New project of TC 16/SC 1:
  - Revision of ISO 3930/OIML R 99 Instruments for measuring vehicle exhaust emissions.

The following work project was withdrawn:
- Project P 6 of TC 3/SC 5: OIML procedure for the review of laboratories to enable mutual acceptance of test results and OIML Certificates of Conformity;

The Committee approved the following proposals:
- When a revision of a publication is published, the previous version remains available on the OIML website, but with an indication that this version has been superseded;
- As long as all the parts of a revised Recommendation included in the Certificate System have not been published, the version referenced in the Certificate System remains applicable;
- When the Certificate System references a revised Recommendation, Certificates may still be issued by reference to the previous version provided the application for a Certificate has been lodged before the publication of the revised version.

<u>MAA Resolutions approved by the CIML in South Africa:</u>

- MAA Resolution 2006-1: The BIML will bear the costs of peer assessments and will subsequently invoice the peer-assessed bodies with a lump sum equal to 1500 € per assessor-day.
- MAA Resolution 2006-2: During the period of transition to the MAA for R 60 and R 76 (provisionally set to end December 31, 2008), Issuing Authorities under the OIML Certificate System for Measuring Instruments (OIML Document B 3) are authorized to continue to issue OIML Certificates of Conformity according to OIML B 3.
  - Issuing Participants in the R 60 and R 76 DoMCs are not authorized to continue to issue basic OIML Certificates for OIML type evaluations unless the application was received before the publication of the DoMC (September 2006).
  - The termination date of this transition period will be reviewed by the CIML at its 43rd Meeting based on a BIML report on operation, experience, and feedback from industry.
- MAA Resolution 2006-3: The R 49 DoMC will continue to move forward despite the fact there is only one potential Issuing Participant.

The CIML instructed TC 3/SC 5 to consider the rules for appointing new Issuing Authorities after the transition period mentioned in the MAA Resolution 2006-2 above, and to propose an appropriate solution for approval by the Committee.

BOD 2007 Final Report
Appendix D – Report on the Activities of the OIML

Report of the Work Group on "Conformity to Type"

The Committee took note of the report given by Mr. Grahame G. Harvey, WG Convener, on the meeting held on October 14, 2006, and instructed the WG to continue its work as proposed during the meeting.

The Committee instructed the Bureau and the TC 3 Secretariat (Metrological control) to review the work and organizational structure of TC 3, including that of its subcommittees and the WG on Conformity to Type.

Positions filled:

The Committee elected Mr. Grahame Harvey (Australia) as CIML Second Vice-President. He will take over his duties immediately.

On the proposal of the CIML President, the Committee appointed Mr. Willem Kool as BIML Assistant Director to fill the position of the retiring Mr. Szilvássy in 2007.

III. Future CIML Meetings

The 42nd CIML Meeting will be hosted by the People's Republic of China in October 2007 in Shanghai, China. The CIML accepted Australia's invitation to hold the 13th Conference and 43rd CIML Meeting in Sydney, Australia, in 2008.

IV. Regional Legal Metrology Organizations

SIM Workshop on Fuel Dispensers

Wayne Stiefel participated in the workshop and made presentations on audit trail security and software developments in OIML and the NWCM. The workshop was held September 15, 2006, at INMETRO Brazil and was attended by 32 representatives from 16 countries: Antigua & Barbuda, Brazil, Chile, Costa Rica, Haiti, Honduras, Jamaica, Mexico, Nicaragua, Paraguai, St. Kitts & Nevis, St. Lucia, St. Vincent, Trinidad & Tobago, United States, and Uruguay. Other topics covered included The Mercosul Draft Directive on Fuel Dispensers – based on OIML R 117 and the Mexican process for prototype fuel dispenser hardware and software approval by CENAM.

Meeting of the SIM General Assembly

ILMG participated in the SIM General Assembly which convened September 16 - 17, 2006, in Rio de Janeiro, Brazil. Dr. Huberto S. Brandi, Director of Scientific and Industrial Metrology at INMETRO Brazil, was elected President. The next SIM General Assembly meeting will be held in September 2007 in Ottawa, Canada.

APLMF Meeting

The 13th APLMF Meeting was held November 15 - 17, 2006, in Singapore. The United States was represented by Dr. Charles Ehrlich, who serves as Chairman of the APLMF Work Group on Mutual Recognition Arrangements. APLMF conducted six training courses/seminars in 2006, including one on the verification of CNG Fuel Dispensers at which the two instructors were from the California Division of Measurement Standards. A seminar on the Singapore Authorized Verifier Scheme was held to announce and describe this new program in Singapore, where private organizations are empowered to conduct verifications under the supervision of the Singapore regulatory authority, SPRING Singapore. A workshop on Metrology of Agricultural Products and Foods was held February 7 - 9, 2007, in Thailand. The Peoples Republic of China announced that it would take over the Presidency and Secretariat of APLMF in 2007. The next meeting of APLMF will be in late October 2007 in Shanghai, China.

Appendix E

Final Report of the
NCWM Associate Member Committee (AMC)

Salt Lake City, UT
Minutes, July 9, 2007

CALL TO ORDER:

Chairman Langford called the meeting to order at 12:12 p.m.

APPROVAL OF JANUARY 21, 2007, MINUTES:

The minutes of the January 21, 2007, meeting were read, Cullen Casey made a motion to approve the minutes, and Bob Reinfried seconded it. A vote was taken, and the minutes were approved.

BOARD OF DIRECTORS REPORT:

Darrell Flocken, the Associate Membership Representative on the NCWM Board of Directors, gave a report about Board activities:

- Automatic temperature compensation is the hot topic of this meeting. Mike Cleary represented the NCWM in a congressional hearing in Washington, DC, a few weeks ago. Since then the NCWM has received several letters from various state representatives voicing their support or opposition to the item.

- Judy Cardin reported that an electronic version of Form 15 is now available on the NCWM website. The form can be completed and submitted online. A few cleanup items are left to complete this task, but they do not impact the use of this form now.

- NIST WMD reported that they have established two directors' workshops to be conducted this year. NIST has also scheduled a Handbook 133 Train-the-Trainer class for later this year.

- The Board has decided to move ahead with a second marketplace survey. While not 100 % complete with the past survey, it was believed they could do the initial development work for the second survey to keep the process moving.

- Management Solutions (Beth) was happy to report that membership levels are up, with current membership of just over 2600. This is the highest level since 2003.

- The Board was asked to develop a position on individual companies or organizations sponsoring NCWM events or individual events occurring at the same time and location as the NCWM conference. The reason for this issue was based on the NCWM's liability and perceived influence - real or not. The Board of Directors did not believe it was their responsibility to limit or prevent such events but agreed these events would not be included in the NCWM agenda and the Conference agenda should include a statement something to the effect that a meeting or event not mentioned in the agenda is not sanctioned by the NCWM. If additional discussions are required, this should be the responsibility of the AMC.

- On a sad note, Darrell Flocken reported that Sam Chappell passed away last week.

BOD 2007 Final Report
Appendix E – Meeting Minutes of the AMC

- To end his report Darrell had some good news; this is his last report as his 3-year term representing the AMC on the Board of Directors ends at the end of this Conference. He would like to thank the AMC for providing him with this opportunity and hopes he met our expectations. Darrell leaves the AMC in the very capable hands of Bob Murnane, our new Board of Directors AMC representative.

FINANCIAL CONDITION

Chairman Langford reported the following fund balance:

Income:	
Balance 1/31/07	$17,999.91
Revenue: 2/1/07 - 6/30/07	345.00
135.00	
120.00	
	75.00
Total Income:	**$18,674.91**
Disbursements:	
2/27/07 Website enhancements	$2,500.00
6/6/07 - 6/30/07 CO Dept of Agriculture training	1,500.00
Total Disbursements:	**$4,000.00**
Ending Balance 6/30/07	**$14,674.91**

$10,000 was set aside for the special event.

AMC FUND DISBURSEMENT REPORTS:

2007 TRAINING FUNDS REPORT
Chairman Langford mentioned a letter from Kristin Macey, Chief, CO Department of Agriculture Measurement Standards, thanking the AMC for the $1500 funds for training. A copy of this letter was made available for anyone to review. (A copy of this letter is printed at the end of the AMC Report, Appendix E.)

TRAINING REQUEST
There were three requests submitted:

1. Craig Leisy, Consumer Affairs Unit, Seattle, WA
   Requested $500 to be used for travel and *per diem* expenses for training and certification for two new weights and measures inspectors.

2. Kirk Robinson, Washington Department of Olympia, WA
   Requested $2084 for the following: $1400 for lodging (*per diem*); $434, travel costs for instructor; $100, training facility rental; and $150, training materials.

3. Charles Carroll, MA Division of Standards
   Requested $1000 to be used for training school held in conjunction with the NEWMA Annual conference.

Chairman Langford suggested that: 1) Craig Leisy's $500 request be denied; however, Craig would be contacted to notify him why his request was denied and give him a chance to resubmit his request for funds for training only; 2) Kirk Robinson's request for $2084 be reduced to $684 for the instructor, training facility rental and training materials; 3) Charles Carroll's $1000 request be approved. Mike Gaspers put Chairman Langford's suggestion in the form of a motion, and Bob Murnane seconded the motion. A vote was taken and the motion passed.

SPECIAL EVENT
A discussion for increasing the Association Membership dues and for increasing the amount given to the special event function was discussed. Darrell Flocken informed the AMC of the number of members for the previous years which were:

Year Members
2003 953
2004 837
2005 829
2006 837
2007 863

Rich Davis made a motion to increase the Association Membership dues by $10, which would raise the Association Membership dues to $25 above the annual dues. Darrell Flocken seconded the motion and the motion passed. Rich Davis made another motion to increase the AMC maximum contribution for the special event from $10,000 to $12,000 or 60 % of the cost, whichever is less. Bob Murnane seconded the motion. A vote was taken and the motion passed.

OLD BUSINESS:

No old business.

NEW BUSINESS:

Dave Wankowski, Kraft Foods Inc., volunteered to fill the vacancy of the AMC member representative on the PDC. Bob Murnane, Seraphin Test Measures, will be the AMC member representative on the BOD.

Non-sanctioned events was discussed. Mike Gaspers make a motion to strongly discourage hospitality suites, and Bob Murnane seconded this motion. A vote was taken and the motion passed by a vote of thirteen to three.

Mike Gaspers was elected to the position of Secretary/Treasurer of the AMC.

Dave Wankowski and Doug Biette were elected to five-year terms on the AMC Board.

ADJOURNMENT:

The meeting was adjourned at 1:00 p.m.

Respectfully submitted,
Stephen Langford, Chair,
Paul Lewis, Secretary-Treasurer

BOD 2007 Final Report
Appendix E – Meeting Minutes of the AMC

Members in Attendance at the
Associate Membership Committee (AMC) Meeting
July 9, 2007

Stephen Langford - Cardinal Scale, Chairman
Chris Guay - Procter & Gamble, Vice Chairman
Paul Lewis - Rice Lake Weighing Systems, Secretary-Treasurer

Doug Biette – Sartorius North America
Cullen Casey – Walz Sclaes
Richard Davis – Georgie-Pacific
Darrell Flocken - Mettler-Toledo
Mike Gaspers – Farmland Foods, Inc.
Jim Hewston – Scale Source
Zina Juroch – Pier 1 Imports
Monica Hammond – DHL Express, Inc.
Tom Herrington - Nestle Foods
Dennis Kolsun – H.J. Heinz Co.
Monte Martinson – Norac, Inc.
Bob Murnane - Seraphin Test Measures
Pete O'Bryan - Foster Farms
Dan Okon – United Parcel Service
Bob Reinfried – Scale Manufacturers Association
Mike Rude – Norac, Inc.
Mark Schwarte – Accu-Sort
Lou Straub - Fairbanks Scales
Dave Wankowski – Kraft Foods Inc.
Nate Wieselquist – Sick, Inc.

*Beth Palys – NCWM Headquarters also attended this meeting

Letter from Kristin Macy

THIS PAGE INTENTIONALLY LEFT BLANK.

Final Report of the
Laws and Regulations Committee

James P. Cassidy, Jr., Chairman
Cambridge, Massachusetts

Reference
Key Number

200 INTRODUCTION

This is the report of the Laws and Regulations Committee (hereinafter referred to as the "Committee") for the 92nd Annual Meeting of the National Conference on Weights and Measures (NCWM). It is based on the Interim Report offered in the NCWM Publication 16, "Committee Reports," testimony at public hearings, comments received from the regional weights and measures associations and other parties, the addendum sheets issued at the Annual Meeting, and actions taken by the membership at the voting session of the Annual Meeting. The Informational items presented below were adopted as presented when this report was approved.

Table A identifies the agenda items in the Report by Reference Key Number, title, and page number. The first three digits of the Reference Key Numbers of the items are assigned from the subject series listed below. Voting items are indicated with a " **V**" after the item number. Items marked with an " **I**" are informational. Items marked with a "**D**" are developing items. The developing designation indicates an item has merit; however, the item is returned to the submitter for further development before any further action is taken by the Committee. Items marked " **W**" have been withdrawn from consideration. Table B lists the appendices to the report, and Table C provides a summary of the results of the voting on the Committee's items and the report in entirety.

This report contains recommendations to amend National Institute of Standards and Technology (NIST) Handbook 130, 2008 Edition, "Uniform Laws and Regulations," or NIST Handbook 133, "Checking the Net Contents of Packaged Goods," Fourth Edition (January 2005). Proposed revisions to the handbook(s) are shown in **bold face print** by ~~striking out~~ information to be deleted and __underlining__ information to be added. New items proposed for the handbooks are designated as such and shown in **bold face print**. Text presented for information only is shown in *italic* print. When used in this report, the term "weight" means "mass."

Subject Series

INTRODUCTION	200 Series
NIST Handbook 130 – General	210 Series
Uniform Laws	220 Series
Weights and Measures Law (WML)	221 Series
Weighmaster Law (WL)	222 Series
Engine Fuels, Petroleum Products, and Automotive Lubricants Inspection Law (EFL)	223 Series
Uniform Regulations	230 Series
Packaging and Labeling Regulation (PLR)	231 Series
Method of Sale Regulation (MSR)	232 Series
Unit Pricing Regulation (UPR)	233 Series
Voluntary Registration Regulation (VRR)	234 Series
Open Dating Regulation (ODR)	235 Series
Uniform National Type Evaluation Regulation (UNTER)	236 Series
Engine Fuels, Petroleum Products, and Automotive Lubricants Regulation (EFR)	237 Series
Examination Procedure for Price Verification	240 Series

L&R Committee 2007 Final Report

Interpretations and Guidelines..250 Series

NIST Handbook 133..260 Series

Other Items..270 Series

Table A
Index to Reference Key Items

Reference Key Number		Title of Item	Page
200		**INTRODUCTION**...	1
232		**METHOD OF SALE REGULATION**...	3
232-1	V	Permissive Temperature Compensation for Refined Petroleum Products and Other Fuels...........	3
232-2	V	Fuel Ethanol Labeling..	10
232-3	I	Biodiesel Labeling..	11
260		**NIST HANDBOOK 133 "CHECKING THE NET CONTENTS OF PACKAGED GOODS"**....	12
260-1	W	2.6. Drained Weight for Glazed or Frozen Seafood...	12
260-2	W	Worksheet for Liquid Volumes..	13
270		**OTHER ITEMS – DEVELOPING ITEMS**..	16
270-1	W	Add to NIST Handbook 130, Method of Sale of Commodities Regulation Section 1.14. Labeling Requirement of Drained Weight for Commodities Packed in a Liquid Medium (foods other than meat or poultry products under USDA jurisdiction)...	16
270-2	W	Amend NIST Handbook 130, Method of Sale Regulation Section 2.13.4. Declaration of Weight..	17
270-3	W	Add Section 2.1.6. to NIST Handbook 130, Interpretations and Guidelines.................................	18
270-4	W	Amend Handbook 133, Chapter 4.7 Polyethylene Sheeting – Test Procedure..............................	23
270-5	I	Amend Section 2.2.1. in Handbook 130 Uniform Engine Fuels Regulation – Premium Diesel Lubricity...	24
270-6	I	Amend Handbook 130 Interpretations and Guidelines Section 2.3.2. Guidelines for the Method of Sale of Fresh Fruits and Vegetables..	26
270-7	D	Amend Handbook 133 Section 2.3, Moisture Allowances to Provide Clearer Guidance.............	30
270-8	D	Laws and Regulations Committee WG on Moisture Loss...	30
270-9	D	Petroleum Subcommittee...	31

Table B
Appendices

Appendix A. L&R Committee Work Group on Moisture Loss..A1

Table C
Voting Results

Reference Key Number	House of State Representatives		House of Delegates		Results
	Yeas	Nays	Yeas	Nays	
232-1	23	16	24	16	Returned to Committee
232-2	40	0	42	0	Passed

Details of all Items
(In order by Reference Key Number)

232 METHOD OF SALE REGULATION

232-1 V Permissive Temperature Compensation for Refined Petroleum Products and Other Fuels

(This item was not adopted and was returned to the Committee)

Sources: The Southern Weights and Measures Association (SWMA), the Western Weights and Measures Association (WWMA), and the Central Weights and Measures Association (CWMA).

Note: This or similar proposals, which have been on the Committee's agenda for several years, were reviewed by each of the regional weights and measures associations. The review process resulted in the submission of several different proposals and numerous comments and suggestions for the Committee to consider. Everyone expressed concern over the scope, cost and impact of establishing a method of sale for petroleum products which required temperature compensation. This subject was widely discussed by the NCWM at public forums dating back more than 30 years. A similar proposal was made by NEWMA as recently as 2000, but the Committee withdrew it in 2001. NEWMA noted at that time that Pennsylvania, New Hampshire, Maine, and Canada permit temperature-compensated sales of products like home heating fuel and retail gasoline. Additional historic and background information is available in previous editions of the Committee's agenda. For recent discussions on this subject see Item 232-1 in the report of the 91st NCWM Annual Meeting in 2006 at www.nist.gov/owm on the Internet. It is also available on a searchable DVD format on NIST Special Publication 979 "Reports of the National Conference on Weights and Measures 1905 to 2006," (November 2006) which is available from the NCWM.

Recommendation: At its 2007 Interim Meeting the Committee received correspondence from consumer groups and other organizations and heard testimony from weights and measures officials, the petroleum industry (including the American Petroleum Institute (API)), consumers and others regarding temperature compensation of refined petroleum products. The Committee appreciates all of the data, discussion and especially the high level of interest. The Committee acknowledges the media attention this item has drawn, and the members were pleased to learn that some agricultural commissioners and other policy makers, as well as some governors and state attorneys general, have expressed interest in temperature compensation.

Proponents for the item spoke of a need to improve the accuracy of measurements of petroleum products because of their cost and of the need to improve accountability, while opponents spoke to the cost of implementing temperature compensation and the potential for confusion in the marketplace. The Committee also was made aware of legislation under consideration in Missouri and Texas that would establish different definitions for a gallon based on the ambient temperature in varied areas of the states. The Committee was especially sensitive to concerns expressed by weights and measures inspectors about the potential cost and increased inspection time they may expend if temperature compensation is allowed in all applications, especially at the retail level.

The Committee duly considered the presentations, discussions, letters, data, media stories, comments received at public hearings and in hallways, and the proposed legislation. The NCWM posted this information at:

http://www.ncwm.net/events/index.cfm?fuseaction=interimagenda07

Following is a list of justifications for adopting a standard that will facilitate the implementation of an orderly yet permissive approach to allowing broader use of temperature compensation in the marketplace:

- Cost of fuel has led to increased consumer and business interest in better methods of measurement, inventory control and accountability. By now everyone has realized or should realize that ambient temperatures are but one factor which impacts the volume of any liquid. Thus, basing a state's temperature-compensation program on regional ambient temperatures is not a technically valid approach to addressing the issue.
- The use of dual-wall storage tanks and deliveries of fuel directly from refineries result in higher temperature product.
- Awareness and concerns over the impact of temperature on the cost of fuel has come about at the same time advances in technology such as electronics and software have made compensation possible in both new and existing measuring devices at lower costs.
- Increased consumer requests that temperature compensation be used, especially in high volume deliveries for improved measurement accuracy.
- The dramatic growth of public interest in recent years is evidenced by articles in many newspapers and widely read magazines such as *Scientific America*. This national conversation about energy has led to greater consumer awareness, as well as interest on the part of political leaders, of energy issues and has contributed to creating an opportunity for change.

After a thorough discussion and polling by its chairman, the Committee was unanimous that it would recommend to the NCWM the adoption of a method of sale for refined petroleum products and other fuels. This would allow industry the option of selling these products on the basis of temperature-compensated sales. While the decision to submit the permissive temperature-compensated method of sale for NCWM consideration was unanimous, the representative from the CWMA supported going forward with the recommendation but did not agree with including retail sales in the scope of the regulation. The Committee ultimately decided it was in the best interest of the U.S. commercial measurement system if the NCWM adopted a standard that would provide guidance to states considering legislation in this area, thus supporting the work of the Specifications and Tolerances Committee, the National Type Evaluation Program (NTEP) and others to develop technical requirements and test procedures for both type approval and field testing for devices equipped with temperature compensation. The Committee believed those efforts were critical to facilitating the introduction of temperature compensation to the marketplace, especially in NTEP states as the NCWM learned there were no retail motor-fuel dispensers available with Certificates of Conformance that included temperature compensation functions.

The following topics/considerations were addressed by the Committee:

1. Temperature compensation was already legal for use in trade unless prohibited by state or local requirements.

The Committee was aware that temperature compensation was already required or permitted in a number of states for vehicle-tank meters, liquefied petroleum gas, and wholesale deliveries to retailers and that it had been used in the marketplace in these applications for decades. At the WWMA Annual Meeting, the State of California reported that for transactions involving 5000 gal or more, purchasers may request temperature compensation; Idaho said that for transactions involving 8000 gal or more, the purchaser had an option to buy, on a yearly basis, temperature-compensated product and that all terminal transactions were temperature compensated; Arizona responded that any transactions involving more than 5000 gal must be compensated for temperature; and currently the State of Hawaii was the only jurisdiction which has taken some action to account for temperature variations in retail sales. The Committee heard enough supportive comments from a broad base of weights and measures directors, inspectors and metrologists to recognize that temperature compensation may find broad acceptance in the marketplace, especially once the potential benefits it offers were realized and implementation costs fall.

The Committee also believed that, unless prohibited by state law, temperature compensation at retail dispensers was already legal in most states. Additionally, the Committee believed it would be difficult to argue against a measurement practice that could only improve the accuracy and reproducibility of a volumetric measurement. The Committee position was that legal metrology must not stand in the way of the marketplace striving to change the way fuels and other products were marketed and sold.

2. Under a permissive approach consumers and businesses will decide where and when to implement temperature compensation.

The Committee was convinced that the marketplace will best determine where and when the benefits from temperature compensation should be implemented to improve accuracy. The Committee recommended the adoption of a method of sale that would allow temperature compensation to be used in sales of petroleum products on a permissive (voluntary) basis, allowing the marketplace (e.g., industry, consumers and other government agencies) to decide if and when it was appropriate to use temperature compensation in specific commercial applications (e.g., sales at truck stops). This recommendation was proposed solely for the purpose of ensuring the delivery of an accurate volume of petroleum at a specific reference temperature. It was not the intent of the Committee to attempt to define a standard energy content of a liter or gallon of gasoline or other engine fuel with this recommendation.

3. Temperature compensation would be permissive, but controlled.

Although the Committee's recommendation allowed for permissive use of temperature compensation, it included mandatory provisions requiring compensation be made by automatic means to ensure the measured quantity was accurately determined. It also defined a temperature-compensated volume for both liters and gallons, requiring the posting of information on dispensers, street signs and on documents to ensure full disclosure and fair competition. Additionally, it required a business location to have all of the devices operating on temperature compensation on a year-round basis unless a written waiver was granted by the Director.

4. The basis of Committee's recommendation was the proposal from the WWMA.

The Committee's recommendation was based on the proposal submitted by the WWMA, which was developed at its 2006 Annual Meeting in Salt Lake City, Utah. The Committee made several amendments to the proposal but found it represented a well-reasoned foundation for the recommendation presented below. The CWMA L&R Committee supported the WWMA's proposal and supported submitting it to the NCWM for a vote. The CWMA agreed with the WWMA that temperature compensation is the most equitable method of sale, which is currently utilized at every step of distribution except for retail sales. Additionally, the CWMA believed the proposal should not be restricted only to petroleum products, but should also include alternative fuels such as E-85, biodiesel and biodiesel blends. The Committee's recommendation incorporated some of the CWMA's suggestions and included additional requirements to address many of the concerns raised issue at the 2007 NCWM Interim Meeting open hearings and discussions. For the purpose of this recommendation the Committee used the definition for "refined petroleum products" as presented in Handbook 130 Uniform Engine Fuels, Petroleum Products, and Automotive Lubricants Inspection Law which reads, "products obtained from distilling and processing of petroleum (crude oil), unfinished oils, recycled oils, natural gas liquids, refinery blend stocks, and other miscellaneous hydrocarbon compounds" with the understanding that its intent was that the requirements would apply when petroleum was blended with other products such as ethanol.

5. Full disclosure will allow informed consumers to make value comparisons.

The Committee believed consumers, when educated through marketing and outreach efforts, will accept new technology and measurement practices. When provided with sound information, consumers will gain confidence that government oversight will prevent deceptive practices. The Committee believed the full disclosure provisions of the method of sale will reduce both unfair competition and consumer confusion. If, for example, a truck stop offers temperature-compensated sales of diesel fuel through high-speed dispensers for truckers, the road signs with price per unit of volume (e.g., gallon or liter) and dispensers must include a declaration that the volume is sold on the basis of temperature compensation. If the price per gallon is higher or lower than the usual price per gallon, consumers will be informed that the volume was compensated to a reference temperature. Several people expressed concern over marketplace confusion if diesel fuel is sold on the basis of both compensated and uncompensated volume. It is incorrect to say that there would be two methods of sale for the same product under this recommendation just as it is inaccurate to say that some consumers will not receive a "full" gallon if temperature compensation is used as some opponents to this method of sale have claimed. The reality is that consumers will be able to compare price per gallon between stations and they will receive a "full" gallon as defined under the Method of Sale of Commodities Regulation. While confusion is possible with any method of sale, the Committee was not deterred by that possibility. If confusion occurs, the proper response is to educate consumers and address any changes identified from the confusion through further refinement of the method of sale. In this application, full disclosure will inform consumers that one product is sold on the basis of temperature compensation and one is not. When consumers are educated, they can make sound value comparisons between these choices just as they already make decisions when choosing between different brand name products, octane ratings, additive offerings, and types of fuels. Business and industry is also well equipped and very experienced in educating its customers whenever it chooses to introduce new products or services; so should they decide to use the method of sale, they are sure to introduce it using an informative marketing effort.

The Committee was urged to clarify that there may be situations in which there is a valid contract where the price is based on the fuel being sold on the basis of uncompensated measurement. The Committee agreed with the comment that if a purchaser operating under such a contract fills up at a location where the dispensers are temperature compensated, the contract should prevail in those transactions. Similarly, the Committee heard from the American Petroleum Institute (API) that it should permit either uncompensated or compensated methods of sale at loading-rack meters when such sales are under contract. The Committee believed its proposal will not interfere with the contracts or understandings that API described.

6. Costs

The Committee heard from some users that the lack of temperature compensation was costing them great sums of money while industry representatives said the cost of equipment and installation will cost industry and, ultimately, consumers even larger amounts of money. The cost of any NCWM action is a concern to the Committee which must defend its actions on both sides of any issue. However, it is very difficult to give each side everything it wants in any recommendation. While the Committee was concerned about cost, it was skeptical of the economic claims from both sides in this debate. For example, at the Interim Meeting one estimate of the cost of implementing temperature compensation dropped nearly $2 billion dollars once industry learned that an alternative technology was available in the marketplace.

That is but one illustration of the weaknesses the Committee saw in cost or damage claims over the years. It dates back to its work in the 1990s on the price verification procedures where some groups claimed that supermarkets were overcharging consumers billions of dollars a year. The Committee never saw data that supported such claims, yet the damage values received wide notice in the media. Some members of the NCWM may remember the claims made during Congressional consideration of the Metric Conversion Act of 1975 that changing to the metric system would cost billions of dollars. In reality those high costs never materialized, which was confirmed through several reliable studies. One reason Congress made conversion to the metric system voluntary was to allow industry to make changes as part of their normal equipment replacement cycle. The automotive industry, for instance, found it cost effective to make the change to metric units when purchasing replacement equipment. Advancements in technology made conversions easier or allowed dual-unit displays on equipment as standard features. These factors were key contributors in reducing costs.

The Committee also heard that no action should be taken pending further studies. The Committee was wary of calls that it take no action pending another study or action by Congress. Each State Director in the NCWM determines whether or not to incorporate what is adopted by the NCWM into his or her state law or regulations, not the Committee. Even states that adopt the Method of Sale of Commodities Regulation by reference or citation can take action to exclude a specific section of a uniform regulation that conflicts with other requirements or policies. As for taking time for additional study, the NCWM record on consideration of the issue of temperature compensation dates back to the mid-1970s and has arisen for consideration every few years since that date. The Committee was aware of the history, the issues, the various points of view, and the potential costs of temperature compensation and believed it was time for the NCWM to move forward on temperature compensation by establishing standards by which this method of sale can be brought into the marketplace on a voluntary, yet controlled, basis.

As one speaker alluded to in his presentation, the marketplace is to some degree "intelligent" in that it helps address many factors through its price-setting function and can generally be trusted to balance costs and prices as well as justify investment in new technology and marketing practices if there is a need, demand or opportunity. A voluntary approach will allow early adopters to develop experience and pull advances in technology into the equipment market while competition and other factors will reduce costs even further if the method of sale is broadly adopted. The Committee believed a permissive approach to temperature compensation turned the choice over to the marketplace where, if consumer demand was sufficient, sellers would make a business decision to invest in the technology and marketing according to the new method of sale when the benefits offset costs.

7. Limiting the option of temperature compensation to specific applications

The Committee received suggestions that temperature compensation be limited to certain applications or not be allowed in retail sales, but it did not hear sufficient justification for taking such positions. Temperature compensation is not new to the commercial measurement system. It is widely used in wholesale transactions in many jurisdictions, and consumers in many states have purchased LPG and oil for heating and other uses for decades on the basis of temperature-compensated sales. No information was presented to the Committee that its use in those applications has been anything but successful. The Committee recognizes that verifying devices with temperature compensation may require additional inspection time and require weights and measures officials to purchase thermometers or other equipment for testing. However, those factors are not sufficient justification to prohibit the marketplace from implementing this method of sale. If a jurisdiction adopts this method of sale and a business decides to use temperature compensation, the weights and measures agency would need to obtain funding to implement appropriate testing procedures to verify devices. However, the Committee would expect that innovation, risk-based testing, and random sampling techniques, as well as technology, would lessen the time required to conduct additional tests just as those factors have reduced the burden of testing many weighing and measuring instruments in the past.

8. Permissive vs. Mandatory Implementation

The Committee heard from the regional associations and others that temperature-compensated sales should be implemented on a permissive basis. The Committee opposed the inclusion of a future mandatory date at this time. The Committee believed temperature-compensated sales should be market driven and that suppliers will conduct sales on a compensated basis when consumers demand it and should not be required to do so before then. The Committee, based on the comments of many jurisdictions, believed the imposition of a mandatory requirement was too burdensome on the industry, requiring upgrades and possibly the replacement of many meters without adequate justification.

The Committee agreed that a mandatory requirement would not be justified at this point in time. The Committee felt it was important to get some form of regulation regarding temperature-compensated sales of petroleum into Handbook 130 and thought that as many barriers as possible should be removed in order to achieve that goal. Although the Committee's recommendation is a permissive requirement for temperature-compensated sales, the Committee was willing to consider establishing future mandatory dates if a justified need was demonstrated after this permissive regulation was implemented and used for a period of time.

9. Comments Reviewed by the Committee

a. The Committee noted that if the proposal was adopted at the 2007 Annual Meeting, it would go into effect January 1, 2008, in the eighteen jurisdictions that indicated they automatically adopt that regulation by reference or citation (see 2006 edition of NIST Handbook 130, "II Uniformity of Laws and Regulations" [page 9] for a list of those states). The Committee also noted that if the recommendation was adopted in July 2007, some jurisdictions might want to delay its implementation or exempt that particular section from being automatically adopted. Since, typically rulemaking takes longer than six months to complete, the Committee debated whether or not it should include a delayed effective date of July 1, 2009, for this regulation.

b. The Committee discussed the subject of unscrupulous retailers artificially heating fuels and the fact that this deceptive practice has occurred from time to time. The State of Arizona actually forbids the practice;

however, the Committee did not address that issue in the following recommendation. The Committee considered if a prohibition on the artificial heating of fuels for the purpose of increasing volume at the time of sale should be added to the recommendation.

c. The Committee asked to receive comments on whether or not the recommendation should allow the state director to grant (and, when justified, revoke) written waivers to some provisions if sufficient justification was provided by the business owner. The Committee discussed whether or not the requirement that all devices that dispense product at a location might result in a hardship for some retailers or difficulties in implementing the new method of sale for specific customers (e.g., over-the-road truckers). For example, if a station decided to sell gasoline and diesel fuel on a temperature-compensated basis but also had a dispenser for K-1 Kerosene (from which limited sales were made), a waiver from the temperature-compensation requirement on all dispensers could be justified. Likewise, if a chain of truck stops decided to sell diesel fuel on a temperature-compensated basis through its high-output dispensers to truckers (e.g., its prime customers), but did not want to implement temperature-compensated sales through its gasoline dispensers, a waiver could also be justified. The purpose of the requirement that all devices at a single location be temperature compensated or not was to prevent a retailer from selling through the compensated or uncompensated dispensers when it benefited him or her. The Committee believed some flexibility was warranted and could make acceptance of the method of sale easier to implement.

At the 2007 Interim Meeting the BOD established an Automatic Temperature Compensation (ATC) Steering Committee to study the issues.

Committee Recommendation: Amend the Method of Sale of Commodities Regulation in Handbook 130 by adding a new Section 2.30. Refined Petroleum Products:

2.30   Refined Petroleum Products – Permissive Temperature Compensation

    2.30.1   Where not in conflict with other statutes or regulations, these products may be sold on the basis of temperature-compensated volume.

    2.30.2   When products are sold on the basis of temperature compensated volume:

        (a) All sales shall be in terms of liters or gallons with the delivered volume adjusted to 15 °C or gallons with the delivered volume adjusted to 60 °F;

        (b) Temperature compensation must be accomplished through automatic means.

    2.30.3.   Full Disclosure Requirements

        2.30.3.1   The primary indicating elements of measuring devices, recording elements, and all recorded or display representations (e.g., receipts, invoices, bills of lading, etc.) shall be clearly and conspicuously marked to show that the product was delivered on the basis of temperature compensated volume;

        2.30.3.2   When a product is offered for sale on the basis of temperature compensated volume, street signs or other advertisements of its unit price must clearly and conspicuously indicate that the volume is temperature compensated.

    2.30.4.   Other Provisions

        2.30.4.1   At a business location all sales on a temperature-compensated basis shall be made continuously and for a period of not less than 12 months (e.g., a person may not engage the automatic temperature compensator on a device only during certain times of the year to prevent the person from taking advantage of temperature compensation).

2.30.4.2 At a business location which offers products for sale on the basis of a temperature compensated volume, all measuring devices shall dispense on the basis of temperature compensated volume (e.g., a person must not operate some devices at a location with automatic temperature compensators and others without compensators to prevent them from taking advantage of temperature variations).

Annotations:

1. As defined in Handbook 130 Engine Fuels, Petroleum Products, and Automotive Lubricants Inspection Law, refined petroleum products are products obtained from distilling and processing of petroleum (crude oil), unfinished oils, recycled oils, natural gas liquids, refinery blend stocks, and other miscellaneous hydrocarbon compounds as well as Biofuels such as E-85 and Biodiesel at various blends.

2. A temperature compensated liter is defined as having a reference temperature of 15 °C and a temperature compensated gallon is defined as 231 cubic inches at a reference temperature of 60 °F;

3. When a product is sold on the basis of a temperature-compensated volume, it is typically called "net" or "net volume," whereas the volume before compensation is called the "gross" or "gross volume."

4. The metric units are shown solely for the purpose of showing metric equivalents in this uniform regulation in this NIST handbook. There is no requirement that dual units be shown in any full disclosure information required under this section.

5. Temperature Compensation may be abbreviated (e.g., Temp Comp, or Compensated to 60 °F) in the interest of space as long as its meaning is clear.

6. The seller is not prohibited from providing both gross and net gallons on receipts, invoices, bills of lading or other documentation as long as it is not misleading or deceptive.

7. A "business location" means a single outlet and should not be interpreted to mean all of the outlets or locations that a business or company operates in a jurisdiction.

Action at 2007 Annual Meeting: The Committee received eighteen comments requesting this item be made Informational to allow the Committee time for additional study and deliberation. The Committee believed the concerns of the commentators were valid but were issues to be addressed by the S&T Committee and NTEP. Additional studies of the method of sale proposal would bring nothing new to the current recommendation that could not be addressed through further revisions next year if needed.

The Committee believed adopting this proposal would provide guidance to policy makers and others currently considering action on temperature compensation at the national, state or local level. Jurisdictions opposing the proposal because their state laws or their policies were against it would not be affected by the adoption of this method of sale because their laws simply prohibited its implementation. The implementation of temperature compensation will be slow primarily because there is no existing nationally approved temperature-compensation device and NIST Handbook 44 must be revised to set forth the specifications, tolerances and other technical requirements for this technology. NTEP will then need to undertake its work where needed. However, the Committee acknowledged that some states may move ahead with their own type approvals to allow temperature compensation. The majority of the Committee believed the proposed method of sale was ready for NCWM adoption as there was not a reasonable justification for delaying the adoption of the proposal as presented. Therefore, the Committee recommended adoption of this item.

This item was subjected to a lengthy discussion at the general voting session and several issues were raised along with calls for further study. On a vote the item did not garner enough support to pass, so the item will be carried forward for reconsideration at the 2008 Interim Meeting.

The ATC Steering Committee will hold a public meeting August 27 - 29, 2007, in Chicago, IL, to address the issues and concerns. The topics to be discussed will include (1) establishing standard product densities; (2) establishing specifications for temperature; (3) response time of thermometer well; (4) referencing 15 °C vs. 60 °F; (5) field test procedures and temperature uncertainties related to the 5 gallon test draft; (6) implementation; (7) labeling/signage/receipts; (8) tax data; (9) temperature data; and (10) NTEP checklists.

For further information on the ATC Steering Committee, please contact:

Don Onwiler, Chairman
Nebraska Weights & Measures Division
PO Box 94757
Lincoln, NE 68509
(402) 471-4292 or at donwiler@agr.ne.gov

232-2　V　Fuel Ethanol Labeling　　　(This item was adopted)

Source: Central Weights and Measures Association (CWMA)

Recommendation: Add a fuel ethanol labeling requirement (Section 2.30.), as recommended by the Petroleum Subcommittee, to the Method of Sale of Commodities Regulation. To ensure agreement, editorially replace the wording in Section 3.8. in the Engine Fuels, Petroleum Products, and Automotive Lubricants Regulation with the following:

> **3.8　E85 Fuel Ethanol**
>
> > **3.8.1　How to Identify E85 Fuel Ethanol.** Fuel ethanol shall be identified as E85.
> >
> > **3.8.2　Labeling Requirements.**
> >
> > > a.　Fuel ethanol shall be labeled with its automotive fuel rating in accordance with 16 CFR Part 306.
> > >
> > > b.　A label shall be posted which states "For Use in Flexible Fuel Vehicles (FFV) Only". This information shall be clearly and conspicuously posted on the upper 50% of the dispenser front panel in a type at least 12.7 mm (½ in) in height, 1.5 mm (1/16 in) stroke (width of type).

Discussion: It was the Committee's view that this proposal did not impose any new requirements. These requirements were adopted by the NCWM and published in the Engine Fuels, Petroleum Products, and Automotive Lubricants Regulation in Handbook 130. However, by adding these requirements in the Method of Sale of Commodities Regulation, the Committee was obligated to give notice that it will become effective on January 1, 2008, in the eighteen jurisdictions which indicate they automatically adopt that regulation by reference or citation (see NIST Handbook 130-2006, "II Uniformity of Laws and Regulations" [page 9] for a list of those states).

Section 2.20. of the Method of Sale of Commodities Regulation in Handbook 130 currently contains requirements for the disclosure of oxygenates in engine fuels. Including requirements for the disclosure of fuel ethanol is consistent with that requirement and should be provided to ensure consumers are fully informed when making purchasing decisions.

While the Committee received numerous comments supporting this item, it also heard some concerns about perceived discrepancies between this item and the Federal Trade Commission's (FTC's) regulation regarding ethanol labeling. These concerns were initially raised when the requirement was being considered for addition to the Engine Fuels, Petroleum Products, and Automotive Lubricants Regulation. In response to the concerns, the Committee reviewed the proposed requirement with the FTC and believes no conflict exists. This proposal has been considered by several regional associations and appears to have the support of most weights and measures officials.

Committee Action at the 2007 Interim and Annual Meetings: At the 2007 Interim Meeting the CWMA and others recommended the Committee separate this item from the Biodiesel Labeling item which is on hold until ASTM finalizes its work on the biodiesel blend specifications (see Item 232-3 below). In response to those suggestions, the Committee agreed to separate the items and recommended the labeling requirement for fuel ethanol be adopted at the 2007 NCWM Annual Meeting. One comment suggested the proposal be amended to clarify that only the maximum volume percentage of ethanol need be declared, but the Committee believed that most officials understood that was the intent of the requirement. The Committee did not make any changes to the proposal above so it would not conflict with the current requirement in the Engine Fuels Regulation. The day after the Committee's discussion, the Petroleum Subcommittee met and began a review of the Engine Fuels, Petroleum Products, and Automotive Lubricants Regulation, which would include this section. The Petroleum Subcommittee made substantive changes to the recommended language at the Annual Meeting and the NCWM adopted the new language and directed NIST to revise Section 3.8. of the Engine Fuel Regulation to maintain consistency between the two sections.

232-3 I Biodiesel Labeling

Source: Central Weights and Measures Association (CWMA)

Recommendation: Add the biodiesel labeling requirements contained in Handbook 130 Engine Fuels, Petroleum Products, and Automotive Lubricants Regulation to the Method of Sale of Commodities Regulation:

<u>2.XX Biodiesel</u>

<u>2.XX.1 Identification of Product. – Biodiesel and biodiesel blends shall be identified by the capital letter B followed by the numerical value representing the volume percentage of biodiesel fuel. (Examples: B10; B20; B100)</u>

<u>2.XX.2 Labeling of Retail Dispensers Containing Between 5 % and 20 % Biodiesel. – Each retail dispenser of biodiesel blend containing more than 5 % and up to and including 20 % biodiesel shall be labeled with either:</u>

<u>2.XX.2.1 The capital letter B followed by the numerical value representing the volume percentage of biodiesel fuel and ending with "biodiesel blend." (Examples: B10 biodiesel blend; B20 biodiesel blend), or;</u>

<u>2.XX.2.2 The phrase "biodiesel blend between 5 % and 20 %" or similar words.</u>

<u>2.XX.3 Labeling of Retail Dispensers Containing More Than 20 % Biodiesel. – Each retail dispenser of biodiesel or biodiesel blend containing more than 20 % biodiesel shall be labeled with the capital letter B followed by the numerical value representing the volume percentage of biodiesel fuel and ending with either "biodiesel" or "biodiesel blend." (Examples: B100 Biodiesel; B60 Biodiesel Blend)</u>

<u>2.XX.4 Documentation for Dispenser Labeling Purposes. – The retailer shall be provided, at the time of delivery, with a declaration of the volume percent biodiesel on an invoice, bill of lading, shipping paper, or other similar document. This documentation is for dispenser labeling purposes only; it is the responsibility of any potential blender to determine the amount of biodiesel in the diesel fuel prior to blending.</u>

<u>2.XX.5 Exemption. – Biodiesel blends containing 5 % or less biodiesel by volume are exempted from requirements 2.XX.1 through 2.XX.4.</u>

Discussion: It is the Committee's view that this proposal did not impose any new requirements. However, by including these requirements in the Method of Sale of Commodities Regulation, the Committee was obligated to give notice that the requirements will become effective on January 1 of the year following adoption in the eighteen jurisdictions which indicate they automatically adopt that regulation by reference or citation (see the 2006 edition of NIST Handbook 130, "II Uniformity of Laws and Regulations" [page 9] for a list of those states). These requirements have already been adopted and are published in the Engine Fuels, Petroleum Products, and Automotive Lubricants Regulation in Handbook 130.

Section 2.20. of the Method of Sale of Commodities Regulation in Handbook 130 currently contains requirements for the disclosure of oxygenates in gasoline blends. Including requirements for the disclosure of biodiesel and biodiesel blends is consistent with this practice and should be required to ensure consumers are fully informed when making purchasing decisions.

The Committee received numerous comments in support of this item and heard from the National Biodiesel Board (NBB) that, in general, supported this item. However, the NBB requested the Committee keep this item on its agenda as an information item until ASTM finalizes its biodiesel specifications. Waiting for the ASTM biodiesel standard before moving this item forward for a vote will ensure there is no conflict with those specifications.

At its 2006 Annual Meeting, the WWMA L&R Committee received no comments regarding this item. The WWMA supported the NBB request to keep this item as Informational pending ASTM action. The WWMA concurred that waiting for adoption of the ASTM specifications will prevent conflicts in the final labeling requirement for biodiesel. At a recent CWMA meeting, a few comments were received that the biodiesel label requirement should include percentages below 5 %. An update on activity within ASTM to develop a stability specification for B 100 was provided. After negative votes were addressed, ballots were circulated to add a B 5 limit to the D 975 diesel specification and to establish a B 20 specification.

Committee Action at the 2007 Interim and Annual Meetings: At the 2007 Interim Meeting, the CWMA and others recommended the Committee keep this proposal on hold until ASTM finalized its work on the biodiesel blend specifications. In response to those suggestions, the Committee agreed to separate this item from the Fuel Ethanol requirements and carried this item forward as an information item. At the Annual Meeting, several people called for this item to be presented for a vote at the 2008 Annual Meeting and encouraged the Petroleum Subcommittee to encourage all stakeholders to move quickly to resolve their concerns so this important consumer protection requirement can be adopted by the NCWM.

260   NIST HANDBOOK 133 "CHECKING THE NET CONTENTS OF PACKAGED GOODS"

260-1   W   2.6. Drained Weight for Glazed or Frozen Seafood

Source: Northeast Weights and Measures Association (NEWMA)

Proposal: Amend Section 2.6 Drained Weight for Glazed or Frozen Foods of NIST Handbook 133 as indicated in *italics:*

1. 2.6 Drained Weight for Glazed or Frozen **Sea**foods.
2. How is the drained weight of frozen ~~shrimp and crabmeat~~ **seafood** determined?
3. Change all references to shrimp and crabmeat to just the word "**seafood**."
4. Delete the glazed section procedure.

Discussion: At its 2006 Interim Meeting, NEWMA addressed the following problems and questions concerning the proposed changes to Section 2.6 of Handbook 133:

1. If the intent was to apply Section 2.6 to just seafood, the heading should just say Frozen Seafoods. It was the opinion of NEWMA that this was the intent. If the intent was to apply this to all frozen food, which is a

very broad category, then the Committee needed to look at the intent of this section. Does it apply to frozen vegetables?

2. The procedure paragraph was too specific. It used just shrimp and crabmeat as examples. It should be generalized by using the term "frozen seafood."

3. The glazed section was not needed. The immersion method will work for glazed products. However, if the committee felt this method was needed, then an editorial change needed to be made. The heading says glazed raw seafood and fish and the next sentence starts that way. The next sentence ended saying, frozen glazed food product. The question was, which one is it – seafood and fish or frozen food products? Does this section cover glazed chicken wings, which is not seafood?

4. If an item was not labeled glazed even though it might be glazed, how would the inspector test the product? It is very hard to tell glazed from simply frozen. Immersion works for both. Supermarkets repack large bags of shrimp and scallops into smaller bags and do not take the tare for the glazing or mark the bags "glazed."

Committee Action at the 2007 Interim Meeting: The Committee withdrew this proposal because it believed the guidance on testing glazed and frozen foods contained in NIST Handbook 133 was consistent with the test procedures prescribed by the Food and Drug Administration.

260-2   W   Worksheet for Liquid Volumes

Proposal: Amend Section 3.2 Gravimetric Test Procedure for Liquids of NIST Handbook 133 to add a worksheet for testing packages labeled by liquid volume.

Source: Central Weights and Measures Association (CWMA)

The proposed worksheet shown on the following page was reformatted from a worksheet created by the CWMA in landscape format. It has been converted to portrait format for use in gravimetric testing as described below.

The CWMA believed the worksheet is a necessary inspection tool for gravimetric testing of packages labeled by liquid volume. The worksheet is used for determining average density, nominal gross weight, converting the MAV from liquid volume to mass units, and converting the average error back to labeled units of volume. A worksheet was included in the third edition of NIST Handbook 133, but was not included in the fourth edition. This proposal is to add the worksheet, with improvements, to the fourth edition of NIST Handbook 133. The new worksheet is one page instead of two. It was modified to provide the added benefit of helping the inspector identify the largest labeled declaration (i.e., fl oz vs. decimal pt vs. ml) and using that declaration to determine the nominal gross weight for the packages.

The worksheet was tested in Nebraska and proved to be an effective and vital tool for package inspectors. The CWMA believed this functional and simple worksheet in Handbook 133 will promote more inspection of packages labeled by liquid volume. Many inspectors currently shy away from those types of packages because they are intimidated by the added complexity of the procedure. This worksheet will greatly reduce that complexity to a process of simply following the steps.

The CWMA believed the only downside of adding the worksheet to the handbook was that, if adopted, it needed to be published in the handbook.

Committee Action at the 2007 Interim Meeting: While the Committee recognized the value of this and other similar worksheets in conducting package inspection, it represented but one way information can be organized and documented to complete the tests. Laptop computers, for example, are gaining wider acceptance and their software can provide similar step-by-step guidance to aid its users. Comments to the Committee at the 2007 Interim Meeting indicated that, while it would be helpful for officials to have worksheets and checklists to use, most officials do not want them added to the printed version of NIST Handbook 133. One reason for not including such forms in the handbook was that if a state adopts the handbook in its entirety, there may be situations where, if the forms or exact steps specified in the handbook are not used or followed (even when they provide similar results), the official could be criticized or have his determinations challenged. The Committee decided to explore creating an Internet site to post Handbook 133 information, references, and even software to assist officials. The Committee agreed the worksheet was useful but decided to withdraw the proposal and pursue the idea of establishing a NIST HB 133 Reference Center on the Internet where documents such as this proposal can be posted.

Worksheet for Packages Labeled by Volume When Using Gravimetric Test Procedure

Label Declaration	Converted to Fluid Ounce	Largest Declaration (Y=Yes, N=No)		Firm:
				Date:
				Commodity:

		1st Package	2nd Package	3rd Package	4th Package	5th Package
1. Gross Weight						
2. Tare Wt	$R_t =$					
Net Wt	$R_c =$					
3. Flask Wt (full)				**Converting MAV to Decimal Pounds**		
4. Flask Wt (empty, wetted)				13. MAV in fl oz (Table 2-6)		
5. Wt of Liquid (step 3 - 4)				14. MAV in lb (step 13 x step 11)		
6. Volume of Flask (fl oz)				**Converting Average Error to Fluid Ounces**		
Temperature of Liquid				15. Avg. Error in lb (Box 18 x Box 2 of Test Report)		
				16. Avg. Error in fl oz (step 15 ÷ step 11)		
7. Liquid Density (step 5 ÷ step 6)						
8. Range of Densities						
9. Are densities within 1 scale division? Yes No						
(If no, use volumetric procedure in Sec. 3.3)						
10. Average Tare Wt (average of step 2)						
11. Average Liquid Density (average of step 7)						
12. Nominal Gross Weight (step 11 x largest labeled volume*) + step 10						
* Use largest labeled volume converted to fl oz from top of page.						

L&R Committee 2007 Final Report

270 OTHER ITEMS – DEVELOPING ITEMS

INTRODUCTION

The NCWM established a mechanism to disseminate information about emerging issues which have merit and are of national interest. Developing items have not received sufficient review by all parties affected by the proposals or may be insufficiently developed to warrant review by the NCWM L&R Committee. The Developing items listed are currently under review by at least one regional association, subcommittee, or work group (WG).

The Developing items are marked according to the specific NIST Handbook into which they fall – Handbook 130 or Handbook 133. The Committee encourages interested parties to examine the proposals included in the appendices and to send their comments to the contact listed in each part.

The Committee asks that the regional weights and measures associations, subcommittees, and WGs continue their work to develop fully each proposal. Should an association, subcommittee, or WG decide to discontinue work on a Developing item, the Committee asks that it be notified. When the status of an item changes because the submitter withdraws the item, the item will be listed in a table below. For more details on items moved from the Developing Items list to the Committee's main agenda, refer to the new reference number in the main agenda.

270-1 W Add to NIST Handbook 130, Method of Sale of Commodities Regulation Section 1.14. Labeling Requirement of Drained Weight for Commodities Packed in a Liquid Medium (foods other than meat or poultry products under USDA jurisdiction)

Source: Western Weights and Measures Association (WWMA)

Proposal: Add Section 1.14. "Labeling Requirement of Drained Weight for Commodities Packed in a Liquid Medium (foods other than meat or poultry products under USDA jurisdiction) ."

Add Section 1.14. to read as follows:

> 1.14 Labeling Requirement of Drained Weight for Commodities Packed in a Liquid Medium. – Drained weight is the appropriate method of sale for products packed in a medium which is inedible or invariably discarded. Food items such as, but not limited to: wet pack shrimp, lobster meat, crabmeat, clams, olives, mushrooms, bamboo shoots, water chestnuts, cocktail onions, roasted peppers, and artichokes shall be labeled with a drained weight declaration.
>
> (a) Drained weight is the weight of the solid food in a container after the packing medium has been drained away.
>
> (b) Packing medium includes water, brine, and acid based liquids. Packing medium should not be construed to include oil based marinades which are generally considered part of the product.

Background: In 1978 the Food and Drug Administration published the Fair Packaging and Labeling Act with interpretations and guidelines. FDA Guide 7563 states that drained weight is the appropriate way to list net weight of contents for products packed in a medium which is inedible or invariably discarded. It lists as examples food items like wet pack shrimp, green olives, ripe olives, canned mushrooms, canned clams, and canned artichokes. Furthermore under Section 403 (d) of the Federal Food, Drug, and Cosmetic Act, a food is considered misbranded if its container is so made, formed, or filled as to be misleading. The FDA guide states it would be regarded as deceptive and in conflict with Section 403 (d) to replace part of the food in the container with excessive packing medium. This is true whether or not the label bears an accurate statement of the drained weight of the food.

Some net weight declarations accurately reflect the usable content while other declarations include the weight of the packing medium, causing an unfair business advantage and making value comparison impossible for the consumer. As markets have changed and more value-added products are being made available to consumers, it is important to specify labeling requirements in order that businesses may compete equally and consumers may have adequate information to facilitate value comparisons. In addition, consumers rely on the weight declarations when deciding which products to buy for recipes and for dietary purposes.

This proposal was initiated because of a consumer complaint.

Discussion: The WWMA L&R Committee received no comments on this item. The WWMA supported forwarding this item, as submitted, to the NCWM L&R Committee for placement on its agenda. The WWMA requested that NIST coordinate discussions with the Federal Food and Drug Administration (FDA) for review and concurrence.

At the 2006 CWMA Interim Meeting, an industry representative mentioned that the wording of the item was problematic because it expected the regulatory jurisdiction to make a judgment call regarding packing medium which is inedible or invariably discarded. Furthermore, the wording was very open-ended with respect to the products covered by this method of sale. Comment from the group was to look at past conference reports in relation to canned clams as guidance.

Committee Action at the 2007 Interim Meeting: The Committee withdrew this proposal because it believed the guidance on testing these products, which is contained in NIST Handbook 133, was consistent with the test procedures prescribed by the Food and Drug Administration and the U.S. Department of Agriculture.

270-2 W Amend NIST Handbook 130, Method of Sale Regulation Section 2.13.4. Declaration of Weight

Source: Western Weights and Measures Association (WWMA)

Proposal: Amend Handbook 130, Method of Sale Regulation Section 2.13.4. "Declaration of Weight." as follows:

> For the purpose of this regulation, <u>when D is not known</u> the minimum density <u>used to calculate the target net weight</u> shall be 0.92 g/cm³ ~~(when D is not known)~~. <u>For products labeled "High Density," "HD," or similar wording, the minimum density (D) used to calculate the target net weight shall be 0.95 g/cm³</u>

Background: Some manufacturers of polyethylene bags labeled as "High Density" or "HD" have been found to package and label products whose labeled net weights met calculated target net mass/weights when employing a factor of 0.92 g/cm³. When a density factor of 0.95 g/cm³ was used, as appropriate, in the calculation for high-density polyethylene materials, products commonly failed to meet the calculated target net mass/weight. Further inspection typically revealed that one or more of the labeled width, thickness, or count statements were inaccurate.

Some manufacturers appeared aware that weights and measures officials were restricted to testing high-density film using the 0.92 g/cm³ value because the actual density value was not stated on the product label and the existing procedural guidelines did not address high-density polyethylene materials. When testing at manufacturing locations, weights and measures officials were able to obtain information regarding the density of the product from the manufacturer. However, at distributor locations, density information was not available and officials tested using the 0.92 g/cm³ designated in Handbooks 130 and 133.

Conversations with manufacturers and review of technical data sheets from various manufacturers indicated that 0.95 g/cm³ is an acceptable minimum density value for HD labeled polyethylene film.

Discussion: The WWMA supported forwarding this item, as amended below, to the L&R Committee for consideration on its agenda.

Recommendation: Amend Handbook 130 Method of Sale Regulation Section 2.13.4. Declaration of Weight as follows:

> For the purpose of this regulation, <u>when the density (D) is not known</u> the minimum density <u>used to calculate the target net weight</u> shall be 0.92 g/cm³ ~~(when D is not known)~~. <u>For products labeled "High</u>

Density," "HD," or similar wording, when D is not known, the minimum density factor used to calculate the target net weight shall be 0.95 g/cm³

When the polyethylene commodity package is labeled with a specific density, the labeled density factor shall be used to calculate the target net weight. If the official determines that the labeled density information is not accurate, the minimum density factors above shall be used to calculate the target net weight.

Committee Action at the 2007 Interim Meeting: The Committee withdrew this proposal because industry representatives supporting the proposal did not agree on the density used by most manufacturers to produce products typically labeled "high-density polyethylene." A state association of film extruders and converters wrote that a density of 0.96 gm/cm³ or higher was generally accepted as the "industry" standard for "high density" sheeting while a letter from a company in that state indicated that resins having densities between 0.946 gm/cm³ to 0.948 gm/cm³ would also be considered to fall under that designation. The Committee believed any proposal to establish a national standard for a product identity should have the support of a large number of manufacturers across the nation. The Committee noted that one significant weakness in this proposal was that an unscrupulous manufacturer could avoid its provisions by simply calling its product by another undefined term. It is unlikely that could be prohibited by saying the official believed it constituted "similar wording" because the language was vague.

270-3 W Add Section 2.1.6. to NIST Handbook 130, Interpretations and Guidelines

Source: Western Weights and Measures Association (WWMA)

Proposal: Add Section 2.1.6. to NIST Handbook 130 Interpretations and Guidelines as follows:

2.1.6 Labeling Requirements for Variable Weight Produce Items Sold in Clear Plastic Bags

Interpretation:

For products, such as broccoli crowns, that are traditionally sold by variable weight as bulk produce items, it is not necessary that these produce items, when single or multiple units are packaged or wrapped in plastic film or bags, be marked with a net weight, unit price, and total price at the time the product is offered for retail sale. The FDA interpretation allows the determination of net weight at the point of sale. Also, a disclaimer statement on the package of "To be weighed at or before time of sale" is required consumer notification, assuming there are scales at the point of sale. In addition, the retail price per weight must be displayed within a reasonable distance to the product when the product is displayed for the consumer at the store level. The customer must be provided with the net weight, unit price, and the total price at the time of sale.

Issue:

The NIST Weights and Measures Division (WMD) has received numerous requests for information regarding the labeling of produce items offered for sale in plastic bags. The bags may be "zip-lock" or not, may be open or closed, and may or may not have some product labeling on the bag. Industry and regulatory officials have requested guidance concerning the packaging and labeling requirements as they apply to these products when offered for sale. A similar issue was raised regarding bunches of bananas wrapped in plastic bags and offered for sale.

Background:

WMD staff reviewed the Uniform Weights and Measures Law, the Uniform Packaging and Labeling Regulation in Handbook 130, and the Food, Drug, and Cosmetic Act. An exemption to some labeling requirements was found in 21 CFR Part 101 that specifically addresses wrapped clusters of bananas. The Food, Drug, and Cosmetic Act preempts state laws where state laws are not identical to the Act for the products covered by the Act. The Food and Drug Administration (FDA) was consulted to obtain their interpretation regarding this issue. The FDA exemption and interpretation are reported below.

Summary:

The Food, Drug, and Cosmetic Act contains a specific exemption to some labeling requirements for wrapped clusters of bananas and allows the net weight to be determined at the time of sale (see wording below). The FDA reported that the exemption probably was written specifically for wrapped clusters of bananas because, most likely, bananas were the only produce item using that method of packaging at the time the exemption was requested (around 1964). The FDA indicated that the sale of other produce items in plastic is analogous to the sale of wrapped clusters of bananas; therefore, the exemption described in 21 CFR Part 100 also applies to other produce items, such as table grapes and broccoli crowns, for example.

References:

The Food, Drug, and Cosmetic Act (FDC Act)   21 CFR, Title 21, Part 101, Subpart G, Section 101.100 (h) provides an explicit statement as it applied to bananas. 21 CFR Title 21, Part 101, Section 101.100 addresses exemptions from food labeling requirements. The text for the exemption is provided below. The exemption mentioned below is to FDC Act Section 403(e)(2), which states that a food package shall be deemed to be misbranded unless it bears a label containing an accurate statement of quantity of contents.

21 CFR Title 21, Part 101, Subpart G, Section 101.100 (h)(3):

> "(i) Wrapped clusters (consumer units) of bananas of nonuniform weight intended to be unpacked from a master carton or container and weighed at or before the point of retail sale in an establishment other than that where originally packed shall be exempt from the requirements of Section 403(e)(2) of the Act during introduction and movement in interstate commerce and while held for sale prior to weighing:
>
> Provided that
> The master carton or container bears a label declaration of the total net weight; and the individual packages bear a conspicuous statement "To be weighed at or before the time of sale" and a correct statement setting forth the weight of the wrapper; using such term as "wrapper tare ___ ounce", the blank being filled in with the correct average weight of the wrapper used.
>
> Provided further, that it is the practice of the retail establishment to weigh the individual packages either prior to or at the time of retail sale.
>
> The act of delivering the wrapped clusters (consumer units) during the retail sale without an accurate net weight statement or alternatively without weighing at the time of sale shall be deemed an act which results in the product's being misbranded while held for sale. Nothing in this paragraph shall be construed as requiring net-weight statements for clusters (consumer units) delivered into institutional trade, provided that the master container or carton bears the required information."

The Act provides an exemption for Identity statements under specified conditions:

Identity:

> "21 Code of Federal Regulations 101.100 (h) (3) for non-meat and non-poultry foods specifically exempts packages from identity statements if the identity of the commodity 'can easily be identified through the wrapper or container'"

~~"A statement of identity is not required if the identity of the product can easily be identified through the wrapper or container. This exemption does not apply to meat and poultry."~~

~~Presently, the NIST Handbook 130 Uniform Packaging and Labeling Regulation addresses responsibility statement requirements as applicable only to packages "kept, offered, or sold at other than the premises where packed" and, furthermore, provides an exemption to quantity statements on packaged commodities intended to be weighed prior to or at time of sale.~~

~~Responsibility:~~

~~UPLR Section 5 states:~~

~~"Any package kept, offered or exposed for sale, or sold, at any place other than the premises where packed shall specify conspicuously on the label of the package the name and address of the manufacturer, packer or distributor."~~

~~This exempts those packages 'kept, offered or exposed for sale, or sold' on the premises where packed from the need for a responsibility statement. When retailers remove wrapped clusters of produce from a shipping container, they often inspect the packages for quality and make adjustments such as removing damaged product before putting them in a bulk display; they are, for all practical purposes, repackaging the produce and assuming responsibility for it.~~

~~Quantity (Exemption for Random Weight Packages): UPLR Section 11.26 states:~~

~~"Individual packaged commodities put up in variable weights and sizes for sale intact, and intended to be weighed and marked with the correct quantity statement prior to or at the time of retail sale, are exempt from a declaration of net quantity."~~

~~"Random weight packages that will be weighed at the time of sale do not need a quantity statement. This regulation does not address package closure and the exemption is not dependent on the package being open or closed."~~

Background/Discussion: In recent years more and more produce items are being packed in clear plastic wrappers of various sizes in order to maintain the integrity and sanitation of the product (i.e., clusters of grapes or broccoli crowns). These products are being shipped to retail stores in fully labeled non-consumer containers. The retail stores take the plastic wrapped produce out of the boxes and stack it in bulk retail displays on the produce counter, advertising it for sale for a certain price per pound. The consumer selects the amount desired and brings it to the checkout counter where it is weighed and the total price is determined.

This interpretation recognizes and clarifies the labeling requirements for an existing retail trade practice that is becoming more and more common. It provides for uniform labeling guidance for both industry and enforcement officials.

NIST Handbook 130 "Uniform Packaging and Labeling Regulation" requires packaged commodities to provide accurate and adequate information as to **identity, quantity** of contents, and the name and address of a **responsible party**. However, if certain conditions exist, there are exemptions from these requirements, as cited under the proposed "Reference" section above.

The WWMA received no comments on this item and supported this item as amended below:

Add Section 2.1.6. to NIST Handbook 130 Interpretations and Guidelines as follows:

> 2.1.6. Labeling Requirements for Variable Weight Produce Items Sold in Clear Bags or Wrapping.

Issue: The NIST Weights and Measures Division (WMD) received numerous requests for information regarding correct labeling of produce items offered for sale in clear bags or overwrapped in clear sheeting. Such bags may or may not have a "zip-lock" feature, may be open or closed, and the bags or sheeting may or may not have some product labeling. Industry and regulatory officials requested guidance concerning packaging and labeling requirements as they apply to these products when offered for sale. A similar issue was raised regarding bunches of bananas wrapped in plastic bags and offered for sale.

Background: WMD staff reviewed the Uniform Weights and Measures Law, the Uniform Packaging and Labeling Regulation (UPLR) in Handbook 130, and the Food, Drug, and Cosmetic Act (FDC Act). A specific exemption to quantity statement labeling requirements is established in Title 21 Code of Federal Regulations (CFR) Part 101, specifically addressing wrapped clusters of bananas. An exemption to identity statement labeling requirements for non-meat and non-poultry products is also established in 21 CFR Part 101. Additional exemptions to responsibility and quantity statements, under specific conditions, are established in the UPLR.

The Food, Drug, and Cosmetic Act preempts state laws when such state laws are not identical to the Act for any products covered by the Act. The Food and Drug Administration (FDA) was consulted to obtain its interpretation regarding this issue. The FDA exemption and interpretation are reported below:

> **Interpretation:** The Food, Drug, and Cosmetic Act contains a specific exemption from quantity statement labeling requirements for wrapped clusters of bananas and allows the net weight to be determined at the time of sale (see wording below). The FDA reported that the exemption was written specifically for wrapped clusters of bananas because, most likely, bananas were the only produce commodity commonly distributed under that method of packaging at the time the exemption was requested (around 1964). The FDA indicated that the sale of other produce items in clear wrapping or bags is analogous to the sale of wrapped clusters of bananas; therefore, the exemption described in 21 CFR Part 100 also applies to other produce items, such as table grapes and broccoli crowns.
>
> Consequently, for products traditionally sold by variable weight as bulk produce items, it is not required that these produce items, when single or multiple units are packaged or wrapped in clear film or bags, be marked with a net weight, unit price, and total price at the time the product is offered for retail sale. The FDA interpretation allows the determination of net weight at the point of sale, provided a scale is available to weigh the commodity at the point of sale. A disclaimer statement on the package stating, "To be weighed at or before time of sale" is required consumer notification. In addition, the retail price per unit of weight is typically displayed to the consumer within a reasonable distance of the product display at the retail store. The customer must be provided with the net weight, unit price, and the total price at the time of sale.
>
> **References:** The Food, Drug, and Cosmetic Act (FDC Act) 21 CFR Title 21, Part 101, Subpart G, Section 101.100 (h) provides an explicit statement applicable to the sale of bananas. 21 CFR, Part 101, Section 101.100 addresses exemptions from food labeling requirements (text provided below). The exemption is from FDC Act Section 403(e)(2), which states that a food package shall be deemed to be misbranded if it does not bear a label containing an accurate statement of quantity of contents.
>
> 21 CFR Title 21, Part 101, Subpart G, Section 101.100 (h)(3) states:
>
> "(i) Wrapped clusters (consumer units) of bananas of nonuniform weight intended to be unpacked from a master carton or container and weighed at or before the point of retail sale in an establishment other than that where originally packed shall be exempt from the requirements of Section 403(e)(2) of the Act during introduction and movement in interstate commerce and while held for sale prior to weighing:
>
> Provided that
> The master carton or container bears a label declaration of the total net weight; and the individual packages bear a conspicuous statement "To be weighed at or before the time of sale" and a correct

statement setting forth the weight of the wrapper; using such term as "wrapper tare _ _ounce", the blank being filled in with the correct average weight of the wrapper used.

Provided further, that it is the practice of the retail establishment to weigh the individual packages either prior to or at the time of retail sale.

The act of delivering the wrapped clusters (consumer units) during the retail sale without an accurate net weight statement or alternatively without weighing at the time of sale shall be deemed an act which results in the product's being misbranded while held for sale. Nothing in this paragraph shall be construed as requiring net-weight statements for clusters (consumer units) delivered into institutional trade, provided that the master container or carton bears the required information."

As discussed above, the FDA indicated that the sale of other produce items in clear wrappings or bags is analogous to the sale of wrapped clusters of bananas, and an exemption to quantity statement requirements applies to other produce items, such as table grapes and broccoli crowns.

The FDC Act provides an exemption from identity statement requirements under specified conditions:

Identity: 21 CFR Section 101.100 (b) (3) for non-meat and non-poultry foods specifically exempts packages from identity statement requirements if the identity of the commodity "can easily be identified through the wrapper or container."

"A statement of identity is not required if the identity of the product can easily be identified through the wrapper or container. This exemption does not apply to meat and poultry."

NIST Handbook 130 Uniform Packaging and Labeling Regulation:

Presently, the NIST Handbook 130 Uniform Packaging and Labeling Regulation (UPLR) addresses responsibility statement requirements as applicable only to packages "kept, offered…or sold at…other than the premises where packed" and, furthermore, provides an exemption to quantity statements on packaged commodities intended to be weighed prior to or at time of sale:

Responsibility: UPLR Section 5 states:

"Any package kept, offered or exposed for sale, or sold, at any place other than the premises where packed shall specify conspicuously on the label of the package the name and address of the manufacturer, packer or distributor."

The responsibility statement requirement in UPLR Section 5 applies only to packages sold from other than the premises where packed. Conversely, when offered, exposed, and/or sold from the premises where packed, the responsibility statement requirement does not apply. When retailers remove wrapped clusters of produce from a shipping container, they often inspect the packages for quality and make adjustments such as removing damaged product before rewrapping and offering the packages for sale. In doing so, these retailers are repackaging the produce and assuming responsibility for it. In such circumstances, packages need not be labeled with a responsibility statement.

Quantity (Exemption for Random Weight Packages): UPLR Section 11.26 states:

"Individual packaged commodities put up in variable weights and sizes for sale intact, and intended to be weighed and marked with the correct quantity statement prior to or at the time of retail sale, are exempt from a declaration of net quantity."

Random weight packages that are to be weighed at the time of sale are not required to be labeled with a quantity statement. This regulation does not address package closure and the exemption is not dependent on the package being open or closed.

Summary:

Variable weight produce commodities sold in clear bags or sheeting are exempt from specific package labeling requirements under specific conditions as follows:

- Exempt from identity statement requirement when the product identity can be readily determined through the packaging;
- Exempt from responsibility statement requirement when packaged or repackaged upon the premises where kept, offered, exposed for sale, or sold;
- Exempt from quantity statement requirement when all of the following applies:
  - Labeled with the statement, "To be weighed at or before the time of sale"
  - Labeled with a statement, "Wrapper tare _ ounce" or similar wording
  - The retailer has approved scale(s) in operation at the point of sale
  - The retailer weighs the commodity and provides net weight information at the time of sale.

Committee Action at the 2007 Interim Meeting: The Committee withdrew this proposal because it believed offering produce for sale in clear plastic bags for which the net weight is determined at the time of sale (e.g., over a point-of-sale system) is an accepted method of sale. It was the Committee's view that this method of sale benefits consumers because, if tare is accurately deducted, they are more likely to receive net weight at time of sale because the loss of weight from prepackaged produce due to moisture loss will not be a factor. The Committee believed that signage adjacent to the display can be used to provide identity, unit price and other information. The Committee recognized that retailers will likely apply a small label to the package which will include a Price Look-Up or Bar Code to assist consumers and store personnel to identify and compute the total price for the product and did not believe the addition of this type of label prevented the package from being considered to be packaged in a "clear plastic bag." Similarly the Committee would not object to the packaging if it bore the statement "To be weighed at time of sale," UPC label, or open dating information. The Committee reminded retailers they are responsible for ensuring net weight is provided in this type of weighing transaction so accurate tare determination and deduction are required.

270-4 W Amend Handbook 133, Chapter 4.7 Polyethylene Sheeting – Test Procedure

Proposal: Amend Handbook 133, Chapter 4.7 Polyethylene Sheeting – Test Procedure

Amend asterisked footnote below Step 3 as follows:

> *Determined by ASTM Standard D 1505-98 <u>(or latest issue)</u> "Standard Method of Test for Density of Plastics by the Density Gradient Technique." For the purpose of this handbook, <u>when the actual density is not known,</u> the minimum density <u>used to calculate the target net weight</u> shall be 0.92 g/cm³ ~~when the actual density is not known. For products labeled "High Density," "HD," or similar wording, the minimum density (D) used to calculate the target net weight shall be 0.95 g/cm³~~

Background: Some manufacturers of polyethylene bags labeled as "High Density" or "HD" have been found to package and label products whose labeled net weights met calculated target net mass/weights when employing a factor of 0.92 g/cm³. When a density factor of 0.95 g/cm³ was used, as appropriate, in the calculation for high-density polyethylene materials, products commonly failed to meet the calculated target net mass/weight. Further inspection typically revealed that one or more of the labeled width, thickness, or count statements were inaccurate.

Some manufacturers appeared aware that weights and measures officials were restricted to testing high-density film using the 0.92 g/cm³ value because the actual density value was not stated on the product label and the existing procedural guidelines did not address high-density polyethylene materials. When testing at manufacturing locations, weights and measures officials were able to obtain information regarding the density of the product from the manufacturer. However, at distributor locations, density information was not available and officials tested using the 0.92 g/cm³ designated in Handbooks 130 and 133.

Conversations with manufacturers and review of technical data sheets from various manufacturers indicated that 0.95 g/cm³ was an acceptable minimum density value for HD labeled polyethylene film.

Discussion: The WWMA L&R Committee received only a few comments on this item and therefore recommended forwarding the item to the NCWM L&R Committee to be placed on its agenda.

Recommendation: Amend Handbook 133, Chapter 4.7 Polyethylene Sheeting – Test Procedure as follows:

> *Determined by ASTM Standard D 1505-98 (or latest issue) "Standard Method of Test for Density of Plastics by the Density Gradient Technique." For the purpose of this handbook, when the actual density (D) is not known, the minimum density used to calculate the target net weight shall be 0.92 g/cm³ when the actual density is not known. For products labeled "High Density," "HD," or similar wording, when D is not known, the minimum density (D) used to calculate the target net weight shall be 0.95 g/cm³. When the polyethylene commodity package is labeled with a specific density, the labeled density factor shall be used to calculate the target net weight. If the official determines that the labeled density information is not accurate, the minimum density factors above shall be used to calculate the target net weight.

Committee Action at the 2007 Interim Meeting: The Committee withdrew this proposal because industry representatives supporting the proposal did not agree on the density used by most manufacturers to produce products typically labeled "high-density polyethylene." (E.g., a state association of film extruders and converters wrote that a density of 0.96 gm/cm³ or higher was generally accepted as the "industry" standard for "high density" sheeting while a letter from a company in that state indicated that resins having densities between 0.946 gm/cm³ to 0.948 gm/cm³ would also be considered to fall under that designation.) The Committee believes that, lacking evidence of a serious national problem with polyethylene labeling, a proposal to establish a national standard for a product identity should have the support of a large number of manufacturers across the nation.

270-5 I Amend Section 2.2.1. in Handbook 130 Uniform Engine Fuels Regulation – Premium Diesel Lubricity

Source: Southern Weights and Measures Association (SWMA)

Proposal: Amend Section 2.2.1. in Handbook 130 Uniform Engine Fuels, Petroleum Products, and Automotive Lubricants Regulation as follows:

2.2.1. **Premium Diesel Fuel.** – All diesel fuels identified on retail dispensers, bills of lading, invoices, shipping papers, or other documentation with terms such a premium, super, supreme, plus, or premier must conform to the following requirements:

  (a) **Cetane Number.** – A minimum cetane number of 47.0 as determined by ASTM Standard Test Method D 613.

  (b) **Low Temperature Operability.** – A cold flow performance measurement which meets the ASTM D 975 tenth percentile minimum ambient air temperature charts and maps by either ASTM Standard Test Method D 2500 (Cloud Point) or ASTM Standard Test Method D 4539 (Low Temperature Flow Test, LTFT). Low temperature operability is only applicable October 1 - March 31 of each year.

  (c) **Thermal Stability.** – A minimum reflectance measurement of 80 % as determined by ASTM Standard Test Method D 6468 (180 min, 150 °C).

  (d) **Lubricity.** – A maximum wear scar diameter of 520 μm as determined by ASTM D 6079. If an enforcement jurisdiction's single test of more than 560 μm is determined, a second test shall be conducted. If the average of the two tests is more than 560 μm, the sample does not conform to the requirements of this part.

Background: A member of the petroleum industry believed the test and associated tolerances for lubricity on premium diesel specified in Section 2.2.1.(d) were inconsistent with that for regular diesel. Effective January 1, 2005, the test tolerance for regular diesel lubricity was the ASTM D 6079 reproducibility of 136 µm (see ASTM D 975-04b). The NCWM chose to accept the ASTM reproducibility limits for all diesel (D 975) and gasoline (D 4814) properties (see Section 7.2.2., Reproducibility), but chose a different reproducibility limit for premium diesel lubricity without providing any explanation as to why the ASTM reproducibility limit was insufficient. If the NCWM intended to impose a stricter lubricity requirement for premium diesel, it should have designated a tighter specification for this property, not a different test tolerance (e.g., for regular and premium gasoline, premium has a different octane specification than for regular, but the test tolerance is the same). ASTM reproducibility limits were, by definition, based on establishing a 95 % probability that product that should pass, will pass. Applying an average test as specified in Section 2.2.1.(d) reduced that probability to 80 %.

The Committee received comments from several members of the Premium Diesel Work Group (WG) who did not support the item as presented by the petroleum industry member. WG members believed the process that led to the current definition was very thorough and complete and the premium diesel lubricity requirements were established with a full understanding of their implications. The WG members felt that knowledgeable individuals provided input to the process, which lead to the consensus position contained in the current regulation. The work being done by the WG was reported at meetings of ASTM Subcommittee E-2 every six months. The current regulation has been endorsed by the American Petroleum Institute, the Engine Manufacturer's Association, and the NCWM.

Prior to this requirement being adopted, the ASTM Lubricity Task Force conducted a great deal of research on this topic. Based on their research, the ASTM Lubricity Task Force concluded that a limit of 520 µm would meet the requirements of equipment in the field. Since the passage of this model regulation, ASTM included a lubricity requirement for No. 1 and No. 2 diesel fuel effective January 1, 2005. The ASTM requirement is also 520 µm.

WG members reported that when this regulation was written, fuels with adequate lubricity provided a functional benefit to the end user. The WG agreed with the ASTM Lubricity Task Force that 520 µm was the correct limit to set for premium diesel. However, the WG's review process also indicated increased pump wear for fuels with High-Frequency Reciprocating Rig (HFRR) values greater than 560 µm. The current reproducibility value of the HFRR test method would have placed enforcement well beyond the 560 µm level, essentially allowing fuels with little lubricity protection to be sold as "Premium." The WG believed they could not recommend a premium fuel standard that would permit excessive pump wear. Using the statistical tools provided in ASTM D 3244, the WG evaluated an enforcement limit of 560 µm. The statistical tools indicated that a single laboratory reporting the assigned test value would have an enforcement limit of approximately 80 % probability of acceptance, while the average of two separate laboratories reporting the assigned test value would have an enforcement limit of approximately 90 % probability of acceptance. It was agreed that for a premium fuel the average of two test results was the best approach given the current test methods and precision available. Therefore, if a test exceeded 560 µm, then a second test must be run. The average of the two tests must exceed 560 µm before a violation would occur. At the 2005 WWMA the Petroleum Subcommittee agreed the proposal was at that time the best approach, and, lacking new information, it continues to hold that position.

Discussion: At the WWMA 2006 Annual Meeting, the WWMA L&R Committee received only one comment regarding this item, acknowledging the ongoing review by the Petroleum Subcommittee. The WWMA noted that the NCWM L&R Committee forwarded the proposal for review by the Petroleum Subcommittee and agreed this item should remain Developmental pending the Subcommittee's recommendation.

At its 2006 Interim Meeting, the CWMA indicated the NCWM Petroleum Subcommittee would make recommendations after ASTM improved the test method's precision and after the conclusion of other tests. The CWMA L&R Committee was awaiting the recommendation from the NCWM Petroleum Subcommittee.

Committee Action at the 2007 Interim Meeting: The Committee carried this item over as an Information item. The Committee sent this proposal to the Petroleum Subcommittee and requested its recommendation on how to proceed with the issue. The Subcommittee suggested this item remain on the agenda as an Information item until further notice and reported that the activities of ASTM International and the Coordinating Research Council were continuing.

Contact: NCWM Petroleum Subcommittee, Ron Hayes, Chairman, (573) 751-2922 or ron.hayes@mda.mo.gov for additional information.

270-6 I Amend Handbook 130 Interpretations and Guidelines Section 2.3.2. Guidelines for the Method of Sale of Fresh Fruits and Vegetables

Source: Northeast Weights and Measures Association (NEWMA)

Proposal: Amend Handbook 130 Interpretations and Guidelines Section 2.3.2. to recognize and support innovation in modern retail food marketing approaches at all forms of outlets from typical grocery stores to the age-old farm markets.

Discussion: The method of sale guidelines for the sale of fresh fruits and vegetables that currently appear in Handbook 130 are outdated and in need of revision. The present guidelines do not recognize current retailing practices and are not expansive enough to cover many exotic and unusual fruits and vegetables that are becoming more common in the marketplace. Additionally, the present guidelines do not take into consideration the necessary limitations experienced by retailers at roadside stands and farmers markets.

The original proposal for this item reflected input from only a single jurisdiction. The Committee was informed that several industry associations requested an opportunity to review and respond to this proposal. The Committee believed there were several factual errors within the classifications of produce provided, and several types of produce still were not covered by the provided proposal. The Committee made this item Developmental so it may be more fully developed with input from jurisdictions throughout the country and from affected industry associations and businesses.

Discussion: At its 2006 Interim Meeting, the CWMA heard a comment that this item should be moved to Informational for a year. The body of the guidelines should be circulated within the CWMA before becoming a Voting item. The WWMA L&R Committee received no comments regarding this item. The committee chairman encouraged all to provide input on this item to the NCWM L&R Committee.

Contact Ross Andersen (NY Bureau of Weights and Measures) at (518) 457-3146 or e-mail at ross.andersen@agmkt.state.ny.us to submit comments or for further information.

2.3.2. Fresh Fruits and Vegetables
(Added 1979, Amended 1980, 1982, and **200X**)

This guideline applies to all sales of fruits and vegetables. There are two tables, one for specific commodities and one for general commodity groups. Search the specific list first to find those commodities that either don't fit into any of the general groups or have unique methods of sale. If the item is not listed, find the general group in the second table. The item may be sold by any method of sale marked with an X.

Specific Commodity	Weight	Count	Head or Bunch	Dry Measure (any size)	Dry Measure (1 dry qt or larger)
Artichokes X	X				
Asparagus X	X				
Avocadoes X					
Bananas X	X				
Beans (green, yellow, etc.) X	X				
Brussels Sprouts (loose) X					
Brussels Sprouts (on stalk) X					
Cherries X	X	X			
Coconuts X	X				
Corn on the Cob X		X			

Specific Commodity	Weight	Count	Head or Bunch	Dry Measure (any size)	Dry Measure (1 dry qt or larger)
Dates X	—				
Eggplant X	X	—			
Figs X	—				
Grapes X	—				
Melons (cut in pieces) X	—				
Mushrooms (small) X	X X			—	—
Mushrooms (Portobello, large) X	X	—			
Okra X	—				
Peas X	X				—
Peppers (bell and other varieties) X	X X	—			
Pineapples X	X				
Rhubarb X	X				
Tomatoes (except cherry) X	X X	—			—

General Commodity Group	Weight	Count	Head or Bunch	Dry Measure (any size)	Dry Measure (1 dry qt or larger)
Berries and Cherry Tomatoes X	X			—	
Citrus Fruits (oranges, grapefruits, lemons, etc.)	X X	X	—		—
Edible Bulbs (onions, garlic, leeks, etc.) X	X X	X	—		—
Edible Tubers (Irish potatoes, sweet potatoes, ginger, horseradish, etc.)	X X				—
Flower Vegetables (broccoli, cauliflower, Brussels sprouts, etc.)	X X		—		
Gourd Vegetables (cucumbers, squash, melons, etc.)	X X	X	—		—
Leaf Vegetables (lettuce, cabbage, celery, etc.) X	X		—		
Leaf Vegetables (parsley, herbs, loose greens) X	X X	—			
Pitted Fruits (peaches, plums, prunes, etc.) X	X	X	—		—
Pome Fruits (apples, pears, mangoes, etc.) X	X	X			—
Root Vegetables (turnips, carrots, radishes, etc.)	X X		—		

Committee Action at the 2007 Interim and Annual Meetings: The Committee carried this item over as Informational and will reconsider it when it receives comments from the regional associations, retailers and other industries affected by the proposed amendments. The Committee also realized the proposed replacement table had been omitted from this item. That oversight has been corrected in this report (see next page).

At the Annual Meeting, concerns were raised that permitting quart sales of some fruits and vegetables would not be useful or practical and the Committee should reconsider that provision of the table.

Comparison of Current and Proposed Tables

The following comparison was prepared for the NCWM Laws and Regulations Committee at the request of the Central Weights and Measures Association. It compares the current Guideline for the Method of Sale of Fresh Fruits and Vegetables in Section 2.3.2. of the Interpretations and Guidelines Section of NIST Handbook 130 with the changes proposed in Item 270-6. A table which lists the commodities included in the current Guideline but which do not appear in the Specific or General Tables is also provided.

Comparison Tables

Key to Tables:

Green rows (dark gray) indicate there is NO change between the current and proposed guideline (i.e., see the rows for Artichokes in the Comparision Table).

Yellow rows (light gray) indicate there is a change between the current and proposed guideline (i.e., see "Dry Measure (1 dry qt or larger) in the header row of the Comparison Table and the cell under the header for count in the row for "Bananas.")

Explanations of the differences or questions to be resolved are provided in the numbered footnotes which are located at the bottom of the table.

Specific Commodity	Weight	Count	Bunch	(any size)	[1]
Artichokes	X	X			
Asparagus	X		X		
Avocadoes		X			
[2]	X	[2]			
Beans (green, yellow, etc.)	X [3]	[3]		X	
[4]			[4]		
[5,6]		X		[6]	[6]
Coconuts	X	X			
Corn on the Cob		X			X
Dates	X				
Eggplant	X	X			
Figs	X				
Grapes	X				
Melons (cut in pieces)	X				
[6,7]	X			[6]	[6]
[7]		X [7]			
Okra	X				
[8]	X				[8]
[9]	X	X			[9]
Pineapples	X	X			
[10]	X		[10]		
[11]	X	[11]			X

[1] This amendment changes the minimum dry measure from 1 peck to 1 dry quart. The equivalents are: one peck = 16 dry pints, 8 dry quarts, ¼ bushel, or 8.810 L.
[2] The current guideline forbids sales of bananas by count (only by weight). However, the NCWM permits individual bananas to be sold under the Ready-to-Eat Food exception in Section 1.12. in the Method of Sale of Commodities Regulation.
[3] The current guideline addresses Brussels sprouts and does not include the "loose" distinction.
[4] This is a new MOS for Brussels sprouts on "stalks" so there is nothing in the current method of sale to compare this with except that the current provision requires Brussels sprouts to be sold by weight.
[5] The reference to Section 4.46. Berry Baskets and Boxes Code in NIST Handbook 44 has been deleted.
[6] If a dry measure of "any size" is ok in Column 3, is an X correct in the 4th Column which limits sales to 1 dry quart or larger?
[7] This proposal distinguishes mushrooms by size between "small" and "large (Portobello)" and introduces the method of sale by count for "large" mushrooms which is not permitted in the current guideline (only by weight or measure).
[8] The current guideline does not allow sales of peas by "dry measure" (only by weight).
[9] The current guideline does not allow sales peppers by "dry measure" (only by weight or count).
[10] The current guideline does not allow sales of rhubarb by "head or bunch" (only by weight).
[11] The current guideline does not allow sales of tomatoes by "count" (only by weight and dry measure).

	26	Weight	Count	Head or Bunch	Dry Measure (any size)	Dry Measure (1 dry qt or larger)
and Cherry Tomatoes		X			X	
, etc.)		X	X			2,3,4
, etc.)		X	7	7		5,6,8
, etc.)		X				9,10
, etc.)		X		X		
, etc.)		X	X			15
, etc.)		X		17,18		
)		X		21	19,21	
, etc.)		X	22			22
, etc.)		X	X			24
, etc.)		X		25		

[1] The reference to Section 4.46. Berry Baskets and Boxes Code in NIST Handbook 44 has been deleted.
[2] The current guideline does not allow sales of oranges by "dry measure" (only by weight or count).
[3] The current guideline does not allow sales of grapefruit by "dry measure" (only by weight or count).
[4] The current guideline does not allow sales of lemons by "dry measure" (only by weight or count).
[5] The current guideline does not allow sales of onions by "dry measure" (see 6).
[6] The current guideline allows sales by weight or bunch for "spring or green" onions and sales by "weight" for dry onions.
[7] The current guideline does not permit sales of garlic by "dry measure" (only by weight or count).
[8] The current guideline does not allow sales of leeks by "count" or "dry measure" (only by weight).
[9] The current guideline does not allow sales of Irish potatoes by "dry measure" (only by weight).
[10] The current guideline does not allow sales of sweet potatoes by "dry measure" (only by weight).
[11] The current guideline does not include ginger.
[12] The current guideline does not include horseradish.
[13] Brussels sprouts are also in the Specific Commodity Table as "loose" and "on stalk."
[14] The current guideline does not allow sales of cucumbers by "dry measure" (only by weight or count).
[15] The current guideline does not include squash.
[16] The current guideline does not allow sales of melons by "dry measure" (only weight or count).
[17] The current guideline does not allow sales by cabbage by "count" (only by weight).
[18] The current guideline allows sales of celery by weight or count so perhaps the Committee should decide whether or not "head or bunch" or "count" is the most appropriate descriptor.
[19] The current guideline does not allow sales of parsley by "dry measure" (only weight or bunch).
[20] The current guideline does not include herbs.
[21] The current guideline does not allow sales of "Greens (all)" by count or dry measure (only by weight).
[22] The current guideline does not allow sales of plums by count (only by weight or dry measure).
[23] The current guideline does not allow sales of prunes by count or dry measure (only by weight).
[24] The current guideline does not allow sales of mangoes by dry measure (only by weight or count).
[25] The current guideline does not allow sales of radishes by "head or count" (only by weight).
[26] While many of these items may fall under the general categories listed above, it may improve uniformity and simplify the use of the table if all of the commodities were placed in a general category instead of the table, saying for instance, "Edible Tubers, etc."

proposed tables.*	
Commodity	Method of Sale
Apricots	Weight
Beets	Weight or Bunch
Cantaloupes	Weight or Count
Cranberries	Weight or Measure
Currants	Weight or Measure
Eggplant	Weight or Count
Escarole	Weight or Bunch
Kale	Weight
Kohlrabi	Weight
Limes	Weight or Count
Nectarines	Weight or Count
Papaya	Weight or Count
Parsnips	Weight
Persimmons	Weight or Count
Pomegranates	Weight or Count
Rutabagas	Weight
Spinach	Weight or Bunch
Tangerines	Weight or Count

The Committee requested this item be considered at upcoming regional meetings and that comments are submitted by November 1, 2007, for inclusion and review at the Interim Meeting in January 2008.

270-7 D Amend Handbook 133 Section 2.3, Moisture Allowances to Provide Clearer Guidance

This item was added to the agenda of the Committee's Work Group (WG) on Moisture Loss (see Appendix A) following the 2007 NCWM Interim Meeting. Also see Item 270-8 for an explanation of the WG's role and responsibilities.

270-8 D Laws and Regulations Committee Work Group (WG) on Moisture Loss

At the 2007 NCWM Interim Meeting, the Committee created a WG to undertake a review of a number of moisture loss and other issues relating to NIST Handbook 133 "Checking the Net Contents of Packaged Goods." NIST recommended the NCWM L&R Committee retain responsibility for this project instead of creating a task force because that would entail additional travel and meeting expenses for all parties. The Board of Directors and the Committee agreed with that proposal because a large portion of this project can be accomplished using e-mail and teleconferences to reduce costs. The Committee also noted the number of items on the Committee's agenda has declined so it has time available during its work sessions at the Interim and Annual Meetings to address this project. If additional meetings are needed, they will be scheduled to coincide with the regional meetings to reduce travel and other costs. Another justification for this approach was that it allowed regional representatives on the Committee to develop a greater understanding of moisture loss and enabled them to better explain the subject matter to their constituents.

Participation in this effort is open to everyone. The first meeting took place on Sunday, July 8, 2007, following the Committee's regular work session at the NCWM Annual Meeting at the Snow Bird Resort near Salt Lake City,

Utah. The first major subject of discussion was the determination of tare using gel-soaker pads. The participants agreed that information on the appropriate test procedures for using gel soaker pads should be distributed to weights and measures officials and industry following the NCWM Annual Meeting, and NIST agreed to publish an article in the upcoming edition of WMD's Newsletter. A discussion of that issue is contained in Item 1 of Appendix A attached to this report. The group developed a formal work plan and addressed additional items listed in Appendix A as time allowed.

To obtain more information on Moisture Loss or to participate in this group, contact Tom Coleman at (301) 975-4004 or by e-mail at t.coleman@nist.gov.

270-9 D Petroleum   Subcommittee

The Petroleum Subcommittee met on January 24, 2007, at the NCWM Interim Meeting in Jacksonville, Florida, to undertake a review of a number of significant issues related to fuel standards. Their first major project was to undertake a major review and update of the Uniform Engine Fuels, Petroleum Products, and Automotive Lubricants Regulation in Handbook 130. The goal of the Subcommittee was to prepare and submit a major revision of this regulation for consideration by the Committee at the 2008 Interim Meeting. The Subcommittee also conducted a review of the Engine Fuels, Petroleum Products, and Automotive Lubricants Law and will prepare suggested changes for that uniform law as well. Another project will be to update and possibly expand the Basic Engine Fuels, Petroleum Products, and Lubricants Laboratory Publication which will then be made available on the Internet. The Subcommittee will undertake other projects as time and resources permit.

The Petroleum Subcommittee also met at the Annual Meeting and continued its work on a number of items in addition to preparing a major revision of the Fuel Ethanol Labeling requirement in Item 232-2.

The Chairman of the Petroleum Subcommittee is Ron Hayes, Missouri, who can be contacted at (573) 751-2922 or at ron.hayes@mda.mo.gov. If you would like to participate in the Petroleum Subcommittee, contact Ron Hayes or Ken Butcher, NIST L&R technical advisor, at (301) 975-4859 or by e-mail at kbutcher@nist.gov.

James P. Cassidy, Jr., Chairman, Cambridge, Massachusetts

Vicky Dempsey, Montgomery County, Ohio
Roger Macey, California
Stephen Benjamin, North Carolina
Joe Benavides, Texas

Ron Hayes, Missouri, Chairman of the Petroleum Subcommittee

Pete O'Bryan, Foster Farms, Associate Member Representative
Doug Hutchinson, Canada, Technical Advisor

Tom Coleman, NIST, Technical Advisor
Ken Butcher, NIST, Technical Advisor
Lisa Warfield, NIST, Technical Advisor

Laws and Regulations Committee

THIS PAGE INTENTIONALLY LEFT BLANK.

Appendix A

L&R Committee Work Group on Moisture Loss

Table A
Table of Contents and Agenda

INTRODUCTION..A2
    Item 1. Gel Soaker Pads...A2
    Item 2. Moisture Loss Guidance in NIST Handbook 133..A3
    Item 3. WMD Package Inspection and Moisture Loss Guidance Letter – Withdrawn.............A9
    Item 4. WMD Suggestions...A9
        a. Seek Greater Recognition of NIST Handbook 133 by FDA and other Federal Agencies...............A9
        b. Create a new supplement or website to NIST Handbook 133 which would provide useful information to administrators, field officials and industry...A9

REFERENCE SECTION I – Excerpts From The Interpretations And Guidelines Section Of Nist Handbook 130..A12

REFERENCE SECTION II – Other Moisture Loss Guidance And Related Documents..............A21
    A. Text from the WMD Memorandum that was issued on January 1, 2006..............................A21
    B. Letter from Kraft Foods Requesting that NIST Withdraw Letter on Moisture Loss*............A28
    C. Chapter 3 from the 3rd Edition of NIST Handbook 133 and 4th Supplement 1994*..............A28

*NOTE: The following documents could not be included in this publication because they are only available in Adobe PDF format; NIST will provide copies on request. Please contact Tom Coleman at (301) 975-4004 or by e-mail at t.coleman@nist.gov.

L&R Committee 2007 Final Report
Appendix A – Committee WG on Moisture Loss

Detail of all Items
(In order by Reference Key Number)

Moisture Loss and Other Issues for Consideration by the NCWM Laws and Regulations Committee and the Board of Directors

INTRODUCTION

The Weights and Measures Division (WMD) prepared this document at the request of Mike Cleary, Chairman of the NCWM, to detail several moisture loss and other package inspection issues to be studied under this project with the goal of developing recommendations for amendments to NIST Handbook 133 (HB 133) in 2008. There are four items listed below and most of the resource material is included to enable this document to serve as an agenda and comprehensive resource.

WMD provided this outline for consideration by the NCWM L&R Committee, the Board of Directors and other interested parties with the goal of developing a consensus on whether or not there was sufficient justification to study the issues described below.

Item 1. Gel Soaker Pads

Several weights and measures officials are concerned that HB 133 does not provide adequate guidance on how to verify the net weight declaration on packages where "gel soaker pads" are used in the package to absorb moisture.

Based on information that WMD has received, this discussion paper is provided as a technical examination of the use of "gel type" soaker pads when determining net weight. Gel soaker pads contain granules of a highly absorbent compound that soak up fluid and retain it so efficiently that the "usual" methods of drying (pressure, wiping and air) do not allow the recreation of "Used Dry Tare." According to two manufacturers, "gel-based soaker pads" can absorb up to 50 times their original weights in fluid compared to "cellulose-based fluff pulp" which absorb only two to four times its weight (see   www.thermasorb.com and www.stockhausen-inc.com). Gel-type soaker pads are used by industry to: (1) extend shelf life thus reducing repackaging costs, (2) reduce bacterial growth, and (3) improve the "presentation of packages" by absorbing blood and fluid, eliminating free flowing liquid in the package.

Inspection problems with this type of tare arise when officials attempt to verify net weight declarations on packages which have been wrapped and labeled at a location other than where the commodity is inspected/tested since officials have no access to "unused dry tare." Some officials report that it is impossible to dry these types of soaker pads using traditional drying procedures and have even attempted to use microwave ovens to establish "used dry tare." WMD discourages the use of microwave ovens or other extreme drying methods for drying tare materials because (1) unused "dry" tare materials have a natural moisture content which cannot be reestablished using most heating methods (e.g., for gel-pads this could be 5 % or more); (2) the intensity/power of microwave ovens varies substantially from device to device so, given the range of variability, it would be impossible to suggest a power setting or heating time that could be considered reasonable, repeatable, and safe; and (3) a more practical concern is that an official could overheat tare material and damage the microwave or cause even more serious problems such as the possibility of fire.

WMD solicits recommendations and comments from all concerned who have interest in this topic. Please consider possible solutions to allow accurate measurement practices that permit officials to safely recreate "used dry tare" for net weight verification on products using "gel-type" material.

WMD believes the requirements of HB 133 are written broadly enough to apply to all types of tare materials including those which are "gel based." Under the definition of "Used Dry Tare" officials use air drying, washing, scraping, pressure, or other techniques which can involve more than normal household procedures but do not go so far as to include laboratory procedures such as oven drying. The field test procedures in HB 133 were developed to provide uniform procedures to enable officials to dry out "used" tare to recreate as close as possible the weight of "unused tare material" that the packager used. When a packager uses a tare material that does not permit the recreation of unused dry tare (and the official does not have access to "unused dry tare" material or to readily accessible reliable information on tare), the official is limited to drying at least two samples of the tare material as best he can using the procedures described by the handbook; he then can use an average tare to determine a net weight. If the packages are then found to be underweight, the packer must be permitted to provide information on whether or not the average tare value used by the official was reasonable or provide other information to the official to defend the net weight claims on the label. Since this is really the same opportunity any packer of any type of tare material has available to him, WMD believes the current guidance in HB 133 is adequate.

A test procedure in HB 133 is necessary to ensure weights and measures can continue to maintain marketplace surveillance to ensure equity and fair competition while still recognizing reasonable moisture loss or gain as required under both federal and state laws and regulations. The relevant sections describing the tare definition and determination procedures from 4th edition of HB 133 (2005) are shown below:

> *Used Dry Tare*
>
> > *Used Dry Tare is defined as follows:* ~~Used tare material that has been air dried, or dried in some manner to simulate the unused tare weight. It includes all packaging materials that can be separated from the packaged product, either readily (e.g., by shaking) or by washing, scraping, ambient air drying, or other techniques involving more than "normal" household recovery procedures, but not including laboratory procedures like oven drying.~~ *Labels, wire closures, staples, prizes, decorations, and such are considered tare. Used Dry Tare is available regardless of where the packages are tested. The net content procedures described in this handbook reference Used Dry Tare.*
>
> *How is a tare weight determined?*
>
> > ~~*Except in the instance of applying unused dry tare, select the packages for the initial tare sample from the sample packages.*~~ *Mark the first two (three or five) packages in the order the random numbers were selected; these packages provide the initial tare sample. Determine the gross weight of each package and record it in block a, "Gross Wt," under the headings "Pkg. 1," "Pkg. 2," "Pkg. 3," etc. on the report form. Except* ~~*for aerosol or other pressurized packages, open the sample packages, empty, clean, and dry them as appropriate for the packaging material.*~~

NIST Handbook 133 is available online at http://ts.nist.gov/WeightsAndMeasures/h1334-05.cfm.

Item 2. Moisture Loss Guidance in NIST Handbook 133

The three items shown below were taken from the L&R Report of the 2004 89th NCWM Annual Meeting Proceedings and later agendas including an item from the Committee's 2007 Interim Meeting agenda. The Committee withdrew two of these items in 2004 and asked NIST to review the moisture loss sections of HB 133, revise them to improve their readability, and, where appropriate, add additional information or clarifications.

NIST conducted the promised review but found there were several suggestions contained in these two items. A few of the suggestions raised substantive questions about what needs to be added to HB 133 and which questions would be the most useful or practical for field officials. NIST believes that responding to some of the suggestions or questions could lead to extensive revisions to the handbook. This level of discussion will take considerable time and effort for the Committee, and WMD would like to ensure everyone has a full understanding of the concerns and agrees to the necessity for change so time and resources will not be wasted. The Committee should review these sections and identify what information administrators need versus what information field officials need to perform their duties.

260-2 W Amend Section 1.2, Package Requirements

(This item was withdrawn.)

Source: Northeastern Weights and Measures Association (NEWMA). (See Item 250-3 on page L&R-18 in the Report of the 88th NCWM Annual Meeting in 2003.)

Recommendation: The Committee reviewed the following proposal to amend the section "Why do we allow for moisture loss or gain?" in Handbook 133, Section 1.2, Package Requirements (page 4) as follows:

Why do we allow for moisture loss or gain?

Some packaged products may lose or gain moisture and, therefore, lose or gain weight or volumes e after packaging. The amount of lost moisture depends upon the nature of the product, the packaging material, the length of time it is in distribution, environmental conditions, and other factors. Moisture loss may occur even when manufacturers follow good distribution practices. Loss of weight "due to exposure" may include solvent evaporation, not just loss of water. ~~Note that allowances for loss or gain of moisture only apply to packages of commodities where the moisture has no value to the consumer (See Jones vs. Rath).~~

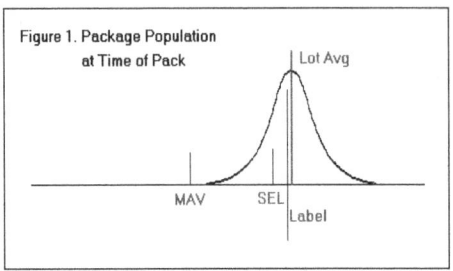

For loss or gain of moisture, ~~you~~ apply the moisture allowances to the maximum allowable variations permitted for individual packages and to the average net quantity of contents before determining the conformance of a lot. ~~You may apply the allowance before measuring the package errors or after. When applying the allowance before the measurements, you essentially correct each package back to theoretical weight at time of pack (see Figure 1 at right). When applying the allowance after measuring the package errors, you correct the MAV and SEL to recognize the moisture loss as in Figure 2 at right. You can find specific directions for applying the allowances in tests in Section 2.3.~~

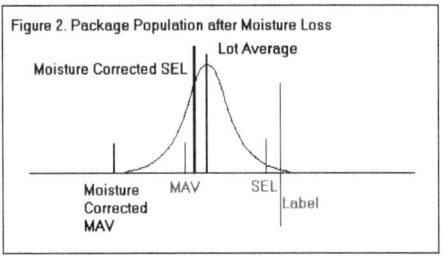

This handbook provides "moisture allowances" for some meat and poultry products, flour, and dry pet food (see "Moisture Allowances" in Chapter 2). These allowances are based on the premise that when the average net weight of a sample is found to be less than the labeled weight, but not by an amount that exceeds the allowable limit, either the lot is declared to be within the moisture allowance or more information must be collected before deciding lot compliance or noncompliance.

Background: The original proponent of this item provided the following written issues and justification. These apply to both this item and the next item (260-3: Amend Section 2.3 Basic Test Procedure):

What products are covered by the requirement to recognize loss/gain of moisture in distribution? The reference to the Rath vs. Jones case in Chapter 1 attempts to find an answer. NEWMA believed this may be premature and should be removed from the item for the short term to help develop a solution. However, this is a battle that will have to be fought some time in the future since regulators get claims of moisture loss from diverse packers as an excuse for packages that fail to have labeled net weight. The claims have ranged from windshield washer fluid in plastic jugs to canned tomato sauce. Where can the official turn to get an answer if not to this handbook? NEWMA would like guidance.

When do you apply the moisture allowance in the test process? Within the handbook itself, the method is either not clear or some of the text is wrong. In Chapter 1 the text indicates that you must apply the allowance before the test (i.e., adjusting by using Box 13a and thus lowering the NGW in Box 14). In Chapter 2, the text appears otherwise. You are directed to add the moisture allowance to the MAV on page 18. You are further directed to compare the difference between sample average and SEL to the moisture allowance on page 19. Both of these instructions can only make sense if the value in Box 13a was not included in the nominal gross weight calculation in Box 14. At the very least these sections fail to provide clear guidance. The proposal attempts to clarify that you can make the correction either before or after measuring the package errors and attempts to provide procedures to do that in each case. Before works great for products with established moisture allowances, but it is not possible to apply a correction before the test when dealing with other products. For these other products, you must do additional investigation to determine the magnitude of the loss and you must apply it <u>after</u> the field official completed the testing. It may also be beneficial to do the adjustment afterwards for products with established moisture loss allowances. Since both before and after methods can provide equivalent results, they should both be recognized in the handbook. The proposal does this in changes for both Chapters 1 and 2.

Shouldn't all the established moisture allowances be listed in one place rather than being listed as separate items? The proposal changes the question from how you apply the allowance for a specific product to what products have established allowances. This brings these all together in one section that is easily found by an inspector.

How do you establish moisture allowances for products not in the list in 3 above? The handbook provides no guidance whatsoever! In the last line at the bottom of page 17, the text directs the inspector to follow steps if the product is listed, but says nothing about the products not listed in the handbook. This is a huge omission that has many officials wondering what to do. The result is that some packers bluff by playing the moisture loss card even when not entitled to a loss (e.g., canned goods) and many officials back away from these products for lack of direction. The proposal included the provision for comparing time-of-pack data with actual field data for moisture content that was in the 3rd edition. It also would permit using data from a scientific study provided by the manufacturer in support of any claim of moisture loss.

Why do we have a different method of evaluating the test results for products with moisture loss than for other products? The basic procedure for evaluating test results calls for evaluating the individual packages against the MAV and evaluating the sample average against the SEL. On page 19 that procedure is no longer used and you have to look at a difference between the sample average and the SEL and not compare it to the moisture allowance. Recently the method of calculating the R_c for tare variability changed to avoid having different methods for different types of packages. Consistency helps inspectors apply the standard uniformly. NEWMA believes that sample average should always be compared to the SEL and this can be accomplished easily by adjusting the SEL rather than looking at differences. Thus we would follow the same process in evaluating the results in all cases. The only difference is in how the SEL and MAV are calculated when applying the moisture loss allowance after the test. If you use Box 13a before the test, this is done automatically. If you follow the proposed procedure after the test, a moisture-corrected MAV and a moisture-corrected SEL are calculated and the original test data are reevaluated. While the result may be the same using the procedure on page 19, a different evaluation process is used, and it is difficult to understand particularly how Box 13a is or is not used in the calculation of NGW.

Discussion: One state believed the explanations provided in HB 133 pertaining to moisture loss were inadequate. In considering this proposal, however, the Committee concluded that the reference to the Jones vs. Rath court case was inappropriate and inaccurate. The Committee considered the additional language provided regarding the application of moisture loss unnecessary and confusing. NIST agreed, however, to review the moisture loss section of HB 133 to see if it can be written more clearly. The Committee has withdrawn this item.

260-3 W Amend Section 2.3 Basic Test Procedure

(This item was withdrawn.)

Source: Northeastern Weights and Measures Association (NEWMA). (See Item 250-4 on page L&R-19 in the Report of the 88th NCWM Annual Meeting in 2003.)

Recommendation: The Committee reviewed the following proposal to delete the current " **Moisture Allowances**" discussion in Handbook 133 (HB 133), Section 2.3, Basic Test Procedure (pages 17 through 19), and replace it as follows:

<u>**Moisture Allowances**</u>
<u>**What products have an established moisture allowance?**</u>

Flour and dry pet food have a moisture allowance of 3 % of the labeled net weight. Note: Dry pet food means all extruded dog and cat foods and baked treat products packaged in Kraft paper bags and/or cardboard boxes with a moisture content of 13 % or less at the time of pack.

Meat and poultry products from a USDA-inspected plant are permitted no moisture allowance when tested under a Category A sampling plan with Used Dry Tare.

Meat and poultry products from a USDA-inspected plant are permitted the following moisture allowances when tested under a Category A sampling plan with Wet Tare. Note: When there is free-flowing liquid or absorbent packaging materials in contact with the product, all free liquid is part of the wet tare.

For packages of fresh poultry that bear a USDA seal of inspection, the moisture allowance is 3 % of the labeled net weight. For net weight determinations only, fresh poultry is defined as poultry above -3.3 °C (26 °F). This is a product that yields or gives when pushed with the thumb.

For packages of franks or hotdogs that bear an USDA seal of inspection, the moisture allowance is 2.5 % of the labeled net weight.

For packages of bacon, fresh sausage, and luncheon meats that bear a USDA seal of inspection, there is no moisture allowance if there is no free-flowing liquid or absorbent materials in contact with the product and the package is cleaned of clinging material. Luncheon meats are any cooked sausage product, loaves, jellied products, cured products, and any sliced sandwich style meat. This does not include whole hams, briskets, roasts, turkeys, or chickens requiring further preparation to be made into ready-to-eat sliced product. When there is no free-flowing liquid inside the package and there are no absorbent materials in contact with the product, Wet Tare and Dried Used Tare are equivalent.

These allowances are based on the premise that when the average net weight of a sample is found to be less than the labeled weight, but not by an amount that exceeds the allowable limit, either the lot is declared to be within the moisture allowance, or more information must be collected before deciding lot compliance or noncompliance.

How do you determine the allowance for products without an established moisture allowance?

For any product subject to moisture loss/gain, you may determine the appropriate moisture loss allowance based on a valid, scientific study. You may not use arbitrarily chosen allowances for moisture loss/gain. Many packers have conducted studies that they can provide in support of any claim that the product lost/gained moisture. Any such study should have included a variety of environments that simulate the potential distribution chains that could be encountered. You may use the moisture loss limits found in such study as an allowance in a compliance test.

What is the accepted method to determine the actual moisture loss for a lot?

Where the packer measures and records the moisture content of product in each lot, you may request a copy of that data to be compared to the moisture content of the product offered for sale. You must select a random sample of the product offered for sale and have it tested for moisture content using a scientifically verified test procedure, e.g. like those in the Official Methods of Analysis of the Association of Official Analytical Chemists (See Appendix D). The actual moisture loss is calculated as the moisture content (percent) at time of pack minus moisture content (percent) at time of sale. Use the difference obtained to calculate the actual moisture loss for the lot by multiplying it times the label quantity. Use this as the moisture allowance in the official test. In the case of moisture gain, this value will be a negative number.

L&R Committee 2007 Final Report
Appendix A – Committee WG on Moisture Loss

Calculations

How do you apply a moisture allowance when conducting a test?

Moisture allowances may be applied either prior to testing or after testing. These two methods are mathematically equivalent means of adjusting both the individual package errors and the sample average. It is common practice to apply the moisture correction prior to the test for those products with established moisture allowances like flour and dry pet food. In most other cases the correction is made after the test since moisture loss data will probably be obtained as part of the follow-up investigation after the initial test has failed.

To compute the moisture loss allowance prior to testing, you correct the nominal gross weight in Box 14 for moisture loss. Find the value of the allowance by multiplying the labeled quantity by the decimal percent value of the allowance. Enter this value in Box 13a on the form. The nominal gross weight is found by adding the average tare (Box 13) to the label quantity (Box 1) and subtracting the moisture allowance (Box 13a). Lot compliance is evaluated in the normal way using decision criteria in Boxes 16 and 24 on the report form.

Example: Labeled quantity of a bag of flour is 2 lb and average tare is 0.04 lb (Box 13). Moisture Allowance is 3 % (0.03) of 2 lb = 0.06 lb.
Nominal Gross Wt. = 2 lb + 0.04 lb – 0.06 lb = 1.98 lb (record this value in Box 14).

To compute the moisture loss allowance after testing, you correct only the MAV and SEL for moisture loss. Perform your initial test with no moisture allowance in Box 13a. When moisture loss data becomes available, find the value of the allowance by multiplying the labeled quantity by the decimal percent value of the moisture loss or allowance. Lot compliance is evaluated using decision criteria in Boxes 16 and 24 on the report form and the moisture corrected MAV and SEL respectively.

Example: Labeled quantity of a package of rice is 2 lb, average tare is 0.04 lb (Box 13), MAV (Box 3) is 0.07 lb, and SEL (Box 23) is 0.023 lb.
Moisture content at time of pack was 13.4 % (packer data).
Moisture content at time of sale is 10.6 % (lab data).
Moisture loss is (13.4 % to 10.6 %) = 2.8 %.
Moisture allowance is 0.028 x 2 lb = 0.056 lb.
Moisture Corrected MAV is 0.07 lb + 0.056 lb = 0.126 lb – Compare each package error measured in the initial test to this moisture corrected MAV using criteria in Box 16.
Moisture Corrected SEL is 0.023 lb + 0.056 lb = 0.079 lb – Compare the sample average error in the initial test to this moisture corrected SEL using criteria in Box 24.

Background: The following information was provided by the original proponent of this item: The products that have established moisture allowances are not clearly stated. Currently the handbook only poses the question, "What is the moisture allowance for flour and dry pet food?" It does not state if any other products have moisture allowances. In addition, the handbook provides no guidance for products that do not have an established moisture allowance.

The "Calculations" section on page 18 is confusing and does not distinguish between applying a moisture allowance before or after testing. The current method of comparing the moisture allowance to the difference between the average error and the SEL is confusing. The current handbook does not address commodities that are packed in sealed containers or how to treat commodities packed on the premises.

Discussion: One state believed the explanations provided in HB 133 pertaining to moisture loss were inadequate. In reviewing this proposal the Committee considered the proposed additional language confusing and inaccurate. The Committee did agree that the "Calculations" section on page 18 needed to do a better job of distinguishing between moisture allowances applied before testing and those applied after testing. The

L&R Committee 2007 Final Report
Appendix A – Committee WG on Moisture Loss

Committee believed there were extensive problems with this proposal as submitted. NIST agreed to review the moisture loss section of HB 133 to see if it can be written more clearly. The Committee withdrew this item.

270-7 Amend NIST Handbook 133 Section 2.3, Moisture Allowances to Provide Clearer Guidance
(This Item was added to the agenda of the WG on Moisture Loss following the 2007 Interim Meeting)

Source: Northeast Weights and Measures Association (NEWMA)

Proposal: Amend NIST Handbook 133 (HB 133) Section 2.3, Moisture Allowances (pages 17 through 19 of Handbook 133) to provide clearer guidance.

Background: The issue of moisture loss is complex. Handbook 133 currently provides specific guidance on the determination and application of moisture allowances for only a limited number of commodities. Concerns have been raised that this guidance is confusing and difficult to understand, particularly with regard to when moisture loss is applied (i.e., at the time of inspection or subsequent to the inspection). Requests have been received to reword this section to make it easier to understand and apply.

In addition, HB 133 provides little guidance on the determination and application of moisture allowances for commodities other than those specifically listed. Weights and measures jurisdictions across the country have been struggling with how to properly handle moisture loss during packaging inspections and need more definite guidance on this issue.

The Committee did not believe it had the time or expertise to address properly the issue of moisture loss within the structure of the NCWM. The Committee decided to request activation of a NIST Moisture Loss WG to establish more effective and extensive guidance to the NCWM regarding the proper determination and application of moisture loss.

Discussion of this Item by the WWMA: The WWMA L&R Committee heard that a meeting was tentatively planned for November 2006; the meeting was delayed to allow time for everyone to identify and agree on the issues to be addressed by the group to ensure that expectations for the meeting results were clear. The Weights and Measures Division (WMD) agreed to fund the travel and attendance of one NCWM representative. Leading issues included providing additional guidance in HB 133 regarding the determination and application of appropriate moisture loss allowances in package inspections, with noted examples including how to address gel soaker pads in poultry/meat packages, as well as how to determine moisture allowances for pasta, rice, and other commodities for which no established moisture loss allowances exist. Additionally, guidance regarding application of moisture loss allowances at the point-of-pack needed to be addressed.

An industry representative urged involvement in the meeting and ensuing work on HB 133 amendments from the Food and Drug Administration (FDA) and the U.S. Department of Agriculture (USDA) to ensure input and consensus from all relevant agencies. He further emphasized the need to review and consolidate all decisions and directives from any and all court rulings regarding moisture loss issues. Factors to be considered in determining and applying appropriate moisture loss allowances and influences upon such losses included commodity stability limits and varying environmental conditions at packing plants such as relative humidity and constant temperature rooms maintained at different temperature levels. The industry representative also urged that guidance be provided to industry members regarding the types of data needed to be tracked and provided by packers/manufacturers in addressing moisture allowance determinations.

Discussion of this Item by the CWMA at its 2006 Interim Meeting: A comment was heard from industry that this needs to be addressed in order for businesses to be competitive. The USDA and FDA need to be involved in the development of this item. A meeting was tentatively scheduled for November prior to the NCWM Interim Meeting. There was general agreement that in order for this meeting to be effective, the USDA and FDA must be present. Comments were heard in support of using the New York proposal to correct the error in HB 133.

Item 3. WMD Package Inspection and Moisture Loss Guidance Letter – Withdrawn

WMD believed there was some useful information for weights and measures officials and industry contained in the 2005 Memorandum that WMD issued to state weights and measures officials and other interested parties, entitled "Verifying the Net Contents of Packaged Goods and Recommended Procedures for Moisture Allowances." WMD withdrew the memorandum at the request of Kraft Foods which detailed a number of concerns about the guidance contained in the WMD communication. The Kraft Foods letter, dated January 31, 2006, was prepared by Steven Steinborn of Hogan and Hartson. WMD recommended the committee review both ___ documents to resolve the corporation's concerns where possible and determine if any information in the WMD letter can be revised and republished to assist weights and measures officials in dealing with net quantity of contents. The WMD memorandum and Kraft's letter are presented in Reference Section II below.

Item 4. WMD Suggestions

a. Seek Greater Recognition of NIST Handbook 133 by FDA and other Federal Agencies.

WMD would like to avoid frequent amendments to HB 133 because, unlike NIST Handbook 44, it is not widely adopted automatically. Many jurisdictions adopt new versions of HB 133 using their Administrative Procedures Acts. Another consideration is that the USDA adopts versions of the handbook which then preempts other versions from being used to verify the net quantity of packages put up under that agency's supervision. In the past, WMD found that several jurisdictions used the wrong edition of HB 133 to take action against USDA-inspected products simply because they used a newer version of the handbook than had been adopted by the USDA. WMD believes that USDA adoption gives a strong endorsement and recognition to the handbook. WMD also believes the 4th edition of HB 133, whose core elements have been in use by the states since 1994, should be recognized by the FDA and all other agencies to eliminate any uncertainty over its use by the states. Perhaps it is time the NCWM consider petitioning the FDA to provide some type of formal recognition of the handbook. WMD believes that establishing a 5-year review cycle for HB 133 may be one way to ensure it is acceptable to other agencies, which will help avoid the confusion over which edition is currently in effect.

b. Create a new supplement or website to NIST Handbook 133 which would provide useful information to administrators, field officials and industry.

WMD would like to explore the possibility and usefulness of creating a new publication or website called NIST Handbook 133-1 which would provide supplementary information and guidance on net quantity of contents testing and moisture loss for administrators and industry. The publication or website would be "informative," thus it would not include regulatory requirements. Instead it would be used to provide additional guidance and more examples than can be included in HB 133 itself. Such a publication or website could also be used to provide complete full-size copies of the various inspection forms and worksheets contained in HB 133 and other useful tools developed by jurisdictions. The publication or website could also include a variety of other information related to net contents verification and random sampling and could include appropriate information from federal regulations and policies as well as frequently asked questions (FAQs). Currently in NIST Handbook 130 (HB 130) Interpretations and Guidelines there are sections related to moisture loss, point-of-pack inspections and administrative procedures which may not be well known or readily accessible. These could be updated and moved to the new publication or website.

For example:

- 2.2.5. Lot, Shipment, or Delivery
- 2.5.6. Guidelines for NCWM Resolution of Requests for Recognition of Moisture Loss in Other Packaged Products
- 2.6.10. Model Guidelines for the Administrative Review Process
- 2.6.11. Good Quantity Control Practices
- 2.6.12. Point-of-Pack Inspection Guidelines

These documents are shown below in Reference Section I.

Another example of the type of package information which could be included in a publication or website for reference purposes is the following report on a meeting held at NIST in 2005 to address concerns over packer supplied tare values.

NIST Weights and Measures Today
November 2005
Report of Meeting on Tare

On November 2, 2005, the Laws and Metric Group at NIST hosted a meeting to discuss ways to improve the communication of tare information between packers and retailers when meat products are packaged at a plant, but weighed and labeled at the retail store. Representatives from the meat packing industry, the retail food industry, and several weights and measures agencies attended the meeting.

The Problem
There is a fundamental change occurring in the retail food marketplace. Retail food stores are shifting from having in-store meat cutters to purchasing already-packaged meat from an outside plant. The supplying plant provides the retail store with packaged meat (including tray, soakers, and overwrap), and the store is then responsible for weighing and labeling the package. In order to weigh and label these products properly, the retail store needs to know the weight of the packaging materials used by the plant (i.e., the tare weight). While this may sound simple and straightforward, it is not.

Retailers
Many retail food chains manage their tare weights from a central location. Tares are maintained at the central or regional office and downloaded to the individual stores on a routine basis. While individual stores may have the ability to override the tare provided in a download (e.g., when an official from weights and measures informs them that they are using an incorrect tare), this correction will be erased when the next download occurs. Several retail food chains believe that the centralized management of tare information is critical to the overall success of their meat departments. With little cutting and packaging being done at the retail level, stores rarely have experienced, professional staff in their meat departments. Without significant expertise at the store level, food retailers are reluctant to leave decisions regarding the use and amount of tare to individual store management.

Weights and Measures Officials
When weights and measures officials find inaccuracies in tares being used, often these inaccuracies are not being communicated to the food retailer's central or regional offices. If the food retailer's central or regional office is not informed that a tare value is inaccurate, then the tare value will not get changed in the next download. While some retail food chains require their store managers to submit copies of inspection reports to the central or regional office, many do not. Some chains leave that decision to the discretion of the individual store managers. Individual store managers may be reluctant to forward disparaging information about their store's performance to the central or regional office. As a result, when weights and measures officials find an inaccurate tare being used in a store and only notify store management of the correction necessary, that information may not be communicated to the people who really need to know—the people at the central or regional office who set the tare values for the entire chain of stores.

Packers
The weight of tare materials used at a meat packing plant varies regularly. Whenever the plant changes suppliers, whether it is suppliers providing soakers, trays, or overwrap, the tare must be reevaluated and changed. Whenever suppliers change the materials used in their products, the tare must be reevaluated and changed. Most meat packers monitor tare continuously and regularly make small adjustments to ensure their packages are accurate. While tare information is routinely shared with retailers, it is difficult to ensure that the correct tare goes on the correct package.

Packers may ship individual packages from several different production lots (lots which may have been packaged using different tare materials) in a single shipment to a retailer's warehouse. The retailer's warehouse then further breaks up these package groups to distribute packages to individual stores. Even if accurate tare information for all packages is provided to the retailer's central or regional office, the retailer has difficulty using this information effectively since not all packages of the same product at the same location will necessarily have the same tare. In addition, new tare information provided to a retailer may only apply to packages still in the retailer's warehouse (and not those presently in the store). This means retailers must coordinate the updating of tare data with the placement of new packages on the store shelves.

Is There a Solution?
The question remains: How do you effectively ensure that the tare information for a particular package "travels" with the package from the point of production to the final retail destination? One suggestion has been to print tare information directly on individual packages. However, packers and retailers all agree that printing tare information on packages, shipping cases, or shipping invoice forms would not be effective. Packers order packaging materials and shipping containers months in advance and at that point could only guess as to what amount of tare would need to be preprinted on these materials. In addition, if tare information were provided on individual packages, shipping cases, or shipping invoices, that information would only be available at the retail store and would never reach the retailer's central or regional office in time to be included in the next download. Most retail food chains do not want individual stores making independent decisions about what tares to use.

Ultimately, the key will be for packers and retailers to communicate more frequently and more effectively. To that end, the American Meat Institute (AMI) has agreed to contact other trade associations representing the retail and meat packing industries to ask for their help in reiterating to their members the importance of accurate net weight labeling at retail. AMI will encourage their packer and processor members to communicate tare values to retail customers whenever changes in tare values occur.

How Can Weights and Measures Officials Help?
Weights and measures agencies can help by sending copies of test reports (especially from failed inspections) to the corporate or regional office of the retailer. While ideally the corporate or regional office will receive this information from the retail store, retailers at this meeting stressed they would rather receive duplicate reports (from the weights and measures agency and the store) than none at all. Retailers consider it absolutely critical that weights and measures officials contact, communicate, and work with the corporate and regional offices early and often. Retailers specifically asked that weights and measures agencies not wait for problems to escalate before they get the corporate or regional offices involved. Weights and measures officials should conduct package inspections in full compliance with NIST Handbook 133 (HB133). Inspectors are encouraged to properly clean tare materials during inspections to avoid imposing tares larger than they should be.

According to HB 133, Used Dry Tare is "tare material that has been air dried, or dried in some manner to simulate the unused tare weight." Before adding this definition to HB 133, members of the NCWM and NIST did extensive testing to compare the weights of Unused Dry Tare (which the packer uses), and Used Dry Tare (which the inspector uses). If Used Dry Tare is dried and cleaned properly, its weight should not vary significantly from the Unused Dry Tare weight. In addition, NIST strongly discourages the use of microwave ovens when drying tare materials, particularly soaker pads. Past tests have shown that excessive heating of soaker pads and other tare materials can significantly alter their weight, and even start a fire as some officials have learned.

REFERENCE SECTION I – EXCERPTS FROM THE INTERPRETATIONS AND GUIDELINES SECTION OF NIST HANDBOOK 130

The following are currently in NIST Handbook 130 (HB 130) Interpretations and Guidelines

2.2.5. Lot, Shipment, or Delivery
(L&R, 1981, p. 95)

Policy
The requirements for the average package net contents to meet or exceed the labeled declaration may be applied to production lots, shipments, or deliveries. Shipments or deliveries are smaller collections of packages than production lots that may or may not consist of mixed lot codes.

Emphasis in inspection activities should be placed on warehouse and in-plant testing without neglecting retail consumer protection.

Background
The Committee heard a petition from the California Brewers Association to define a lot as:

> "a selection of containers under one roof produced by a single company of the same size, type and style, manufactured or packed under similar conditions with a minimum number to be equivalent to one production line shift."

The intention of the petition is to focus Weights and Measures enforcement on production lots as opposed to small collections of packages on retail shelves, because the production lot is under the control of the packager.

An alternative proposal was made that would require mingling of lot and date codes in package inspection at warehouse locations.

The Committee has reviewed the proposals in light of § 7.6. and § 12.1. of the Uniform Packaging and Labeling Regulation which refers to "shipment, delivery, or lot." If the petition is approved, the terms "shipment" and "delivery" would have to be dropped from this Uniform Regulation.

The Committee recognizes the inherent value of in-plant and warehouse inspection and is of the opinion that, wherever possible, such inspections should be carried out. At the same time, the Committee recognizes the need for the state and local weights and measures officials to protect the consumer at the level where the ultimate sale is made. Therefore, the Committee recommends no change to the Uniform Regulation.

The Committee looks forward to the work of the Special Study Group on Enforcement Uniformity of the NCWM which will be exploring the mechanisms that might be instituted to make in-plant inspection workable.

2.5.6. Guidelines for NCWM Resolution of Requests for Recognition of Moisture Loss in Other Packaged Products
(Exec, 1988, p. 94)

The Task Force on Commodity Requirements limited its work to only a few product categories, using these categories as models for addressing moisture loss. The gray-area concept is the result of this work.

Recognizing several candidates for future work in moisture loss, the Task Force recommends that the following guidelines for moisture loss be followed as far as possible by any industry requesting consideration:

1. There should be reasonable uniformity in the moisture content of the product category. For example, since pet food has final moisture contents ranging from very moist to very dry, some subcategorization of pet food needs to be defined by industry before the NCWM study of the issue.

2. The predominant type of moisture loss (whether into the atmosphere or into the packaging materials) must be specified.

3. Different types of packaging might make it necessary to subcategorize the product. For example, pasta is packaged in cardboard, in polyethylene, or other packaging more impervious to moisture loss. The industry should define the domain of packaging materials to be considered.

4. "Real-world" data is needed on the product as found in the retail marketing chain—not just laboratory moisture-loss data.

5. The industry requesting consideration of moisture loss for its product should collect data on an industry-wide basis (rather than from only one or two companies).

   Information concerning the relative fractions of imported and domestically produced product should be available, for example, in order to assess the feasibility of interacting with the manufacturer on specific problem lots.

6. Moisture loss may occur either:
   - during manufacturing or
   - during distribution.

   Data will be needed to show the relative proportion of moisture loss in these different locations since moisture loss is permitted only under good distribution practices. Geographical and seasonal variations may apply.

7. A description of the processing and packaging methods in use in the industry will be of great value, as will a description of the distribution system and time for manufacturing and distribution. A description of the existing net quantity control programs in place should be given, together with information on how compliance with Handbook 133 is obtained. A description of maintenance and inspection procedures for the scales should be provided, together with information on suitability of equipment and other measurements under Handbook 44.

8. A description of federal and local agency jurisdiction and test should be given, as well as any regulatory history with respect to moisture loss and short weight. Has weights and measures enforcement generated the request? What efforts have addressed the moisture loss issue prior to approaching the NCWM? Are the appropriate federal agencies aware of the industry's request to the NCWM?

9. The industry should propose the type of compliance system and/or moisture determination methodology to be used. The compliance scheme, if it contains industry data components, should be susceptible to verification (examples: USDA net weight tests for meat; exchange of samples with millers for flour) and should state what the companies will do to provide data to field inspection agencies in an ongoing fashion (as the gray-area approach requires). If in-plant testing is to be combined with field testing, who is to do such testing, and how is this to be accomplished? It should be possible to incorporate the proposed testing scheme into Handbook 133 to be used with Category A or B sampling plans.

When all the preliminary information recommended above has been collected, a field test of the proposed compliance scheme should be conducted by weights and measures enforcement officials to prove its viability. See the plan diagrammed on the next page.

L&R Committee 2007 Final Report
Appendix A – Committee WG on Moisture Loss

Plan For NCWM Resolution of Individual Requests For Recognition of Moisture Loss

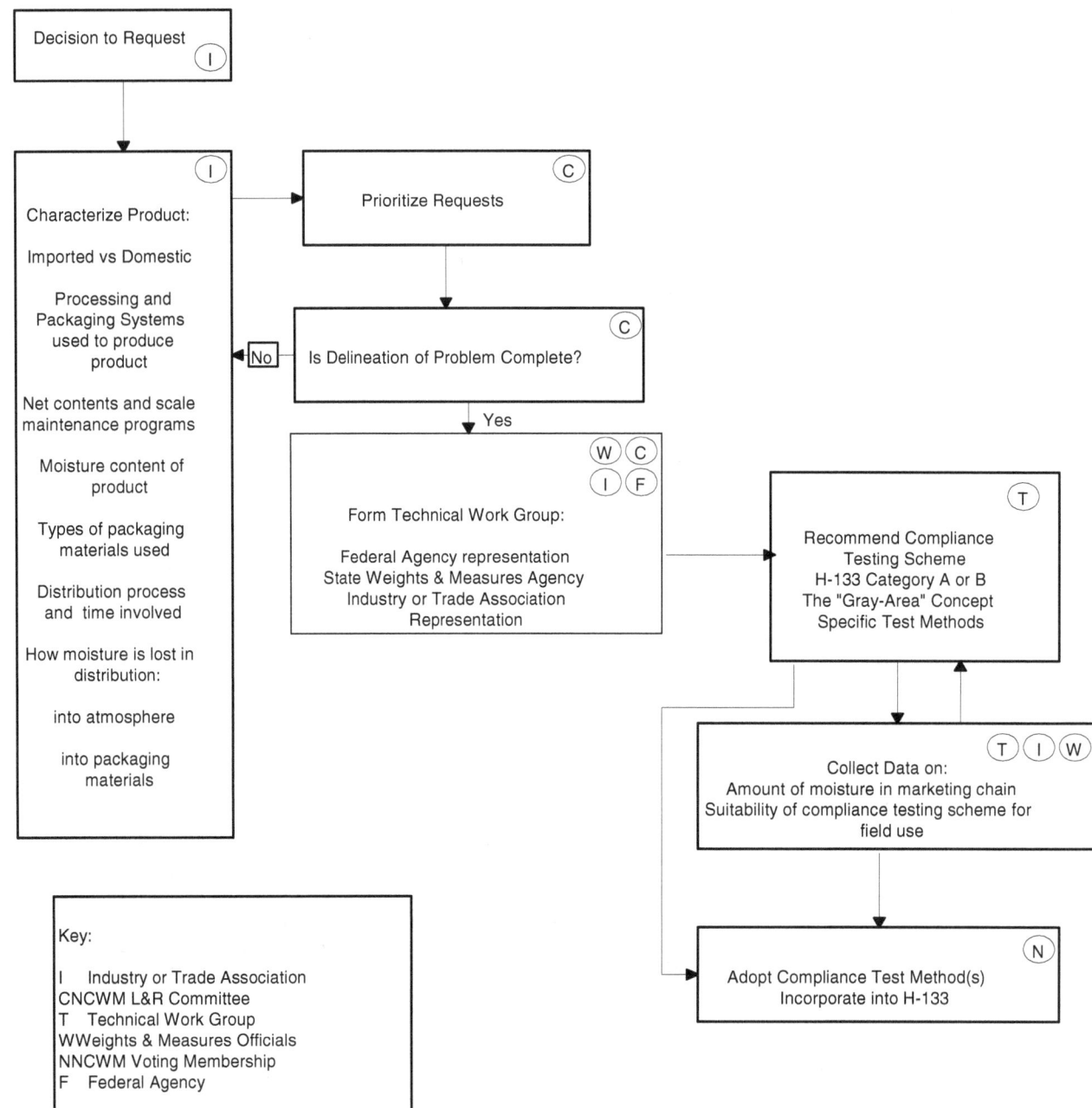

L&R - A14

2.6.10. Model Guidelines for the Administrative Review Process

Purpose
These guidelines are provided to assist weights and measures programs in establishing an administrative review process. They are not intended to be the only process an agency may use nor are they intended to supersede any agency's existing process. Before implementing ANY process, it should be approved by legal counsel.

These guidelines ensure that persons affected by "inspection findings" (e.g., price misrepresentations or shortweight packages), or who are deprived of the use of their property (devices or packages placed under "stop" or "off-sale" order), are provided a timely-independent review of the action. The process enables affected persons to provide evidence which could be relevant in determining whether the enforcement action was proper. The purpose of the process is to ensure that a person's ability to conduct business is not hindered by improper enforcement actions. This process is independent of any other action (e.g., administrative penalties, prosecutions, etc.) that may be taken by the enforcement agency.

Background
In the course of their work, weights and measures officials take enforcement actions that may prohibit the use of devices or the sale of packaged goods (e.g., "stop-sale" or "off-sale" orders for packages and "stop-use" or "condemnation" tags issued on devices). Improper actions (e.g., not following prescribed test procedures, enforcing labeling requirements on exempted packages, or incorrectly citing someone for a "violation") place the official and the jurisdiction in the position of being liable for the action if it is found that the action was "illegal." In some cases, weights and measures jurisdictions could be ordered to pay monetary damages to compensate the affected party for the improper action.

This process is one way to provide affected persons an opportunity to present evidence which may be relevant in determining whether the order or finding has been properly made to an independent party. The procedure enables business operators to obtain an independent review of orders or findings so that actions affecting their business can be evaluated administratively instead of through litigation. This ensures timely review, which is essential because of the impact that such actions may have on the ability of a business to operate and in cases where perishable products may be lost.

Review Provisions
Parties affected by enforcement actions must be given the opportunity to appeal enforcement actions.

Inspectors are the primary contacts with regulated firms and thus are in the best position to ensure that the enforcement actions they take are "proper." "Proper" means that inspections are conducted (1) within the scope of the authority granted by law, (2) according to recognized investigative or testing procedures and standards, and (3) that enforcement actions are lawful. The "burden" for proving that actions are "proper" falls on the weights and measures program, not on regulated firms.

Weights and measures officials are law enforcement officers. Therefore, they have the responsibility to exercise their authority within the "due process" provisions of the U.S. Constitution. As weights and measure programs carry-out their enforcement responsibilities in the future, more and more challenges to their actions and authority will occur. It is in the best interest of any program to establish strict operational procedures and standards of conduct to prevent the occurrence of improper actions which may place the jurisdiction in an untenable position in a court challenge of an enforcement action. The foundation for ensuring "proper" actions is training, clear and concise requirements, and adoption of, and adherence to uniform test procedures and legal procedures.

Prior to taking enforcement actions, the inspector should recheck test results and determine that the information on which the action will be taken is accurate.

Inspections shall be conducted with the understanding that the findings will be clearly and plainly documented and reviewed with the store's representative.

During the review of the findings, the firm's representative may provide information which must be used by the inspector to resolve the problems and concerns before enforcement actions are taken. In some cases, the provided information may not persuade the inspector to forego the action. In some cases the inspector and business representative may not understand the circumstances surrounding the violations, or there may be a conflict between the parties that they cannot resolve. In other cases, the owner or manufacturer may not learn that an enforcement action has occurred until long after the inspector leaves the establishment.

Steps:

1. Provide a framework that will help in resolving most of these situations where "due process" is of concern. Make sure that the responsible party (e.g., as declared on the package label) is notified of violations and receives copies of inspection reports. Establish standard operating procedures to assure the affected party of timely access to a representative of the weights and measures program so that the firm can provide the relevant information or obtain clarification of legal requirements.

2. Make the process as simple and convenient as possible. Especially in distant or rural areas where there are no local offices, the review should be conducted by a supervisor of the official taking the action if agreed to by the person filing the request for review.

3. The process should include notice that the firm can seek review at a higher level in the weights and measures program or an independent review by a third party. The following procedures are recommended:

    (a) Any owner, distributor, packager, or retailer of a device ordered out of service, or item or commodity ordered "off-sale," or inspection finding (e.g., a price misrepresentation or a shortweight lot of packages) shall be entitled to a timely review of such order, to a prompt, impartial, administrative review of such off-sale order or finding.

    A notice of the right to administrative review should be included on all orders or reports of findings or violations and should be communicated to the responsible firm (e.g., person or firm identified on the product label):

    (b) The administrative review shall be conducted by an independent party designated by the Director or before an independent hearing officer appointed by the Department. The officer shall not be a person responsible for weights and measures administration or enforcement.

    (c) No fees should be imposed for the administrative review process.

> **Sample Notice**
>
> You have the right to Administrative Review of this order or finding. To obtain a review, contact the Director of Weights and Measures by telephone or send a written request (either postmarked, faxed, or hand delivered) to:
>
> (Name, Address or Fax Number of the Director or other Designated Official)
>
> Your request should reference any information that you believe supports the withdrawal or modification of the order or finding.

    (d) The firm responsible for the product or the retailer may introduce any record or other relevant evidence.

For example:

> (i) Commodities subject to the off-sale action or other findings were produced, processed, packaged, priced, or labeled in accordance with applicable laws, regulations or requirements.
>
> (ii) Devices subject to the "stop-use" order or "condemnation" were maintained in accordance with applicable laws, regulations or requirements.
>
> (iii) Prescribed test procedures or sampling plans were not followed by the inspector.
>
> (iv) Mitigating circumstances existed which should be considered.

(e) The reviewer must consider the inspector's report, findings, and actions as well as any evidence introduced by the owner, distributor, packager, or retailer as part of the review process.

(f) The reviewer must provide a timely written recommendation following review unless additional time is agreed to by the department and the petitioner.

(g) The reviewer may recommend to the Department that an order be upheld, withdrawn or modified. If justified the reviewer may recommend other action including a reinspection of the device or commodity based upon information presented during the review.

(h) All actions should be documented and all parties advised in writing of the results of the review. The report of action should be detailed in that it provides the reasons for the decision.

2.6.11. Good Quantity Control Practices

Good Quantity Control Practices means that the plant managers should take all reasonable precautions to ensure the following quantity control standards or their equivalent are met:

1. A formal quantity control function is in place with authority to review production processes and records, investigate possible errors, and approve, control, or reject lots.

2. Adequate facilities (e.g., equipment, standards and work areas) for conducting quantity control functions are provided and maintained.

3. A quantity control program (e.g., a system of statistical process control) is in place and maintained.

4. Sampling is conducted at a frequency appropriate to the product process to ensure that the data obtained is representative of the production lot.

5. Production records are maintained to provide a history of the filling and net content labeling of the product.

6. Each "production lot" contains on the average the labeled quantity and the number of packages exceeding the specified maximum allowable variation (MAV) value in the inspection sample shall be no more than permitted in Tables 2-1 and 2-2 in NIST Handbook 133.

7. Packaging practices are appropriate for specific products and measurement procedures (e.g., quantity sampling, density and tare determinations) and guidelines for recording and maintaining test results are documented.

8. Personnel responsible for quantity control follow written work instructions and are competent to perform their duties (e.g., background, education, experience and training). Training is conducted at sufficient intervals to ensure good practices.

9. Recognized procedures are used for the selection, maintenance, adjustment, and testing of filling equipment to insure proper fill control.

10. Weighing and measuring devices are suitable for their intended purpose, and measurement standards are suitable and traceable to national standards. This includes a system of equipment maintenance and calibration to include recordkeeping procedures.

11. Controls over automated data systems and software used in quantity control ensure that information is accessible, but changeable only by authorized personnel.

12. Tare materials are monitored for variation. Label changes are controlled to ensure net quantity matches labeled declaration.

2.6.12. Point-of-Pack Inspection Guidelines

A. Weights and Measures Officials' Responsibilities

1. Conduct inspections during hours when the plant is normally open for business. Open the inspection by making contact with the plant manager or authorized representative (e.g., the quality assurance manager or the production manager).

2. Present the proper credentials and explain the reason for the visit (e.g., routine or follow-up inspection or consumer complaint, etc.).

3. Request access to quantity measurement equipment in the packing room, moisture testing equipment in the laboratory or in the packing room, and product packed on premise or stored in warehouse areas.

4. Obtain permission from a plant representative prior to using a tape recorder or a camera.

5. Conduct inspection-related activities in a professional and appropriate manner and, if possible, work in an area that will not interfere with normal activities of the establishment.

6. Abide by all the safety and sanitary requirements of the establishment and clean the work area upon completion of the inspection/test. Return borrowed equipment and materials.

7. To close the inspection, recheck inspection reports in detail and ascertain that all information is complete and correct.

8. Sample questions and tasks for Inspectors:

   a. Inside Buildings and Equipment:

      (i) Is all filling and associated equipment in good repair?

      (ii) Are net content measurement devices suitable for the purpose being used?

      (iii) Are standards used by the firm to verify device accuracy traceable to NIST?

   b. Packing Room Inspection:

      (i) Observe if the program for net quantity of content control in the packing room is actually being carried out.

      (ii) Ensure that the weighing systems are suitable and tare determination procedures are adequate. If there are questions regarding tare determination, weigh a representative number of tare and/or filled packages.

(iii) For products labeled and filled by volume and then checked by weight, ensure that proper density is used.

   c. Warehouse Inspection:

      If an inspection is conducted:

      (i) Select lot(s) to be evaluated.

      (ii) Determine the number of samples to be inspected. Use the appropriate sampling plan as described in NIST Handbook 133.

      (iii) Randomly select the number of samples or use a mutually agreed on plan for selecting the samples.

      (iv) Determine the average net quantity of the sample and use the standard deviation factor to compute the Sample Error Limit (SEL) to evaluate the lot.

      (v) Look for individual values that exceed the applicable Maximum Allowable Variation as found in NIST Handbook 133.

      (vi) Apply moisture allowances, if applicable.

      (vii) Review the general condition of the warehouse relevant to package integrity, good quantity control, and distribution practices.

      (viii) Prepare an inspection report to detail findings and actions.

9. Close the inspection – Review findings with Plant Representative.

After the inspection, meet with the management representative to discuss inspection findings and observations. Provide additional information as needed (e.g., information on laws and regulations or explanations of test procedures used in the inspection). Be informative, courteous and responsive. If problems/violations are found during the inspection/test, bring them to the attention of the appropriate person.

B. Plant Management Responsibilities

1. Recognize that inspectors are enforcing a federal, state or local law.

2. Assist the official in conducting inspection activities in a timely and efficient manner.

3. During the initial conference with the inspector, find out whether the inspection is routine, a follow-up, or the result of a consumer complaint. If a complaint, obtain as much information as possible concerning the nature of the complaint, allowing for an appropriate response.

4. The plant manager, quality assurance manager, or any designated representative should accompany the inspector.

5. Plant personnel should take note of the inspector's comments during the inspection and prepare a detailed write-up as soon as the inspection is completed.

6. When an official presents an inspection report, discuss the observations and, if possible, provide explanations for any changes deemed necessary as a result of the inspection/test.

Plant Management: information that must be shared with the inspector.

1. Establishment name and address.

2. Type of firm and information on related firms or applicable information (e.g., sub-contractor, servant or agent).

3. General description and location of shipping and storage areas where packaged goods intended for distribution are stored.

4. Commodities manufactured by or stored at the facility.

5. Names of responsible plant officials.

Plant Management: information that may be shared with the inspector.

1. Simple flow sheet of the filling process with appropriate net content control checkpoints.

2. Weighing or measuring device maintenance and calibration test records.

3. Type of quantity control tests and methods used.

4. Net content control charts for any lot, shipment, or delivery in question or lots which have previously been cited.

5. Method of date coding the product to include code interpretation.

6. Laboratory reports showing the moisture analysis of the products which are in question or have been previously cited.

7. Product volume of lot sizes or related information.

8. Distribution records related to any problem lots including names of customers.

REFERENCE SECTION II – OTHER MOISTURE LOSS GUIDANCE AND RELATED DOCUMENTS

This section contains the text from a WMD memorandum to state weights and measures directors and other interested parties and a letter from Kraft General Foods stating the reasons justifying a withdrawal of the WMD memorandum.

A. Text from the WMD Memorandum that was issued on January 1, 2006

Memorandum for State Weights and Measures Directors and Other Interested Parties

Subject: Verifying the Net Contents of Packaged Goods and Recommended Procedures for Moisture Allowances

This memo supersedes the April 3, 1995, memorandum from the Weights and Measures Division (WMD) concerning the impact of the Nutrition Labeling and Education Act of 1990 (NLEA) on net content testing by State and local weights and measures officials.

I am revising the earlier correspondence primarily in response to the National Conference on Weights and Measures' (NCWM) adoption of the 4th edition (January 2005) of the National Institute of Standards and Technology's Handbook 133 "Checking the Net Contents of Packaged Goods" (Handbook 133). Recent inquiries from State officials on the status of package inspection programs that test products subject to Food and Drug Administration (FDA) jurisdiction have further prompted a response. This memorandum describes guidance provided by FDA. Since 1985 that agency has advised NIST that Handbook 133 has not ___ been in conflict with that agency's practices enforcing net quantity of content on packaged foods.

I. Recommendations for Verifying the Net Quantity of Contents of Packages Subject to FDA Jurisdiction

WMD recommends that weights and measures officials use the 4th edition of Handbook 133 (January 2005) for all products <u>except</u> those subject to regulation by the U.S. Department of Agriculture (USDA), which has adopted the 3rd edition of Handbook 133 and its 4th Supplement.[1] NIST recently learned that the USDA may adopt the 2005 edition of Handbook 133 in the near future. These publications are available on the Internet.[2]

The Category A Sampling Plans in Handbook 133 provide a statistically valid sampling scheme and sample correction factors to enable you to determine if a sample passes or fails a test with a confidence level of at least 97 %. The test methods prescribed for foods are consistent with those used by the FDA.[3]

Weights and measures officials must apply both the "average" and "individual package" requirements in Handbook 133 to the packages they inspect because Federal and State laws and regulations relating to net quantity of content require officials to allow reasonable variations (both plus and minus errors in net contents) from the labeled net contents. By applying both requirements, officials avoid the appearance

---

[1] See 9CFR317.19 and 9CFR381.121b for the applicable meat and poultry regulations.

[2] The 3rd Edition and 4th Supplement required by USDA and the January 2005 4th Edition of Handbook 133 are free at **http://ts.nist.gov/WeightsAndMeasures/h1334-05.cfm** on the Internet.

[3] Historically, the FDA has used enforcement procedures based on a 95 % confidence level that findings of underfill are accurate. The Category A Sampling Plans in the 4th edition of Handbook 133 are based on an approximate 97 % confidence level that the findings are accurate; therefore, these plans should be acceptable to use in testing packages under FDA jurisdiction.

they are imposing a "minimum" net content system [4] while providing a high level of protection for consumers and ensuring fair competition in the marketplace.

Weights and Measures Officials should continue to test packages at retail and should consider Section 1.1. of Handbook 133 before taking enforcement action on small inspection lots of package:

> Testing packages at retail outlets evaluates the soundness of the manufacturing, distributing, and retailing processes of the widest variety of goods at a single location. It is an easily accessible, practical means for State, county and city jurisdictions to monitor packaging procedures and to detect present or potential problems. Generally, retail package testing is not conducive to checking large quantities of individual products of any single production lot. Therefore, follow-up inspections of a particular brand or lot code number at a number of retail and wholesale outlets, and ultimately at the point-of-pack are extremely important aspects in any package-checking scheme. After the evaluation of an inspection lot is completed, the jurisdiction should consider what, if any, further investigation or follow-up is warranted. At the point-of-sale, a large number of processes may affect the quality or quantity of the product. Therefore, there may be many reasons for any inspection lot being out of compliance. A shortage in weight or measure may result from mishandling the product in the store, or the retailer's failure to rotate stock. Shortages may also be caused through mishandling by a distributor, or failure of some part of the packaging process. Shortages may also be caused by moisture loss (desiccation) if the product is packaged in permeable media. Therefore, being able to determine the cause of an error in order to correct defects is more difficult when retail testing is used.

It is important to realize that the Category A Sampling Plans in Handbook 133, while statistically valid, may fail lots that contain the labeled net quantity of content approximately three times out of 100 tests. By basing enforcement actions on samples from multiple lots of the same product from the same manufacturer tested at different locations, you will have a better indication of whether or not an enforcement action is necessary. When a lot fails an inspection, NIST recommends you contact the manufacturer to obtain quantity control records and other production information on the lot to assist in your decision process. To ensure due process, we encourage jurisdictions to follow the NCWM's Section 2.6.10. Model Guidelines for the Administrative Review Process in NIST Handbook 130 "Uniform Laws and Regulations in the area of legal metrology...." (Those guidelines are shown below this memorandum) for reference but, your agency's general counsel may of course have you follow other procedures. When following up on possible violations with manufacturers, recognize they are required under Federal and State laws or regulations to follow current good manufacturing practices. The NCWM has also adopted guidelines in Section 2.6.11. on "Good Quantity Control Practices" that officials can use as a tool to assess quantity control systems. (These are provided below).

Weights and Measures officials should conduct inspections at the point of pack whenever possible so they will have access to larger lots of packages and can also assess the packager's entire packaging system. The NCWM adopted guidelines in Section 2.6.12. on "point-of-pack inspections" to help officials conduct these inspections, (See below this memorandum).

We encourage jurisdictions to collaborate on conducting marketplace surveys to determine the level of compliance of commodity groups (e.g., store-packed random weight items, mulch, polyethylene sheeting, flour, milk, soft drinks, animal food, etc.) and to work together to follow up on possible problems at the point-of-pack where the packaging plant or distribution point is located in a jurisdiction other than where the packages failed to pass a test. The State of California conducts a wide variety of marketplace surveys which can serve as model for other states to follow. NIST encourages all states to follow the example set by California's Division of Measurement Standards for monitoring compliance in the all areas of weights

---

[4] Under a "minimum" net content system (these systems are common in European countries), no package in a sample may contain less than the net quantity of contents stated on the package label.

and measures enforcement. NIST will provide assist to states who want to conduct or collaborate in surveys...

Ensure that all samples are selected randomly. The statistical reliability of the sampling plans is valid only when the sample has been randomly selected from the inspection lot.

To be consistent with FDA inspection activities, utilize used dry tare when taking enforcement actions. The handbook permits unused dry tare to be used to conduct audits and to verify net weights of packages put up in retail stores.

Apply the average and individual package requirements to products tested at any point in distribution. Over the last ten years several jurisdictions have contacted WMD concerning industry claims that States can only take action on production lots. FDA advises that there are no provisions in the Federal Food, Drug, and Cosmetic Act or its legislative history that support this claim. Another issue that WMD has been asked about is the claim that the FDA has a "1 %" tolerance that States must permit. FDA advises that they have a policy for their field compliance staff to use in determining whether or not to request enforcement actions by the U.S. Justice Department. The only purpose for the policy is for FDA to prioritize agency resources, not to set a limit for State enforcement actions. The FDA also reports that it did not establish this policy as a statistical allowance or tolerance that could be easily abused by an unscrupulous packager.

Allow for reasonable moisture loss.

The following Federal regulation preempts any State or local requirement that is not identical:

21 CFR § 101.105

> (q) The declaration of net quantity of contents shall express an accurate statement of the quantity of contents of the package. Reasonable variations caused by loss or gain of moisture during the course of good distribution practice or by unavoidable deviations in good manufacturing practice will be recognized. Variations from stated quantity of contents shall not be unreasonably large.

State and local jurisdictions must allow reasonable variations in net contents caused by the loss or gain of moisture in food products that occurs during good distribution practice. If not, a jurisdiction may be questioned if enforcement action is taken against the product. The moisture loss issue has challenged weights and measures officials and industry since the Federal Food, Drug, and Cosmetic Act allowing for moisture loss was passed more than 75 years ago. However, the fact that FDA has not adopted specific moisture allowances is not justification for not making reasonable allowances for moisture loss.

The NCWM has adopted moisture allowances (also called "gray areas") for flour, dry pet food, chicken, and hot dogs. Under the "gray area" concept, any food found short in excess of the allowance is subject to enforcement action. If the product is found short, but within the allowance, the official would take additional steps (such as comparing the moisture content of a sample from the lot to the time-of-pack moisture content provided by the packer) to determine if the product is short because of underweighing at the time of pack, or if the shortage is due to "reasonable" moisture loss that occurred during distribution. WMD recommends that officials use the following guidelines with the "gray area" approach to allow reasonable moisture loss for the listed foods.

WMD only recommends moisture allowances. It is the individual jurisdiction's responsibility to make the final decision concerning appropriate moisture allowances. Final decisions should be made after considering moisture loss data provided by the packager.

II. Recommended Moisture Allowances for Some Foods

WMD has consulted with State and local weights and measures agencies and affected industries on moisture loss problems associated with hygroscopic foods. The following moisture allowances, beyond those already addressed by the NCWM, are recommended. WMD used data from the FDA's Quantity of Contents Compendium as the major source for the numerical values for gray area recommendations. Moisture loss has been identified with flour, pasta, rice, cheese and cheese products, dried fruits and vegetables, fresh and frozen fruits and vegetables, coffee beans, and bakery products. Of all of these commodities, the extent of moisture loss variations is greatest for flour and pasta. Very little current data are available for many other commodities. However, WMD considers the need for allowances for affected commodities to be pressing and believes that States must make some allowance for these commodities until other data can be obtained for the respective commodities. If a recommended allowance is perceived as too lenient, weights and measures agencies may prevent abuses of the allowance through inspections at the point of pack. Allowances if too lenient provide are a disadvantage for firms with products in competition with packers where point-of-pack inspections may not be possible; consequently, such firms may wish to provide information to WMD so that we can recommend a more stringent allowance. Where allowances are too stringent, firms may also provide information justifying a more appropriate allowance. WMD suggests that firms desiring such an allowance be encouraged to work closely with the NCWM in view of its experience in this area. Even though the process of developing moisture allowances is time-consuming, affected firms will be provided some relief during the interim period if State and local agencies implement the following recommendations:

III. Moisture Allowances at Point of Pack

WMD recommends that moisture allowances at the point of pack not be made for packages taken immediately off the production line. However, regulatory officials may often encounter product at the point of pack that has been stored by the packer prior to shipment to other locations. In the past, moisture allowances have not been recognized in tests until the food is "introduced into interstate commerce;" however, since many manufacturers store the product for extended periods at the packing location, moisture loss should be recognized. It is recognized that moisture loss is a natural phenomenon that is not controlled or delayed by any specific schedule, and WMD recommends that, at some point during such storage, allowances be permitted for moisture loss. But, considering the multiplicity of foods, differences in packing materials, and the various environmental factors that affect moisture loss, it would be impossible for WMD to determine moisture loss that occurs on the packaging line or in the first few hours or days following the packaging of any one product type, let alone the tens of thousands of products that might be inspected at the point of pack. Certainly, some products begin to lose moisture immediately after packaging, but there must be some definitive guidance provided for weights and measures officials and industry.

This problem is not unique to the United States where we are trying to encourage State and local officials to focus more on point-of-pack inspections. WMD is aware that point-of-pack inspections are one of the primary tools used in European countries to control net contents in packaged goods. We have learned that in some of these countries officials make no allowance for moisture loss within the first 7 days of the date of pack for some products. As this is the only documented guidance on the issue available, WMD recommends that States consider a similar approach until other guidance on this issue is available. This will provide packers and officials with guidance on when moisture loss allowances must be applied and will enable officials to conduct inspections at point of pack to ensure that packers are not taking advantage of recognized allowances for moisture loss. To minimize the possibility of moisture loss considerations, officials should inspect the most recently packed items.

In 1995 WMD received comments on the 7-day recommendation from the Food Industry Weights and Measures Task Force (Task Force) of the Grocery Manufacturers of America. The Task Force was concerned the 7-day period was not reasonable because the data submitted to the NCWM to develop the gray areas for flour, dry pet food, and other products clearly showed that some products lose as much as 0.5 % to 1 % of their weight due to moisture loss in the first few days of packing. WMD acknowledged the industry's concerns about the 7-day period but believed then and now that the concerns can be addressed without dropping the recommendation. WMD believes it is crucial to have specific guidelines on moisture loss for use in point-of-pack inspections.

WMD recommends an exception to the 7-day period if the packer can provide daily moisture loss data collected using the following procedures. We have developed the following guidelines in collaboration with industry for packers to use the results of the short-term moisture loss studies at the point of pack. To be acceptable, the data must be computed using the average moisture loss determined on a daily basis (e.g., the weight of each package in each of the sample control lots is determined everyday for 7-days) in environmental conditions similar to those that exist when the product is being inspected. For example, an inspector visits a pet food plant in Ohio in the middle of July to conduct a point-of-pack inspection. If the product tested had been packaged 5 days before the inspection and is found underweight; the moisture loss data must reflect the loss that would occur in July not January. At least three sample control lots, consisting of at least 48 randomly selected packages, must be used to develop the moisture loss data. Each sample lot must be stored under the same conditions that are typical for the product (e.g., if the product is typically placed in a sealed case on a pallet and shrink wrapped, the sample lots must be stored under the same conditions. Moisture loss data obtained by removing the individual packages from the shipping case and storing them in a laboratory would not be acceptable). The three-sample control lots must be placed at various locations in the storage site. The average moisture loss value must be computed from the three-sample control lots with a 95 % prediction interval.

Since point-of-pack inspections are not routinely done in most jurisdictions at this time, there will be many situations where packers may not have "acceptable" moisture loss data for a particular product found to be underweight at the time of a point-of-pack inspection. In these cases, WMD recommends the packer be allowed to conduct a study using the criteria specified above. This data could then be provided to the weights and measures official for use in making a final determination whether or not moisture loss caused the product to be underweight. One benefit of this approach is that the moisture loss study can be conducted within a few days of the inspector finding the inspection lot underweight so the test will more closely reflect the environmental conditions under which the original inspection lot was subject.

A similar recommendation is included for fresh bakery products weighed within 1 day following the end of the day of pack (in this case the moisture loss data would have to be based on the amount of moisture lost on an hourly basis under the same conditions listed above for the 7-day period). WMD will provide technical assistance on request to any jurisdiction to resolve these individual moisture loss cases by working with you and the packer and will seek FDA assistance in resolving these situations.

IV. Recommended Moisture Allowances for Use at Point of Pack and Testing at Any Other Location

Provide the following allowances for moisture loss (expressed as a percentage of the labeled net quantity of contents):

1. No allowance for moisture loss should be made if:

    (a) A food, other than a fresh bakery product, while stored by the packer, is weighed within 7 days following the end of the day of pack, except when the packer provides acceptable (see note below) documentation of the moisture loss for the product in storage at the point-of-pack, or

    (b) A fresh bakery product, while stored by the packer, is weighed within 1 day following the end of the day of pack, except when the packer provides acceptable (see note below) documentation of the moisture loss for the product in storage at the point of pack, or

    (c) The food is not subject to moisture loss, or

    (d) The food is packaged in an air-/moisture-tight container (e.g., cans, glass bottles, enclosed in paraffin, etc).

2. Allow 1 % for the following foods: frozen fruits and frozen vegetables, and fresh baked breads, buns, rolls and muffins.

3. Allow 3 % for the following foods: flour, dry pet food, pasta, rice, cheese and cheese products, dried fruits and vegetables, fresh fruits and vegetables, coffee beans, and bakery products other than fresh baked breads, buns, rolls and muffins.

Note for Moisture Allowances at Point of Pack: The data must be computed using the average moisture loss determined on a daily basis (e.g., the weight of each package in each of the sample control lots is determined everyday for 7 days) in environmental conditions similar to those that exist when the product is being inspected. For example, an inspector visits a pet food plant in Ohio in the middle of July to conduct a point-of-pack inspection. If the product tested had been packaged 5 days before the inspection and is found underweight; the moisture loss data must reflect the loss that would occur in July, not January. At least three sample control lots consisting of at least 48 randomly selected packages must be used to develop the moisture loss data. Each sample lot must be stored under the same conditions that are typical for the product (e.g., if the product is typically placed in a sealed case on a pallet and shrink wrapped, the sample lots must be stored under the same conditions. Moisture loss data obtained by removing the individual packages from the shipping case and storing them in a laboratory would not be acceptable). The three-sample control lots must be placed at various locations in the storage site. The average moisture loss value must be computed from the three-sample control lots with a 95 % prediction interval. If the packer does not provide the information, no additional moisture allowance should be permitted.

V. Moisture Loss for Products Not Listed in NIST Handbook 133

When officials test product for which no moisture loss guidance has been provided NIST can provide technical assistance. In the past NIST has published recommended moisture allowances for use at all locations including Point-of-Pack. If moisture loss studies are required NIST will assist in the completion of such studies. If studies are a necessity they should be a collaborative effort between officials and industry and can be very time consuming depending on the product. Because of the potential impact on interstate commerce, studies must be completed on a nationwide basis and not by individual jurisdictions unless circumstances justify only local consideration.

The amount of moisture lost from a package is a function of many factors not the least of which is the product itself (e.g., moisture content), packaging, storage conditions (e.g., temperature, humidity, air flow), time, handling and others. If a packaged product is subject to moisture loss officials must allow for "reasonable" variations caused by moisture either evaporating or draining from the product. Officials cannot set arbitrary moisture allowances based solely on their experience or intuition. Moisture allowances must be based on scientific data and must be "reasonable." Reasonable does not mean that all of the weight loss caused by moisture evaporation or draining from the product must be allowed. As a result of product and moisture variability the approach used by official must be developed on a case-by-case basis depending on many factors to include, but not be limited to, the manufacturing process, packaging materials, distribution, environmental influence and the anticipated shelf life of the product.

NIST Handbook 130 provides a starting point for developing a workable procedure in Section 2.5.6. in the Interpretation and Guideline Section regarding "Resolution for Requests for Recognition of Moisture Loss in Other Packaged Products." NIST WMD has worked and will continue to work extensively with the NCWM, The Laws and Regulations Committee, and industry to develop protocol for determining moisture allowances that can serve as models for future studies. Most studies involving nationally distributed products will require that products be tested during different seasons of the year and in different geographic locations to develop a nationally recognized moisture allowance. Some studies may require the development of laboratory tests used for inter-laboratory comparisons to establish moisture content in products at time-of-pack or at the time-of-inspection.

In some cases manufacturers can and may provide valid moisture loss data for officials to consider in lieu of conducting studies. In cases like this, WMD will provide assistance to determine if the information is complete or if further documentation is required. For example, a major producer of bar soap has provided moisture loss evidence for consideration by officials to determine what if any moisture loss could be expected to occur, in some cases this information has proven to be accurate thus avoiding the need for national data collection.

Moisture loss or gain is a critical consideration for any net content enforcement effort and one that, in most cases, cannot be addressed by a field official. If moisture loss issues are to be deliberated, it is the regulatory official's responsibility to resolve the packers concern utilizing available resources and due process procedures.

To fulfill this obligation officials may be required to utilize specialized test equipment and specific laboratory procedures. Additionally, the collection of adequate test data may require product examination over a broad geographical area and consideration of a wide range of environmental factors. If a national effort is required a coordinated effort involving industry, trade associations, weights and measures officials and federal agencies may be required. NIST will provide technical support upon request.

VI. Background Information on Federal Preemption

In the previous memorandum we reported that FDA was expected to adopt regulations identical to those contained in the 4th Supplement of the 3rd Edition of Handbook 133 adopted by the NCWM in 1994. The FDA published proposed regulations regarding net quantity of contents test procedures for packaged food under its jurisdiction in the March 4, 1997, issue (62 FR 9826) of the Federal Register. FDA subsequently withdrew that proposal on November 26, 2004 (69 FR 68831). FDA based the withdrawal on its need to reduce its regulatory backlog and focus its resources on current public health issues. The withdrawal did not speak to the merits of the proposal. Based on the experience reported since the adoption of the substantive revisions in 1994, WMD believes that the latest edition of Handbook 133 provides the basis for nationally uniform test methods and other requirements consistent with the requirements in Federal laws relating to net quantity of contents. Therefore, WMD recommends that State and local authorities test products according to the procedures outlined in the latest edition of Handbook 133 unless future FDA guidance or regulations specify otherwise. Moreover, it is extremely important that State and local jurisdictions continue to provide regulatory oversight so businesses can compete in a fair marketplace and consumers can depend on the representations of quantity upon which they make purchasing decisions.

a. Federal Preemption under the Nutrition Labeling and Education Act (NLEA) of 1990

The NLEA was signed into law on November 8, 1990, to amend Title 21 Section 343 of the Federal Food, Drug, and Cosmetic Act (FDCA). The Act requires nutrition labeling on foods and regulates health claims about food nutrients to help consumers select a more healthful diet. Under the Act, State and local laws not "identical" to corresponding FDA requirements are preempted. According to regulations under FDA [21 CFR Part 100.1 (c)(4)], the phrase "not identical" does not refer to the specific words in the requirement. Instead it means that the State or local requirement directly or indirectly imposes obligations or contains provisions that (1) are not imposed by or contained in an FDA requirement, or (2) differ from those specifically imposed by or contained in an FDA requirement or implementing regulation.

The preemption ensures uniformity in labeling requirements and prohibits non-uniform State and local laws, regulations, formal and informal policies, and other enforcement practices that prevent firms from conducting efficient and cost-effective business in all 50 States. Congress recognized that even though federal requirements may preempt more restrictive state requirements in certain instances, the net benefits from national uniformity in these aspects of the food label outweigh any loss in consumer protection that may occur as a result.

The ultimate goal of the NLEA is uniformity in laws, regulations, and test procedures—a goal shared by the NCWM and NIST alike. Under NLEA, state and local labeling requirements must be identical to many of the regulations promulgated under the Federal Food, Drug and Cosmetic Act, as amended by the NLEA, in Title 21 - Code of Federal Regulations, Parts 100 to 169 (current edition). Jurisdictions may continue to enforce state or local regulations on foods where there is no federal requirement and continue to enforce existing state and local laws if they are "identical" to FDA regulations.

b. Defining what is "Identical"

Federal preemption of the net quantity of contents regulations and test procedures occurred on November 8, 1991. On that date, state and local regulations on quantity of contents (e.g., net quantity of contents regulations, sampling plans, and test procedures) were preempted under the NLEA if they were not "identical" to federal requirements. The question is, what is "identical?" Both State and FDA regulations require packers to express an "accurate" statement of the quantity of contents of packaged food while permitting "reasonable" variations. The most common questions WMD receives are "do the test procedures used by the states and FDA provide identical results" (e.g., do the sampling plans have equal confidence levels, and are the products weighed or measured using recognized procedures) and "are the criteria for defining reasonable variations (e.g., the values of maximum allowable variations, the sample correction factors, and allowances for moisture loss) consistent with those used by FDA?"

FDA's test procedures are based on those contained in "Official Methods of Analysis" of the Association of Official Analytical Chemists International (AOAC). Based on information provided by FDA, WMD believes the test procedures contained in the 4th edition of Handbook 133 are identical to the AOAC procedures. If officials implement the recommendations in this memo, they should be using test procedures equivalent to FDA's.

c. Preemption Extends Beyond Food Packages Introduced into Interstate Commerce

Federal courts have ruled that the FDA has jurisdiction over all food products made from ingredients shipped in interstate commerce, regardless of the amount of the ingredient present, even though the finished product has not moved in interstate commerce. Products that have not entered interstate commerce (e.g., bakery products offered for sale in the food store where they are baked and packaged) that are made of ingredients shipped in interstate commerce to the store are subject to the Food, Drug, and Cosmetic Act and, therefore, should only be tested according to the following recommendations in this memorandum until final regulations are adopted by the FDA.

This memorandum is not legal advice. I encourage you to review this memo with your State Attorney General or staff attorney before implementing any policy on these issues or before you take enforcement action against a product that falls under FDA or other federal jurisdiction.

Training and Technical Support

WMD is committed to supporting state and local jurisdictions in their package inspection programs by providing technical assistance and training classes on Handbook 133. If you need assistance, please contact Tom Coleman at (301) 975-4004 or by e-mail at t.coleman@nist.gov.

NOTICE

The following documents could not be included in this publication because they are only available in Adobe PDF format. They are available from NIST upon request. Please contact Tom Coleman at (301) 975-4004 or by e-mail at **t.coleman@nist.gov** or Lisa Warfield at (301) 975-3308 or at **lisa.warfield@nist.gov** to obtain copies.

B. Letter from Kraft Foods Requesting that NIST Withdraw Letter on Moisture Loss

C. Chapter 3 from the 3rd Edition of NIST Handbook 133 and 4th Supplement 1994

Report of the
Specifications and Tolerances Committee

Michael J. Sikula, Chairman
Assistant Director
New York Bureau of Weights and Measures

Reference
Key Number

300 INTRODUCTION

This is the final report of the Committee on Specifications and Tolerances (S&T) (hereinafter referred to as the "Committee") for the 92nd Annual Meeting of the National Conference on Weights and Measures (NCWM). The report is based on the Interim Report offered in the NCWM Publication 16, "Committee Reports," testimony at public hearings, comments received from the regional weights and measures associations and other parties, the addendum sheets issued at the Annual Meeting, and actions taken by the membership at the voting session of the Annual Meeting.

Table A identifies the agenda items in the report by Reference Key Number, Item Title, and Page Number. The item numbers are those assigned in the Interim Meeting agenda. Voting items are indicated with a " **V**," or if the item was part of the Voting Consent calendar by the suffix " **VC**" after the item number. Items marked with an " **I**" after the reference key numbers are Information items. Items marked with a " **D**" after the key numbers are Developing items. The Developing designation indicates that an item, while it has merit, may not be adequately developed for action at the national level. Items marked " **W**" have been withdrawn from consideration. Items marked with a " **W**" will generally be referred to the regional weights and measures associations because they either need additional development, analysis, and input or did not have sufficient Committee support to bring them before NCWM.
Table B lists the appendices to the report, Table C identifies the acronyms for organizations and technical terms used throughout the report, and Table D provides a summary of the results of the voting on the Committee's items and the report in entirety.

This report contains recommendations to amend National Institute of Standards and Technology (NIST) Handbook 44, 2008 Edition, "Specifications, Tolerances, and Other Technical Requirements for Weighing and Measuring Devices." Proposed revisions to the handbook are shown in **bold face print** by ~~striking out~~ information to be deleted and __underlining__ information to be added. New items proposed for the handbook are designated as such and shown in **bold face print**.

Note: The policy of NIST is to use metric units of measurement in all of its publications; however, recommendations received by the NCWM technical committees have been printed in this publication as submitted. Therefore, the report may contain references to inch-pound units.

Table A
Index to Reference Key Items

Reference Key Number			Title of Item	Page
300			INTRODUCTION	1
310			GENERAL CODE	5
	310-1A	V	G-S.2. Facilitation of Fraud	5
	310-1B	I	Appendix D – Definition of Equipment	6
	310-2	VC	G-S.5.6.1. Recorded Representation of Metric Units on Equipment with Limited Character Sets and Table 1. Recorded Representation of Metric Units on Equipment with Limited Character Sets	6

S&T Committee 2007 Final Report

310-3	VC	G-S.8.1. Multiple Weighing or Measuring Elements that Share a Common Provision for Sealing	8
320	**SCALES**		**10**
320-1	W	S.1.1.(c) Zero Indication; Requirements for Markings or Indications for Other than Digital Zero Indications	10
320-2	I	S.1.1.1.(b) Digital Indicating Elements	13
320-3	I	S.1.2.1. Weight Units and T.N.2.1. General	16
320-4	D	S.1.4.6. Height and Definition of Minimum Reading Distance, UR.2.10. Primary Indicating Elements Provided by the User, UR.2.11. Minimum Reading Distance, and Definitions of Minimum Reading Distance and Primary Indications	19
320-5	W	S.2.1.7. Tare Rounding on a Multiple Range Scale	19
320-6	V	N.1.3.1. Bench or Counter Scales, N.1.3.8. All Other Scales Except Crane Scales, Hanging Scales, Hopper Scales, Wheel–Load Weighers, and Portable Axle-Load Weighers, and Appendix D, Definitions of Bench Scale and Counter Scale	23
320-7	VC	N.1.3.6.1. Dynamic Monorail Weighing Systems	29
320-8	W	Table 4. Minimum Test Weights and Test Loads	30
320-9	I	Appendix D; Definitions for Tare Mechanism, Gross Weight Value, Net Weight, Net Weight Value, Tare, and Tare Weight Value	32
321	**BELT-CONVEYOR SCALE SYSTEMS**		**35**
321-1	I	UR.2.2.(n) Belt Alignment	35
324	**AUTOMATIC WEIGHING SYSTEMS**		**36**
324-1	I	S.1.2. Value of Division Units and T.2.1. General	36
324-2	VC	Note 5 Table S.7.b. Notes for Table S.7.a.; Temperature Range	38
324-3	I	Appendix D; Definitions for Tare Mechanism, Gross Weight Value, Net Weight, Net Weight Value, Tare, and Tare Weight Value	41
330	**LIQUID-MEASURING DEVICES**		**42**
330-1	VC	S.1.2.3. Value of the Smallest Unit	42
330-2	V	S.1.6.5.5. Display of Quantity and Total Price and S.1.6.5.6. Display of Quantity and Total Price, Aviation Refueling Applications	44
330-3	V	S.3.1. Diversion of Measured Liquid	46
330-4	I	Temperature Compensation for Liquid Measuring Devices Code	47
331	**VEHICLE-TANK METERS**		**50**
331-1	V	Temperature Compensation	50
356(A)	**GRAIN MOISTURE METERS**		**53**
356(a)-1	VC	S.1.2. Grain or Seed Kind and Class Selection and Recording and Table S.1.2. Grain Types Considered for Type Evaluation and Calibration and Minimum Acceptable Abbreviations	53
357	**NEAR-INFRARED GRAIN ANALYZERS**		**56**
357-1	VC	S.1.2. Selecting Grain Class and Constituent and Table S.1.2. Grain Types Considered for Type Evaluation and Calibration and Minimum Acceptable Abbreviations	56
360	**OTHER ITEMS**		**58**
360-1	I	International Organization of Legal Metrology (OIML) Report	58
360-2		Developing Items	60

Table B
Appendices

Appendix Title	Page
A	Item 360-2: Developing Items..........A1

Part 1, Item 1, Scales: S.1.4.6. Height and Definition of Minimum Reading Distance, UR.2.10. Primary Indicating Elements Provided by the User, UR.2.11. Minimum Reading Distance, and Definitions of Minimum Reading Distance and Primary Indications..........A1
Part 2, Item 1, Belt-Conveyor Scale Systems: UR.3.2.(c) Maintenance; Zero Load Tests..........A4
Part 3, Item 1, Liquid-Measuring Devices: T.5. Predominance – Retail Motor-Fuel Devices..........A5
Part 3, Item 2, Liquid-Measuring Devices: Price Posting and Computing Capability and Requirements for a Retail Motor-Fuel Dispenser (RMFD)..........A6
Part 4, Item 1, Water Meters: UR.2.1. Accessibility for Reading..........A7

Table C
Glossary of Acronyms

AWS	Automatic Weighing Systems	NCWM	National Conference on Weights and Measures, Inc.
CC	Certificate of Conformance	NEWMA	Northeastern Weights and Measures Association
CWMA	Central Weights and Measures Association	NIST	National Institute of Standards and Technology
EPO	Examination Procedure Outline	NTEP	National Type Evaluation Program
GS	Grain Analyzer Sector	NTETC	National Type Evaluation Technical Committee
GMM	Grain Moisture Meters	RMFD	Retail Motor-Fuel Dispenser
GPMA	Gasoline Pump Manufacturers Association	SI	International System of Units
HB 44	NIST Handbook 44	SMA	Scale Manufacturers Association
HB 130	NIST Handbook 130	SWMA	Southern Weights and Measures Association
LMD	Liquid-Measuring Device	WMD	NIST Weights and Measures Division
LPG	Liquefied Petroleum Gas	WS	Weighing Sector
MDMD	Multiple Dimension Measuring Devices	WWMA	Western Weights and Measures Association
MFM	Mass Flow Meter	USNWG	NIST/OIML U.S. National Work Group
MMA	Meter Manufacturers Association	WG	Work Group
MS	Measuring Sector	VTM	Vehicle-tank Meters
OEM	Original Equipment Manufacturer		

"Handbook 44" (HB 44) means the 2008 Edition of NIST Handbook 44 "Specifications, Tolerances, and Other Technical Requirements for Weighing and Measuring Devices"
"Handbook 130" (HB 130) means the 2008 Edition of NIST Handbook 130 "Uniform Laws and Regulations in the Areas of Legal Metrology and Fuel Quality."

Note: NIST does not imply that these acronyms are used solely to identify these organizations or technical topics.

Table D
Voting Results

Reference Key Number	House of State Representatives		House of Delegates		Results
	Yeas	Nays	Yeas	Nays	
300 (Consent Calendar)	42	0	38	0	Passed
310-1A	41	0	39	0	Passed
320-6	30	10	32	7	Passed
330-2	42	1	38	0	Passed
330-3	27	15	30	9	Passed
331-1	34	6	35	3	Passed
300 (Report in its Entirety Voice Vote)	All Yeas	No Nays	All Yeas	No Nays	Passed

Details of All Items
(In Order by Reference Key Number)

310 GENERAL CODE

310-1A V   G-S.2. Facilitation of Fraud

(This item was adopted)

Source: Western Weights and Measures Association (WWMA)

Recommendation: Amend HB 44, Section 1.10. General Code paragraph G-S.2. as follows:

> **G-S.2. Facilitation of Fraud.** - All equipment and all mechanisms **, software,** and devices attached ~~thereto~~ **to** or used in ~~connection~~ **conjunction** therewith shall be so **designed,** constructed, assembled, and installed for use such that they do not facilitate the perpetration of fraud.

Background/Discussion: This proposal modified the language in paragraph G-S.2. to clarify that the prohibition against facilitating fraud applied to the electronically programmed and coded components of weighing and measuring devices. Some argued the existing language in Section 1.10. General Code. Paragraph G-S.2. Facilitation of Fraud was intended to address only hardware components of weighing and measuring devices. That is, "equipment, mechanisms, and devices" and the mechanics of how they are "constructed, assembled, and installed" appeared to deal with tangible components. Fraud issues in the past ten years involved: (1) altering, manipulating, or interfering with software interfaced with or installed in equipment; (2) microprocessor issues such as additional pulser units hidden in gas pumps and taximeters; and (3) software programs permitting manipulation of vehicle scale data used to generate weighmaster certificates.

The CWMA, SWMA, and WWMA recommended this item move forward for a vote.

NEWMA recommended this item be referred to the NTETC Software Sector for review and input.

At the 2007 NCWM Interim Meeting, the Committee considered the WWMA proposal and an alternate proposal developed by the SMA. The Committee acknowledged that neither proposal was reviewed by the NTETC Software Sector. The Committee agreed that updating the requirement could be accomplished by adding general terms to address the types of electronic and software-based technology being fraudulently used today. The WWMA proposed language naming specific software applications that should not facilitate fraud. Whereas, the SMA alternate proposal included broader language that is intended to prohibit fraudulent use of software, wireless connections, and all future technology "without limitation." The Committee agreed the SMA proposal encompasses all possible equipment configurations and more appropriately addressed the problem at hand. Therefore the Committee agreed to present the SMA proposal for a vote at the 2007 NCWM Annual Meeting.

At the 2007 NCWM Annual Meeting, the Committee considered multiple alternate proposals from the regional weights and measures associations, NTETC Software Sector, SMA, and NTEP participating laboratories to modify paragraph G-S.2. and agreed on the above proposal that maintained the original intent of the design specification and also clearly expanded the scope of the requirement to apply to software and wireless connections affecting metrological parameters. The Committee also considered a proposal to define the term "equipment" which has a unique meaning to requirements in HB 44, making it difficult to determine which part of a device or system must meet paragraph G-S.2. The proposed new definition of equipment was based on paragraph G-A.1. Commercial and Law-Enforcement Equipment and clarifies the various types and portions of a device or system used to establish a weight or measure that must comply with paragraph G-S.2. However, because the definition had just been introduced to the Conference, the Committee recommended splitting the proposal so that the proposed definition became a separate Information item presented as Item 310-1B. The proposal to modify paragraph G-S.2. was renumbered to become 310-1A and was presented for a vote.

310-1B I Appendix D – Definition of Equipment

Source: NIST Weights and Measures Division

Recommendation: Add a new definition for "equipment" to Appendix D as follows:

equipment. Weights, measures, and weighing and measuring devices, instruments, elements, and systems or portion thereof used or employed in establishing the size, quantity, value, extent, area, composition, constituent value, or measurement of quantities, things, produce, or articles for distribution or consumption, purchased, offered, or submitted for sale, hire, or award, or in computing any basic charge or payment for services rendered on the basis of weight or measure.[1.10, 2.20, 2.21, 2.22, 2.24, 3.30, 3.31, 3.32, 3.33, 3.34, 3.35, 3.38, 4.40, 5.51, 5.56.(a), 5.56.(b), 5.57, 5.58, 5.59]

Discussion: The Committee agreed there is a need to define the term "equipment" since the term is used throughout HB 44 device codes. The term may be misinterpreted in paragraph G-S.2. unless there is a specific definition added to Appendix D to clarify which parts or portions of a device or system must comply. The Committee split S&T Item 310-1 into two separate items: S&T Item 310-1A (a proposal to modify paragraph G-S.2.) and S&T Item 310-1B (an Information item that recommends a new definition for "equipment" as used in HB 44). The Committee noted that the term "equipment" does not appear in all HB 44 Codes. The Committee recommended that Item 310-1B be carried over to allow sufficient time for a review of the proposed definition.

310-2 VC G-S.5.6.1. Recorded Representation of Metric Units on Equipment with Limited Character Sets and Table 1. Recorded Representation of Metric Units on Equipment with Limited Character Sets

Source: Southern Weights and Measures Association (SWMA)

(This item was adopted)

Recommendation: Amend paragraph G-S.5.6.1. and Table 1. as follows:

Modify paragraph G-S.5.6.1. and Table 1. as follows:

G-S.5.6.1. Indicated and Recorded Representation of ~~Metric Units on Equipment with Limited Character Sets.~~ – Appropriate Abbreviations.

(a) For equipment manufactured after January 1, 2008, the appropriate defining symbols are shown in NIST Special Publication SP 811 "Guide for the Use of International System of Units (SI)" and Handbook 44 Appendix C – General Tables of Units of Measurement.

Note: SP 811 can be viewed or downloaded at http://physics.nist.gov/cuu/pdf/sp811.pdf. (Added 2007)

(b) The appropriate defining symbols on equipment manufactured prior to January 1, 2008, with limited character sets are shown in Table 1. ~~Representation of SI Units on Equipment Manufactured prior to January 1, 2007, with Limited Character Sets~~.
(Added 1977) (Amended 2007)

Table 1. ~~Recorded~~ Representation of ~~Metric~~ SI Units on Equipment Manufactured prior to January 1, 2008, with Limited Character Sets				
Representation			**Form I**	**Form II**
Name of Unit	**International symbol (common use symbol)**	**(double case)**	**(single case lower)**	**(single case upper)**
Base SI units				
meter kilogram	m m m M kg kg kg KG			
Derived SI units				
newton N N n N pascal Pa Pa pa PA watt W W w W volt V V v V degree Celsius	°C	°C	°c	°C
Other units				
liter gram metric ton bar bar bar bar BAR	l or L g g g G t	L t	l tne	L TNE

Background/Discussion: At its fall 2006 Annual Meeting, the SWMA reviewed a proposal from the Weighing Sector to amend paragraph G-S.5.6.1. The amendment would require abbreviations for SI units for both indications and recorded representations on new technology as specified in NIST Special Publication 811 "Guide for the Use of International System of Units (SI) and HB 44 Appendix C – General Tables of Units of Measurement. The amendment would continue to permit exceptions to those guidelines for older equipment with limited character sets. WMD has received inquiries from device manufacturers regarding how to apply the requirements in Table 1 for the abbreviation of SI units. There appears to be confusion about the intent of Table 1 unless one is directed to review paragraph G-S.5.6.1. in conjunction with Table 1. Additionally, there are instances where abbreviations for SI units may be confused with other abbreviations; for example, in devices designed with or capable of indicating and/or recording in additional units of measurement (e.g., inch-pound units) or when used with identifiers for measurement values such as gross, tare, and net (G, T, N).

HB 44 paragraph G-S.5.6.1. was originally added to HB 44 in 1977 to address concerns about equipment with limited printing capabilities, that is, with either upper or lower case characters only. For example, a recording element, interfaced with a weighing system, which is equipped with upper case characters only; it will print the symbol for kilogram as "KG." It was the NCWM S&T Committee's view at that time that to require a lower case character capability solely to provide the appropriate symbol in lower case character (e.g., "kg") would be cost prohibitive. Further, the Committee saw no problem in identifying "KG" as representing kilograms just as there is no problem in identifying the abbreviation for pound as "LB" or "lb." The Committee also reviewed the International Standard Organization's ISO 2955, which sets forth guidelines for the representation of SI and other units for use in systems with limited character sets. ISO 2955 "Representations of SI and other Units in Systems with Limited Character Sets," an information processing standard, was withdrawn in 2001.

WMD believes that permitting exceptions for abbreviations of SI units of measure is no longer necessary when considering advances in printer and display technology.

SWMA supported the proposal and agreed to forward it to the NCWM S&T Committee with a recommendation that it be a Voting item on the Committee's 2007 agenda.

At the 2007 NCWM Interim Meeting, the Committee made two editorial changes to the SWMA proposal as shown above. The Committee notes that the requirement includes units from multiple systems of measurement; therefore, it is not appropriate to name only metric units in the paragraph's title. The proposal more appropriately lists the requirements that apply for SI units in a separate subparagraph. The Committee agreed there is precedence for citing a website where a reference document is available. The Committee agreed to present the item as modified for a vote at the 2007 NCWM Annual Meeting.

At the 2007 NCWM Annual Meeting, the Committee also recognized that HB 44 was inconsistent in how it designates titles of paragraphs and tables where only table and paragraph numbers are referenced. Since there was no convention or document style guideline, the Committee agreed with WMD that the title or name of the corresponding paragraph or table (including a shortened title where appropriate) should be included when referencing the paragraph number, and that this could be done editorially throughout HB 44 as necessary.

310-3 VC G-S.8.1. Multiple Weighing or Measuring Elements that Share a Common Provision for Sealing

(This item was adopted)

Source: Carryover Item 310-3. (This item originated from the Western Weights and Measures Association (WWMA) and first appeared on the Committee's 2006 agenda.)

Recommendation: Add a new paragraph G-S.8.1. as follows:

~~G-S.8.1. Multiple Weighing or Measuring Elements that Share a Common Provision for Sealing. – A change to any metrological parameter (calibration or configuration) of any weighing or measuring element shall be individually identified.~~
~~[Nonretroactive as of January 1, 2010]~~

Note: For devices that utilize an electronic form of sealing, in addition to the requirements in G-S.8.1., any appropriate audit trail requirements in an applicable specific device code also apply. Examples of identification of a change to the metrological parameters of a weighing or measuring element include, but are not limited to,:

(1) a broken, missing, or replaced physical seal on an individual weighing, measuring, or indicating element or active junction box;
(2) a change in a calibration factor or configuration setting for each weighing or measuring element;
(3) a display of the date of calibration or configuration event for each weighing or measuring element; or
(4) counters indicating the number of calibration and/or configuration events for each weighing or measuring element.

(Added 2007)

Remove the existing Section 3.30. paragraph S.2.2.1. Multiple Measuring Elements with a Single Provision for Sealing when G-S.8.1. becomes effective; add a note to S.2.2.1. to indicate its removal date.

S.2.2.1. Multiple Measuring Elements with a Single Provision for Sealing. – A change to the adjustment of any measuring element shall be individually identified.
[Nonretroactive as of January 1, 2005]

Note 1: Examples of acceptable identification of a change to the adjustment of a measuring element include, but are not limited to:

(a) a broken, missing, or replaced physical seal on an individual measuring element;

(b) a change in a calibration factor for each measuring element;

(c) a display of the date of or the number of days since the last calibration event for each measuring element; or

(d) a counter indicating the number of calibration events per measuring element.
(Added 2004)

Note 2: S.2.2.1. will be removed in the 2010 edition of Handbook 44 when General Code paragraph G-S.8.1. Multiple Weighing or Measuring Elements with a Single Provision for Sealing becomes effective.
(Note 2 Added 2007)

Background/Discussion: The Committee believes a General Code requirement for identification of adjustments to individual weighing or measuring elements is appropriate, regardless of the device type, when systems have multiple weighing or measuring elements with a single provision for sealing. Initially, this proposal was developed to add to all the liquid-measuring device codes a requirement for identifying when an adjustment is made to _any_ measuring device which has multiple measuring elements, but which is equipped only with a single provision for sealing the adjustment mechanism or access to the adjustment mechanism(s). After rejecting a meter for not meeting performance requirements, jurisdictions reported difficulty in determining whether or not repairs or adjustments were made to that meter. During the subsequent inspection, an official might have to test multiple grades or blends to confirm the rejected meter had been corrected. The proposed requirement is similar to the existing requirement in Section 3.30. paragraph S.2.2.1. Multiple Measuring Elements with a Single Provision for Sealing.

The Committee heard from the weighing industry that the proposal was not appropriate for all devices. The Committee believed it was important to be sure no specific HB 44 codes would be adversely affected by placing the requirements in the General Code; therefore, the Committee originally agreed to make the proposal an Information item to provide the opportunity for the National Type Evaluation Technical Committee Sectors and the regional weights and measures associations to evaluate the item further, especially for any adverse impact on a particular device type(s).

A General Code requirement would address all possible device types, including weighing systems, and any scenario where metrological parameters (calibration or configuration) have a single means for security. The list of acceptable means for individually identifying a change to a metrological parameter includes provisions for devices where features are accessed through an indicator or active junction box, but the list was not meant to be all-inclusive. Examples of weighing systems that have multiple weighing elements connected to a single indicator such that the calibration of each is controlled by a single seal include "in-and-out" weighing systems, shipping scale systems equipped with at least two platforms with different capacities connected to a single indicator, and multiple platform vehicle scales and axle-load weighers used for highway load enforcement or for truck operators' use such as "CAT Scales." Additionally, NTEP has evaluated indicators with the ability to support up to as many as ten weighing elements.

At their fall 2006 meetings, CWMA, NEWMA, SWMA, and WWMA agreed the proposal should move forward for a vote as written. The CWMA agreed that if this item was adopted, LMD Code paragraph S.2.2.1. would become redundant and should be deleted. The WWMA agreed the proposal should apply to all device technologies where multiple components with metrological functions are secured by a single seal. The WWMA also heard there were weighing devices with multiple load-receiving elements interfaced to a single indicator (where sealing occurs) that have the ability to track changes to metrological parameters through an audit trail. Devices with an event logger would comply with the proposal. Devices utilizing only common counters for calibration and configuration parameters that increment one time when one or more weighing or measuring elements have been accessed would still need an additional means, such as a calibration factor for each element, to identify that changes were made to a particular element.

At the 2007 NCWM Interim Meeting, the Committee agreed that modifications were needed to the title to clarify that the provision applies when elements share a security seal. Changes were also needed to the proposed language in the paragraph to eliminate the example allowing the display of the number of days to identify a change to metrological parameters in proposed new paragraph G-S.8.1. to eliminate any potential conflict with existing audit trail criteria. The Committee also agreed that if proposed paragraph G-S.8.1. was adopted, then Section 3.30. paragraph S.2.2.1. would no longer be needed and should be removed.

At the 2007 NCWM Annual Meeting, the Committee agreed with industry comments that it was appropriate that the proposal to modify paragraph G-S.8.1. have a 2010 enforcement date to lessen the impact of the requirement on device manufacturers needing to modify equipment. Rather than delete paragraph S.2.2.1. Multiple Measuring Elements with a Single Provision for Sealing from the Liquid Measuring Devices Code at this time, the Committee agreed to recommend the inclusion of a second note in paragraph S.2.2.1. to indicate that paragraph S.2.2.1. will be removed from HB 44 when new proposed paragraph G-S.8.1. becomes effective in 2010. On January 1, 2010, paragraph G-S.8.1. will apply to all classes of devices in the specific device codes.

For additional background information, refer to the Committee's 2006 Final Report.

320 SCALES

320-1 W S.1.1.(c) Zero Indication; Requirements for Markings or Indications for Other than Digital Zero Indications

(This item was withdrawn)

Source: Carryover Item 320-1. (This item originated from the Committee and first appeared on its 2004 agenda.)

Recommendation: Amend paragraph S.1.1.(c) as follows:

S.1.1. Zero Indication.

(a) On a scale equipped with indicating or recording elements, provision shall be made to either indicate or record a zero-balance condition.

(b) On an automatic-indicating scale or balance indicator, provision shall be made to indicate or record an out-of-balance condition on both sides of zero.

(c) A zero-balance condition may be indicated by other than a continuous digital zero indication, provided that an effective automatic means is provided to inhibit a weighing operation or to return to a continuous digital indication when the scale is in an out-of-balance condition **and is marked or includes supplemental indications to indicate that the "other than continuous digital zero indication" represents a no-load condition of the scale.**
(Added 1987) (Amended 1993 **and 200X**)

**Note: The markings or supplemental indications in S.1.1.(c) are not required if, prior to the start of a transaction: (1) operator intervention is required to verify the zero-balance condition with a digital zero indication, or (2) for a scale equipped to indicate a zero-balance condition by a digital zero indication, the scale automatically resets to a digital zero indication.
(Added 200X)**
(Amended 1987)

Background/Discussion: The proposed changes to the requirement are intended to clarify that all primary indicators on scales using anything other than a digital zero indication (e.g., scrolling messages, dashes, etc.) to indicate zero require additional markings or indications to inform customers the scale is at a zero-balance condition. No markings are necessary on these devices when operator intervention is required to return the indication to a digital zero before conducting a transaction. The proposal addresses instances where the OEM elects to display rather than mark the information (i.e., supplemental indications) on the device. The proposed changes are meant to be applied retroactively and, therefore, apply to all equipment including self-service applications that have undergone type evaluation.

The proposal is more than a simple clarification or housekeeping item. The proposed language is not in conflict with type evaluation procedures in NCWM Publication 14 (a document derived from HB 44 requirements). The proposal is warranted because of ongoing disagreements between NTEP laboratories at type evaluation on whether or not a scale complies with paragraph S.1.1.(c). If the proposal is adopted, the labs will find that Publication 14 and

HB 44 agree and there is no vagueness in the wording of either document or room for misinterpretation. Since field officials may not have access to Publication 14, they need definitive guidelines in their working documents on how to apply the requirement should devices be modified after type evaluation.

In 2004 the Committee interpreted General Code paragraph G-S.6. Marking Operational Controls, Indications, and Features and Scales Code paragraph S.1.1. Zero Indication as requiring weighing devices to be marked or provide an indication stating the zero balance is represented by other than a digital zero indication. This position is supported by the 1993 amendment to paragraph S.1.1.(c) as well as type evaluation requirements and other HB 44 requirements adopted to ensure customers have sufficient information about displays and recorded transaction information in order to make an informed decision during a direct sale transaction.

In 2005 the Committee heard opposition to the proposal from several regional associations, the Weighing Sector, and scale manufacturers. These groups cited the following reasons for taking this position: (1) current HB 44 language provides sufficient guidelines, (2) labeling criteria applied during type evaluation offers adequate protection from fraud, (3) the type evaluation laboratory determines that labeling is not necessary if a scale has an automatic means to inhibit a transaction when it is out of balance or returns to a continuous digital indication when in an out-of-balance condition, and (4) several jurisdictions have indicated they are not receiving any complaints because equipment lacks explanatory marking information.

The Committee believes provisions should be in place for all devices to indicate clearly a zero-balance condition either with a digital zero, an annunciator, or using some other accepted means. The Committee is concerned there are no definitive guidelines available for the field official to verify a zero-balance condition particularly on software-based devices modified after type evaluation but also on devices that do not return to a digital zero. It is the continued belief of the Committee that the proposal has some merit but modified the language in response to comments that there is confusion about the language that addresses markings and indications. The Committee made changes to S.1.1.(c) to: (1) specify that markings and indications must be visible to the customer, and (2) clarify one instance where markings and indications are not required.

In spring 2006 the Committee heard further opposition to the proposal from the public and private sector members who believe the wording in paragraph S.1.1.(c) is adequate to prevent fraud. However, one jurisdiction in support of the proposal noted that an indication other than zero would not be acceptable for devices such as a retail motor-fuel dispenser since it found dispensers in the field with no zero indication as a result of software changes made to indications after type evaluation. Because of varied positions, the Committee changed the status of the proposal from a Voting item to an Information item. The Committee asked that the regional weights and measures associations consider the proposal during their 2006 fall sessions, being mindful that there are installations where the operator is not present to verify a zero-balance condition.

In the fall of 2006, the WWMA agreed it should be clear that a scale starts a transaction at zero. The WWMA believes the proposed modifications to (c) are sufficient and the note that describes when markings are not necessary is redundant. The WWMA further asserted that part (2) of the note describing how the device must function is not clearly worded. Consequently, the WWMA supported the proposal as a Voting item, but without the addition of the proposed note. The SWMA supports the WWMA alternate proposal.

The CWMA and NEWMA recommend this proposal be withdrawn because the current wording in NIST HB 44 is sufficient.

In fall 2006 the SMA restated its opposition to this proposal because it believes the current provisions of paragraph S.1.1.(c), are sufficient to prevent facilitation of fraud. The SMA continues its support of the Weighing Sector's 2005 analysis of the proposal.

During the 2007 Interim Meeting, WMD continued to support the 1993 and 2004 Committee's position in favor of using markings that explain when indications other than a digital zero indication represent a zero-balance condition and making the requirement readily available to current and future field officials. WMD recommended a modified proposal eliminating proposed new subparagraph (2), which seemed to create some difficulty for manufacturers in the setup of the automatic sequence for resetting the scale to a digital zero indication.

The Committee acknowledged that the weights and measures community is still divided on whether or not markings are needed to identify that an other-than-digital zero indication represents a zero-load condition on a scale. The Committee also heard a suggestion from both private and public sector members to modify the language to require a zero-balance indication that would clarify any ambiguity about the scale's zero-balance condition. The Committee agreed the proposal as worded does not get to the source of the problem that can occur should a device be set up to start a transaction when a zero condition does not exist. The Committee believes the proposal must go beyond a marking requirement. Consequently, the Committee kept the proposal as an Information item and recommends that rather than solve the problem with a marking requirement, the Weighing Sector and others affected in the weights and measures community provide input on possible modifications to arrive at a proposal that is a nonretroactive requirement that specifies the scale must start at a zero indication or have a center-of-zero indicator.

In response to the Committee's request, WMD submitted an alternative proposal for consideration by the community as follows:

S.1.1. Zero Indication.

(a) On a scale equipped with indicating or recording elements, provision shall be made to either indicate or record a zero-balance condition.

(b) On an automatic-indicating scale or balance indicator, provision shall be made to indicate or record an out-of-balance condition on both sides of zero.

(c) **For Scales Manufactured Between January 1, 1993, and January 1, 200X.** – A zero-balance condition may be indicated by other than a continuous digital zero indication, provided that an effective automatic means is provided to inhibit a weighing operation or to return to a continuous digital indication when the scale is in an out-of-balance condition.
(Added 1987) (Amended 1993 **and 200X**)

(d) For Scales Manufactured On or After January 1, 200X. – A zero-balance condition may be indicated by other than a continuous digital zero indication, provided that:

　i) an effective automatic means is provided to inhibit a weighing operation when the scale is out of balance until a digital zero-balance indication is displayed, or

　ii) a "center-of-zero" is displayed when the scale is within ± ¼ of a scale division of zero and returns to a continuous digital indication when the scale is in an out-of-balance condition more than ± ¼ of a scale division.
(Added 200X)

During its development of the alternate proposal, WMD concluded that the "center-of-zero" language in paragraph S.1.1.1. Digital Indicating Elements would also need to be amended since the current language in paragraph S.1.1.1. does not require the "center-of-zero" indications if the automatic zero-tracking mechanism (AZT) maintains the zero-balance condition within ± ¼ d. Therefore, WMD also developed a separate alternate proposal to amend paragraph S.1.1.1. in S&T Item 320-2 to require that the "center-of-zero" indication always be provided when the zero-balance condition is within ± ¼ d, even when AZT maintains the zero-balance condition within ± ¼ d. WMD's alternate proposal to amend paragraph S.1.1.1. is similar to an OIML R 76 recommendation in Section 4.4.5. that requires a "center-of-zero" indication at all times when the zero balance is within "0.25 e" (and for a center-of-zero indication to be allowed after tare has been taken and the device is displaying a "net" zero). WMD recommended that the Committee may also want to consider combining S&T Items 320-1 and 320-2 into a single proposal because they are so closely related.

The Committee requested input on this alternate proposal from the weights and measures community.

At the 2007 NCWM Annual Meeting, the Committee heard testimony from the CWMA, NEWMA, and SMA recommending this item be withdrawn since the current technologies allowed by paragraph S.1.1.(c). are sufficient to prevent facilitation of fraud.

The Committee also heard comments at both the 2007 NCWM Interim and Annual Meetings from an NCWM member that, as a consumer and weights and measures professional, she believes consumers have a right to have adequate information about a transaction, including information to indicate the scale is starting on zero.

WMD commented that NCWM Publication 14 Digital Electronic Scale (DES) Section 11.8.4 and Electronic Cash Registers Interfaced with Scales (ECRS) Section 8 were amended in 2004 to specify that a label is required if the scale or electronic cash register (ECR) display returns to a live weight when the scale which is not at a zero-balanced condition are to be used. These changes to Publication 14 were based on a position taken by the 89th S&T Committee (2004) after a review of the 78th NCWM S&T Committee (1993) discussions on paragraph S.1.1.(c). Zero Indication.

WMD also provided the Committee with information on the Canadian Type Evaluation and Field Manual requirements that defined the term "sleep mode;" and WMD also provided conditions when a scale could enter a sleep mode and the procedures to verify the correct operation of the sleep mode. The Canadian requirements state that "the device must bear, adjacent to the weight display, the following marking: 'The device is at zero when in sleep mode' or equivalent statement if the device is allowed to go into a sleep mode with a load on the scale" (Specifications Relating to Non-automatic Weighing Devices (1998) Sections 30 to 33, and 41, and Laboratory Manual for the Evaluation of Non Automatic Weighing Devices dated January 1997, Sections 10.9 to 10.12, Sleep Mode or Displaying Non Metrological Information.

The Committee agreed there has been significant advancement in technology since the topic of "other than digital zero indications" was discussed, and weights and measures officials are more familiar with the technology. The Committee also heard from regional associations that officials in their region have not received complaints from the general public regarding the lack of a display of digital zero at the start of a transaction. The Committee believes the opinion of the 1993 S&T Committee interpretation that requires a label stating a screen saver or scrolling message represents zero is no longer valid or necessary. Therefore, a label is not required if the scale is capable of displaying non-zero information when it is in the sleep mode if the requirement for an effective and automatic means is provided to inhibit a weighing operation or to return to a continuous digital indication when the scale is in an out-of-balance condition, thereby meeting the provision of paragraph S.1.1.(c).

Therefore, the Committee agreed to withdraw the item from its agenda.

For additional background information, refer to the Committee's 2004, 2005, and 2006 Final Reports.

320-2   I   S.1.1.1.(b) Digital Indicating Elements

Source: National Type Evaluation Technical Committee (NTETC) Weighing Sector

Recommendation: At the 2007 Annual Meeting, the Committee modified the proposed language developed after the 2007 Interim Meeting. The recommendation (as modified by the Committee) currently under consideration by the Committee is to amend S.1.1.1. as follows:

S.1.1.1. Digital Indicating Elements.

(a) A digital zero indication shall represent a balance condition that is within ± ½ the value of the scale division.

(b) A digital indicating device shall either automatically maintain a "center-of-zero" condition to ± ¼ scale division or less, or have an auxiliary or supplemental "center-of-zero" indicator that defines a zero balance condition to ± ¼ of a scale division or less.
[Nonretroactive as of January 1, 1993]

Note: The "center-of-zero" indication may also work when zero is indicated for gross load zero or after a tare operation.

(Amended 1992 **and 200X**)

Discussion: Scales Code requirements do not include sufficiently detailed language to identify all types of tare, define how tare features must operate, or specify the net and tare values a scale must indicate and record. Current HB 44 requirements that address tare include paragraphs S.2.1.6. Combined Zero-Tare ("0/T") Key, S.2.3. Tare, S.2.3.1. Monorail Scales Equipped with Digital Indications, and T.N.2.1. General (Tolerances). This Weighing Sector proposal is the first of several proposed modifications to HB 44 requirements intended to clarify the suitability of tare features already widely used in commercial applications.

The Weighing Sector developed criteria used to type evaluate tare features based on General Code paragraph G-S.2. Facilitation of Fraud and other requirements that apply to indicating and recording elements and recorded representations. NTEP laboratories find that it has become increasingly difficult to base its compliance decisions on paragraph G-S.2. solely because the general nature of the language results in multiple interpretations. Type evaluation criteria are published in NCWM Publication 14; however, this document is not in wide distribution in the weights and measures community and only a limited number of weights and measures officials, device manufacturers, and device owners and operators are regular participants in Weighing Sector meetings where tare evaluation criteria are developed and discussed. Additionally, it is difficult for parties responsible for the design, use, and test of the tare feature to interpret and apply technical requirements published in Publication 14. This results in differing interpretations of HB 44 requirements.

In 2006, the NTETC Weighing Sector formed a Tare Work Group (WG) to review existing tare requirements and make recommendations about how tare is to operate on a single range scale, a multiple range scale, and a multi-interval scale. The WG was also asked to develop, where necessary, recommendations for changes to Publication 14, HB 44, and HB 130 and to provide guidance to the Weighing Sector on type evaluation requirements.

The WG is currently developing proposals to amend HB 44 requirements to:

(1) ensure that a tare feature operates in a manner that increases the accuracy of net weight determinations,
(2) clearly state what information and values are permitted and required for indicated and recorded representations of net weight and tare weight, and
(3) identify the types (e.g., semiautomatic and stored tares) of tare weight values that are determined at the time objects are weighed or tare weight values that are determined prior to the time objects are weighed.

The Weighing Sector agreed the WG's proposal to amend paragraph S.1.1.1.(b) further clarifies that an auxiliary or supplemental "center-of-zero" indication is permitted with a load on the scale provided tare material is zero-balanced off by the tare mechanism and prescribes that the acceptable limits of accuracy are within ± ¼ scale division for the resulting zero net indication. The Weighing Sector recommends the adoption of the proposal as an important step in promoting the development of specific language in HB 44 for specifications, test notes, and tolerances for different types of tare (e.g., tare, preset tare, percentage tare, etc.).

The Committee considered the Weighing Sector's proposal to modify paragraph S.1.1.1. as follows:

S.1.1.1. Digital Indicating Elements.

(a) A digital zero indication shall represent a balance condition that is within ± ½ the value of the scale division.

(b) A digital indicating device shall either automatically maintain a "center-of-zero" condition to ± ¼ scale division or less, or have an auxiliary or supplemental "center-of-zero" indicator that defines a zero balance condition to ± ¼ of a scale division or less. **The auxiliary or supplemental "center-of-zero" indicator may be operable with a zero net weight indication.**
[Nonretroactive as of January 1, 1993]
(Amended 1992 **and 200X**)

The SWMA supported the intent of the Weighing Sector's proposal, but agreed some modifications to the text in paragraph S.1.1.1. were needed to clarify that the center-of-zero indicator may be operable when a zero condition exists in the net weight mode. The SWMA recommended its alternate proposal move forward as a Voting item.

The Committee considered the SWMA's alternate proposal as follows:

S.1.1.1. Digital Indicating Elements.

(a) A digital zero indication shall represent a balance condition that is within ± ½ the value of the scale division.

(b) *A digital indicating device shall either automatically maintain a "center-of-zero" condition to ± ¼ scale division or less, or have an auxiliary or supplemental "center-of-zero" indicator that defines a zero balance condition to ± ¼ of a scale division or less.* **The auxiliary or supplemental "center-of-zero" indicator may be operable with a zero condition in the net weight mode.**
[Nonretroactive as of January 1, 1993]
(Amended 1992 **and 200X**)

During the Committee's review of the SWMA alternate proposal, WMD recommended the Committee consider there may be a possible conflict between the SWMA proposal and 2006 NCWM Publication 14 criteria for zero indications in Section 41.5 that prohibits a minus sign from preceding a zero indication.

The SMA supported the Weighing Sector's proposal.

The Committee discussed the possibility of using language in the Weighing Sector's and the SWMA's proposals to modify paragraph S.1.1.(b) because together the proposals included two of three conditions that must be met for a center-of-zero indication when the scale is in a zero balance condition.

The Committee agreed the best approach to developing language to address the operation of a center-of-zero indication was to request the NIST technical advisor to the Weighing Sector rework paragraph (b) using language similar to Publication 14 criteria that specifies how the center-of-zero must operate at zero gross weight or defines when there can be a zero indication of net weight. The Committee received the alternate proposal to amend S.1.1.1. as shown below and made it a Voting item in its 2007 Interim Report since this tare-related item focuses only on clarifying how the center-of-zero indication operates.

S.1.1.1. Digital Indicating Elements.

(a) ~~A digital zero indication shall represent a balance condition that is within ± ½ the value of the scale division.~~ **A digital indicating device shall automatically maintain a "center-of-zero" condition to ± ¼ scale division and have an auxiliary or supplemental "center-of-zero" indicator that defines a zero balance condition to ± ¼ of a scale division or less. The "center-of-zero" indication may also work when zero is indicated for:**

i. gross load zero, or
ii. after a tare operation.
~~[Nonretroactive as of January 1, 2007]~~

(b) **For** ~~A~~ **Digital Indicating Elements Manufactured Before January 1, 2007. –** ~~device shall either automatically maintain a "center-of-zero" condition to ± ¼ scale division or less, or have an auxiliary or supplemental "center-of-zero" indicator that defines a zero-balance condition to~~ ± ¼ ~~of a scale division or less.~~ **A digital zero indication shall represent a balance condition that is within ± ½ the value of the scale division**

(c) **For Digital Indicating Elements Manufactured Between January 1, 1993, and January 1, 2007. – A digital indicating device shall either automatically maintain a "center-of-zero" condition to**

± ¼ **scale division or less, or have an auxiliary or supplemental "center-of-zero" indicator that defines a zero balance condition to ± ¼ of a scale division or less.**
[Nonretroactive as of January 1, 1993]
(Amended 1992 **and 2007**)

At the 2007 NCWM Annual Meeting, the Committee heard testimony from the CWMA, NEWMA, and SMA stating this item has changed from the original intent to verify that zero tracking could be operable in the net mode, to now include the addition of other language which alters the requirement even more. For example, in paragraph S.1.1.1.(a), by stating "and" instead of "or" would make both requirements mandatory. If "or" is used instead of "and," then this proposal lowers the current requirement of ½ e to ¼ e. The SMA further stated that proposed paragraph (a) adds a dual requirement that is not consistent with Canadian and OIML requirements. Therefore, the CWMA, NEWMA, and SMA recommended the status of the proposal be changed to Informational to allow time for further consideration.

WMD agreed with the CWMA, NEWMA, and SMA and recommended deleting the additional changes added to the proposal (changing "or" to "and," in addition to requiring all electronic indicators maintain zero to ¼ e). WMD suggested the Committee consider amending the proposal as shown in the recommendation to be more consistent with the original intent of the NTETC Weighing Sector. WMD also provided the Committee with a second proposal to consider at a later date to define the zero condition of a scale with a "center-of-zero" annunciator while the scale is in a "sleep mode" if the Committee had chosen to recommend agenda Item 320-1 for a vote.

The Committee agreed that comments shown in its 2007 Interim report significantly change the original intent of the proposal. Additionally, the changes to the center-of-zero indication requirements are in conflict with OIML recommendations and Canadian requirements.

The Committee agreed the status of the item should be changed to Informational and the first alternate proposal from WMD become a carry-over item for the 2008 Committee agenda since that text is consistent with the intent of the original proposal from the NTETC Weighing Sector.

320-3   I   S.1.2.1. Weight Units and T.N.2.1. General

Source: National Type Evaluation Technical Committee (NTETC) Weighing Sector

Recommendation: Add a new note to paragraph S.1.2.1. and amend paragraph T.N.2.1. as follows:

S.1.2.1. Weight Units. - *Except for postal scales, a digital-indicating scale shall indicate weight values using only a single unit of measure. Weight values shall be presented in a decimal format with the value of the scale division expressed as 1, 2, or 5, or a decimal multiple or sub-multiple of 1, 2, or 5.*
[Nonretroactive as of January 1, 1989]

Note: The requirements that the value of the scale division be expressed only as 1, 2, or 5, or a decimal multiple or submultiples of only 1, 2, or 5 does not apply to net weight indications and recorded representations that are calculated from gross and tare weight indications where the scale division of the gross weight is different from the scale division of the tare weight(s) on multi-interval or multiple range scales.

For example, a scale indicating a tare weight of 2 kg in the lower range or segment and a gross weight of 5 kg in the higher range or segment may indicate a net weight of 3 kg, or a scale indicating a tare weight of 20 lb in the lower range or segment and a gross weight of 50 lb in the higher range or segment may indicate a net weight of 30 lb.
[Nonretroactive as of January 1, 1989]
(Added 1987) **(Amended 200X)**

S.2.3. Tare. – *On any scale (except a monorail scale equipped with digital indications* ~~and multi-interval scales or multiple range scales when the value of tare is determined in a lower range~~), *the value of the tare division shall be equal to the value of the scale division.* ∗ The tare mechanism shall operate only in a backward

direction (that is, in a direction of underregistration) with respect to the zero-load balance condition of the scale. *A device designed to automatically clear any tare value shall also be designed to prevent the automatic clearing of tare until a complete transaction has been indicated.**
(Amended 1985)

[Note: On a computing scale, this requires the input of a unit price, the display of the unit price, and a computed positive total price at a readable equilibrium. Other devices require a complete weighing operation, including tare, net, and gross weight determination]*
[*Nonretroactive as of January 1, 1983]
(Amended 200X)

T.N.2.1. General. – The tolerance values are positive (+) and negative (-) with the weighing device adjusted to zero at no load. When tare is in use, the tolerance values are applied from the tare zero reference **(zero net indication)**; the tolerance values apply to **the net weight indication for any possible tare load using** certified test loads ~~only~~.
(Amended 200X)

Discussion: In 2006, the NTETC Weighing Sector formed a Tare WG to review existing tare requirements and make recommendations about how tare is to operate on a single range scale, multiple range scale, and multi-interval scale. The WG was also asked to develop, where necessary, recommendations for changes to Publication 14, HB 44, and HB 130 and to provide guidance to the Weighing Sector on related type evaluation requirements.

This proposal, which was developed by the Tare WG and supported by the Weighing Sector, adds a new note to paragraph S.1.2.1. The note recognizes display and printing of net weight values in divisions other than the scale division used in the display of gross weight, resulting in a more accurate net weight determination.

The proposal also amends paragraph T.N.2.1. to clarify that tolerances also apply to net weight indications regardless of the gross load on the scale. The Tare WG reviewed OIML R 76 "Nonautomatic Weighing Instruments" for corresponding requirements to determine if there were areas where HB 44 could be aligned with international recommendations. Based on that review, the WG agreed that HB 44 paragraph T.N.2.1. should be modified to state that tolerances also apply to net load indications.

The Tare WG discussed problems associated with determining the appropriate direction to round tare on multi-interval scales and multiple range scales whenever gross and tare weights fall in different weighing segments on a multi-interval scale or in different weighing ranges on multiple range scales. In these cases, the scale division size for the gross and tare weights differ; however, the net weight must be in mathematical agreement with the gross and tare weights that are indicated and recorded by the device (i.e., gross weight - tare weight = net weight).

The problem arises when the tare weight is rounded up to the next larger scale division where the net weight falls in the higher segment or range. For example, a 0.004 lb tare weight in a weighing range or segment with 0.002 lb intervals in the lower weighing range or segment may round to zero when the net weight falls in the upper weighing range with 0.01 lb intervals:

      10.05 lb Gross Weight
    – 0.004 lb Tare Weight
      10.046 lb the Mathematically Correct Net Weight;

However, due to rounding of tare weight the device indicates 10.05 lb Net Weight

This results in a transaction where a commodity is bought or sold on the basis of gross weight or an insufficient amount of tare weight is taken and results in a misrepresentation of net weight for the transaction. Essentially, the rounding of tare that falls in a smaller division in either direction (e.g., a 0.015 lb tare weight rounded down to zero or to 0.01 lb or up to 0.02 lb) provides a less accurate net weight.

S&T Committee 2007 Final Report

The Tare WG developed a corresponding proposal for the Automatic Weighing Systems Code to clarify the appropriate scale division values and the application of tolerances to tare weights for those devices (see S&T Item 324-1).

The SWMA supports the recommendation; however, the SWMA also agreed that an additional note should be added to paragraph S.2.3. Tare. The new note proposed for paragraph S.2.3. clarifies that the requirement does not apply to multi-interval scales or multiple range scales when tare is determined in the lower range of those scales.

WMD agreed it might be more appropriate if the proposed new note explains that gross weight and calculated tare weight are expressed as an "indicated weight value" rather than as a "scale value." WMD notes that the proposed SWMA text is necessary to clarify that tare weights are excluded from the requirement that specifies weight values must be the same as the scale division value. However, the SWMA's proposal needs further work to better explain if only part or the entire paragraph does not apply to tare weights indicated on either a multi-interval or multiple range scale and to clarify the relationship of paragraph S.1.2.1. to corresponding paragraph S.2.3. WMD also asked if it was the SWMA's intent that this newly proposed note be a retroactive or nonretroactive requirement, and if nonretroactive, then what is an appropriate effective date?

The SMA supports the Weighing Sector's proposal, but recommended the proposed new note become a subparagraph of paragraph S.1.2.1. and include a modification to the proposed new text in paragraph T.N.2.1. to require the net weight indication for "any" rather than "every" possible tare load using certified test loads. The Committee agreed to the SMA's recommended changes to paragraph T.N.2.1. and modified the proposal accordingly.

The Committee deliberated at length on this item and S&T Items 320-5 and 320-9, which are all meant to clarify the distinct differences in how various tare features are permitted to operate. The Committee agreed that ultimately neither the buyer nor seller should incur a loss as a result of an inaccurate calculation of a tare weight. Much of the weights and measures community has not had the opportunity to discuss these proposals nor has the Tare WG or Weighing Sector had time to analyze feedback on these proposed changes to the Scales Code and corresponding proposals to change the AWS Code (see Items 324-1 and 324-3). The Committee agreed that all proposals related to the operation of the tare feature should be Information items to ensure all aspects of the operation of tare features are adequately addressed and clearly defined for both the public and private sector.

During the 2007 NCWM Annual Meeting, the Committee heard comments from the CWMA and NEWMA supporting this item with recommendations to change the word "value" to "division" and incorporating the SWMA recommendation to modify paragraph S.2.3.

NEWMA pointed out that the proposed amendment to S.1.2.1. appears to be permissive and not a requirement and asked if the intent was to prohibit multi-interval and multiple range scales from rounding and indicating calculated net weights in scales divisions to only 1, 2, or 5 when appropriate or if rounding the scale divisions of 1, 2, or 5 was still allowed? The WMD representative to the NCWM Tare WG stated that the intent is for the language to be permissive because there are a significant number of devices with an NTEP CC in the marketplace that round the tare values before calculating net weights.

The Committee made several modifications to the proposal:

- to clarify the examples in the proposed note to paragraph S.1.2.1., and
- to clarify that the SWMA proposed modification to the language in S.2.3 for an exception for multi-interval and multiple range scales only applies to the requirement that the value of tare shall be equal to the value of the scale division.

The Committee also agreed that the words "scale value" should be changed to "scale division" to be consistent with the terminology currently used in HB 44 and recommends that the NIST technical advisor forward the amended proposal to the Tare WG and NTETC Weighing Sector for their consideration and comment.

320-4   D   S.1.4.6. Height and Definition of Minimum Reading Distance, UR.2.10. Primary Indicating Elements Provided by the User, UR.2.11. Minimum Reading Distance, and Definitions of Minimum Reading Distance and Primary Indications

(The status of this item was changed to "Developing" during the January 2007 NCWM Interim Meeting and was moved to Appendix A as Item 360-2: Developing Items Part 1, Item 1 Scales.)

During the 2007 NCWM Annual Meeting, the Committee was informed that the NTETC Weighing Sector intends to continue developing this item before asking the Committee to consider the issue on its agenda.

320-5   W   S.2.1.7. Tare Rounding on a Multiple Range Scale

(This item was withdrawn)

Source: Southern Weights and Measures Association (SWMA)

Discussion: The Committee considered an SWMA proposal to add a new paragraph S.2.1.7. to the Scales Code as follows:

S.2.1.7. Tare Rounding on a Multiple Range Scale. – A multiple range scale with tare capability must indicate and record values that satisfy the equation:

net = gross - tare

and round the tare value up to the larger division size when entering the larger division. (Added 200X)

A recent reversal of a 10-year-old NTEP policy now permits the operation of tare on multiple range scales to round down, thus overstating the quantity. The SWMA believes the Weighing Sector's decision to round tare down should be addressed by all members of the NCWM. The proposal was developed to eliminate any conflict in the operation of the tare function on multiple range scales in the determination of a net weight.

Currently, there may be a conflict between HB 44 requirements and NCWM Publication 14 policy for rounding tare values on multiple range scales. HB 44 General Code paragraph G-S.5.2.2.(c) Digital Indication and Representation requires that digital values round off to the nearest minimum unit that can be indicated or recorded. Also in question is a possible conflict with NIST HB 130 guidelines for Packaging and Labeling Regulations Section 6.13. Rounding, which specifies that in no case shall rounded values result in overstating the net quantity. NTEP is also revising its tare criteria through its Tare WG to ensure no further conflict with HB 44.

At their fall 2006 meetings, the regional weights and measures associations considered this SWMA proposal as part of ongoing work by the Weighing Sector Tare WG. However, the SWMA intended it to be a separate proposal that addressed only tare rounding policies and procedures for multiple range scales. The WWMA believes the issue of tare capability is complex and the proposal also needs to address the suitability of the tare division size, the current prohibition of division sizes other than 1, 2, and 5, the scale application (buying or selling), and other issues that relate to tare. For these reasons, the WWMA believes the proposal should be thoroughly developed in the NTETC Weighing Sector prior to forwarding it to the NCWM S&T Committee for action. Consequently, the WWMA recommended withdrawing the SWMA proposal. The CWMA and NEWMA opposed this proposal as presented and agreed to await further input from the Weighing Sector Tare WG.

During its 2006 meeting, the SWMA considered its proposal an urgent matter warranting an upgrade in status from Developing to an item that is ready for national consideration. The SWMA reported that a majority of the Weighing Sector believes the criteria noted in Publication 14 for use in type evaluation of devices with the tare feature are not supported by HB 44 requirements. The SWMA agreed that the decision to permit rounding keyboard tare down on multiple range scales is facilitation of fraud. For example, the customer and the operator observe that a tare weight was entered in the lower range of a multiple range scale, yet when the gross weight is in a higher weighing range, the customer is not provided with "clear, definite, accurate" indications that tare has been reduced.

The SWMA recognizes that OIML permits rounding tare down, but believes that customers are not able to make adjustments in unit prices to compensate for losses when tare is rounded down, whereas businesses can adjust the price to compensate for overhead expenses and losses that occur if tare is rounded up.

The SWMA provided discussion and examples to support its position as follows:

History

The operation of "tare" on a weighing device was first addressed in detail in 1971. In the 1971 Committee's Final Report (see NIST Special Publication (SP) 358, Page 170), the rationale for adding paragraph S.2.3. Tare Mechanism to HB 44 was to ensure net weight was represented for commodities sold directly over computing scales and to recognize new developments in device technology. Tare capability and its operation were again addressed in S&T Item 301-3 Tare in the 1980 Committee's Final Report (see NIST SP 599, page 216). The report noted "a key factor is the requirements in paragraphs G-S.2. Facilitation of Fraud and G-S.5.1. Indicating and Recording Elements, General specify the indications to be clear, definite, accurate, and easily read by all parties involved in the weighing operation."

The SWMA notes that some believe General Code paragraph G-S.5.2.2. Digital Indication and Representation is intended to address the rounding of tare to the nearest minimum unit when it was amended in 1973. However, the Committee's 1980 Final Report notes only General Code paragraphs G-S.2. and G-S.5.1. Furthermore, there is no evidence in any of the Final Reports that the Committee agreed that the practice of rounding tare up, which has been NTEP policy, is in conflict with HB 44.

In 2006, the NIST technical advisor to the Weighing Sector contacted two members of the 1980 NCWM S&T Committee and determined that the focus of tare discussions were on single range scales, rather than multi-interval scales and multiple range scales, and followed rounding rules listed in HB 44. Consequently, specific interpretations or proposals were needed to determine how requirements apply to multi-interval and multiple range devices.

The SWMA provided an example to make its point that if no tare is taken, the store has sold less than the quantity represented. Consider an example where a store's deli is selling cheese for $7/lb and the weight of the roll of wrapping paper used in the deli is 40 lb. Sections of the wrap used in individual transactions are not heavy enough to register on the scale during a single transaction; however, if no tare is taken, the store collects an extra $280 (40 lb x $7/lb). The store controls the unit price for the commodity and selects the tare material and the resolution for the scale that it uses. The SWMA heard the argument that the store is losing money if it is forced to round tare up. The SWMA's response to that argument is to remind everyone that businesses view such losses as part of overhead expenses, which they most typically compensate for by making adjustments to their unit prices. The customer does not have the ability to adjust or bargain on the unit price.

The SWMA notes that the loss to the customer when tare is rounded down is larger when scale error is on the plus side, even though the scale is within accuracy tolerances. In this case, the SWMA does not believe scale error is a justification for selling less than the quantity represented. For example, given a 30 lb x 0.01 lb scale:

The scale has an internal error of plus (+) 0.012 lb, which is displayed as 0.01 lb, which is within maintenance tolerance. However, if the tare material used weighs 0.004 lb, there is an increased loss to the customer from 0.01 lb to 0.02 lb since 0.012 lb + 0.004 lb = 0.016 lb would be displayed as 0.02 lb on the scale.

OIML

Historically, weights and measures officials have been against rounding tare down. But what should occur if you are rounding to the nearest division? Is zero considered a division? The SWMA acknowledges that zero is a division. The OIML Secretariat of TC 9/SC 1 for Nonautomatic Weighing Instruments R 76 noted in his response to the U.S. inquiry on that same question that "of course, rounding the tare value to zero is possible if it is less than 0.5 e_i (interval of the weighing segment) of the actual range i (interval)." Multiple range scales meet R 76 rounding criteria when they round to zero. However, R 76 Section 4.13.3.2 Semi-automatic Tare Device specifies that an instrument may be fitted with semi-automatic tare devices if the action of the tare device *does not permit a reduction of the value of tare*.

The SWMA notes that there is not consensus within the international weighing and measuring community to allow tare to round down. A direct quote of The Netherlands' position on the latest draft of R 76 (in regard to 4.6.12.5. Multi-interval instrument with a preset tare device) was "In principle the conclusion that with e = 2 g the value of 3 g can be rounded to 2 g or 4 g is correct. However could we not agree in this Recommendation that 1 g or 3 g always will be rounded up (because in the case where e = 1 g, a tare value of 0.5 g is always rounded up)."

Application of Tare Rounding Criteria

On multi-interval scales tare is restricted to the smallest division, thus eliminating the possibility of rounding tare below its actual weight. For example, criteria for rounding tare on a multiple range scale results in a tare value of 12 lb in Range 1 (e = 1 lb), but when the net weight causes the scale to switch to Range 2 (e = 10 lb), the tare value would become 10 lb.

The Tare WG considered that the problems of tare rounding can be demonstrated in the following which illustrates some of the losses that can occur to parties involved in a transaction that is conducted on a multiple range scale where different rules for rounding are applied:

Given a multiple range scale where,

Capacity of the first range = 60 lb; scale division of the first range = 0.01 lb
Capacity of the second range = 300 lb; scale division of the second range = 0.1 lb

	No Rounding of Tare or Net	Tare Rounded Down to Nearest Division in the 2nd Range	Tare Rounded Up to Nearest Division in the 2nd Range
Gross	266.2 lb (falls in 2nd range)	266.2 lb (falls in 2nd range)	266.2 lb (falls in 2nd range)
Tare	53.44 lb (falls in 1st range)	53.4 lb (falls in 2nd range)	53.5 lb (falls in 2nd range)
Net	212.76 lb	212.8 lb	212.7 lb
Rounding Error	0.0 lb	0.04 lb (consumer's loss)	0.06 lb (store's loss)

A multiple range scale is viewed as two separate scales even though it has two or more weighing ranges with different maximum capacities and different scale intervals, each extending from zero to its maximum capacity all on the same load receptor. A multiple range scale is basically multiple scales in a single housing. Current practices do not allow rounding of tare to zero with completely separate scales when the results of weighments on both scales are used to determine the gross, net, and tare weight. Indicators totalizing multiple weighing elements are required to calculate the total weight based on the smallest scale division to eliminate problems with inaccurate net weights.

Conclusion

The SWMA agreed that, if the real issue is protecting both the retailer and the consumer, perhaps what should be looked at is: (1) the suitability of the scale division based on unit price and/or application, (2) limiting the multiple of the scale division difference between the weighing ranges, (3) reducing the allowable tolerance, and (4) limiting the initial determination of the tare, gross, and net to the same weighing range.

The SWMA believes all multiple range scales currently evaluated by NTEP should not round tare down when changing to a higher scale division. For over ten years, the NTEP checklist test criteria for multiple range and multi-interval devices in NCWM Publication 14 has always been that tare will round up to the nearest scale division.

The SMA supports the proposal provided the last sentence is modified to reflect the rounding requirements in HB 44 Appendix A – Fundamental Considerations, Section 10 "Rounding Off Numerical Values."

WMD agreed with the SWMA concern that the resulting net weight may be inaccurate when tare is rounded down or to zero. A device owner is still responsible for ensuring accurate net weight at time of sale regardless of how a scale operates. Device requirements in HB 44 are not meant to create conflicts with weights and measures law or the principles of NIST Handbook 133. WMD believes that part of the solution to this problem is addressed in S&T Item 320-3, which is a proposal to permit tare to be expressed in a value other than the scale division value of 1, 2, or 5. Furthermore, the equipment selected for use in the transaction must be suitable for that application and, therefore, must not facilitate inaccuracies when rounding weight values and must not misrepresent the net weight at the time of sale. The following table shows an example where the tare is 0.004 lb and the scale division is 0.01 lb. The table compares the results of weighments when tare is rounded up or down to the nearest division:

No Tare Rounding (lb)		Tare Rounding to the Nearest Scale Division (lb)		Tare Rounding Up (lb)	
10.05	Gross Weight	10.05	Gross Weight	10.05	Gross Weight
0.004	Tare Weight	0.00	Tare Weight	0.01	Tare Weight
10.046	Actual Net Weight	10.05	Net Weight	10.04	Net Weight
10.05	Displayed Net Weight				
Results in an accurate tare weight, because the tare weight is indicated in a value other the scale division of 1, 2, or 5 as proposed in S&T Item 320-3. This is only a partial solution because even though the tare weight is accurate, the net weight is rounded to the nearest division, which results in overstating the net weight. Rounding will occur and depending on its direction can result in either overstating or understating the net weight.		Results in an error of 0.004 lb in the net weight, if existing General Code paragraph G-S.5.2.2.(c) is applied. No tare is deducted.		Results in an error of 0.006 lb as proposed in S&T Item 320-5.	

The Committee considered the conflicts with this proposal where tare is rounded up and the proposed language in S&T Items 320-3 and corresponding Automatic Weighing Systems Item 324-1 where no tare rounding is permitted. The proposal in Item 320-5 will frequently result in an inaccurate net weight. In cases where tare is rounded up, the losses that occur in a transaction will depend on whether the commodity is bought (operator loss) or sold (customer loss) based on that inaccurate net weight. The Committee agreed the most appropriate method for calculating weight values during a transaction was to permit tare to have a value other than that of a scale division of 1, 2, or 5 when that increment more accurately represents the tare value. The Committee believes this provision will, at least in part, address the concerns of the SWMA. Consequently, the Committee withdrew this proposal from its agenda since the proposal forces the scale to always round up regardless if the scale owner is a seller or buyer and it treats tare rounding differently between single range and multiple range scales. The Committee also requested the Weighing Sector continue its work on Items 320-3, 320-9, 324-1, and 324-3 to develop procedures and associated terminology that results in a more accurate determination of net weight and a better understanding of tare features and functions.

320-6 V N.1.3.1. Bench or Counter Scales, N.1.3.8. All Other Scales Except Crane Scales, Hanging Scales, Hopper Scales, Wheel–Load Weighers, and Portable Axle-Load Weighers, and Appendix D, Definitions of Bench Scale and Counter Scale

(This item was adopted)

Source: Carryover Item 320-3. (This item originated from the National Type Evaluation Technical Committee (NTETC) Weighing Sector and first appeared on the Committee's 2005 agenda.)

Recommendation: Delete paragraph N.1.3.1. and renumber subsequent paragraphs.

N.1.3. Shift Test.

> ~~N.1.3.1. Bench or Counter Scales. A shift test shall be conducted with a half-capacity test load centered successively at four points equidistant between the center and the front, left, back, and right edges of the load-receiving element.~~

Add new paragraph N.1.3.3. as follows:

> N.1.3.~~4~~.3 Vehicle Scales, Axle-Load Scales, and Livestock Scales.
>
> **N.1.3.3. Prescribed Test Patterns and Test Loads for Two-Section Livestock Scales.** A shift test shall be conducted using the following prescribed test loads and test patterns, provided the shift test load does not exceed one-half the rated section capacity or one-half the rated concentrated load capacity, whichever is applicable, using either:
>
> (a) a one-quarter nominal capacity test load centered as nearly as possible, successively, over each main load support as shown in N.1.3.7. Figure 2; or
>
> (b) a one-half nominal capacity test load centered as nearly as possible, successively, at the center of each quarter of the load-receiving element as shown in N.1.3.7. Figure 1.

Renumber and amend paragraph N.1.3.8. as follows:

> **N.1.3.~~8~~7. All Other Scales Except Crane Scales, Hanging Scales, Hopper Scales, Wheel-Load Weighers, and Portable Axle-Load Weighers.** A shift test shall be conducted using the following prescribed test loads and test patterns. **A single field standard weight used as the prescribed test load shall be applied centrally in the prescribed test pattern. When multiple field standard weights are used as the prescribed test load, the load shall be applied in a consistent pattern in the shift test positions throughout the test and applied in a manner that does not concentrate the load in a test pattern that is less than when that same load is a single field standard weight on the load-receiving element.** ~~For livestock scales, shift test shall not exceed one-half the rated section capacity or one-half the rated concentrated load capacity, whichever is applicable. A shift test shall be conducted using either:~~
>
> (a) For scales with a nominal capacity greater than 500 kg (1000 lb), a shift test may be conducted by either using a one-third nominal capacity test load (defined as test weights in amounts of at least 30 % of scale capacity, but not to exceed 35 % of scale capacity) centered as nearly as possible at the center of each quadrant of the load-receiving element using the prescribed test pattern as shown in Figure 1 below, or by using a one-quarter nominal capacity test load centered as nearly as possible, successively, over each corner of the load-receiving element using the prescribed test pattern as shown in Figure 2 below.
>
> (b) For scales with a nominal capacity of 500 kg (1000 lb) or less, a shift test shall be conducted using a one-third nominal capacity test load (defined as test weights in amounts of at least 30 % of scale capacity, but not to exceed 35 % of scale capacity) centered as nearly as possible at the

<u>center of each quadrant of the load-receiving element using the prescribed test pattern as shown in Figure 1 below.</u>

~~(a) A one-quarter nominal capacity test load centered as nearly as possible, successively over each main load support as shown in the diagram below; or~~

~~(b) A one-half nominal capacity test load centered as nearly as possible, successively at the center of each quarter of the load-receiving element as shown in the diagram below.~~

(Amended 1987~~, and~~ 2003<u>, and 2007</u>)

Delete the diagrams that correspond to existing paragraphs N.1.3.8.(a) and (b) and add new Figures 1 and 2 to correspond with proposed revisions to N.1.3.8. as follows:

Figure 1

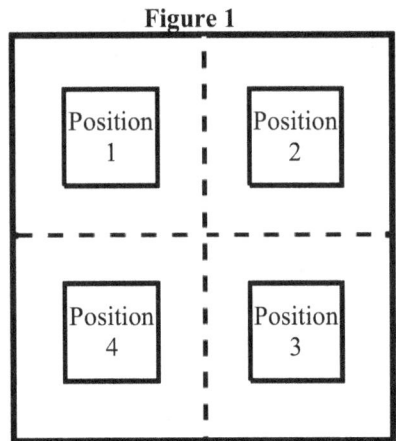

Figure 2

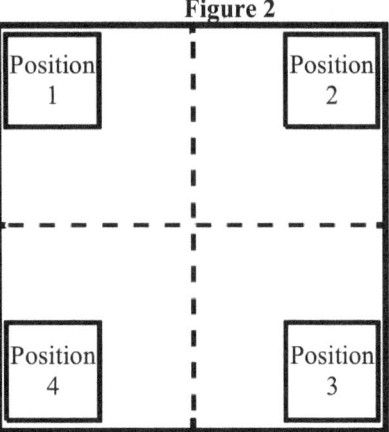

(Added 2003)
(Amended 2007)

Delete Appendix D definitions for "bench scale" and "counter scale" as follows:

~~bench scale. See "counter scale." [2.20]~~

~~counter scale. One that, by reason of its size, arrangement of parts, and moderate nominal capacity, is adapted for use on a counter or bench. Sometimes called "bench scale." [2.20]~~

Discussion: The proposal was intended to clarify the appropriate shift test pattern and test loads for scales currently designated as bench/counter scales and other platform-type scales. Currently, bench and counter scale shift tests are conducted with a one-half capacity test load centered successively at four points equidistant between the center and the front, left, back, and right edges of the load-receiving element. Shift tests for other platform scales are conducted with a one-half capacity test load centered, as nearly as possible, successively at the center of each quadrant. The proposal eliminates references to bench and counter scales and instead prescribes that the shift test load and test pattern used for those and all scales other than livestock be based on the scale's nominal capacity. For livestock scales the proposal further clarifies, but does not change, the existing requirements for shift tests.

In 2005, the proposal was kept on the agenda as an Information item. This was in response to comments indicating that data should be collected on shift tests to verify that the proposed test loads and positions are equivalent to existing test patterns and to allow the data to be reviewed by the Weighing Sector, NIST, and the NTEP laboratories.

During the 2006 NCWM Interim Meeting, the Committee received data comparing shift tests conducted using current shift test requirements and shift tests on the same scales using the proposed test requirements (a test load of one-third the scale's capacity). There was no demonstrated difference in scale performance based on the location of the scale, thus the terms "bench" and "counter" should be eliminated. In response to that data, comments were received from the public and private sectors in support of the proposal.

In response to comments from the weights and measures community, the Committee modified the entire proposal to include language that is technically correct and consistent in its description of how to conduct a shift test on all types of scales. The Committee modified the language to: (1) clarify what defines "acceptable" weight values for a test load that is one-third of the scale's nominal capacity, (2) ensure uniform procedures are followed when applying test weights on the load-receiving element, (3) eliminate instances where test weights are concentrated in a pattern that overload the load-bearing points as illustrated in the example below, and (4) change the scale capacity that is used as the basis for the shift test load from 150 kg (300 lb) to 500 kg (1000 lb) to align the proposed one-third capacity shift test load requirement with existing minimum test weight requirements for the greater of 25 % device capacity or 300 lb for devices with 1000 lb capacity already specified in Table 4. Minimum Test Weights and Test Loads.

The Committee considered an example of a livestock scale with a section capacity of 1000 lb: a shift test is performed as shown in Figure 1 using a test load of 500 lb. While 100 lb test weights are not commonly used or available, they are used in this example to illustrate the concept of uniformity when applying a test load in a specified pattern on the load-receiving element.

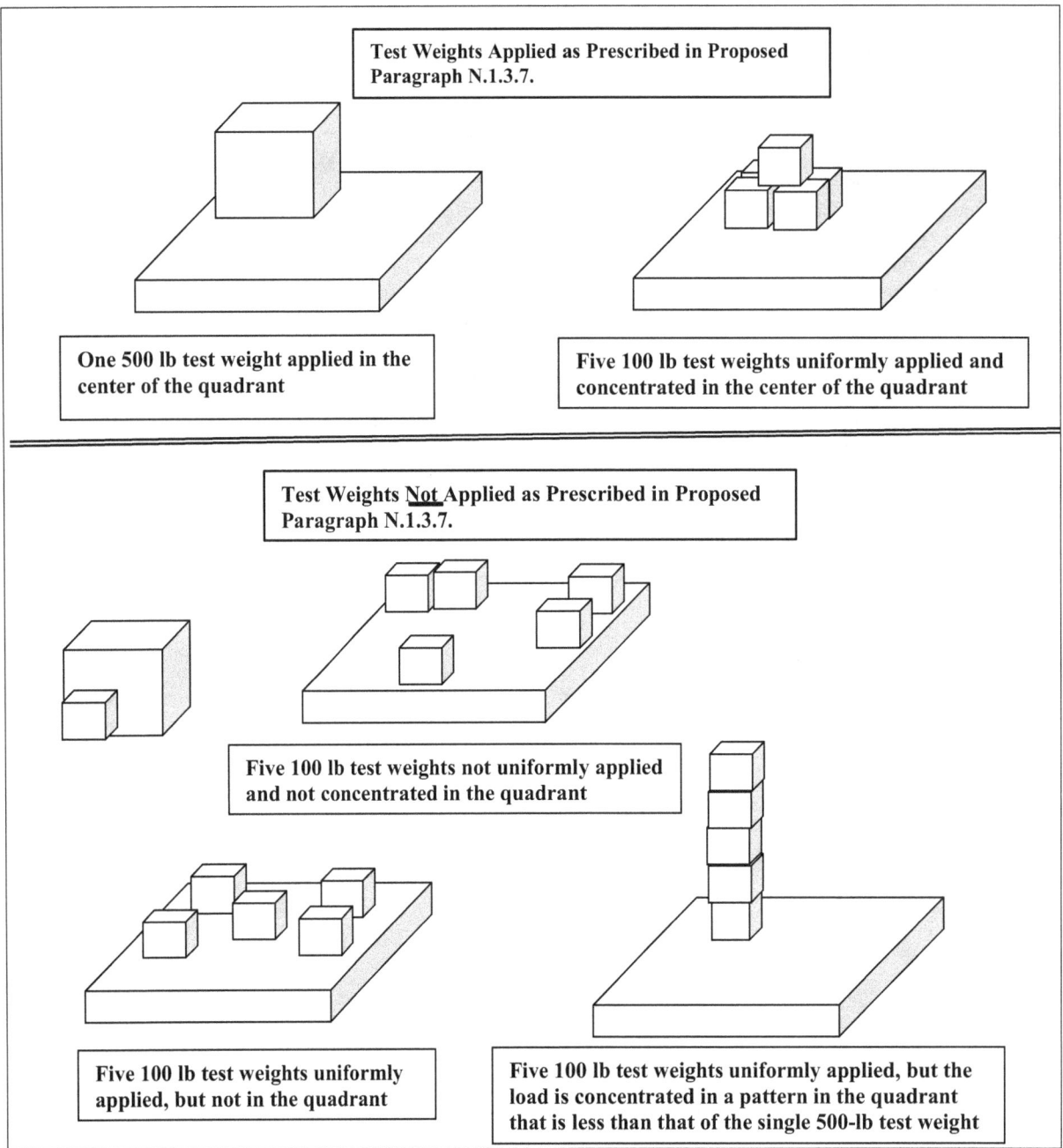

Figure 1: Application of Test Weights

At the 2006 NCWM Annual Meeting, the Committee agreed there was sufficient data and a consensus for presenting the proposal for a vote at the meeting. During the voting session, the Committee heard concerns that substantive changes were made to the livestock scale requirements and it should revisit earlier proposed language. The Committee explained those changes were only a reorganization of the text. The vote on the item did not yield a sufficient number of positive or negative votes for the item to be accepted or defeated and, therefore, the proposal was returned to the Committee for further action. The Committee requested jurisdictions to review carefully the consistency that exists between the proposed language and current HB 44 requirements for livestock scales and to provide input on alternate language that might be more appropriate and/or further clarify the shift tests and test loads for these devices.

The WWMA S&T Committee had the opportunity to review an alternate proposal that was to be presented to the NTETC Weighing Sector in September 2006. The WWMA S&T Committee liked the direction of the Weighing Sector's alternate proposal, which clarified shift test procedures in livestock scale applications, addressed shift test patterns for circular platforms, and eliminated some of the redundant text. Since the Weighing Sector members would not have the opportunity to review and agree on the alternate language until after the WWMA meeting, the WWMA recommended the proposal as an Information item.

The CWMA supported most of the Committee's 2006 recommendation, but suggested some alternate wording to modify and renumber paragraph N.1.3.8.(b) to read as follows:

N.1.3.87. All Other Scales Except Crane Scales, Hanging Scales, Hopper Scales, Wheel-Load Weighers, and Portable Axle-Load Weighers.

(b) For scales with a nominal capacity of 500 kg (1000 lb) or less, a shift test shall be conducted using up to 50 % nominal capacity test load (defined as test weights in amounts of at least 30 % of scale capacity, but not to exceed 50 % of scale capacity) centered as nearly as possible at the center of each quadrant of the load-receiving element using the prescribed test pattern as shown in Figure 1 below.

The CWMA developed this alternate recommendation with the intent that jurisdictions would have more flexibility in using their existing test weights.

Based on the comments received during the 2006 NCWM Annual Meeting, the NIST technical advisor to the Weighing Sector amended the proposal as summarized below to:

(1) Make it clear that no significant changes are being made to requirements for two-section livestock scales;
(2) Simplify the language for the shift test on "Other" scales;
(3) Group the livestock scale shift test requirements together;
(4) Change the order of the "test notes" so that the more common type of scales are listed first; and
(5) Include minor editorial suggestions on existing language.

The Weighing Sector considered this alternate proposal along with a comment solicited from the PTB and one industry consultant indicating there is a higher risk of overloading one of the (multiple) supports by using a one-half capacity load in an eccentric loading test pattern than by using a one-third capacity load. This appears to stem from the difference in test method between HB 44 and OIML R 76. In other words, HB 44 more or less assumes a rectangular platform and places the load at a point on a line halfway from the center to the edge as illustrated in Figure 1.

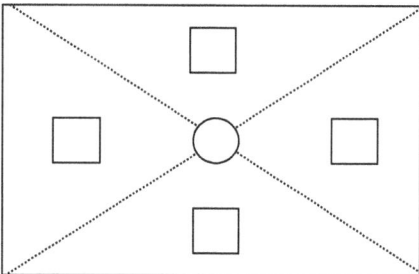

Figure 1: NIST Handbook 44 Shift Test at One-Half Capacity

OIML R 76 recognizes that platforms exist in other shapes (e.g., square, triangular, or circular platforms) as illustrated in Figure 2.

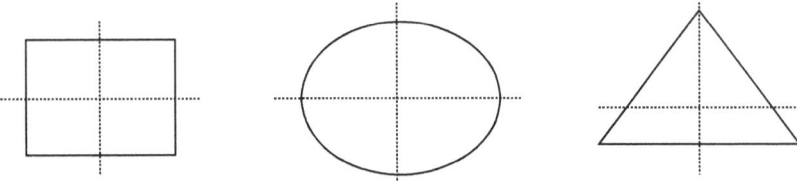

Figure 2: OIML R 76 – Quadrants shown for platforms of devices with four or fewer points of support

Thus, since OIML R 76 depends more on placing the eccentric load in a prescribed section of the total area of the platform rather than on a specific line, they more or less trust the load will be placed at the center of the quadrant according to the figures illustrated in OIML R 76 for scales with four or fewer supports. The end result of both methods, especially for rectangular platforms, is more or less the same.

During subsequent discussions, several Weighing Sector members stated that the proposed language was unnecessary since there was no technical justification to change the current language in HB 44. Additionally, the proposed language would prohibit weights and measures officials from using one-half capacity even though the scale could be weighing loads up to one-half scale capacity that are not in the center of the platform. In contrast, the NIST technical advisor stated that there was no technical reason to use procedures different than those in R 76. (Note: Manufacturers have stated in past discussions that they have to adjust the scales differently for scales intended for North America and scales intended for countries that adopt OIML recommendations.)

Another industry consultant cited text from the 1915 edition of the precursor to HB 44 (see Section 10 for Counter Balances and Scales, page 19), noting that the shift test loads and positions have not changed in 91 years.

Measurement Canada reported that the proposal to amend HB 44 would be in conflict with their current requirements; however, in the past they have indicated a commitment to align their requirements with OIML R 76.

One scale manufacturer reminded the Sector that the test load positions were also changed in the proposal and that the proposed change to one-third scale capacity puts a different torque on the load cell that is roughly equivalent to current forces when using current HB 44 test loads and positions.

Based on a vote of 11 in favor of and 8 against withdrawing the proposal to amend current HB 44 shift test procedures and shift test loads, the Weighing Sector agreed to withdraw their support for the proposal and recommended that the proposal be withdrawn from the Committee's agenda.

The SMA and NEWMA supported the Committee's 2006 proposal.

The SWMA recommended withdrawing this proposal from the S&T Agenda, but provided no rationale for this position.

WMD recommended the next step should be to ascertain if manufacturers have sufficient data to support the changes in test procedures for devices equipped with single and multiple load cells.

The Committee agreed the proposal includes suitable requirements for a minimum test load and test patterns for off center loading based on field data and input from manufacturers and officials. In response to concerns about changes to shift test requirements for livestock scales, the Committee deleted all references in its 2006 proposal to livestock scales in paragraph N.1.3.8. and placed those requirements in a proposed new paragraph N.1.3.3.3. Keeping livestock scale requirements under one heading seemed a more appropriate approach since paragraph N.1.3.4. is proposed to be renumbered to N.1.3.3. and already addresses the shift test procedures for all other types of livestock scales. The Committee considered the NIST recommendation for OEM data to support the proposal from an engineering standpoint. As of the 2007 NCWM Interim and Annual Meetings, the Committee had heard opposition from OEMs and wanted to move in the direction of harmonization where the proposal is an accepted practice.

During the 2007 NCWM Annual meeting, the Committee heard comments from a jurisdiction that the current test is more stringent than the proposed shift tests and recommended the proposal be amended to permit an optional shift test to be conducted with a test load of:

- one-half scale capacity centered successively at four points equidistant between the center and the front, left, back, and right edges of the load-receiving element, and
- one-half scale capacity centered as nearly as possible, successively, at the center of each quarter of the load-receiving element.

Another jurisdiction commented that the proposed shift test loads and positions are equivalent with the current HB 44 shift tests for scales with one load support and may be less stringent with scales with four load supports.

Manufacturers concurred that the proposed shift test loads and positions are equivalent with the current HB 44 shift tests for scales with one load support and may be less stringent with scales with four load supports. Manufacturers also expressed concerns with the comment that both types of shift tests should be performed on scales and would prefer that the proposal be withdrawn rather than having two different methods for conducting shift tests.

The Committee considered the comments and concluded that both methods for conducting shift tests are equivalent. Additionally, the Committee opposes having two different methods, noting this would promote nonuniformity of tests between service agents, weights and measures officials, and among weights and measures jurisdictions.

The Committee believed there is sufficient support for this item with the correction of the references to Figures 1 and 2 in proposed paragraphs N.1.3.3.3.(a) and N.1.3.3.3.(b). The Committee further modified paragraph N.1.3.3.3. to reverse the order of the paragraphs (a) and (b) so each paragraph appears in the same order as its corresponding figures 1 and 2.

Consequently, the Committee agreed to present the item for a vote.

For more background information, refer to the Committee's 2005 and 2006 Final Reports.

320-7   VC N.1.3.6.1. Dynamic Monorail Weighing Systems

(This item was adopted)

Source: Central Weights and Measures Association (CWMA)

Recommendation: Modify paragraph N.1.3.6.1. as follows:

N.1.3.6.1. **Dynamic Monorail Weighing Systems.** – Dynamic tests with livestock carcasses **shall** ~~should~~ be conducted **during normal plant production** ~~to duplicate actual use conditions~~. No less than 20 test loads using carcasses or portions of carcasses of the type normally weighed **shall** ~~should~~ be used in the dynamic test ~~; two additional test loads may be included in the test run for use in the event that one or two test loads are rendered unusable during the dynamic test. Prior to starting the dynamic test, the test carcasses must be positioned far enough ahead of the scale so that their swaying motion settles to duplicate the normal sway of a continuously running plant chain~~. If the plant conveyer chain does not space or prevent the carcasses **or portions of carcasses** from touching one another, dynamic tests **shall** ~~should~~ not be conducted until this condition has been corrected.

All carcasses **or portions of carcasses** shall be individually weighed statically on either the same scale being tested dynamically or another monorail scale with the same or smaller divisions and in close proximity. (The scale selected for **static** weighing **of** the carcasses **or portions of carcasses** shall first be tested statically with **certified** test weights **that have been properly protected from the harsh environment of the packing plant to ensure they maintain accuracy**.)

If the scale being tested is used for weighing freshly slaughtered animals, (often referred to as a "hot scale") care must be taken to get a static weighment as quickly as possible before or following the dynamic weighment to avoid loss due to shrink. If multiple dynamic tests are conducted using the same carcasses **or portions of carcasses**, static weights shall be obtained before and after multiple dynamic tests. If the carcass **or portion of a carcass** changes weight between static tests, the amount of weight change **shall** ~~should~~ be taken into account, or the carcass **or portion of a carcass shall** ~~should~~ be disregarded for tolerance purposes.

(**Note:** For a dynamic monorail test, the reference scale shall comply with the principles in the Fundamental Considerations paragraph 3.2. Tolerances for Standards.)
(Added 1996) (Amended 1999 **and 2007**)

Discussion: The CWMA supported this item and recommended it move forward for national consideration. The CWMA heard testimony from the USDA Packers and Stockyards Administration that the proposal clarifies that the device should be tested while in production and the extra two carcasses referenced in the current language are only for replacement purposes in cases where carcass weight loss occurs as a result of influences other than from the device being tested. The extra carcasses were not intended to replace erroneous or outlying device readings.

The Committee supported the proposal along with the SWMA recommendation to include a requirement for the use of certified weights in paragraph N.1.3.6.1. (2nd paragraph) to clarify the appropriate procedures to test the scale used for the static weighing of carcasses.

During the 2007 NCWM Annual Meeting, the Committee heard testimony from the submitters of this item that some applications weigh portions of carcasses. The submitters made the following recommendations: (1) the proposed language be amended to clarify that the tests also apply to portions of carcasses; (2) the requirements that the tests be conducted during normal plant operation should be mandatory and not permissive; and (3) the word "should" be changed to "shall."

The Committee agreed with comments that the test of a dynamic monorail scale be conducted during normal plant operation because tests conducted when the plant is not in normal operation may not represent an "as used" condition. Therefore, the Committee changed all references to the word "should" in paragraph N.1.3.6.1. to "shall" to clarify when the test must be performed. The Committee also agreed with a comment that the words "or portions of carcasses" should be inserted where appropriate in the proposed text to recognize that carcasses are frequently split in half prior to normal weighing.

Consequently, the Committee agreed to present the modified item for a vote.

320-8 W Table 4. Minimum Test Weights and Test Loads

(This item was withdrawn)

Source: Carryover Item 320-4. (This item originated from the Northeastern Weights and Measures Association (NEWMA) and first appeared on the Committee's 2006 agenda.)

Discussion: The Committee considered an earlier NEWMA proposal to modify Table 4. Minimum Test Weights and Test Loads as follows:

Discussion: The Committee considered an earlier NEWMA proposal to modify Table 4. Minimum Test Weights and Test Loads as follows:

Table 4.
Minimum Test Weights and Test Loads [1]

Device capacity	Minimums (in terms of device capacity)		(where practicable)
	Test weights (greater of)	Test loads[2]	
0 to 150 kg (0 to 300 lb)	100 %		
151 to 1 500 kg (301 to 3 000 lb)	25 % or 150 kg (300 lb)	75 %	Test weights to dial face capacity, 1 000 d, or test load to used capacity, if greater than minimums specified. During initial verification a scale should be tested to capacity.
1 501 to 20 000 kg (3 001 to 40 000 lb)	12.5 % or 500 kg (1 000 lb)	50 %	
20 001 kg **to 250 000 kg** (40 001 lb **to 500 000 lb**)	12.5 % or 5 000 kg (10 000 lb)	25 %[3]	
250 001 kg+ (500 001 lb+)	12.5 % OR 30 000 KG (62 500 LB)	**25 %**[3]	

[1] If the amount of test weight in Table 4 combined with the load on the scale would result in an unsafe condition, then the appropriate load will be determined by the official with statutory authority.

[2] The term "test load" means the sum of the combination of field standard test weights and any other applied load used in the conduct of a test using substitution test methods. Not more than three substitutions shall be used during substitution testing, after which the tolerances for strain load tests shall be applied to each set of test loads.

[3] The scale shall be tested from zero to at least 12.5 % of scale capacity using known test weights, and then to at least 25 % of scale capacity using either a substitution or strain load test that utilizes known test weights of at least 12.5 % of scale capacity. Whenever practical, a strain load test should be conducted to the used capacity of the scale. When a strain load test is conducted, the tolerances apply only to the test weights or substitution test loads.
(Amended 1988, 1989, 1994, and 2003)

[**Note:** GIPSA requires devices subject to their inspection to be tested to at least "used capacity," which is calculated based on the platform area of the scale and a weight factor assigned to the species of animal weighed on the scale. "Used capacity" is calculated using the formula:

Used Scale Capacity = Scale Platform Area x Species Weight Factor

Where species weight factor = 540 kg/m^2 (110 lb/ft^2) for cattle, 340 kg/m^2 (70 lb/ft^2) for calves and hogs, and 240 kg/m^2 (50 lb/ft^2) for sheep and lambs]

(Amended 200X)

Field officials are faced with determining the minimum test load necessary to verify the performance of scales with nominal capacities that exceed 1 000 000 lb. Since January 2006, the Committee has considered several proposed modifications to Table 4, which included listing the minimum and maximum test weights and test loads for devices with capacities that exceed 500 001 lb. However, this action has not resulted in any new guidelines beyond the existing minimum test load requirements in Table 4.

The Committee further acknowledged that officials might have difficulty placing the recommended minimum 25 % test load on some load-receiving elements such as railway track scales with two small platforms with a dead space between them because this configuration limits the size of each platform. In its earlier reviews of this item, the Committee agreed that until the submitter develops alternate language and data to justify specific minimum load requirements that warrant a change to existing HB 44 requirements, the proposal should remain an Information item.

The WWMA discussed the proposal and heard one comment that recommended the proposal specify only 62 500 lb of minimum test weights in the proposed new device capacity range that exceeds 500 001 lb. The WWMA believes that the carryover proposal does not change the requirements in Table 4, even though the proposed text specifies the amount of test weights for scale capacities that exceed 500 000 lb. The WWMA also believes that data may be needed to demonstrate what is an adequate amount of test weight for scales with capacities that exceed 500 000 lb. Consequently, the WWMA recommended the proposal be withdrawn.

The CWMA recommended this proposal be withdrawn, but provided no rationale for its position.

NEWMA recommended that HB 44 provide flexible guidelines for determining the minimum acceptable test load when testing high-capacity scales. At its October 2006 meeting, NEWMA developed an alternate proposal which modified Table 4 as follows to address devices with a capacity up to 500 000 lb and to allow some flexibility by eliminating the last column.

Table 4. Minimum Test Weights and Test Loads [1]			
Device capacity	**Minimums (in terms of device capacity)**		~~(where practicable)~~
	Test weights (greater of)	**Test loads [2]**	
0 to 150 kg (0 to 300 lb)	100 %		
151 to 1 500 kg (301 to 3 000 lb)	25 % or 150 kg (300 lb)	75 %	
1 501 to 20 000 kg (3 001 to 40 000 lb)	12.5 % or 500 kg (1 000 lb)	50 %	~~Test weights to dial face capacity, 1 000 d, or test load to used capacity, if greater than minimums specified.~~
20 001 kg~~-~~ **to** **250 000 kg** (40 001 lb~~-~~ **to 500 000 lb**)	12.5 % or 5 000 kg (10 000 lb)	25 % [3]	~~During initial verification, a scale should be tested to capacity.~~
250 001 kg (500 001 lb)	**12.5 % OR 30 000 KG (62 500 LB)**	**25 % [3]**	

[1] If the amount of test weight in Table 4 combined with the load on the scale would result in an unsafe condition, then the appropriate load will be determined by the official with statutory authority.

.
.

Where species weight factor = 540 kg/m^2 (110 lb/ft^2) for cattle, 340 kg/m^2 (70 lb/ft^2) for calves and hogs, and 240 kg/m^2 (50 lb/ft^2) for sheep and lambs]

The SMA supported the carryover proposal with modifications for removing the proposed new minimum requirement for "12.5 %" test weights and any reference to the original footnote 3 from the fifth row of the table.

At the 2007 NCWM Interim Meeting, the Committee determined there was insufficient support at the national level for this proposal and the data that supported adopting the proposed minimum test weight and test loads for devices that exceed 500 001 lb capacities had not been provided. Therefore, the Committee withdrew this proposal from its agenda.

320-9   I   Appendix D; Definitions for Tare Mechanism, Gross Weight Value, Net Weight, Net Weight Value, Tare, and Tare Weight Value

Source: National Type Evaluation Technical Committee (NTETC) Weighing Sector

Recommendation: Modify the definition for "tare mechanism" and add new definitions for "gross weight value," "net weight," "net weight value," "tare," and "tare weight value" to Appendix D.

Amend the following definition for "tare mechanism:"

> tare mechanism. A mechanism (including a tare bar) designed for determining or balancing out the weight of packaging material, containers, vehicles, or other materials that are not intended to be included in net weight determinations **and for setting the indication to zero when the tare object is on the load-receiving element:**
>
> 1. **by reducing the weighing range for net loads (e.g., subtractive tare where Net Weight + Tare Weight ≤ Gross Weight Capacity), or**
> 2. **without altering the weighing range for net load on mechanical scales (e.g., additive tare mechanism such as a tare bar on a mechanical scale with a beam indicator).**
>
> **The tare mechanism may function as:**
> 1. **a non-automatic mechanism (load balanced by an operator),**
> 2. **a semi-automatic mechanism (load balanced automatically following a single manual command),**
> 3. **an automatic mechanism where the load is balanced automatically without the intervention of an operator. An automatic tare mechanism is only suitable for indirect sales to the customer (e.g., prepackaging scales).**
>
> [2.20**, 2.24**]
> **(Amended 200X)**

Add the following new definitions to Appendix D:

gross weight value. Indication or recorded representation of the weight of a load on a weighing device with no tare mechanism in operation.[2.20, 2.24]
(Added 200X)

net weight. The term "net mass" or "net weight" means the weight of a commodity excluding any materials, substances, or items not considered to be part of the commodity. Materials, substances, or items not considered to be part of the commodity include, but are not limited to, containers, conveyances, bags, wrappers, packaging materials, labels, individual piece coverings, decorative accompaniments, and coupons, except that, depending on the type of service rendered, packaging materials may be considered to be part of the service. For example, the service of shipping includes the weight of packing materials.[2.20, 2.24]
(Added 200X)

net weight value. Indication or recorded representation of the weight of a load placed on a weighing device after the operation of a tare mechanism.[2.20, 2.24]
(Added 200X)

tare. The weight of packaging material, containers, vehicles, or other materials that are not intended to be part of the commodity included in net weight determinations.[2.20, 2.24]
(Added 200X)

tare weight value. The weight value of a load determined by a tare mechanism.[2.20, 2.24]
(Added 200X)

Discussion: This Weighing Sector proposal is one of several proposed modifications to HB 44 requirements intended to clarify the acceptable tare features already recognized for use in commercial applications. Scales Code requirements do not include sufficiently detailed language to identify all types of tare, define how tare features must operate, or specify the net and tare values a scale must indicate and record. Current HB 44 requirements that address tare include paragraphs S.2.1.6. Combined Zero-Tare ("0/T") Key, S.2.3. Tare, S.2.3.1. Monorail Scales Equipped with Digital Indications, and T.N.2.1. General (Tolerances).

The Weighing Sector has developed criteria used to type evaluate tare features based on General Code paragraph G-S.2. Facilitation of Fraud and other requirements that apply to indicating and recording elements and recorded representations. NTEP laboratories find that it has become increasingly difficult to base its compliance decisions solely on paragraph G-S.2. because the general nature of the language results in multiple interpretations. Type evaluation criteria are published in NCWM Publication 14; however, this document is not in wide distribution in the weights and measures community. In addition, only a limited number of weights and measures officials, device manufacturers, and device owners and operators are regular participants in Weighing Sector meetings where tare evaluation criteria are developed and discussed. Additionally, it is difficult for parties responsible for the design, use, and test of the tare feature to interpret and apply technical requirements published in Publication 14. This results in differing interpretations of HB 44 requirements.

In 2006 the NTETC Weighing Sector formed a Tare WG to review existing tare requirements and make recommendations on how tare should operate on a single range scale, a multiple range scale, and a multi-interval scale. The WG also was asked to develop, where necessary, recommendations for changes to Publication 14, HB 44, and HB 130 and to provide guidance to the Weighing Sector on type evaluation requirements.

The WG is currently developing proposals to amend HB 44 requirements to:

(1) ensure that a tare feature operates in a manner that increases the accuracy of net weight determinations,
(2) clearly state what information and values are permitted and required for indicated and recorded representations of net weight and tare weight, and
(3) identify the types of tare weight values (e.g., semiautomatic and stored) determined at the time objects are weighed or tare weight values are determined prior to the time objects are weighed.

At its 2006 meeting, the Weighing Sector agreed to submit a proposal to the NCWM S&T Committee to amend HB 44 Appendix D by amending the term "tare mechanism" and adding new tare definitions to ensure a uniform understanding of the terminology used in HB 44.

The SWMA supported the proposal, but also believed the wording of the definition for "net weight" (which referenced the HB 130 definition of tare) should appear in Appendix D rather than have the reader refer to NIST HB 130 for that information. Consequently, the SWMA recommended adding the complete definition of "net weight" from HB 130 to the proposal as shown in the recommendation above.

The SMA supported the intent of the proposal, but recommended the proposal be returned to the Weighing Sector for further development and subsequent review by the regional weights and measures associations.

WMD noted there should be a corresponding proposal in the Automatic Weighing Systems (AWS) Code since the terms also apply to those devices. Both proposals should be discussed and eventually voted on as a block.

The Weighing Sector submitted a single proposal (S&T Item 320-9), which included modified and new definitions for tare and related weight values that referenced HB 44 Sections 2.20. Scales and 2.24. Automatic Weighing Systems. The Committee agreed that for procedural reasons, a separate corresponding proposal should have appeared in its 2007 S&T Agenda in Section 3.24. for AWS. A separate item is more appropriate because some in the community, due to time constraints and interests, will focus only on specific device sections in the agenda. Therefore, the Committee developed a separate proposal for automatic weighing systems that now appears in this report as new S&T Item 324-3. For the sake of brevity, the Committee kept the proposed text for both applications under S&T Item 320-9 to ensure a similar outcome since devices in both Code Sections 2.20. and 2.24. are affected by the definitions. The Committee will consider this item and new S&T Item 324-3 jointly during all future sessions.

The Committee further modified the proposed formula for subtractive tare in subparagraph one that appears in the definition of "tare mechanism" to clarify that the combined net and tare net weight value should not exceed the permissible gross weight capacity. The Committee agreed that lengthy discussions on all of the tare proposals demonstrate that, although it is necessary to address tare, the matter is too complex to move forward without a more thorough review of all related proposals by the Weighing Sector and weights and measures jurisdictions. Consequently, the Committee recommended this proposal and other related proposals addressing tare features remain as Information items for further review and development. The Committee also agreed that all tare related items, when ready, should be presented for voting as a block.

321 BELT-CONVEYOR SCALE SYSTEMS

321-1   I   UR.2.2.(n) Belt Alignment

Source: Southern Weights and Measures Association (SWMA)

Recommendation: Modify paragraph UR.2.2.(n) as follows:

UR.2.2. Conveyor Installation

(n) Belt Alignment. – The belt shall be centered on the idlers in the weighing area and shall track in practically the same position whether empty or loaded.   The belt shall not extend beyond the edge of the idler roller in any area of the conveyor.
(Amended 1998 **and 2007**)

Background/Discussion: During the 2006 NCWM Interim Meeting, the Committee considered the recommendation from the NCWM review panel's recommendations and comments from industry. The review panel indicated the proposal should have included national data that demonstrated a need for modifying paragraph UR.2.2. and should be a Developing item until such data is provided. At that time, one representative from the belt-conveyor scale service industry indicated there are too many factors that influence belt tracking to ensure a belt is centered at all times. The service representative recommended that the belt should not extend beyond the edge of the idler roller in any area of the conveyor on the carrying side or touch holding brackets on the return side to reduce any detrimental effects on accuracy. Industry representatives indicated the design of idlers and scales are such that the belt is not intended to stay in the exact center. Industry also indicated no mechanism is available to monitor the belt's tracking 24 hours a day, 7 days a week. Industry requested specifications for what constitutes either "center" or an acceptable "range of center" for belt tracking. Although the 2005 SWMA reported the proposal was ready for national consideration, the Committee agreed it was more appropriate to make the proposal a Developing item until there is some clear indication that belt alignment can be tracked for maintenance and accuracy purposes.

At its 2006 meeting, the WWMA agreed with concerns about the difficulties in tracking belt alignment and agreed it should first be determined if there are mechanisms capable of monitoring this feature before establishing device requirements. Consequently, the WWMA recommended this item be withdrawn from the agenda.

The CWMA does not believe this proposal should move forward without more information from industry.

In 2006 the SWMA recommended the proposal remain a Developing item, but indicated if industry provides no additional input, the item should be withdrawn from the Committee's agenda.

During the 2007 Interim Meeting, the Committee heard comments that the BCS Code requirements are far too prescriptive when compared to the language in other scale code sections and device operators, manufacturers, and officials are able to detect improper belt alignment either through belt wear or in the system's performance. The Committee agreed the proposed language was sufficiently developed and should be upgraded from a Developing item to an Information item in this report in order to receive additional input and national data demonstrating the need for amending paragraph UR.2.2. The Committee requested input from all stakeholders, including a review by the National Weighing and Sampling Association by the 2007 Annual Meeting, before it will consider the proposal ready for adoption.

During the 2007 NCWM Annual Meeting, the Committee heard testimony that a work group of the National Weighing and Sampling Association is working on this item and will have a recommendation for the Committee prior to the 2008 NCWM Interim Meeting.

324 AUTOMATIC WEIGHING SYSTEMS

324-1　I　S.1.2. Value of Division Units and T.2.1. General

Source: National Type Evaluation Technical Committee (NTETC) Weighing Sector

Recommendation: Add a new note to paragraph S.1.2. and amend paragraph T.2.1. as follows:

> **S.1.2. Value of Division Units.** – The value of a division d expressed in a unit of weight shall be equal to:
>
> (a)　1, 2, or 5; or
>
> (b)　a decimal multiple or submultiple of 1, 2, or 5.
>
> **Note: The requirements that the value of the scale division be expressed only as 1, 2, or 5, or a decimal multiple or submultiples of only 1, 2, or 5 does not apply to net weight indications and recorded representations that are calculated from gross and tare weight indications where the scale division of the gross weight is different from the scale division of the tare weight(s) on multi-interval or multiple range scales.**
>
> **For example, a scale indicating a tare weight of 2 kg in the lower range or segment and a gross weight of 5 kg in the higher range or segment may indicate a net weight of 3 kg, or a scale indicating a tare weight of 20 lb in the lower range or segment and a gross weight of 50 lb in the higher range or segment may indicate a net weight of 30 lb.**
> **(Note Added 200X)**
>
> **S.2.2. Tare.** – On any automatic weighing system ~~(except for multi-interval scales or multiple range scales when the value of tare is determined in a lower range)~~ the value of the tare division shall be equal to the value of the scale division. The tare mechanism shall operate only in a backward direction (i.e., in a direction of underregistration) with respect to the zero-load balance condition of the automatic weighing system. A device designed to automatically clear any tare value shall also be designed to prevent the automatic clearing of tare until a complete transaction has been indicated.
>
> **Note:** On a computing automatic weighing system, this requires the input of a unit price, the display of the unit price, and a computed positive total price at a readable equilibrium. Other devices require that a transaction or lot run be completed.
> **(Amended** 2004 and **200X)**
>
> **T.2.1. General.** – The tolerance values are positive (+) and negative (-) with the weighing device adjusted to zero at no load. When tare is in use, the tolerance values are applied from the tare zero reference **(zero net indication)**; the tolerance values apply to **the net weight indication for any possible tare load using** certified test loads~~only~~.
> **(Amended 200X)**

Discussion: In 2006 the NTETC Weighing Sector formed a Tare WG to review existing tare requirements and make recommendations on how tare is to operate on a single range scale, multiple range scale, and multi-interval scale. The WG was also asked to develop, where necessary, recommendations for changes to Publication 14, HB 44, and HB 130 and to provide guidance to the Weighing Sector on type evaluation requirements.

This proposal developed by the Tare WG and supported by the Weighing Sector adds a new note to paragraph S.1.2. The note recognizes display and printing of net weight values in divisions other than the scale division used in the display of gross weight, resulting in a more accurate net weight determination.

The proposal also amends paragraph T.2.1. to clarify that tolerances also apply to net weight indications regardless of the gross load on the scale. To determine if there were areas where HB 44 could be aligned with international recommendations, the Tare WG reviewed OIML R 76 "Nonautomatic Weighing Instruments" for corresponding requirements. Based on that review, the WG agreed that HB 44 paragraph T.2.1. should be modified to state that tolerances also apply to net load indications.

The Tare WG discussed problems associated with determining the appropriate direction to round tare on multi-interval scales and multiple range scales whenever gross and tare weights fall in different weighing segments on a multi-interval scale or in different weighing ranges on multiple range scales. In these cases, the scale division size for the gross and tare weights differ; however, the net weight must be in mathematical agreement with the gross and tare weights indicated and recorded by the device (i.e., gross weight - tare weight = net weight).

The problem arises when the tare weight is rounded up to the next larger scale division, where the net weight falls in the higher segment or range. For example, a 0.004 lb tare weight in a weighing range or segment with 0.002 lb intervals in the lower weighing range or segment may round to zero when the net weight falls in the upper weighing range with 0.01 lb intervals:

      10.05   lb   Gross Weight
     − 0.004 lb   Tare Weight
      10.046 lb   the Mathematically Correct Net Weight;

However, because the tare weight will be rounded to zero in the upper range, the device indicates 10.05 lb Net Weight.

This results in a transaction where a commodity is bought or sold on the basis of gross weight (as shown in the example above) or when an insufficient amount of tare weight is taken and results in a misrepresentation of net weight for the transaction. Essentially, the rounding of tare that falls in a smaller division in either direction provides a less accurate net weight than if the tare weight were not rounded.

The Tare WG developed a corresponding proposal for the Scales Code to clarify the appropriate scale division values and the application of tolerances to tare weights for those devices (see S&T Item 320-3).

The SWMA supports the recommendation; however, the SWMA also agreed that an additional note should be added to paragraph S.2.2. Tare (as shown in the recommendation above) to eliminate any conflict with proposed changes to paragraph S.1.2. The new note proposed for paragraph S.2.2. clarifies that the requirement does not apply to multi-interval scales or multiple range scales when tare is determined in the lower range of those scales.

WMD agreed that it might be more appropriate if the proposed new note explains that gross weight and calculated tare weight are expressed as an "indicated weight value" rather than as a "scale value." WMD notes that the proposed SWMA text is necessary to clarify that tare weights are excluded from the requirement that specifies tare weight values must be the same as the scale division value. However, the SWMA's proposal needs further work to clarify that only part of the entire paragraph applies to tare weights indicated on either a multi-interval or multiple range scale and to clarify the relationship of paragraph S.1.2. to corresponding paragraph S.2.2. WMD also asked if it was the SWMA's intent that this newly proposed note be a retroactive or nonretroactive requirement, and if nonretroactive, then what is an appropriate effective date?

The SMA supports the Weighing Sector proposal, but recommends the proposed new note become a subparagraph of paragraph S.1.2. and a modification to the proposed new text in paragraph T.2.1. to require the net weight indication for "any" rather than "every" possible tare load using certified test loads. The Committee agreed to the SMA's recommended changes to paragraph T.2.1. and modified the proposal accordingly.

The Committee deliberated at length on this item and S&T Items 320-5, 320-9, and 324-3, which are all meant to clarify the distinct differences in how various tare features are permitted to operate. The Committee agreed that ultimately neither the buyer nor seller should incur a loss as a result of inaccurate calculation of a tare weight. Much of the weights and measures community has not had the opportunity to discuss these proposals nor has the Tare WG or Weighing Sector had time to analyze feedback on these proposed changes and corresponding proposals to 320-3 and 324-3 to make changes to the Scales Code and the AWS Code, respectively. The Committee agreed that all proposals related to the operation of the tare feature should be Information items to ensure all aspects of the operation of tare features are clearly defined for the public and private sectors and its operation is adequately addressed.

During the 2007 NCWM Annual Meeting, the Committee heard comments from the CWMA and NEWMA supporting this item with recommendations to change the word "value" to "division" and incorporate the SWMA recommendation to modify paragraph S.2.2.

NEWMA pointed out that the proposed change to paragraph S.2.1. appears to be permissive and not a requirement and asked if the intent was to prohibit multi-interval and multiple range scales from rounding and indicating calculated net weights in scale divisions to only 1, 2, or 5 when appropriate or if rounding the scale divisions of 1, 2, or 5 was still allowed? The WMD representative to the NCWM Tare WG stated that the intent was for the language to be permissive because there are a significant number devices with NTEP CCs in the marketplace that round the tare values before calculating net weights.

The Committee made several modifications to the proposal:

- to clarify the examples in the proposed note to paragraph S.1.2., and
- to clarify the SWMA proposed modification to the language in S.2.2. for an exception for multi-interval and multiple range scales only applies to the requirement that the value of tare shall be equal the value of the scale division.

The Committee also agreed that the words "scale value" should be changed to "scale division" to be consistent with the terminology currently used in HB 44 and recommends that the NIST technical advisor forward the amended proposal to the Tare WG and NTETC Weighing Sector for their consideration and comment.

324-2 VC Note 5 Table S.7.b. Notes for Table S.7.a.; Temperature Range

(This item was adopted)

Source: National Type Evaluation Technical Committee (NTETC) Weighing Sector

Recommendation: Amend Note 5 in Table S.7.b. as follows:

5. Required only on automatic weighing systems if the **temperature** range **on the NTEP CC** is ~~other~~ **narrower** than **and within** –10 °C to 40 °C (14 °F to 104 °F). **(Amended 2007)**

Add new paragraph T.2.X. as follows:

T.2.3. Subsequent Verification Examination. – For subsequent verification examinations, the tolerance values apply regardless of the influence factors in effect at the time of the conduct of the examination. (Also see G-N.2.)
(Added 2007)

Background/Discussion: Questions periodically arise about whether or not a device is suitable for field operation based on the limited temperature range the device is subjected to under type evaluation. In other cases a device's suitability is questioned when the temperature limits marked on the device are narrower or wider than the –10 °C to 40 °C (14 °F to 104 °F) temperature range referenced in HB 44. In 2005, the NTETC Weighing Sector established a policy where its laboratories will only test and issue approvals over the –10 °C to 40 °C (14 °F to 104 °F) temperature range because of the limitations of its environmental chambers and safety concern for laboratory staff working in high temperature environments. In 2006 the Weighing Sector asked for the Committee's interpretation of how to apply temperature limits given the climatic conditions developed in the laboratory and those that exist in real-world environments.

Most HB 44 Section 2 and Section 5 device codes include requirements for marking equipment with temperature limits. Many of those codes include specific conditions for marking a temperature range on commercial equipment.

Weighing devices are required to perform within tolerance over the temperature range of –10 °C to 40 °C (14 °F to 104 °F). The temperature range of –10 °C to 40 °C was selected as the low and high climatic limits of operation to: (1) align U.S. and International Organization of Legal Metrology (OIML) environmental conditions for performance tests, (2) keep within a range that represents at least 80 % of the climatic conditions for meeting performance requirements in military specifications for electronic equipment, and (3) duplicate the conditions typically found in most outdoor environments. Current OIML recommendations for temperature test levels for electronic equipment are left to each nation based on the severity of climatic conditions where the instrument is typically in use.

In 1991 the NCWM S&T Committee provided guidelines on how to apply temperature range marking requirements and the appropriate use of a scale that is marked for use in a temperature range narrower or wider than –10 °C to 40 °C. Device manufacturers are required to mark the equipment's working temperature range when it is narrower or wider than –10 °C to 40 °C. Device codes also specify the minimum difference between the lower and upper limits of the temperature range based on the device's accuracy class.

The following text is excerpted from Item 320-3 of the 1991 Final S&T Report and includes the Committee's interpretation on marking requirements for temperature ranges on scales that should be included in the training modules for scales:

Temperature Range of –10 °C to 40 °C (14 °F to 104 °F):

This case has two parts. The conclusion is the same whether or not the temperature range is marked on the device.

If a temperature range is not marked on the scale, the device must be accurate over the range of –10 °C to 40 °C (14 °F to 104 °F). If a temperature range is not marked on a device with an NTEP Certificate of Conformance, it was tested over a temperature range of –10 °C to 40 °C (14 °F to 104 °F).

If a device is marked with a temperature range of –10 °C to 40 °C (14 °F to 104 °F), the marking is not considered to be a limitation to its application. The device may be used outside the specified temperature range, but the device must be accurate in the environment in which it is used since Scales Code paragraph T.N.2.3. Subsequent Verification Examination applies. The marking of the temperature range -10 °C to 40 °C (14 °F to 104 °F) is optional.

Marked Temperature Range **Less** *Than –10 °C to 40 °C (14 °F to 104 °F):*

If a device is marked with a temperature range less than –10 °C to 40 °C (14 °F to 104 °F), then the environment in which the device is used must be evaluated to determine if the device is suitable for use in that application. The device cannot be used in an environment in which the temperatures exceed the temperature limits marked on the device.

Marked Temperature Range **Greater** *Than –10 °C to 40 °C (14 °F to 104 °F):*

If a device is marked with a temperature range greater than –10 °C to 40 °C (14 °F to 104 °F) this indicates a scale of higher quality than a scale without a temperature marking for devices within the same accuracy class and of the same scale division value. This fact may be used as a marketing tool in the same manner as the maximum number of scale divisions, n_{max}. A scale marked with a wider temperature range is tested during type evaluation over the marked temperature range.

No changes were made to HB 44 temperature marking requirements until 1998 when the Weighing Sector identified a discrepancy between HB 44 and Publication 14 National Type Evaluation Program Administrative Procedures, Technical Policy, Checklists, and Test Procedures in the requirement for marking temperature ranges on scales. HB 44 required that Class III, III L, and IIII devices be marked with a temperature range if the temperature limits are *other* than –10 °C to 40 °C (14 °F to 104 °F). However, some sections of Publication 14 stated that these devices must be marked with a temperature range if the temperature range is *narrower* than –10 °C to 40 °C (14 °F to 104 °F).

In 1998 the Weighing Sector discussed instances where is it permissible to use a device if the device is marked with a specific temperature range or a range is listed on a CC. The Sector agreed that, if possible, the requirement should harmonize with OIML. OIML R 76 Clause 3.9.2.1. Prescribed Temperature Limits states, "If no particular working temperature is stated in the descriptive markings of an instrument, this instrument shall maintain its metrological properties within the following temperature limits: –10 °C to 40 °C (14 °F to 104 °F)."

Subsequently, the Committee considered a proposal to modify Scales Code Table S.6.3.b. Notes for Table S.6.3.a., Note 5. to read as follows:

> 5. *Required only on Class III, III L, and IIII* ~~scales~~ **devices** *if the* ~~temperature~~ *range* **on the NTEP CC** ~~is other~~ **narrower** *than* ~~and within~~ *–10 °C to 40 °C (14 °F to 104 °F).*
> *[Nonretroactive as of January 1, 1986]*

The Committee agreed that although the modifications to Note 5 are less restrictive, they appear to more adequately describe the temperature marking requirements and eliminate any conflict between HB 44 and Publication 14. During the 1999 Annual Meeting, hearing no unfavorable comments on this proposal, the Conference adopted the item, and it remains the same today.

In 2006 the Sector questioned why requirements that address equipment operating at temperatures outside the -10 °C to 40 °C temperature range, such as Scales Code paragraph T.N.2.3. Subsequent Examination Verification, are not included in all weighing device codes. The Sector also noted there are inconsistencies in the language that specifies temperature requirements throughout the weighing device codes. The Weighing Sector agreed this is an important issue and recognized that the Committee needed time to research the codes and policies established on this topic. Consequently, the Weighing Sector request became a Developing item on the Committee's 2006 agenda.

The Weighing Sector agreed that no evaluation would be conducted for temperature ranges outside of laboratory capabilities, which are –10 °C to 40 °C while it awaited input from the Committee. The Weighing Sector's *ad hoc* policy is contrary to an earlier 1991 NTEP policy where NTEP agreed to require testing to demonstrate compliance with the manufacturer's specified temperature range, including accepting data from recognized and approved laboratories for tests performed under the oversight of an NTEP lab at temperature ranges that exceeded the –10 °C to 40 °C temperature range.

At their fall 2006 meetings, the regional weights and measures associations reviewed the proposal in its former status as a Developing item (Part 4, Item 1) that did not include any recommendation to modify HB 44. The WWMA agreed the proposal is predominantly a type evaluation laboratory issue and should be considered at the next meeting of the Automatic Weighing System WG. The WWMA may revisit the issue at a later date if it is deemed necessary to modify HB 44 to adequately address temperature requirements. The WWMA recommended the issue remain a Developing item while the NCWM S&T Committee and Weighing Sector develop a position that can be published for review.

The CWMA recommended that the Automatic Weighing Systems Code reflect HB 44 Scales Code T.N.8. Influence Factors. NEWMA supported the CWMA recommendation.

At the conclusion of its 2006 meeting, the Weighing Sector agreed that the NIST technical advisor would prepare and submit to the SWMA proposed changes to Note 5 as shown in the recommendation above. The Sector agreed that any corresponding changes to other codes should first be evaluated by the appropriate NTETC sector.

The Weighing Sector believes that its 2005 technical policy defining the scope of temperature testing conducted by NTEP is not in conflict with the 1991 S&T Committee's position since the 1999 modification to Note 5 resulted in a link of the temperature range marking requirement to the range listed on the CC. The Sector also agreed that the CC does not cover devices marked with a larger temperature range than what is listed on the CC. For example, an NTEP CC that lists a temperature range of –5 °C to +30 °C would not cover a device that was not marked with a temperature range or a device marked with a –5 °C to +45 °C temperature range.

The Sector agreed with the concerns from the NTEP laboratories that testing over increasing temperature ranges may become a health and safety issue and that existing temperature chambers are limited in their capabilities to perform temperature tests over wider ranges. Additionally, the Sector recommended the NCWM S&T Committee reconsider amending the Committee's 1991 position on temperature requirements to correspond with the Sector's current marking requirement policy that recognizes health and safety concerns and the limitations of NTEP laboratory testing equipment.

The SWMA agreed the Weighing Sector's proposal should move forward as a Voting item on the NCWM S&T Committee's agenda. However, both the SWMA and WMD recommended including in the proposal a new paragraph T.2.X. Subsequent Verification Examination that was inadvertently overlooked by the Weighing Sector. A new paragraph T.2.X. Subsequent Verification Examination, which now appears in the recommendation, clarifies how field devices must operate under temperature conditions outside of the range for type evaluation.

The Committee agreed it is appropriate to include a new tolerance paragraph based on Scales Code paragraph TN.2.3. Subsequent Verification Examinations to address what tolerances must apply during subsequent verification of the device when temperature conditions are outside of those during initial verification. The Committee made one editorial revision to text that appeared in its January 2007 agenda changing "or the examination" to "of the examination" in proposed new paragraph T.2.X. as shown in the above recommendation. The Committee believed the proposal with these modifications was ready for a vote at the July 2007 NCWM Annual Meeting.

During the 2007 NCWM Annual Meeting, the Committee heard comments that there may be some confusion with the use of the word "subsequent verification" and that the proposed tolerance paragraph would not be applicable to the initial verification after the device was installed.

The Committee believed that "subsequent verification" as used in the AWS Code is any test other than type evaluation examinations, and the Committee has not received any comments of problems with similar terminology and language in Scales Code paragraph T.N.2.3. Subsequent Verification. The Committee noted that the definition for "initial verification" in HB 44 Appendix D may be the source of confusion. This definition, however, is only applicable to Section 2.21 Belt-Conveyor Scale Systems.

Additionally, the Committee agreed to recommend numbering the proposed paragraph as shown above and renumbering current paragraph T.2.3. Multiple Range and Multi-Interval Automatic Weighing Systems to T.2.4.

Consequently, the Committee agreed to present the modified item for a vote.

324-3　I　Appendix D; Definitions for Tare Mechanism, Gross Weight Value, Net Weight, Net Weight Value, Tare, and Tare Weight Value

Source: S&T Committee

Recommendation: Modify the definition for "tare mechanism" and add new definitions for "gross weight value," "net weight," "net weight value," "tare," and "tare weight value" to Appendix D that apply to Section 2.24. Automatic Weighing Systems. These are the definitions shown in the "Recommendation" for Item 320-9.

Discussion: At the 2007 Interim Meeting, the Committee agreed that for procedural reasons a separate corresponding proposal should have appeared on its 2007 S&T Agenda in Section 324 for Automatic Weighing Systems. Therefore, the Committee developed a separate proposal for automatic weighing systems that now appears in this report as new S&T Item 324-3. The Committee recommends that new S&T Item 324-3 along with a corresponding proposal to apply these definitions to devices that fall under the Scales Code S&T Item 320-9, be discussed and considered jointly during all deliberations. In the interest of brevity, the Committee placed all recommendations, discussion, and background information for this proposal in S&T Item 320-9 because the proposed definitions apply to both applications; this ensures both proposals are addressed collectively.

330 LIQUID-MEASURING DEVICES

330-1 VC S.1.2.3. Value of the Smallest Unit

(This item was adopted)

Source: Carryover Item 330-2. (This item originated from the National Type Evaluation Technical Committee (NTETC) Measuring Sector and first appeared on the Committee's 2006 agenda.)

Recommendation: Modify NIST HB 44 paragraph S.1.2.3. as follows:

> **S.1.2.3. Value of Smallest Unit.** – The value of the smallest unit of indicated delivery, and recorded delivery if the device is equipped to record, shall not exceed the equivalent of:
>
> > (a) 0.5 L (~~1 pt~~ **0.1 gal**) on ~~retail~~ devices **with a maximum rated flow rate of 750 L/min (200 gal/min) or less;**
> >
> > (b) 5 L (1 gal) on ~~wholesale~~ devices **with a maximum rated flow of more than 750 L/min (200 gal/min);**~~.~~
> >
> > **(c) 5 L (1 gal) on meters with a rated maximum flow rate of 375 L/min (100 gal/min) or more used for jet fuel aviation refueling systems.**
>
> This requirement does not apply to manually operated devices equipped with stops or stroke-limiting means. (Amended 1983, 1986, and 2007)

Background/Discussion: In 2004 the definition of a "retail device" in HB 44 was modified to include all devices used to measure product for the purpose of sale to the end user. At that time, the Committee believed all affected parties were aware of the proposal and there was no opposition to the change. The Committee had not considered applications where very large deliveries were made to the end user, typically at high flow rates. After the 2005 edition of HB 44 was published and distributed, NIST WMD received input from a weights and measures jurisdiction that routinely tests large meters used to deliver fuel to fishing fleets and other large ocean-going boats. The jurisdiction stated that the average fuel delivery was approximately 300 000 gal and may be as much as 1 000 000 gal. Prior to the revision of the definition of "retail," these deliveries were classified as "wholesale" and the value of the smallest unit of the indicated delivery for these devices was permitted to be 1 gal. Most of these devices have mechanical registers which make it impractical to have a smallest indicated unit of 0.1 gal at the high flow rates used for such large deliveries. Because the fuel was being delivered to the end user, after January 2005 with the revisions to the definition of retail device, HB 44 would define these meters as making retail deliveries and would require a smallest unit of delivery of not more than 0.5 L (1 pt or 0.125 gal) for these devices.

To remedy this issue the NTETC Measuring Sector developed the original recommendation in the Committee's 2006 agenda. The Measuring Sector believed that, because the maximum flow rate for many applications has increased, 200 gal/min is an appropriate "break point" for determining what the smallest unit of measurement should be.

At the 2006 NCWM Interim Meeting, it was suggested the Committee revisit the discussion on suitability of liquid-measuring devices discussed by the NCWM from 1991 through 1993. In these earlier discussions, the NCWM was unable to reach a consensus on any changes to HB 44, and the item was withdrawn from the Committee's agenda. The Committee was informed there was interest expressed at the 2005 NTETC Measuring Sector meeting in developing new criteria addressing suitability as it relates to flow rate, minimum measured quantity (MMQ), and smallest unit of measure for applications using liquid-measuring devices. The Committee encouraged the NTETC Measuring Sector to pursue the development of suitability requirements for the Committee's consideration and was interested in input from the weights and measures community on this approach.

During the 2006 NCWM Annual Meeting, the Committee received input from several aircraft refueling equipment manufacturers regarding a safety concern with stationary refueling systems capable of delivering jet fuel through two different sized hoses at different flow rates using two different meters. In this scenario, the operators of the refueling facility wanted both meters to have the same unit of indication, that is, 5 L (1 gal). The Committee understood the concern, but was reluctant to modify the recommendation based on the limited information available at the meeting. The Committee recommended the aircraft refueling industry propose a change to HB 44 during the next Conference cycle through the NTETC Measuring Sector and the regional associations. However, the Committee recognized that a legitimate problem might exist with existing jet aircraft refueling equipment and encouraged weights and measures jurisdictions to consider safety implications before taking official action on existing jet aircraft refueling devices that may not meet the requirements of paragraph S.1.2.3. During the voting session there appeared to be concern that, if this item were adopted, weights and measures officials could be perceived as ignoring safety issues for aircraft refueling. There was lack of support for the proposal without an exemption for jet aircraft refueling; therefore, the Committee changed the status of the proposal from a Voting item to an Information item to allow sufficient time to address these areas of concern.

At its fall 2006 meeting, the CWMA agreed with the original recommendation, but proposed an accompanying user requirement be added to HB 44 to address aircraft refueling applications. The intent of the CWMA proposal was to require a 0.1 gal increment for equipment used to fuel smaller aircraft.

At its fall 2006 meeting, the WWMA discussed the proposed amendment to paragraph S.1.2.3. and also discussed the issues the aviation industry has when refueling aircraft using a combination of meters that register in 0.1 gal and 1 gal increments. The aviation industry was not present at that meeting, but the WWMA was made aware of the aviation industry's safety concerns about under-filling fuel tanks and tanks with an unbalanced load because of misread meter indications. The WWMA recognized industry's concerns but believes this is a training issue for aircraft refuelers. The WWMA agreed there is an immediate need to provide guidelines for fishing fleet and similar applications; therefore, it recommended the proposal move forward as written as a Voting item even if an exemption for aircraft fueling is not added.

At their fall 2006 meetings, the NTETC Measuring Sector and the SWMA reviewed a proposal to add a new subparagraph (c) to the original proposal to address the smallest acceptable unit of measure for jet aircraft refueling applications. The Measuring Sector considered the proposed marked maximum flow rate of 575 L/min (150 gal/min), but agreed it should be changed to 375 L/min (100 gal/min) to harmonize with a similar requirement in HB 44 Section 3.31. paragraph S.1.1.3. Value of the Smallest Unit (c). The Measuring Sector and the SWMA supported the modified proposal as shown above. The SWMA agreed to forward the proposal to the NCWM S&T Committee with the recommendation that the new subparagraph (c) be added to the original proposal.

At the 2007 NCWM Interim Meeting, the Committee considered the SWMA proposal which included a new paragraph (c) as shown above and a proposal from the CWMA for a corresponding user requirement as follows:

UR.XX Value of Smallest Unit. – The value of the smallest unit of indicated delivery, and recorded delivery if the device is equipped to record, shall not exceed the equivalent of:

(a) 0.5 L (0.1 gal) on devices with a flow rate of 750 L/min (200 gal/min) or less;

(b) 5 L (1 gal) on devices with a flow rate of more than 750 L/min (200 gal/min);

(c) 5 L (1 gal) on meters with a rated maximum flow of 375 L (100 gal/min) or more used for aviation turbine fuels.

This user requirement allows high-volume meters to sell in 1 gal increments to the end user and requires 0.1 gal increment deliveries only from meters delivering at less than 200 gal/min.
(Added 200X)

The Committee did not believe that the user requirement proposed by the CWMA would provide the desired result of providing a smaller display increment for applications fueling smaller aircraft. If a metering device is installed with two different sized hoses and nozzles for fueling different sized aircraft or for over-the-wing and under-the-wing fueling, the flow rate of the meter would be based on the size of the larger hose. Even though the rate of flow through the smaller hose might fall into the category intended to require a 0.1 gal increment, the "rated flow" for the meter would allow an increment of 1 gal. Therefore, the Committee did not include the CWMA proposal. The Committee agreed to forward the SWMA proposal without additional changes for a vote at the 2007 NCWM Annual Meeting.

330-2   V   S.1.6.5.5. Display of Quantity and Total Price and S.1.6.5.6. Display of Quantity and Total Price, Aviation Refueling Applications

(This item was adopted)

Source: Southern Weights and Measures Association (SWMA)

Recommendation: Modify HB 44 Section 3.30. paragraph S.1.6.5.5. and add a new paragraph S.1.6.5.6. as follows:

S.1.6.5.5. Display of Quantity and Total Price. – Except for aviation refueling applications, W~~w~~hen *a delivery is completed, the total price and quantity for that transaction shall be displayed on the face of the dispenser for at least 5 minutes or until the next transaction is initiated by using controls on the device or other customer-activated controls.*
[Nonretroactive as of January 1, 1994]
(Added 1992) (Amended 1996 **and 2007**)

~~S.1.6.5.6. Display of Quantity and Total Price, Aviation Refueling Applications.~~

~~(a) The quantity shall be displayed throughout the transaction.~~

~~(b) The total price shall also be displayed under one of the following conditions:~~

~~i   The total price can appear on the face of the dispenser or through a controller adjacent to the device.~~

~~ii   If a device is designed to continuously compute and display the total price, then the total price shall be computed and displayed throughout the transaction for the quantity delivered.~~

~~(c) The total price and quantity shall be displayed for at least 5 minutes or until the next transaction is initiated by using controls on the device or other customer-activated controls.~~

~~(d) A printed receipt shall be available and shall include, at a minimum, the total price, quantity, and unit price.~~
[Nonretroactive as of January 1, 2008]
(Added 2008)

Background/Discussion: The typical self-serve installation for aviation fuels does not use an analog or digital "gasoline dispenser" that simultaneously displays money and volume or that is equipped with a unit price display. In most cases the self-serve user interface is a credit card console/controller that handles the transaction. These devices display only quantity and are not set up for the simultaneous display of quantity and total price. This proposal provides an exemption for aviation refueling based on the position that the information provided by equipment that complies with the proposal is sufficient for the customers using these devices. The submitter stated that pilots are an informed group of customers that necessarily pay attention to the quantity of fuel put onboard the aircraft during a refueling operation, but are less concerned about the total cost of the commodity until the end of the transaction. As long as a unit price is posted, they have the ability to verify that the total price is correct on the receipt that is available at the end of the transaction.

Some designs of aviation self-serve dispensing systems use a meter-register that is a PD meter that can have a mechanical register and pulser, an electronic register with pulse output, or an "industrial" dispenser with a "volume only display" and a pulse output. The meter-register sends pulses to the credit card console/controller. In the example given all three components including the console/controller have separate NTEP certificates, but were not evaluated as a system.

In June 2006 a jurisdiction reviewed a couple of planned installations at airports and completed installations that had received grant funds to upgrade their fueling equipment. The jurisdictions informed the installing company that the equipment was required to be a "retail motor-fuel dispenser" (RMFD) that included a continuous display of "quantity and total sale." At some other airports "card-lock systems" were opened to other self-serve customers. This started a series of exchanges of information among several parties including two console/controller manufacturers, several equipment suppliers, and the weights and measures jurisdiction.

The manufacturer of the equipment used in some of these installations stated that neither high-flow diesel dispensers nor typical "retail gasoline dispensers" that have the simultaneous display of quantity and total price capability are designed, in terms of materials of construction, for aviation gasoline or jet fuel, and neither have the appropriate flow-rate capability for stationary jet refueling applications.

One company that assembles dispensers could make a unit to meet the materials of construction and minimum flow requirements of aviation refueling applications. Their NTEP certificate currently covers diesel and gasoline applications on their simultaneous display dispenser. They could use the appropriate aviation-approved materials of construction components for applications up to 50 gal/min and simultaneously display quantity and total price. However, these devices are not commonly used in the aviation industry and the maximum flow rate of the meter might be inadequate for some jet fuel applications.

At their fall 2006 meetings, the NTETC Measuring Sector and the SWMA reviewed a proposal to allow devices used in aircraft refueling to either display or print the total price and quantity delivered at the end of the transaction. The Measuring Sector took no position on the proposal because most members did not feel qualified to make an informed recommendation concerning the proposal. The SWMA believed that a printed receipt containing, at a minimum, the quantity, unit price, and total price should be required for all deliveries; therefore, the SWMA modified the above proposal to allow devices used in aircraft refueling to display the total price either throughout the transaction or at the end of the transaction provided a printed receipt was available. The SWMA agreed to forward the modified proposal to the NCWM S&T Committee with the recommendation that it be a Voting item on the Committee's 2007 agenda.

At the 2007 NCWM Interim Meeting, the Committee received letters from the National Air Transportation Association (NATA), the Aircraft Owners and Pilots Association (AOPA), and Alabama Weights and Measures. The NATA supported the modification of paragraph S.1.6.5.5. and the addition of a new paragraph S.1.6.5.6. The AOPA did not believe the new paragraph S.1.6.5.6. was needed if the proposed exemption in S.1.6.5.5. was adopted. However, if S.1.6.5.6. is adopted the exemption in S.1.6.5.5. for aircraft refueling becomes a necessity and should also be adopted. Alabama Weights and Measures opposed the exemption for aircraft refueling because it could limit the amount of transaction information available to the consumer. The Committee heard a concern that if the exemption is adopted, other RMFD users could ask for the same exemption. The Committee also heard concerns that if many small airports throughout the United States were required to replace their existing equipment, they might stop providing fueling services for small aircraft. That would cause considerable inconvenience and possible safety issues for small aircraft pilots. The Committee also heard a concern that if a dispenser was designed with full computing capability, that function should not be allowed to be disabled. The Committee agreed that computing capability should not be disabled on a full computing device and modified the proposal accordingly. The Committee discussed all of the testimony and input received. The Committee also reviewed a series of photographs of the equipment in question at an actual installation at an airport, as well as similar equipment installed on a VTM for aircraft refueling at the same airport. The Committee agreed there was little difference in the two devices. The primary difference was that the VTM was operated by airport personnel and the stationary meter was operated by the pilot of the aircraft. The Committee agreed to present the modified proposal for a vote at the 2007 NCWM Annual Meeting.

At the 2007 NCWM Annual Meeting, the Committee recognized that the term "full computing capability" as used in the SWMA recommendation was not defined in HB 44. Even though the SWMA had what most would describe as a "typical RMFD" in mind when this proposal was developed, the Committee believed some officials might not understand the intent. Therefore, the Committee agreed with the WMD recommendation to modify the proposed paragraph S.1.6.5.6. (as shown above) to make it clear what was intended by "full computing" and change the formatting to facilitate reading and understanding of the proposal.

This wording also addressed concerns that language that appeared in the 2007 NCWM Publication 16 could be misinterpreted as allowing scrolling messages on aircraft refueling devices (e.g., weather information) in place of the continuous computation and display of the total price during a delivery.

330-3   V   S.3.1. Diversion of Measured Liquid

(This item was adopted)

Source: Carryover Item 330-4. (This item originated from the Central Weights and Measures Association (CWMA) and first appeared on the Committee's 2006 agenda.)

Recommendation: Amend paragraph S.3.1. as follows:

> **S.3.1. Diversion of Measured Liquid.** – No means shall be provided by which any measured liquid can be diverted from the measuring chamber of the meter or its discharge line. Two or more delivery outlets may be installed only if automatic means are provided to ensure that:
>
> (a) liquid can flow from only one outlet at a time, and
>
> (b) the direction of flow for which the mechanism may be set at any time is clearly and conspicuously indicated.
>
> A**n** ~~manually controlled~~ outlet that may be opened for purging or draining the measuring system or for recirculating, **if recirculation is required in order to maintain the** product in **a deliverable state,** ~~suspension~~ shall be permitted   **only when the system is measuring food products, or agri-chemicals, biodiesel, or biodiesel blends.** Effective **automatic** means shall be provided to prevent passage of liquid through any such outlet during normal operation of the measuring system and to inhibit meter indications (or advancement of indications) and recorded representations while the outlet is in operation.

(Amended 1991, 1995, ~~and~~ 1996, and 2007)

Background/Discussion: The CWMA noted that the requirements in paragraph S.3.1. in Section 3.30. of the Liquid-Measuring Devices Code and paragraph S.4.1. Diversion of Measured Product in Section 3.37. of the Mass Flow Meters Code of HB 44 are not consistent with each other. Paragraph S.3.1. bans manual valves for recirculating product or for purging or draining the measuring system, except for foods and agri-chemicals. Paragraph S.4.1. allows manual and automatic valves and it makes no distinction for types of products measured as long as the system meets the specified requirements.

Cold weather and physical characteristics make recirculation necessary for a number of products not currently recognized in paragraph S.3.1., for example, #6 fuel oil and B100 biodiesel. Liquid-measuring devices exist which have NTEP CCs for these high viscosity products; however, the current wording of HB 44 forces vendors of these products to use mass flow meters if they wish to recirculate their product in order to keep it in a deliverable state. This inconsistency appears to be the unintended result of the fact that the two codes were written at different times with input from different segments of industry. The CWMA does not believe retailers of these products should be restricted to using only mass flow meters for commercial measurements if other suitable technologies are available. Likewise, the CWMA believes both manual and automatic valves are suitable for recirculating products in discharge lines of liquid-measuring devices, and the requirements for either type of meter should be the same.

The Committee believes the means to prevent passage of liquid through any such outlet during normal operation of the measuring system and to inhibit meter indications should be automatic. Therefore, the Committee modified the proposal accordingly.

At the 2006 NCWM Annual Meeting, this proposal, along with a corresponding proposal to modify the Mass Flow Meters Code, was presented for a vote. The Committee received input regarding the inappropriateness of allowing diversion of product on all types of liquid-measuring device applications. The vote on this item did not yield a sufficient number of positive or negative votes for the item to be accepted or defeated and, therefore, it was returned to the Committee for further action. The corresponding proposal under 2006 S&T Agenda Item 337-2, S.4.1. Diversion of Measured Product to similarly modify the Mass Flow Meters Code was adopted.

At its fall 2006 meeting, the CWMA affirmed that this proposal was drafted primarily to address an inequity between mass flow meters and other liquid-measuring devices in metering biodiesel and #6 fuel oil at terminals and marine fuelers. The objections to the proposal at the 2006 NCWM Annual Meeting seemed to center on the idea that passage of this proposal would lead to widespread recirculation at retail motor-fuel pumps and in applications with products other than biodiesel and #6 fuel oil. Minnesota, which adopted this proposal by rule in 2005, has experienced neither of these phenomena.

It has been Minnesota's experience that, because recirculation systems are expensive to install and operate, industry has utilized it only as a last resort. Recirculation has been confined to the marine fuelers on Lake Superior; a handful of terminals in the coldest regions of the state; and milk meters where recirculation has always been allowed. Minnesota has received no complaints about these installations and has seen no evidence that allowing recirculation has led to the facilitation of fraud.

The WWMA discussed an objection to the proposal because it would allow diversion and recirculation of all products. The WWMA believes it may not be appropriate to recirculate some products and might facilitate fraudulent practices. The WWMA recognizes that jurisdictions are preparing for sales of alternate fuels, but is uncertain at what point biodiesel products and blends need recirculating (low temperature limits or specific blend ratios). The WWMA S&T Committee agreed the list of products should be limited but should recognize all biodiesel products and blends. Consequently, the WWMA developed an alternate proposal as shown in the recommendation above and recommended it move forward as a Voting item on the 2007 S&T Committee's agenda.

The SWMA agreed with the WWMA's alternate proposal.

NEWMA supported the original proposal as shown in the 2007 NCWM Publication 15.

At the 2007 NCWM Interim Meeting, the jurisdiction that originally developed the proposal stated they were willing to support that proposal if the WWMA proposed text were more acceptable to having biodiesel included as a product allowed to be recirculated. The Committee agreed to present the WWMA alternate proposal for a vote at the 2007 NCWM Annual Meeting.

330-4 I Temperature Compensation for Liquid Measuring Devices Code

Source: 2007 S&T Committee

Discussion/ Background: The Committee is considering a proposal to make the following modifications to Section 3.30. Liquid-Measuring Devices (LMD) Code to recognize temperature compensation for retail devices as follows:

S.1.6.8. Recorded Representations from Devices with Temperature Compensation. – Receipts issued from devices or systems with automatic temperature compensation must include a statement that the volume of the product has been adjusted to the volume in liters at 15 °C for liters or the volume in gallons at 60 °F for gallons.
[Nonretroactive as of January 1, 200X] (Added 200X)

S.1.6.89. Lubricant Devices, Travel of Indicator. – The indicator shall move at least 2.5 cm (1 in) in relation to the graduations, if provided, for a delivery of 0.5 L (1 pt).

S.2.6. Temperature Determination and Wholesale Devices. – *For test purposes, means shall be provided to determine the temperature of the liquid either:*

(a) in the liquid chamber of the meter, or

(b) immediately adjacent to the meter in the meter inlet or discharge line.
[Nonretroactive as of January 1, 1985]
(Added 1984) (Amended 1986 **and 200X**)

S.2.7. ~~Wholesale~~ **Devices Equipped with Automatic Temperature Compensators.**

S.2.7.1. Automatic Temperature Compensation. – A device may be equipped with an **adjustable** automatic means for adjusting the indication and registration of the measured volume of product to the volume at 15 °C **for liters or** ~~(~~60 °F~~)~~ **for gallons.**

~~S.2.7.2. Display of Net and Gross Quantity. – A device equipped with automatic temperature compensation shall indicate or record, both the gross (uncompensated) and net (compensated) volume for testing purposes. It is not necessary that both net and gross volume be displayed simultaneously. [Nonretroactive as of January 1, 200X]~~

S.2.7.~~2~~3. Provision for Deactivating. – On a device **or system** equipped with an automatic temperature-compensating mechanism that will indicate or record only in terms of **liters** compensated to 15 °C **or gallons compensated to** ~~(~~60 °F~~)~~, provision shall be made for deactivating the automatic temperature-compensating mechanism so that the meter can indicate, ~~and record if it is equipped to~~ **or** record, in terms of the uncompensated volume.
(Amended 1972 **and 200X**)

S.2.7.~~3~~4. Provision for Sealing Automatic Temperature-Compensating Systems. – Provision shall be made for applying security seals in such a manner that an automatic temperature-compensating system cannot be disconnected and that no adjustment may be made to the system without breaking the seal **or providing a record of the action.**

S.2.7.~~4~~5. Temperature Determination with Automatic Temperature-Compensation. – For test purposes, means shall be provided (e.g., thermometer well) to determine the temperature of the liquid either:

~~S.4.3. Wholesale Devices.~~

~~S.4.3.1. Discharge Rates. – A wholesale device shall be marked to show its designed maximum and minimum discharge rates. However, the minimum discharge rate shall not exceed 20 % of the maximum discharge rate.~~

S.4.3.~~2~~. Temperature Compensation. – If a device or system is equipped with automatic temperature compensation, the primary indicating elements, recording elements, or recorded representation shall be clearly and conspicuously marked to show that the volume delivered has been adjusted to the volume at 15 °C **for liters or** ~~(~~60 °F~~)~~ **for gallons.**
(Amended 200X)

S.4.~~3~~4. Wholesale Devices, Discharge Rates. – A wholesale device shall be marked to show its designed maximum and minimum discharge rates. However, the minimum discharge rate shall not exceed 20 % of the maximum discharge rate.

Renumber successive paragraphs S.4.4. to S.4.5.

N.4.1.1. ~~Wholesale~~ **Devices Equipped with Automatic Temperature-Compensating Systems.** – On ~~wholesale~~ devices equipped with automatic temperature-compensating-systems, normal tests shall be conducted:

(a) by comparing the **net** (compensated) volume indicated or recorded to the actual delivered volume ~~corrected~~ **adjusted** to 15 °C **for liters or 60 °F for gallons, and**

(b) ~~with the temperature-compensating system deactivated,~~ comparing the **gross** (uncompensated) volume indicated or recorded to the actual delivered volume. **(For some devices this may require that the temperature compensator be deactivated.)**

The first test shall be performed with the automatic temperature-compensating system operating in the "as found" condition. On devices that indicate or record both the compensated and uncompensated volume for each delivery, the tests in (a) and (b) may be performed as a single test.
(Amended 1987 **and 200X**)

N.5. Change in Product Temperature ~~Correction on Wholesale Devices.~~ – ~~Corrections~~ **Adjustments** shall be made for any changes in volume resulting from the differences in liquid temperatures between time of passage through the meter and time of volumetric determination in the prover **or test measure**. When adjustments are necessary, appropriate petroleum measurement tables should be used.
(Amended 1974 **and 200X**)

UR.3.6. Temperature Compensation.

UR.3.6.1. Automatic.

UR.3.6.1.1. ~~When to be~~ **Use**d of Automatic Temperature Compensation. – If a device is equipped with ~~a mechanical~~ automatic temperature ~~compensator~~**compensation**, it shall be connected, operable, and in use at all times. An electronic or mechanical automatic temperature-compensating system may not be removed, nor may a compensated device be replaced with an uncompensated device, without the written approval of the ~~responsible~~ weights and measures jurisdiction **with statutory authority over the device**.
[**Note**: This requirement does not specify the method of sale for product measured through a meter.]
(Amended 1989)

UR.3.6.1.2. **Recorded Representation**s **(Invoices, Receipts, and Bills of Lading).**

(a) A **n** ~~written~~ invoice based on a reading of a device **or recorded representation issued by a device or system** that is equipped with an automatic temperature compensator shall show that the volume delivered has been adjusted to the volume at 15 °C **for liters or** ~~(~~60 °F~~)~~ **for gallons and decimal subdivisions or fractional equivalents thereof.**

(b) The invoice issued from an electronic wholesale device equipped with an automatic temperature-compensating system shall also indicate: (1) the API gravity, specific gravity or coefficient of expansion for the product; (2) product temperature; and (3) gross reading.

(c) On request, the owner or operator of a retail device equipped with an active automatic temperature compensator shall provide the official with statutory authority the bills of lading for at least the last two deliveries.
(Amended 1987 and 200X)

UR.3.6.1.3. Temperature Determination. – Means for determining the temperature of measured liquid in an automatic temperature-compensating system shall be so designed and located that, in any "usual and customary" use of the system, the resulting indications and/or recorded representations are within applicable tolerances.
(Added 200X)

UR.3.6.4. Temperature Compensated Sale. – All sales of products, when the quantity is determined by an approved measuring system with temperature compensation, shall be in terms of the liter at 15 °C or the U.S. gallon of 231 in^3 at 60 °F.
(Added 200X)

Prior to the 2007 NCWM Interim Meeting, the Committee recognized via reports from the regional L&R committees and other sources that there was increasing support within the weights and measures community to address temperature compensation features for the retail sale of petroleum products in the Liquid-Measuring Devices Code. In response to these concerns and to encourage uniformity in applications where temperature compensation is being used, the Committee developed this proposal to provide design and performance requirements and testing criteria for retail metering systems that incorporate temperature compensation capability. The Committee was also concerned that if the current L&R Committee proposed language for the Method of Sale of Commodities in NIST HB 130 is adopted, retail motor-fuel devices could be placed in service with no guidelines in HB 44 for type approval and field testing. The L&R proposed language would permit the temperature-compensated sale of petroleum products at all levels of distribution.

At the 2007 Interim Meeting, the L&R Committee moved forward with a Method of Sale proposal containing permissive language for retail sales of petroleum products using automatic temperature compensation (see L&R Item 232-1). Although the Committee recognized this S&T item was still not fully developed, it felt it could resolve the remaining issues in time for the 2007 NCWM Annual Meeting; therefore, the Committee unanimously voted to make this item a "priority" Voting item as described in Section H of the Introduction of HB 44 since it felt it was very important for there to be a corresponding S&T item that provided HB 44 guidance if the L&R item passed. Following the Committee vote, the Committee chairman went before the NCWM Board of Directors (BOD) for their input. The BOD instructed the Committee to make this an Information item. Irrespective of the concerns about the timing of adoption of language in HB 130, the Committee, after further deliberation, concurred with the BOD and added the proposal to its agenda as an Information item. The BOD further informed the Committee of its plan to form a steering committee to provide guidance and give support to both the S&T and L&R Committees on temperature compensation issues. The Committee looks forward to working with the steering committee on this important issue.

This item is still in development. Some of the issues the Committee is currently working on are outlined below.

Recorded Representations (S.1.6.7.): What, if any, abbreviations are acceptable for devices equipped with ATC (e.g., gal at 60 °F)?

API Gravity: How should the API gravity be entered in the device and what API gravity should the inspector use during a test? Should an average API gravity be used (national or state)? The Committee will work on gathering API data in order to resolve this issue.

Difference between Net and Gross (T.4.): Is the current tolerance of 0.1 % (electronic) appropriate for field-testing of retail devices with ATC? Will maintaining our current tolerances mean taking extra drafts to obtain a stable temperature? The Committee will work on gathering data concerning temperature measurement.

The Committee will continue work on this issue and will seek input from the regions and other interested parties in the weights and measures community.

331 VEHICLE-TANK METERS

331-1 V Temperature Compensation

(This item was adopted)

Source: Carryover Item 331-3. (This item originated from the Western Weights and Measures Association (WWMA) and first appeared on the Committee's 2000 agenda.)

Discussion/Background: The Committee considered a proposal to modify Section 3.31. Vehicle-Tank Meters (VTM) Code by adding the following new paragraphs to recognize temperature compensation as follows:

S.2.5. Automatic Temperature Compensation for Refined Petroleum Products.

S.2.5.1. Automatic Temperature Compensation for Refined Petroleum Products. – A device may be equipped with an automatic means for adjusting the indication and registration of the measured volume of product to the volume at 15 °C for liters or the volume at (60 °F) for gallons and decimal subdivisions or fractional equivalents thereof where not prohibited by state law.

S.2.5.2. Provision for Deactivating. – On a device equipped with an automatic temperature-compensating mechanism that will indicate or record only in terms of liters (gallons) compensated to 15 °C (60 °F), provision shall be made for deactivating the automatic temperature-compensating mechanism so the meter can indicate and record, if it is equipped to record, in terms of the uncompensated volume.

S.2.5.3. Gross and Net Indications. – A device equipped with automatic temperature compensation shall indicate or record, if equipped to record, both the gross (uncompensated) and net (compensated) volume for testing purposes. It is not necessary that both net and gross volume be displayed simultaneously.

S.2.5.4. Provision for Sealing Automatic Temperature-Compensating Systems. – Adequate provision shall be made for an approved means of security (e.g., data change audit trail) or physically applying security seals in such a manner that an automatic temperature-compensating system cannot be disconnected and no adjustment may be made to the system.

S.2.5.5. Temperature Determination with Automatic Temperature Compensation. – For test purposes, means shall be provided (e.g., thermometer well) to determine the temperature of the liquid either:

    (a) in the liquid chamber of the meter, or

    (b) immediately adjacent to the meter in the meter inlet or discharge line.
(Added 2007)

S.5.6. Temperature Compensation for Refined Petroleum Products. – If a device is equipped with an automatic temperature compensator, the primary indicating elements, recording elements, and recorded representations shall be clearly and conspicuously marked to show the volume delivered has been adjusted to the volume at 15 °C for liters or the volume at (60 °F) for gallons and decimal subdivisions or fractional equivalents thereof.
(Added 2007)

N.4.1.3. Automatic Temperature-Compensating Systems for Refined Petroleum Products. – On devices equipped with automatic temperature-compensating systems, normal tests shall be conducted:

    (a) by comparing the compensated volume indicated or recorded to the actual delivered volume corrected to 15 °C for liters or (60 °F) for gallons and decimal subdivisions or fractional equivalents thereof; and

    (b) with the temperature-compensating system deactivated, comparing the uncompensated volume indicated or recorded to the actual delivered volume.

The first test shall be performed with the automatic temperature-compensating system operating in the "as-found" condition. On devices that indicate or record both the compensated and uncompensated volume for each delivery, the tests in (a) and (b) may be performed as a single test.
(Added 2007)

N.5. Temperature Correction for Refined Petroleum Products. – Corrections shall be made for any changes in volume resulting from the differences in liquid temperatures between the time of passage through the meter and the time of volumetric determination in the prover. When adjustments are necessary, appropriate petroleum measurement tables should be used.
(Added 2007)

    T.2.1. Automatic Temperature-Compensating Systems. – The difference between the meter error (expressed as a percentage) for results determined with and without the automatic temperature-compensating system activated shall not exceed:

        (a) 0.4 % for mechanical automatic temperature-compensating systems; and

        (b) 0.2 % for electronic automatic temperature-compensating systems.

    The delivered quantities for each test shall be approximately the same size. The results of each test shall be within the applicable acceptance or maintenance tolerance.
(Added 2007)

    UR.2.5. Temperature Compensation for Refined Petroleum Products.

        UR.2.5.1. Automatic.

            UR.2.5.1.1. When to be Used. – In a state that does not prohibit, by law or regulation, the sale of temperature-compensated product, a device equipped with an operable automatic-temperature compensator shall be connected, operable, and in use at all times. An electronic or mechanical automatic temperature-compensating system may not be removed, nor may a compensated device be replaced with an uncompensated device, without the written approval of the responsible weights and measures jurisdiction.

            [Note: This requirement does not specify the method of sale for products measured through a meter.]

            UR.2.5.1.2. Invoices. – An invoice based on a reading of a device that is equipped with an automatic temperature compensator shall show that the volume delivered has been adjusted to the volume at 15 °C for liters or the volume at (60 °F) for gallons and decimal subdivisions or fractional equivalents thereof).
(Added 2007)

This proposal was developed to provide design requirements and testing criteria for vehicle-tank metering systems that incorporate temperature-compensation capability. When this item was originally submitted, several officials reportedly were confused about the specific applications of a meter covered by an NTEP CC that included a temperature-compensation feature. The WWMA acknowledged some jurisdictions permit temperature-compensated deliveries in applications not addressed by HB 44. Some states do not allow the use of automatic temperature compensation for the delivery of products using a VTM. At the 2002, 2003, and 2004 NCWM Annual Meetings, this proposal did not achieve a majority vote to pass or fail and, therefore, was returned to the Committee for further consideration.

At the 2006 NCWM Interim Meeting, the Committee agreed to leave the proposal on its agenda as an Information item because the L&R Committee was close to fully developing a corresponding method of sale requirement that was acceptable to most jurisdictions. The Committee encouraged the weights and measures community to review the newly modified L&R item along with the proposal shown in the recommendation above and provide input to the Committee prior to the 2007 January NCWM Interim Meeting.

At their 2006 fall meetings the CWMA, NEWMA, the SWMA, and the WWMA supported the proposal as a Voting item on the 2007 NCWM S&T Committee's agenda. The SWMA recommended the development of an additional requirement that the device have the ability to display both gross and net indications, but did not have a specific proposal to offer at the time. The WWMA reiterated that temperature-compensated devices were already in use in some jurisdictions.

At the 2007 NCWM Interim Meeting, the L&R Committee agreed to propose additional language in L&R Item 232-1 for a corresponding Method of Sale of Commodities requirement in HB 130 that permits the temperature-compensated sale of petroleum products at all levels of the distribution chain, provided it does not conflict with existing laws and regulations in a jurisdiction. The Committee believed that if the L&R proposal was adopted, there should be appropriate language in the VTM Code to assist weights and measures officials in conducting tests of devices or systems that include automatic temperature-compensation capability. To address concerns over the additional time required to test devices equipped with automatic temperature compensation, the Committee modified paragraph S.2.5.3. to require that, for test purposes, devices or systems must indicate or record both a "net" and a "gross" volume for each test draft. The Committee agreed to present Item 331-1 as modified for a vote at the 2007 NCWM Annual Meeting.

At the 2007 NCWM Annual Meeting, the Committee stated that this proposal supported jurisdictions that currently permit the use of or have automatic temperature-compensated vehicle-tank meters. The proposal provided both the weights and measures official and the NTEP laboratories with the proper criteria to use when evaluating a VTM with automatic temperature compensating capability.

For additional background on this item, see the 2000 through 2006 S&T Final Reports.

356(a)   GRAIN MOISTURE METERS

356(a)-1   VC S.1.2. Grain or Seed Kind and Class Selection and Recording and Table S.1.2. Grain Types Considered for Type Evaluation and Calibration and Minimum Acceptable Abbreviations

(This item was adopted)

Source: NTETC Grain Analyzer Sector

Recommendation: Modify HB 44 Section 5.56.(a) Grain Moisture Meters paragraph S.1.2. and Table S.1.2. to include minimum acceptable abbreviations for "multi-class" grain moisture calibrations as follows:

> **S.1.2. Grain or Seed ~~Kind~~ Type and Class Selection and Recording.** – Provision shall be made for selecting and recording the ~~kind~~type and class **or multi-class group** (as appropriate) of grain or seed to be measured. The means to select the ~~kind~~type and class **or multi-class group** of grain or seed shall be readily visible and the ~~kind~~type and class **or multi-class group** of grain or seed selected shall be clearly and definitely identified. Abbreviations for grain types **and multi-class groups** indicated on the meter must meet the minimum acceptable abbreviations listed in Table S.1.2. ~~Meters shall have the capability (i.e., display capacity) of indicating the grain type using a minimum of four characters in order to accommodate the four character abbreviations listed in Table S.1.2.~~
> (Amended 1993, ~~and~~1995, **and 2007**)

Table S.1.2. Grain Types and Multi-Class Groups Considered for Type Evaluation and Calibration and Their Minimum Acceptable Abbreviations

Grain Type	Grain Class	Minimum Acceptable Abbreviation
Wheat	Durum Wheat	DURW
	Soft White Wheat	SWW
	Hard Red Spring Wheat	HRSW
	Hard Red Winter Wheat	HRWW
	Soft Red Winter Wheat	SRWW
	Hard White Wheat	HDWW
	All-Class Wheat*	WHEAT
	Wheat Excluding Durum*	WHTEXDUR
Corn ---		CORN
Sunflower seed (Oil)	---	SUNF
Grain Sorghum	---	SORG or MILO
Soybeans ---		SOYB
Barley	Two-Rowed Barley	TRB
	Six-Rowed Barley	SRB
	All-Class Barley*	BARLEY
Oats ---		OATS
Rice	Long Grain Rough Rice	LGRR
	Medium Grain Rough Rice	MGRR
	All-Class Rough Rice*	RGHRICE
Small Oil Seeds (under consideration)	--- ---	

[Note: Grain Types marked with an asterisk (*) are "Multi-Class Calibrations"]

[Nonretroactive as of January 1, 1998]
(Table Added 1993) (Amended 1995, 1998, and 2007)

Add new definitions to Appendix D as follows:

multi-class. A description of a grouping of grain classes, from the same grain type, in one calibration. A multi-class grain calibration may include (1) all the classes of a grain type (all-class calibration), or (2) some of the classes of a grain type within the calibration.[5.56.(a)]
(Added 2007)

all-class. A description of a multi-class calibration that includes all the classes of a grain type.[5.56.(a)]
(Added 2007)

grain class. Different grains within the same grain type. (For example, there are six classes for the grain type "wheat": Durum Wheat, Hard Red Spring Wheat, Hard Red Winter Wheat, Soft Red Winter Wheat, Hard White Wheat and Soft White Wheat.)[5.56(a)]
(Added 2007)

grain type. See "kind of grain."[5.56.(a)]
(Added 2007)

Background/Discussion: The GMM type evaluation criteria in Publication 14 were amended to allow multi-class moisture calibrations. "Multi-class" describes the grouping of grain classes in a calibration. There are a total of 15 NTEP grains, which include wheat, rice, and barley, all of which have different classes. There are six classes of wheat, two classes of barley, and two classes of rice. A manufacturer may decide to have: (1) a separate calibration for each individual class of wheat, rice, or barley; or (2) have a single calibration for all the classes of wheat, rice, or barley ("All-Class Wheat, All-Class Rice, or All-Class Barley"); or (3) have a calibration that includes all the classes of wheat except durum wheat ("WHTEXDUR," Wheat Excluding Durum). Examples (2) and (3) are "multi-class" calibrations. Currently, the acceptable abbreviations (and grain types) in Table S.1.2. of HB 44 do not address the groupings and the types acceptable for use when selecting and recording "multi-class" calibrations. At its August 2006 meeting, the NTETC Grain Analyzer Sector agreed "multi-class" groups should be added to Table S.1.2. Grain Types Considered for Type Evaluation and Calibration and Minimum Acceptable Abbreviations by grain type and their corresponding minimum acceptable abbreviations for each "multi-class" group, and paragraph S.1.2. Grain or Seed Kind and Class Selection and Recording should be modified to recognize "multi-class" groupings.

Paragraph S.1.2. Grain or Seed Kind and Class Selection and Recording specifies that the means to select the kind and class of grain or seed be readily visible and that the kind and class of grain or seed selected be clearly and definitely identified. A multi-class grain calibration that includes all the NTEP classes of a given grain type (e.g., two-rowed barley and six-rowed barley) can be clearly and definitely identified by a single type name (e.g., BARLEY). Similarly, both long-grain and medium-grain rough rice could be identified as "rough rice." However, a multi-class grain calibration that does not include all of the NTEP classes of a grain type may not be identified using a single grain type name (e.g., WHEAT). For example, a calibration for "all wheat except durum" cannot be labeled "WHEAT" because the grain type "WHEAT" (i.e., "All-Class Wheat") includes "Durum Wheat."

At its August 2006 meeting the NTETC Grain Analyzer Sector agreed the originally suggested multi-class groups (soft wheat, hard wheat, red wheat, and white wheat) were confusing and subject to potential misuse. Only the following multi-class groups should be considered for type evaluation:

    All-Class Wheat
    Wheat Excluding Durum
    All-Class Barley
    All-Class Rough Rice

A poll of manufacturers present at the 2006 NTETC Grain Analyzer Meeting revealed that increasing the four-character display requirement of paragraph S.1.2. to eight characters would not be a problem with instruments in current production; therefore, it was agreed that up to eight characters could be used for multi-class group abbreviations. The Sector agreed that the sentence specifying the display capacity was not needed because the necessary display capacity was obvious from the number of characters in the longest minimum acceptable abbreviation listed in Table S.1.2.

The Sector agreed to modify paragraph S.1.2. and Table S.1.2. as shown above and forward its recommendation to the 2007 NCWM S&T Committee for consideration.

The SWMA recommended the proposal move forward to the NCWM S&T Committee as a Voting item on its 2007 agenda.

The NIST technical advisor to the Grain Analyzer Sector proposed adding new definitions for "multi-class" and "all-class" to the proposal to assist weights and measures officials in understanding the differences between those classes of grain. Prior to the 2007 Interim Meeting, the technical advisors balloted the Sector and received its approval to include three new definitions and have the term "grain type" cross reference "kind of grain" in Appendix D.

At the 2007 NCWM Interim and Annual Meetings, the Committee received no comments opposing this item and, therefore, agreed to present it for a vote.

357 NEAR-INFRARED GRAIN ANALYZERS

(This item was adopted)

357-1 VC S.1.2. Selecting Grain Class and Constituent and Table S.1.2. Grain Types Considered for Type Evaluation and Calibration and Minimum Acceptable Abbreviations

Source: NTETC Grain Analyzer Sector

Recommendation: Modify NIST HB 44 Section 5.57. Near-Infrared (NIR) Grain Analyzers paragraph S.1.2. Selecting Grain Class and Constituent and Table S.1.2. Grain Types Considered for Type Evaluation and Calibration and Minimum Acceptable Abbreviations to include minimum acceptable abbreviations for "multi-class" constituent (protein, starch, and oil) calibrations as shown below.

S.1.2. Selecting ~~and Recording~~ Grain Class and Constituent. – *Provision shall be made for selecting, and recording the type or class **or multi-class group** of grain and ~~the~~ constituent(s) to be measured. The means to select the grain type or class **or multi-class group** and ~~the~~ constituent(s) shall be readily visible and the type or class **or multi-class group** of grain and the constituent(s) selected shall be clearly and definitely identified in letters (such as HRWW, HRSW, **WHEAT**, etc. or PROT, etc.). A symbol to identify the display of the type or class **or multi-class group** of grain and constituent(s) selected is permitted provided that it is clearly defined adjacent to the display. Minimum acceptable abbreviations are listed in Table S.1.2. ~~Meters shall have the capability (i.e., display capacity) of indicating the grain type using a minimum of four characters in order to accommodate the abbreviations listed in Table S.1.2.~~*
[Nonretroactive as of January 1, 2003]

If more than one calibration is included for a given grain type, the calibrations must be clearly distinguished from one another.
[Nonretroactive as of January 1, 2004]

Table S.1.2. Grain Types and Multi-Class Groups Considered for Type Evaluation and Calibration and Their Minimum Acceptable Abbreviations		
Grain Type	**Grain Class**	**Minimum Acceptable Abbreviation**
Wheat	Durum Wheat	DURW
	Soft White Wheat	SWW
	Hard Red Spring Wheat	HRSW
	Hard Red Winter Wheat	HRWW
	Soft Red Winter Wheat	SRWW
	Hard White Wheat	HDWW
	All-Class Wheat*	WHEAT
	Wheat Excluding Durum*	WHTEXDUR
Barley	Two-Rowed Barley	TRB
	Six-Rowed Barley	SRB
	All-Class Barley*	BARLEY
Corn ---		CORN
Soybeans ---		SOYB

[Note: Grain Types marked with an asterisk (*) are "Multi-Class Calibrations"]
[Nonretroactive as of January 1, 1998]
(Table Added 1993) (Amended 1995, 1998, and 2007)

(Amended 2003 **and 2007**)

Add new definitions to Appendix D as follows:

> **multi-class. A description of a grouping of grain classes, from the same grain type, in one calibration. A multi-class grain calibration may include (1) all the classes of a grain type (all-class calibration), or (2) some of the classes of a grain type within the calibration.[5.57.]**
> (Added 2007)
>
> **all-class. A description of a multi-class calibration that includes all the classes of a grain type.[5.57.]**
> (Added 2007)
>
> **grain class. Different grains within the same grain type. (For example, there are six classes for the grain type "wheat": Durum Wheat, Hard Red Spring Wheat, Hard Red Winter Wheat, Soft Red Winter Wheat, Hard White Wheat and Soft White Wheat.)[5.57.]**
> (Added 2007)
>
> **grain type. See "kind of grain."[5.57.]**
> (Added 2007)

Background/Discussion: At its August 2006 Sector meeting, the NTETC Grain Analyzer Sector agreed to amend the NIR type evaluation criteria in Publication 14 and the NIST Handbook (HB 44) NIR Code to allow multi-class calibrations. These changes correspond to amendments to the GMM type evaluation criteria in Publication 14 to allow multi-class moisture calibrations. "Multi-class" describes the grouping of grain classes in a calibration. There are several NTEP grains, including wheat and barley, many of which have different classes. There are six classes of wheat, two classes of barley, and two classes of rice. (Note: Rice is only a grain type in the GMM code of NIST HB 44). A manufacturer may decide to have: (1) a separate calibration for each individual class of wheat, rice, or barley; (2) have a single calibration for all the classes of wheat, barley, or rice ("All-Class Wheat, All-Class Barley, or All-Class Rice"); or (3) have a calibration that includes all the classes of wheat except durum wheat ("WHTEXDUR," Wheat Excluding Durum). Examples (2) and (3) are "multi-class" calibrations. Currently, the acceptable abbreviations (and grain types) in Table S.1.2. of HB 44 do not address the groupings and the names that are acceptable for use when selecting and recording "multi-class" calibrations. At its August 2006 meeting, the NTETC Grain Analyzer Sector agreed that "multi-class" groups should be added to Table S.1.2. Grain Types Considered for Type Evaluation and Calibration and Minimum Acceptable Abbreviations by grain type and the corresponding minimum acceptable abbreviations for each "multi-class" group, and paragraph S.1.2. Selecting Grain Class and Constituent should be modified to recognize "multi-class" groupings.

The Sector recommended changes to the GMM and the Near-Infrared Code to recognize specific multi-classes of grains and to provide minimum acceptable abbreviations that identify multi-class groupings when user selection of a multi-class group is performed using the group name or an abbreviation of the name.

The Sector agreed to modify paragraph S.1.2. and Table S.1.2. as shown above and forward its recommendation to the 2007 NCWM S&T Committee for consideration.

The SWMA recommended the proposal move forward to the NCWM S&T Committee as a Voting item on its 2007 agenda.

The NIST technical advisor to the Grain Analyzer Sector proposed adding new definitions for "multi-class" and "all-class" to the proposal to assist weights and measures officials in understanding the differences between those classes of grain. Prior to the 2007 Interim Meeting, the technical advisors balloted the Sector and received its approval to modify the Sector's original proposal to include three new definitions and have the term "grain type" cross reference "kind of grain" in Appendix D.

At the 2007 NCWM Interim and Annual Meetings, the Committee received no comments opposing this item and agreed to present it for a vote.

360 OTHER ITEMS

360-1   I   International Organization of Legal Metrology (OIML) Report

Many issues before the OIML, the Asian-Pacific Legal Metrology Forum (APLMF), and other international groups are within the purview of the Committee. Additional information on OIML activities will appear in the Board of Directors Agenda and Interim and Final Reports and on the OIML website at   http://www.oiml.org. NIST WMD staff provided the latest updates on OIML activities during the open hearing sessions at NCWM meetings. For more information on specific OIML-related device activities, contact the WMD staff listed in the table below. The OIML projects listed below represent only currently active projects. For additional information on other OIML device activities that involve WMD staff, please contact WMD using the information listed below:

NIST Weights and Measures Division (WMD) Contact List for International Activities	
Contact Information	**Responsibilities**
Postal Mail and Fax for All Contacts:	NIST WMD 100 Bureau Drive MS 2600 Gaithersburg, MD 20899-2600 Tel: (301) 975-4004 Fax: (301) 975-8091
Mr. Kenneth Butcher (LMG) (301) 975-4859 kenneth.butcher@nist.gov	• D 1 "Elements for a Law on Metrology" • TC 3 "Metrological Control" • TC 3/SC 1 "Pattern Approval and Verification" • TC 3/SC 2 "Metrological Supervision" • TC 6 "Prepackaged Products"
Mr. Steven Cook (LMDG) (301) 975-4003 steven.cook@nist.gov	• R 50 "Continuous Totalizing Automatic Weighing Instruments (Belt Weighers)" • R 51 "Automatic Catchweighing Instruments" • R 60 "Metrological Regulations for Load Cells" • R 76 "Non-automatic Weighing Instruments"
Dr. Charles Ehrlich (ILMG) (301) 975-4834 charles.ehrlich@nist.gov	• CIML Member • B 10 "Framework for a Mutual Acceptance Arrangement (MAA) on OIML Type Evaluations" • TC 3/SC 5 "Expression of Uncertainty in Measurement in Legal Metrology Applications," "Guidelines for the Application of ISO/IEC 17025 to the Assessment of Laboratories Performing Type Evaluation Tests," & "OIML Procedures for Review of Laboratories to Enable Mutual Acceptance of Test Results and OIML Certificates of Conformity"
Mr. Richard Harshman (LMDG) (301) 975-8107 richard.harshman@nist.gov	• R 106 "Automatic Rail-weighbridges" • R 107 "Discontinuous Totalizing Automatic Weighing Instruments" (totalizing hopper weighers) • R 134 "Automatic Instruments for Weighing Road Vehicles In-Motion and Measuring Axle Loads"
Ms. Diane Lee McGowan (LMDG) (301) 975-4405 diane.lee@nist.gov	• R 59 "Moisture Meters for Cereal Grains and Oilseeds" • R 92 "Wood Moisture Meters-Verification Methods and Equipment" • R 121 "The Scale of Relative Humidity of Air Certified Against Saturated Salt Solution" • TC 17/SC 8 "Measuring Instruments for Protein Determination in Grains"
Mr. Ralph Richter (ILMG) (301) 975-3997 ralph.richter@nist.gov	• R 35 "Material Measures of Length for General Use" • R 49 "Water Meters" (Cold Potable Water & Hot Water Meters) • R 71 "Fixed Storage Tanks" • R 80 "Road and Rail Tankers" • R 85 "Automatic Level Gauges for Measuring the Level of Liquid in Fixed Storage Tanks" • R 105 & R 117 "Measuring Systems for Liquids Other Than Water" (all measuring technologies) • R 118 "Testing Procedures and Test Report Format for Pattern Examination of Fuel Dispensers for Motor Vehicles" • TC 3/SC 4 "Verification Period of Utility Meters Using Sampling Inspections" • TC 8/SC 7 P1 "Measuring Systems for Gaseous Fuel" (i.e., large pipelines) • TC 8/SC 7 P2 "Compressed Gaseous Fuels Measuring Systems for Vehicles" • TC 8/SC 8 "Gas Meters" (Diaphragm, Rotary Piston, & Turbine Gas Meters)

NIST Weights and Measures Division (WMD) Contact List for International Activities	
Contact Information	**Responsibilities**
Dr. Ambler Thompson (ILMG) (301) 975-2333 ambler@nist.gov	• D 16 "Principles of Assurance of Metrological Control" • D 19 "Pattern Evaluation and Pattern Approval" • D 20 "Initial and Subsequent Verification of Measuring Instruments and Processes" • D 27 Initial Verification of Measuring Instruments Using the Manufacturer's Quality Management System" • R 34 "Accuracy Classes of Measuring Instruments" • R 46 "Active Electrical Energy Meters for Direct Connection of Class 2" • TC 5/SC 2 "General Requirements for Software Controlled Measuring Instruments"
Ms. Juana Williams (LMDG) (301) 975-3989 juana.williams@nist.gov	• R 21 "Taximeters"

LIST OF ACRONYMS			
ILMG – International Legal Metrology Group	LMDG – Legal Metrology Devices Group LMG – Laws and Metrics Group	B – Basic Publication CIML – International Committee of Legal Metrology D – Document	P – Project R – Recommendation SC – Subcommittee TC – Technical Committee

360-2 Developing Items

The NCWM established a category of items called "Developing Items" as a mechanism to share information about emerging issues which have merit and are of national interest, but that have not received sufficient review by all parties affected by the proposal or that may be insufficiently developed to warrant review by the Committee. These items are currently under review by at least one regional association, technical committee, or organization.

Developing items are listed in Appendix A according to the specific HB 44 code section under which they fall. Periodically, proposals will be removed from the Developing item agenda without further action because the submitter recommends it be withdrawn. Any remaining proposals will be renumbered accordingly.

The Committee encourages interested parties to examine the proposals included in Appendix A and send their comments to the contact listed in each item. The Committee asks that the regional associations and NTETC Sectors continue their work to develop fully each proposal. Should an association or Sector decide to discontinue work on an item, the Committee asks that it be notified.

Michael J. Sikula, New York, Chairman (1)

Carol P. Fulmer, South Carolina (2)
Todd R. Lucas, Ohio (3)
Brett Saum, San Luis Obispo County, California (4)
Kristin Macey, Colorado (5)

Ted Kingsbury, Measurement Canada, Technical Advisor
Steven Cook, NIST, Technical Advisor
Richard Suiter, NIST, Technical Advisor
Juana Williams, NIST, Technical Advisor

Specifications and Tolerances Committee

Appendix A

Item 360-2: Developing Items

Part 1, Item 1 Scales: S.1.4.6. Height and Definition of Minimum Reading Distance, UR.2.10. Primary Indicating Elements Provided by the User, UR.2.11. Minimum Reading Distance and Definitions of Minimum Reading Distance and Primary Indications

Source: NTETC Weighing Sector

Note: This proposal was Carryover Item 320-2 in the Committee's 2006 Agenda and appeared on the Committee's 2007 Agenda as Item 320-4. (This item originated from the 2005 NTETC Weighing Sector and first appeared on the Committee's 2006 agenda.) Although the Committee believed the proposal has merit, there was not a consensus on the size and quality of primary indication information on devices used in direct and indirect sales transactions or an enforcement date for such requirements. Therefore, the Committee moved Item 320-4 from its agenda and made it a Developing item 360-2 Part 1, Item 1 to allow sufficient time for the community to fully develop requirements acceptable to those affected.

Recommendation: The Committee considered the Weighing Sector's first attempt at a proposal that adds new paragraphs S.1.4.6., UR.2.10., and UR.2.11. to the Scales Code.

S.1.4. Indicators.

~~S.1.4.6. Height. – All primary indications shall be indicated clearly and simultaneously.~~

(a) ~~On digital devices that display primary indications during direct sales to the customer, the numerical figures displayed to the customer shall be at least 9.5 mm (0.4 in) high.~~

(b) ~~The units of mass and other descriptive markings or indications, such as lb, kg, gross, tare, net, etc., shall be clearly and easily read and shall be at least 2 mm (0.08 in) high.~~
[Nonretroactive as of January 1, 200X]
(Added 200X)

UR.2. Installation Requirements

UR.2.10. Primary Indicating Elements Provided by the User. – Primary indicating elements that are not the same as the primary indicating elements provided by the original equipment manufacturer (e.g., video display monitors) shall comply with the following:

(a) On digital devices that display primary indications during direct sales to the customer, the numerical figures displayed to the customer shall be at least 9.5 mm (0.4 in) high.

(b) The units of mass and other descriptive information, such as gross, tare, net, etc., shall be displayed or marked on the device and shall be at least 2 mm (0.08 in) high.
(Added 200X)

UR.2.11. Minimum Reading Distance – On digital devices that display primary indications, the height of the numbers expressed in millimeters should be not less than three times the minimum reading distance expressed in meters, without being less than 2 mm (0.08 in). (Example: If the height of the primary indications is 10 mm, then the minimum reading distance should not be greater than 30 m).
(Added 200X)

S&T Committee 2007 Final Report
Appendix A – Item 360-2: Developing Items

Add new definitions of "minimum reading distance" and "primary indications" to Appendix D as follows:

<u>**minimum reading distance. The shortest distance that an observer is freely able to approach the indicating device to take a reading under normal conditions of use. This approach is considered to be free for the observer if there is a clear space of at least 0.8 m in front of the indicating device. However, if the minimum reading distance "S" in Figure X below is less than 0.8 m, then the minimum reading distance is "L" in Figure X.[2.20]**
(Added 200X)</u>

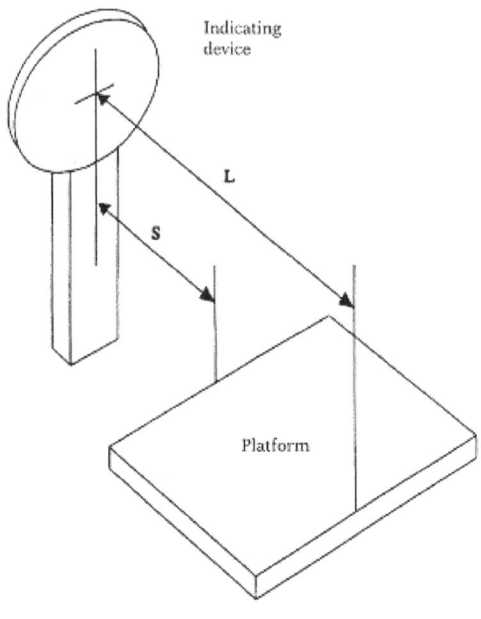

<u>**Figure X**</u>

<u>**primary indications. Weight or other units of measurement values that are displayed by a primary indicating element. The primary indications are used as the determining factor in arriving at the sale representation when the device is used commercially. (Examples of primary indications include the measurement value, unit price or count, and total price on instruments capable of price computing. Primary indications do not include indications from auxiliary indicating devices such as totalizing registers and pre-determined stop mechanisms.)[1.10], [2.20]**
(Added 200X)</u>

This proposal was developed to address a growing problem with the readability of weight indications and the values that define transaction information. Field and laboratory officials indicate both are becoming increasingly smaller, as demonstrated in the following example of a weight display where the actual size of the weight values are 23 mm in height, but the unit of measurement (g) is 4 mm in height.

S&T Committee 2007 Final Report
Appendix A – Item 360-2: Developing Items

Field and laboratory officials need more specific requirements to consistently determine if indications are suitable for the environment in which the device is used. Currently only the Taximeters, Grain Moisture Meters, and Near-Infrared Grain Analyzers Codes include requirements that specify the minimum height of figures, words, and symbols. The size requirements for all three device technologies were developed primarily because of concerns about the visibility of indications from the customer's position. HB 44 and NCWM Publication 14 include no uniform size requirements or specific guidelines on how to evaluate display information for clarity and readability for equipment other than these three device types.

The Committee agreed that although the clarity and readability of indications is a growing issue, the current proposal has only limited support from the public and private sectors. The Committee recognized the proposal requires a significant amount of work before the language is clear, technically correct, and deemed applicable to the different types of installations and technologies in current use. The Committee has concerns about whether or not the proposed 2 mm height requirements for units of measurement and other markings are adequate. The Committee also questioned the clarity of the proposed user requirements for the minimum reading distance.

The Committee recommends the submitter consider several points in its review of the current proposal:

- The proposed 2 mm height limits in the proposal may possibly be an error due to a miscommunication within the Weighing Sector. The value was intended to be closer to that of the figure in the example display which was 4 mm.

- Any specification and corresponding user requirement should provide laboratory and field officials with uniform guidelines:

    - to determine if the required markings on a new equipment design from the manufacturer or a device recently modified by the owner or a service company are suitable for continued use in a particular application; and

    - to remove all ambiguity or subjectivity when assessing if primary indications can be observed from a reasonable customer and operator position.

- A size requirement for figures and their corresponding descriptive symbols and characters that are specified as a percentage might be a good approach. This approach was explored by the 2006 Weighing Sector in its review of the relationship of size requirements for taximeter indications. The legibility of primary indications is dependent upon or relative to not only the distance the reader is from the information, but also the total area (square footage) of the display panel where those markings are posted. For example, a 9.5 mm figure is not a suitable size for a primary indication on a typical vehicle scale scoreboard because of the distance of the scoreboard from the typical customer position.

- Corresponding new language in HB 44 similar to that which exists in HB 130 for labels might be needed. This language may be necessary to provide guidelines to ensure sufficient contrast between the color and illumination of all required markings and their background. For example, a requirement might specify, "all required markings shall be prominent, definite, plain, and conspicuous as to size and style of symbols, letters, and numbers and as to color that is in contrast to the background and presented so that there is adequate free area surrounding those markings." This language would be consistent with current General Code requirements or might be added to a specific code section of HB 44.

- A recognized vision standard such as those used to determine visual acuity (eye exam charts, etc.) might be a good source for establishing specific distance limits.

- When the size of indications becomes a selectable configuration parameter, access to this feature must be sealed.

For more background information refer to the Committee's 2006 Final Report.

During the 2007 NCWM Annual Meeting, the Committee was informed that the NTETC Weighing Sector will continue to develop this item.

To comment on this proposal, contact Steven Cook, NIST technical advisor to the NTETC Weighing Sector, by e-mail at steven.cook@nist.gov, by telephone at (301) 975-4003, by fax at (301) 975-8091, or by postal mail at NIST WMD, 100 Bureau Drive MS 2600, Gaithersburg, MD 20899-2600.

Part 2, Item 1 Belt-Conveyor Scale Systems: UR.3.2.(c) Maintenance; Zero Load Tests

Source: 2005 Western Weights and Measures Association (WWMA)

Recommendation: Modify UR.3.2.(c) as follows:

UR.3.2. Maintenance. – Belt-conveyor scales and idlers shall be maintained and serviced in accordance with manufacturer's instructions and the following requirements:

(c) **Zero-load and load (simulated or material) tests.** ~~Ssimulated load tests, or material tests, and zero load tests~~ shall be conducted at periodic intervals between official tests in order to provide reasonable assurance that the device is performing correctly.
(Amended 200X)

The action to be taken as a result of the zero-load tests is as follows:
(Added 2000X)

- **if the change in zero is less than ± 0.1 %, make no adjustment, record results and proceed to simulated load tests; or**

- **if the change in zero is ± 0.1 % to ± 0.25 %, inspect the conveyor and weighing area for compliance with UR.2. Installation Requirements and retest.**
(Added 200X)

The action to be taken as a result of the simulated load or material tests ~~or simulated load tests~~ is as follows: ~~(Amended 2002)~~

- if the error is less than 0.25 %, no adjustment is to be made;

- if the error is at least 0.25 % but not more than 0.6 %, **inspect the conveyor and weighing area for compliance with UR.2. Installation Requirements and repeat the test** ~~adjustment may be made if the official with statutory authority is notified;~~
(Amended 1991 **and 200X**)

S&T Committee 2007 Final Report
Appendix A – Item 360-2: Developing Items

- **if the result of tests, after compliance with UR.2. Installation Requirements is verified, remain greater than ± 0.25 %, a span correction shall be made and the official with statutory authority notified;**

- if the error is greater than 0.6 % but does not exceed 0.75 %, **inspect the conveyor and weighing area for compliance with UR.2. Installation Requirements and repeat the test;**
(Amended 1991 **and 200X**)

- **if the result of tests, after UR.2. Installation Requirements compliance is verified, remains greater than ± 0.25 %, a span correction shall be made, the official with statutory authority shall be notified, and an official test shall be conducted;**

- if the error is greater than 0.75 %, an official test is required.
(Amended 1987 **and 200X**)

Discussion: HB 44 gives limited guidance on what to do with zero-load test results. Belt loss is not the only factor which may require the scale operator to make physical adjustments to the belt-conveyor system to correct for deficiencies. For example, a dirty scale structure or a worn belt scraper will increase the zero-reference number and the test results may exceed tolerances.

The scale user/owner has to protect his interest between weighing transactions. At present, some belt-conveyor systems may have errors greater than 0.5 % in zero reference over a 24-hour period. The belt is part of tare (net load) on any empty running system, and the system must be maintained to within tolerance at all times.

During its 2006 meeting, the WWMA recommended the alternate industry proposal shown above. The WWMA also recommended the alternate proposal be considered at a future meeting of the USNWG on Belt-Conveyor Scale Systems. The WWMA recommended the alternate proposal remain a Developing item to allow sufficient time for a review by the WG. The CWMA and the SWMA concur with the WWMA's recommendation.

During the 2007 NCWM Annual Meeting, the Committee heard testimony that a work group of the National Weighing and Sampling Association is working on this item and will have a recommendation for the WWMA prior to their 2007 Annual Technical Conference.

To comment on this proposal, contact Steven Cook, NIST technical advisor to the NTETC Belt-Conveyor Scales Sector, by e-mail at steven.cook@nist.gov, by telephone at (301) 975-4003, by fax at (301) 975-8091, or by postal mail at NIST WMD, 100 Bureau Drive MS 2600, Gaithersburg, MD 20899-2600.

Part 3, Item 1, Liquid-Measuring Devices: T.5. Predominance – Retail Motor-Fuel Devices

Source: Central Weights and Measures Association (CWMA)

Recommendation: The CWMA recommends withdrawing its earlier proposal (to add a new paragraph G-UR.4.1.1. to the General Code) and replacing it with the following new proposal developed by the Nebraska Weights and Measures Division to add a new paragraph T.5. to HB 44 Section 3.30. as follows:

T.5. Predominance – Retail Motor-fuel Devices. – The retail motor-fuel devices in service at a single place of business shall be considered maintained in proper operating condition when evaluation of normal test results indicate the following parameters are met:

(a) **The number of meters with minus test errors in excess of one-half maintenance tolerance shall be less than 60 % of the meters at the location, and**

(b) When there are three or more meters of a single grade or type of fuel, the average error of the meters shall not be a minus value exceeding one-half maintenance tolerance. Meter test results that exceed maintenance tolerance shall not be included in determining the average meter error of a single grade or type of fuel.

(Added 200X)

In 1991 this same topic was brought before the NCWM as an Information item. The intent of the proposal at that time was to provide guidance to states in the interpretation of General Code paragraph G-UR.4.1. Maintenance of Equipment. In 1993 the State of Wisconsin adopted a policy that defined "predominance" as shown in the proposal. That policy was similar to the one proposed in 1991, except Wisconsin felt that one-third ac*ceptance* tolerance was too stringent because there was a need to take into account normal variability in testing procedures, equipment, and environmental conditions found in the field. Wisconsin, therefore, adopted a "greater-than-one-third" ma*intenance* tolerance guideline. In 2003 the Wisconsin policy was further refined by deleting the language "all __ devices are found to be in error in a direction favorable to the device user." The new guideline for permissible errors was "60 % or more of the devices are found to be in error in favor of the device owner/user by more than one-third of the maintenance tolerance." Both of these criteria were seldom used in the field because they made the policy confusing.

Recently NIST conducted a national survey of retail motor-fuel dispenser testing, and the results pointed to a need to gain more uniformity in the application of tolerances. There is a wide variation in how different states handle the "predominance" question. Strides should be continually made to gain uniformity. Adoption of the proposed new paragraph G-UR.4.1.1. would be one step toward gaining greater uniformity. With more than five years of history using the proposed criteria, Wisconsin saw a relatively low number of devices rejected on the basis of "predominance," and most station owners and all service companies have a working understanding of predominance.

In 2005 the CWMA agreed to submit the modified proposal to the NCWM S&T Committee with a recommendation that it be placed on the Committee's agenda as a Developing item.

At their fall 2006 meetings, NEWMA, the SWMA, and the WWMA considered an earlier CWMA proposal to modify a General Code requirement and set limits on how to determine predominance in favor of the device operator. NEWMA believed the item was addressed adequately in HB 44 and recommended it be withdrawn from the NCWM S&T Committee's 2007 agenda. The SWMA recommended this item remain "developing" as a user requirement in the General Code. The SWMA encouraged the jurisdictions to review the proposed policy and use it on a trial basis. The WWMA considered the limits in the proposal too stringent given the effects of temperature and other uncertainties. The WWMA was concerned dispensers will be set to the limits in the proposal rather than as close as practical to zero error. Since the current General Code adequately addresses predominance, and jurisdictions may establish policy to gain uniformity in determining predominance, the WWMA recommended this proposal be withdrawn from the agenda.

At the 2007 NCWM Interim Meeting, the Committee considered proposals to withdraw this item from its agenda. However, because a jurisdiction involved in developing the current proposal indicated their intent to provide the Committee with considerable data and continue further development of the item, the Committee agreed to keep Part 2, Item 1 on its agenda as a Developing item through 2007.

Part 3, Item 2 Liquid-Measuring Devices: Price Posting and Computing Capability and Requirements for a Retail Motor-Fuel Dispenser (RMFD)

Source: WMD and all Regional Associations

Recommendation: Review and update NIST HB 44 requirements that address RMFD pricing and computing capability. This issue is under development and not ready for committee action.

Background/Discussion: In the early 1990s, various sections of the Liquid-Measuring Devices Code in HB 44 (including paragraphs S.1.6.4. Display of Unit Price and Product Identity, S.1.6.5.4. Selection of Unit Price, UR.3.2. Unit Price and Product Identity, and UR.3.3. Computing Device) were modified to address multi-tier pricing applications such as cash-credit. Since that time, marketing practices have evolved and recent years have seen the addition of new practices such as frequent shopper discounts and club member discounts. Numerous questions have been posed to WMD regarding the requirements for posting unit prices, calculation of total price, customer-operated controls, and other related topics such as the definitions for associated terminology.

It was clear from these questions that changes were needed to HB 44 to ensure the requirements adequately address current marketplace conditions and practices. WMD raised this issue with the NCWM S&T Committee and also discussed a variety of pricing practices with individual state and local weights and measures jurisdictions.

NIST WMD is now in the process of reviewing the existing requirements and their application to current market practices. WMD collected information on a number of scenarios, including the following:*

(1) Frequent shopper discounts
(2) Club member discounts
(3) Discount for prepaying cash (to prevent "drive-offs")
(4) Prepay at the cashier for credit sales
(5) Discounts for purchasing store products
(6) Discounts for purchasing a service (e.g., carwash)
(7) Targeted group discounts (e.g., Tuesday-Ladies 5 cents off per gallon)
(8) Full Service
(9) Self Service
(10) Progressive discounts based on volume of motor-fuel purchased
(11) Coupons for discounts on immediate or future purchases
(12) Rebates (e.g., use of oil company credit card)
(13) Day-of-the-Week Discounts

*(Note: The conditions under some of these scenarios may not typically fall under the authority of weights and measures jurisdictions.)

WMD is interested in receiving input from the weights and measures community about the various practices and pricing structures in use. Working with input from the weights and measures community, WMD plans to introduce proposed modifications to current requirements through the regional weights and measures associations and technical committees. In the meantime, WMD welcomes opportunities to discuss this issue at regional weights and measures associations to ensure the issue is adequately addressed.

The WWMA acknowledged that marketing practices change on a daily basis and the task to ensure HB 44 codes address each scenario is monumental. However, the WWMA encourages NIST in its efforts to tackle this ongoing issue. Therefore, the WWMA recommends this issue be considered and move forward to the national level as a Developing item.

The CWMA recommends that State Directors compile information regarding whether or not they are enforcing the Liquid-Measuring Devices Code in HB 44 (including paragraphs S.1.6.4. Display of Unit Price and Product Identity, S.1.6.5.4. Selection of Unit Price, UR.3.2. Unit Price and Product Identity, and UR.3.3. Computing Device). If jurisdictions are not enforcing the specific code requirement, it should be stated why not (for example, overriding state statute). Information is to be sent to:

James Truex, Chief
Division of Weights and Measures
8995 E. Main Street
Reynoldsburg, Ohio 43068

Phone: (614) 728-6290
Fax: (614) 728-6424
E-mail: truex@mail.agri.state.oh.us

NEWMA looks forward to further development of this item.

The SWMA recommends adding this item to the NCWM S&T Committee's 2007 Agenda as a Developing item.

At the 2007 NCWM Interim Meeting, the Committee agreed to add this proposal to its agenda as a Developing item.

S&T Committee 2007 Final Report
Appendix A – Item 360-2: Developing Items

To comment on this proposal, contact NIST technical advisors to the NCWM S&T Committee: Steve Cook at steven.cook@nist.gov or by telephone at (301) 975-4003; Richard Suiter at richard.suiter@nist.gov or by telephone at (301) 975-4406; or either by fax at (301) 975-8091 or by mail at NIST WMD, 100 Bureau Drive, MS 2600, Gaithersburg, MD 20899-2600.

Part 4, Item 1 Water Meters: UR.2.1. Accessibility for Reading

Recommendation: Add a new paragraph UR.2. to HB 44, Section 3.36. Water Meters, as follows:

> **UR.2. Accessibility for Reading. – A water meter shall be so located that there is reasonable access to obtain a reading by means of the primary indicating element or a remote indicating element. Otherwise, it shall be the responsibility of the device owner or operator to make available, within 24 hours of a request being received by the owner or operator from a current lessee, mortgagee, or titleholder, the necessary labor and support to provide the consumer a means to obtain a meter reading, provided such requests are made with a frequency consistent with the normal billing cycle of the utility.**

The WWMA also considered an alternate proposal developed by the California Division of Measurement Standards (DMS) to add new paragraph UR.2.1. to the Water Meters Code as follows:

> **UR.2.1. Accessibility of Customer Indication. – An unobstructed standing space of at least 30 in wide, 36 in deep, and 78 in high shall be maintained in front of an indication intended for use by the customer to allow for reading the indicator. The customer indication shall be readily observable to a person located within the standing space without necessity of a separate tool or device.**

Industry Position: The industry proposal is intended to assist enforcement personnel in properly and uniformly enforcing the applicable regulations for obtaining meter readings. The proposed language is more appropriate than (1) trying to define inherently ambiguous and subjective terms like "reasonable" and "ordinary circumstances," or (2) defining specific height requirements that insure visibility for customers and/or officials. Proposed new paragraph UR.2.1. Accessibility for Reading should be added to Section 3.36. Water Meters Code of HB 44 because of the need for language to describe acceptable and applicable provisions.

Industry members stated that existing language in General Code paragraphs G-UR2.1.1. and G-UR.3.3. includes terms such as "reasonable" and "readily observable" which are subjective requirements; it is not possible to understand the installation requirements without relying on each local authority's interpretation of these terms, which varies even within the same jurisdiction.

Water submetering locations in a vast majority of cases are NOT chosen by the service agency or the property/meter owner, but are dictated by the engineers and architects who use both national and state building and plumbing codes as their primary guide.

The regulation which is most commonly cited on notices of violation for register visibility issues is paragraph G-UR.3.3. Position of Equipment. HB 44 defines dir<u>ect sale</u> as " *a sale in which both parties in the transaction are present when the quantity is being determined ….*" Industry notes that paragraph G-UR.3.3. is being misapplied and should have no bearing on a water submeter since both parties are **not** present when the quantity is determined. Furthermore, the antonym of a direct sale would be an indirect sale. NIST HB 130, Packaging and Labeling, Section 11. Exemptions, Subsection 11.1.1. Indirect Sale of Random Packages gives examples of indirect sales, several of which are exact examples of how water-submetering bills are paid. Examples of such indirect methods include on-line bill payments, phone bill payments, fax bill payments, and bill payments by mail.

Since water submetering is typically billed on a monthly cycle and since water submetering is not a direct sale where both parties are present at the time of the transaction, accessibility requirements for reading water meters should not be the same as those enforced on direct sale devices where transactions take place frequently and with both parties present.

If the interpretation of the terms "reasonable and readily observable" continue to be enforced as they are currently, many meter owners will choose to abandon their systems for alternative billing methods such as "remote utility billing service" (RUBS) because re-plumbing existing water lines within walls is costly to building and coop/condo owners. Since there is no framework in place to know how to perform such a plumbing retrofit, the work will be compliant with all interpretations of "reasonable" and "readily observable."

A detailed 12-month sampling of call center complaints from California properties showed that not a single complaint about the difficulty in obtaining a water meter reading had been received.

Regional Association Positions:

HB 44, Water Meters Code paragraph S.1.1.1. General permits a remote display as long as it is "readily accessible to the customer."

The industry proposed language is no more definitive than existing language. The industry proposal removes the requirement for providing a readily accessible customer indicator. The California DMS alternative language would remove the vagueness from the current requirement while providing flexibility to installers.

Property owners do not read the indicators on each meter or they would be placed in a more convenient reading location. With remote reading, however, many meters are now being placed in inaccessible locations. Hardware is being installed to permit remote readings for billing purposes, but not for customers' use.

Complaints have been lodged where the remote billing did not match the meter readings and customers should be able to monitor easily their actual use without involving the property owner. Occasionally disputes exist between the property owner or manager and tenants that make requesting assistance a less desirable solution to reading a meter for verification.

The industry in California has been advised that remote customer indications are permissible. However, industry has not submitted devices for California DMS type evaluation. Between better planning for the installation of future meters and submitting remote indicators to be approved for use by customers, this problem can be resolved in a manner more consistent with other device applications.

The WWMA considered a proposal developed by industry and an alternate recommendation developed by California DMS. The industry proposal permits access to indications either through a primary indicator or a remote indicator, or requires the operator to provide a means for customer access to meter indications when given 24-hour notice within a billing cycle. The California DMS proposal specifies the dimensions for a clear, unobstructed perimeter surrounding the device to ensure accessibility for viewing meter indications.

The WWMA acknowledged that a device used to submeter a utility service is commercial equipment that presents a unique set of circumstances because the customer making the purchase does not observe the entire measurement operation but receives a bill on a periodic cycle based on meter indications. In some cases the operator/meter owner may be offsite and not required to observe primary meter indications, and may not be familiar with the unusual plumbing configurations that make it difficult to install an accessible meter and read a meter. Consequently, no one General Code or Water Meter Code requirement appears to provide a complete and uniform set of guidelines that specifies all conditions for making meter indications available so the consumer can verify the measurement and allow the official to conduct an inspection. Some jurisdictions have developed policies to address this situation. In 2002 paragraph S.1.1. was modified to ensure remote indications remain accessible to the customer.

In any case, requirements and jurisdiction policies should address the needs of the customer and the official for access to meter indications without placing an undue burden on the operator or customer, and they should not deter a customer from making a legitimate complaint. In the marketplace it is essential to have all components used in determining utility charges transparent; this includes meter indications that are available to all parties involved in the transaction.

The WWMA agreed that each proposal has some elements necessary to address meter accessibility and indicator accessibility. Therefore, the WWMA recommends the proposal become a Developing item to allow time to rework the text to establish uniform guidelines to fully address accessibility. The guidelines should include the following points: (1) installation and location is such that there is no obstruction of the meter or indications, and

(2) indications are accessible for viewing by the customer and official without the use of tools separate from the device.

The WWMA encouraged the California DMS and industry to work together to develop a proposal for regional consideration.

At the fall 2006 CWMA meeting, there was discussion that LP gas, natural gas, and electric meters should be included in this proposal; however, the CWMA did not submit any additional language at this time.

The SWMA supported the proposal moving forward as a Developing item on the NCWM S&T Committee's 2007 Agenda.

At the 2007 NCWM Interim Meeting, the Committee agreed to add this proposal to its agenda as a Developing item.

To comment on this proposal, contact Ken Lake, California Division of Measurement Standards, by e-mail at klake@cdfa.ca.gov or by telephone at (916) 229-3047.

Final Report of the
Professional Development Committee (PDC)[1]

Agatha Shields, Chairman
Franklin County Weights and Measures
Columbus, Ohio

Reference
Key Number

400 INTRODUCTION

This is the report of the Professional Development Committee (hereinafter referred to as the "Committee" or PDC) for the 92nd Annual Meeting of the National Conference on Weights & Measures (NCWM). This report is based on the Interim Report offered in NCWM Publication 16, testimony heard at public hearings, comments received from the Regional Weights and Measures Associations and other parties, the Addendum Sheets issued at the Annual Meeting, and actions taken by the membership at the Voting Session of the Annual Meeting. The informational items presented below were adopted as presented when the Committee's report was approved.

Table A identifies the agenda items in the Report by Reference Key Number, Item Title, and Page Number. Item numbers are those assigned in the Interim Meeting Agenda. A voting item is indicated with a "✓" after the item number. An item marked with an "I" after the reference key number is an information item. An item marked with "D" after the reference key number is a developing item. The developing designation indicates an item has merit; however, the item was returned to the submitter for further development before any action can be taken at the national level. Table B lists the Appendix to the Agenda.

Table A
Index to Reference Key Items

Reference Key Number		Title of Item	Page
400		INTRODUCTION	1
401		EDUCATION	2
401-1	I	National Training Program (NTP)	2
401-2	I	Create a Curriculum Plan	3
401-3	D	Instructor Improvement	4
401-4	D	Certification	5
401-5	D	Recommended Topics for Conference Training	6
402		PROGRAM MANAGEMENT	7
402-1	I	Safety Awareness	7
402-2	V	Standard Categories of Weighing and Measuring Devices	8
402-3	D	PDC Publication	9

Table B
Appendix

Appendix	Title	Page
A	Strategic Direction for the Professional Development Committee	A1
B	Curriculum Package (Guideline for Creating a Basic Inspector Curriculum)	B1
C	National Training Curriculum Outline	C1
D	NCWM Curriculum Work Plan	D1

---

[1] Note: Report content is published as received with the exception of minor editorial and format changes.

Table C
Voting Results

Reference Key Number	House of State Representatives		House of Delegates		Results
	Yeas	Nays	Yeas	Nays	
402-2 41		0	41	0	Passed

Details of All Items
(In Order by Reference Key Number)

401 EDUCATION

401-1   I   National Training Program (NTP)

Source: The Committee (2003)

Background: The Board of Directors established the Committee at the 2003 NCWM Annual Meeting in Sparks, Nevada. The first critical charge given to the Committee was to develop a National Weights and Measures Professional Development Program in cooperation with its partners including:

- State and local weights and measures departments;
- Private industry at all levels; and
- Technical advisors from NIST Weights and Measures Division and Measurement Canada

The NTP will address the following tasks in order of priority:

(a) The education and professional development of weights and measures officials and the promotion of uniformity and consistency in the application of weights and measures laws and regulations;
(b) The education of industry personnel with regard to weights and measures laws and regulations, including all areas from device manufacturer to service technician;
(c) Quality standards for weights and measures activities and programs;
(d) Safety awareness for weights and measures-related activities; and
(e) Development of a firm partnership with the state and local weights and measures departments, private industry, and the NCWM. It is critical that NIST Weights and Measures Division (NIST WMD) partner with the Committee, and, where appropriate, provide technical advice. Measurement Canada is also encouraged to participate in Committee activities.

The Committee began developing the concept of a National Certification Program for weights and measures officials during the 2004 NCWM Annual Meeting. The Committee's continued work on this issue is reported in Item 401-4 of this report.

The Committee's overall strategic direction is summarized in Appendix A.

Discussion: The regions continue to support the proposed direction of the NTP. In addition, the Western Weights and Measures Association (WWMA) suggested that the PDC establish an action plan and timeline to identify those tasks which must be completed for the establishment of the NTP. The regions have submitted curricula for several topic areas, and the PDC is in the process of developing curriculum guidelines and certification models for review by the jurisdictions.

The Committee reviewed the WWMA's suggestion to establish an action plan and timeline. The Committee agreed that timelines need to be established; however, the Committee believes it is premature to establish timelines for the tasks until the curricula for the core areas are completed.

PDC 2007 Final Report

401-2 I Create a Curriculum Plan

Source: The Committee (2003)

Background: The Committee agreed the following steps must be addressed for the NTP to be viable:

(a) Develop and maintain a curriculum plan in cooperation with our partners that establishes uniform and consistent training objectives for weights and measures professionals in all fields and at all levels.
(b) Develop objectives of the curriculum plan representative of a consensus of our partners and organize those objectives by scope, sequence, and level of complexity to assist those developing the curriculum materials.

The development of a training program should follow the steps below:

(a) Study training programs of state and local weights and measures jurisdictions and outside agencies.
(b) Establish knowledge goals for weights and measures officials and administrators.
(c) Develop curriculum based upon the findings and results of steps (a) and (b) above.
 (1) Coordinate the development of curriculum materials to be used in the delivery of training (i.e., lesson plans, digital presentations, slide shows, testing guides, etc.) using a variety of formats (e.g., self-study, traditional instruction).
 (2) Consider creating a network of interested parties to establish priorities, share training resources, foster cooperation to reduce redundancy, and promote uniformity and consistency.
(d) Develop examinations, quizzes, or tests based on the content of the materials developed under step (c)(1).
(e) Gather and share information from trainers on highly effective training techniques, visual aids, and other materials that have been used to facilitate learning. Use as many of these resources as available.

The Committee reviewed the notes from the NIST-sponsored administrators' workshops held in Denver, Colorado, and Baltimore, Maryland, and plans to explore many of these ideas.

During the 2004 Annual Meeting, the Committee discussed the idea of using work groups to develop courses that could be used for self-study or for traditional classroom settings. The Committee agreed that the initial priority should be high profile devices (e.g., motor-fuel dispensers and retail computing scales). The Committee studied the survey results to focus on the memberships' needs and desires.

There were several recommendations submitted by the regional associations. The CWMA commented that the Committee should draw upon other sources, both external and internal, for establishment of curricula. The WWMA recommended the Committee review current training courses on the NIST website at http://www.nist.gov/owm to establish and identify various levels of training. The WWMA also suggested the Committee review and update all existing NIST training courses, and recommended that WMD post them on the NIST website. The Northeast Weights and Measures Association (NEWMA) recommended the Committee set standards for education that include provisions for field tests.

During the 2005 Interim Meeting, recommendations were made to develop course curriculum with specific learning objectives and development of tests to determine mastery of the learning objectives. Training responsibility to meet the objectives would rest with the jurisdictions. It was recommended that the Committee oversee development of the tests to be administered for each course. Upon successful testing, certificates would be issued. Protocol for preserving the integrity of the tests and the testing system would need to be developed.

Following the 2006 Annual Meeting, the PDC forwarded to the regional associations a small-scale example format developed in 2002 by the prior Administration and Public Affairs Committee (A&P) and the documents provided by New York as example formats. These documents were also posted to the PDC page on the NCWM website. The regional associations began work on their designated curriculum plans. The regional committee responsible for developing the curriculum segment was reminded to focus on a level of competency expected of the entry-level inspector. As the regions developed the curriculum, they were encouraged to begin development of the written certification questions needed to verify that the curriculum goals were met.

Discussion: The Committee thanks the following regions for submitting curricula for consideration: the Southern Weights and Measures Association (SWMA), Class III and III L scales; WWMA, Retail Motor-fuel Dispensers; the NEWMA, Small Scales; and CWMA, Package Checking. Based on comments from several of the regions and its own assessment, the Committee decided that it is essential to have a standardized format to ensure the end product is uniform. Based on a collective review of samples received, the Committee is working to create a sample template and example for regions to use in developing other curricula. The Committee also supports the general approach used in the "California Core Competency Model for the First Course in Accounting," which provides a model for improving the quality of education in a select discipline. The Committee plans to include this information as a general guideline for the regions to use as they develop other curriculum topics. In addition, the Committee will ask those jurisdictions that have already submitted curricula to make revisions based on the Committee's recommendations for formatting.

The Committee prioritized those subjects of interest based on survey results collected in 2004. The four main topics of interest are: Retail Motor-fuel Dispensers, Small-capacity Scales, Handbook 44, and Safety. The Committee is pleased that the work in progress covers the first three of these main areas of interest. Regional workgroups are encouraged to work with the PDC on the next highest prioritized subjects. The Committee is also pursuing efforts in conjunction with Item 402-1 of its agenda to respond to the interest expressed in safety training. Since the needs of weights and measures officials and service companies change over time, the Committee also encourages continued input from these groups to ensure that changing priorities are addressed as the Committee's work proceeds.

The Committee is working on a curriculum package to send to the regions, which will include the following:

- Cover Memorandum (guide to curriculum development);
- California Accounting Core Competency Guide Model (emphasis on the Introduction and the three Appendices);
- NCWM Curriculum Template (curriculum guideline);
- NCWM Sample Curriculum (examples of desired format);
- Guide to Writing Test Questions (including examples);
- National Training Curriculum Outline (updated from 2004 version); and
- NCWM Curriculum Work Plan (2007)

The Cover Memorandum, California Accounting Core Competency Guide Model, and Guide to Writing Test Questions are included in Appendix B.

The Committee is working to agree upon and refine the model template and examples which will be posted to the PDC page of the NCWM website as soon as they are complete.

After the Committee reviews the revised curricula, they will be forwarded to the State Certification Coordinators (SCC) and selected organizations, industry, or individuals for review and comment.

At the NCWM Annual Meeting, the Committee revisited the original "National Training Curriculum Outline" from its 2004 NCWM final report. The Committee prepared an accompanying "NCWM Curriculum Work Plan," which is intended to assist in the management of curriculum development. The original outline and the new accompanying Work Plan are included in Appendices C and D. The Committee is making revisions to the original curriculum outline to match the Work Plan and will include the revised version in the Curriculum Package. The Committee will agree upon a final format for the curriculum and will distribute the template along with the complete package to the development team in each region following the 2007 Annual Meeting.

401-3 D Instructor Improvement

Source: The Committee (2003)

Background: One Committee goal is to work with all interested parties to improve the competence of instructors and the uniformity of curriculum delivery.

The Committee concluded there are two parts to the instructor improvement strategy. The first part is educating trainers in effective methods of instruction. A variety of courses and training methods are available from state, federal, and private sources to develop instructional skills and techniques. Jurisdictions are encouraged to seek out and send selected staff to participate in this type of training.

The second area of instructor improvement is to provide trainers with the knowledge of the technical aspects of all types of devices. The Committee believes that NIST WMD continued leadership and participation is a valuable asset in this area and recommends that WMD continue to provide the technical training for instructors. The Committee invites and looks forward to working with WMD as a resource to consult with trainers and to work with the Committee to keep the curricula current as changes to the handbooks occur, new technologies are developed, and emerging issues evolve.

Industry has continued to support and sponsor training on their new technology for weighing and measuring devices. NIST has assured the committee they will continue their work towards providing technical training for the trainers.

Discussion: The Committee, while recognizing the importance of this item, is maintaining it as a "Developing" item on its agenda until progress is made in other areas of the NTP plan.

401-4 D Certification

Source: The Committee (2003)

Background: In December 2004 several Committee members met in Harrisburg, Pennsylvania, to further develop the concept of a National Certification Program. The participants agreed the NTP should take the following directions:
   (a) Responsibility of training remains with the state and local jurisdictions;
   (b) Administrator training must be added to the curriculum; and
   (c) Training and structure used by agencies outside the NCWM should be explored and used as models.

The participants also acknowledged that: (1) the CWMA offered to assist the Committee in determining what knowledge and prerequisites are required for beginning and advanced inspectors; and (2) the WWMA recommended course outlines for shorter training courses.

The Committee believes an NCWM certification program should be developed based on a curriculum plan with measurable levels of competency. The Committee agrees that weights and measures officials must pass written examinations to receive certification. Certificates could be presented at the Annual Meeting to administrators and weights and measures officials who complete training classes and pass the course examination. In 2004, then Chairman Dennis Ehrhart indicated the Board of Directors would consider requests to fund training.

The WWMA and CWMA submitted extensive comments and recommendations regarding this item prior to the 2004 NCWM Annual Meeting. The 2005 NCWM Certification Proposal was redrafted to reflect the NCWM's role in issuance of the certificates and was posted on the PDC page on the NCWM website.

Subsequent to the 2006 NCWM Annual Meeting, all states not previously contacted were sent a letter requesting the name of their State Certification Coordinator (SCC). The state director will be deemed the default SCC in the absence of a designated contact. The list of SCC contacts is posted on the PDC page of the NCWM website.

Discussion:

The Committee continues to hear support from the regions concerning the establishment of a certification program. In addition to expressing support for this effort, the WWMA stated its support for having the states meet the requirements established by the NCWM. The WWMA commented that after demonstrating competency, the NCWM would be the appropriate entity to issue the certificate.

PDC 2007 Final Report

By exposing weights and measures inspectors to standardized training methodology, this certification process will lead to uniformity. However, the Committee believes it is time to begin the process of building the infrastructure of the program. We must determine what the program will look like and establish the roles of the states and the NCWM. It is unrealistic for the NCWM to fund a complete certification program. It is critical that the states take an active role in the process if the program is to be successful. The WWMA also recommends that the certification program not be limited to weights and measures personnel. NCWM certification could be offered for a fee to manufacturers, service companies, or individuals providing they meet the criteria set forth by the PDC.

The Committee will be contacting the SCC of each state to gather information on its current training and certification programs. The Committee will develop model certification programs that will be presented to the jurisdictions to determine workability. The Committee appreciates comments received from the regions and will consider these as it develops possible models.

The Committee will include a guide for writing test questions in the curriculum package referenced in Item 401-2. Test questions subsequently generated by the regional volunteers should provide a bank of questions, which can be used in a certification program and in training activities. NEWMA has provided an example of a draft statute, based on the Massachusetts statute, to establish a certification program. The Committee will study the sample with the possibility that it might ultimately be used to establish model criteria for a certification program.

The Committee agreed to maintain this issue as a Developing item on its agenda as it continues work on this issue.

401-5 D Recommended Topics for Conference Training

Source: The Committee (2003)

Background: The Board has charged the Committee with responsibility for selecting appropriate topics for the technical sessions at future Annual Meetings. The Board asked that the Committee review and prioritize possible presentations and submit those to the chairman. The chairman would then work with NCWM staff to make the arrangements and schedule the sessions.

The Committee continues to carry the following list and recommends these topics for possible training seminars, roundtables, or symposia for presentation at the NCWM meetings:

   (a) Risk-based Inspections (Robert Williams, Tennessee, volunteered to present his state's RMFD testing program);
   (b) Marketplace Surveys;
   (c) Auditing the Performance of Field Staff (Will Wotthlie, Maryland, volunteered to lead the session);
   (d) Alternative Fuels (including motor-fuel trends and technology updates);
   (e) Device Inspections Using a Sampling Model; and
   (f) Emerging Issues.

Discussion: The Committee received the following additional suggestions (listed in no particular order) for educational topics at the 2007 Annual Meeting:

   (a) Nebraska 52-week Dispenser Field Study (offered by presenters Steve Malone, Nebraska, and Henry Oppermann, Weights and Measures Consulting, LLC);
   (b) Temperature Compensation Report (presenter Ross Andersen, New York);
   (c) Training session on BioDiesel Issues (offered by presenter Paul Hoar, AgriFuels LLC)
   (d) Proper Lifting Techniques (recommended by Ken Deitzer, Pennsylvania);
   (e) Overview of OIML and its Relationship to Standards Development (recommended by Julie Quinn, Minnesota);
   (f) Back and Stress Techniques (recommended by Don Onwiler);
   (g) Public Relations, specifically dealing with aggressive/angry people (recommended by the SWMA);
   (h) Inspector Investigative Procedures (recommended by the SWMA),
   (i) General Safety Issues (recommended by the WWMA);
   (j) Defensive Driving (recommended by the WWMA);

(k) Administrative Civil Penalty Process (recommended by the WWMA);
(l) Price Verification (recommended by the WWMA); and
(m) Customer Service (recommended by the WWMA).

The Committee also received comments from the CWMA that high fuel prices make cheating on quantity a lucrative business for unscrupulous station owners. Some jurisdictions have uncovered retail motor-fuel fraud schemes that operate at nonstandard hours or that employ difficult-to-detect technology. The CWMA is recommending that industry and knowledgeable jurisdictions conduct a technical/information session at the Annual Meeting to apprise everyone of all the known retail motor-fuel fraud schemes. All jurisdictions would then have the knowledge to determine the best approach for fraud detection and deterrence.

The Committee acknowledged the value and anticipated interest by NCWM members of the many topic ideas submitted. For the 2007 NCWM Annual Meeting Technical Education Sessions, the Committee recommended using Steve Malone and Henry Oppermann's results from the Nebraska 52-week Dispenser Field Study, and Ross Andersen's Temperature Compensation Report. The Committee was pleased that both of these sessions were selected for presentation at the 2007 Annual Meeting. At the January 2008 NCWM Interim Meeting, the Committee will discuss ideas for educational sessions to be presented the July 2008 NCWM Annual Meeting and encourages people to submit ideas for the sessions to the Committee Chair, c/o NCWM Headquarters, before the Interim Meeting.

402 PROGRAM MANAGEMENT

402-1 I Safety Awareness

Source: The Committee (2003)

Background: In the past, the Committee's responsibility extended to the identification of safety issues in the weights and measures field and included efforts to increase safety awareness.

At the 2005 Annual Meeting, Past-Chairman Dennis Ehrhart recommended the committee make training its highest priority. The Voluntary Quality Assurance Assessment program, NCWM Associate Membership Scholarships, and safety awareness efforts were carryover items from the Committee on Administration and Public Affairs (A&P) and not PDC items.

Jurisdictions should send their safety reports and issues to their regional safety liaison, who in turn will forward them to Charles Gardner, the NCWM Safety Coordinator. Charles recommends the reports or report summaries be published in the NCWM newsletter. At the 2005 Interim Meeting, a CD-ROM on safety produced for the U.S. Environmental Protection Agency was made available for review. The Committee believes safety awareness should be a part of every aspect of training for NCWM stakeholders.

Discussion: The Committee reiterated the importance of safety awareness and education in weights and measures inspection and service activities. In an effort to continue emphasizing this issue, the Committee will reach out to the regional safety liaisons to ask that they write newsletter articles designed to raise safety awareness within and provide safety tips to the weights and measures community. These articles will also be archived on the PDC page of the NCWM website. The NCWM newsletter is published three times a year and all articles should be e-mailed to the NCWM headquarters office, at ncwm@mgmtsol.com, by the deadline dates listed below. The Committee has suggested the following schedule:

Association	Issue Article	Deadline
CWMA	2007, Issue 2	March 15, 2007
NEWMA	2007, Issue 3	July 15, 2007
SWMA	2008, Issue 1	November 15, 2007
WWMA	2008, Issue 2	March 14, 2008

PDC 2007 Final Report

The Committee is pleased to report that the CWMA submitted an article for Issue 2 of the 2007 NCWM newsletter, and has been advised that NEWMA will be submitting an article for Issue 3.

402-2   V   Standard Categories of Weighing and Measuring Devices

(This item was adopted)

Source: Western Weights and Measures Association (WWMA) (2005)

Recommendation: The Committee recommends the following standardized category codes be adopted for use in NCWM studies and other data collection efforts.

NCWM DEVICE CATEGORY CODES			
DEVICE CODE	**CATEGORY**	**CAPACITY**	**EXAMPLES**
SP	Scale, Precision	< 5 g scale division	jewelry, prescription scales
SS	Scale, Small	< 300 lb	retail computing scales
SM	Scale, Medium	301 to 5 000 lb	dormant, platform scales
SL	Scale, Large	> 5 001 lb	livestock, recycler scales, hopper scales, belt conveyor
SV	Scale, Vehicle	> 40 000 lb	vehicle, railway track scales
MS	Meter, Small	< 30 gpm[1]	retail motor-fuel dispensers
MM	Meter, Medium	30 to 200 gpm	vehicle-tank meters
ML	Meter, Large >	200 gpm	agri-chemical meters, bulk oil meters, loading rack meters
MF	Meter, Mass Flow	All	heated tanks of corn syrup (soft drinks)
MW	Meter, Water	All	water sub-meters for mobile homes & apartments
MG	Meter, LPG	All propane	sales
MT	Meter, Taxi All taximeters		
DT	Device, Timing	All	clocks in parking garages
DL	Device, Length Measuring	All cordage	meters
GM	Grain Moisture Meter	All	
GA	Grain Analyzer All		
MD	Multiple Dimension Measuring Device	All	
MC	Meter, Cryogenic All		

[1] Retail motor-fuel dispenser counts are based on meters.

Background: The WWMA A&P Committee recommended that standard categories of weighing and measuring devices be adopted to facilitate development of technical standards, inspector training, data collection, and program management.

The final report of the *Survey of Inspection Statistics Collected by State Weights and Measures Programs (2003)*, conducted during mid-2002, observed the absence of standard categories for weighing and measuring devices was a serious obstacle to data collection. For example, the way weights and measures programs categorize scales by type, use, or capacity often varies considerably. Retail motor-fuel dispensers are currently being counted either by dispenser, grade, or number of hoses or meters. The need for reliable weights and measures statistics is summarized in the final report conclusion as follows:

> Accurate statistics would be helpful in many ways at both the state and national level. For instance, performance measures are difficult to develop without statistics. Also, work plans

require accurate and detailed statistics. In addition, budget, staffing, and other elements of each state program demand statistics on inspection workloads. Finally, neither individual states nor the NCWM will be able to estimate and advertise the value of the nation's weights and measures programs unless reliable statistics are available.

To correct this problem, the WWMA developed *Standard Categories for Weighing and Measuring Devices,* and recommends that standard categories for weighing and measuring devices be adopted to facilitate the development of technical standards, inspector training, inspection data collection, and weights and measures program management.

At the 2005 Interim Meeting, the Committee agreed this item should remain Informational to allow for additional input on standardized categories of weighing and measuring devices.

Discussion: During its deliberations at the 2007 NCWM Interim Meeting, the Committee agreed that interested parties have had adequate time to review and comment on the proposed device category codes. Consequently, the Committee agreed to propose the category codes for a vote at the 2007 NCWM Annual Meeting. The Committee heard some confusion about how the codes would affect the recordkeeping procedures currently in use in individual weights and measures jurisdictions. The purpose of agreeing on and adopting standardized codes is to facilitate the collection and comparison of data across weights and measures jurisdictions. Thus, jurisdictions participating in NCWM studies and other data collection efforts would need to submit data to the NCWM using the standardized codes. While the Committee encourages jurisdictions to consider using these codes in their own jurisdiction's recordkeeping procedures, jurisdictions are under no obligation to use these codes.

402-3 D PDC   Publication

Source: The Committee (2005)

Many of the PDC items will continue to be carryover items from year to year as the broad scope of the Committee's work progresses. To help NCWM members follow the history and work of the PDC, the Committee has created a PDC document archive. The NCWM will maintain the archive. To eliminate the cost of reprinting the more lengthy items in their entirety and to preserve the important aspects of the PDC work, a legacy document was developed. Following the 2006 Annual Meeting, the documents listed below were archived on the PDC page of the NCWM website for easy access and downloading as needed.

- History of the PDC
- Formal Scope of the PDC
- NCWM Board of Directors Charge to the PDC
- The PDC's Role in the NCWM Strategic Plan
- The PDC's Strategic Plan
- National Training Curriculum Outline
- Suggested Topics for the NCWM Annual Conference
- Standard Categories of Weighing and Measuring Devices
- Safety Liaison Contact Information
- List of State Certification Coordinators and Contacts
- NCWM Issued Certification Program
- Voluntary Quality Assurance Assessment Program

When completed, the Committee's revised "Curriculum Package (Guideline for Creating a Basic Inspector Curriculum)" will also be posted to the PDC page of the NCWM website. The PDC page will continue to be utilized and updated.

PDC 2007 Final Report

Agatha Shields, Chair, Franklin County, Ohio
Kenneth Deitzler, Pennsylvania
Ross Andersen, New York
John Sullivan, Mississippi
Stacy Carlsen, Marin County, California
Tina Butcher, NIST Weights and Measures Division
C. Gardner, New York, Safety Liaison
Linda Bernetich, NCWM Staff Liaison

Professional Development Committee

Appendix A

Strategic Direction for the Professional Development Committee

The Committee developed their strategic direction to define its roles and responsibilities to the NCWM and the weights and measures community. The Committee members wrote principles to guide them in their deliberations and defined four main areas to focus their efforts. The Committee recognizes that its direction and responsibilities may be changed by the Board of Directors.

The guiding principles of the group were:

- Keep things simple;
- Develop programs that are realistic and achievable;
- Minimize redundancy and administrative tasks;
- Recognize that no one size fits all; and
- Meet the needs of weights and measures officials, service companies, industry, and manufacturers.

The four main areas for focusing their efforts were:

National Training Program – The focus of the National Training Program (NTP) would be to increase technical knowledge, strengthen credibility, and improve the professionalism of the individual weights and measures official. A strong NTP would work to promote uniformity across the nation.

National Certification System – A national certification system would be developed to recognize or accredit weights and measures programs as competent or capable. The program would include requirements around individual training, proper test standards, use of national handbooks, and a data gathering system.

Conference Training Topics – The Committee would be the focal point for gathering and recommending workshops or symposia on leadership, management, and emerging issues to be presented during the annual conference. These topics would provide a forum for the exchange of ideas and discussion of changes in the marketplace.

Uniformity of Data – The Committee would work to develop standard categories for devices and inspection areas so that such things as the number of devices, compliance rates, frequency of inspection and other areas could be compiled and compared at the national level. These statistics could be used to benchmark organizations and to communicate the value of weights and measures to the public and to decision makers (see Item 402-4).

THIS PAGE INTENTIONALLY LEFT BLANK

Appendix B

Curriculum Package

National Conference on Weights and Measures

"United by common purpose we can and shall prevail in all that we do."

15245 Shady Grove Rd.• Rockville, MD 20850 (300) 632-9454 FAX (301) 990-9771 E-mail: ncwm@mgmtsol.com Web: www.ncwm.ne

February 2007

To: Curriculum Development Volunteers
From: NCWM Professional Development Committee (PDC)
Re: Guideline for Creating a Basic Inspector Curriculum

Thank you for volunteering to work on the curriculum for a Basic Level Inspector. We define "basic" as the competency level required for the inspector to operate without direct supervision. In this work, we are moving to an outcome-based approach for setting educational standards and away from a textbook approach. The outcome approach is widely used in primary and secondary education and in the training of many professionals. Under this model, we focus on the outcomes and use these to describe the organization and coverage of the training course. The course materials become a means to an end rather than the end itself. The approach encourages innovation and creativity because it does not limit the trainer to a specific textbook or course presentation. The outcomes and milestones in the curriculum also will directly drive the certification program that we envision as the logical next step in the process.

The curriculum lists the outcomes in terms of the specific knowledge and skills we expect the basic inspector to possess at the end of the training. Each outcome will be further defined by a set of milestones, or competencies, that specify the activities and tasks that will be used to measure the student's mastery of the knowledge and skills, i.e., outcomes. The milestones must specify a single, clear objective, stating what the student will be able to do after the training. Milestones must be measurable and should lead to obvious test questions. Your task is to create the curriculum for a small segment of our profession.

Since many groups will be working on selected pieces of the overall curriculum, the Committee has selected a format for the curriculum materials based on work of the California Society of Certified Public Accountants (CACPA). In their publication, The California Core Competency Model for the First Course in Accounting, they provide a model accounting curriculum, a discussion of their methodology, and the rationale for using that methodology. Before beginning your work, we strongly recommend you read the short introduction to that publication and the Appendices. This common format will ensure that the pieces that get developed mesh together without extensive reformatting and editing.

The Committee is also asking that you review the three curriculum segments leading to small capacity retail scales prepared by New York State. These serve as a W&M example of the format we want to use and were prepared using the CACPA model. These segments also demonstrate the level of detail we want to see in the final product. As in the CACPA model document, our goal is to set standards rather than create a "lesson plan."

Please note the layered approach used in the small scale materials and how this limits redundancy in the curriculum. The first segment on general device inspection should be considered a prerequisite for the second segment on basic scales. Both are prerequisites for the segment on small capacity scales. The first segment is also a prerequisite for any other measuring device area. For some devices, like timing devices, only one layer below this first layer is necessary. For liquid measuring devices, we would expect there to be two layers, a general layer that applies to all dynamic volume measuring and then a number of specific disciplines below that. Above all of these is a much broader segment that will include state and local laws and regulations, administrative procedures, enforcement policies, etc. that need not be included with each specific device segment. Please refer to Appendix A from the Profession Development Committee Final Report for the 2004 NCWM for a complete outline of the curriculum plan.

Your task will be to identify the outcomes and the milestones that are pertinent to the area of Weights and Measures you chose to work on.

We suggest a process that involves the following steps:

1. **Brainstorm.** Create a bullet list of knowledge and skills expected. Ask simple questions. What should the inspector know? What should the inspector understand? What should the inspector be able to do?

2. **Group the bullets to define a broad outcome.** For a device segment, consider groupings like technology and terminology, classification and performance standards, markings and operational controls, technical requirements, user requirements, and test procedures. As a guideline, you should aim to have three to eight milestones under each outcome.

3. **Create a concise outcome statement for each outcome.** See Appendix B in the CACPA document and the New York samples for explanation and examples.

4. **Group similar milestones to the extent practical into a broader category**. For example, instead of listing expectations for use of zero, tare, units buttons, state a single expectation regarding typical controls on the device and consider listing specific controls parenthetically.

5. **Create a milestone statement, i.e. competency, using a verb from the list based on the levels of cognitive learning in Bloom's Taxonomy in Appendix C of the CACPA document**. For the basic inspector we recommend you limit your milestones primarily to the first three levels, i.e., knowledge, understanding, and application. The higher levels of learning in Bloom's Taxonomy, analysis, synthesis, and evaluation, typically require practical experience not expected in the basic inspector.

In Bloom's Taxonomy:

- Knowledge refers to the ability to recall facts, terms, and basic concepts.
- Understanding refers to the ability to interpret or explain concepts using your own words.
- Application refers to the ability to put knowledge/understanding to practical use and demonstrate skills required actually to perform specific acts.

As part of the process of developing curriculum segments, the Committee is asking work groups to draft sample test questions that evaluate whether the milestones in the segment have been met. The Committee has prepared a guide to developing test questions to aid in that process and will circulate that to the work groups and become part of the curriculum development package. The test questions will be used both as instructional tools in training but also for future certification programs.

As a curriculum segment draft is completed, the Committee will do a quick review and suggest editing for uniformity of format. When it is ready, we will circulate the draft for review and comment. The critical questions we will ask are: What is missing from this curriculum segment and what should be removed or moved to another segment in another level? With this review process, we hope to build a consensus of agreement on the standards being set. The same would apply to sample questions.

The Committee greatly appreciates your willingness to contribute to this project. Please send your comments or questions on the project to the current chair of the PDC committee with a carbon copy to Linda Bernetich at NCWM

Inc, lbernetich@mgmtsol.com. Ross Andersen has agreed to help with questions about the format and the CACPA model. Please contact him at ross.andersen@agmkt.

Curriculum Package

THE CALIFORNIA CORE COMPETENCY MODEL
FOR THE FIRST COURSE IN ACCOUNTING

California Society of CPAs Committee on Accounting Education

July 1995

This document may be copied without restriction.

The California Society of CPAs Committee on Accounting Education is proud to present this White Paper entitled *The California Core Competency Model for the First Course in Accounting.*

The idea for this model began with a grassroots movement of accounting educators who wanted to reverse a deteriorating articulation process for the first course in accounting. This movement gained significant momentum when Bob Knox of the California Society of CPAs formed the Task Force on the First Course in Accounting in December of 1993. This Task Force's efforts were successfully completed when the California Society of CPAs Committee on Accounting Education formally approved the model on April 24, 1995. During this two-year period, Paul Solomon of San Jose State University led the effort to improve articulation, develop the competencies, and secure their adoption.

The model presented here is the result of the tireless efforts of Task Force members and extensive input from the Committee on Accounting Education, as well as the input of several hundred accounting educators, accounting and business professionals, and non-accounting business educators. This input was collected from a combination of nearly 30 presentations, workshops, panels, and receptions throughout the state over a period of two years.

The hundreds of hours of time volunteered for this project is an impressive example of professional volunteerism at its best. Even more impressive is the fact that when conflicts arose, educators searched for creative solutions that would meet the needs of more than one point of view. Clearly, accounting educators consistently subordinated their individual views of the course to the greater good-the long-run improvement of accounting education.

If you are an accounting educator in California, you are urged to share this model with your faculty and help improve accounting education state-wide by working for the model's endorsement. If you are an accounting educator outside California, we hope that this model will help you to facilitate the types of changes encouraged by the Accounting Education Change Commission in its Position Statement No.2 entitled *The First Course in Accounting.*

PDC 2007 Final Report
Appendix B – Curriculum Package

THE CALIFORNIA CORE COMPETENCY MODEL
FOR THE FIRST COURSE IN ACCOUNTING

BACKGROUND

The first course in accounting offered at California's institutions of higher education represents a sizable expenditure of money for the State. It has been conservatively estimated that the instructional costs of this course - taught at 107 community colleges, 20 California State Universities (CSU), and a majority of the 9 universities within the California University system (UC) - are over $50 million! Additional costs for this course are incurred at a significant number of private universities.

The first course in accounting has several major stakeholders. For example, one major stakeholder is non-accounting faculty who rely on the first course to provide part of the foundation knowledge required of all business students by the American Assembly of Collegiate Schools of Business. Since over 80% of all students enrolled in the first course are non-accounting majors, it is reasonable that these non-accounting faculty have input into the design of this course. Another major stakeholder is the accounting community, in other words, accountants in industry, government, and public accounting.

The California Society of CPAs (CSCPA), with approximately 29,000 members, has strongly urged accounting educators to deliver better prepared students to the accounting profession. The CSCPA believes that if students' first exposure to accounting is positive, then more high quality students are likely to choose accounting as their major. Because of the interest of these stakeholders, the CSCPA, through its Committee on Accounting Education, established the Task Force on the First Course in Accounting.

THE MISSION OF THE TASK FORCE ON THE FIRST COURSE IN ACCOUNTING

The mission of this task force is to improve the quality of education in the first accounting course by helping faculty implement the changes recommended in the AECC's Position Statement Number Two entitled *The First Course in Accounting*. Like the AECC, our task force defines the first course in accounting to mean the full introductory accounting sequence commonly taught over two semesters or three quarters.

Since the California community colleges are such an integral part of the accounting education system-teaching as many as 90 % of the students who take introductory accounting in California and over 50 % of the students who enroll in the California State University system-our mission includes facilitating first course articulation among two-year and four-year accounting programs.

Although our focus is on accounting education in California, we hope that our approach will also help accounting programs outside of California.

ACCOMPLISHING OUR MISSION

We have accomplished our mission by identifying expected student outcomes and core competencies as a basis for articulation agreements. The diversity of emerging instructional models for the first course in accounting has made the process of articulation very difficult for the great majority of California's institutions of higher learning. To reduce the severity of this problem requires a dramatic change in how course equivalencies between institutions are measured. It is, therefore, proposed that the basis for articulation agreements shift from the current textbook/topic approach to one that focuses on identifying desirable outcomes students should achieve and core competencies that measure their achievement. The current version of these outcomes and core competencies-referred to as the "California Core Competency Model" or CCCM-is included in this *White Paper*. Milestones for accomplishing this part of our mission as well as definitions of "outcome" and "competency" are included in Appendices A and B.

THE TASK FORCE MEMBERS

The members of the Task Force on the First Course in Accounting were:

Curtis DeBerg	California State University - Chico [Co-Chair]
Roger Gee	San Diego Mesa College
Ken Harper	De Anza Community College

PDC 2007 Final Report
Appendix B – Curriculum Package

Bob Hurt	Cal-Poly Pomona
Patrick Kelly	Price Waterhouse LLP
Bob Knox	California Society of CPAs (CSCPA), Director, Relations with Educators
Joe Mori	San Jose State University CSCPA Chair, Committee on Accounting Education
Jim Peters	Ernst & Young LLP
Bonnie Slager	Rancho Santiago College (Orange)
Paul Solomon	San Jose State University [Co-Chair]

GENERAL PHILOSOPHY ABOUT HOW TO USE THIS MODEL

Identifying outcomes and core competencies is an important step in the process of improving accounting education. How accounting educators help students master these outcomes and competencies and how they simultaneously measure student mastery are equally important tasks. Thus, our next task will be to publish a *Guide to Competency Implementation and Assessment.* The *Guide* will be based on input collected from hundreds of educators and business professionals at numerous CSCPA-sponsored workshops conducted throughout the state in 1994 and 1995 and will be presented at the 1996 California Colloquium on Accounting Education.

Our intention is *not* to develop a "statewide lesson plan" for the first course in accounting. Instead, we want individual faculty to be creative in implementing the common set of outcomes and core competencies described in this *White Paper.* Moreover, as Appendix B explains, we hope each accounting program will develop a set of outcomes and special competencies that will reflect the unique perspective of its faculty and the special needs of its students. Thus, our philosophy encourages diversity. Although we want students to attain the educational objectives of the Accounting Education Change Commission, we do not expect them to attain these objectives in a prescribed manner.

SOME SPECIFIC NOTES ABOUT THE CALIFORNIA CORE COMPETENCY MODEL

- The outcomes and core competencies you see are derived from the Accounting Education Change Commission's Position Statement Number Two entitled *The First Course in Accounting.* We strongly recommend that you study this document as background preparation before you view our model.

- Like the AECC, our task force defines the first course in accounting to mean the full introductory accounting sequence commonly taught over two semesters or three quarters.

- Do not interpret the user *orientation* of our financial accounting outcomes and competencies to mean that students should no longer prepare statements. Although we do not include the traditional detailed treatment of debits and credits in the core competencies, we do want students to develop the skills needed to intelligently use such financial reports as are found in an annual report. Accordingly, students must be able to prepare simple financial statements.

- Our model contains twelve outcomes divided into three categories of competencies: financial accounting (31 competencies), managerial accounting (29 competencies), and active learning (9 competencies). The active learning skills are intended to facilitate accounting content. That is, whenever possible, instructors should require their students to use active learning skills to master both financial and managerial outcomes. For example, a student should be able to identify the assumptions and possible positions underlying an ethical issue for any of the financial and managerial outcomes. Also, these active learning competencies are not designed to be mutually exclusive. That is, when a student analyzes a case study in a group setting, the assignment may also involve one or more communication skills and problem solving skills.

- Each competency in the model contains a concrete verb that denotes action. An inventory of such concrete verbs is included in Appendix C.

- The model is a "living document." It will be re-evaluated annually to consider the evolving content and pedagogy of the first course in accounting. Thus, if you wish to comment on any aspect of the model, please contact Paul Solomon at:

Phone Number:	(408) 924-3487
Fax Number:	(408) 252-6882

E-mail Address: psolomon@sjsuvm1.sjsu.edu
Mailing Address: 1210 Stafford Drive, Cupertino, CA 95014

THE CALIFORNIA CORE COMPETENCY MODEL

The primary objective of this course is to help students learn how accounting meets the information needs of various users by developing and communicating information that is useful for decision-making. This objective will be achieved by requiring the following outcomes and core competencies.

Financial Accounting Outcomes with Core Competencies

[1] Accounting's Role in Society

Part A: How does accounting meet the information needs of investors and creditors?

- identify the types of decisions investors and creditors make and describe what information in the financial statements and/ or related disclosures meets the information needs of each group. [lA-I]

- discuss what role ethics plays in the preparation of financial statements. [1A-2]

- identify and discuss examples of how U.S. accounting measurement techniques and financial statements differ from the measurement techniques and financial statements of other countries. [1A-3]

Part B: How does accounting meet the information needs of regulatory agencies and taxing authorities?

- describe how information sources other than the annual report (e.g., SEC Form 10-K) can be used to learn more about the nature of an entity's business. [1B-1]

- identify some of the differences between the objectives of tax accounting and financial accounting and at least one difference between taxable income and financial accounting income. [lB-2]

- explain how a tax return is actually a special version of the income statement. [1B-3]

[2] Fundamental Business Concepts: How do businesses operate and how does accounting serve them?

- explain the meanings of key business terms (e.g., assets, budget, collateral, financing, limited liability, and lease). [2-1]

- distinguish among profit, governmental and other nonprofit entities by identifying their respective goals and by looking at the content of their financial reports. [2-2]

- identify the characteristics of the corporate, partnership, and sole proprietorship forms of entity and discuss the advantages and disadvantages of each form. [2-3]

- classify business transactions into operating, investing, and financing activities. [2-4]

- describe the key differences in the financial statements of merchandisers, manufacturers, non-financial service companies (e.g. United Air Lines), and financial service companies; and explain how these differences reflect the operating, investing, and financing activities of each type of entity. [2-5]

[3] Fundamental Accounting Concepts Underlying Financial Statements: What are the elements of, the relationships among, and the accounting concepts underlying the primary financial statements?

- discuss what information is typically found in the balance sheet, income statement, statement of owners' equity, and statement of cash flows. [3-1]

- apply the fundamental accounting equation ($A = L + OE$) to:

    (a) analyze the effects of accounting transactions on the elements of the balance sheet. [3-2a]

    (b) prepare a balance sheet that reports the financial condition of any entity (e.g., a person, sole proprietorship, partnership, corporation, etc.). [3-2b]

- apply the income statement equation ($R - E = NI$) to:

(a) discuss the criteria used to determine when revenue is recognized, and apply these criteria to a specific entity to determine when its revenue should be recognized. [3-3a]

(b) discuss the process used to recognize expense. [3-3b] prepare an income statement that reports the results of operations for any entity. [3-3c]

(c) prepare an income statement that reports the results of operations for any entity. [3-3c]

- distinguish between the accrual and the cash basis of income measurement by preparing both an accrual basis and a cash basis income statement from the same set of business transactions. [3-4]

- differentiate the balance sheet from the income statement by being able to classify account titles into asset, liability, owners' equity, and non-balance sheet accounts. [3-5]

- describe how the amounts reported on the income statement and balance sheet are determined by:

    (a) distinguishing among the following valuation methods: historical cost, current cost, current market value, and the present value of cash flows. [3-6a]

    (b) identifying the generally accepted valuation method for each of the major asset and liability accounts. [3-6b]

    (c) describing how the balance in each major asset, liability, owners' equity, revenue, and expense account is calculated (e.g., accounts receivable and depreciation expense). [3-6c]

- link the following related financial statements-balance sheet, income statement, statement of cash flows, and statement of owners' equity. [3-7]

- classify cash receipt and cash payment transactions as well as significant non-cash transactions into the appropriate statement of cash flow activity. [3-8]

[4] Uses and Limitations of Financial Statements:
What are the uses and limitations of financial statements and related information in making both business and personal financial decisions?

- identify several ways in which financial accounting information is used to make business and personal decisions. [4-1]

- calculate at least one financial statement ratio within each of the following four categories and discuss its usefulness and limitations in making decisions:

    (a) liquidity-e.g., current ratio and acid test ratio

    (b) activity or turnover-e.g., average collection period

    (c) financial leverage-e.g., debt to equity ratio

    (d) profitability-e.g., profit margin ratio and return on equity (e) valuation-e.g., price-earnings ratio and dividend yield [4-2]

    (e) valuation-e.g., price-earnings ratio and dividend yield [4-2]

- explain how percentage analysis can be used to uncover important relationships and trends in the financial statements. [4-3]

- explain how inventories and accounts receivable can be mismanaged and describe how a manager can use financial statement analysis to monitor and control them. [4-4]

- explain the relationship between net income and cash flows and discuss how a highly profitable, fast-growing business might face liquidity problems that could force it into bankruptcy. [4-5]

- identify several limitations of the financial statements found in the annual report. [4-6]

- discuss the basic principles of internal control and describe the attributes of an effective and efficient internal control system. [5A-2]

- identify the strengths and weaknesses of an internal control system and, if appropriate, suggest improvements to this system. [5A-3]

Part B: How are business transactions input, processed by an accounting information system, and output by that same system to produce financial statements? To appreciate the role of technology in this process, students should work with one or more of the following tools: a spreadsheet, an accounting software package, a database, or other technology.

- identify and apply the essential conditions necessary for a business event to qualify as an accounting transaction and, therefore, be recorded in the accounting information system. [5B-1]

- distinguish between the recording phase and the reporting phase of the accounting process or cycle by being able to:

    (a) record the effects of accounting transactions in an accounting information system. [5B-2a]

    (b) transfer the effects of these explicit transactions to individual asset, liability, and owners' equity accounts. [5B-2b]

    (c) analyze whether an adjustment or correction is needed in a particular situation. [5B-2c]

    (d) record and transfer the effects of adjustments and corrections to individual asset, liability, and owners' equity accounts. [5B-2d]

    (e) prepare the financial statements. [5B-2e]

- explain the significance of debits and credits as they are used in an accounting information system. [5B-3]

Managerial Accounting Outcomes with Core Competencies

[6] Role of the Management Accountant

Part A: How does management accounting differ from that of financial accounting and what role does the management accountant play as a member of the management team?

- distinguish between the usefulness of managerial and financial accounting by considering the activities of planning, evaluating, controlling, and decision making. [6A-1]

- explain why managerial accounting applies to all types of industries (e.g., merchandising, manufacturing, non-financial services, financial services, government and other nonprofit entities). [6A-2]

- describe different ways in which the management accountant's advice can help an entity to operate more effectively. [6A-3]

- analyze a company's financial statements and/or management reports and identify several strengths and several weaknesses of the company from this analysis. [6A-4]

Part B: Why do management accountants need to have both a broad and in-depth understanding of their entity to fully participate in decisions about the products and services provided?

- discuss, using specific examples, the cause and effect relationship between expenses and revenues and how they affect operating decisions. [6B-1]

- discuss the need for and uses of a management control system and how accounting information facilitates control. [6B-2]

- explain how the operating philosophies of continuous improvement, total quality management and just-in-time manufacturing are used to manage optimal inventory levels; and discuss how the accounting function can be used to support their implementation. [6B-3]

[7] Using Accounting Information to Make Decisions

Part A: How is accounting information used to make and communicate short-term management decisions needed to run the entity?

- distinguish between fixed costs, variable costs, and mixed costs by categorizing various costs of an entity into these three categories. [7A-l]
- explain the usefulness and discuss the limitations of Cost-Volume Profit (CVP) analysis as a decision making tool. [7 A-2]
- read a CVP graph and explain the significance of the components illustrated. [7 A-3]
- calculate fixed and variable costs, contribution margin, contribution margin ratio, break-even point in sales dollars and units, and target sales volume in dollars and units. [7 A-4]
- calculate the effects of changes in sales volume, sales price, variable costs and/or fixed costs on company contribution margin, breakeven point, and operating income for both multi-product and single product situations. [7 A-5]
- explain how pricing decisions are made, including transfer pricing decisions. [7 A-6]
- identify the relevant costs in a make-or-buy decision and discuss both the qualitative and quantitative factors considered in this decision. [7 A-7]

Part B: How is accounting information used to make and communicate long-term strategic decisions needed to position the firm for competitive advantage?

- identify and explain the long-term strategic decisions that management needs to make. [7B-l]
- calculate both return on investment (ROI) and residual income (RI) and explain how each method is used. [7B-2]

[8] Using Accounting Information To Analyze and Improve Operational Efficiency: How is accounting information used to analyze and improve efficiency in operating, financing, and administering the entity?

- explain the purposes of budgets and prepare both a simple operating budget and a simple cash budget. [8-1]
- explain the relationship between budgeting and strategic planning. [8-2]
- discuss the limitations of budgets in managing organizations. [8-3]
- explain the relationship between accounting budgets and nonfinancial performance measures, e.g. cycle time, defect rate, and ontime delivery. [8-4]
- explain how the concept of responsibility accounting applies to cost centers, profit centers, and investment centers. [8-5]
- distinguish between controllable and non-controllable costs and discuss why the distinction is important. [8-6]
- explain how the concept of cost control is used to compare budgeted to actual amounts and to interpret any significant variances. [8-7]

[9] Processing Managerial Accounting Information: What is the importance and proper use of automated information processing in managerial accounting?

- identify alternative ways costs are tied to inventory and expense accounts (including the systematic and rational allocation associated with financial accounting). [9-1]
- trace the flow of costs in both a job order cost and process cost manufacturing system. [9-2]

- explain the causes and appropriate dispositions of over-applied and under-applied manufacturing overhead. [9-3]
- distinguish between a periodic and a perpetual inventory system for a merchandiser and a manufacturer. [9-4]
- describe the information benefits of maintaining a perpetual inventory. [9-5]
- distinguish between an activity-based cost accounting system and a traditional cost accounting system. [9-6]

Active Learning Outcomes With Core Competencies

[10] Communication Skills: How can students demonstrate their ability to communicate effectively in both oral (speaking and listening) and written form?

- engage in one or more of the following in-class speaking activities:

    (a) summarize an accounting-related newspaper or magazine article

    (b) present an accounting concept or homework problem applying a concept

    (c) debate at least one side of an accounting issue

    (d) present an analysis of an assigned case

    (e) present the results of a research assignment or project [10-1]

- engage in one or more of the following in-class listening activities:

    (a) listen to someone speak, summarize what they say, and ask them for feedback about your summary

    (b) listen to someone's response to a question or assignment and compare it to your own

    (c) compare notes you have taken to those taken by another student and evaluate the effectiveness of your listening skills [10-2]

- engage in one or more of the following written communication activities:

    (a) accumulate a written record of the concepts and terminology learned in the course, e.g. a writing journal

    (b) summarize the content of assigned readings, e.g. a reading log

    (c) describe what was learned in class, e.g. a one-minute response

    (d) submit questions about concepts or problems

    (e) submit potential exam questions

    (f) respond to discussion questions or cases

    (g) respond in essay form to questions in quizzes and exams

    (h) submit an essay describing a particular issue [10-3]

[11] Group Work Skills: How can students demonstrate their ability to work effectively in groups?

- participate in groups whose task is to do one or more of the following:

    (a) solve problems

    (b) discuss readings from the financial press

    (c) analyze financial statements

    (d) analyze case studies [11-1]

- perform the following tasks that are commonly associated with collaborative or cooperative learning:
    - (a) facilitate the discussion and keep the group on task
    - (b) record the group's results
    - (c) report the results of the group's work to the class
    - (d) keep time, assist the leader, and fill vacant roles [11-2]

[12] Problem Solving Skills: How can students demonstrate their ability to reason creatively and critically rather than to memorize?

- identify the problem, alternate ways of solving the problem, alternate positions, and position arguments for a controversial issue. [12-1]
- identify the assumptions and possible positions underlying an ethical issue. [12-2]
- evaluate a speaker's or writer's content for the appearance of underlying assumptions and of facts versus opinions. [12-3]
- analyze an unstructured problem that has no single correct answer. [12-4]

APPENDIX A: MILESTONES FOR IMPLEMENTING COMPETENCY-BASED ARTICULATION

The intent of the Committee on Accounting Education is to promote the widespread acceptance of essential student outcomes and competencies, while encouraging individual programs to implement these outcomes and competencies in ways that best suit their own students. The following milestones are used to evaluate progress in implementing this competency-based articulation system:

MILESTONE 1: Derive expected student outcomes (knowledge and skills) from AECC Position Statement No.2.

MILESTONE 2: Create core competencies (activities expressed in behavioral terms) that are logically derived from the expected student outcomes. The core competencies are developed from the input of the CSCPA Task Force and extensive feedback from both accounting educators and accounting practitioners.

MILESTONE 3: Promote a competency-based articulation approach by conducting workshops for interested faculty on how to implement and assess core competencies. The purpose if these workshops is to:

1. explain how the use of core competencies reduces the volume of material covered in the first course and provides:
    - (a) more time to develop the communication, group work and critical thinking skills of students.
    - (b) more flexibility to cover special topics that individual accounting programs or faculty believe their students must learn (i.e. special competencies).
2. describe how faculty at each school can develop their own special competencies to clearly communicate the unique aspects of their first course in accounting.
3. provide numerous examples of how faculty can test the degree to which their students have mastered the core competencies. This effort will culminate in the distribution of a *Guide to Competency Implementation and Assessment*.

MILESTONE 4: Establish acceptance of a single set of outcomes and core competencies–The California Core Competency Model–as the basis for articulation among all California four-year and two-year accounting programs.

APPENDIX B: DEFINITIONS: OUTCOMES AND COMPETENCIES

HOW DO YOU DISTINGUISH AN OUTCOME FROM A COMPETENCY?

An outcome is "what" you expect your students to achieve, whereas a competency demonstrates "how" your students can achieve that outcome. Think of an outcome as an end and a competency as a means to that end.

Outcomes are the knowledge and skills recommended in the AECC's Position Statement Number Two entitled The First Course in Accounting. Competencies are the specific activities used to measure a student's mastery of the knowledge/skills or outcomes.

The outcome/competency approach is different from the traditional textbook/topic approach to accounting instruction. First, the choice of a textbook no longer dictates the organization and coverage of the course. Instead, the outcomes and competencies become the driver and the textbook becomes their vehicle. A related difference is that the course is driven by an output measure (outcomes/competencies) rather than an input measure (textbook/topics). Finally, students more clearly know the content they are expected to study and the precise activities they must perform on examinations and other forms of evaluation by studying the outcome/competency pairings and working problems that reflect them.

AN EXAMPLE OF THE DISTINCTION

Outcome: Students completing the first accounting course should understand the elements of, the relationships among, and the accounting concepts underlying the primary financial statements. This understanding will be implemented if students can:

> Competency 1: discuss what information is typically found in the balance sheet, income statement, statement of owners' equity, and statement of cash flows.
>
> Competency 2: apply the fundamental accounting equation ASSETS = LIABILITIES + OWNERS' EQUITY– to prepare a balance sheet that reports the financial condition of any entity (e.g., a person, sole proprietorship, partnership, corporation, etc.).

HOW DO YOU DISTINGUISH CORE COMPETENCIES FROM SPECIAL COMPETENCIES?

Our task force's articulation approach includes both core competencies and special competencies.

Core competencies are competencies required of students in all accounting programs that subscribe to the outcome/competency articulation approach. Special competencies are competencies that are required by an individual accounting program to meet the special needs of its students.

It is expected that faculty at each school will identify and develop special competencies to communicate clearly the unique aspects of their first course in accounting.

WHAT COMPETENCIES ARE REQUIRED FOR ARTICULATION?

As the name implies, a core competency is an essential component of an articulation agreement, whereas a special competency is not. If a two year program can document that its students are required to satisfy all of the core competencies, its course fulfills the articulation agreement. It is not required to fulfill any of the four-year program's special competencies. For a more concrete understanding, consider the following example:

> Core Competency: Record the effects of accounting transactions in an accounting information system.
>
> Special Competency: Record accounting transactions in journal entry form (i.e., debit-credit form).

Notice that two-year programs that teach debits and credits in their first course through the special competency can articulate with four-year programs that do not teach debits and credits. All the two-year program has to do is document that its students are required to comply with the core competency above and all other core competencies.

If, instead, the four-year program teaches debits and credits in its first course through the special competency, it cannot deny articulation to a two-year program that teaches the core competency but not the special competency. Instead, the four year program will have to provide transferring students some vehicle (e.g. software materials or a one-unit bridge course) to master this special competency.

APPENDIX B: CHARACTERISTICS OF WELL-CONSTRUCTED COMPETENCIES

A well constructed behavioral learning objective or competency has the following characteristics:

- it expresses one objective;
- it is specific;
- it states what the student will be able to do after the learning experience; and
- it uses a concrete verb to specify the desired activity that must be performed by the student to demonstrate competency.

INVENTORY OF CONCRETE VERBS DENOTING ACTION TAKEN IN COMPETENCIES

The following suggested verbs are arranged in the six cognitive domains identified in Bloom's Taxonomy.

1. Knowledge		2. Comprehension		3. Application	
arrange	order	classify	record	apply	operate
define	recognize	describe	report	choose	practice
duplicate	relate	discuss	restate	demonstrate	schedule
label	recall	explain	review	dramatize	sketch
list	repeat	express	select	employ	solve
memorize	reproduce	identify	tell	engage	transfer
name		indicate	translate	illustrate	use
		locate		interpret	

4. Analysis		5. Synthesis		6. Evaluation	
analyze	differentiate	arrange	organize	appraise	evaluate
appraise	discriminate	assemble	plan	argue	judge
calculate	distinguish	collect	prepare	assess	predict
categorize	examine	compose	present	attach	rate
compare	experiment	construct	propose	choose	score
contrast	inventory	create	setup	compare	select
convert	question	design	suggest	debate	support
criticize	test	formulate	summarize	defend	value
diagram		justify	write	estimate	
		manage			

The model is a "living document." It will be re-evaluated annually to consider the evolving content and pedagogy of the first course in accounting. Thus, if you wish to comment on any aspect of the model, please contact:

Paul Solomon, Chair
Task Force on the California Core Competency Model
1210 Stafford Drive
Cupertino, CA 95014
Phone: (408) 924-3487
Fax: (408) 252-6882
psolomon@Sjsuvm1.sjsu.edu

PDC 2007 Final Report
Appendix B – Curriculum Package

Guide for Developing Test Questions
For the National Training and Certification Program
Prepared by the
NCWM Professional Development Committee
First Draft - January 2007

This guide was prepared to assist those work groups preparing curriculum materials as they prepare test questions. These test questions will be used both as aids to training delivery and also as a measuring stick in any future certification effort. If the certification program is to have credibility, it is vital that the test questions adequately evaluate that the student has achieved the multiple milestones in each curriculum area.

As you write your questions, please remember that we have set the bar at a level of application, the third in Bloom's taxonomy. Thus, we expect that the trainee will KNOW certain things, UNDERSTAND other things, and be able to APPLY the remainder. We are not looking for higher learning levels in Bloom's Taxonomy for basic inspectors and we will not be testing for analysis, integration, or evaluation.

Testing for Knowledge – A test question for knowledge is usually in the form of a true/false, multiple choice, or fill-in-the blank question. At this point, the Committee is suggesting that developers focus on multiple choice and fill-in-the blank questions, such as questions 1 and 2 below. With true/false the person has a 50-50 chance of guessing and getting the right answer. Please note that at this level the trainee need only demonstrate that he/she knows the information and not necessarily that he/she understands it or can apply it.

1. **Which statement best describes the legal standing of NIST Handbook 44?** (Answer: B)

    A. Handbook 44 is a federal regulation published by the National Institute of Standards and Technology that preempts the states.
    B. Handbook 44 is adopted either by act of the state legislature or through promulgation in regulation by the state.
    C. Handbook 44 is amended each year and all states agree to abide by the actions of the National Conference on Weights and Measures.
    D. Handbook 44 is adopted as part of the administrative policy by order of the state director.

2. **A paragraph beginning with "S." in any of the NIST Handbook 44 Codes is a _____.**
    (Answer: Specification)

Testing for Understanding – A test question for understanding is usually a multiple choice question, such as questions 3 and 4 below. Questions concerning understanding often ask the trainee to pick the best response in situations where more than one answer could be correct in some respect. For example, in Question 3, answer B could be a correct answer if the equipment was manufactured after the effective date. Answer C. is a better answer since it is more specific and also includes items brought into the state after the effective date. Please note for understanding the trainee needs to demonstrate that he/she knows and understands the information and not necessarily that he/she can apply it.

3. **A nonretroactive requirement is best described by which of the following statements?** (Answer: C)

    A. A nonretroactive requirement is enforceable on all equipment up to the terminal date.
    B. A nonretroactive requirement is enforceable only on new equipment after the effective date.
    C. A nonretroactive requirement is enforceable on equipment manufactured after the effective date or brought into the state after the effective date.
    D. A nonretroactive requirement is enforceable on equipment with an NTEP Certificate granted after the effective date.

4. Which of the following best describes the difference between "d" and "e" in the Scales Code?
(Answer: D)

A. The value of "e" is always displayed while "d" may or may not be.
B. The value of "d" is always smaller than or equal to "e".
C. The display of values for "d" must always be different in size or character from "e".
D. When "d" does not equal "e," the tolerances are applied to the value of "e".

Testing for Application – A test question for application should be either be a multiple-choice question or a "Yes/No with reason" question, such as questions 5 and 6 below. Questions concerning application will usually require the trainee to perform multiple steeps to reach the correct answer. In the field, they will not be guided to the correct section of the handbook, but will have to find it based on their knowledge and experience. For example, the question may provide information about the situation and some test results. The trainee must then decide whether to apply maintenance or acceptance tolerances and then evaluate the test results against the appropriate tolerances for that test. In question 5 below, the person must see that the scale is subject to the non-retroactive requirement in Scales Code S.1.7.(b) and then correctly deduce that the only correct response is an overload error. The Yes/No with reason question (question 6) also requires several steps but goes further in that it also requires the trainee to state the nature of any violation and cite the section of the Handbook that is violated. This is critical as this reason and citation would have to be indicated on any official stop-use order issued for the violation. Please note that the trainee needs to demonstrate that he/she knows, understands, and can apply the requirements.

5. You are inspecting a new price-computing sale (30 x 0.01 lb) in a deli that was placed in service last week. It has an NTEP CC # 99-205. You place a 1 lb weight on the scale and press the tare key. You then place an additional 29.2 pounds of test weights on the scale. Which of the following is an acceptable indication for this test load? (Answer: A)

A. Overload error
B. 29.24 lb
C. 29.18 lb
D. 29.16 lb

6. You are inspecting the scale at right and find that it has no zero tracking. With the scale at zero as indicated, you add 0.1 d (0.002 lb) to the platform and the scale indicates a stable 0.02 lb. Is this acceptable?

Yes or No (No must include reason and citation)

_____

Capacity 100 x 0.02 lb

0.00 lb

| Power | Zero | Tare | Print |

Answer: No – The digital zero indication must be maintained accurate within +/- ¼ d of true zero or the scale must have a center zero indicator. Scales Code S.1.1.1.

Initially the Committee is looking to build a bank of test questions that evaluate if the trainee has reached the milestones in each curriculum segment and cover a range of difficulty. Any exam that is prepared will include a mix of questions at each appropriate level in Bloom's Taxonomy from the curriculum, and varying levels of difficulty from easy to challenging. In that way, the test can be fair yet still differentiate those that really have mastered the discipline from those that haven't.

After the questions are prepared and tested (testing method to be developed), the Committee would then split the questions into two groups. The first group, called "sample questions," would be widely circulated for use in training programs. Instructors could use the sample questions in their training or as part of quizzes or final exams to measure effectiveness of the training. Most important, trainees would be exposed to the kinds of questions and the range of difficulty that would be included in a certification exam.

The second group of questions would be secured for use in a certification exam program. The Committee envisions charging some group to administer the certification exam and assist in the grading. That group would also create alternative exams or periodically change the questions so the exam is not the same for candidates that fail to pass the first time. Please look to set the bar so it is fair yet represents the high level of ability you want working for you.

A long journey begins with one-step. We are counting on our curriculum development teams to start generating our bank of test questions (with an answer key) based on the milestones they choose in the curriculum segment(s) they are preparing. If we work together to create a good range of difficulty in those questions, we can be well on our way toward that certification program we are shooting for. There is plenty of room for creativity in this effort, including the use of graphics and photographs.

Thanks again for your willingness to contribute. Please call or email Ross Andersen, New York, with questions or comments at (518) 457-3146 or ross.andersen@agmkt.state.ny.us.

Appendix C

National Training Curriculum Outline
2004 Version

Weights & Measures General/State Policies

- State Administrative Issues
  - Completion of administrative forms
  - Review of rules and policies
- History
- Roles in Society
- Need for W&M
- System of W&M
- W&M in U.S. & Your State
- Metrology
- State Laws
- Relationship to National & International W&M
- Associations
  - Regional, State, Federal
- Federal Agencies

Market Practices Laws and Regulations NIST Handbook 130

Price Verification
- Terminology
- NIST H-130 Specifications & Requirements
- Safety
- Support Equipment
- General Enforcement Guidelines

Test Purchases
- Examination Specifications
- EPO
- Purchasing Process
- Check for Validity of Purchase
- Field/Practical Exercises

E-Commerce
- Terminology
- NIST H-130 Requirements & Specifications
- Packaging & Labeling Regulations
- Exemptions
- Indirect Sale of Random Packages

Fuel Quality
- Terminology
- NIST H-130 Specifications & Requirements
- Uncertainty
- Safety
- Support Equipment
- Sampling
- General Enforcement Guidelines

General Devices NIST Handbook 44

Weights & Measures Administration

Laboratory Metrology

Commodities General
- Terminology
- Wet/Dry Tare
- NIST H-133 Specifications & Requirements
- Uncertainty
- Safety
- Support Equipment
- General Enforcement Guidelines

Standard Pack (WT)
- Examination Specifications
- Contents of EPO
  - Test Equipment
  - Examination
  - Test Specifications
  - Evaluation
- Field/Practical Exercises

Random Pack (wt)
- Examination Specifications
- Contents of EPO
  - Test Equipment
  - Examination
  - Test Specifications
  - Evaluation
- Field/Practical Exercises

Sale by Volume
- Examination Specifications
- Contents of EPO
  - Test Equipment
  - Examination
  - Test Specifications
  - Evaluation
- Field/Practical Exercises

Sale by Count
- Examination Specifications
- Contents of EPO
  - Test Equipment
  - Examination
  - Test Specifications
  - Evaluation
- Field/Practical Exercises

General Devices NIST Handbook 44
- Terminology
- NIST Handbook 44
- Fundamental Consideration
- Uncertainty
- Safety
- Support Equipment
- Seals
- Supports
- General Enforcement Guidelines

PDC 2007 Final Report
Appendix C – National Training Curriculum Outline

Weighing Devices
- Terminology
- Scale Types
- Technology
- Suitability
- User Requirements
- Operation/Markings
- Scale Classes & Tolerances
- Basic Scale Test Procedures
- Basic Inspection

Measuring Devices
- Terminology
- Measuring Device Types
- Technology
- Suitability
- User Requirements
- Operation & Markings
- Tolerances for LMDs
- Basic LMD Test
- Basic LMD Inspections

Other Devices
- Terminology
- Other Device Types
- Technology
- Suitability
- User Requirements
- Operation & Markings
- Tolerances for LMDs
- Basic Test
- Basic Inspections

Retail Computing Scales
- Common traits
- Examination Specifications
- Test Equipment
- Examination, Installation, & Maintenance
- Test Specifications
- Evaluation
- Field/Practical Exercises

Platform Scales
- Common traits
- EPO
  - Examination Specifications
  - User Requirements
  - Suitability
  - Test Equipment
  - Examination, Installation, & Maintenance
  - Test Specifications
  - Evaluation
- Field/Practical Exercises

Vehicle Scales
- Common traits
- Contents of EPO
  - Examination Specifications
  - User Requirements
  - Suitability
  - Test Equipment
  - Examination, Installation, & Maintenance
  - Test Specifications
  - Evaluation
- Field/Practical Exercises

Vehicle Scales Advanced
- Initial Verification

Railroad Track
- Common traits
- Contents of EPO
  - Examination Specifications
  - User Requirements
  - Suitability
  - Test Equipment
  - Examination, Installation, & Maintenance
  - Test Specifications
  - Evaluation
- Field/Practical Exercises

Hopper
- Common traits
- Contents of EPO
  - Examination Specifications
  - User Requirements
  - Suitability
  - Test Equipment
  - Examination, Installation, & Maintenance
  - Test Specifications
  - Evaluation
- Field/Practical Exercises

Point-of-Sale Scales
- Common traits
- Examination Specifications
- User Requirements
- Suitability
- Test Equipment
- Examination, Installation, & Maintenance
- Test Specifications
- Evaluation
- Field/Practical Exercises

Precision Scales Class I/II
- Common traits
- Examination Specifications
- User Requirements
- Suitability
- Test Equipment
- Examination, Installation, & Maintenance
- Test Specifications
- Evaluation
- Field/Practical Exercises

PDC 2007 Final Report
Appendix C – National Training Curriculum Outline

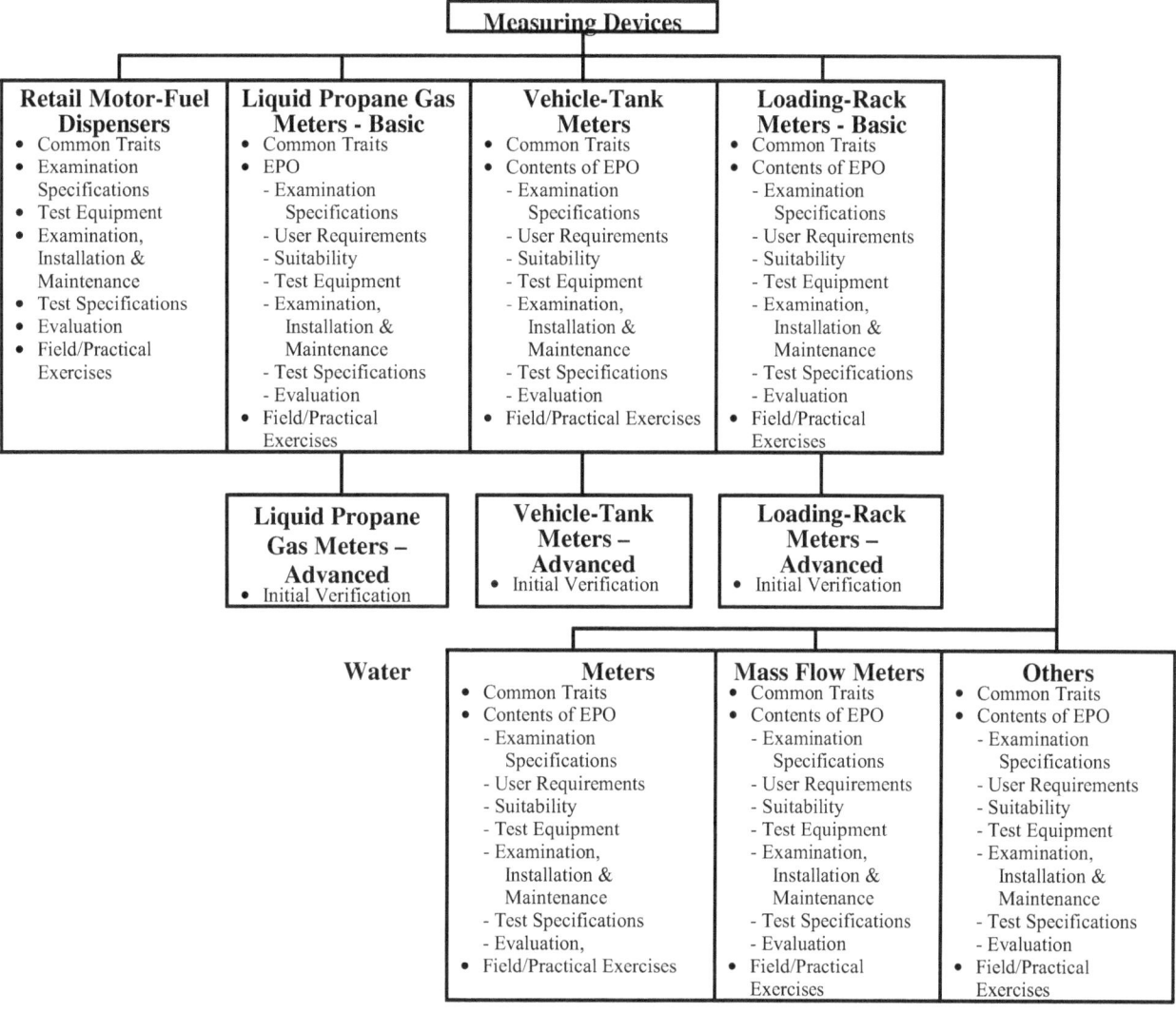

PDC - C3

PDC 2007 Final Report
Appendix C – National Training Curriculum Outline

Weights & Measures Administration

Weights & Measures Administration
- Understanding the Commercial Measurement System
- Responsibilities of W&M Regulatory Official
  - Consumer Protection
  - Fair Competition
  - Facilitating Value Comparisons
- Funding Considerations
  - Licensing of W&M Devices
  - Licensing of Service Agencies
  - Conflicts of Interest
- Roles of Stakeholders
  - Manufacturers
  - Packagers
  - Retailers
  - Service Agencies
- Powers & Duties of Officials
  - Weighmaster Considerations
- Type Evaluation, Initial Verification & Subsequent Inspection
  - Economic Impact
- Complete Scope of Weights & Measures Inspections
- Concurrent Federal & State Jurisdiction
- Federal Pre-emption
- Organizational Structure
- Budget
- Personnel
  - Knowledge, Skills & Abilities
  - Training
- Strategic Planning & Goals
- Education
  - Officials
  - Administrative Staff
  - Public
- Publicity
- Public Relations
- Communication
- Record Keeping
- Forms
- Legal Considerations
  - Due Process
  - Stop Orders
  - Standards Development
  - Prosecution
  - Court

Laboratory Metrology Administration
- Purpose of the Laboratory
- Responsibilities of the Metrologist
- NIST Expectations of the Laboratory
- Rationale for the Requirements for Recognition of the Laboratory
- Important Considerations for Laboratory Operation
- Factors Driving Changes in Laboratory Requirements
- Quality System
- NVLAP Accreditation
- Hierarchy of Laboratory Standards
- Calibration Intervals for All Standards
- Annual RMAP Round Robins & Training
- Laboratory Facility Requirements
- Uncertainty Analysis
- Management Review of Laboratory Operations

Laboratory Metrology

Concepts - Basic
- Introduction
- Statistics
- Uncertainty
- Measurement Assurance
- Standard Operating Procedures
  - Mass
  - Volume
- Calibration
- Calculations
- Traceability

Concepts – Advanced
- Program Philosophy
- New Technology
- Calibration Design Concepts
- Computerized Workshops
- Statistics for Quality
  - t-tests
  - F-tests
- Workshop on Errors
- Advanced Uncertainties
- Software Workshop
- Integration of Advanced Concepts

THIS PAGE INTENTIONALLY LEFT BLANK

Appendix D

NCWM Curriculum Work Plan
Revised July 9, 2007

Segment / Subject

Level 1 /Level 2/ Level 3

0.   W&M General/State Policies
0.1   Introduction to W&M Programs
0.2   W&M Laws and Regulations
0.3   Official Powers & Duties
0.4   Field Standards & Test Equipment
0.5   State Program Scope and Overview

1. W&M Administration
1.1 Program Organization
1.2   Administration Functions (Personnel, Management, Budget, Safety, etc.)
1.3   Legislation and Regulations (Interaction with legislature, stakeholders, industry)
1.4   Regulatory Control (Device inspection, commodities, complaints)

2. Laboratory Metrology
2.1   NIST Basic Metrology
2.2   NIST Advance Metrology

3.   Device Control Program
3.0   Introduction to Device Control
3.0.a Safety Considerations
3.1 Weighing Systems General
3.1.1   Static Electronic Weighing Systems, General
3.1.2   Static Mechanical and Hybrid Weighing Systems, General
3.1.3   Dynamic Weighing Systems, General
3.1.4   Precision Weighing Systems Class I and II
3.1.5   Small Capacity Weighing Systems Class I
3.1.6   Medium Capacity Weighing Systems Class III
3.1.7   Vehicle Scale Class III or IIIL
3.1.8 Railroad Track Scales
3.1.9 Hopper Scale Systems
3.1.10   Automatic Bulk Weighing Systems
3.1.11 Automatic Weighing Systems
3.1.12   Belt Conveyor Weighing Systems
3.1.13   Multiple Dimension Measuring Systems
3.1.14   In-Motion Railroad Track Scales
3.1.15 In-Motion Monorail Scales
3.1.16   Other Specialty Weighing Systems
3.2   Dynamic Volume Measuring Systems, General
3.2.1   Retail Motor Fuel Dispensers
3.2.2   Loading Rack and Other Stationary Metering Systems
3.2.3   Vehicle Tank Meter Systems
3.2.4 Milk Metering Systems
3.2.5 Water Meters
3.2.6   LPG/Anhydrous Ammonia Liquid Metering Systems

3.2.7 LPG Vapor Meter Systems
3.2.8 Mass Flow Metering Systems
3.2.9 Other Metering Systems (Cryogenics, Carbon Dioxide, etc.)
3.3 Static Volume Measuring Systems, General
3.3.1 Liquid Measures
3.3.2 Farm Milk Tanks
3.3.3 Dry Measures
3.4 Other Measuring Systems
3.4.1 Taximeters and Odometers
3.4.2 Wire and Cordage Measuring Systems
3.4.3 Linear Measures
3.4.4 Timing Devices
3.4.5 Weights
3.5 Quality Measuring Devices
3.5.1 Grain Moisture Meters
3.5.2 NIR Grain Analyzers
3.5.3 Fat Measuring Devices

4. Market Practices, Laws and Regulations (NIST HB 130)
4.0.a Safety Considerations
4.1 General Provisions of NIST Handbook 130
4.1.1 Packaging and Labeling Regulations
4.1.2 Method of Sale Regulations
4.1.3 Price Verification
4.1.4 Test Purchases
4.1.5 E-Commerce
4.1.6 Quality of Automotive Fuels and Lubricants
4.2 Package Net Contents Control, NIST HB 133 (General)
4.1.1 Packages Labeled by Weight, Standard and Random
4.1.2 Packages Labeled by Weight, Special
4.2.3 Packages Labeled by Liquid Volume, Volume and Gravimetric
4.2.4 Packages Labeled by Liquid Volume, Special
4.2.5 Packages Labeled by Length/Area
4.2.6 Packages Labeled by Count
4.2.7 Other Package Types

Note: Initial Verification has been intentionally left off this listing and will be addressed later.

NTEP Committee 2007 Final Report

Report of the
National Type Evaluation Program (NTEP) Committee

Don L. Onwiler, Chairman
Program Manager
Nebraska Department of Weights and Measures

Reference
Key Number

500 INTRODUCTION

The National Type Evaluation Program (NTEP) Committee (hereinafter referred to as "Committee") submits its report for consideration by the 92nd National Conference on Weights and Measures (NCWM). This consists of the Interim Report presented in NCWM Publication 16 as amended in the Addendum Sheets issued during the Annual Meeting that was held July 8 - 12, 2007, in Salt Lake City, Utah. The Committee considered communications received prior to and during the 92nd Annual Meeting that are noted in this report.

Table A identifies the agenda items in the report by Reference Key Number, Item Title, and Page Number. The item numbers are those assigned in the Committee's Interim Meeting Agenda. A voting item is indicated with a **"V"** after the item number or, if the item was part of the consent calendar, by the suffix " **VC**." An item marked with an **"I"** after the reference key number is an information item. An item marked with a **"W"** was withdrawn by the Committee and generally will be referred to the regional weights and measures associations because it either needs additional development, analysis, and input or does not have sufficient Committee support to bring it before the NCWM. Table B lists the appendices to the report, and Table C provides a summary of the results of the voting on the Committee's items and the report in entirety.

This report contains many recommendations to revise or amend National Conference on Weights and Measures (NCWM) Publication 14, Administrative Procedures, Technical Policy, Checklists, and Test Procedures or other documents. Proposed revisions to the publication(s) are shown in **bold face print** by ~~striking out~~ information to be deleted, and __underlining__ information to be added. Requirements that are proposed to be nonretroactive are printed in *italics*.

Note: The policy of NIST is to use metric units of measurement in all of its publications; however, recommendations received by the NCWM technical committees have been printed in this publication as they were submitted and may, therefore, contain references to inch-pound units.

Table A
Index to Reference Key Items

Reference Key Number	Title of Item	Page
500	**INTRODUCTION**	1
1.	Test Data Exchange Agreements	3
2.	NTEP Participating Laboratories and Evaluation Reports	4
3.	NTETC Sector Reports	5
4.	NTEP Participation in U.S. National Work Group on Harmonization of NIST Handbook 44, NCWM Publication 14, and OIML R 76 and R 60	7
5.	Software Sector	7
6.	Conformity Assessment Program	9
7.	NTEP Certification of Residential-type Water and Vapor Meters	9
8.	Use of NTEP Logo	10
9.	NTEP Certification of Medical Scales	15

Table B
Appendices

Appendix	Title	Page
A	NTEP Certification Mark License	A1
B	NTETC Grain Analyzer Sector Meeting Summary	B1
C	NTETC Measuring Sector Meeting Summary	C1
D	NTETC Weighing Sector Meeting Summary	D1
E	NTETC Software Sector Meeting Summary	E1

Table C
Glossary of Acronyms*

Acronym	Definition	Acronym	Definition
BIML	Bureau of International Legal Metrology	IR	International Recommendation
BOD	NCWM Board of Directors	MAA	Mutual Acceptance Arrangement
CC	NTEP Certificate of Conformance	NCWM	National Conference on Weights and Measures
CD	Committee Draft[1]	NTETC	National Type Evaluation Technical Committee
CIML	International Committee of Legal Metrology	OIML	International Organization of Legal Metrology
CPR	Committee on Participation Review	PTB	Physikalisch-Technischen Bundsanstalt
DD	Draft Document[2]	R	Recommendation
DR	Draft Recommendation[2]	SC	Subcommittee
DV	Draft Vocabulary[2]	TC	Technical Committee
DoMC	Declarations of Mutual Confidence	WD	Working Document[3]

[1] CD: a draft at the stage of development within a technical committee or subcommittee; in this document, successive drafts are numbered 1 CD, 2 CD, etc.

[2] DD and DR: draft documents approved at the level of the technical committee or subcommittee concerned and sent to BIML for approval by CIML.

[3] WD: precedes the development of a CD; in this document, successive drafts are number 1 WD, 2 WD, etc.

* Explanation of acronyms provided by OIML.

Table D
Voting Results

Reference Key Number	House of State Representatives		House of Delegates		Results
	Yeas	Nays	Yeas	Nays	
500 (In its entirety) voice vote	All Yeas	No Nays	All Yeas	No Nays	Passed

---
Details of All Items
(In Order by Reference Key Number)
---

1. Test Data Exchange Agreements

Background/Discussion: This item was included on the Committee's agenda in 1998 to provide an update on NTEP's work to establish bilateral and multilateral agreements. Under such agreements and arrangements, manufacturers would be able to submit their equipment to any of the participating countries for testing to OIML-recommended requirements. The resulting test data would be accepted by other participants as a basis for issuing each country's own type approval certificate. Following is a report on the three types of test data exchange agreements:

Mutual Acceptance Arrangement (MAA):

Background: During the 2006 NCWM Interim Meeting, the full NCWM Board carefully considered this issue and the recommendation of the NTEP Committee. Significant discussion was held on this issue with the primary focus on the desire to become a utilizing member (Country B) for the DoMC that will cover OIML R 60 Load Cells. Significant comments also came from the full membership during the 2006 NCWM Interim Meeting open hearings on this issue. In addition, a very large group attended a late evening meeting on this topic. The participants in this meeting asked many important questions and demonstrated a high level of interest in the NCWM's direction regarding MAAs. The NTEP Committee acknowledges and thanks this group of participants for their significant contributions in discussing this issue.

The decision of the Board was to accept the recommendation of the NTEP Committee and indicate the intention of signing the DoMC for OIML R 60 Load Cells as a utilizing participant. The NCWM Board indicated no interest at this time in being an issuing participant for OIML R 76 "Non-automatic Weighing Instruments" (NAWI). The intent is to investigate various alternatives and determine if a laboratory can be established that will allow the NCWM to be an issuing participant in the DoMC for OIML R 76. It was clearly stated that this laboratory would have to be "viable" and that the NCWM must fully understand the effect such a signing may have on NTEP, existing NTEP labs, and our standards development process in the NCWM. It was also stated that it is not clear at this time if funding for such a laboratory is available.

The DoMC for OIML R 60 was signed by NCWM Chairman Don Onwiler at the 2006 NCWM Annual Meeting.

During the 2007 NCWM Interim Meeting, it was reported that on September 29, 2006, the International Bureau of Legal Metrology (BIML) issued a circular notifying CIML members and OIML Issuing Authorities that the first two Declarations of Mutual Confidence (DoMCs) for OIML R 60 (Load Cells) and R 76 (Non-automatic Weighing Instruments) have been officially published on the MAA pages of the OIML website (www.oiml.org). The publication is in the form of two summaries of the individual registration forms signed by each participant. Five countries signed the R 60 DoMC as both Issuing and Utilizing Participants (an 'Issuing Participant' is one that performs tests and issues certificates under the DoMC), and another eleven countries signed as only Utilizing Participants (Country B's). The United States (National Conference on Weights and Measures, Inc.) is listed as a Utilizing Participant. Seven countries signed the R 76 DoMC as both Issuing and Utilizing Participants, and another eight countries signed as only Utilizing Participants. The United States did not sign the R 76 DoMC. The complete listing can be found on the OIML website.

The NCWM and NTEP look forward to the opportunity to work with our international partners in the DoMC for OIML R 60. The NTEP director reported that NTEP is now prepared to accept OIML MAA Evaluation Reports for R 60 submitted along with an appropriate NTEP application. After review of the information contained in the OIML Evaluation Report and any additional requirements that may be required, and provided that all requirements have been met, an NTEP Certificate of Conformance (CC) will be issued.

Now that the DoMCs for R 60 and R 76 have been signed, the 'definitive' CPR is established (the NCWM is a member). All Issuing Participants of the DoMC must now issue OIML MAA Certificates for R 60 and R 76 devices, except for what are being called 'basic' (old-style) certificates that had already been applied for earlier. A termination date for issuing 'basic' certificates was discussed at the 41st CIML meeting in Cape Town, South Africa, in October 2006 and was provisionally set for December 31, 2008. The final termination date will establish when NTEP can no longer issue 'basic' OIML certificates.

OIML TC 3/SC 5 will start revising both publication B 10-1 (MAA) and publication B 3 "OIML Certificate System for Measuring Instruments " in 2007 based on issues that have arisen and been discussed in the CPR and CIML meetings. A number of these issues were discussed at the Cape Town CIML meeting, and several MAA-related resolutions were approved at that time (see the OIML Report in the NCWM Board of Directors' Committee Report, Appendix A) since it was agreed that decisions were needed before the revision process could be completed. TC 3/SC 5 is also circulating to its members for comment and vote a Draft Guide for the application of ISO/IEC 17025 to legal metrology and a 2 CD of the OIML Guide for the application of ISO/IEC Guide 65 to legal metrology.

The BIML has also announced a new CPR and DoMC for OIML R 49 (water meters) with the 'provisional' CPR to be established by January 31, 2007. At this time, it is not anticipated the United States will take part in this CPR.

During the 2007 NCWM Annual Meeting, it was reported that the NTEP director attended the third meeting of the Committee on Performance Review (CPR) in Tsukuba, Japan on June 7 and 8, 2007. One of the agenda items focused on the change in the current policy of the MAA to permit data submitted by a manufacturer to be included in the Evaluation Report. The NTEP Committee views such data as a conflict of interest and unacceptable. The NTEP director strongly expressed this position to the attendees of that meeting. There was no consensus from the CPR to recommend a change in the current policy of not accepting manufacturer's data.

NTEP anticipates having an Evaluation Report submitted soon for a load cell evaluation conducted under the MAA R 60 DoMC.

For further information on the MAA and its implementation, please contact Mr. Steve Patoray, NTEP Director, at (828) 859-6178 or spatoray@mgmtsol.com or Dr. Charles Ehrlich at charles.ehrlich@nist.gov, at (301) 975-4834, or by fax at (301) 975-8091.

Bilateral Agreements: No additional discussions have been held on this topic, pending the outcome of the MAA discussions.

NTEP-Canada Mutual Recognition Program During the 2007 NCWM Annual Meeting, it was reported that both Measurement Canada and the NTEP Labs are engaged in dialog to improve the data exchange under the Mutual Recognition Arrangement (MRA). During the recent NTEP lab meeting, an entire day was spent exchanging information regarding the current MRA for weighing devices. Several areas of improvement were identified, including initial review of new applications to establish an agreed upon test plan for the evaluation. In addition, a training session was conducted to improve the consistency of data collected by the labs. This will help improve the ability of the various labs to more consistently exchange data.

2. NTEP Participating Laboratories and Evaluation Reports

At the 2007 NCWM Interim Meeting, Stephen Patoray, NTEP Director, updated the Committee on NTEP laboratory and administrative activities since October 1, 2006.

The NTEP weighing laboratories met in September 2006 before the meeting of the Weighing Sector in Annapolis. The NTEP measuring laboratories also met in October 2006 prior to the Measuring Sector meeting in Annapolis.

Julie Quinn (MN) reported that Minnesota is interested in becoming an NTEP-authorized laboratory for weighing devices evaluated in the field (e.g., weighing/load-receiving elements, such as vehicle, livestock, hopper). The state has begun to prepare for the required training. It was reported that some final details are now being worked out.

Steve Patoray reported that all the laboratories are now operating with full staff and have completed all equipment upgrades and physical moves and that there have been no other changes in the number of authorized laboratories.

During the 2007 NCWM Annual Meeting, the NTEP Committee Chair announced that Minnesota has been authorized by NCWM as a field laboratory to conduct evaluation on Weighing/Load Receiving Elements.

The NTEP director reported the NTETC Software Sector held its third meeting in May 2007 followed by a joint meeting of the NTEP weighing and measuring laboratories in Sacramento, California. The NTEP director also reported that the backlog in the NTEP labs is now below historical levels and is approximately 25 % below the peak backlog seen during the past year. NTEP continues to assign devices to the appropriate laboratory to distribute the evaluations more evenly and continue to reduce the backlog.

These developments are consistent with the continuing efforts of NTEP to improve the level of service and responsiveness to the industries it serves.

Upcoming meetings:

Grain Analyzer Sector	August 2007	Kansas City, Missouri
Weighing Sector	September 2007	Sacramento, California
Measuring Sector	October 2007	Little Rock, Arkansas

NTEP Participating Laboratories and Evaluations Report

NTEP Application Statistics 10/01/06 - 06/15/2007			
	Previous Quarter	Current Quarter	Total To Date
	10/01/2005 - 06/15/2006	10/01/2006 - 06/15/2007	10/01/2000 - 06/15/2007
Applications Processed	176	179	1649
Applications Completed	194	160	1422
New Certificates Issued	194	160	1523
Certificates Distributed to State Directors	218	154	1523
Certificates Posted to Website	196	164	4067
Current Active NTEP Certificates (12/31/2006)	-	-	1638
	Average Median		
Time for NCWM to Assign an Evaluation	12		8
Time for NCWM to Review a Draft Certificate	9		7
Time for Complete Evaluation (Completed NCWM Assignments)	185 133		

3. NTETC Sector Reports

Background:

Grain Analyzer Sector: The NTETC Grain Analyzer Sector held a meeting in Kansas City, Missouri, August 23 - 24, 2006. A draft of the final summary was provided to the Committee for review and approval prior to the 2007 NCWM Interim Meeting.

The next meeting of the Grain Analyzer Sector is scheduled for August 2007 in Kansas City, Missouri. For questions on the current status of sector work or to propose items for a future meeting, please contact the sector technical advisors:

Diane Lee
NIST WMD
100 Bureau Drive, Stop 2600
Gaithersburg, MD 20899-2600
Phone: (301) 975-4405
Fax: (301) 975-8091
e-mail: diane.lee@nist.gov

Jack Barber
J.B. Associates
10349 Old Indian Trail
Glenarm, IL 62536
Phone: (217) 483-4232

e-mail: jbarber@motion.net

Measuring Sector: The NTETC Measuring Sector met October 20 - 21, 2006, in Annapolis, Maryland. A draft of the final summary was provided to the NTEP Committee for review and approval during the 2007 NCWM Interim Meeting.

The next meeting of the Measuring Sector is scheduled for October 2007 in Little Rock, Arkansas, in conjunction with the Southern Weights and Measures Association's Annual Meeting. For questions on the current status of sector work or to propose items for a future meeting, please contact the sector technical advisor:

Richard Suiter
NIST WMD
100 Bureau Drive, Stop 2600
Gaithersburg, MD 20899-2600

Phone: (301) 975-4406
Fax: (301) 975-8091
e-mail: rsuiter@nist.gov

Weighing Sector: The NTETC Weighing Sector met September 26 - 28, 2006, in Annapolis, Maryland. A final draft of the meeting summary was provided to the NTEP Committee for review and approval during the 2007 NCWM Interim Meeting.

The next Weighing Sector meeting is scheduled for September 2007 in Sacramento, California. For questions regarding the current status of sector work or to propose items for a future meeting, please contact the sector technical advisor:

Steven Cook
NIST WMD
100 Bureau Drive, Stop 2600
Gaithersburg, MD 20899-2600

Phone: (301) 975-4003
Fax: (301) 975-8091
e-mail: stevenc@nist.gov

Steve Patoray reported that the previous year's sector reports could be found on the NCWM website. He also reported that, if contacted, he could supply anyone interested with all previous sector reports.

During the 2007 NCWM Annual Meeting, the NTEP Committee heard the 2007 NCWM Interim Report of each NTETC Sector. This was presented by Steven Cook, technical advisor, and Stephen Patoray, NTEP director. The NTEP Committee also heard and considered several other items recommended by the Multiple Dimension Measuring Device (MDMD) Work Group (WG) and the Automatic Weighing Systems (AWS) WG. In addition, one item related to the laboratory method of test for automatic zero-setting mechanism (AZSM) was also heard and considered. Several items regarding the taximeter checklist also were heard and considered.

All items submitted by the Weighing, Measuring, and Grain Analyzer Sectors were accepted with one exception. The NTEP Committee considered additional comments on the recommendation of the Weighing Sector to change the term "designation" to "identifier." Based on those comments and additional discussion on this item, the NTEP Committee determined the term "designation" currently in NCWM Publication 14 is more precise and the use of this word did not deviate from the intent of NIST Handbook 44.

Recommendations for changes to the NCWM Publication 14 taximeter checklist were also accepted. The review of the taximeter checklist indicated there may need to be a clarification in NIST Handbook 44 and NCWM

Publication 14 regarding taximeters with multiple rate capabilities. The NIST technical advisor will begin to gather information on this item and will keep all appropriate parties informed of any needed changes or clarifications.

The NTEP labs reported that the testing criteria listed in NCWM Publication 14 Digital Electronic Scales regarding Auto Zero-Setting Mechanism is not consistent with the method currently used by all of the authorized NTEP laboratories, Measurement Canada, or OIML R 76. It was the decision of the NTEP Committee that an *ad hoc* procedure be documented for the NTEP labs to reflect the current methods now being used. This item will be submitted to the Weighing Sector for consideration at the next regular meeting in September 2007.

4. NTEP Participation in U.S. National Work Group on Harmonization of NIST Handbook 44, NCWM Publication 14, and OIML R 76 and R 60

Background: The Secretariat for OIML TC 9/SC 1 recently submitted the 2 CD of OIML R 76-1 "Non-automatic Weighing Instruments" to the participating members of TC 9/SC 1 for review, comment, and vote. The 2 CD was developed based on an analysis of the 1992 edition OIML R 76, answers from OIML TC 9/SC 1 members to a questionnaire distributed in May 2002, and comments on the December 2003 WD for R 76. The 2 CD includes the changes to the December 2003 WD and the December 2004 1 CD based upon comments and recommendations of the U.S. National Work Group (USNWG) and other countries on R 76.

The United States submitted 27 recommendations and requests for clarifications to the secretariat of TC 9/SC 1 on the 1 CD and opposed the 1 CD being elevated to a Draft Recommendation. Eighteen of the U.S. recommendations and requests for clarification were accepted by the secretariat, four recommendations resulted in alternate language proposed by the secretariat, and five recommendations were not accepted by the secretariat. The Secretariat provided the United States with a reason why the remaining comments were not accepted.

The Secretariat has already registered the 2 CD of R 76-1 as a DR in order not to prolong the revision process at the technical committee level provided the 2 CD receives approval.

During the 2005 Annual Meeting, NIST WMD asked the USNWG for R 76 and other interested individuals, organizations, and associations to review the 2 CD and submit any comments, along with recommended language and technical justifications to NIST WMD. During the 2006 NCWM Interim Meeting, Steven Cook, NIST WMD, provided the committee with an update to the revision of R 76 and indicated that the United States would vote in favor of the 2 CD.

At its October 2006 meeting in Cape Town, South Africa, the 41st CIML approved DR 7: R 76-1 Non-automatic weighing instruments, Part 1: Metrological and technical requirements – Tests. The DoMC for R 76 will need to be updated to reflect the changes included in the new revision of R 76. Although the review of R 76 has been completed, OIML has indicated a willingness to revisit the Recommendation to consider including a large-capacity class similar to the current Handbook 44 Class III L and the Canadian Class III HD, plus other additional requirements that were identified in the DoMC deliberations. WMD will be working with its Canadian counterparts to develop a North American Heavy-Duty Device Class and Tolerance if R 76 is reopened.

5. Software Sector

Background: The first meeting of the Software Sector was April 5 - 7, 2006, in Annapolis, Maryland.

At this time, the recommended scope of the Software Sector is to:

- Develop a clear understanding of the use of software in today's weighing and measuring instruments.

- Develop NIST Handbook 44 specifications and requirements, as needed, for software incorporated into weighing and measuring devices. This may include tools for field verification, security requirements, identification, etc.

- Develop NCWM Publication 14 checklist criteria, as needed, for the evaluation of software incorporated into weighing and measuring devices, including marking, security, metrologically significant functions, etc.

- Assist in the development of training guidelines for weights and measures officials in verifying software as compliant to applicable requirements and traceable to an NTEP Certificate. Educational material for manufacturers, designers, service technicians, and end users may also be considered.

SOFTWARE SECTOR
Meeting Summary
Annapolis, Maryland
April 5 - 7, 2006

Note: Underlined "D-SW" sections refer to International Document (OIML D-SW) "General Requirements for Software Controlled Measuring Instruments."

Action items:

1. Software identification (model/version, help screen, etc.)
   a. Built-for-purpose
   b. Not-built-for-purpose
   c. Version number or greater
2. Software protection/security D-SW 5.1.3
   a. Identification of unapproved/unauthorized software
3. Storage of data, D-SW5.2.3 and subsections, automatic storing and transmission
4. Software maintenance and reconfiguration D-SW5.2.6
5. D-SW Section 7. verification in the field—needs work
6. Manufacturer documentation to be submitted, change to the NTEP application D-SW 6.1.1
7. Definitions of software-based device, etc.

The group agreed Jim Truex should continue on as Software Sector chairman. Mr. Truex asked Steve Patoray to continue on as technical advisor to the Software Sector. It was requested that NIST consider the role of technical advisor in the future as they currently do with other sectors.

The Software Sector met for a second time on October 18 - 19, 2006, in Annapolis, Maryland. Much discussion was held on the above action items. It was clear that additional work is needed to find consensus on these various items. Additional meetings are needed to complete the work of this Sector. There will be a request to the NCWM Board for additional funding for future meetings.

During the 2007 Interim Meeting, the NCWM BOD reviewed a request from the Software Sector Committee chair, Jim Truex, for funding an additional meeting of the Software Sector during the 2006 - 2007 fiscal year. After considering this item and the potential cost savings with holding the Software Sector meeting in conjunction with the NTEP Lab meeting in May 2007, the NCWM BOD agreed to fund this meeting and direct the Software Sector to begin meeting on a yearly cycle in conjunction with the NTEP lab meeting.

This item will be removed from future NTEP Committee reports. Further updates on the progress of the Software Sector will be found in the annual NTEP Sector Reports in the NCWM Interim Agenda and the Interim and Annual Reports of the sector to the NTEP Committee.

During the 2007 Interim Meeting, the Software Sector chair submitted a request for funding an additional meeting of the Software Sector in the fall of 2007. This request was considered and approved by the NCWM Board. The location and date of this meeting is yet to be determined.

The Software Sector report is included in this Annual Report as Appendix E.

6. Conformity Assessment Program

Background: The Conformity Assessment Program was established to ensure that devices produced after the device has been type evaluated and certified by NTEP continue to meet the same requirements. This program has three major elements: (1) Certificate Review (administrative), (2) Initial Verification (inspection and performance testing); and (3) Verified Conformity Assessment (influence factors). This item is included on the Committee's agenda to provide an update on these elements.

Certificate Review: The question is how this would be accomplished given the limited resources of the NCWM. Work on this item may need to be delayed until resources can be clearly identified in order to proceed in an efficient, thorough, and accurate manner.

Steve Patoray reported that this item continues on the "back burner" until funding can be identified for this project.

Initial Verification: During the 2007 NCWM Interim Meeting, the WG chairman, Lou Straub, received data from several states on small-capacity price computing scales and reported that the pilot of Initial Verification for small-capacity scales has been completed. There were several state and local jurisdictions that submitted information. All data has been forwarded to NCWM staff for safekeeping. It was also reported that Steve Malone, Nebraska, is working on a database format for logging in the data. In addition, Lou Straub reported that the WG continues to develop a checklist for vehicle scales and retail motor-fuel dispensers.

During the 2007 Annual Meeting, the WG chairman, Lou Straub, reported the WG is currently looking for direction from the NTEP Committee on how to proceed to the next step since they have completed work on the checklists for both vehicle scales and retail motor-fuel dispensers (RMFD). The WG has received some data for the vehicle scales checklist. The WG is seeking volunteers for RMFD at this time. Mr. Straub clarified that not all states or jurisdictions need to participate in submitting information to NCWM on initial verification. A subset of states would be sufficient. NTEP Committee chair, Don Onwiler, instructed the WG to proceed with development of additional checklists. The NTEP committee will also consider how to process the data that will be generated from initial verification.

Verified Conformity Assessment Program (VCAP): The WG chairman provided the NCWM Board with a final version of the WG report at the 2006 NCWM Annual Meeting. This report will form the basis of the technical policy. Additional work will be needed. Steve Patoray reported that the NCWM Board at its October 2006 meeting directed him to form a small WG to develop the necessary details to define the program based on the final report of the VCAP WG. Steve reported that the WG had met one time and had identified seven action items. The information will be developed over the next several months and will be sent to others for comment and review. It was reported that the WG plans to make a formal presentation on its progress at the NCWM Annual Meeting in 2007.

During the 2007 Annual Meeting, NTEP Director, Steve Patoray, reported that further meetings of the WG did not occur. He further explained that, based on additional information the WG received, the initial direction of developing a detailed checklist for VCAP was not the correct direction. With this new insight, actual progress on VCAP should begin over the next several months with development of final material based on the current information available and some additional information regarding the selection of a certified auditor. Mr. Patoray anticipates that beta testing of VCAP will take place over the next several months and a report will be given on the status at the Interim Meeting in January 2008.

7. NTEP Certification of Residential-type Water and Vapor Meters

Background: A request was received from one state for NTEP to conduct evaluations and certify residential-type water meters and vapor meters. The main usage of such devices is in sub-metering. A discussion was held on this item at the Measuring Sector meeting in October 2006. There was insufficient representation from the manufacturers of these types of devices to come to a consensus on this item; however, two WGs were formed consisting of interested parties regarding these device types. The Sector chairman, Mike Keilty, wrote a letter to be sent to device manufacturers of these device types with a request for comments, recommendations, and additional information on sub-metering standards and policies from other agencies and municipalities.

At the 2007 NCWM Interim Meeting, Steve Patoray reported that these items were discussed at the most recent Measuring Sector meeting in October 2006. Mike Keilty, Measuring Sector Chair, reported that he had begun to contact interested parties and other associations interested in this type of certification. Comments during the open hearing during the meeting suggested that NTEP might also need to be concerned with other federal or state agencies that may also regulate these types of devices. The Measuring Sector will continue to work on this item.

The NTEP Committee reported that this item will be removed from its agenda, but information may be found in future Measuring Sector reports.

During the 2007 NCWM Annual Meeting, the NTEP Committee agreed on the following position regarding the evaluation of water meters:

> Due to the need for certification of these types of devices in sub-metering applications, NTEP should proceed with development of a checklist for these types of devices. It has been noted that California currently has checklists for both of these device types and has many years of experience certifying these devices at the state level. NTEP will utilize these current checklists as much as possible in developing checklists for Publication 14.

The NTETC Measuring Sector chair, Michael Keilty, reported to the NTEP Committee that he has been in contact with the American Waterworks Association (AWWA) and has attended a recent meeting of this organization. He has passed along information regarding NCWM and NTEP, along with contact information, to this organization.

8. Use of NTEP Logo

Background: The NTEP logo is a registered trademark of the NCWM. NCWM Publication 14 Administrative Policy provides some parameters on the appropriate use of the logo. Over the past several months, NTEP has been attempting to resolve an issue of misuse of the NTEP logo. During this time, the NTEP Committee and the NCWM Board have discussed developing a systematic method of addressing misuse of the NTEP logo in the future. A WG was formed during the 2006 Annual Meeting with the charge to develop draft form letters that could be used by NTEP to inform anyone believed to be misusing the NTEP logo. Additionally, NCWM staff was directed by the Board to obtain advice from legal counsel as to the appropriate methods of deterring misuse of the logo. Legal counsel recommended that a license agreement be implemented between the NCWM and anyone wishing to use the NTEP logo. This agreement would provide allowances and limitations on the use of the logo. The license agreement, along with form letters drawn up by legal counsel, was submitted to the NCWM Board for discussion. The Board has recognized that this change in policy relating to the use of the NTEP logo is significant. Therefore, the NTEP Committee presented the proposed license agreement for review and requested comments from NCWM membership during the 2007 Interim Meeting. A draft copy of the license agreement can be found in Appendix A.

During the NCWM Interim Meeting, the NCWM Board and NTEP Committee reported they received and reviewed several comments, suggestions, and questions submitted prior to the NCWM Interim Meeting. These questions and comments were forwarded to legal counsel for review and comment. The comments from legal counsel were all forwarded to the BOD members for review. Several comments were heard by the NTEP Committee during the open hearings. All of these comments were considered and discussed fully.

One suggestion was that the act of agreeing to NTEP policy for use of the NTEP logo could be incorporated into the application for an NTEP evaluation rather than signing a separate license agreement. The NTEP Committee agreed this approach would be much simpler, but that it only addressed holders of NTEP CCs and would apply only to a single CC. After additional discussion and suggestions from members, the NTEP Committee decided to use the invoice for annual maintenance fees as the vehicle to reaffirm agreement by holders of CCs to adhere to NTEP policy for use of the logo. No additional fees will be applied. For those who do not hold an active CC, but still wish to use the NTEP logo, they will be required to sign a license agreement. A one-time fee will be assessed to non-holders of certificates to obtain the privilege to use the NTEP logo in the marketing of goods or services. The amount of the fee is yet to be determined.

Additional work will be required for the NCWM BOD to review and approve the final language of the NTEP Logo License Agreement. This additional work will take place at the BOD meeting in May 2007. Appendix A provides information on current proposed changes to the NTEP Administrative Policy, a list of questions about the license agreement from the BOD with response from counsel, an amended license agreement, and a list of questions from an NCWM member with responses from counsel.

Note: There may be additional changes to NCWM Publication 14 Administrative Policy based on the input from the members at the NCWM Interim Meeting and advice of counsel to implement these suggestions.

During the open hearings of the 2007 NCWM Annual Meeting, the NTEP Committee presented the "NTEP Logo Usage Guideline" to the membership for comment. The final document, approved by the NTEP Committee, is below:

NTEP Logo Usage Guideline

The NTEP Logo is much more than a certification mark - it is the public face of our organization. It is a mark that clients covet and consumers seek out. It is a powerful symbol, which represents both a company's concern and regard for its consumers, and recognition that the device type has demonstrated the capability of meeting the requirements of NIST Handbook 44.

A. Use the NTEP Logo

Manufacturers use the NTEP Logo to demonstrate to clients their commitment to meeting the requirements of NIST Handbook 44.

1. The NTEP Logo increases the acceptance of your product or service. Your clients, potential clients, regulators, retailers, and dealers are all more inclined to accept products, advertising and promotion that bear the NTEP Logo.

2. The NTEP Logo builds confidence and trust in your product. When your clients see the NTEP Logo on your product or in an advertisement, they know that the product has been evaluated by a third-party, non-biased organization and has successfully demonstrated its capability to meet the requirements of NIST Handbook 44.

3. The NTEP allows for easier entry into new markets. Whether it is a new industry segment or a new international market, the NTEP Logo on product packaging, advertising and literature makes it easier to reach potential clients.

4. The NTEP Logo provides a faster communications tool. The challenge for any company is to communicate product performance quickly and effectively. The NTEP Logo is one tool that does this. It is a small mark with a giant message.

5. The NTEP Logo reassures clients. Per NIST Handbook 44, NTEP Certified devices must be identified with the NTEP CC Number, Make, Model and Serial/Version Number.

B. Language Guidelines

An Explanation of the NTEP Logo will help clarify the meaning of "NTEP Certified." Effective use of the NTEP Logo in advertising and promotional materials is a matter of repetitive and consistent visual design. Following these guidelines allows you to reinforce the importance of NTEP Certification and gain valuable benefits for your organization in the marketplace.

Please consult the NTEP Director or NCWM Headquarters for guidance on specific products.

NTEP Committee 2007 Final Report

~~Acceptable/Unacceptable~~ **Preferred** Language for Use with the NTEP Logo in Advertising or Promotional Materials

Note: The "C" in "Certified" and in "Certification" should be capitalized when used immediately before or after NTEP and when referring to NTEP Certification.

~~Acceptable~~ **Preferred** Language: (in addition to that found in NCWM Publication 14 Administrative Policy

NTEP Certified
NTEP Certification
NTEP CC
Certified by NTEP
Evaluated and Certified by NTEP
ABC's ~~(company)~~ product is ~~c~~**C**ertified by NTEP to applicable requirements of NIST Handbook 44.

~~Unacceptable Language~~

~~NTEP Approved~~
~~Approved by~~
~~Verified by~~
~~Seal or Seal of Approval~~
~~Meets NTEP requirements~~
~~Legal-for-Trade or LFT~~
~~Best in Class~~
~~Implying NCWM, Inc. or NTEP are government agencies/organizations~~

C. Guidelines for Literature and Advertising

NOTE: Whenever the NTEP Logo or language related to NTEP is used, NCWM suggests that the applicable NTEP Certificate of Conformance Number (NTEP CC) be provided.

For use on letterhead, business cards, placards, print ads, Internet, and other promotional materials.

Size
For visibility and legibility, it is recommended that the NTEP Logo be reproduced no smaller than 3/8 inches (.9525 cm) in diameter in print materials.

Position
The NTEP logo should not be angled or rotated

Visibility
The NTEP Logo shall not be cropped. The mark must be 100 % visible and the NTEP letters must be legible.

NOT ACCEPTABLE
The mark shall not appear in a manner that may directly or indirectly represent non-certified products/systems as Certified by NTEP.

Color Options

The NTEP Logo comes in two versions:

Black and White
The NTEP Logo may appear White and Black

Screen
The black and white NTEP Logo can be screened back in color if desired. ~~(this may need an example)~~

Or

Color
The Pantone colors are Pantone Black, Pantone Red 032, Pantone Yellow 018

No variations in the color scheme are allowed.

No other color schemes or styles are acceptable.

Photo ready artwork is available from NCWM Headquarters.

Additional Guidelines:

1. These NTEP Logo guidelines apply when using the NTEP Logo directly on a product.

2. Please contact the NTEP Director if you have questions regarding the use of the NTEP Logo on a specific product line.

3. The NTEP logo is a registered trademark of NCWM, INC. No company or person shall apply or use the NTEP Logo or language related to NTEP in connection with a product or represent in any way that the product is certified until an NTEP Certificate of Conformance is issued for that device. NCWM may pursue legal recourse if the mark is misused.

4. Rectangular Box under the NTEP Logo: When it is necessary to explain details regarding a specific certification, or include the NTEP CC Number, a rectangular box ~~shall~~ **may** be placed under the NTEP Logo.

The example~~s~~ below demonstrate~~s~~ use of a rectangular box.

Size Text in proportion to the NTEP Logo.

Specifications for text in the box:
Font: Text in the box should be Arial bold and legible
Gotham may be substituted for Arial
Color: Black
Box Dimensions: Typically, the text in the box should not exceed the diameter of the circle

NTEP CC yy-yyyA1

Changes to information in the current Content of NCWM Publication 16

Changes to recommended revisions to NTEP Policies

Page NTEP – **A3**

C. Section U.2 Permissible Use of Statements and NTEP Logo – revise paragraph "b" to state,

> b. The NTEP statement or logo shall only be used by person(s) or organization(s) that have been granted a license by NCWM to use the statements and logo. All holders of Certificates of Conformance and companies that distribute goods that include certified devices may apply for a license. ~~The license is provided without fee or royalty.~~ All licensees must use the statements and logo only in conjunction with products that have been certified in accordance with this publication and NIST Handbook 44. The statement or logo shall never be used in any manner that could suggest or imply that certification extends to a product that is not NTEP certified.

Page NTEP – **A4**

NCWM, in its sole discretion, determines whether its certified mark and statements are properly used in conformance with the license agreement and these policies. Direct questions to the NTEP Director or refer to the NTEP Logo Use Guideline at www.ncwm.net.

After the final section, add the following sentence:

There will be the need to add a reference to Appendix B. of the NCWM Publication 14 Administrative Policy regarding the license fee that will be charged to non-holders of NTEP CC's.

Changes to the Agreement

Page NTEP – **A9**

3. **License requirements and limitations** · The license granted in section 1 is granted subject to the following requirements and limitations:

   a. **Compliance with the NCWM National Type Evaluation Program Administrative Policy, Publication 14 ("Publication 14").** Licensee shall comply with all requirements in Publication 14, as currently existing or later revised. Licensee is solely responsible for keeping itself informed of the current requirements in Publication 14 by reviewing from time to time **the information** posted on the NCWM website.

Page NTEP – **A10**

4. **License fees and royalties** · This license is granted NCWM reserves the right to charge fees or royalties in the future.

Wording has not been finalized for this section. The section will contain information stating that current NTEP CC holders will have no fee or royalty. It will further state that non-holders of NTEP CC's will be charged a one-time license fee for use of the NTEP logo.

Note: A separate document containing answers to frequently asked questions is currently under development and will be posted to the NCWM website when complete.

New Item:

9. NTEP Certification of Medical Scales

The NTEP Committee reported that they had received a request from a manufacturer for NTEP to certify weighing instruments used in the medical field. After discussing this item, the NTEP Committee determined this may be an area for NTEP to consider. Several issues related to these types of devices were discussed briefly, and it was quickly determined that it would be best to instruct the Weighing Sector to begin to review this device type and contact interested parties and other agencies interested in these types of devices. The manufacturer informed the NTEP Committee chair that it will contact other interested parties and will report to the Weighing Sector at the next meeting in September 2007.

This item will not appear in future NTEP Committee agendas but will be reported in the Weighing Sector Summaries.

During the 2007 NCWM Annual Meeting, the NTEP Committee discussed the request and was interested in the concept of providing type evaluation certification for medical weighing devices. The NTEP Committee needs to know if the medical industry wants a standard to reference for these types of devices. The NTEP Committee does not foresee inspection of medical devices by weights and measures officials. One concept would be to provide a unique class marking for medical scales, separating them from commercial devices. This would clarify for the inspector that these devices are not NTEP certified for "commercial" use and are limited to use in the healthcare industry.

This item is presented simply as a concept item. Any further development will be upon the initiative of the manufacturers.

Don Onwiler, Nebraska, NTEP Committee Chair

Mike Cleary, California, NCWM Chair
Judy Cardin, Wisconsin, NCWM Chair-Elect
Charles Carroll, Massachusetts
Randy Jennings, Tennessee

NTEP Technical Advisor: S. Cook, WMD
NTEP Technical Advisor: S. Patoray, NTEP Director

National Type Evaluation Program Committee

THIS PAGE INTENTIONALLY LEFT BLANK

Appendix A

NTEP Certification Mark License

THIS PAGE INTENTIONALLY LEFT BLANK

PFAU ENGLUND
NONPROFIT LAW , P.C.

3213 Driftwood Drive, #622 ♦ Alexandria, VA 22314
Phone: 703/304-1204 ♦ Fax: 252/336-4821
Internet: SPFAU@NONPROFITLAW.COM
ADMITTED IN VA AND DC

EMAIL MEMORANDUM

TO: Stephen Patoray, NCWM

FROM: Sandra Pfau Englund

RE: Recommended revisions to NTEP policies

DATE: August 24, 2006

You asked that I review and provide recommendations on how to strengthen compliance with NCWM's administrative policies regarding use of the NTEP certification mark. Following are my recommendations for revisions to the NCWM administrative policies. I previously provided and recommended NCWM use a certification license to regulate use of the mark. Attached are draft letters that may be used to transmit and request execution of the recommended certification mark license.

Let me know if you have questions or if I can assist further with this matter.

Recommended modifications to NCWM Administrative Policies

A. Section N.5 Withdrawn Status -- add to the *Reasons for Withdraw*
   (4) Use of the NTEP certification mark without a license from NCWM;
   (5) Misuse of the NTEP certification mark.

B. Section N.7 Reactivitation of Certificates of Conformance – revise paragraph "a" to state,
   a. An application for reactivation.... This will require an application, processing fee and evidence that the applicant is in full compliance with all NCWM administrative policies.

C. Section U.2 Permissible Use of Statements and NTEP Logo – revise paragraph "b" to state,

   b. The NTEP statement or logo shall only be used by person(s) or organization(s) that have been granted a license by NCWM to use the statements and logo. All holders of Certificates of Conformance and companies that distribute goods that include certified devices may apply for a license. ~~The license is provided without fee or royalty.~~ All licensees must use the statements and logo only in conjunction with products that have been certified in accordance with this publication and NIST Handbook 44. The statement or logo shall never be used in any manner that could suggest or imply that certification extends to a product that is not NTEP certified.

When reference is made to the NTEP logo or an NTEP CC; it is essential to clearly identify which products are NTEP certified if a copy also includes products that are not certified. References to NTEP must always be located in close proximity to any references to a certified product when non-certified products are shown on the same page.

NCWM, in its sole discretion, determines whether its certified mark and statements are properly used in conformance with the license agreement and these policies. **Direct questions to the NTEP Director or refer to the NTEP Logo Use Guideline at www.ncwm.net.**

D. Section T. Appeal and Review Process – revise the first bullet under T.1 by deleting the initial phrase, "At any stage in the evaluation process." Add a fourth bullet that states, "A licensee may appeal withdrawal of the NTEP Certification Mark License Agreement"

Revise the last sentence of section T.2 (e) to state,
"A copy of the Director's decision shall be delivered or mailed to the appellant, the Committee Chair, and (if appropriate) the laboratory."

NTEP Committee 2007 Final Report
Appendix A – NTEP Certification Mark License

Questions from members of the BOD to Counsel with responses from Counsel:

Issues of Language in License:

- Item 3a on page two - This mentions that the only notification of changes to the contents of Pub 14 is changes placed on the website. I feel this should state that a notification of changes would be placed on the website. As currently worded, it could be read that the actual change or the contents of Pub 14 will be placed on the website. I do not think it is our intention to publish Pub 14 on the web.

    Revised to provide that only a notice that Publication 14 has been revised will be included on the website. Licensees are responsible for obtaining a current copy of, and abiding by the rules included in, Publication 14 at all times.

- Item 3a on page two – first sentence: Strike "as currently exists or later revised." They simply must comply with Pub 14.

    I do not recommend that this change be made. Without this language, it is not as clear that licensees must comply with the publication, even if later revised.

- Item 3a on page two – last sentence: There should not be a conflict between Pub 14 and the license agreement, but if there is, Pub 14 is our standard and it should prevail.

    I disagree. The license agreement is much easier to revise than Publication 14. The license may include minor procedural or other matters not specifically addressed in Publication 14. This language allows more flexibility for the organization.

- Item 3b on page two – first sentence: Change "device" to "type." This term would be more appropriate for software, as an example.

    I made this change. I am concerned, however, about the definition of "device" versus the definition of a "type." Does "types" include all "devices"?

- Item 3b on page two – third sentence: "...in close proximity to the certified product" is ambiguous. Would "in conjunction with the certified product" be better?

    I disagree with this change. The word "proximate" refers to the nearness or location of the logo to the product. The word "conjunction" can be interpreted as merely including the logo with the advertisement. The NCWM has had concerns with advertisement not including the logo near enough to the device/type to which the logo refers.

- Item 3d on page two – I am concerned about the statement of no changes to the mark. What about size, color, etc? See comment on Exhibit A below.

    I do not believe the language of this provision needs to be changed. If NTEP has particular size/color requirements, these items can be included with Exhibit A. If there are no size or color requirements, this also can be stated with Exhibit A. However, the language of this provision makes clear that the logo itself...its design...cannot be changed by the licensee.

- Item 3d on page two and Item 5 on page four – Strike the word "confusingly."

    The phrase "confusingly similar" is a legal term of art with respect to trademarks. Therefore, I did not make this change.

- Item 3f on page two - Providing a sample of all logo usage could be a major effort. I would like to see the request limited to any documentation being reported as misusing the logo. I know this may sound lame but this open a statement makes me nervous. It simply states that copies of all usages could be requested without any additional justification. I know this is not the intent but a small clarification would help.

  I recommend that this provision remain to enable the NCWM to request materials if needed to determine compliance with the license. The license is written for the NCWM's best interests and needs to "police" its trademark. I do not believe that the NCWM is going to abuse the need to get copies.

- Item 3f on page three – Do we need to define "third party"? Also, would our policy require a third party to have an agreement prior to use of the logo?

  The phrase "third party" is a legal term of art to refer to any party not a party to this agreement. I believe any party using the logo needs to sign a license agreement.

- Item 4 on page three – Should all reference to royalties be omitted? What if we decide at a later date to charge royalties? Should we be considering fees now?

  This provision was revised to reserve the right to the NCWM to charge fees or royalties in the future if desired.

- Item 6e on page four - The requirement to update all usage of the logo in 30 days would be very difficult and expensive. While I understand and agree with the intent of this requirement, for some of us it may be very difficult to change all documentation in the 30 days. In some cases we may have thousands of copies of documents that would need to be destroyed. I would suggest the wording be softened a little to provide flexibility.

  This provision was revised to require any materials created or distributed after the rules have changed to be in compliance with the rules.

- Item 6e on page four – The implication here is compliance with all subsequent changes to any portion of Publication 14. Is that the intent or should it be specific to Pub 14 Administrative Policy?

  My understanding is that the NCWM wants NTEP logo users to comply with all provisions of Publication 14.

- Item 10.c. Termination. – Should the license agreement be terminated if a CC holder fails to pay maintenance fees?

  Yes. Is the requirement to pay maintenance fees a part of the requirements found in Publication 14? Or is this a new provision that should be added to the license agreement?

- Item 12.a. – Since the NCWM is incorporated in Virginia, should we reference Virginia law instead of Maryland law?

  The choice of law is based on where the drafter, the NCWM, would like lawsuits handled. Montgomery County, Maryland was chosen because this is where the NCWM's management offices are located.

- Exhibit A – This needs to provide additional information such as size requirements like minimum size, limited colors, and font size. Also, I would suggest that the NTEP offer a "photo ready" logo to limit documentation use.

  All sounds fine.

- Should there be an expiration of the license agreement?

Currently the license is written as "evergreen"...allowing it to continue until terminated. Including an expiration date would entail more administration...requiring staff to contact each license holder at the license expiration date to get them to sign a new license.

Issues of Implementation/Enforcement of License:

- If Handbook 44 changes and a device no longer meets Handbook 44, what happens to devices in the field bearing the logo? I can see changing advertising materials, etc, but what about manuals that came with the device, etc.?

  Changes to Section 6e may handle this concern...requiring only that new manuals be revised.

- In general law-making you can't make a statute ex post facto (after the fact) so I agree that whatever we do now with regard to a license agreement will only have an impact on those who are willing to sign it today. Those who refuse to sign will not be subject to the provisions of the agreement.

  I disagree. What this license does is clarify that the requirements of Publication 14 apply to all users of the NTEP logo. My recommendation is that any organization that wants to continue using the NTEP logo MUST sign the license agreement. The license is being created to enable the NCWM better enforcement of its current policies. It is not changing the requirements of Publication 14.

- My concern is the same enforceability. Who will find the violator and who will enforce the agreement after the violator is found? Are all companies that distribute NTEP devices required to sign the agreement? If not, what if they are the people putting on the logo.

  NCWM staff, I assume, will be the "enforcers." When a new user of the logo is found, or a violator is found, a contact will be made. To maintain its trademark rights in its logo, the NCWM must show that it is using its best efforts to "police" its mark.

- What do we do with the people that are using the logo that are not part of the program?

  This is part of the reason for the license agreement. I understand that there are many users of the logo that are not Certificate holders. By requiring any user of the logo to sign the license, the NCWM has a way to bring all logo users into compliance with its rules.

- To simplify matters when a COC is issued to the applicant we should also include an application for use of the NTEP logo stating the conditions of use, which must be signed and returned if the applicant intends to use the logo.

  Yes, agreed.

- Item 6.e. requires compliance with Pub 14 changes within one month of those changes being made. How will the NCWM notify agreement holders of changes to Pub 14 that may affect the license agreement?

  See change to 3a. The suggestion is that only a notice on the NCWM's website stating that a change to Pub 14 has been made be required.

Sandra Pfau Englund
Pfau Englund Nonprofit Law, P.C.

Revised Draft document based on information above from January 6, 2007

National Conference on Weights and Measures (NCWM)
NTEP Certification Mark License Agreement

This License Agreement ("License") is entered into by and between the National Conference on Weights and Measures, Inc., a Virginia nonprofit, tax-exempt corporation with its principal office located at 1524 Shady Grove Road, #130, Rockville, Maryland 20850 (known in this License as "NCWM"), and

Company name: _____
Company address: _____
Contact name: _____ Contact phone: _____
Contact email: _____
known in this License as the "Licensee".

Background

The NTEP (National Type Evaluation Program) name and logo (the "Certification Mark") is a Certification Mark registered with the United States Patent and Trademark Office and owned by the National Conference on Weights and Measures ("NCWM"). As the owner of the Certification Mark, NCWM has the exclusive right to authorize the parties that may use the Certification Mark and how the Certification Mark may be used. NCWM also is required to prevent the misuse of the Certification Mark.

Generally NCWM authorizes holders of Certificates of Conformance, and third party purchasers of certified devices, to use the Certification Mark provided such parties enter into a Certification Mark licensing agreement with NCWM and agree to use the Certification Mark in conformance with NCWM's policies.

WHEREAS, NCWM is the owner of the trademark shown in Exhibit A and referred to as the "Certification Mark" in this agreement, which Certification Mark is registered with the United States Patent and Trademark Office (Registration No. 2397670) and is used to certify that an apparatus has been found through the National Type Evaluation Program to conform to the design requirements and be capable of meeting the performance requirements for goods of the particular type as set forth in *Handbook 44, Specifications, Tolerances, and Other Technical Requirements for Weighing and Measuring Devices*, of the National Institute of Standards and Technology; and,

WHEREAS, Licensee desires to obtain a license to use the Certification Mark with respect to the distribution or sale of a certified device;

NOW THEREFORE, the parties agree as follows:

AGREEMENT

1. **License grant.** Provided Licensee complies with all the terms, conditions and policies relating to the use of the Certification Mark, NCWM grants Licensee a limited, non-exclusive, world-wide, revocable, non-transferable royalty-free license to use the Certification Mark on or in connection with a certified device.

2. **Reservation of rights.** Except for the limited license rights granted in this agreement, NCWM reserves to itself all right, title and interest in and to the Certification Mark.

3. **License requirements and limitations.** The license granted in Section 1 is granted subject to the following requirements and limitations:

    a. **Compliance with the NCWM National Type Evaluation Program Administrative Policy, Publication 14 ("Publication 14").** Licensee shall comply with all requirements in Publication 14, as currently existing or later revised. Licensee is solely responsible for keeping itself informed of the current requirements in Publication 14 by reviewing from time to time the version the information posted on the NCWM website. NCWM is under no obligation to inform Licensee of changes to Publication 14 other than by posting a notice on its website that the publication has been revised. If Licensee does not agree with any changes to Publication 14, Licensee's sole remedy is to terminate this Agreement as provided herein. If the provisions of Publication 14 and this License conflict, the terms of this License shall control.

    b. **Certification Mark used with certified devices only.** Licensee shall only use the Certification Mark in conjunction with devices types that have been certified in accordance with Publication 14 and NIST Handbook 44, and that hold an active NTEP Certificate of Conformance. It is essential that when a device is included as part of a product that it be clear that only the device, and not the entire product, is certified. When a certified product is shown on the same page with a non-certified product, the Certification Mark must be located in close proximity to the certified product. Licensee understands and agrees that NCWM shall determine, in its sole discretion, if use of the Certification Mark is inappropriate or unclear, and Licensee agrees to revise the use or placement of the Certification Mark, or remove the Certification Mark, as directed by NCWM.

    c. **Advertising Statements.** Licensee understands and agrees that all statements used in conjunction with the Certified Mark must comply with Appendix C of Publication 14. Licensee understands and agrees that NCWM shall determine, in its sole discretion, if the statements used comply with NCWM's policies, and Licensee agrees to revise or remove statements that NCWM determines do not comply with its policy.

    d. **Certification Mark may not be modified.** Licensee shall not modify, enhance or change the Certification Mark or combine it with another mark, or use, adopt or register any marks confusingly similar to the Certification Mark.

    e. **Certification Mark may not be used:** (i) in any manner that is likely to reduce, diminish or damage the goodwill, value or reputation associated with the Certification Mark; (ii) in any manner as would violate the rights of any third parties; (iii) in any manner as would result in any third party claim or any governmental investigation, claim or proceeding alleging unlawful or improper use of the Certification Mark; (iv) on or in connection with any products or services other than the certified devices and promotional materials pertaining to the certified devices; or (v) in any manner other than as a certification mark.

f. **Inspection.** Licensee will, upon NCWM's request and at no cost to NCWM, provide NCWM with samples of all uses of the Certification Mark by Licensee.

g. **Withdrawn Certification.** If at any time the Certificate of Conformance is withdrawn from a device, Licensee will immediately cease all use of the Certification Mark. Licensee also will notify all distributors and customers who may have or promote formerly certified devices that the Certificate of Conformance has been withdrawn and the use of the Certification Mark must cease immediately.

h. **Noncompliance.** Licensee shall immediately and at its sole cost and expense correct any usage of the Certification Mark that NCWM regards as failing to comply with the requirements of this Agreement or Publication 14.

i. **Third-Party Infringement.** Licensee will promptly notify NCWM if it becomes aware of any infringement of the Certification Mark by a third party. Licensee shall have neither the right nor the obligation to prosecute any infringement claims against third-party infringers.

j. **Use of NCWM.** Nothing in this Agreement gives Licensee the right or license to use the marks "National Conference of Weights and Measures" or "NCWM" apart from the Certification Mark as shown in Exhibit A.

k. **Unauthorized Use.** Licensee acknowledges that if it engages in any unauthorized use or reference to the Certification Mark, its right to continue using the Certification Mark may be terminated and that irreparable injury will occur if such unauthorized use continues.

4. **License fees and royalties.** While this license is granted ~~fully paid and without royalty,~~ NCWM reserves the right to charge fees or royalties in the future.

5. **NCWM ownership of Certification Mark.** Licensee acknowledges the National Conference of Weights and Measures exclusive right, title and interest in and to the Certification Mark and acknowledges that nothing in this Agreement shall be construed to provide to Licensee any rights in the Certification Mark except as expressly provided in the Agreement. Licensee acknowledges that its use of the Certification Mark will not create in it any right, title or interest in the Certification Mark other than the limited license rights granted to Licensee in this Agreement and that all such use of the Certification Mark and the goodwill generated thereby will inure to the benefit of the NCWM. Licensee warrants and represents that: (a) it will not at any time challenge the NCWM's right, title or interest in the Certification Mark or the validity of the Certification Mark or any registration of the Certification Mark; (b) it will not do or cause to be done or omit to do anything, the doing, causing, or omitting of which would contest or in any way impair or tend to impair the rights of the NCWM in the Certification Mark; (c) it will not represent that it has any ownership in or rights with respect to the Certification Mark; and (d) it will not, either during or subsequent to the term of this Agreement, adopt, use or register any certification mark, trademark, service mark, trade name, insignia or logo that is confusingly similar to or a colorable imitation of the Certification Mark or any of the NCWM's other marks.

6. **Representations of Licensee.** Licensee represents and warrant that:
   a. It is duly organized and in good standing under the laws of its jurisdiction of organization;
   b. Licensee has taken all actions that are necessary or advisable in order for it to enter into this Agreement;
   c. The person executing this Agreement on behalf of Licensee is authorized to do so;

d. The Agreement, upon its execution by Licensee (and assuming due execution by NCWM) shall be the binding obligation of Licensee, enforceable in accordance with its terms;
e. Licensee will immediately take all necessary action to comply with all changes to Publication 14. All materials and publications will comply with the requirements of Publication 14 at the time that the publications are developed, printed and distributed. Any advertisements that include the NTEP logo must at all times comply with the requirements of Publication 14 in effect at the time the advertisement is published. within one (1) month from the date such changes are made;
f. Licensee will not challenge NCWM's rights under its National Type Evaluation Program, Publication 14, or this Agreement and will not challenge the validity of any NCWM mark.

7. **No warranty by the NCWM. The NCWM provides the license granted in this Agreement without warranty of any kind. TO THE MAXIMUM EXENT PERMITTED BY LAW, THE NCWM DISCLAIMS ALL EXPRESS, IMPLIED AND STATUTORY WARRANTIES.**

8. **Limitation of Liability.** IN NO EVENT SHALL NCWM BE LIABLE FOR LOST PROFITS OR SPECIAL, INCIDENTAL OR CONSEQUENTIAL DAMAGES ARISING OUT OF OR IN CONNECTION WITH THIS AGREEMENT REGARDLESS OF THE LEGAL THEORY UPON WHICH SUCH CLAIM IS BASED AND EVEN IF THE NCWM HAS BEEN ADVISED OF THE POSSIBILITY THEREOF.

9. **Indemnity.** Licensee agrees to defend, indemnify and hold NCWM and its respective representatives, employees, officers, directors and agents harmless against all claims, suits, cost, damages, judgments, attorney's fees, settlements or expenses incurred, caused by, arising from or relating to any breach of this Agreement by Licensee or claimed, obtained or sustained by any third party, whether for personal injury, misrepresentation, or otherwise arising out of or relating to the manufacture, advertising, promotion, use, marketing or sale of the certified devices, provided such claims are not caused by NCWM's negligence or breach of this Agreement.

10. **Effective date, term and termination.**
    a. **Effective date.** This Agreement shall commence and the license granted under the Agreement shall become effective (the "Effective Date") upon the execution of this agreement by both parties.
    b. **Term.** The term of this Agreement shall commence on the Effective Date and shall continue until terminated by a party as provided in this Agreement.
    c. **Termination.**
        i. **Termination by Licensee.** Licensee may terminate this Agreement at any time by providing written notice to NCWM and by discontinuing all use of the Certification Mark. Termination in this manner shall be effective upon receipt of the written notice by NCWM or at such time (not to exceed 30 days after the date notice is received) specified in the notice from Licensee.
        ii. **Termination by NCWM.** NCWM may terminate this Agreement upon thirty (30) days notice if Licensee breaches any provision of this Agreement and fails to cure such breach within such thirty (30) day period. NCWM also may terminate this Agreement upon thirty (30) days notice if it discontinues use of the Certification Mark or modifies the design of the Certification Mark.

iii. **Consequences of termination.** Upon termination of this Agreement, the license granted shall immediately terminate. Licensee will immediately discontinue all use of the Certification Mark and shall destroy all materials in their possession containing the Certification Mark and shall certify to the destruction of such materials if the NCWM requests that they do so.

11. **Compliance with laws.** Licensee will at all times comply with all laws, regulations, ordinances, rules and orders that are applicable to it in connection with its manufacture and sale of NTEP certified devices and the operation of its business generally.

12. **Miscellaneous.**
    a. **Governing Law.** This Agreement will be governed by and construed in accordance with the laws of the State of Maryland as applied to agreements entered into and fully performed therein by residents thereof. Both parties submit to jurisdiction in Maryland and further agree that any cause of action arising under this Agreement shall be brought in a court in the County of Montgomery, Maryland.
    b. **Severability; Headings.** If any provision within this Agreement is held to be invalid or unenforceable for any reason, the remaining provisions will continue in full force without being impaired or invalidated in any way. Headings are for reference purposes only and in no way define, limit, construe or describe the scope or extent of such section.
    c. **Independent contractors.** The parties are independent contractors, and no agency, partnership, joint venture, employee-employer or franchisor-franchisee relationship is intended or created by this Agreement. Neither party shall make any warranties or representations on behalf of the other party.
    d. **Notice.** NCWM may give notice to Licensee by personal delivery, mail, courier, facsimile or e-mail to Licensee's address as identified in this Agreement. Licensee may give notice to NCWM by personal delivery, mail, courier, or facsimile to NCWM's physical address as identified at www.ncwm.net or electronically by e-mail to ncwm@mgmtsol.com. Notice shall be deemed given: upon personal delivery; if sent by fax, with confirmation of correct transmission, on the next business day after it was sent; upon the courier's confirmed delivery if sent by courier; and if sent by mail with proper postage prepaid, five (5) days after the date of mailing. Notices by e-mail shall be deemed given by the end of the business day on which they are sent.
    e. **Entire agreement; Waiver.** This Agreement sets forth the entire understanding and agreement of the parties and supersedes any and all oral or written agreements or understandings between the parties as to the subject matter of this Agreement. This Agreement may be changed only by a writing executed by both parties that expressly states that it is changing the provisions of this Agreement. The waiver of a breach of any provision of this Agreement will not operate or be interpreted as a waiver of any other or subsequent breach.
    f. **Assignment.** Licensee may not transfer its rights or obligations under this Agreement in whole or in part to any third party without the prior written consent of NCWM and any attempt to do so is void.
    g. **Counterparts.** This Agreement may be executed in two or more counterparts, each of which shall be deemed an original, but all of which shall constitute one and the same instrument,

IN WITNESS WHEREOF, the parties have caused this Agreement to be executed by their duly authorized representatives.

For LICENSEE: **For NCWM:**

Signature: _____   Signature: _____

Name: _____   Name: _____

Title: _____   Title: _____

Date: _____   Date: _____

Question from NCWM member with responses from Counsel January 15, 2007

- Paragraph 3 – notice of changes to Publication 14 – a proposed revision to this section provides that notice of any changes to Publication 14 will be placed on the NTEP website. NTEP may also want to consider placing the wording of any changes on the website.

- However, it should be noted that the use of the NTEP logo by certificate holders and others is a privilege, not a right. Therefore, I would not consider requiring licensees to periodically purchase the manual to keep abreast of the requirements for certificate holders to be overly burdensome. This is made truer by the fact that there is currently no fee associated with the license. NTEP must have methods in place to cover its costs of administering the program.

- Paragraph 3(i) – requiring licensees to notify a licensor of any known misuse of a mark is common to license agreements. The value of the NTEP mark is only as good as the enforcement of its proper use. Certificate holders may be more aware of the misuse of the mark by third parties than NTEP. Requiring licensees to call, e-mail or write NTEP if they become aware of a misuse is not overly burdensome and protects the value of the NTEP mark for all users of the mark.

- Paragraph 6(e) – a proposed revision has been made regarding the timeframe for revising publications.

- Paragraph 6(f) – this provision requires licensees, who are gaining the privilege to use the NTEP registered trademark, not to challenge NCWM's rights under its National Type Evaluation Program, Publication 14, or the license agreement and also not to challenge the validity of any NCWM mark. Most license agreements require the licensee not to challenge the licensor's rights to its trademarks. This requirement, at a minimum, should remain in the agreement. NCWM may consider whether to remove the broader requirements not to challenge NCWM's rights under the program itself or Publication 14. It should be noted, however, that using the NTEP trademark is a privilege not a right.

- Paragraph 10(c)(iii) – Once the license is revoked, NCWM must require that the Certification Mark no longer be used. Language regarding deleting the mark from any new materials, particularly advertising materials, similar to paragraph 6(e) may be considered.

    Sandra Pfau Englund
    Pfau Englund Nonprofit Law, P.C.
    Admitted in VA and DC. Practice otherwise limited to matters before federal agencies such as the IRS.

Exhibit A

Certification Mark

Appendix B

National Type Evaluation Technical Committee
Grain Analyzer Sector

August 23 - 24, 2006, Kansas City, Missouri
Meeting Summary

Agenda Items
1. Report on the 2006 NCWM Interim and Annual Meetings..2
2. Report on NTEP Type Evaluations and OCP (Phase II) Testing...2
3. Review of On-going Calibration Program (Phase II) Performance Data....................................3
4. Proposed Change to Publication 14 – Bias Tolerances for Test Weight per Bushel....................3
5. Proposed Amendment to Handbook 44 Section 5.56.(a) to Address Minimum Acceptable Abbreviations for Multi-Class Grain Moisture Calibrations..7
6. Proposed Changes to Handbook 44 and Publication 14 to Address Multi-Class Calibrations (other than moisture) for Near Infrared Grain Analyzers...8
   (a) Proposed Changes to Section 5.57 of NIST Handbook 44:..8
   (b) Proposed Changes to the NIR Grain Analyzer Chapter in the 2006 Edition of Publication 14:...............9
7. Proposed Change to the GMM Chapter of Publication 14 to Avoid Reducing a Previously Evaluated Approved/Pending Moisture Range Due to Lack of Data..13
8. Proposed Changes to Handbook 44 Section 5.56.(a), Paragraph S.4. and to the GMM Checklist of Publication 14 to Modify Operating Instruction Requirements..16
9. Report on "Basis of Determination" in Official Grading Standards..16
10. Report on OIML TC 17/SC 1 IR 59 "Moisture Meters for Cereal Grains and Oilseeds"...........18
11. Report on OIML TC 17/SC 8 Protein Draft Recommendation..18
12. Report on OIML TC 5/SC 2 Document D-SW, "General Requirements for Software Controlled Measuring Devices" and NTEP Software Sector Activities..18
13. Time and Place for Next Meeting..19
14. Encouraging Participation by State Weights and Measures Personnel......................................19
15. Questions Regarding NIR Calibration for Enhanced Nutrient Corn..19

Details of All Items
(In Order by Reference Key Number)

1. Report on the 2006 NCWM Interim and Annual Meetings

The 91st Interim Meeting of the National Conference on Weights and Measures (NCWM) was held January 22 - 25, 2006, in Jacksonville, Florida. Steve Patoray, NTEP Director, reported that the NTEP Committee accepted the Sector's recommended amendments and changes to the 2005 edition of the Grain Moisture Meter (GMM) chapter of Publication 14. These changes appear in the 2006 edition. For additional background, refer to *Committee Reports for the 91st Annual Meeting,* NCWM Publication 16, April 2006.

Amendments and Changes to the 2005 Edition of the Grain Moisture Meter Chapter of Publication 14			
Section Number	**Amendment/Change**	**Page**	**Source**
Section IV. Tolerances for Calibration Performance	Correct language	GMM-7	08/05 GMM Sector Item 8
Section V. Criteria for NTEP Moisture Calibration Review	Add language for Multi-Class Calibration in Case VIII	GMM-9	08/05 GMM Sector Item 8
Appendix D. Sample Temperature Sensitivity	Correct table	GMM-44	08/05 GMM Sector Item 9

The 91st Annual Meeting of the NCWM was held July 9 - 13, 2006, in Chicago, Illinois. No Grain Moisture Meter (GMM) or Near Infrared (NIR) Grain Analyzer items were presented for consideration by the NCWM at the 2006 Annual Meeting.

Steve Patoray reported that the Board of Directors, on behalf of NCWM, Inc., had signed a Declaration of Mutual Confidence (DoMC) with the International Organization of Legal Metrology (OIML) as a "utilizing participant" for OIML R 60 (Load Cells). He explained that a DoMC is an agreement, signed by various bodies in charge of legal metrology activities in different countries, by which a signing country declares it will voluntarily accept test results of type evaluations conducted according to the OIML Recommendations for a specific category of instruments. A "utilizing participant" accepts OIML Evaluation Reports validated by OIML Certificates but does not issue any OIML Test Reports or OIML Certificates under the DoMC. While this specific action does not directly affect grain analyzers, Mr. Patoray pointed out it does show why the harmonization of International Standards (OIML) and U.S. Standards (NIST Handbook 44 and NCWM Publication 14) is increasingly important. Instrument manufacturers may eventually be able to facilitate the type approval of their instruments in various countries, using the "one-stop testing" concept.

2. Report on NTEP Type Evaluations and OCP (Phase II) Testing

Cathy Brenner of the Grain Inspection, Packers, and Stockyards Administration (GIPSA), the NTEP participating laboratory for grain analyzers, reported on NTEP type evaluation activity. In addition to regular grain moisture meter calibration updates, evaluations are currently underway for two additional devices: one for test weight per bushel (an add-on to a currently approved grain moisture meter); and one for a new grain moisture meter. She also reported that the following device types would be enrolled in the OCP (Phase II) for the 2006 harvest:

[Note: Models listed on a single line are considered to be of the same "type".]
    DICKEY-john Corporation   GAC2000, GAC2100, GAC2100a, GAC2100b
    DICKEY-john Corporation   OmegAnalyzer G
    Foss North America   Infratec 1241
    Foss North America   Infratec 1227, Infratec 1229
    Seedburo Equipment Company   1200A
    The Steinlite Corporation   SL95

Ms. Brenner noted that there are now six devices, and the cost to manufacturers for Phase II has increased from $ 5,300 to $ 7,730 per meter type.

NTEP On-Going Calibration Program Fee Schedule For Fiscal Years 2005-2009							
(1) Total Meters (including official meter)	(2) Meters in NTEP Pool	(3) Cost per NTEP Pool Meter	(4) Total Program Cost	Funding Contribution from Participants			(8) Cost per Meter Type
^	^	^	^	(5) NIST	(6) GIPSA	(7) Manufacturers (total funding from mfg's)	^
2	1	$ 19,875	$ 19,875	$ 6,625	$ 6,625	$ 6,625	$ 3,315
3	2	19,875	39,750	13,250	13,250	13,250	4,415
4	3	19,875	59,625	19,875	19,875	19,875	4,970
5	4	19,875	79,500	26,500	26,500	26,500	5,300
6	5	19,875	99,375	26,500	26,500	46,375	7,730
7	6	19,875	119,250	26,500	26,500	66,250	9,465
8	7	19,875	139,125	26,500	26,500	86,125	10,765
9	8	19,875	159,000	26,500	26,500	106,000	11,775

3. Review of On-going Calibration Program (Phase II) Performance Data

At their August 2005 meeting, the Sector agreed that comparative OCP performance data identifying the Official Meter and listing the average bias for each NTEP meter type should be available for annual review by the Sector. Accordingly, Cathy Brenner, representing GIPSA, the NTEP participating laboratory for grain analyzers, presented data showing the performance of NTEP meters compared to the air oven. These data were based on the last 3 crop years (2003 - 2005) using calibrations updated for use during the 2006 harvest season. Noting that the X-axis for Durum Wheat covered a range of 8 % to 18 % moisture although no samples had been received in the 16 % to 18 % interval, Ms. Brenner explained that the moisture intervals (ranges) shown for each grain are the same as those listed on GIPSA Program Directive 9180.61 for the Official Meter. Using a fixed X-axis for individual grain types makes it easier to make meaningful visual comparisons in the results for successive 3-year periods.

In response to a question of why the "sustained bias" rule hadn't been applied to the Official Meter's calibration for corn, Dr. Richard Pierce, GIPSA, explained that as long as the meters are within the allowed tolerance for "sustained bias" there is no requirement to change the calibration.

The Sector acknowledged the effort that had gone into the compilation and presentation of the comparative performance data and thanked Cathy Brenner for a job well done.

4. Proposed Change to Publication 14 – Bias Tolerances for Test Weight per Bushel

Background: This is a carry-over item from the Sector's August 2005 meeting; see the summary of that meeting for additional information.

The Grain Moisture Meter (GMM) Chapter of Publication 14 calls for testing the automatic test weight per bushel (TW) measuring feature of GMMs for accuracy, repeatability (precision), and reproducibility using 12 selected samples of each grain type (for which the meter has a pending or higher moisture calibration). The two tests for accuracy between the meter and the standard reference method are bias (meter versus the standard reference method) and the standard deviation of the differences (SDD). Publication 14 states that, "The manufacturer may adjust the calibration bias to compensate for differences from the type evaluation laboratory in reference methods or sample sets."

Recent NTEP tests revealed that the results of the bias test, which uses only 12 selected samples, are sample set dependent. Because of this, the NTEP Lab did not list specific bias terms for each grain type on the Certificate of

Conformance (CC) for instruments recently evaluated for test weight (TW). Instead, the CC simply indicated that the meter is approved for test weight per bushel measurements for each grain type verified for test weight.

NIST Handbook 44, Section 5.56.(a) Grain Moisture Meters Code, stipulates:

> **S.2.4.3. Calibration Transfer** - *The instrument hardware/software design and calibration procedures shall permit calibration development and the transfer of calibrations between instruments of like models without requiring user slope or bias adjustments.*

This requirement applies to both moisture and TW calibrations. In devices where grain-dependent TW calibration coefficients are imbedded in the CC listing of grain moisture calibration coefficients, there is no problem. Any change in coefficients affecting TW will require a change in the moisture calibration and an amendment to the CC. The concern is with devices that do not treat grain-dependent TW coefficients as part of the moisture calibration. In that case, unless TW coefficients are listed on the CC, there is no way for field inspectors to know if the most recent adjustment coefficients are being used for test weight. The Sector agreed that if TW calibration coefficients are not part of the moisture calibration coefficients then they must be listed on the CC.

The Sector was in general agreement that TW data from the On-going Calibration Program (OCP), (Phase II, was the best measure of how closely a meter is biased to the standard quart kettle method. In response to a question of whether or not Phase II TW data for corn for the entire moisture range or for a restricted (and lower) moisture range should be used, Dr. Pierce replied that TW data above 20 % moisture would not be used.

At its August 2005 meeting, the Sector agreed that the Grain Moisture Meter chapter of Publication 14 should be amended using the following guidelines:

1. The bias test for TW accuracy will be retained.
2. Data from the Phase II On-going Calibration Review Program may be used at the manufacturer's discretion to support a grain-specific TW bias-adjustment change in a TW calibration. TW data for corn will be limited to samples with oven moistures not exceeding 20 %.
3. A new Phase I evaluation is NOT required for a grain-specific TW bias-adjustment change in a TW calibration supported by Phase II data.
4. Any change in a grain-specific TW calibration must be reflected on the CC in a manner obvious to field inspectors.
5. The bias results for TW accuracy for each of the two instruments of like-type submitted for evaluation must agree with each other by the same tolerance that they must agree with the reference method.

The Sector's co-technical advisor, Mr. Jack Barber, was directed to draft proposed wording for the amendment for consideration by the Sector at its August 2006 meeting.

Discussion: The Sector reviewed the proposed amendments to Section VII of Publication 14 to address criteria for TW calibration, which was provided in the 2006 meeting agenda. Cathy Brenner, representing GIPSA, the NTEP Participating Laboratory for Grain Analyzers, reported that based on historical data, meters passing the existing Phase I Test Weight per Bushel (TW) test for bias also passed the proposed test for Δ bias (see guideline 5, above). Furthermore, the majority of the times a meter failed the existing test for TW Bias they passed the test for Δ bias. The few times when a meter also failed the proposed Δ bias test, there was a problem with one of the instruments. The Sector concluded that the proposed test for Δ bias was both redundant and ineffective. Portions of the proposed amendment related to Δ bias were deleted.

One sector member questioned if it was really possible to identify how a meter was configured to measure TW or if there was an identifiable TW calibration on a meter. Mr. Barber explained that the steps involved in arriving at a TW value include: 1) measuring the weight of the grain in the meter's test cell (or separate test "cup"); and 2) converting the measured weight into an equivalent pounds per bushel figure assuming that the test cell volume is constant. Unfortunately, the conversion step is grain specific. The packing density of grain is influenced by the size and shape of the kernels of grain; by the size and shape of the test cell; by the surface condition of the grain; by the distance the grain drops as it loads into the cell; and by the size of the sample being dropped. Additionally, the effective volume of grain being weighed will vary by grain type due to the way the device "strikes off" or removes excess grain from the top of the test cell. As a result, meters use empirically determined grain-specific constants to convert the measured weight into pounds per bushel. The constant is typically a "slope" term in the TW calibration. An additional grain-specific constant, a "bias" or "intercept" term, is sometimes used to provide a "best fit" over the range of available samples.

Answering manufacturer's questions concerning how to handle device-specific adjustments/parameters that were also grain specific, the co-technical advisor, Diane Lee, cited the following paragraphs from Section 5.56.(a) of NIST Handbook 44, noting that the code differentiates between "grain calibrations" (typically the grain specific constants that are identical for all devices of like type) and "standardization adjustments" (the device specific adjustments or software parameters that make all devices of like type respond identically to the grain being measured when using the same calibrations.)

S.2.4. Calibration Integrity

S.2.4.1. Calibration Version. - A meter must be capable of displaying either calibration constants, a unique calibration name, or a unique calibration version number for use in verifying that the latest version of the calibration is being used to make moisture content and test weight per bushel determinations. (Added 1993) (Amended 1995 and 2003)

S.2.4.2. Calibration Corruption. - If calibration constants are digitally stored in an electronically alterable form, the meter shall be designed to make automatic checks to detect corruption of calibration constants. An error message must be displayed if calibration constants have been electronically altered. (Added 1993) (Amended 1995)

S.2.4.3. Calibration Transfer. - *The instrument hardware/software design and calibration procedures shall permit calibration development and the transfer of calibrations between instruments of like models without requiring user slope or bias adjustments.*

*[**Note**: Only the manufacturer or the manufacturer's designated service agency may make standardization adjustments on moisture meters. This does not preclude the possibility of the operator installing manufacturer-specified calibration constants under the instructions of the manufacturer or its designated service agency.] Standardization adjustments (not to be confused with grain calibrations) are those physical adjustments or software parameters which make meters of like type respond identically to the grain(s) being measured.*
[Nonretroactive as of January 1, 1999]
(Added 1994) (Amended 1998)

The Sector engaged in a lengthy discussion. One faction was of the opinion that the Type Evaluation for TW (Phase I) was a one-time evaluation and should not be extended into Phase II with a required annual report. They suggested that manufacturers be permitted to make TW calibration changes at their own discretion supported by existing Phase II or manufacturer-supplied data. Field-testing of TW could be used to determine if individual devices were in compliance. The opposing faction was equally firm in believing if it was important enough for a manufacturer to change a TW calibration, it was important enough to set tolerance limits for performance based on the largest set of data available and to ensure that it could be verified in the field that the calibration changes have been made to all devices of like type in use.

An attempt was made to find a common ground between these two positions. The compromise proposal eliminated performance tolerances but retained the following paragraphs:

Test-weight-per-bushel data from Phase II may be used at the manufacturer's discretion to support a grain-specific bias adjustment change in a test weight per bushel calibration. A repeat of the basic instrument tests and the accuracy, precision, and reproducibility tests cited previously is not required for a grain-specific bias-adjustment change in a test weight per bushel calibration supported by Phase II data.

Any change in a grain-specific test-weight-per-bushel calibration (including changes in grain-specific bias adjustments) must be reflected on the CC in a manner obvious to field inspection personnel.

Steve Patoray, NTEP Director, pointed out that as far as NTEP Publication 14 was concerned, Phase II TW data doesn't exist. [Editor's note: The TW data currently being supplied to manufacturers along with Phase II moisture results are being collected by GIPSA as an internal matter and are being provided to manufacturers as a courtesy.] Consequently, the compromise proposal cannot refer to "Test-weight-per-bushel data from Phase II." With that revelation the Sector agreed by consensus to the original proposal modified only by reducing the tolerances of paragraph III.C.b. to 0.40 for corn and oats; 0.25 for wheat; and 0.35 for all other grains.

It was suggested that CCs include a note telling field inspectors how to determine if the most recent TW calibration had been installed. For example, should the inspector be looking for a specific calibration identifier, or were TW calibration coefficients embedded in the listed moisture calibration coefficients?

Recommendation: Amend Section VII. Additional Type Evaluation Test Procedures and Tolerances for Grain Moisture Meters Incorporating an Automatic Test Weight per Bushel Measuring Feature of the 2006 edition of the GMM chapter of NCWM Publication 14 as follows, to define calibration performance requirements on the basis of data collected as part of the on-going national moisture calibration program.

VII. Additional Type Evaluation Test Procedures and Tolerances for Grain Moisture Meters Incorporating an Automatic Test Weight per Bushel Measuring Feature

A. Basic Instrument Tests:

B. Accuracy, Precision, and Reproducibility

C. Tolerances for Test Weight per Bushel Calibration Performance:

In addition to the Basic Instrument Tests and the Accuracy, Precision, and Reproducibility Tests cited previously, test weight per bushel calibration performance will be monitored using test weight per bushel data collected as part of the on-going national moisture calibration program (Phase II). Evaluation of test weight per bushel performance for corn will be limited to data collected on samples with moisture content not exceeding 20 % as determined by the USDA air-oven reference method.

For up to 3 years of available test weight per bushel data:

a. The difference between the average bias to quart kettle for all samples in a given year and the average bias to quart kettle for any other year shall not exceed 0.80 for corn and oats; 0.50 for wheat; and 0.70 for all other grains.

b. The average calibration bias with respect to quart kettle shall not exceed 0.40 for corn and oats; 0.25 for wheat; and 0.35 for all other grains calculated using the most recent calibration and all available raw data collected within the last 3 years for the entire moisture range (data for corn samples above 20 % moisture will be excluded.)

Failure to meet the requirements in either item a. or b. above will cause removal of test weight per bushel approval status for the affected grain type(s) on the NTEP Certificate of Conformance (CC) for that instrument.

Test weight per bushel data from Phase II may be used at the manufacturer's discretion to support a grain-specific bias adjustment change in a test weight per bushel calibration. A repeat of the basic instrument tests and the accuracy, precision, and reproducibility tests cited previously is not required for a grain-specific bias-adjustment change in a test weight per bushel calibration supported by Phase II data.

Any change in a grain-specific test weight per bushel calibration (including changes in grain-specific bias adjustments) must be reflected on the CC in a manner obvious to field inspection personnel.

5. Proposed Amendment to Handbook 44 Section 5.56.(a) to Address Minimum Acceptable Abbreviations for Multi-Class Grain Moisture Calibrations

Discussion: NIST Handbook 44, Section 5.56.(a) paragraph S.1.2. Grain or Seed Kind and Class Selection and Recording requires that, "The means to select the kind and class of grain or seed shall be readily visible and the kind and class of grain or seed selected shall be clearly and definitely identified." The GMM chapter of NCWM Publication 14 was recently amended to allow multi-class moisture calibrations. A multi-class grain calibration that includes all the NTEP classes of that grain type (e.g., two-rowed barley and six-rowed barley) can clearly and definitely be identified by a single type name (e.g., barley). Similarly, both long grain and medium grain rough rice could be identified unambiguously as "rough rice". However, a multi-class grain calibration that does not include all of the NTEP classes of a grain type may not be clearly and definitely identified using a single grain type name (e.g., wheat). For example, a calibration for "all wheat except durum" cannot be labeled "wheat" because the grain type "wheat" does not include "durum wheat." The acceptable abbreviations (and grain names) in Table S.1.2. of Handbook 44 do not address the groupings and the names that might be used for selecting and recording multi-class calibrations.

Conclusions and Recommendation: The Sector decided that the originally suggested multi-class groups (soft wheat, hard wheat, red wheat, and white wheat) were thought to be confusing and subject to potential misuse. Only the following multi-class groups should be considered for type evaluation:

> All-class Wheat
> Wheat excluding Durum
> All-class Barley
> All-class Rough Rice

A poll of manufacturers present at the meeting revealed that increasing the four-character display requirement of paragraph S.1.2. to eight characters would not be a problem with instruments in current production; therefore, up to eight characters could be used for multi-class group abbreviations. The Sector decided that the sentence specifying the display capacity was not needed because the necessary display capacity was obvious from the number of characters in the longest minimum acceptable abbreviation listed in Table S.1.2.

The Sector agreed that the above multi-class groups should be added to Table S.1.2. and that paragraph S.1.2. should be modified as necessary to accommodate multi-class grain moisture calibrations.

The Sector agreed to recommend the following modifications to paragraph S.1.2. Grain or Seed Kind and Class Selection and Recording and Table S.1.2. of Section 5.56.(a) of NIST Handbook 44 to include minimum acceptable abbreviations for multi-class grain moisture calibrations.

> **S.1.2. Grain or Seed Kind and Class Selection and Recording.** – Provision shall be made for selecting and recording the kind and class *or multi-class group* (as appropriate) of grain or seed to be measured. The means to select the kind and class *or multi-class group* of grain or seed shall be readily visible and the kind and class *or multi-class group* of grain or seed selected shall be clearly and definitely identified. Abbreviations for grain types *and multi-class groups* indicated on the meter must meet the minimum acceptable abbreviations listed in Table S.1.2. ~~Meters shall have the capability (i.e., display capacity) of indicating the grain type using a minimum of four characters in order to accommodate the four-character abbreviations listed in Table S.1.2.~~
> (Amended 1993, ~~and~~ 1995, and 2008)

Table S.1.2. Grain Types and MultiClass Groups Considered for Type Evaluation and Calibration and Their Minimum Acceptable Abbreviations

Grain Type	Minimum Acceptable Abbreviation	Grain Type	Minimum Acceptable Abbreviation
Corn CORN		Soybeans SOYB	
Durum Wheat	DURW	Two-rowed Barley	TRB
Soft White Wheat	SWW	Six-rowed Barley	SRB
Hard Red Spring Wheat	HRSW	All-class Barley*	BARLEY
Hard Red Winter Wheat	HRWW	Oats OATS	
Soft Red Winter Wheat	SRWW		
Hard White Wheat	HDWW		
All-Class Wheat*	WHEAT		
Wheat excluding Durum*	WHTEXDUR		
Sunflower seed (Oil)	SUNF	Long Grain Rough Rice	LGRR
		Medium Grain Rough Rice	MGRR
		All-class Rough Rice*	RGHRICE
Grain Sorghum	SORG or MILO	Small oil seeds (under consideration)	

[Note: Grain Types marked with an asterisk (*) are "Multi-class Calibrations"]

[Nonretroactive as of January 1, 1998]
(Table Added 1993) (Amended 1995, ~~and~~ 1998, 2008)

[Editors Note: In preparing this item for the NCWM S&T review it was determined that the term "Multi-class" is not a widely used term. The Sector may want to consider developing a definition for multi-class calibrations.]

6. Proposed Changes to Handbook 44 and Publication 14 to Address Multi-Class Calibrations (other than moisture) for Near Infrared Grain Analyzers

Background: The GMM chapter of NCWM Publication 14 was recently amended to allow multi-class moisture calibrations. In conjunction with agenda Item 5, the Sector recommends modifications to the GMM Code of Handbook 44 to specify allowed multi-class groupings when user selection of a multi-class group is performed using the group name or an abbreviation of the name. The NIR Grain Analyzer program allows for either individual-class calibrations or "all-class" calibrations for constituents other than moisture, but does not have any provisions for multi-class calibrations for those constituents.

Conclusions/Recommendation: The Sector agreed that modifications should be made to the NIR Grain Analyzer Code of Handbook 44 and the corresponding sections of Publication 14 to correspond with changes recommended in agenda Item 5 in order to cover multi-class moisture calibrations.

The Sector recommends the following modifications to item (a) below in paragraph S.1.2. *Selecting and Recording Grain Class and Constituent* and Table S.1.2. of Section 5.57 of NIST Handbook 44, and to item (b) to amend Section III. Accuracy, Precision, and Reproducibility Requirements in the 2005 edition of the GMM chapter of NCWM Publication 14 to add criteria applicable to "multi-class" calibrations. Proposed additions and changes are shown below:

(a) **Proposed Changes to Section 5.57 of NIST Handbook 44:**

S.1.2. Selecting and Recording Grain Class and Constituent. - *Provision shall be made for selecting and recording the type or class of grain and the constituent(s) to be measured. The means to select the grain type or class and the constituent(s) shall be readily visible and the type or class of grain and the constituent(s) selected shall be clearly and definitely identified in letters (such as HRWW, HRSW, WHEAT etc. or PROT, etc.). A symbol to identify the display of the type or class of grain and constituent(s) selected is permitted provided it is clearly defined adjacent to the display. Minimum acceptable abbreviations are listed in*

Table S.1.2. ~~*Meters shall have the capability (i.e., display capacity) of indicating the grain type using a minimum of four characters in order to accommodate the abbreviations listed in Table S.1.2.*~~
[Nonretroactive as of January 1, 2003]

If more than one calibration is included for a given grain type, the calibrations must be clearly distinguished from one another.
[Nonretroactive as of January 1, 2004]

Table S.1.2. Grain Types Considered for Type Evaluation and Calibration and Minimum Acceptable Abbreviations	
Grain Type	**Minimum Acceptable Abbreviation**
Durum Wheat	*DURW*
Hard Red Spring Wheat	*HRSW*
Hard Red Winter Wheat	*HRWW*
Hard White Wheat	*HDWW*
Soft Red Winter Wheat	*SRWW*
Soft White Wheat	*SWW*
All-Class Wheat*	*WHEAT*
Wheat excluding Durum*	*WHTEXDUR*
Soybeans	*SOYB*
Two-rowed Barley	*TRB*
Six-rowed Barley	*SRB*
All-Class Barley*	*BARLEY*
Corn	*CORN*

[Note: Grain Types marked with an asterisk (*) are "Multi-class Calibrations"]

[Nonretroactive as of January 1, 2003]
(Table Amended 2001 and 2008)
(Amended 2003 and 2008)

(b) Proposed Changes to the NIR Grain Analyzer Chapter in the 2006 Edition of Publication 14:

III. Accuracy, Precision, and Reproducibility Requirements

Grain analyzers will be tested for accuracy, repeatability (precision), and reproducibility over the applicable constituent concentration ranges shown in Table 1. Instrument and calibration performance will be individually tested for each grain type and constituent.

Table 1. Constituent Ranges for Type Evaluation				
Grain Type	**Constituent**	**Constituent Range (%) at Moisture Basis (M.B.) Shown**	**Low Moisture Range**	**High Moisture Range**
Durum Wheat	Protein	10 to 18 at 12 % M.B.	10 % - 12 %	13 % - 15 %
Hard Red Spring Wheat	Protein	10 to 19 at 12 % M.B.		
Hard Red Winter Wheat	Protein	8 to 18 at 12 % M.B.		
Hard White Wheat	Protein	9 to 16 at 12 % M.B.		
Soft Red Winter Wheat	Protein	9 to 12 at 12 % M.B.		
Soft White Wheat	Protein	8 to 15 at 12 % M.B.		
"All Class" Wheat Calibration*	Protein	8 to 19 at 12 % M.B.		
Wheat Excluding Durum*	Protein	8 to 19 at 12 % M.B.		
Two-rowed Barley	Protein	8 to 17 at 0 % M.B.	10 % - 12 %	13 % - 15 %
Six-rowed Barley	Protein	8 to 17 at 0 % M.B.		
"All Class" Barley Calibration*	Protein	8 to 17 at 0 % M.B.		
Corn	Protein	8 to 12 at 0 % M.B.	11 % - 13 %	14 % - 16 %
Corn	Oil	3 to 9 at 0 % M.B.		
Corn	Starch	67 to 73 at 0 % M.B		
Soybeans	Protein	30 to 40 at 13 % M.B.	10 % - 12 %	13 % - 15 %
Soybeans	Oil	16 to 21 at 13 % M.B.		

[Note: Calibrations marked with an asterisk (*) are "Multi-class calibrations.]

Grain Type	Constituent	Sample Temperature Sensitivity Test Tolerance	Accuracy Tolerance	Repeatability Tolerance	Reproducibility Tolerance
Durum Wheat	Protein	± 0.35	0.30	0.15	0.20
Hard Red Spring Wheat	Protein	± 0.35	0.30	0.15	0.20
Hard Red Winter Wheat	Protein	± 0.35	0.30	0.15	0.20
Hard White Wheat	Protein	± 0.35	0.30	0.15	0.20
Soft Red Winter Wheat	Protein	± 0.35	0.30	0.15	0.20
Soft White Wheat	Protein	± 0.35	0.30	0.15	0.20
"All Class" Wheat Calibration*	Protein	± 0.35	0.30	0.15	0.20
Wheat Excluding Durum*	Protein	± 0.35	0.30	0.15	0.20
Two-rowed Barley	Protein	± 0.45	0.40	0.20	0.25
Six-rowed Barley	Protein	± 0.45	0.40	0.20	0.25
"All Class" Barley Calibration*	Protein	± 0.45	0.40	0.20	0.25
Corn	Protein ±	0.45	0.50	0.25	0.30
Corn	Oil ±	0.45	0.50	0.20	0.25
Corn	Starch ±	0.45	1.0	0.30	0.35
Soybeans	Protein ±	0.45	0.55	0.25	0.30
Soybeans	Oil ±	0.45	0.45	0.20	0.25

[Note: Calibrations marked with an asterisk (*) are "Multi-class calibrations."]

Two instruments will be tested using test sets consisting of no less than 50 samples for each grain type to be used on the instrument submitted for type approval. (Note: In cases where grain types have multiple constituent calibrations, more than 50 samples may be required to satisfy the range requirements for each constituent associated with that grain type.) The sample set will be screened using the GIPSA official instrument model and reference method. Samples where the official instrument model disagrees from the reference method by more than the Handbook 44 acceptance tolerance will be deleted and another sample will be selected to replace it. No sample set will be used where the standard deviation of the differences between the GIPSA official instrument model and the reference method exceeds one-half the Handbook 44 acceptance tolerance applied to individual samples. Finally, any sample result not within three standard deviations of the mean for the test instrument will be dropped before analysis of the data.

Three replicates will be run on each instrument for each sample, resulting in a minimum of 300 observations per constituent calibration (2 instruments x 50 samples [minimum] x 3 replicates).

Accuracy. The first replicate for each sample will be used to calculate the Standard Error of Performance (SEP) for each instrument with respect to the reference method. Each instrument will be tested individually. The equation to calculate SEP is:

where
$$SEP = \sqrt{\frac{\sum_{i=1}^{n}(y_i - \bar{y})^2}{n-1}}$$

x_i = predicted constituent concentration for the first replicate of sample i

r_i = reference constituent concentration for sample i

$y_i = x_i - r_i$

$\bar{y}$ = average of y_i

n = number of samples in the test set for the constituent calibration being evaluated (n = 50, see Note 1 below regarding "all class" calibrations.)

The tolerance for SEP is shown in Table 2.

If requested by the applicant, data from a 20-sample slope set will be provided for adjusting calibration slope and bias prior to the start of type evaluation testing. No further standardization adjustments will be made during type evaluation testing.

Note 1: ~~"All-class"~~ "Multi-class" *calibrations will be tested using full test sets for all included classes (50 x number of classes). In addition to meeting accuracy requirements (SEP) for the test sets of each individual class, for publication* ~~"all class"~~ *"Multi-class" calibrations must meet the accuracy requirements (SEP) when the data from all included classes are pooled.*

Note 2: A single slope and bias will be used for ~~"all-class"~~ *"multi-class" calibrations.*

Repeatability. The Standard Deviation (SD) of the three replicates will be calculated and pooled across samples for each class. Each instrument will be tested individually. The equation used to calculate SD is:

where
$$SD = \sqrt{\frac{\sum_{i=1}^{n}\sum_{j=1}^{3}(P_{ij} - \bar{P}_i)^2}{2n}}$$

P_{ij} = predicted constituent concentration for sample i and replicate j

$\bar{P}_i$ = average of the three predicted constituent concentration values for sample i

n = number of samples in the test set for constituent calibration being evaluated (n = 50, see Note below regarding "all class" calibrations.)

The tolerance for repeatability is shown in Table 2.

Note: ~~"All-class"~~ *"Multi-class" calibrations will be tested using full test sets for all included classes.* ~~"All-class"~~ *"Multi-class" calibrations must meet the repeatability requirements (SD) for the test sets of each individual class.*

Reproducibility. The results for each of the three replicates obtained for samples in the test set will be averaged for each instrument and the Standard Deviation of the Differences (SDD) between instruments will be calculated using the following equation:

where
$$SDD = \sqrt{\frac{\sum_{i=1}^{n}(d_i - \bar{d})^2}{n-1}}$$

$d_i = \bar{P}_{1_i} - \bar{P}_{2_i}$

$\bar{P}_{1_i}$ = average of three replicates for sample i on instrument 1

$\bar{P}_{2_i}$ = average of three replicates for sample i on instrument 2

$\bar{d}$ = average of d_i

n = number of samples in the test set for constituent calibration being evaluated (n = 50, see Note below regarding "all class" calibrations.)

The tolerance for reproducibility is shown in Table 2.

Note: ~~"All class"~~ "Multi-class" calibrations will be tested using full test sets for all included classes. ~~"All class"~~ "Multi-class" calibrations must meet the reproducibility requirements (SDD) for the test sets of each individual class.

7. Proposed Change to the GMM Chapter of Publication 14 to Avoid Reducing a Previously Evaluated Approved/Pending Moisture Range Due to Lack of Data

Background: At the Sector's August 2005 meeting, Dr. Richard Pierce, GIPSA (the NTEP laboratory), mentioned that the NTEP laboratory is having problems increasing and decreasing "approved" or "pending" ranges of grain moisture meters depending on the data available in the most recent 3 year period. Most Sector members agreed that it didn't seem logical to reduce a range solely because data previously used to justify the range classification had to be dropped from the most recent 3 year period. Further discussion of the issue at that time was dropped because of time constraints.

The present system for determining the range of 2 % moisture intervals eligible for "approved" status uses only the most recent 3 years of NTEP data. An "approved" range cannot be extended by including manufacturer data. When the "approved" and "pending" moisture ranges were originally proposed, it was believed that after a meter had been in the Phase II on-going calibration program for 3 years the "pending" classification would go away because there would always be sufficient data in the 2 % intervals at the end of the calibration data range. Experience has shown that this is not the case. In fact, to maintain even a "pending" classification at the ends of the calibration data range, manufacturers often have to supply archived Phase II data to supplement the most recent 3 years used for the initial NTEP calibration report. With that data, moisture intervals listed as "not approved" on the initial calibration report can be upgraded to "pending" if the bias to air oven is within the approval tolerance for that moisture interval. Confidence intervals are not applied to approval tolerances for use in determining "pending" ranges when manufacturer data are used.

For calibration performance comparison purposes, it seems logical to continue using data from the most recent 3 year period. As new models are added to the On-going Calibration Program (Phase II), comparisons between meters become meaningful sooner than they would have if a longer period had been chosen.

At first glance, it also appears logical to recommend, provided a calibration has not changed, that moisture ranges previously evaluated as "pending" or "approved" not be reduced due to lack of data in subsequent 3-year periods. However, hard to find samples are only one issue. The NTEP laboratory has reported instances where there were quite a few samples in a moisture interval with the samples coming from only one or two growing locations. This resulted in meter to oven biases that varied from year to year depending on the source of the samples. In one meter and one moisture interval, the meter was out of NTEP tolerance using the last 3 years of data but biased within 0.08 of air oven result when using the last 5 years of data.

When it comes to determining how to set operating limits for an individual meter, one would think that using 5 years of available Phase II data would increase the number of samples across the entire moisture range and reduce the number of inadequately represented moisture intervals. However, for some grains no samples have been received in some moisture ranges within the last 3 years or even the last 5 years. There are cases where only one sample is available in a 2 % interval.

Eliminating or even reducing the problems encountered in determining "approved" or "pending" calibration ranges may require not only using more than the most recent 3 years or even 5 years of Phase II data but also limiting the moisture range over which an "approved" or "pending" rating can be granted. In practice, the present distinction between "approved" and "pending" classifications is lost to the user. The upper and lower moisture limits for a device are set using the "pending" range, so any "out-of-limits" warning printed or displayed appears only when the "pending" range is exceeded. Limiting the use of "pending" to a new device that has not been evaluated in Phase II could simplify the administration of Phase II and the annual re-issuing of CCs.

Discussion: The Sector discussed recommending major revisions to the GMM Chapter of Publication 14 that would be based on the following points:

1. Redefine "Pending" to read: A new calibration that has not been validated by on-going calibration data collected as part of the national calibration program.

2. The upper and lower moisture limits for a new device are to be set using the standard 6 % moisture ranges used in device evaluation.

3. Retain the present GMM comparison report based on the most recent 3 years of Phase II data. This report will be used for comparison purposes and for review by the Sector.

4. Limit the use of manufacturer data to the initial type evaluation and first complete season while enrolled in Phase II.

5. Prepare a second calibration report using all available Phase II data on file at GIPSA. This report is to be used to determine "approved" ranges. "Approved" ranges are to be used to set the upper and lower moisture limits for a GMM.

6. The maximum upper moisture interval and the minimum lower moisture interval that can be given "approved" status will be defined for each grain. These upper and lower limits are to be fixed values that do not change from year to year.

Consideration of the above points prompted a lively discussion. Although most Sector members were generally in favor of either redefining or eliminating the "Pending" classification, this approach implied that another method had to be found to determine operating ranges, because "Pending" moisture ranges have traditionally been used to set the upper and lower moisture limits (operating range) for each calibration. Manufacturers objected to using a single fixed range for all types of devices, noting that some technologies were more accurate than others at high moistures. They preferred an option that would allow them to extend competitively the operating range and objected to being restricted by limitations in the Phase II sample collection system. The suggestion that CCs carry the notation, "Evaluated over the moisture range of __ % to __ %, and certified for use over the range of __ % to __ %," was rejected on the grounds that an NTEP certificate was not intended to be a marketing tool. The Sector was also of the opinion that a 6 % operating range was too restrictive for a new device.

The question of how operating limits should be determined was temporarily set aside to consider fixed ranges for certification/verification of moisture calibrations. There was general agreement that the ranges had to be wide enough to encompass the moisture ranges used in the market, but there was concern that choosing ranges that were too wide would lead to the present problem of insufficient samples. Dr. Richard Pierce, GIPSA, distributed a page from the USDA/GIPSA Moisture Handbook that listed the moisture ranges supported by GIPSA for each grain type, suggesting that these moisture ranges might be considered for use as the fixed ranges for NTEP Phase II verification. Many Sector members believed that these ranges were too wide to be supported by 3 years (or even 5 years) of NTEP Phase II data. Durum Wheat, with a "GIPSA supported" range of 7 % to 20 %, had only four samples in the 6 % to 8 % moisture interval and only one sample in the 18 % to 20 % interval for the most recent 3 years of Phase II data. Similar sample shortages were noted for most of the other NTEP grains. A decision on the specific fixed ranges to be used for certification/verification of moisture calibrations was left for further study.

Several "what if" questions were asked regarding how fixed certification/verification ranges might work under certain circumstances. These questions and the Sector's response are outlined below.

> Question: What "Certified/Verified" range should be listed for a new device?
> Answer: New devices would be certified/verified over the basic 6 % moisture ranges listed for Phase I tests.
>
> Question: What happens if not enough samples are available to certify the new device for the full range after one year in Phase II?
> Answer: The certified/verified range remains at 6 % until enough samples have been collected in a 3-year period to certify the device for the full range.
>
> Question: Will confidence intervals still be used?
> Answer: Yes, a 95 % confidence interval will be added to the maximum tolerance for each 2 % moisture interval outside of the basic 6 % moisture range.
>
> Question: What happens if a meter is outside of tolerance (even with the confidence interval) on any of the upper 2 % moisture intervals of the full range? Does the whole calibration get rejected?
> Answer: Yes, the manufacturer must submit a new calibration with re-predicted moistures showing that tolerances are met for all 2 % intervals in the full range.
>
> Question: What happens to an existing calibration if not enough samples are available in any of the upper 2 % intervals?
> Answer: A previously verified calibration would not be forced to re-calibrate due to lack of samples.

With these questions answered, it was suggested that the manufacturer should specify the operating moisture range for each grain. This range would NOT be listed on the CC, but would be used to determine when warnings would be displayed and printed to indicate that the displayed/printed moisture content of a sample being measured was beyond the operating range of the device. [See NIST Handbook 44, Section 5.56.(a)., paragraphs S.1.1.(f) and S.1.3.(c).] Steve Patoray, NTEP Director, noted that there was a precedent for evaluation ranges that differed from operating ranges. There are devices that are tested by the NTEP lab over one range of conditions but used over a wider range of conditions. The Sector agreed that allowing individual manufacturers to specify the operating moisture ranges for their devices would make adoption of fixed evaluation/verification ranges for all CCs more acceptable.

Conclusion: The Sector decided that additional study was needed before a final recommendation could be made on this issue. This item will be carried over to the Sector's August 2007 meeting. The following points summarize the Sector's thinking at the close of the August 2006 meeting:

1. The "pending approval" classification will be eliminated. Operating ranges (upper and lower moisture limits) will be specified by the manufacturer. Operating ranges will NOT be listed on CCs.

2. The three most recent years of Phase II data will continue to be used to evaluate calibration performance.

3. Certificates will list a single "standard" moisture range for each grain calibration. These ranges will not vary from year to year. They will be the same for all instruments. (See exception for new instruments.) The "standard" ranges have to be wide enough to encompass the moisture ranges most commonly used in the market (to be determined) but narrow enough to assure sufficient Phase II data will be available (over a 3-year period) to:

   a. permit a new meter's calibrations to be "verified" over those ranges by the end of its third year in Phase II; and

   b. permit existing NTEP certified meters' calibrations to be "verified" over those ranges using the most recent 3 years of Phase II data when the new rules are first adopted.

4. Once a calibration has been "verified," a recalibration will not be forced due to lack of samples.

5. New instruments will be "evaluated" over the basic 6 % moisture ranges for corn, soybeans, and hard red winter wheat. Certificates for new instruments will continue to list the 6 % moisture ranges as the "evaluated" or "verified" ranges until sufficient Phase II data has been collected to allow the new instrument to achieve "verified" status for the full moisture range.

6. Outside the basic 6 % moisture range, tolerances used to require a change in calibrations will continue to include the application of a 95 % confidence interval to the maximum tolerance for each 2 % moisture interval.

8. Proposed Changes to Handbook 44 Section 5.56.(a), Paragraph S.4. and to the GMM Checklist of Publication 14 to Modify Operating Instruction Requirements

Background: Item (d) of paragraph S.4. in Handbook 44, Section 5.56.(a) Grain Moisture Meters requires that operating instructions for the device specify "the kinds or classes of grain or seed for which the device is designed to measure moisture content and test weight per bushel." Item (e), which requires declaring a device's "limitations of use" in the operating instructions, includes "kind or class of grain or seed" in the list of limitations to be declared and also requires that the "moisture measurement range" be shown, presumably, for each grain or seed. These requirements are redundant, considering paragraph S.1.3. Operating Range specifies that "A meter shall automatically and clearly indicate when the operating range of the meter has been exceeded," and with Item (c) of that paragraph further stating, "Moisture and test weight per bushel values may be displayed when the moisture range is exceeded if accompanied by a clear indication that the moisture range has been exceeded." The requirements of paragraph S.4. are also unnecessarily burdensome to manufacturers selling their GMMs in markets outside the United States. In those markets, the kinds and classes of grain or seed for which the GMM is to be used may not be the same as in the United States and may include non-NTEP grain or seed. In the United States, information pertaining to the kinds and classes of grain or seed for which the device is designed to measure moisture and TW are included in the NTEP CC along with the moisture measurement range of each NTEP grain or seed. Furthermore, the kinds and classes of grain are listed on the device's "menu" of included calibrations.

Discussion: The Sector considered the amendments and changes proposed in the agenda. Ms. Cassie Eigenmann, Dickey-john, was concerned that the above requirements applied to the "Instruction Manual." A review of the Grain Moisture Meter code in Handbook 44 indicated that the handbook mentions only "operating instructions" and makes no reference to an "Instruction Manual."

Conclusion: The Sector concluded that the "operating instructions" referred to in Handbook 44 could take many forms, including those displayed on the device's menu of installed calibrations. No change to Handbook 44 was deemed necessary.

9. Report on "Basis of Determination" in Official Grading Standards

Discussion: The principles governing application of official grain grading standards include definitions of the "basis of determination" to be used for each of the individual official tests. The "basis of determination" identifies whether a measurement will be made on the whole grain sample, also referred to as the entire or original grain sample, or on a grain sample after dockage has been removed and/or after the sample has been cleaned.

The various "basis of determination" requirements are part of the U.S. grain grading standards and most have not been changed since USDA began implementing official standards in 1916. Current standards require that:

- official moisture measurements be made on the whole (uncleaned) grain sample;
- test weight measurements be made on the whole grain sample for some grain types while for other grain types test weight measurements be made on grain samples with dockage removed; and
- protein and oil determinations be made using clean grain samples.

Largely because conflicting "basis of determination" requirements are a barrier to adoption of multi-use instruments in official inspections, GIPSA is investigating the potential for establishing a common "basis of determination" for determining moisture, test weight, protein, and oil. Also, there is concern that moisture and test weight measurements on uncleaned grain samples may yield results that are not accurate for either the grain portion of the sample or the dockage in the sample.

Dr. Richard Pierce, GIPSA, presented a brief historical overview of inspection practices; a review of the levels of foreign material (FM), dockage, etc. measured in samples officially inspected in recent years; and preliminary data indicating how moisture and test weight measurements are affected as different levels of dockage are added to a clean sample.

Early test results on corn found no major effect on either moisture or TW as up to 12 % BCFM (broken corn and foreign material) was re-introduced in increments of approximately two percentage points to a clean sample from which the BCFM had been removed.

Soybeans were tested for the effects of added Splits (soybeans that are split/broken) and added FM.

Effect on Moisture and TW
- Moisture results showed negligible change with up to 10 % added Splits.
- Beyond 10 % Splits, moisture increased with added Splits.
- At 35 % Splits, percent moisture had increased by 0.8 %.
- Moisture results appear to be more variable with added Splits.
- TW decreases (2.0 lbs/bu) with 35 % added Splits.

Although moisture results seemed to be more variable with added FM, a recognizable pattern for moisture due to added FM was not found. Test weight decreased almost linearly with added FM to a loss of 5.5 lb/bu at 10 % added FM.

Wheat was tested for the effects of added SHBN (shrunken and broken kernels) and added DKG (dockage).

Effect on Moisture and TW
- Added SHBN below 3 % had no major effect on either moisture or TW.
- Levels of SHBN above 3 % were virtually nonexistent in the database.
- Percent moisture decreased with increasing DKG (-0.6 % with 2 % DKG).
- Moisture results seemed to become more variable.
- TW also decreased with increased DKG to a loss of 2 lb/bu at 2 % added DKG.

Dr. Pierce stressed that this study was in the early stages. Test procedures will be refined and additional data will be obtained on the effects of testing unclean grain samples. Although the early results seem to indicate that moisture results may not be greatly affected by moderate levels of dockage, the Sector agreed unanimously that clean samples must always be used for NTEP evaluations, calibration development, and state field-testing.

NTEP Committee 2007 Final Report
Appendix B – NTETC Grain Analyzer Sector

As additional data become available on the effects of testing unclean grain samples, and as GIPSA considers possible changes in "basis of determination" requirements, the Sector may want to discuss the possible implications for state-regulated commercial transactions.

10. Report on OIML TC 17/SC 1 IR 59 "Moisture Meters for Cereal Grains and Oilseeds"

Background: This item was included on the Sector's agenda to provide a summary of the activities of OIML TC 17/SC 1. Since June 22, 2001, an international work group (IWG) of TC 17/SC 1 has been meeting to review revision to OIML R 59. The most recent meeting of the TC 17/SC 1 work group (WG) was held on September 20 - 21, 2004, at the Laboratory National D'Essais (LNE) in Paris, France.

Discussion: Ms. Diane Lee, NIST/WMD, reported that the 4 CD, dated July 2006, along with U.S. comments on the 3 CD had been distributed to the United States National Work Group (USNWG). The USNWG is for the most part a subset of the NTEP Grain Analyzer Sector. Ms. Lee asked Sector members to review the changes included in the latest draft and forward comments to her by November 1, 2006. To assist in identifying and locating changes that have been made to the 3 CD for inclusion in the 4 CD, a copy of the collated comments to the 3 CD from all participating countries has been requested and will be forwarded to the USNWG upon receipt. [Editor's note: A copy of comments to the 3 CD from all participating countries was e-mailed to the USNWG on September 5, 2006.] The USNWG comments on the 4 CD of OIML R 59 will be collated and forwarded to the TC 17/SC 1 secretariat for inclusion in the next draft of the document.

11. Report on OIML TC 17/SC 8 Protein Draft Recommendation

Background: This item was included on the Sector's agenda to provide a summary of the activities of OIML TC 17/SC 8, the subcommittee responsible for developing a Recommendation for Grain Protein Measuring instruments. Since May 2004, an IWG of TC 17/SC 8 has been meeting to develop a new OIML Recommendation for instruments that measure grain protein. The most recent meeting of the TC 17/SC 8 WG was held in June 2005 in Berlin, Germany to discuss the latest round of comments on the 3 WD of the Recommendation.

Discussion: Diane Lee, NIST/WMD, reported that a 1 CD of "Protein Measuring Instruments for Cereal Grain and Oil Seeds" dated May 1, 2006, addressing comments received on the 3 WD had been distributed to the USNWG and related parties for comment. A meeting of the IWG was held in Ottawa, Canada, September 25 - 26, 2006, to discuss the comments to the 3 WD and the resulting 1 CD. The TC 17/SC 8 secretariat will make changes to the 1 CD according to discussion during the September 2006 meeting and develop a 2 CD that will be forwarded to the USNWG for comment when it is available.

12. Report on OIML TC 5/SC 2 Document D-SW, "General Requirements for Software Controlled Measuring Devices" and NTEP Software Sector Activities

Background: This item was included on the Sector's agenda to provide a summary of the activities of OIML TC 5/SC 2. In 2004, all OIML TCs and SCs that were revising an OIML Recommendation were contacted to ensure that software aspects are considered in revised Recommendations. All OIML Documents and Recommendations published since 1990 were reviewed for terms and requirements related to software. A pre-draft of the document "Software in Legal Metrology" was circulated in October 2004 by the Secretariats (Germany and France). When complete, this document will serve as guidance for OIML technical committees addressing software requirements in Recommendations for software-controlled instruments. NIST submitted U.S. comments on an early draft in February 2005. The 1 WD of this document, titled "General Requirements for Software Controlled Measuring Instruments," was received in February 2006, after which comments from U.S. interested parties were solicited. U.S. comments on this draft were sent to the secretariat May 30, 2006. The 1 WD and the U.S. comments can be viewed on the NIST/WMD website at http://ts.nist.gov/ts/htdocs/230/235/TC5-SC2.htm.

Discussion: After the report on OIML TC 5/SC 2, Steve Patoray, NTEP Director, called the Sector's attention to the recently formed NTETC Software Sector. This new Sector held its first scheduled meeting April 5, 6, and 7, 2006, in Annapolis, Maryland, where several subcommittee WGs were formed to focus on various aspects relating to the use of software in today's weighing and measuring instruments. Mr. Patoray mentioned that the Software Sector's work initially would not affect the Grain Analyzer Sector because grain analyzers, at present, are "built-for-purpose" devices. Looking to the future, however, a system in which a local instrument obtains optical data on the sample to be measured, transmits it to an off-site computer that calculates the result and transmits the result back to the local instrument for display and printout would most likely have to comply with standards developed by the Software Sector. Interested parties wishing to participate in this Sector should direct their requests to Steve Patoray who will see that they are forwarded to the appropriate individual for processing.

13. Time and Place for Next Meeting

The next meeting is tentatively planned for the week of August 20, 2007, in the Kansas City, Missouri, area. Meetings will be held in one of the meeting rooms at the National Weather Service Training Center if available. The meeting room will be reserved for Wednesday and Thursday, August 22 and 23. Sector members are asked to hold both these days open pending determination of agenda items, exact meeting times, and meeting duration. Final meeting details will be announced by late April 2007.

If you would like to submit an agenda item for the 2007 meeting, please contact Steve Patoray, NTEP Director, at spatoray@mgmtsol.com; G. Diane Lee, NIST Technical Advisor, at diane.lee@nist.gov; or Jack Barber, Technical Advisor, at jbarber@motion.net by April 2, 2007.

[Note: The following items were not on the original agenda, but were added at the meeting on an "as time permits" basis.]

14. Encouraging Participation by State Weights and Measures Personnel

Discussion: Noting that only one state W&M representative was able to attend the current Sector meeting, several Sector members wondered what could be done to encourage additional states to send representatives to Sector meetings. At present, five states are represented on the Grain Analyzer Sector: Arkansas, Nebraska, New York, North Carolina, and Missouri. Of those five states, only three participate on a regular basis. For the current meeting, family illness and travel budget restrictions cut the participation to one. Budget cuts and a significant increase in travel costs (gasoline, airfares, and lodging) seem to be the major underlying causes for the drop in participation. With limited personnel and limited budgets, state W&M administrators have had to make hard choices on how best to utilize the people and dollars available.

It is current NCWM policy to provide funding for travel to a Sector meeting to one participant from each state NTEP laboratory active in evaluating the device type(s) which will be discussed at the particular Sector meeting. Unfortunately, GIPSA is the sole participating NTEP laboratory for grain analyzers. GIPSA is a federal agency not a state agency; therefore, no state W&M representative receives funding from NCWM, Inc., for travel to Grain Analyzer Sector meetings.

According to the 2002 Census of Agriculture, the states of Illinois, Indiana, Iowa, Minnesota, and Nebraska grew 67 % of the corn and 60 % of the soybeans grown in the entire United States. Only one of these states is listed as having a representative on the Grain Analyzer Sector, and it has been four years since that representative has attended a Sector meeting.

The Sector took no action on this issue.

15. Questions Regarding NIR Calibration for Enhanced Nutrient Corn

Discussion: Dr. Stuart Kaplan, BASF Plant Science, explained that BASF contracts with select area grain elevators to receive and store BASF enhanced nutrient corn grown by farmers who are also under contract with BASF. To verify that incoming BASF corn meets contract specifications, elevators test the corn using Foss Infratec 1241 NIR analyzers that BASF has placed in the elevators for this purpose. Because the present NTEP corn calibration for the Foss 1241 does not accurately measure the constituents of the BASF germplasm, BASF developed a calibration specifically for their enhanced nutrient corn. Dr. Kaplan was concerned that their NIR instruments might be "tagged" by state W&M field inspectors. He asked the Sector what might be done to avoid problems of this sort.

Sector members offered a number of suggestions. Steve Patoray, NTEP Director, suggested that Dr. Kaplan contact the director of each related state weights and measures division to see how this would be handled in that jurisdiction. A state W&M member explained that his state had an "implied use" regulation. If an inspector encountered a measuring instrument in a location where buying and selling took place, it was implied that the instrument was in "commercial use" and would be subject to test. Another member suggested that notice be placed on the instrument to indicate that it was the property of BASF and was to be used exclusively for testing corn grown under contract with BASF. (Note: Although an instrument may be used for contract sales, it is still commercial and subject to weights and measures regulation.)

Noting that paragraph S.1.2. of Section 5.57. of Handbook 44 states, "If more than one calibration is included for a given grain type, the calibrations must be clearly distinguished from one another," Mr. Jack Barber, the co-technical advisor, suggested that the BASF calibration be installed on the NIR instrument with a name that clearly differentiated their proprietary variety from common yellow dent corn. If the NTEP corn calibration is also installed on the instrument, normal regulatory field inspection of the instrument could be performed using the NTEP calibration. Nothing in Handbook 44 prohibits using proprietary calibrations for specialty crops grown under contract. Field inspection of the instrument with standard corn samples could offer BASF assurance that the instrument was functioning properly.

Change Summary

Recommended Amendments to the 2006 Edition of NIST Handbook 44			
Section Number	Amendment/Change	Page	Source
5.56.(a) Grain Moisture Meters	Modify paragraph S.1.2. and Table S.1.2. to include minimum acceptable abbreviations for multi-class grain moisture calibrations.	5-28	08/06 Grain Analyzer Sector – Item 5
5.57. Near Infrared Grain Analyzers	Modify paragraph S.1.2. and Table S.1.2. to add criteria applicable to "multi-class" calibrations.	5-42	08/06 Grain Analyzer Sector – Item 6(a)

Recommended Amendments/Changes to the Grain Moisture Meters Chapter to the 2006 Edition of NCWM Publication 14			
Section Number	Amendment/Change	Page	Source
VII. Additional Type Evaluation Test Procedures and Tolerances for Grain Moisture Meters Incorporating an Automatic Test Weight per Bushel Measuring Feature	Add paragraph C. Tolerances For Test Weight per Bushel Calibration Performance [Note: Paragraph C should immediately follow the table of tolerances for reproducibility on page GMM-16.]	GMM-16	08/06 Grain Analyzer Sector – Item 4

Recommended Amendments/Changes to the Near Infrared Grain Analyzers Chapter to the 2006 Edition of NCWM Publication 14			
Section Number	Amendment/Change	Page	Source
III. Accuracy, Precision, and Reproducibility Requirements	Amend to add criteria applicable to "multi-class" calibrations.	NIR-3 thru NIR-6	08/06 Grain Analyzer Sector – Item 6(b)

Appendix C

National Type Evaluation Technical Committee
Measuring Sector

October 20 - 21, 2005, Annapolis, Maryland
Meeting Summary

National Type Evaluation Technical Committee 1
   1. Recommendations to Update to NCWM Publication 14 to Reflect Changes to NIST Handbook 44 2
      A. Checklist and Test Procedures (LMD – 11) 2
      B. Philosophy for Sealing (LMD – 17- 20) 3
      C. Checklist and Test Procedures for Retail Motor-Fuel Dispensers 5
      D. Checklist and Test Procedures for Specific Criteria for Vehicle Tank Meters 6
      E. Checklist for LPG Liquid Measuring Devices 7
      F. Checklist for Mass Flow Meters 8

Carry-over Items: 9
   2. Reorganize Publication 14 to Clarify Tests of ECRs for RMFDs 9
   3. Add Magnetic Flowmeters to Product Family Table 9
   4. Value of the Smallest Unit for LMD Code 18

New Items: 19
   5. Product Families for Meters 19
   6. Table of Key Characteristics of Products in Product Families Table for Meters 20
   7. NTEP Checklist for Water Meters in Sub-metering Application 21
   8. NTEP Checklist for LPG Vapor Meters in Sub-metering Applications 21
   9. Testing Electronic Indicators Using Simulated Inputs 22
   10. Next Meeting 23

Additional Items for Discussion if Time Permits 23
   11. Display of Quantity and Unit Price for Self-serve Aviation Dispensers 23
   12. S.1.2.3. Value of the Smallest Unit for Aviation Turbine Fuel 24
   13. Testing Meters Made of Different Metals 25

Additional Items Added at the Meeting 27
   14. Number of Tests Required for Permanence Test 27
   15. Permanence Tests for RMFD 29

List of Appendices: 31
   Appendix A – Reorganized Publication 14 – LMD Checklist 31
   Appendix B – Reorganized Publication 14 – ECR Interfaced with RMFD Checklist 31
   Appendix C – Domestic Cold Water Meters 31
   Appendix D – Hydrocarbon Gas Vapor Meters 31

*For copies of the Appendices contact Richard Suiter at NIST, (301) 975-4406 or by e-mail: richard.suiter@nist.gov.

NTEP Committee 2007 Final Report
Appendix C – NTETC Measuring Sector

Details of All Items
(In Order by Reference Key Number)

---

1. Recommendations to Update to NCWM Publication 14 to Reflect Changes to NIST Handbook 44

Source: NIST/WMD

Background: The 90th National Conference on Weights and Measures (NCWM) adopted the following items that will be reflected in the 2006 edition of NIST Handbook 44 and NCWM Publication 14. These items are part of the agenda to inform the Measuring Sector of the NCWM actions and recommend changes to NCWM Publication 14.

Recommendation: The Sector will review and, if acceptable, recommend to the NTEP Committee adoption of the following changes to Publication 14 based on changes to NIST Handbook 44:

A. Checklist and Test Procedures (LMD – 11)

Code Reference G-S.1. (~~e~~g). Effective January 1, 2003 (LMD – 13)

1.1.5. The NTEP Certificate of Conformance (CC) Number or a corresponding CC addendum number for devices that have a CC. The number shall be prefaced by the terms "NTEP CC", "CC", or "Approval". These terms may be followed by the word "Number" or an abbreviation for the Word "Number". The abbreviation shall as a minimum begin with the letter "N" (e.g., No or No.).	Yes	No	N/A

The device must have an area, either on the identification plate or on the device itself, suitable for the application of the CC Number. If the area for the CC Number is not part of an identification plate, note its intended location and how it will be applied.

Location of CC Number if not located with the identification:

_____

_____

Code Reference: G-S.1.1. <u>Location of Marking Information for</u> Not-Built-for-Purpose Devices, Software-Based (LMD – 13)

1.2. For not built-for-purpose, software-based devices the following shall apply:

1.2.1. <u>The required information in G-S.1 Identification. (a), (b), (d), and (e) shall be permanently marked or continuously displayed on the device; or</u>   Yes   No   N/A

~~the manufacturer or distributor and the model designation shall be continuously displayed or marked on the device (see note below), or~~

1.2.2.	<s>The Certificate of Conformance (CC) Number shall be:</s> <s>1. permanently marked on the device;</s> <s>2. continuously displayed; or</s> <s>3. accessible through an easily recognized menu and, if necessary, a submenu. Examples of menu and submenu identification include, but are not limited to "Help," "System Identification," "G-S.1 Identification," or "Weights and Measures Identification."</s> <s>the Certificate of Conformance (CC) Number shall be continuously displayed or marked on the device (see note below), or</s>	Yes	No	N/A
<s>1.2.3.</s>	<s>all required information in G-S.1. Identification. (a), (b), (c), (e), and (h) shall be continuously displayed. Alternatively, a clearly identified view only System Identification, G-S.1. Identification, or Weights and Measures Identification shall be accessible through the "Help" menu. Required information includes that information necessary to identify that the software in the device is the same type that was evaluated.</s>	Yes	No	N/A

<u>Note: For (b), clear instructions for accessing the information required in G-S.1. (a), (b), and (d) shall be listed on the CC, including information necessary to identify that the software in the device is the same type that was evaluated.</u> <s>Clear instructions for accessing the remaining required G-S.1. information shall be listed on the CC. Required information includes that information necessary to identify that the software in the device is the same type that was evaluated.</s>

1.3.	The identification badge must be visible after installation.	Yes	No	N/A
1.4.	The identification badge must be permanent.	Yes	No	N/A

B. Philosophy for Sealing (LMD – 17- 20)

Category 1 Devices (Devices with No Remote Configuration Capability):

• The device is sealed with a physical seal or it has an audit trail with two event counters (one for calibration, the second for configuration).	Yes	No	N/A
• A physical seal must be applied without exposing electronics.	Yes	No	N/A
• Event counters are non-resettable and have a capacity of at least 000 to 999.	Yes	No	N/A
• Event counters increment appropriately.	Yes	No	N/A
• The audit trail information must be capable of being retained in memory for at least 30 days while the device is without power, or must be retained in nonvolatile memory.	Yes	No	N/A
• Accessing the audit trail information for review shall be separate from the calibration mode.	Yes	No	N/A
• Accessing the audit trail information must not affect the normal operation of the device.	Yes	No	N/A
• Accessing the audit trail information shall not require removal of any additional parts other than normal requirements to inspect the integrity of a physical security seal. (e.g., a key to open a locked panel may be required).	Yes	No	N/A

Category 2 Devices (Devices with Remote Configuration Capability but Controlled by Hardware):

- ~~Category 2 applies only to devices manufactured prior to January 1, 2005. Devices with remote configuration capability manufactured after that date must meet the sealing requirements outlined in Category 3. Devices without remote configuration capability manufactured after that date will be required to meet the minimum criteria outlined in Category 1.~~ Yes No N/A
- ~~The physical hardware enabling access for remote communication must be on-site.~~ Yes No N/A
- ~~The physical hardware must be sealable with a security seal or~~ Yes No N/A
- ~~The device must be equipped with at least two event counters: one for calibration, the second for configuration parameters~~
   - ~~calibration parameters event counter~~
   - ~~configuration parameters event counter~~
  Yes No N/A
- ~~Adequate provision must be made to apply a physical seal without exposing electronics.~~ Yes No N/A
- ~~Event counters are non-resettable and have a capacity of at least 000 to 999.~~ Yes No N/A
- ~~Event counters increment appropriately.~~ Yes No N/A
- ~~Event counters may be located either:~~
   - ~~at the individual measuring device or~~
   - ~~at the system controller~~
  Yes No N/A
- ~~If the counters are located at the system controller rather than at the individual device, means must be provided to generate a hard copy of the information through an on-site device.~~ Yes No N/A
- ~~An adequate number (see table below) of event counters must be available to monitor the calibration and configuration parameters of each individual device.~~ Yes No N/A
- ~~The device must either:~~
   - ~~clearly indicate when it is in the remote configuration mode or~~
   - ~~the device shall not operate while in the remote configuration mode.~~
  Yes No N/A
- ~~If capable of printing in the calibration mode, it must print a message that it is in the calibration mode.~~ Yes No N/A
- ~~The audit trail information must be capable of being retained in memory for at least 30 days while the device is without power.~~ Yes No N/A
- ~~The audit trail information must be readily accessible and easily read.~~ Yes No N/A

Minimum Number of Counters Required		
	Minimum Counters Required for Devices Equipped with Event Counters	**Minimum Event Counter(s) at System Controller**
Only one type of parameter accessible (calibration or configuration)	One (1) event counter	One (1) event counter for each separately controlled device, or one (1) event counter, if changes are made simultaneously.
Both calibration and configuration parameters accessible	Two (2) event counters	Two (2) event counters for each separately controlled device, or two (2) or more event counters if changes are made to all controlled devices simultaneously.

Category 3 Devices (Devices with Unlimited Remote Configuration Capability):

Category 3 devices have virtually unlimited access to sealable parameters or access is controlled though a password.

- For devices manufactured after January 1, 2001, the device must either:
  - clearly indicate when it is in the remote configuration mode, or
  - the device shall not operate while in the remote configuration mode

  Yes No N/A

- The device is equipped with an event logger   Yes No N/A

- The event logger automatically retains the identification of the parameter changed, the date and time of the change, and the new value of the parameter.   Yes No N/A

- Event counters are nonresettable and have a capacity of at least 000 to 999.   Yes No N/A

- The system is designed to attach a printer, which can print the contents of the audit trail.   Yes No N/A

- The audit trail information must be capable of being retained in memory for at least 30 days while the device is without power or must be retained in nonvolatile memory.   Yes No N/A

- The event logger must have a capacity to retain records equal to ten times the number of sealable parameters in the device, but not more than 1000 records are required.   Yes No N/A

- The event logger drops the oldest event when the memory capacity is full and a new entry is saved.   Yes No N/A

- Describe the method used to seal the device or access the audit trail information. _____

- ~~Note: All devices with remote communication that are manufactured after January 1, 2005 must meet the requirements outlined for Category 3.~~

C. Checklist and Test Procedures for Retail Motor-Fuel Dispensers
Code Reference S.1.2. Units (LMD – 26)

S.1.2. Units. – A liquid-measuring device shall indicate, and record if the device is equipped to record, its deliveries in liters, gallons, quarts, pints, **fluid ounces,** or binary-submultiples or decimal subdivisions of the liter or gallon.

Code Reference: S.1.2. Units

7.23.	A liquid-measuring device shall indicate, and record if the device is equipped to record, its deliveries in liters, gallons, quarts, pints, fluid ounces, or binary-submultiples or decimal subdivisions of the liter or gallon.	Yes No N/A

D. Checklist and Test Procedures for Specific Criteria for Vehicle Tank Meters

Code Reference: S.1.1.3. Value of Smallest Unit

If the meter is equipped to record, the value of the smallest unit of indicated delivery and recorded delivery shall not exceed the equivalent of:

24.4.	0.5 L (0.1 gal) or 0.5 kg (1 lb) on milk-metering systems and on meters with a rated maximum flow rate of ~~500~~ **700** L/min (~~100~~ **200** gal/min) or less used for ~~retail~~ deliveries ~~of liquid fuel~~, **or**	Yes No N/A
24.5.	~~5 L (1 gal) on meters with a rated maximum flow of 575 L/min (150 gal/min) or more used for jet fuel aviation refueling systems, or (Added 2006)~~	~~Yes No N/A~~
24.6	5 L (1 gal) on other meters	Yes No N/A

(Renumber succeeding paragraphs)

Code Reference S.1.4.1. Display of Unit Price (LMD – 43)

Code Reference: S.1.4.1. Display of Unit Price

25.1.	Means must be provided to display the unit price at which the device is set to compute in proximity to the total computed price display. **(In a device of the computing type, means shall be provided for displaying, in a manner clear to the operator and an observer, the unit price at which the device is set to compute. The unit price is not required to be displayed continuously.)**	Yes No N/A
25.2.	The unit price shall be expressed in dollars and decimals of dollars using a dollar sign. A common fraction shall not appear in the unit price (e.g., $1.299 not $1.29 9/10).	Yes No N/A

Code Reference Measuring Element (LMD – 44)

Code Reference: S.2.2. Provision for Sealing

Measuring elements shall be designed with a provision for sealing such that an adjustment to the measuring element or the flow rate control (if the flow rate affects the accuracy of deliveries) cannot be made without breaking the security seal. **These provisions can be an approved means of security (e.g., data change audit trail) or physically applying a security seal which must be broken before adjustments can be made.** ~~Milk meters are exempt from this requirement.~~ **When applicable, t**~~T~~he adjusting mechanism shall be readily accessible for the purposes of affixing a security seal.

26.1.	A measuring element shall have provision for sealing its adjustable components.	Yes No N/A

26.2. Any adjustable element controlling the delivery rate shall provide for sealing if the flow rate affects the accuracy of deliveries.   **Yes   No   N/A**

26.3. The adjusting mechanism shall be readily accessible to affix a security seal.   **Yes   No   N/A**

E. Checklist for LPG Liquid Measuring Devices

31. Measuring Element (LMD – 49)

Code Reference: S.2.2. Provision for Sealing

Measuring elements shall be designed with a provision for sealing such that an adjustment to the measuring element or the flow rate control (if the flow rate affects the accuracy of deliveries) cannot be made without breaking the security seal. <u>These provisions can be an approved means of security (e.g., data change audit trail) or physically applying a security seal which must be broken before adjustments can be made. When applicable, t</u>~~T~~he adjusting mechanism shall be readily accessible for the purposes of affixing a security seal.

31.1. A measuring element shall provide for sealing its adjustable components.   **Yes   No   N/A**

31.2. Any adjustable element controlling the delivery rate shall provide for sealing if the flow rate affects the accuracy of deliveries.   **Yes   No   N/A**

31.3. The adjusting mechanism shall be readily accessible to affix a security seal.   **Yes   No   N/A**

33. Marking

Code Reference: S.4. Marking Requirements

Code Reference: S.4.3. Location of Marking Information; Retail Motor-Fuel Dispenser

33.4. <u>The marking information required in the General Code, paragraph G-S.1. Identification shall appear as follows</u>:   **Yes   No   N/A**

    (a) <u>within 60 cm (24 in) to 150 cm (60 in) from the base of the dispenser;</u>

    (b) <u>either internally and/or externally provided the information is permanent and easily read; and</u>

    (c) <u>on a portion of the device that cannot be readily removed or interchanged (i.e., not on a service access panel).</u>

    <u>Note: The use of a dispenser key or tool to access internal marking information is permitted for retail liquid-measuring devices.</u>
    <u>[Nonretroactive as of January 1, 2003]</u>
    <u>(Added 2006)</u>

Code Reference: S.4.3. Temperature Compensation

33.~~4~~<u>5</u>. If a device is equipped with an automatic temperature compensator, the primary indicating elements, recording elements, and recorded representations shall be clearly and conspicuously marked to show that the volume delivered has been adjusted to the volume at 15 °C (60 °F).   **Yes   No   N/A**

NTEP Committee 2007 Final Report
Appendix C – NTETC Measuring Sector

F. Checklist for Mass Flow Meters

38. Marking (LMD – 57)
Code Reference: S.5. Marking Requirements

38.1. The dispenser shall have the following information on the identification plate:

a.	pattern approval mark (i.e., type approval number);	Yes	No	N/A
b.	name and address of the manufacturer or his trademark and, required by the weights and measures authority, the manufacturer's identification mark in addition to the trademark;	Yes	No	N/A
c.	model designation or product name selected by the manufacturer;	Yes	No	N/A
d.	non-repetitive serial number;	Yes	No	N/A
e.	accuracy class of the meter as specified by the manufacturer consistent with Table T.2;	Yes	No	N/A
f.	maximum and minimum flow rates in pounds per unit of time;	Yes	No	N/A
g.	maximum working pressure;	Yes	No	N/A
h.	applicable temperature range if other than –10 °C to +50 °C;	Yes	No	N/A
i.	minimum measured quantity (MMQ);	Yes	No	N/A
j.	product limitations if applicable.	Yes	No	N/A

Code Reference: S.5.1. Location of Marking Information; Retail Motor-Fuel Dispensers.

38.2. ~~The marking information required in General Code, paragraph G-S.1. Identification shall appear as follows:~~   Yes   No   N/A

   (a) ~~within 60 cm (24 in) to 150 cm (60 in) from the base of the dispenser;~~

   (b) ~~either internally and/or externally provided the information is permanent and easily read; and~~

   (c) ~~on a portion of the device that cannot be readily removed or interchanged (i.e., not on a service access panel).~~

   ~~Note: The use of a dispenser key or tool to access internal marking information is permitted for retail liquid-measuring devices.~~
   ~~[Nonretroactive as of January 1, 2003]~~
   ~~(Added 2006)~~

Code Reference: S.5. ~~1~~2. Marking of Gasoline Volume Equivalent Conversion Factor

A device dispensing compressed natural gas shall have either the statement "1 Gasoline Liter Equivalent (GLE) is Equal to 0.678 kg of Natural Gas" or "1 Gasoline Gallon Equivalent (GGE) is Equal to 5.660 lb of Natural Gas" permanently and conspicuously marked on the face of the dispenser according to the method of sale used.

Conclusion: The Sector reviewed and agreed to recommend to the NTEP Committee adoption of the changes to Publication 14 shown above based on changes to the 2007 edition of NIST Handbook 44.

Carry-over Items:

2. Reorganize Publication 14 to Clarify Tests of ECRs for RMFDs

Source: NTEP Laboratories

Background: At the 2005 NTEP laboratory meeting, one of the measuring labs stated that the LMD section of Publication 14 was not well organized. During an NTEP evaluation, the evaluator must continuously flip from one section of the publication to another to find all the requirements applicable to the device under test. The lab also stated that the evaluation of an ECR interfaced with a RMFD required the use of both the ECR Checklist and the LMD Checklist in order to find all the applicable requirements. The California laboratory volunteered to provide a draft reorganization of the LMD Checklist and a draft of a revised ECR Checklist with the applicable requirements added from the LMD Checklist. The drafts of the reorganized LMD Checklist and the revised ECR Checklist are in Appendices A and B, respectively. At the 2005 Sector Meeting, the Sector supported the concept, provided all NTEP laboratories and other interested parties conducted a thorough review of the proposed changes before they are incorporated into NCWM Publication 14.

Recommendation: The Sector reviewed the drafts submitted and received input from the NTEP laboratories for possible forwarding to the NTEP Committee for approval as revisions to the 2007 version of Publication 14.

Conclusion: The Sector discussed the reorganized checklists which were reorganized with the intent to make them more user friendly. Although the draft reorganized checklists have not been used extensively, the NTEP laboratories had no problems to report. The Sector agreed to forward the drafts to the NTEP Committee for inclusion in the next edition of Publication 14.

3. Add Magnetic Flowmeters to Product Family Table.

Source: Magnetic Meters Work Group (WG)

Background: At the 2002 Sector Meeting, a Work Group (WG) was formed to address the issue of product family criteria. Prior to the 2003 Sector Meeting the technical advisor was informed that this WG was not ready to present a recommendation; however the WG requested that the item remain on the agenda for further development.

At the 2003 Sector Meeting, the Sector agreed that a new WG should be formed to develop family product tables for Mag Meters for consideration by the Sector at its next meeting. The members of the new WG are: Charlene Numrych (Liquid Controls), Chair, Richard Miller (FMC); Joe Buxton (Daniel Measurement & Control); Randy Byrtus (Measurement Canada). Charlene volunteered to contact other manufacturers to invite them to participate in the WG.

The WG formed at the 2003 Sector Meeting identified four Turbine Meter manufacturers that could provide data on a variety of products measured using this type of meter. For the 2004 Measuring Sector Meeting, only one Mag Meter manufacturer of three manufacturers was identified as having a certificate for products other than milk. No information had been gathered regarding manufacturers of Ultrasonic Meters. The WG did not have a proposal to present at that time, but planned to continue its work. A new chairman was needed for the WG because Charlene Numrych (Liquid Controls) was no longer available to perform that function. The WG had nothing to provide for the 2005 Measuring Sector Meeting.

The WG is submitting a proposal to add Magnetic Meters to the Family Products table with additional background information, for discussion at the 2006 Sector Meeting.

The proposed Product Family table adding magnetic flowmeters has been reviewed by manufacturer representatives holding magnetic flowmeter NTEP Certificates of Conformance (CC). Those comments were included in the organization of this proposal.

NTEP Committee 2007 Final Report
Appendix C – NTETC Measuring Sector

Operation: Magnetic flowmeters determine the velocity of an electrically conductive liquid in a known diameter tube section of the piping. The gross volumetric flow rate of the liquid is calculated in the electronic transmitter. The delivered volumetric quantity is displayed on the transmitter and/or scaled pulses are transmitted to a compatible register.

Influence factors: The magnetic flowmeter determines the gross volume. The magnetic flowmeter is not influenced by the density of the liquid.

The magnetic flowmeter has no moving mechanical components that would rely on close tolerances and capillary fluid action. The magnetic flowmeter is not influenced by the viscosity of the liquid.

Magnetic flowmeters determine the velocity of electrically conductive liquids. The conductivity of the liquid must be above a minimum threshold value determined in the engineered design of the flowmeter and specified by the manufacturer. The value of the conductivity is not significant to the determination of the volumetric flow rate.

The Product Family Table: The table has been edited to add a column for magnetic flowmeters.

The Water Mixes of Alcohol and Glycols and Water categories have been combined for magnetic flowmeters. Juices and Beverages have been added to this category.

The Agricultural Chemical Liquids and Chemicals categories have been combined for magnetic flowmeters.

Test D is required for Agricultural Chemical Liquids, Chemicals, Water, Beverages and Juices. The conductivity of the liquids in these categories is not significant to the performance of the magnetic flowmeter.

A new Test F has been added that is specific to magnetic flowmeters. Test F is required for liquids in product categories where the liquids commonly have low conductivity. The manufacturer submits the flowmeter to be tested at a specified conductivity. The specified conductivity is listed on the certificate. All liquids in the same category with conductivity above the conductivity of the liquid tested will be included.

The following copyrighted documents can be referenced for as supporting documentation:

ASME Draft MFC-16M: Measurement of Fluid Flow in Closed Conduits, with Electromagnetic Flowmeters.

AWWA Draft Committee Report: Magnetic Inductive Flowmeters

Recommendation: The Sector will review the following proposal for possible forwarding to the NTEP Committee for approval and addition to the 2007 edition of Publication 14.

Add magnetic flowmeters to the Product Family Table as follows:

Tests to be Conducted

Test A - Products must be individually tested and noted on the CC.

Test B - To obtain coverage for a range of products within a family: Test with one product having a low specific gravity; test with a second product having a high specific gravity. The CC will cover all products in the family within the specific gravity range tested.

Test C - To obtain coverage for a range of products within a family: Test with one product having a low viscosity; test with a second product having a high viscosity. The CC will cover all products in the family within the viscosity range tested.

Test D - To obtain coverage for a product family: Test with one product in the product family.

Test E - To obtain coverage for a range of products within a family: Test with one product having a low kinematic viscosity; test with a second product having a high kinematic viscosity. The CC will note coverage for all products in the family within the kinematic viscosity range tested.

Test F - To obtain coverage for a range of products within a family: Test with one product having a specified conductivity. The CC will note coverage for all products in the family with conductivity equal to or above the conductivity of the tested liquid.

Mass Meter Product Family & Test Requirements (Test B unless otherwise noted)	Magnetic Flow Meter Product Family & Test Requirements (Test D unless otherwise noted)	PD Product Family & Test Requirements (Test C unless otherwise noted)	Turbine Product Family & Test Requirements (Test A unless otherwise noted)	Typical Products[1]	Viscosity[5] (Centipoise) (Centistokes)	Specific Gravity[2]
Normal Liquids	Test E	Fuels, Lubricants, Industrial and Food Grade Liquid Oils	Fuels, Lubricants, Industrial and Food Grade Liquid Oils (Test E permitted)	Diesel Fuel[3], Distillate, Gasoline[4], Fuel Oil, Kerosene, Light Oil, Spindle Oil, Lubricating Oils, SAE Grades, Bunker Oil, 6 Oil, Crude Oil, Asphalt, Vegetable Oil, Biodiesel above B20, Avgas, Jet A, Jet A-1, Jet B, JP4, JP5, JP7, JP8, Cooking Oils, Sunflower Oil, Soy Oil, Peanut Oil, Olive Oil, etc.	0.3 to 2500 0.44 to 2270	0.68 to 1.1
	Test E	Solvents General	Solvents General (Test E permitted)	Acetates, Acetone, Esters, Ethylacetate, Hexane, MEK, Naphtha, Toluene, Xylene, etc.	0.3 to 7 0.5 to 4.38	0.6 to 1.6
	Test E	Solvents Chlorinated	Solvents Chlorinated	Carbon Tetra. Chloride, Methylene Chloride, Perchloro. Ethylene, Trichloro. Ethylene, etc.	0.3 to 7 0.5 to 4.38	0.6 to 1.6
Pure Alcohols & Glycols, Water (Demineralized & Deionized) Test E	Alcohols, Glycols, & Water Mixes Thereof	Alcohols, Glycols, & Water Mixes Thereof (Test E permitted)	Ethanol, Methanol, Butanol, Isopropyl, Isobutyl, Ethylene glycol, Propylene glycol, etc.	0.3 to 7 0.5 to 4.38	0.6 to 1.6
Water (Tap, Potable & Nonpotable), Water (Mixes of Alcohols & Glycols), Juices, Beverages, (Test D)		Water (Test D permitted)	Water (Test D permitted)	Tap Water, Deionized, Demineralized, Potable, Nonpotable	1.0	1.0

Mass Meter Product Family & Test Requirements (Test B unless otherwise noted)	Magnetic Flow Meter Product Family & Test Requirements (Test D unless otherwise noted)	PD Product Family & Test Requirements (Test C unless otherwise noted)	Turbine Product Family & Test Requirements (Test A unless otherwise noted)	Typical Products[1]	Viscosity[5] (Centipoise) (Centistokes)	Specific Gravity[2]
	Clear Liquid Fertilizers, Crop Chemicals, Suspensions Fertilizers, Liquid Feeds, Chemicals Test D	Clear Liquid Fertilizers	Clear Liquid Fertilizers	Nitrogen Solution: 28 %, 30 % or 32 %; 20 % Aqua Ammonia; Urea; Ammonia Nitrate; N, P, K solutions: 10-34-0; 4-10-10; 9-18-9; etc.	10 to 400 10 to 275	1.0 to 1.45
		Crop Chemicals	Crop Chemicals	Herbicides: Round-up, Touchdown, Banvel, Treflan, Paraquat, Prowl, etc.	4 to 400 5.7 to 333	0.7 to 1.2
		Crop Chemicals	Crop Chemicals	Fungicides, Insecticides, Adjuvants, Fumigants	0.7 to 100 1 to 83	0.7 to 1.2
		Flowables	Flowables	Dual, Bicep, Marksman, Broadstrike, Doubleplay, Topnotch, Guardsman, Harness, etc.	20 to 900 20 to 750	1 to 1.2
		Crop Chemicals	Crop Chemicals	Fungicides		
		Crop Chemicals	Crop Chemicals	Micronutrients		
		Suspensions Fertilizers	Suspensions Fertilizers	3-10-30; 4-4-27, etc.	20 to 900 20 to 560	1.0 to 1.6
		Liquid Feeds	Liquid Feeds	Liquid Molasses; Molasses plus Phos Acid and/or Urea; etc.	10 to 50 000 8 to 33 000	1.2 to 1.5
		Chemicals	Chemicals	Sulfuric Acid, Hydrochloric Acid, Phosphoric Acid, etc.	1.0 to 296 0.9 to 160	1.1 to 1.85
Heated Products (above 50 °C)	Test E	Heated Products (above 50 °C)	Heated Products (above 50 °C)	Bunker C, Asphalt, etc.		0.8 to 1.2

Mass Meter Product Family & Test Requirements (Test B unless otherwise noted)	Magnetic Flow Meter Product Family & Test Requirements (Test D unless otherwise noted)	PD Product Family & Test Requirements (Test C unless otherwise noted)	Turbine Product Family & Test Requirements (Test A unless otherwise noted)	Typical Products[1]	Viscosity[5] (Centipoise) (Centistokes)	Specific Gravity[2]
Compressed Liquids (Test D)	Not Applicable (conductivity too low)	Fuels and Refrigerants	Fuels and Refrigerants (Test E)	LPG, Propane, Butane, Ethane, Freon 11, Freon 12, Freon 22, etc.	0.1 to 0.5 / 0.3 to 0.77	0.3 to 0.65
		NH_3	NH_3	Anhydrous Ammonia Note: If a meter is certified for anhydrous ammonia, the same meter type may also be certified for LPG without further testing.	0.1 / 0.2	0.56 to 0.68
Compressed Gases (Test D)	Note: CNG is only included in Section 3.37 Mass Flow Meters of Handbook 44			CNG	0.6 to 0.8	
Cryogenic Liquids and Liquefied Natural Gas (Test D)	Not Applicable (conductivity too low)	Cryogenic Liquids and Liquefied Natural Gas (Test A)	Cryogenic Liquids and Liquefied Natural Gas (Test D)	Liquefied Oxygen, Nitrogen, etc.	0.07 to 1.4	

[1] NOTE: The Typical Products listed in this table are not limiting or all-inclusive; there may be other products and product trade names, which fall into a product family. Water and a product such as stoddard solvent or mineral spirit may be used as test products in the fuels, lubricants, industrial, and food-grade liquid oils product family.

[2] The specific gravity of a liquid is the ratio of its density to that of water at standard conditions, usually 4 °C (or 40 °F) and 1 atm. The density of water at standard conditions is approximately 1000 kg/m³ (or 998 kg/m³).

[3] Diesel fuel blends (biodiesel) with up to 20 % vegetable or animal fat/oil.

[4] Gasoline includes oxygenated fuel blends with up to 15 % oxygenate.

[5] Kinematic viscosity is measured in centistokes. $$Centistokes = \frac{Centipoise}{SpecificGravity}$$

Source for some of the viscosity value information is in the Industry Canada - Measurement Canada "Liquid Products Group, Bulletin V-16-E (rev. 1) August 3, 1999."

Conclusion: There was considerable discussion of the proposal to add magnetic flowmeters to the Product Families table. Most of the discussion centered on a determination of what product characteristics were most important when evaluating a magnetic flow meter. The members of the WG present at the meeting agreed that the most important product characteristic is conductivity. During the discussion, a member stated that the column for magnetic flowmeters could be simplified similar to the column for mass meters. The Sector agreed and modified the Product Families table to add Magnetic Flow Meters as follows:

Tests to be Conducted

Test A - Products must be individually tested and noted on the CC

Test B - To obtain coverage for a range of products within a family: Test with one product having a low specific gravity; test with a second product having a high specific gravity. The CC will cover all products in the family within the specific gravity range tested.

Test C - To obtain coverage for a range of products within a family: Test with one product having a low viscosity; test with a second product having a high viscosity. The CC will cover all products in the family within the viscosity range tested.

Test D - To obtain coverage for a product family: Test with one product in the product family. The CC will cover all products in the family.

Test E - To obtain coverage for a range of products within a family: Test with one product having a low kinematic viscosity; test with a second product having a high kinematic viscosity. The CC will note coverage for all products in the family within the kinematic viscosity range tested.

Test F - To obtain coverage for a range of products within a family: Test with one product having a specified conductivity. The CC will note coverage for all products in both of the families with conductivity equal to or above the conductivity of the tested liquid.

Mass Meter Product Family & Test Requirements (Test B unless otherwise noted)	Magnetic Flow Meter Product Family & Test Requirements (Test D unless otherwise noted)	PD Product Family & Test Requirements (Test C unless otherwise noted)	Turbine Product Family & Test Requirements (Test A unless otherwise noted)	Typical Products[1]	Viscosity[5] (Centipoise) (Centistokes)	Specific Gravity[2]
Normal Liquids (Test E permitted) Fuels, Lubricants, Industrial and Food Grade Liquid Oils, Solvents General, Solvents Chlorinated, Pure Alcohols & Glycols, Water (De-mineralized & deionized), Heated Products (above 50 °C)		Fuels, Lubricants, Industrial and Food Grade Liquid Oils	Fuels, Lubricants, Industrial and Food Grade Liquid Oils (Test E permitted)	Diesel Fuel[3], Distillate, Gasoline[4], Fuel Oil, Kerosene, Light Oil, Spindle Oil, Lubricating Oils, SAE Grades, Bunker Oil, 6 Oil, Crude Oil, Asphalt, Vegetable Oil, Biodiesel above B20, Avgas, Jet A, Jet A-1, Jet B, JP4, JP5, JP7, JP8, Cooking Oils, Sunflower Oil, Soy Oil, Peanut Oil, Olive Oil, etc.	0.3 to 2500 0.44 to 2270	0.68 to 1.1
		Solvents General	Solvents General (Test E permitted)	Acetates, Acetone, Esters, Ethylacetate, Hexane, MEK, Naphtha, Toluene, Xylene, etc.	0.3 to 7 0.5 to 4.38	0.6 to 1.6
		Solvents Chlorinated	Solvents Chlorinated	Carbon Tetra-Chloride, Methylene-Chloride, Perchloro-Ethylene, Trichloro-Ethylene, etc.	0.3 to 7 0.5 to 4.38	0.6 to 1.6

Mass Meter Product Family & Test Requirements (Test B unless otherwise noted)	Magnetic Flow Meter Product Family & Test Requirements (Test D unless otherwise noted)	PD Product Family & Test Requirements (Test C unless otherwise noted)	Turbine Product Family & Test Requirements (Test A unless otherwise noted)	Typical Products[1]	Viscosity[5] (Centipoise) (Centistokes)	Specific Gravity[2]
		Alcohols, Glycols, & Water Mixes Thereof	Alcohols, Glycols, & Water Mixes Thereof (Test E permitted)	Ethanol, Methanol, Butanol, Isopropyl, Isobutyl, Ethylene glycol, Propylene glycol, etc.	0.3 to 7 0.5 to 4.38	0.6 to 1.6
	Test D Water (Tap, Potable & Nonpotable), Water (Mixes of Alcohols & Glycols), Juices, Beverages, Clear Liquid Fertilizers, Crop Chemicals, Suspensions Fertilizers, Liquid Feeds, Chemicals	Water (Test D permitted)	Water (Test D permitted)	Tap Water, Deionized, Demineralized, Potable, Nonpotable	1.0	1.0
		Clear Liquid Fertilizers	Clear Liquid Fertilizers	Nitrogen Solution: 28 %, 30 % or 32 %; 20 % Aqua-Ammonia; Urea; Ammonia Nitrate; N.P. K solutions: 10-34-0; 4-10-10; 9-18-9; etc.	10 to 400 10 to 275	1.0 to 1.45
		Crop Chemicals	Crop Chemicals	Herbicides: Round-up, Touchdown, Banvel, Treflan, Paraquat, Prowl, etc.	4 to 400 5.7 to 333	0.7 to 1.2
		Crop Chemicals	Crop Chemicals	Fungicides, Insecticides, Adjuvants, Fumigants	0.7 to 100 1 to 83	0.7 to 1.2
		Flowables	Flowables	Dual, Bicep, Marksman, Broadstrike, Doubleplay, Topnotch, Guardsman, Harness, etc.	20 to 900 20 to 750	1 to 1.2
		Crop Chemicals	Crop Chemicals	Fungicides		
		Crop Chemicals	Crop Chemicals	Micronutrients		
		Suspensions Fertilizers	Suspensions Fertilizers	3-10-30; 4-4-27, etc.	20 to 900 20 to 560	1.0 to 1.6
		Liquid Feeds	Liquid Feeds	Liquid Molasses; Molasses plus Phos Acid and/or Urea; etc.	10 to 50 000 8 to 33 000	1.2 to 1.5
		Chemicals	Chemicals	Sulfuric Acid, Hydrochloric Acid, Phosphoric Acid, etc.	1.0 to 296 0.9 to 160	1.1 to 1.85
Heated Products (above 50 °C)		Heated Products (above 50 °C)	Heated Products (above 50 °C)	Bunker C, Asphalt, etc.		0.8 to 1.2

Mass Meter Product Family & Test Requirements (Test B unless otherwise noted)	Magnetic Flow Meter Product Family & Test Requirements (Test D unless otherwise noted)	PD Product Family & Test Requirements (Test C unless otherwise noted)	Turbine Product Family & Test Requirements (Test A unless otherwise noted)	Typical Products[1]	Viscosity[5] (Centipoise) (Centistokes)	Specific Gravity[2]
Compressed Liquids (Test D)	Not Applicable (conductivity too low)	Fuels and Refrigerants	Fuels and Refrigerants (Test E)	LPG, Propane, Butane, Ethane, Freon 11, Freon 12, Freon 22, etc.	0.1 to 0.5 0.3 to 0.77	0.3 to 0.65
		NH^3	NH^3	Anhydrous Ammonia Note: If a meter is certified for anhydrous ammonia the same meter type may also be certified for LPG without further testing.	0.1 0.2	0.56 to 0.68
Compressed Gases (Test D)	Note: CNG is only included in Section 3.37 Mass Flow Meters of Handbook 44			CNG	0.6 to 0.8	
Cryogenic Liquids and Liquefied Natural Gas (Test D)	Not Applicable (conductivity too low)	Cryogenic Liquids and Liquefied Natural Gas (Test A)	Cryogenic Liquids and Liquefied Natural Gas (Test D)	Liquefied Oxygen, Nitrogen, etc.	0.07 to 1.4	

[1] NOTE: The Typical Products listed in this table are not limiting or all-inclusive; there may be other products and product trade names, which fall into a product family. Water and a product such as stoddard solvent or mineral spirits may be used as test products in the fuels, lubricants, industrial, and food- grade liquid oils product family.

[2] The specific gravity of a liquid is the ratio of its density to that of water at standard conditions, usually 4 °C (or 40 °F) and 1 atm. The density of water at standard conditions is approximately 1000 kg/m³ (or 998 kg/m³).

[3] Diesel fuel blends (biodiesel) with up to 20 % vegetable or animal fat/oil.

[4] Gasoline includes oxygenated fuel blends with up to 15 % oxygenate.

[5] Kinematic viscosity is measured in centistokes. $$Centistokes = \frac{Centipoise}{SpecificGravity}$$

Source for some of the viscosity value information is in the Industry Canada -Measurement Canada "Liquid Products Group, Bulletin V-16-E (rev. 1), August 3, 1999."

NTEP Committee 2007 Final Report
Appendix C – NTETC Measuring Sector

4. Value of the Smallest Unit for LMD Code

Source: NCWM S&T Committee

Background/Discussion: In 2004 the definition of a "retail device" in NIST Handbook 44 was modified to include all devices used to measure product for the purpose of sale to the end user. At that time the Committee believed all affected parties were aware of the proposal and there was no opposition to the change. The Committee had not considered applications where very large deliveries are made to the end user, typically at high flow rates. After the 2005 edition of the Handbook was published and distributed, WMD received a comment from a weights and measures jurisdiction that routinely tests large meters used to deliver fuel to fishing fleets and other large ocean-going boats. The jurisdiction stated that the average delivery is approximately 300 000 gal and may be as much as 1 000 000 gal. Prior to the revision of the definition of "retail," the value of the smallest unit of the indicated delivery for these devices was permitted to be 1 gal. Most of these devices have mechanical registers which make it impractical to have a smallest unit of 0.1 gal at the high flow rates used for such large deliveries. Because the fuel is being delivered to the end user, the jurisdiction believes this is a retail delivery. However, with the revisions to the definition of retail device, NIST Handbook 44 now requires a smallest unit of delivery of not more than 0.5 L (1 pt or 0.125 gal) for these devices.

At its October 2005 meeting, the NTETC Measuring Sector developed a proposal and agreed to forward it to the Committee for consideration. The Measuring Sector believed that, because the maximum flow rate for many applications has increased, 200 gal/min is an appropriate "break point" for determining what the smallest unit of measurement should be. At its October 2005 meeting, the SWMA agreed with the Measuring Sector's proposal and recommended that the item move forward to the Committee.

At the 2006 NCWM Interim Meeting, it was suggested that the Committee should revisit the discussion on suitability of liquid-measuring devices that was discussed by the NCWM in 1991 through 1993. In these earlier discussions, the NCWM was unable to reach a consensus on any changes to NIST Handbook 44, and the item was withdrawn from the Committee agenda. The Committee was informed that there was interest expressed at the 2005 NTETC Measuring Sector meeting in developing new criteria addressing suitability as it relates to flow rate, minimum measured quantity (MMQ), and the smallest unit of measure for applications using liquid-measuring devices. The Committee encourages the NTETC Measuring Sector to pursue development of suitability requirements for submission to the Committee for consideration. In the meantime, the Committee heard no opposition to Item 330-2 and agreed to present the item for a vote at the 2006 NCWM Annual Meeting.

At the 2006 NCWM Annual Meeting, the Committee received input from several manufacturers of aircraft refueling equipment that there is a safety concern with stationary refueling systems that are capable of delivering jet fuel through two different sized hoses at different flow rates using two different meters. In this scenario, the operators of the refueling facility want both meters to have the same unit of indication; that is, 5 L or 1 gal. The Committee understood the concern, but was reluctant to modify the recommendation based on the limited information available at the meeting. The Committee believed that the aircraft refueling industry should propose a change during the next Conference cycle through the NTETC Measuring Sector and the regional associations. However, the Committee recognized that a legitimate problem may exist with existing jet aircraft refueling equipment and encouraged weights and measures jurisdictions to consider safety implications before taking official action on existing jet aircraft refueling devices that may not meet the requirements of paragraph S.1.2.3. During the voting session, there appeared to be concern that if this item was adopted, weights and measures officials could be perceived as ignoring safety issues for aircraft refueling. There was an evident lack of support for the item without an exemption for jet aircraft refueling; therefore, the Committee changed the status of Item 330-2 to an information item to provide sufficient time for development of appropriate language to address the safety concerns with jet aircraft refueling equipment. The Committee requested that the Measuring Sector provide comments or changes to the proposal as appropriate.

Recommendation: The Sector reviewed the following proposal and provided comments to the S&T Committee for consideration at the 2007 NCWM Interim Meeting.

Proposal: Modify Handbook 44, Section 3.30., S.1.2.3. Value of the smallest unit as follows:

S.1.2.3. Value of Smallest Unit. – The value of the smallest unit of indicated delivery, and recorded delivery if the device is equipped to record, shall not exceed the equivalent of:

(a) 0.5 L (~~1 pt(1 gal)~~ on ~~retail~~ devices <u>with a maximum rated flow rate of 750 L/min (200 gal/min) or less</u>

(b) 5 L (1 gal) on ~~wholesale~~ devices <u>with a maximum rated flow of more than 750 L/min (200 gal/min)</u>

This requirement does not apply to manually operated devices equipped with stops or stroke-limiting means.
(Amended 1983, ~~and~~ 1986, <u>and 200X</u>)

See agenda Item 12.

Conclusion: The Sector continued to support its recommended changes to S.1.2.3. as shown above but agreed to consider the addition of a paragraph (c) to allow a larger minimum unit for aircraft jet refueling, during the discussion of agenda Item 12.

New Items:

5. Product Families for Meters

Source: NTEP Director

Background/Discussion: During several NTEP evaluations conducted since the last Sector meeting, there have been concerns that the Product Families tables for meters needs to be revised and updated to reflect changes in metering designs being submitted for evaluation and products currently found in the market place. One meter manufacturer wanted to know what testing was required to include "biodiesel" on a CC: Must the evaluation be conducted using biodiesel fuel with the highest specific gravity available or can testing be conducted using a product, with very similar characteristics, that is available in the manufacturer's lab?

Recommendation: The Sector reviewed and discussed possible changes to clarify the Product Families table for Positive Displacement Meters in the LMD Technical Policy of Publication 14 to be forwarded to the NTEP Committee for approval and addition to the 2007 edition of Publication 14.

The NTEP Director, Steve Patoray, offered the following list of concerns with the current Product Families table:

1. The table as it currently exists is still very confusing.
2. It is not clear which tests are actually required.
3. Instead of the "Tests" being listed in the header of the table, they should be listed with each product group.
4. Typical products should be listed in ascending order (if possible) based on one of the key characteristics or have a method to ID key characteristics.

Conclusion: The Sector agreed that it would be appropriate to consider reorganizing the Product Families table by meter technology considering the most important product characteristics for each. The Sector formed a WG to develop a proposal for consideration at the next meeting. The WG will work primarily through e-mail and conference calls. The chairman appointed the following individuals as members of the WG:

Alex Gutierrez	MEGGITT Fueling Products, Whittaker Controls
Maurice Forkert	Tuthill Transfer Systems
Mark Buttler	Emerson Process Management – Micro Motion
Rodney Cooper	Actaris Neptune
Charlene Numrych	Liquid Controls LLC

NTEP Committee 2007 Final Report
Appendix C – NTETC Measuring Sector

Paul Glowacki	Murray Equipment Inc.
Wade Mattar	Invensys/Foxboro
Richard Suiter	NIST/WMD
Ross Andersen	New York Bureau of Weights and Measures
Richard Miller	FMC Measurement Solutions
Mike Keilty	Endress & Hauser Flowtec AG
Richard Wotthlie	Maryland Weights and Measures
Joe Buxton	Daniel Measurement & Control

6. Table of Key Characteristics of Products in Product Families Table for Meters

Source: NTEP Director

Background/Discussion: Prior to the Sector Meeting the NTEP Director, Steve Patoray submitted the following comments for Sector consideration.

> This is a developing item. Probably all of you reading this know more about this topic than I ever will. I have had discussions with several different people on this topic over the past several months. The Product table in NCWM Publication 14 has been improved over the past several years. Currently, Mass Flow Meters have a key characteristic of specific gravity. PD meters have a key characteristic of viscosity. We list in the table numbers; however, these numbers are without reference. These are normally tied to some temperature. None is listed; also, there is no cross reference for anyone to identify what products might fall within those ranges. I had a very difficult time finding specific information on even some very basic products that we normally use in evaluations. Several of the folks on the sector helped to locate various tables and charts to help identify these values. The information in these charts varies for the "same" product.
>
> As an example of the potential confusion, there are both dynamic (absolute) and kinematic viscosity. The values for these are not the same for the same product; the unit for these, respectively, is centipoises (cP) and centistokes (cSt).
>
> Quoting from the Engineering Tool Box: The viscosity of a fluid is highly temperature dependent and for either dynamic or kinematic viscosity to be meaningful, the reference temperature must be quoted.
>
> In the table on page LMD-3 there are numbers for both Viscosity and Specific Gravity (S.G.) but no temperatures. While S.G. may not be as temperature dependant, some reference should still be cited.
>
> To expand on this in the table in the publication on page LMD-3, we have Test C which just states viscosity, while Test E states specifically kinematic viscosity. This may be very important for the device that uses these tests, but I would suggest that it be clarified and consistent. The use of just the term "viscosity" could be misinterpreted.
>
> What I am proposing is that this group considers listing specific values for each of the typical products listed in this table. It may need to be a separate table. With this information, the NTEP evaluator would then be able to look to the chart and find the correct value for the critical characteristic. This could be listed on the CC and the range could clearly be identified. Additional products could be added as necessary when they are used for an evaluation. The main point is that the same values will be used.
>
> Also, there are four different product groups for crop chemicals. Without further information, this can lead to confusion.
>
> Trying to follow all of the special notes is very difficult.

There still seems to be product families that are based on some other factor that is not specified, not just viscosity or specific gravity (first page of table); many of the different products' values overlap.

This should be enough to get the discussion started. I hope that I have been clear in the fact that I would like to see this table continue to be revised and if possible condensed.

Recommendation: The Sector discussed the NTEP director's concern and explored the concept of having a table of product characteristics. The Sector considered appointing a WG to develop this item for presentation and discussion at the next meeting.

Conclusion: The Sector agreed that further development of key characteristics should be included in the tasks of the WG formed to develop a new product families table approach, as discussed in agenda Item 5.

7. NTEP Checklist for Water Meters in Sub-metering Application

Source: NTEP Director

Background/Discussion: The NTEP Committee has asked the Measuring Sector to consider and develop a checklist for residential water meters. These devices will most likely be used for sub-metering. Several states have recently contacted NTEP regarding these devices. California already has evaluation and certification of these devices in their state. It is recommended that the Sector review the procedures used by California and rework them into a format acceptable to NCWM Publication 14.

Comments from the California NTEP Laboratory: California has found an electronic version and copied the specific section. California uses this as an EPO for field enforcement, follows the same guidelines in approval, does three tests at three flow rates, and does check repeatability. It also has a basic form you can print and do water meter tests. This also follows Handbook 44 Sections 1.10 and 3.36.

In type evaluation, we have a procedure (not a checklist) but it is for the evaluator and starts with application review and other directives not pertaining to actual testing. We also have an electronic form, which is specific for our provers, and as previously stated, follow the testing criteria of the EPO. It probably would not take a whole lot of work (I'm guessing) to format it to the Publication 14 format.

The Sector members can review the California checklist for Domestic Cold Water Meters in the attached Appendix C.

Recommendation: The Sector discussed the NTEP director's concern and explored the concept of adding a checklist for evaluation of water meters in sub-metering applications to Publication 14. The Sector considered appointing a WG to develop this item for presentation and discussion at the next meeting.

Conclusion: The Sector agreed that the best approach for developing a Publication 14 checklist for water meters would be the utilization of a WG made up of technical experts and other interested parties. The members present at the meeting who volunteered to serve on the WG were Dan Reiswig, California NTEP Laboratory; Jim Welch, Measurement Canada; and Rodney Cooper, Actaris Neptune. The Sector chairman, Mike Keilty, will also invite participation by water meter manufacturers AMR, Badger Meter, and Neptune Water Meter Division.

8. NTEP Checklist for LPG Vapor Meters in Sub-metering Applications

Source: NTEP Director

Background/Discussion: The NTEP Committee has asked the Measuring Sector to consider and develop a checklist for LPG Vapor meters. These devices will most likely be used for sub-metering. Several states have

NTEP Committee 2007 Final Report
Appendix C – NTETC Measuring Sector

recently contacted NTEP regarding these devices. California already has evaluation and certification of these devices in their state. It is recommended that the Sector review the procedures used by California and rework them into a format acceptable to NCWM Publication 14.

The Sector members can review the California type evaluation checklist for LPG vapor meters in the attached Appendix D.

Recommendation: The Sector discussed the NTEP director's concern and explored the concept of adding a checklist for evaluation of LPG vapor meters in sub-metering applications to Publication 14. The Sector considered appointing a WG to develop this item for presentation and discussion at the next meeting.

Conclusion: The Sector agreed that the best approach for developing a Publication 14 checklist for LPG vapor meters would be the utilization of a WG made up of technical experts and other interested parties. Dan Reiswig, California NTEP Laboratory, will provide a list of vapor meter manufacturers to be contacted for participation on the WG.

9. Testing Electronic Indicators Using Simulated Inputs

Source: FMC

Background/Discussion: It was stated at the 2004 Measurement Sector meeting that the reason for allowing fixed indicators to use simulated inputs was the fact that durability testing was not required due to the limited vibration associated with their intended use, and vehicle-mounted indicators could not be tested with simulated inputs for the same reason. The intended use was a severe environment; therefore, testing in the field following the permanence requirements was needed to test the durability of the device. In other words to make sure the device would function in its intended environment without failures due to its usage.

The rational of allowing simulated inputs for revisions to an existing CC regardless of installation type is the fact that the device has already undergone the durability phase of the testing. Software revisions will not affect the durability of a device; software changes do however affect the functionality of a device. Therefore, testing with simulated inputs offers a sufficient test to verify software functionality.

Recommendation: The Sector reviewed the following proposal for possible forwarding to the NTEP Committee for consideration at the 2007 NCWM Interim Meeting.

Proposal: Modify Publication 14 Technical Policy Section U. as follows: (LMD – 9)

U. Testing Electronic Indicators ~~for Stationary Installations~~ Utilizing Simulated Inputs.

a. When evaluating electronic indicators for stationary installations, submitted separate from a measuring element, indicators may be evaluated using simulated inputs (i.e., meter pulse, temperature, pressure, density, communications, etc.).

b. <u>When evaluating electronic indicators (regardless of installation type) for revisions to an existing CC for metrological significant software revisions, indicators may be evaluated using simulated inputs (i.e., meter pulse, temperature, pressure, density, communications, etc.).</u>

Conclusion: The submitter explained the background for the original proposal as discussed above. A member asked if the current language in "a." would prevent being able to do some testing with simulated inputs and additional field testing using "live meter" input. During the meeting the Sector developed new language for Publication 14 Technical Policy Section U. as follows and agreed to forward it to the NTEP Committee for addition to the 2007 edition of Publication 14.

U. Evaluating electronic indicators submitted separate from a measuring element.

   When evaluating electronic indicators submitted separate from a measuring element, simulated inputs (i.e., meter pulse, temperature, pressure, density, communications, etc.) may be used as follows:

   1) For the initial testing of the indicator.

   2) For the evaluation of stationary indicators.

   3) For software changes to a device with an existing CC.

10. Next Meeting

Recommendation: The Sector was asked to discuss the time and location for its next meeting.

Conclusion: The Sector discussed the time and location for its next meeting and agreed that the meeting would be scheduled immediately prior to the October 2007 SWMA Meeting, in Little Rock, Arkansas. The exact dates were yet to be determined. The Sector also agreed that any items to be included on the agenda for the 2007 Sector Meeting must be submitted not less than 30 days prior to the meeting in order for the agenda to be distributed to the membership at least 2 weeks prior to the meeting.

Additional Items for Discussion if Time Permits

11. Display of Quantity and Unit Price for Self-serve Aviation Dispensers

Source: Veeder-Root

Background/Discussion: The normal self-serve installation for aviation fuels does not use an analog or digital "gasoline dispenser" that simultaneously displays money and volume. In most cases the self-serve user interface is a credit card console/controller that handles the transaction. These devices are not set up for the simultaneous display.

Aviation self-serve dispensing systems use a base meter-register that is a PD meter with a mechanical register and pulser or an electronic register with pulse output, or an industrial dispenser with volume only and a pulse output. The meter-register part sends pulses to the credit card console/controller. All three components including the consol/controller have NTEP certificates.

In June, the State of Alabama Weights and Measures reviewed a couple of planned installations and informed the installing company that the equipment was "Retail Motor Fuel," and "simultaneous display of Quantity and Sale was required." This started a series of exchanges of information between several parties including two consol/controller manufacturers, several equipment suppliers, and the State of Alabama.

The typical "retail gasoline dispenser" that has the display capability is not designed in terms of materials of construction for aviation gasoline or jet fuel, nor does it have the flow rate capacity. Higher capacity diesel dispensers have the materials of construction problem. Moreover, in jet fuel applications, the dispensers do not have the flow rate capacity required.

There is one small company that assembles dispensers that could today put together a unit to meet the materials of construction and minimum flow requirements. Their NTEP certificate currently is for diesel and gasoline on their simultaneous display dispenser. They could use the appropriate aviation-approved materials of construction components for applications up to 50 gpm and simultaneously display price and currency. These units, however, are not now commonly used in the aviation industry, which means the experience is not there for wide acceptance, and would not be adequate for jet fuel flow rates.

NTEP Committee 2007 Final Report
Appendix C – NTETC Measuring Sector

Recommendation: The Sector reviewed the following proposal for possible forwarding to the NCWM S&T Committee for consideration.

Proposal: Modify Handbook 44, Section 3.30., paragraph S.1.6.5.5. as follows:

S.1.6.5.5. Display of Quantity and Total Price.

> (a) *When a delivery is completed, the total price and quantity for that transaction shall be displayed on the face of the dispenser for at least 5 minutes or until the next transaction is initiated by using controls on the device or other customer-activated controls.*
> *[Nonretroactive as of January 1, 1994]*
> (Added 1992)(Amended 1996)
>
> (b) **For aviation fuel dispensing, the quantity and total price need not be displayed simultaneously as long as the total price and quantity delivered can be viewed by interacting with the display or controller, or the total price and quantity is available on a printed receipt as specified in S.1.6.7.**

Conclusion: The Sector reviewed the proposal to allow devices used in aircraft refueling to either display or print the total price and quantity delivered at the end of the transaction. The Sector took no position on the proposal because most members did not feel qualified to make an informed recommendation concerning aircraft refueling.

12. S.1.2.3. Value of the Smallest Unit for Aviation Turbine Fuel

Source: Veeder-Root

Background/Discussion: At the NCWM Annual Meeting in July, the VTM code Section 331-1, S.1.1.3. Value of Smallest Increment was changed to make the smallest increment 1 gal for aviation jet fuel metering. This item is a follow-on to that item for recognizing the normal installations and operations of the aviation industry for jet fuel. The aviation industry meters and registers jet fuel in whole gallons in fixed applications as it does on aviation refueling vehicles (VTM code). Jet fuel consumers normally expect whole gallon increments.

In most applications, 2 in or larger (150 gal/min or greater) PD meters are used. Retail sale of jet fuel from a fixed fueling system is done in the industry, and there are self-serve jet aviation installations. The minimum flow rate of 150 gal/min relates to a 2 in meter that is not mounted in a dispenser housing. If "self-contained" dispensers were available and used for jet fuel, it would use a smaller meter with less flow rate and the expected minimum increment would be 0.1 gal.

The "exemption" requested for jet fuel is not for "dispensers," but for 2 in and above meters.

See agenda Item 4.

Recommendation: The Sector reviewed the following proposal for possible forwarding to the NCWM S&T Committee for consideration.

Proposal: Modify Handbook 44, Section 3.30., paragraph S.1.2.3. Value of the smallest unit as follows:

> **S.1.2.3. Value of Smallest Unit.** - The value of the smallest unit of indicated delivery, and recorded delivery if the device is equipped to record, shall not exceed the equivalent of:
>
> (a) 0.5 L (1 pt) on retail devices;
>
> (b) 5 L (1 gal) on wholesale devices.
>
> **(c) 5 L (1 gal) on meters with a rated maximum flow rate of 575 L (150 gal/min) or more used for aviation turbine fuels.**

This requirement does not apply to manually operated devices equipped with stops or stroke-limiting means.
(Amended 1983, 1986, and 200X)

Conclusion: The Sector discussed the Veeder-Root proposal to add an exemption for jet aircraft refueling to S.1.2.3. to allow the smallest unit required to be 1 gal on meters with flow rates of 575 L (150 gal/min) or more. One member noted that the similar exemption to the requirements in the VTM Code lists the flow rate as 375 L (100 gal/min) and suggested that the flow rate be the same in both codes. The Sector agreed and modified the proposal as follows:

S.1.2.3. Value of Smallest Unit. - The value of the smallest unit of indicated delivery, and recorded delivery if the device is equipped to record, shall not exceed the equivalent of:

(a) 0.5 L (~~1 pt 0.1 gal)~~ on ~~retail~~ devices <ins>with a maximum rated flow rate of 750 L/min (200 gal/min) or less</ins>

(b) 5 L (1 gal) on ~~wholesale~~ devices <ins>with a maximum rated flow of more than 750 L/min (200 gal/min)</ins>

(c) <ins>5 L (1 gal) on meters with a rated maximum flow rate of 375 L (100 gal/min) or more used for jet fuel aviation refueling systems</ins>

The Sector agreed to forward the modified proposal to the SWMA and NCWM S&T Committees for consideration.

13. Testing Meters Made of Different Metals

Source: California NTEP Laboratory

Discussion/Background: The California NTEP Laboratory is conducting an NTEP evaluation of a family of meters using multiple products in different product families. The meter family includes meters made of aluminum and stainless steel. Because Publication 14 does not specifically address this scenario, the laboratory is asking for input from the Sector before testing starts.

Recommendation: The Sector discussed the scenario described above. The following proposal was offered as a possible solution. The Sector reviewed the proposal for possible forwarding to the NTEP Committee for inclusion in Publication 14.

Proposal: Add a new Section F. to the Publication 14 Technical Policy as follows and renumber subsequent sections:

<ins>L. Meters Within the Same Family Made of Different Materials</ins>

<ins>When multiple meters within a meter family, made of different materials, are submitted for evaluation, all meters will be tested with at least one product from each product family to be included on the CC and at least one meter will be tested with the range of products required in the product family table for the meter type (e.g., positive displacement, turbine, mass meter, etc.) submitted for evaluation.</ins>

The MMA provided the following white paper for Sector consideration during the discussion:

Meter Manufacturers Association

Speaking as experienced manufacturers of PD Meters, Turbine Meters, and Mass Meters; it is our experience that the materials of construction do not affect the quality of measurement over the specified operating range of a particular metering technology, as these have been considered and accounted for during the design phase of the meter.

It is the manufacturers responsibility to ensure that the meter meets type additionally material selection is the manufacturer's responsibility and is typically driven by the requirements of chemical compatibility with the liquid products that are being measured or by industry regulations. (i.e., non ferrous meters for aircraft refueling).

Materials are not selected or modified for reasons of accuracy. The market does identify and eliminate the inferior products through the normal surveillance process as well as the manufacturers' warranty process.

It is normal industry practice to include material varieties such as Stainless Steel, Aluminum, cast Iron, Plastic, etc. into one meter, for example some of our PD meters have cast steel outer housings, stainless steel bearings, cast iron rotors, anodized aluminum blades or cast Iron blades or Plastic blades. Non-ferrous aircraft meters will utilize aluminum cast components and Stainless Steel bearings. We manufacturer turbine meters with stainless steel housings and aluminum rotors, the point being the measurement accuracy is a function of the manufacturing process, not the materials used.

It is not the intent of Handbook 44 to differentiate between measurement technologies, only the intended application.

Doesn't material selection fall under measurement technology?

Where do you draw the line on NTEP lab decisions on the materials of construction?

The manufacturers believe that the answer to the question is in the **LONG** history of meters themselves. There are hundreds of thousands of meters in service in the United States used for direct sales (i.e., home heating oil delivery, loading rack wholesale deliveries, aircraft refueling, agriculture chemical deliveries, etc.). These meters are verified routinely by the local Weights and Measures agencies, if problems are detected (accuracy out of range) then they are taken out of service.

Summary:

The meter manufacturers make determination of materials of construction.

Meter manufacturers make the determination of what particular attributes of a meter enable it to be considered as "part of a family."

Questions that need to be answered in order to make an informed decision:

1. Is there a real world problem that requires a solution by the inclusion of a new section specifically aimed at materials in Publication 14?

2. Is there an inequity in the market, facilitation of fraud?

One of the NTEP laboratories stated that during an evaluation of a mass flow meter, the performance was different for two meters with different "tube" materials. Two mass flow meter manufacturers stated that if both meters were calibrated for the product being measured, there should be no difference in performance due to "tube" material. Another laboratory stated that the permanence test of a meter conducted after 30 days is not a true indicator of long-term permanence. Another member stated that NTEP should be interested in testing key characteristics and metrologically significant components.

Conclusion: The Sector agreed that the best approach for resolving the issue of what components are "metrologically significant" and require additional evaluation, was to include the discussion and development of a proposal for Sector consideration in the tasks of the WG formed to develop a new Product Families table approach, as discussed in agenda Item 5.

Additional Items Added at the Meeting

14. Number of Tests Required for Permanence Test

Source: Endress & Hauser Flowtec AG

Background/Discussion: An application was submitted for evaluation of mass flow meter. During the initial test, not only was the meter tested and met all requirements for the 10 to 1 turndown ratio, but it also passed at 12 to 1 turndown ratio. Following the required time and throughput, the permanence testing was conducted. The meter passed testing for the 10 to 1 turndown ratio but failed at the 12 to 1 ratio. The question was: Should a CC be issued for the meter limited to only a 10 to 1 turndown ratio or should the device fail and testing begin over?

Conclusion: The Sector discussed the issue at length and agreed that the device should have a CC issued for the required 10 to 1 turndown ratio. During the meeting, the Sector proposed changes to Publication 14 as shown below to clarify how this situation should be addressed if it happened again in the future. The Sector agreed to forward its recommendations to the NTEP Committee for consideration at the 2007 NCWM Interim Meeting.

Publication 14 Page – LMD – 64

Permanence Test Procedures for Meters

A. Field Evaluation and Permanence Test of New-Design Meters in Retail Motor-fuel Dispensers

All new-design meters are subject to a permanence test. If a meter is the same as one in a previously tested dispenser, a permanence test is not required. NTEP reserves the right to require a permanence test based on the result of the initial examination.

Initial Examination

1. All meters of the new type ---------------

2. At least one meter -------------------------

3. All meters must ---------------------------

4. Repeatability - When consecutive -------

Subsequent Examination

1. Following the period of use, the tests listed above are to be repeated. All results within the range of flow rates to be included on the CC must be within the ~~acceptance~~ applicable tolerances. Extended flow range testing performed at the manufacturer's discretion may be included on the CC provided the results are within the acceptable tolerances.

2. The examination --------------------------

3. Five tests ----------------------------------

4. Repeatability - When consecutive -------

C. Field Evaluation and Permanence Test for Vehicle-Tank; Except for LPG, Cryogenic and CO$_2$ Meters

The following tests are considered -----------------

Only one meter is required ---------------------------

Following the period of use, the tests listed above are to be repeated. All results within the range of flow rates to be included on the CC must be within the ~~acceptance~~ applicable tolerances. <u>Extended flow range testing performed at the manufacturer's discretion may be included on the CC provided the results are within the acceptable tolerances.</u>

D. Initial Evaluation and Permanence Tests for Wholesale Positive Displacement (PD) Meters

The following tests are considered to be appropriate for metering systems on Wholesale PD Meters:

1. Four test drafts at each of five flow rates.

2. Only one meter ---------------------------

3. Following the period of use, the tests listed above are to be repeated. All results within the range of flow rates to be included on the CC must be within the ~~acceptance~~ applicable tolerances. <u>Extended flow range testing performed at the manufacturer's discretion may be included on the CC provided the results are within the acceptable tolerances.</u>

E. Field Evaluation and Permanence Test for LPG and Cryogenic Meters

The following tests are considered to be appropriate for metering systems on LPG and cryogenic meters:

1. Four test drafts at each of five flow rates.

Only one meter is required ---------------------------

Following the period of use, the tests listed above are to be repeated. All results within the range of flow rates to be included on the CC must be within the ~~acceptance~~ applicable tolerances. <u>Extended flow range testing performed at the manufacturer's discretion may be included on the CC provided the results are within the acceptable tolerances.</u>

Repeatability on LPG & NH3 Meters (Code Reference T.3.)

When multiple tests -----------------------------------

Tests of Automatic Temperature Compensating Systems - LPG & NH$_3$ Meters

The difference between ------------------------------

F. Field Evaluation and Permanence Test for LPG Vapor Meters

The following tests are to be run on an LPG vapor meter as part of the permanence test:

1. Three tests at the maximum discharge rate.

2. Three slow-flow tests.

3. One low-flame test.

Only one meter will be required ----------------------

Following the period of use, the tests listed above are to be repeated. All results within the range of flow rates to be included on the CC must be within the ~~acceptance~~ applicable tolerances. <u>Extended flow range testing performed at the manufacturer's discretion may be included on the CC provided the results are within the acceptable tolerances.</u>

G. Repeatability on Milk Meters (Code Reference N.4.1.1. and T.3.)

Technical Advisors Note: At the meeting, Section G. was identified for inclusion in the recommended changes; however, it speaks only to repeatability. Publication 14 does not have a section on Field Evaluation and Permanence Tests for Milk Meters other than vehicle-tank.

H. Field Evaluation and Permanence Test for Turbine Meters

The following tests are considered to be appropriate for turbine meters:

1. Meters tested in a laboratory -----------------

2. At least one meter is required for each product type for the initial test.

3. If the meter is to be ---------------------------

4. To indicate meter performance ---------------

5. Following the initial test, ----------------------

6. Following the period of use, the tests listed above are to be repeated. All results within the range of flow rates to be included on the CC must be within the ~~acceptance~~ applicable tolerances. <u>Extended flow range testing performed at the manufacturer's discretion may be included on the CC provided the results are within the acceptable tolerances.</u> Following evaluation of test data and analysis of the data presented by the manufacturer for meter performance over temperature and viscosity ranges, the evaluating laboratory may require additional testing prior to issuing a CC for the meter.

I. Field Evaluation and Permanence Tests for Mass Flow Meters

The following tests are considered to be appropriate for mass flow meters:

Type evaluation. The gravimetric test method shall ----------------------

Test Data. Meters tested in a laboratory environment will ---------------

Following the initial test, the meters will be placed into service for the permanence test. The minimum throughput criterion recommended for these meters are 60 days, or 2000 x maximum rated flow in units per minute. Following the period of use, the tests listed above are to be repeated. All results within the range of flow rates to be included on the CC must be within the ~~acceptance~~ applicable tolerances. <u>Extended flow range testing performed at the manufacturer's discretion may be included on the CC provided the results are within the acceptable tolerances.</u>

15. Permanence Tests for RMFD

Source: Gilbarco

Background/Discussion: During a recent evaluation the measuring element from a device with an existing CC was installed in a new frame. For the permanence test, the evaluator required a throughput of 20 000 gal and a minimum of 20 days use before conducting the follow-up tests. The manufacturer believes that the permanence criteria for RMFDs in Publication 14 should be separated into a 20-day requirement for electronics and a 20 000 gal throughput for metering elements. The Meter Manufacturers Association (MMA) developed a proposal to modify

Publication 14 to distinguish between electronics and measuring elements and between elements covered by an existing CC and new equipment being evaluated for the first time.

Conclusion: The Sector reviewed the MMA's proposed changes and agreed to forward them to the NTEP Committee with the recommendation that they be approved as revisions to the 2007 edition of Publication 14.

Publication 14 Page - LMD – 65

A. Field Evaluation and Permanence Test of New-Design Meters in Retail Motor-fuel Dispensers

All new-design meters are subject to a permanence test. If a meter is the same as one in a previously tested dispenser, a permanence test is not required. NTEP reserves the right to require a permanence test based on the result of the initial examination.

Initial Examination

1. All meters of the new type -----------------------

2. At   least one meter --------------------------------

3. All   meters must -----------------------------------

4. Repeatability   - When consecutive ---------------

Subsequent Examination

1. All meters of the new type installed at the type evaluation location must perform within acceptance tolerance throughout the time and volume period specified below.

2. ~~The examination will be conducted no sooner than 20 days after the initial examination and not before the previously chosen meters have measured at least 20 000 gallons for throughput testing.~~
   The examination will be conducted as applicable:

   - No sooner than 20 days for electronic changes of metrological significance.

   - 20 000 gal for throughput testing for mechanical changes of metrological significance.

3. Five   tests --

4. Repeatability   - When consecutive ---------------

B. Field Evaluation Test of Previously Evaluated Components Retail Motor-Fuel Dispensers ~~Using Different Previously Evaluated Meters~~

Different Previously Evaluated Meter

Previously evaluated dispensers using a previously type evaluated meter and indicator (register) will be subject to an initial test. Based on the test results of the initial test, NTEP may require a permanence test.

Nonmetrological Changes

An administrative review shall be conducted to issue a new CC or revise an existing CC for previously evaluated devices because of non metrological changes. Based on the results of the administrative review, NTEP may require an initial test.

List of Appendices:

For copies of the following listed documents, contact Richard Suiter at NIST, (301) 975-4406 or by e-mail richard.suiter@nist.gov.

Appendix A – Reorganized Publication 14 – LMD Checklist
Appendix B – Reorganized Publication 14 – ECR Interfaced with RMFD Checklist
Appendix C – Domestic Cold Water Meters
Appendix D – Hydrocarbon Gas Vapor Meters

THIS PAGE INTENTIONALLY LEFT BLANK.

Appendix D

National Type Evaluation Technical Committee
Weighing Sector

September 26 - 28, 2006, Annapolis, Maryland
Meeting Summary

Carry-over Items D3

    1. Recommended Changes to Publication 14 Based on Actions at the 2006 NCWM Annual Meeting..........D3
        1(a). G-S.1. (d) Identification and G-S.1.1. Location of Marking Information for Not-Built-for-Purpose Devices..D3
        1(b). Time Dependence – Non-automatic Weighing Instruments...D3
        1(c). Time Dependence – Load Cells..D4
    2. S.1.1.(c). Zero Indication (Marking Requirements)..D4
    3. Bench/Counter Scale Shift Test and Definitions..D4
    4. Publication 14 Force Transducer (Load Cell) Family and Selection Criteria – Report of the Load Cell Work Group (WG)..D6
    5. Report of the Tare Work Group (Tare on a Multiple Range Scales)..D6
    6. Minimum Size of Weight and Units Indications..D8
    7. AWS Influence Factor Temperature Ranges that Exceed -10 °C to 40 °C...............................D9

New Items D11

    8. GIPSA Grain Test Scale Requirements..D11
    9. *Ad Hoc* Procedures for Wireless Communication of Metrological Information....................D12
    10. Procedures for Percentage and Proportional Tare..D13
    11. Permanence of Identification When an Audit Trail is the "Security Means"........................D13
    12. e_{min} and Other Markings on Load-Receiving Elements...D15

Railway Track Scale Items D15

    13. CLC Type Evaluation Tests on Railway Track/Vehicle Scales – Technical Policy.................D15
    14. Railway Track Scales with a Rotary Dump Feature Technical Policy...................................D16
    15. In-Motion Railway Track Scale Technical Policy – Developing Item....................................D17
        15(a). Permanence Test for Indicators/Controllers (Note: This was listed as agenda Item 15 (b) in the original agenda.)...D17
        15(b). Permanence Test Criteria for Railway Track Scales Used to Weigh In-Motion.............D20
    16. Added Item – Tare Annunciator at a Zero Net Load Indication..D20

Next Sector Meeting D21

Appendix A. Recommendations for Amendments to Publication 14 ....D23

    Attachment for Agenda Item 1(a) (Ballot Item and comments):..D23
    Attachment for Agenda Item 1(b)...D27
    Attachment for Agenda Item 1(c)...D27
    Attachment for Agenda Item 4..D29
    Attachment for Agenda Item 5..D34
    Attachment for Agenda Item 8..D36
    Attachment for Agenda Item 10..D38
    Attachment for Agenda Item 12..D40
    Attachment for Agenda Item 13..D42
    Attachment for Agenda Item 14..D43
    Attachment for Agenda Item 16..D43

Appendix B. 2006 NTETC Weighing Sector Meeting Attendees D44

Appendix C. Attachments D46
    Attachment for Agenda Item 5 ....D46
    Attachment for Agenda Item 7 ....D52

<td colspan="4" align="center">**Glossary of Acronyms**</td>			
AWS	Automatic Weighing Systems	NTETC	National Type Evaluation Technical Committee
CC	NTEP Certificate of Conformance	OIML	International Organization of Legal Metrology
CIM	Coupled-in-Motion (Railway Track Scales)	S&T	NCWM Specifications and Tolerances Committee
CLC	Concentrated Load Capacity	SWMA	Southern Weights and Measures Association
EPO	Examination Procedure Outline	W/LRE	W/LRE
GIPSA	Grain Inspection Packers and Stockyards Administration	WG Work	Group
NCWM	National Conference on Weights and Measures	WMD	Weights and Measures Division
NIST	National Institute of Standards and Technology	WWMA	Western Weights and Measures Association
NTEP	National Type Evaluation Program		
<td colspan="4">Unless Otherwise Stated: - "Handbook 44" (HB 44) means the 2006 Edition of NIST Handbook 44 "Specifications Tolerances, and Other Technical Requirements for Weighing and Measuring Devices" - "Handbook 130" (HB 130) means the 2006 Edition of NIST Handbook 130 "Uniform Laws and Regulations in the areas of legal metrology and fuel quality." - "Publication 14" (Pub. 14) means the 2006 Edition of NCWM Publication 14 - Weighing Devices - Technical Policy • Checklists • Test Procedures - "Sector" means the NTETC Weighing Sector.</td>			
<td colspan="4">Note: NIST does not imply that these acronyms are used solely to identify these organizations or technical topics.</td>			

Details of All Items
(In Order by Reference Key Number)

Carry-over Items:

1. Recommended Changes to Publication 14 Based on Actions at the 2006 NCWM Annual Meeting

The NIST Technical Advisor, Steve Cook, provided the Sector with specific recommendations for incorporating test procedures and checklist language based upon actions of the 2006 Annual Meeting of the 91st NCWM. The Sector was asked to briefly discuss each item and provide general input on the technical aspects of the issues.

1(a). G-S.1. (d) Identification and G-S.1.1. Location of Marking Information for Not-Built-for-Purpose Devices

Background: See the Report of the 2006 NCWM, S&T Committee agenda Item 320-1 for additional background information. During its 2006 Annual Meeting, NCWM agreed to addend NIST Handbook 44 Section 1.10. paragraph G-S.1.(d) Identification to include requirements for identifying the required software version designation for not-built-for-purpose devices using acceptable words, abbreviations, or symbols and amend G-S.1.1. to clarify the location requirements for the required information in G-S.1.

Discussion: The Weighing Sector discussed a proposal from the NIST Technical Advisor to consider amending NCWM Publication 14 Technical Policy, Checklists, Test Procedures for Weighing Devices, Electronic Cash Registers Interfaced to Scales, Automatic Bulk-Weighing Systems, and AWS. The Technical Advisor reported that the language adopted by the NCWM was edited by NIST after the proposed amendments to Publication 14 were developed. As a result, the language drafted by the Technical Advisor required substantial revisions and were not ready to be reviewed by the Sector. Additionally, the NTEP Director, Stephen Patoray, recommended that the proposed changes to Publication 14 AWS type evaluations procedures be considered by the AWS Work Group (WG) instead of the Sector.

Recommendation: The Weighing Sector recommends that the proposed amendments in the agenda be revised and presented to the Sector as a ballot item on the Publication 14 Scales and Electronic Cash Registers Interfaced with Scales checklists as shown in Appendix A – Attachment for agenda Item 1(a). The result of the ballot will be forwarded to the NTEP Committee prior to the January 2007 NCWM Interim Meeting. The Sector also recommended that the proposed amendments to the type evaluation procedures to the AWS checklist be forwarded to the AWS Work Group for their consideration.

1(b). Time Dependence – Non-automatic Weighing Instruments

Background: See the Report of the 2006 NCWM, S&T Committee agenda Item 320-6 for additional background information regarding the discussions to amend Handbook 44 requirements for load cell time dependence tests. During its 2006 Annual Meeting, the NCWM agreed to amend NIST Handbook 44 2.20. Scales Code paragraph T.N.4.5.1. Time Dependence; Class II, III, and IIII Non-automatic Weighing Instruments as follows to harmonize further the type evaluation test conditions with procedures included in OIML requirements.

Discussion/Recommendation: The Sector recommends that amendments proposed in Appendix A – agenda Item 1(b) be incorporated into NCWM Publication 14 DES Section 58. Time Dependence Test.

1(c). Time Dependence – Load Cells

Background: See the Report of the 2006 NCWM, S&T Committee agenda Item 320-7 for additional information on the discussion to add creep test tolerances, procedures, and corresponding terminology and definitions. During its 2006 Annual Meeting, the NCWM agreed to amend NIST Handbook 44 2.20. Scales Code paragraph T.N.4.6. Time Dependence (Creep) for Load Cells During Type Evaluation, Table T.N.4.6., and add a new paragraph T.N.4.7. Creep Recovery for Load Cells during Type Evaluation. These changes are intended to harmonize further the type evaluation test conditions with procedures included in OIML recommendations; add creep recovery requirements and the appropriate apportionment factors for Class III L load cells that were inadvertently omitted from the language added to NIST Handbook 44 in 2005; and add definitions for the terms and abbreviations used in new paragraph T.N.4.7.

Discussion/Recommendation: The Sector recommends that amendments proposed in Appendix A for agenda Item 1(c) be incorporated into NCWM Publication 14 FT (Force Transducers), Sections 13 and 14 "Determination of Creep."

2. S.1.1.(c) Zero Indication (Marking Requirements)

Source: 2004 Weighing Sector agenda Item 4 - S.1.1.(c). Zero Indication (Marking Requirements).

Background: See the Report of the 2006 NCWM, S&T Committee agenda Item 320-1 for additional background information regarding the justifications for and against the proposed language to amend Scales Code paragraph S.1.1.(c) Zero Indication (Marking Requirements).

Discussion/Recommendation: This item was included in the agenda to provide the Sector with an update on the status of this item. The Sector was asked if there was any new information that could be forwarded to the S&T Committee on agenda Item 320-1. Members of the Sector stated that there is no recommended change to their 2005 position that stated that the Sector does not support the proposal, and that they continue to agree that additional markings should not be required on devices that have an effective means to inhibit a weighing operation or return the device to a continuous digital indication when the scale is in an out-of-balance condition.

3. Bench/Counter Scale Shift Test and Definitions

Source: NIST WMD and 2005 NTETC Weighing Sector (Carryover Item)

Background: This item has been added to the agenda as an update to the 2005 Weighing Sector agenda Item 4. Please refer to the 2005 NTETC Weighing Sector Meeting Summary agenda Item 4 and the 2006 NCWM S&T Committee Final Report on agenda Item 320-3 for additional background information.

Based on the comments received during the 2006 NCWM Annual Meeting, the NIST Technical Advisor to the Weighing Sector amended the language in the proposal as summarized below:

Summary of Proposed Changes

1. Made it clear that no significant changes are being made to two-section livestock scales,
2. Simplified the language for the shift test on "Other" scales,
3. Grouped the livestock scale shift test requirements together,
4. Changed the order of the "test notes" so that the more common type of scales are listed first, and
5. Made minor editorial suggestions on the existing language.

Discussion: The Sector considered e-mail comments from the PTB and John Elengo stating that there is a higher risk of overloading one of the (multiple) supports by using a ½ capacity load in an eccentric loading test pattern than by using a ⅓ capacity load. This appears to stem from the difference in test method between Handbook 44 and OIML R 76. Handbook 44 more or less assumes a rectangular platform and places the load at a point on a line half way from the center to edge, whereas OIML R 76 acknowledges that platforms might exist in other shapes, such as in square, triangular, or circular platforms. Thus, OIML R 76 depends more on placing the eccentric load in a prescribed section of the total area of the platform rather than on a specific line; they more or less trust the load will be placed at the center of the quadrant according to the figures in OIML R 76 for scales with four or less supports. The conclusion made by these comments is that off-center moment (load times distance) in both methods, especially with rectangular platforms, is more or less the same.

Otto Warnloff noted that the use of the term "known test load" in paragraph N.1.1. should be consistently used in the proposed language instead of "test weights." A motion to withdraw this item from the Sector agenda was proposed by Otto Warnloff and seconded by Bob Feezor. During the subsequent discussion, several members of the Sector stated that the proposed language was unnecessary since there was no technical justification to change the current language in Handbook 44. Additionally, the proposed language would prohibit weights and measures officials from using ½ capacity even though the scale could be weighing loads up to ½ scale capacity that are not in the center of the platform. The NIST Technical Advisor stated that there was no technical reason to use procedures that are different than those in R 76. (Note: Manufacturers have stated in past discussion that they have to adjust the scales differently for scales intended for North America and scales intended for countries that adopt OIML recommendations).

Otto Warnloff stated that the current procedures for both shift test loads and positions in Handbook 44 are the same that were included in the 1915 Edition of the National Bureau of Standards Handbook titled "Tolerances and Specifications for Weights and Measures and Weighing and Measuring Devices." Page 19 of the handbook states:

> project over the edge of the weight plate or the commodity plate, pan, or scoop.

Measurement Canada reported that the proposal to amend Handbook 44 would be in conflict with their current requirements; however, they have stated in the past their commitment to align their requirements with OIML R 76.

Darrell Flocken (Mettler Toledo) reminded the Sector that the test load positions are also changed in the proposal and that ⅓ scale capacity in the proposed change puts a different torque in the load cell that is roughly equivalent to current forces when using current Handbook 44 test loads and positions.

Recommendation: The Sector recommends that this item be withdrawn from the Sector agenda and that the Sector withdraws their support for the proposal to amend Handbook 44 shift test positions and test loads. The result of the vote on the motion was:

- **11 votes in favor of withdrawing the item from the Sector agenda and reporting to the S&T Committee that the Sector no longer supports S&T Item 320-3.**

- **8 votes against withdrawing the item from the Sector agenda and reporting to the S&T Committee that the Sector no longer supports S&T Item 320-3.**

- **0 abstentions.**

4. Publication 14 Force Transducer (Load Cell) Family and Selection Criteria – Report of the Load Cell Work Group (WG)

Source: NTEP Committee Technical Advisor (Carryover Item)

Background: During the 2005 NTETC Weighing Sector Meeting Summary discussion of agenda Item 5, Publication 14 Force Transducer (Load Cell) Family and Selection Criteria, Stephen Patoray, NTEP Director, described a proposal that has been forwarded to the Load Cell WG. In summary, the proposal has the potential for an applicant to submit only one load cell for a basic load cell family to be covered on an NTEP CC. However, taking into consideration possible groups within the family (e.g., material construction, methods of mounting, strain gauge bonding, output rating, input impedance, supply voltage, cable details, etc.), there will be no significant difference in the number of load cells that have to be submitted for evaluation.

One of the questions that must be addressed in any proposed change to the selection criteria is how the criteria will affect applications to amend and expand existing Certificates of Conformance.

Discussion: NTEP director Stephen Patoray updated the Sector on the status of the project and provided a copy of the proposed family and selection procedures for Publication 14. See Appendix A – agenda Item 4 for a copy of the proposed language presented by the NTEP Director. He stated that there are only a few companies in the Sector that are affected by the proposed language and recommended that it be sent to other holders of NTEP CC for review. He further requested that any comments be submitted to him no later than December 1, 2006. He also confirmed that the proposed language is similar to the current OIML R 60 selection criteria and that what appears to be additional language is in fact improvements to parts of OIML R 60 that may be subject to different interpretations. He did add that the selection requirements are similar for typical families of load cells and that a small family of load cells may require an additional load cell to be submitted for NTEP because of the current policy of evaluating additional load cells with more than 5000 divisions.

In an e-mail, John Elengo stated that proposed language goes a long way towards alignment with OIML. He further agreed that the added language which clarifies language in OIML R 60 is an improvement and that it should be submitted for consideration during the next revision on the OIML recommendation.

Recommendation: The Sector agrees with the suggestion for the NTEP Director to forward the proposal in Appendix A – agenda Item 4 to holders of NTEP CCs for review and comment by December 1, 2006. The comments will be summarized and if necessary the proposal will be amended and submitted to the NTEP Committee as a recommendation to incorporate them into NCWM Publication 14.

5. Report of the Tare Work Group (Tare on a Multiple Range Scales)

Source: NTEP Participating Laboratories (Carryover Item):

Background: See the 2005 NTETC Weighing Sector Meeting Summary agenda Item 10, Tare on Multiple Range Scales, for additional background information on the earlier Sector discussions and WG developing items and recommendations.

During its 2005 meeting, the Sector voted 13 to 4 in favor of modifying Publication 14 to make tare rounding consistent with Handbook 44 General Code paragraph G-S.5.2.2.(c) Digital Indication and Representation for multi-interval and multiple range scales. The NIST technical advisor developed amendments to Publication 14 Sections 31, 32, and 45 to 51 for Tare and other possible sections that would consistently apply the rounding of tare throughout the digital electronic scales checklist. The Sector was to be balloted on the proposed modifications to Tare in Publication 14. The Sector also agreed to consider the OIML R 76 examples of tare rounding at a later date once the revision of R 76 has been completed.

During the development of the letter ballot language, it was noted that some items (e.g., tare annunciator and terminology) required further discussion by the Sector. Additionally, there is a developing (D) item in the 2006 NCWM S&T Agenda that may have an impact on the Sector recommendation. The NIST technical advisor developed an alternate proposal that would address the operation of the "tare entered" annunciators, give examples demonstrating tare rounding in different scenarios, and add definitions clarifying the differences between semi-automatic tare and preset tare. Based on the concerns above, the NIST Technical Advisor did not believe that the language to amend Publication 14 was sufficiently developed to be submitted to the Sector as a letter ballot.

The NIST technical advisor consulted with the NCWM Chairman, Don Onwiler, NTEP Committee Chairman, Jim Truex, Sector Chairman, Darrell Flocken, and NTEP Director, Stephen Patoray, on both proposals to amend Publication 14 tare requirements. Because of the differing views and complexity of the issue, it was recommended that a small WG be established to review the proposals, review tare operation and requirements in general, and make recommendations on how tare is applied to single range, multiple range and multi-interval scale operation. The WG was specifically asked to develop a recommendation(s) for changes to Publication 14 (based on the Sector's 2005 recommendation), Handbook 44, and Handbook 130 (if necessary) and provide the Weighing Sector guidance on checklist requirements. It was anticipated that the group could perform the tasks though the use of e-mail correspondence and conference calls. The members of the WG are:

> Scott Davidson, Chairman (Mettler Toledo) Andrea Buie (Maryland NTEP Laboratory)
> Jim Truex (Ohio NTEP Laboratory) Todd Lucas (Ohio NTEP Laboratory)
> Steve Cook (NIST Technical Advisor) Stephen Patoray (NTEP Director)

The WG, having met on five occasions through conference calls, developed a list of action items which is summarized below with the proposed amendments to Publication 14 Sections 31, 32, and 45 to 51 based on the recommendation in the 2005 Weighing Sector Summary for agenda Item 10. A full copy of the report of the Tare WG, including the status of the action items, can be found in Appendix C – Attachment to Item 5.

1. Amend Publication 14 Sections 31, 32, and 45 to 51.
2. Discuss a request that the S&T Committee revisit the 1980 discussion.
3. Propose adding definitions of "Tare" and "Preset tare" to Handbook 44.
4. Propose adding a definition of "net" based on Handbook 130.
5. Propose adding requirements for "Tare" and "Preset tare" to Handbook 44.
6. Propose adding indication and printing requirements for tare values to Handbook 44.
7. Propose adding a tolerance for scale accuracy in the net mode to Handbook 44.
8. Consider the OIML allowance for 1e deviation of (calculated) indicated and printed net weights due to the rounding of tare.
9. Propose amending Scales Code paragraph S.1.2.1. to clarify that indicated and printed net weights calculated from gross and tare weights on multi-interval scales, multiple range scales, and weights determined from two different scales may have an apparent interval other than 0, 1, 2, or 5.
10. Agree on a position that paper/plastic zeroed off by an automatic zero-tracking mechanism (AZT) be interpreted as net weight without a net or tare indication based on the definition of net in Handbook 130 (e.g., When a bag or paper is placed on the scale it is balanced off by the AZT mechanism. The product is then added to the scale without removing the tare material).
11. Discuss recommending policy on tare less than 0.5 e for:
    - Single range scales, and/or
    - Multi-interval and multiple range scales.

    Alternatively discuss recommending suitability criteria and minimum number of tare intervals. (e.g., 2 e for single range scales and 5 e_1 for multi-interval and multiple range scales)
12. Discuss and develop a position on Southern Weights and Measures Association (SWMA) Developing S&T agenda Item 360-4 Part 2, Item 1 Scales: S.2.1.7. Tare Rounding on a Multiple Range Scale.

Discussion: The Sector reviewed and discussed Action Item 1 to amend Publication 14 Sections 31 and 32. Additionally, the Sector reviewed the remaining action items and the status of the "Tare" WG. The NIST technical advisor stated many of the proposed definitions in Appendix D; proposed amendments to the Scales Code paragraphs S.1.1.1. Digital Indicating Elements, S.1.2.1. Weight Units, and T.N.2.1. General and AWS Code paragraphs S.1.2. Value of Division Units and T.2.1. General, were sufficiently developed and could be submitted to the NCWM S&T Committee through SWMA for consideration.

Recommendation: The Sector recommends that the amendments to Publication 14 Sections 31 to 32 and 45 to 51 in Appendix A – agenda Item 5 be submitted to the NTEP Committee for approval. The Sector further recommended that the NIST Technical Advisor submit to the SWMA S&T Committee the Tare WG recommendations that propose:

- Adding new and amended definitions to facilitate a uniform understanding of the terms already used in Handbook 44 (e.g., "tare mechanism," "tare," "net," etc.) in Handbook Appendix D – Definitions;
- Amending Scales Code and AWS Code paragraph S.1.1.1. Digital Indicating Elements. Clarifying that a scale can display a "center-of-zero" indication with a load on the platform provided it has been balanced off by a tare mechanism while the scale is in the net mode of operation,
- Amending Scales Code paragraph S.2.2.1. Weight Units. and AWS Code paragraph S.2.1. Value of Division Units. by adding a note that permits calculated net weights from multi-interval and multiple range scales to be in units other than 0, 1, 2, and 5 in order to maintain the accuracy of tare weights when the gross weights are in a weighing range with a larger scale division, and
- Amending Scales Code tolerance paragraph T.N.2.1. General and AWS Codes paragraph T.2.1. General to clarify that tolerances are also applied to net weight indications from a net indication of zero using any possible tare load.

Copies of the proposals submitted to SWMA are included in Appendix C – Attachment to Item 5.

6. Minimum Size of Weight and Units Indications

Source: New York NTEP Participating Laboratory (Carryover Item)

Background: See the 2006 NCWM Specifications and Tolerance Committee Final Report on Item 320-2 for additional background information.

This proposal was originally developed to address a growing problem with the readability of weight indications and the values that define transaction information. Field and laboratory officials indicate that both are becoming increasingly smaller, as demonstrated in the following example of a weight display where the actual size of the weight values are 23 mm in height, but the unit of measurement (g) is 4 mm in height.

During its 2005 meeting, the Sector agreed that any proposal to specify the height of the weight display and units indications in NIST Handbook 44 should be limited to the Scales Code and should align with OIML R 76 to the extent possible. The size requirements should be limited to weight indications visible to the customer in direct sale applications; the weight display should be no smaller than 9.5 mm; and the units display or marking should be no smaller that 2 mm.

Discussion: The Weighing Sector reviewed the background information and the original proposal. Many of the public Sector members believed the 2 mm height specification for the units of measures was too small. Other Sector members commented that the language, while permitting larger display heights for the weight, would still allow a 2 mm display of the units. For example, a scoreboard display with a 155 mm (6 in) weight display could still have a unit display of 2 mm (¼ in). Otto Warnloff stated that the proposed language is not needed since Handbook 44 General Code paragraph G-S.5.1. General (Indicating and Recording Elements) states the primary indicating indications shall be clear, definite, and easily read under any conditions of normal use. The Sector discussed a recommendation to state that the minimum units display height shall be related to the height of the weight display similar to the relationship between the display height and the unit of measure height as specified in Handbook 44 Taximeter Code paragraph S.1.3.1. Minimum Height of Figures, Words, and Symbols which states:

> **S.1.3.1. Minimum Height of Figures, Words, and Symbols.** The minimum height of the figures used to indicate the fare shall be 10 mm and for extras, 8 mm. The minimum height of the figures, words, or symbols used for other indications, including those used to identify or define, shall be 3.5 mm.

It was recognized that the ratio of the 3.5 mm requirement for figures, words, and symbols to the 10 mm for indication of the fare equates to 35 %. The Sector supported the concept of specifying a ratio for this relationship of the weight display and the "units" indication and discussed what might be an appropriate limit. The current language in the proposal would equate to a 21 % relationship. Some public Sector members believed that the ratio should be 60 %. The manufacturers stated that they could not suggest a current relationship at this time since they need to check with their suppliers and verify available sizes and display specifications.

The NTEP Director, Stephen Patoray, suggested that the Sector not discuss or comment on the proposed user requirements at this time since NTEP typically does not evaluate user requirements during type evaluation.

Recommendation: The Sector did not reach a consensus on where to set the minimum height of the units. However, the Sector still supports the proposed specifications and recommends that the minimum height of the units indication be stated as a percentage of the height of the weight display. The NIST technical advisor amended the proposed language to state that the minimum height of the units display be written in terms of as a percentage ratio (starting at 21 %) of the height of the weight display as shown below. The percentage may be changed based on research and input from manufacturers prior the January 2007 NCWM Interim Meeting.

> S.1.4.6. Height. - All primary indications shall be indicated clearly and simultaneously.
>
> (a) On digital devices that display primary indications during direct sales to the customer, the numerical figures displayed to the customer shall be at least 9.5 mm (0.4 in) high.
>
> (b) The units of mass and other descriptive markings or indications, such as lb, kg, gross, tare, net, etc., shall be clearly and easily read and shall be at least 21 % on the height of the primary weight indications.
>
> [Nonretroactive as of January 1, 2007]
> (Added 200X)

The Sector did not have sufficient time at the end of its meeting to discuss and provide recommendations to the S&T Committee on the proposed user requirements for "Minimum Reading Distance" and "Primary Indicating Elements Provided By The User" and the definition for minimum reading distance.

7. AWS Influence Factor Temperature Ranges that Exceed -10 °C to 40 °C

Source: Ohio NTEP Participating Laboratory. (Carryover Item)

Background: See the 1991 and 1999 NCWM S&T Committee Reports and the 2005 NTETC Weighing Sector Meeting Summary agenda Item 18 for additional background information.

Juana Williams (NIST), Steve Cook (NIST), and Darrell Flocken (Mettler Toledo) agreed to develop a summary paragraph, with points that need to be addressed (e.g., temperature testing at the time of the NTEP evaluation vs. ambient temperature during subsequent verifications and the marked temperature range).

During the research of this item for the summary paragraph, NIST WMD discovered that the technical policy recommended by the 2005 Weighing Sector conflicts with the position of the 1991 S&T Committee Item 320-3 (I) S.6.3. Marking Requirements; Temperature Range that states:

> "If a device is marked with a temperature range greater than 14 °F to 104 °F, then the device is tested over the wider range during type evaluation."

Discussion: The Sector reviewed the background information provided in the agenda and considered the following two parts regarding:

Part 1. Developing a recommendation for the NCWM S&T Committee to amend the temperature requirements in the Belt-Conveyor Scale Systems, Automatic Bulk-Weighing Systems, AWS, Multiple Dimension

Measuring Devices, and Grain Moisture Meter (GMM) codes to be similar to the following Scales Code paragraphs T.N.8.1.4. and Table S.6.3.b.

The Sector noted that any proposal to amend the AWS, Belt-Conveyor Scale Systems, and Grain Codes should be submitted to the appropriate Sectors.

Part 2. Developing and recommending a technical policy to address the 1991 S&T position for devices submitted with a temperature range where the minimum and/or maximum temperature exceeds the limit specified in Scales Code paragraph T.N.8.1. Temperature.

Many Sector members reiterated their concerns that the larger temperature ranges listed on the NTEP CC may infer higher quality devices and that applicants would consider submitting these devices in order to gain a potential marketing advantage. The NTEP laboratories were concerned that testing devices to the wider temperature ranges could be a potential safety issue when the evaluator has to spend a significant amount of time in their environmental chamber while devices are tested at the temperature extremes. Additionally, not all the laboratories have environmental chambers that are rated or capable of operating with the larger temperature ranges. The Sector believes that this will result in one or two laboratories receiving the majority of NTEP applications requesting temperature testing using the larger temperature ranges.

The NTEP Director noted that the current language in Handbook 44 Scales Code Table S.6.3.b. Note 5 states that the temperature range marking on the device is only required if **"the temperature range stated on the CC is narrower than and within'**the standard temperature range. Don Onwiler added that a higher range marked on the device would not be supported or covered by the NTEP CC if the CC listed that standard range.

The Sector briefly discussed the possibility of utilizing the provision in the NTEP Administrative Policy to allow "Provisional" NTEP CCs on devices where NTEP evaluated with the larger temperature range submitted by the applicant. This was not recommended because of concerns that the larger temperature range issue may be used as a marketing issue inferring that it is a better quality device.

Recommendation for Part 1: The NIST Technical Advisor will prepare a proposal to SWMA to amend the AWS Code Table S.7.b. Note for Table S.7.a. to align Note 5 with the Scales Code for only the AWS Code. The Sector agreed that the other codes listed by the NIST Technical Advisor need further evaluation by the appropriate NTETC Sector. A copy of the proposal to amend the AWS Code is in Appendix C – Attachment to Item 7.

Recommendation for Part 2: The Sector believes that the technical policy defining the scope of temperature testing conducted by NTEP that was adopted by the 2005 Weighing Sector is not in conflict with the 1991 S&T Committee since the 1999 revision to Scale Code Table S.6.3.b. amended Note 5 by linking the temperature range marking requirement to the range listed on the CC. The Sector also believes the CC would not cover devices that are marked with a larger temperatures range than what is listed on the CC. For example, an NTEP CC that lists a temperature range of -5 °C to $+30$ °C would not cover a device that was not marked with a temperature range, or marked with a -5 °C to $+45$ °C temperature range.

The Sector agrees with the concerns from the NTEP laboratories that testing over larger and larger temperature ranges may become a health and safety issue and that existing temperature chambers are limited in their capabilities to perform temperature tests over wider ranges.

Additionally, the Sector asks that the NCWM S&T Committee review and amend the Committee's 1991 position considering changes to the marking requirements, health and safety concerns, and limitations of NTEP laboratory testing equipment.

New Items

8. GIPSA Grain Test Scale Requirements

Source: GIPSA and the NTEP Committee

Background: GIPSA is responsible for approval of equipment used to inspect grain under the USDA official system. GIPSA has reviewed the NTEP requirements for official grain test scales in an effort to simplify and harmonize with NTEP requirements for commercial grain test scales.

GIPSA, in consultation with the American Association of Grain Inspection and Weighing Agencies, Ohaus, Mettler Toledo, and Seedburo Equipment Company, revised its rules for official grain test scales and user requirements in the GIPSA Equipment Handbook Chapter 2, Grain Test Scales (page 6) effective February 2002. This can viewed at the USDA web site using the following internet address: http://archive.gipsa.usda.gov/reference-library/handbooks/equipment/eq2-scal.pdf

GISPA submitted recommended amendments for NCWM Publication 14 DES Section 37. Grain Test Scales to the Sector in order to align Publication 14 with their requirements for the suitability of scales used to weigh grain samples.

Discussion: The Sector reviewed the proposed amendments submitted by GIPSA and discussed the following to clarify information requested by GISPA in order for an NTEP Certified Grain Test Scale to be used in GISPA supervised applications:

- GISPA reviews a scale's parameters, such as accuracy class, capacity, and "e" or "d" before a scale can be used in a GISPA supervised application. In other words, a suitable scale may be used even if it does not have all the features of a grain test scale as defined in Handbook 44 Appendix D and grain associated calculations (i.e., bushel weight) are not required to be part of the scale.
- Scale manufacturers reported that the availability of suitable scales has improved since the requirements for grain test scales were first revised in the GIPSA Equipment Handbook.
- The GIPSA classifications for "Precision," "Moisture," and "General" are no longer used when applying scales suitability requirements on scales marked with an accuracy class. GIPSA currently determines suitability based on the intended loads called a "Work Portion" in the proposed amendments to Publication 14, and the values of "d" and if applicable "e" for Class II and Class III NTEP certified scales.
- DRAFT NTEP CCs with references to GIPSA shall be submitted to GIPSA for review and comment.
- The "Work Portion" column in the proposed is the range of weights for particular grain samples. Grain samples within a range specified the proposed table must meet the requirements for "d." This can be accomplished by using scales with expanded resolution, multi-interval and multiple range scales, a precision scale scales that covers the anticipated sample weights, or by using more than one scale.
- The GIPSA requirement permits the use of "d" when "d" is smaller than "e."

There were additional discussions about the suitability of Class II or III grain test scales used for other Class II or III applications such as gem and jewelry weighing. Sector members stated that the current Class II or III scales intended for either application are able to be configured to be suitable for direct sale commercial weighing by disabling the grain associated features or making "e" equal to "d" and that the use of grain test scales in other non grain weighing applications is not within the scope of NTEP.

Recommendation: The Sector made some editorial changes to the proposal and recommends that the amended proposed changes in Appendix A – agenda Item 8 be incorporated into Publication 14.

9. Ad Hoc Procedures for Wireless Communication of Metrological Information

Source: NTEP Laboratories

Background: NTEP has received several inquiries about the suitability of scales with wireless communication capability between the W/LRE and the indicating element (and recording element, if applicable). Several NTEP applicants had this feature reviewed, evaluated, and listed on their CCs according to NTEP Technical Policy in Publication 14 Section A that states that "All options and features to be included on the CC must be submitted for evaluation. Nonmetrological features may be listed on a CC, but only if the feature has been evaluated and operates as intended." Other holders of NTEP CCs did not have the feature evaluated and listed on the CC. Because of this discussion, it was noted that there are no specific procedures in Publication 14 and that the participating laboratories were evaluating this feature based on interpretations of language in Publication 14 Section 11. Indicating and Recording Elements - General. Therefore, the Participating Laboratories developed **ad hoc** procedures specifically for weighing devices using wireless communication to transmit weight values between the load-receiving element and a receiver (i.e., indicating element and/or printing element).

The Sector was asked to:

1. Review and recommend the proposed **ad hoc** language in the agenda be added to Publication 14 Section 11. Indicating and Recording Elements – General; and

2. Discuss installations where scale owners or third parties are adding wireless communication capability to weighing equipment that already has an NTEP CC, and whether or not additional NTEP policies or procedures are needed to address this type of modification.

Part 1 Discussion/Recommendation: The Sector made several editorial suggestions for formatting and clarification to the proposed ad hoc procedures. The Sector agreed that the ad hoc procedures in the agenda are sufficiently developed and recommends that the proposed amended ad hoc procedures in Appendix A – agenda Item 9 be incorporated into Publication 14.

Part 2 Discussion/Recommendation: The Sector discussed several scenarios where a device owner or third party replaces cables between the various weighing/load-receiving, indicating, and recording elements, and if the original device would still be traceable to the NTEP CC for the device. The Sector Chairman, Darrell Flocken, asked the Sector about the following scenario.

> **Does the NTEP CC still cover an NTEP certified scale with a third party wireless printer on a scale that was originally evaluated with a cable between the scale (printer output) and a printer or a remote display that was not used as the primary indictor (i.e., a transmitter would be installed on the scale and a receiver would be installed on the printer or slave display)?**

Many of the Sector members believed that this would be a non-metrological modification to the device since the NTEP CC does not state that the "printer output" feature is limited to printers that are physically connected to the device. Therefore, the CC would still apply to installations with printer outputs that have already been evaluated by NTEP where the printer cable is replaced by a wireless communication device. Although the dumb printers and auxiliary displays should not be subject to NTEP evaluation, they are typically verified for agreement of indications during normal inspections. Other Sector members disagreed and stated that this would not be covered by the NTEP CC since it needs to be verified that there is no metrological effect on the measurement when metrological information is sent to the printer via the wireless communication.

- **The Sector agreed that the devices would no longer be traceable to the NTEP CC when wireless communication is added between metrological elements and is not listed on the NTEP CC.**
- **The Sector also recommended that the discussion on wireless communication between a metrological element and a non-metrological element be carried over as an item to be further developed and discussed for the 2007 meeting of the Sector.**

10. Procedures for Percentage and Proportional Tare

Source: NTEP Laboratories

Background: During the April 2000 NTEP Participating Laboratories Technical Session, the weighing devices laboratories discussed the use of percentage and proportional tare. A WG was formed to develop proposed additions to Publication 14. The 2000 WG developed the following definitions and type evaluation procedures for consideration by the Sector in order to facilitate a consistent understanding of the terms used in the proposals. However, the proposals did not get placed on the 2001 Weighing Sector Agenda:

Discussion: The Sector reviewed proposed definitions and Draft Publication 14 type evaluation procedures. A few of the Sector members stated that the terms "proportional tare" and "percentage tare" are not in Handbook 44, and therefore, the proposed type evaluation procedures should not be used in Publication 14. The NTEP Director stated that evaluations of percentage tare are currently being conducted by the NTEP laboratories and that procedures need to be included in Publication 14. Andrea Buie, Maryland, stated that the procedures and definitions are consistent with those used by Measurement Canada and that NTEP uses those procedures for U.S./Canada mutual recognition type evaluations.

Recommendation: The Sector believes that it needs additional time to study the proposed language developed by the NTEP laboratories and recommends that the proposed Publication 14 language be submitted to the Sector as a ballot item prior to the January 2007 NCWM Interim Meeting.

The Sector voted nine to zero to approve and recommend that the 2000 WG proposal in Appendix A - Agenda Item 10 to evaluate weighing devices with percentage and proportional tare be included in NCWM Publication 14.

11. Permanence of Identification When an Audit Trail is the "Security Means"

Source: New York NTEP Laboratory

Background: The New York NTEP Laboratory has stated that audit trails may not always be the appropriate method of sealing for a scale or indicator to ensure permanence of the identification information. This is true if the identification information marked on the device is on a removable part of the weighing (or measuring) device such as a cover or outer case. The identification information marked on the device should not be considered "permanent" according to NIST Handbook 44 paragraph G-S.3. Permanence if it is on a removable part of the device unless the cover can be physically sealed to an integral part of the scale.

1. If an audit trail is the means of sealing, then the outer case or cover containing the identification information can be removed and replaced with that of another scale or indicator, making the information not permanent. This is true of some scales with physical seals where the security seal is located on a cover that is not on an integral part of the scale.

2. If an audit trail is the approved method of sealing for this case, the case base containing the ID plate can be switched with the ID plate on another case.

NTEP Committee 2007 Final Report
Appendix D – NTETC Weighing Sector

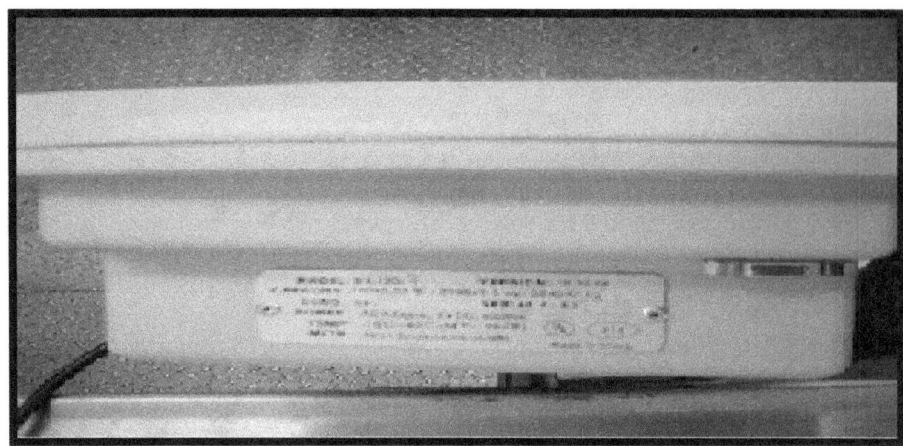

The New York NTEP Laboratory recommends that a scale with the identification located on an easily removed cover and electronic means of sealing still should have a physical security means to seal the cover to an integral part of the scale.

The NIST Technical Advisor provided the Sector additional information on this subject from the June 1989 Weighing Sector NTETC-Weighing Sector meeting discussions on agenda Item 4 regarding identification information located on a removable part of a scale, such as a cover. During that meeting, the Sector recommended that:

> ". . . the fraud aspects of manipulating identification badges were not valid. Many other possibilities exist for fraud and are easier to perpetrate if someone chooses to do so. Tampering was not considered significant relative to the marking requirement. The consensus of the Committee was that "permanent" should mean that the identification information must be sufficiently durable to withstand normal wear and tear throughout the life of the device. An identification badge must be difficult to remove. Blind rivets to attach a badge to a device are acceptable, but removable screws are not...
>
> "The Committee concluded that the sentence (*It may be installed on a removable cover if the cover can be fitted with a security seal.*) in the second paragraph on page 69 of NCWM Publication 14 (1989) shall be deleted."

Discussion: The Sector reviewed the background information and discussed whether there is sufficient justification for this subject to be revisited. During the discussions, the New York and Maryland participating laboratories stated that sealing a cover to the base of the scale is a deterrent and is intended to indicated that a security seal that has been broken or removed from the scale indicates that something has happened to the device. Maryland stated that they have experienced a situation where a cover (and the identification information) was removed from a rejected scale and placed on a sealed scale thereby inferring that the rejected scale was corrected.

Other Sector members agreed with the 1989 Sector discussions that the fraud aspects of manipulating identification badges were not valid. Many other possibilities exist for fraud and are easier to perpetrate if someone chooses to do so. Tampering was not considered significant relative to the marking requirement.

The New York laboratory suggested that the serial number of the scale could be made part of the electronic method of sealing and available in a similar fashion as other forms of audit trails. The manufacturers stated that adding serial numbers to event counters and event loggers would add a significant cost to the scale since the audit trail components would require unique programming for every scale.

The NTEP Director, Stephen Patoray, commented that the identification information and serial number are currently not considered sealable parameters and do not fall within the "Philosophy for Sealing" in Publication 14. He also suggested that the Sector consider developing language similar to Handbook 44 Liquid-Measuring Devices Code paragraph S.4.4.2. Location of Marking Information; Retail Motor-Fuel Dispensers that requires the identification information on a portion of the device that cannot be readily removed or interchanged and allows the information be located internally provided there is easy access through the use of a key or tool. However, the words "easily" and "readily" used in the referenced LMD code paragraph are too subjective. The manufacturers responded that there is no part of a computing scale that is not removable and added that the platter support is an integral part of a scale which can be removed with two screws.

Recommendation: The Sector did not reach a consensus on this item and stated that there was no proposed language to be reviewed in order for the Sector to comment on a proposal to amend Handbook 44 or Publication 14. The New York laboratory was requested to consider the comments made during the discussion and if they still believe that there is sufficient justification, develop a specific proposal to be considered by the Sector or the S&T Committee.

12. e_{min} and Other Markings on Load-Receiving Elements

Source: California NTEP Laboratory

Background: The California NTEP Laboratory has reported that applicants are using incorrect abbreviations for minimum verification scale interval, maximum number of scale division, and load cell verification interval that are used in NIST Handbook 44 Scales Code Table S.6.3.a. and in the applicable definitions in Appendix D. That is, the applicants are using the letters in both upper and lower text cases and without the appropriate subscript. The incorrect case and lack of the subscript "min" or "max" completely changes the definition of the symbol or abbreviation. For example, a lower can "n" by itself indicates the number of divisions configured for a specific instrument and not the maximum number of divisions (n_{max}) and an uppercase "E" is a symbol used for load cells to define the dead load of a load cell in a specific instrument.

Discussion/Recommendation: The Sector considered a proposal to amend NCWM Publication 14 Section 4. Additional Marking Requirements – W/LREs and Section 76. List of Acceptable Abbreviations/Symbols. The NIST technical advisor suggested that the Sector may want to review other sections of Publication 14 for other symbols and abbreviations that are not permitted in Handbook 44 such as markings for load cells and separable indicating elements and clearly state that "Class IV" is or is not an acceptable Marking for Class IIII instruments.

The Sector recommends that the proposed amendments in Appendix A – agenda Item 12 be added to Publication 14 DES Sections 4 and 76. Additionally, the Sector recommends that the proposed amendments to Section 76 be added to the "List of Acceptable Abbreviations/Symbols" that was adopted by the 2006 NCWM during its 91st Annual Meeting.

Railway Track Scale Items

13. CLC Type Evaluation Tests on Railway Track/Vehicle Scales – Technical Policy

Source: Brechbuhler Scales Inc. (Carryover Item)

Background: During its 2005 meeting, the NTETC Weighing Sector agreed that NCWM Publication 14 Technical Policies and Test Criteria for vehicle scales and railway track scales should be reviewed and that separate test criteria should be developed for combination vehicle/railway track scales. The new criteria should include technical policies and test procedures for:

1. New NTEP applications,
2. Amendments to existing Certificates of Conformance (CCs) for railway track scales to include the vehicle weighing feature including:
   a. CLC ratings,
   b. CLC testing using field standard weights (center vs. off-center),
   c. Permanence tests, and
3. Tests using the vehicle scale e_{min} for new NTEP applications and existing CCs.

Ed Luthy developed a draft proposal and distributed it for review and comment to Stephen Langford, Darrell Flocken, and Bob Feezor prior to it being placed on the Sector agenda.

Discussion: The Sector reviewed the proposed amendment to Publication 14 technical policies in Section 8.e., and made some editorial suggestions to the proposed language in Appendix A – Attachment to Item 13, and recommends that it be incorporated into Publication 14 Section 8.e.

The NTEP Director, Stephen Patoray, noted that the proposed amendment to Section 8.e. applies only to devices submitted for evaluation and could not be applied to previous evaluations without additional testing as it is currently worded. The Sector discussed the impact of the proposal to accept a vehicle scale application on an existing NTEP CC for railway track scales.

Some of the Sector members commented that vehicles are wider than the width of the rails and that they may travel along one side of the scale or the other; consequently, it may not be appropriate to include vehicle weighing applications without additional testing since the evaluation of the railway track scale applies test loads directly on the rail and cannot be conducted side-to-side. (**NOTE:** *Side to side testing is not required for an evaluation of a single platform vehicle scale that is less than 14 ft wide)*. Additionally, it was noted that Publication 14 Section 69.5 Increasing Load and Section Test does not specifically state that sections are to be tested up to 100 000 lb although it is implied.

The NTEP Director asked the Sector to confirm that railway track scale section and strain load tests were similar to and had the same impact as vehicle scale evaluations. The Sector stated that the tests are equivalent although the language in Section 69. Performance and Permanence Tests for Railway Track Scales Used to Weigh Statically is not the same as Section 66.a. Performance and Permanence Tests for "Single Load-Receiving Element" Legal for Highway Vehicle Scales and Permanently-Installed Axle-Load Weighing Elements.

The NTEP Director suggested and the Sector agreed that Publication 14 Section E. Modification of Type could be amended to update existing railway track scale CCs to include vehicle-weighing applications without additional testing if:

- the section test on the railway track scale was performed with 100 000 lb of certified test weights or weight carts;
- strain load tests were conducted during the original railway track scale evaluation;
- the design of the load-receiving element is no wider than 12 ft; and
- the design of the weighing element is "beam and girder" design (this would not be applicable to other scale designs such as composite designs where the strength of the deck is dependent on several individual elements being combined in the design of the scale deck). (See SAP suggestions)

Recommendation: The Sector recommends that Section 8.e. as amended by the Sector in Appendix A – Attachment to Item 13 be incorporated into Publication 14 Section 8.e.

The Sector also recommends that specific language for Publication 14 Section E. Modifications be developed as a carryover item based on the above discussion. Stephen Patoray, Todd Lucas and Steve Beitzel agreed to review Section E and develop language to be considered by the Sector during its 2007 Annual Meeting.

14. Railway Track Scales with a Rotary Dump Feature Technical Policy

Source: Bob Feezor, Norfolk Southern Corporation (Carryover Item)

Background: The following is from the 2005 Annual Meeting of the NTETC Weighing Sector, agenda Item 19 which included a discussion and recommendation on the lack of documentation and test procedures for railway track scales with the rotary dump feature that facilitates emptying loose bulk material (e.g., coal) from a railway car while still on the load-receiving element.

> Manufacturers of rotary dump mechanisms for railway track cars offer a weighing option where a railway track scale is built into, or installed in the rotary dump mechanism. The manufacturers of these systems frequently believe that the railway track scale is approved for this application (or in some cases, just the load cells and indication elements), and is covered by an NTEP CC. Additionally, there are many existing rotary dump mechanisms that were installed prior to the formation of NTEP that are nearing the end of their useful life, and the users of these devices are requesting that the railway track scales be covered by NTEP CCs. The submitter of this item is concerned there are no documented policies and test criteria for these devices, and therefore promotes inconsistent enforcement of the NTEP requirements on these devices.
>
> NTEP and the laboratories have consistently stated that a railway track scale CC must include the rotary dump mechanism and must be verified by NTEP and subsequently listed on the CC. The problem is that this policy is not documented in NCWM Publication 14, nor are there any documented procedures to test the rotary dump scales.
>
> Robert Feezor recommended that *ad hoc* policies and test criteria should be developed to add the rotary dump mechanism as a feature on the.
>
> **Recommendation:** The Sector agreed with the submitter that the rotary dump option should be included on CCs for railway track scales, and that NTEP Technical Policies and test criteria are needed for Publication 14. Robert Feezor and Steve Cook agreed to draft technical policies and test criteria will be developed and submitted for the 2006 meetings of the NTEP Labs and Weighing Sector.

Bob Feezor and William Bates (GIPSA) submitted a test form and procedures for testing railway track scales with a "rotary dump" feature.

The NIST Technical Advisor recommended that the "Railway Track Scale Rotary Unloading (Dump)" feature be added to the "Features and Options - Characteristics of Each Model(s)/Type(s) or Sub-Group(s)" section of the NTEP application for scales.

Discussion/Recommendation: The Weighing Sector reviewed the proposed amendment to Section E. Modification of Type and recommends that Section E, as amended by the Sector in Appendix A – Attachment to Item 14, be incorporated into NCWM Publication 14.

15. In-Motion Railway Track Scale Technical Policy – Developing Item

Source: NTEP Director

15(a). Permanence Test for Indicators/Controllers (Note: This was listed as agenda Item 15 (b) in the original agenda.)

Background: During recent months, there has been extensive discussion by the NTEP Committee, the NTEP Director, and several NTEP CC holders regarding this device type. The question has been raised as to the necessity of a permanence test, or more appropriately, the value of a permanence test, for this device type.

The current Section 68 appears to be written to evaluate an entire system, including a previously NTEP-certified W/LRE and NTEP-certified indicating element.

It has been suggested that the CIM device is actually an electronic device that is software-based, which in many cases, is added onto the existing indicating element. It has been further suggested that other electronic devices such as separable indicating elements or POS systems are not required to be subjected to a permanence test in Publication 14. So the question is raised: Should this type of device be required to go through a permanence test when both the W/LRE and indicating element already have an NTEP CC and the W/LRE has already gone through a permanence test?

Discussions on the permanence requirements for the W/LRE indicate that the method of loading does not change with this type of device whether it is a static or a CIM device. The rail car must still travel on the rail over the scale.

However, arguments against the above position indicate that the CIM device is subject to other factors that 1) can only be evaluated as an actual system; 2) cannot be simulated in the laboratory; and 3) must be subjected to some type of actual performance tests and permanence tests to determine if the device can gather and perform the necessary calculations to estimate the weight of both the individual cars and the unit train. Other factors may include, but are not limited to, something in the W/LRE "working loose" in the time between the initial performance test and the permanence test causing additional vibrations that would not effect static weighing, but would have an impact on the software's ability to determine a weight while the railway car is in motion.

In summary, questions that need to be addressed are:

1. Should an in-motion type of device be required to go through a permanence test when the W/LRE is covered by an NTEP CC and has already been tested for permanence for static weighing applications?

2. Should there be different permanence test requirements for W/LRE that are evaluated for static or CIM weighing applications?

3. Should there be different permanence test requirements for CIM or uncoupled in-motion weighing applications?

Additionally, it may be necessary to review the entire Section 68 to clarify several sections applicable to the in-motion indicators and controllers that are not currently clear (e.g., the three sentences before the recording Data table on page DES 113 in the *Actual In-Motion Test* paragraph that state that the system is to be tested under normal operating conditions and then specifies tests that are outside of the normal operation conditions).

Jim Truex submitted the following comments in an e-mail to Stephen Patoray dated September 9, 2006:

> As you are aware, the NTEP Committee ruled on an issue pertaining to the need for a permanence test on a CIM railway system controller. Section 68 of Publication 14, in present form, appears to require a full permanence test (initial and follow-up). The decision by the NTEP Committee was that a full permanence test was not necessary. A one time test, if the controller passed, would be sufficient. In effect, the decision was an **ad hoc** type decision as it needs to be addressed and "red stamped" by the NTETC Weighing Sector. Ohio NTEP laboratory personnel discussed the issue and provided input prior to the decision of the NTEP Committee. The Ohio NTEP laboratory agrees with the decision of the NTEP Committee and is recommending a change to Publication 14 to reflect the decision of the NTEP Committee. The following represents our position and rationale.
>
> 1. The manufacturer is requesting an evaluation and CC for the controller only. If the request was for a complete railway system CC, a permanence test would be necessary.
>
> 2. If the manufacturer was requesting to have their CC for the weighing element amended to cover in-motion weighing, a permanence test would be necessary. It is our understanding that a CC will only be issued for the controller upon successful completion of the evaluation. NTEP does not perform permanence tests on scale indicators and controllers (e.g., hopper scale controllers, vehicle scale controllers/weigh-in & weigh-out system controllers, cash registers, etc.) in the laboratory.
>
> 3. Yes, in this case we are evaluating and testing a system, as necessary to evaluate the performance of the controller in the system, but in this case, we are only issuing a CC for the controller. We do not perform permanence tests on electronics.
>
> 4. What purpose would the permanence test serve? If the system fails the permanence test, but we determine the system failed because a load cell went haywire, what would be our rationale for failing the controller and refusing to issue a CC?

5. It goes without saying Publication 14 needs to be addressed and clarified. It is appropriate to direct any changes to Publication 14 through the appropriate Sector – in this case the Weighing Sector.

Discussion: The NTEP Director provided the Sector with additional background information stating that this item arose from an appeal from a manufacturer to the NTEP Committee regarding permanence testing for a coupled in-motion indicator/controller. The NTEP Committee stated that permanence testing was not needed for the "controller electronics and software." As a result, other manufacturers and the railroads believed that it was an incorrect decision.

Steven Beitzel, Systems Associates provided the Sector with their justification as to why permanence testing is required on both the weighbridge and electronics. He indicated that NTEP Publication 14 Section 68. Performance and Permanence Tests for Railway Track scales Used to Weigh-In-Motion clearly states that a permanence test shall be performed. To issue a certificate with the knowledge that required testing had not been performed cannot be allowed. There can be only one interpretation of the word "shall" under the permanence-testing requirement in the "Permanence Test" paragraph of the procedure.

With regards to modifying the test procedure, Steven Beitzel added that the permanence testing cannot be eliminated. The weight-processing unit of an in-motion railcar weighing system uses a set of filters or algorithms to differentiate the railcar's weight from the extraneous information from the load cell data being generated as the railcar passes over the weigh rail. These algorithms are trade secrets and confidential and not open for evaluation except by performance and permanence testing. These algorithms must determine the true weight while filtering out the erroneous signals generated by impacts of steel wheels on steel rail. As the nature of the "noise" generated by the railcar traffic changes with use of the weighing system and the cars being tested, the follow up test is critical to insure the system can continue to differentiate the actual weight with a system that has seen the effects of time and traffic. This permanence test cannot be eliminated.

Many of the railroads support permanence testing for controllers since Publication 14 Section 68 is intended for the system regardless if the W/LRE has already passed a permanence test and they question the waiving of the requirements without receiving input from the Sector.

Other Sector members stated that many of the arguments presented by Steve Beitzel and the railroads in the previous paragraph are legitimate concerns but that they are mechanical influences of the various part of the track and are installation-related, and not related to the controller electronics and software. NTEP has several examples where permanence testing is waived for electronics and software and that permanence testing is limited to the mechanical portion of a weighing system.

The NTEP Director stated that the comments made by the Sector are all good points, but the language in Section 68 is unclear as to what constitutes a permanence test. Is it intended to evaluate the permanence of the installation?

Otto Warnloff added that permanence testing is based on Handbook 44 General Code paragraph G-S.3. Permanence. which states that __all equipment__ shall be of such materials, design, and construction as to make it probable that, under normal service conditions, accuracy will be maintained, operating parts will continue to function as intended, and adjustments will remain reasonably permanent. Prior to the establishment of NTEP, NBS (now NIST) Report of Tests for all weighing and measuring devices clearly stated that the report did not verify permanence.

Stephen Langford added that the results of permanence testing reflect a device's ability to maintain its accuracy over a period of time established by NTEP. Electronic elements historically demonstrated that permanence testing was not required and the cost of the additional testing provided no benefit to the evaluation.

The Sector was unable to come to a consensus, and the Sector Chairman asked for a vote to see if the Sector agrees with the NTEP Committee decision to waive permanence testing for indicators and controllers used in CIM railway track scale type evaluations.

NTEP Committee 2007 Final Report
Appendix D – NTETC Weighing Sector

- 8 Sector members voted *to support* the NTEP Committee decision.
- 9 Sector members voted *not to support* the NTEP Committee decision.
- 1 Sector member *abstained* from voting.

Recommendation: The Sector did not make a specific recommendation on this item and will forward the discussion and voting results to the NTEP Committee. This item will be carried over to the 2007 Weighing Sector agenda.

15(b). **Permanence Test Criteria for Railway Track Scales Used to Weigh In-Motion**

Source: NTEP Director (**Note:** This was listed as agenda Item 15(b) in the original agenda.)

Background: There are no criteria specified in the permanence test paragraph on page DES-100 of Section 68 of NCWM Publication 14 - Performance and Permanence Tests for Railway Track Scales Used to Weigh-In-Motion, other than the requirements to repeat the tests after a minimum of 20 days after the initial performance test. There needs to be specific "minimum use" requirements in the permanence test similar to permanence test requirements for other weighing devices. For example, the permanence section should include a minimum number of cars (or hours) to be run across the device during the 20-day period.

Discussion/Recommendation: The Sector discussed this item in conjunction with the previous item. During the discussion, the question arose if a WG was needed to better answer the technical issues, propose NTEP technical policies, and develop specific permanence test procedures for CIM performance and weighbridge, and possibly CIM indicators/controllers.

The Sector made no recommendation on this item since Don Onwiler reported that the NTEP Committee would reconsider their decision during their October 2006 meeting. This item will be carried over to the 2007 Weighing Sector Agenda.

16. Added Item – Tare Annunciator at a Zero Net Load Indication

Source: California NTEP Laboratory

Background: This item was inadvertently left off the agenda.

The California NTEP laboratory has reported that some scales submitted for evaluation have a "TARE" annunciator in lieu of Gross or Net annunciators, which do not have a labeled "GROSS" or "NET" display. The scale operates as follows:
- With no weight on the scale, the display shows 0.000 lb with the words STABLE and ZERO on the display underneath the weight.
- With 5 lb on the load-receiving element, the scale displays 5.000 lb with the word STABLE on the display below the weight indication.
- When the TARE button is pressed, the scale displays 0.000 lb and the words STABLE and TARE are displayed below the weight indication. (See picture.)

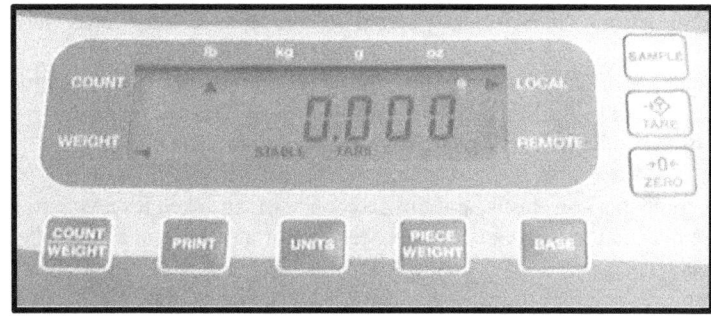

- With 10 lb added to the load-receiving element, the scale displays 10.000 lb with STABLE and TARE displayed below the weight indication.
- When all weights are removed, the scale displays −5.000 with STABLE and TARE displayed below the weight indication.

The California NTEP laboratory is asking the Sector if the word "TARE" is considered to be similar to "TARE ENTERED" according to paragraph 46.1.5. in Publication 14 which states:

| 46.1.5. | A lighted legend or annunciator of TARE ENTERED or **similar statement** is used to indicate that a tare value has been entered and the display indicated net weight. |

The California NTEP laboratory recommended that the language be amended as follows:

| 46.1.5. | A lighted legend or annunciator of TARE ENTERED or words that clearly state ~~similar statement is used to indicate~~ that a tare value has been entered and the display indicated net weight. |

The other NTEP laboratories agreed that "TARE" should not be considered to be a similar statement as "TARE ENTERED" during their April 2006 meeting. Steve Cook and Jim Truex provided background information and stated that they, too, had questioned the use of the term "TARE" back in the late 1970's. The response was given that it had been accepted as "TARE ENTERED" since the 1970's on devices evaluated under NBS Reports of Test (prior to NTEP). The NTEP laboratories believe that both terms "TARE" and "TARE ENTERED" alone do not clearly describe that net weights are being displayed. The laboratories also asked that the Tare WG discuss this item and which terms should and should not be used when the scale is displaying net weight.

The Tare WG has not discussed this item and was not able to provide the Sector with their position prior to the Sector meeting.

The Sector was asked to review the background information and the current language in Publication 16 Section 46.1. If the Sector agrees with the NTEP laboratories, they should review the following proposal to delete Publication 14 paragraph 46.1.5. to clarify that the terms TARE or TARE ENTERED alone are not acceptable as indication of the displayed net weight:

Discussion/Recommendation: The Sector agreed that an indication of "zero" in the net mode should not be identified as "tare" as shown in above picture. Additionally, this example is not consistent with the intent of Handbook 44 General Code paragraphs G-S.5.1. (Indicating and Recording Elements). and General, G-S.5.2.4. Values. that state that primary indications shall be clear, definite, and adequately defined by a sufficient number of figures, words or symbols.

The Sector recommends that NCWM Publication 14 be amended as shown in Appendix A – Attachment to Item 16.

Editorial Note: The NIST Technical Advisor also recommends that Publication 14 Section 46. Tare Operation – Facilitation of Fraud code references include Handbook 44 General Code paragraph G-S-5-2.4. Values and that paragraph 46.2. be amended by deleting the words "TARE ENTERED" and is shown in Appendix A – Attachment to Item 16.

Next Sector Meeting

Discussion/Recommendation: The Sector recommends that the 2007 meeting be held in conjunction with the WWMA Annual Technical Conference in Nevada. The WWMA is considering two different times for their technical conference; September 10 - 14 or October 1 - 4. The Sector prefers to meet after the conference if it is held in September or before the conference if it is held in October to keep it in the 2007 fiscal year.

THIS PAGE INTENTIONALLY LEFT BLANK

Appendix A

Recommendations for Amendments to Publication 14 [1]

Attachment for Agenda Item 1(a) (Ballot Item and comments):

The results of the ballot are:

- 8 *affirmative* votes in favor of the proposed language,

- 3 *negative* votes against the proposed language unless amended to eliminate the word "identifier," and

- 1 member *abstained* from voting.

The three members who voted against the proposed language (and one other non voting member) commented that the use of the word "identifier" was inappropriate although it was adopted into HB 44 by the 91st NCWM during their 2006 Annual Meeting. Other Sector members that voted for the proposed language commented that they also agreed that the word "identifier" was not appropriate, but stated that the language in Publication 14 should reflect the language adopted into HB 44.

During the 2007 Interim Meeting, the NTEP Committee reviewed the ballot language and results. They also considered all comments that were received during the balloting process regarding the use of the word "identifier" that was adopted during the NCWM 2006 Annual Meeting. The Committee concurred with the three sector members who voted against the proposed language and agreed that the word "designation" will remain in Publication 14.

(DES 2) B. Certificate of Conformance Parameters

Certificates of Conformance (CC) shall detail the main elements, load cells, and auxiliary devices used during an evaluation, including model d~~esignation~~ identifier and other significant parameters, under the "Test Conditions" portion of the CC. Only the standard features and options that have been evaluated will be included on the CC.

(DES 6) 8. Weighing Systems, Scales or Weighing/load-receiving elements Greater than 30 000 lb Capacity

In the case of a weighbridge design where the deck is integrated into the weighbridge to be structurally significant, both concrete and steel decks must be tested separately to cover both options on an NTEP Certificate of Conformance. Full NTEP tests are required on both options unless NTEP decides otherwise. A composite scale consisting of a minimum of two decks, (i.e., two spans), one span deck being of steel construction and the other of concrete may be submitted and tested to include both types of decks. Concrete-deck and steel-deck scales should be marked with unique model ~~designations~~ identifier to indicate the difference in platform material.

(DES 17) 1. Marking - Applicable to Indicating, Weighing/Load-Receiving Elements and Complete Scales
Virtually all weighing and measuring equipment (except separate parts necessary to the measurement process but not having any metrological effect) must be clearly and permanently marked with the manufacturer's name or trademark, model ~~designation~~ identifier, and serial number. "Permanent" markings addresses two aspects: (1) the printed information will withstand wear and cleaning, and (2) if the markings are on a plate or badge, then the marking badge must be "permanently" attached to the device. Permanence of it must be obvious that the badge or plate containing this information has been removed. All markings must be clear and attachment of the badge means that the identification information required by G-S.1. is not easily removed, if it is removed, then easily readable. The following test procedure shall be used to determine the permanence of the identification markings.

---

[1] Recommended changes to Publication 14 are indicated in shaded, ~~strike-out,~~ and underlined text.

The system must be clearly and permanently marked on an exterior surface, visible after installation, as follows:				
1.1	The name, initials, or trademark of the manufacturer or distributor. A remote display is required to have the manufacturer's name or trademark and model ~~designation~~ **identifier**. (Code Reference G-S.1.)	Yes	No	N/A
1.2	A model ~~designation~~ **identifier** that positively identifies the pattern or design of the device. The Model ~~designation~~ **identifier** shall be prefaced by the word "Model," "Type," or "Pattern." These terms may be followed by the term "Number" or an abbreviation of that word. The abbreviation for the word "Number" shall, as a minimum, begin with the letter "N" (e.g., No or No.). The abbreviation for the word "Model" shall be "Mod" or "Mod." (Code Reference G-S.1.)	Yes	No	N/A

(DES 23) 3. Additional Marking Requirements - Not Built-for-Purpose Software-Based Devices
References: G-S.1. (c) and G-S.1.1.

~~For software-based, not built-for-purpose devices, the required G-S.1. marking information shall be:~~
- ~~permanently marked on the device, or continuously displayed, or~~
- ~~displayed in a clearly identified "System Identification", "G-S.1. Identification", or~~
- ~~Weights and Measures Identification" that is accessible through the "Help" menu or submenu.~~

3.1.	**2006 language was amended and moved to new Section 3.3.**	Yes	No	N/A
	For software-based, not built-for-purpose devices, the required G-S.1. marking information shall include the current version or revision identifiers in G-S.1. (d) instead of non repetitive serial numbers in G-S.1. (c). The words "version" or "revision" shall be prefaced by words, an abbreviation, or a symbol that clearly identifies the number as the required version or revision.			
3.2.	**2006 language was deleted and replaced with language in 3.32.**	Yes	No	N/A
	If an abbreviation is used for the words "version" or "revision," the abbreviation shall begin with an uppercase "V" or "R" followed by the number. Acceptable examples include, "Ver. 1234," "V 1234," "REV 1234," and "R 1234." Unacceptable abbreviations include "v 1234," "ver 1234," "r 1234," and "rev 1234."			
3.3~~1~~.	At least one of the following methods in 3.3.1. or 3.3.2. must be used:			
3.3.1.	The required information in G-S.1. (a), (b), (d), and (e) ma~~nufacturer or distributor and the model identifier designation are~~shall be (check all that apply):	Yes	No	N/A
	permanently marked on the device according to Section 1 Markings - Applicable to Indicating, Weighing/Load-Receiving Elements and Complete Scales~~.~~, or			
	continuously displayed, or			
	accessible through an easily recognized menu, and if necessary, a sub menu. Examples of menu and submenu include, but are not limited to "Help," "System Identification," "G-S.1. Identification," or "Weights and Measures Identification."			
3.3.1.1.	If the "~~Help"~~ menu or submenu is used to access the required marking information, the "~~Help"~~ menu or submenu must be a part of the main operator screen that is used during normal operation of the device.	Yes	No	N/A
3.3.1.2.	If the "~~Help"~~ menu or submenu is used to access required marking information it must be limited to view-only access.	Yes	No	N/A

3.3.2.	The Certificate of Conformance number may be permanently marked or displayed on the device. If this method is used then clear instructions for accessing the information required in G-S.1. (a), (b), and (d) shall be listed on the CC, including information necessary to identify that the software is the same type that was evaluated.	Yes	No	N/A

List instructions for accessing the required G-S.1. markings using a menu or submenu, or by referencing the information on the CC:

_____

_____

	~~3.1.2.~~	~~The manufacturer or distributor and the model designation are continuously displayed on the device.~~	~~Yes~~	~~No~~	~~N/A~~
	~~3.1.3.~~	~~The manufacturer or distributor and the model designation are accessible through the "Help" menu. Clear instructions for accessing the remaining required information shall be listed on the CC.~~	~~Yes~~	~~No~~	~~N/A~~
~~3.2.~~	~~At least one of the following methods must be used:~~				
	~~3.2.1.~~	~~The Certificate of Conformance (CC) Number is permanently marked on the device.~~	~~Yes~~	~~No~~	~~N/A~~
	~~3.2.2.~~	~~The Certificate of Conformance (CC) Number is continuously displayed on the device.~~	~~Yes~~	~~No~~	~~N/A~~
	~~3.2.3.~~	~~The Certificate of Conformance (CC) Number is accessible through the "Help" menu or submenu. Clear instructions for accessing the remaining required information shall be listed on the CC.~~	~~Yes~~	~~No~~	~~N/A~~
~~3.3.~~	~~All required marking information that is not permanently marked on the device or not continuously displayed must be accessible in an easily recognized clearly identified "System Identification", "G-S.1. Identification", or "Weights and Measures Identification" that is accessible through the "Help" menu or submenu.~~		~~Yes~~	~~No~~	~~N/A~~
~~3.4.~~	Moved to 3.3.1.1.		~~Yes~~	~~No~~	~~N/A~~
~~3.5.~~	~~The software is identified with a software version that is sufficient to identify that the software is the same type evaluated.~~		~~Yes~~	~~No~~	~~N/A~~
~~3.6.~~	Moved to 3.3.1.2.		~~Yes~~	~~No~~	~~N/A~~
~~3.7.~~	~~Clear instructions for accessing the remaining required information shall be listed on the CC.~~		~~Yes~~	~~No~~	~~N/A~~

~~List instructions for accessing the required G-S.1. markings:~~

ECRS – 6

5.7.	**(Delete Existing paragraphs 5.7. through 5.7.4).**	Yes	No	N/A
	For software-based, not built–for–purpose devices, the required G-S.1. marking information shall include ~~be the~~ current version or revision identifiers in G-S.1. (d) instead of non repetitive serial numbers in G-S.1. (c). The words "version" or "revision" shall be prefaced by words, an abbreviation, or a symbol that clearly identifies the number as the required version or revision.			
5.8.	If an abbreviation is used for the words "version" or "revision," the abbreviation shall begin with an uppercase "V" or "R" followed by the number. Acceptable examples include, "Ver. 1234," "V 1234," "REV 1234," and "R 1234." Unacceptable abbreviations include "v1234," "ver1234," "r1234," and	Yes	No	N/A

	"rev 1234."				
5.9.	At least one of the following methods in 5.7. or 5.8. must be used:				
	5.9.1.	The required information in G-S.1. (a), (b), (d), and (e) ~~manufacturer or distributor and the model identifier designation are~~shall be (check all that apply:	Yes	No	N/A
		permanently marked on the device according to Section 1 Markings - Applicable to Indicating, Weighing/Load-Receiving Elements and Complete Scales~~.~~, or			
		continuously displayed, or			
		accessible through an easily recognized menu, and if necessary, a sub menu. Examples of menu and submenu include, but are not limited to "Help," "System Identification," "G-S.1. Identification," or "Weights and Measures Identification."			
5.9.1.1.		If the "~~Help~~"menu or submenu is used to access the required marking information, the "~~Help~~"menu or submenu must be a part of the main operator screen that is used during normal operation of the device.	Yes	No	N/A
5.9.1.2.		If the "~~Help~~"menu or submenu is used to access required marking information it must be limited to view only access.	Yes	No	N/A
5.9.2.		The Certificate of Conformance number may be permanently marked or displayed on the device. If this method is used then clear instructions for accessing the information required in G-S.1. (a), (b), and (d) shall be listed on the CC, including information necessary to identify that the software is the same type that was evaluated.	Yes	No	N/A
List instructions for accessing the required G-S.1. markings using a menu or submenu, or by referencing the information on the CC:					

NTEP Committee 2007 Final Report
Appendix D – NTETC Weighing Sector - Appendix A. Recommendations

(ECRS 8-9) 7. Marking Requirements

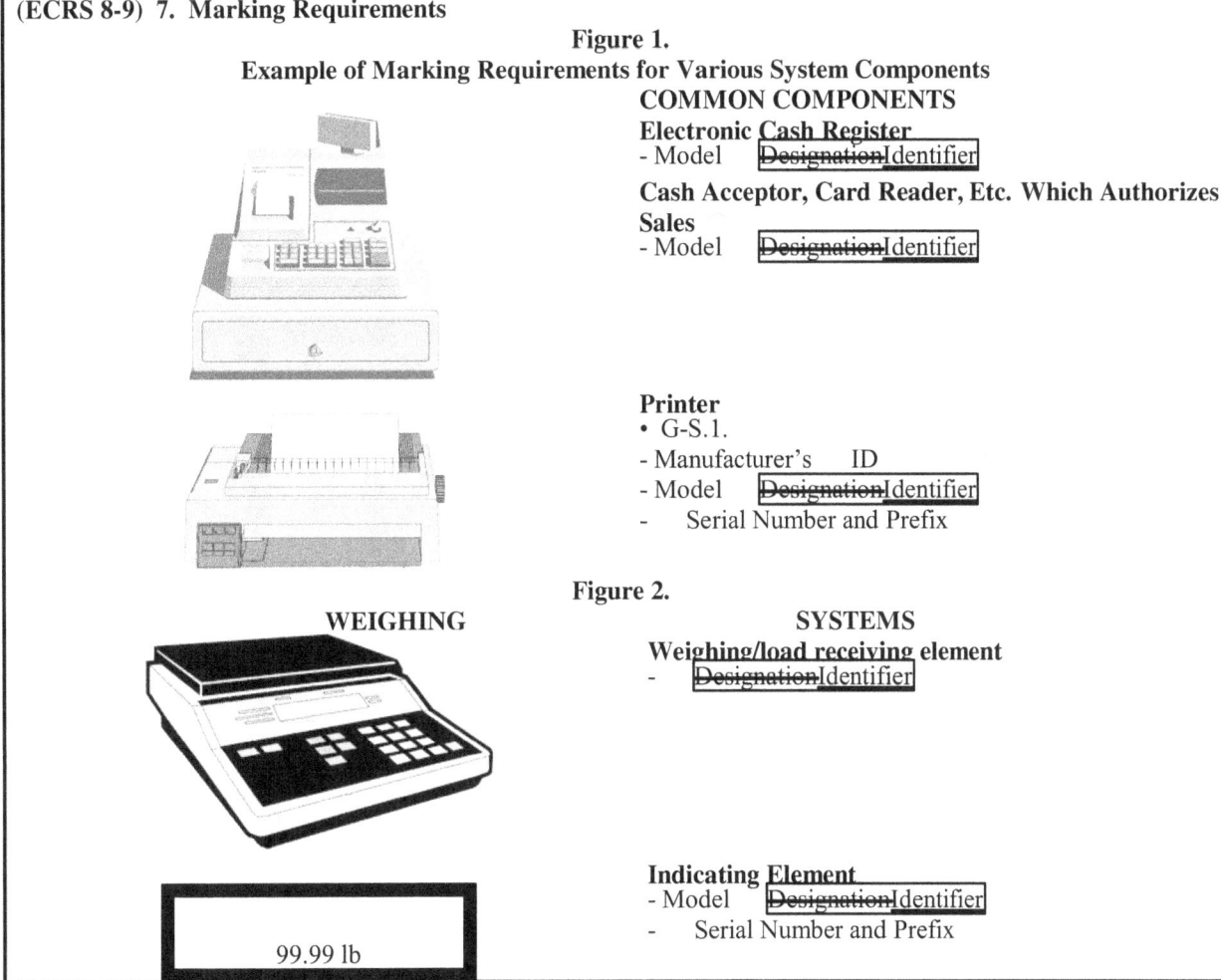

Figure 1.
Example of Marking Requirements for Various System Components

COMMON COMPONENTS

Electronic Cash Register
- Model   ~~Designation~~ Identifier

Cash Acceptor, Card Reader, Etc. Which Authorizes Sales
- Model   ~~Designation~~ Identifier

Printer
- G-S.1.
- Manufacturer's ID
- Model   ~~Designation~~ Identifier
- Serial Number and Prefix

Figure 2.

WEIGHING   SYSTEMS

Weighing/load receiving element
- ~~Designation~~ Identifier

Indicating Element
- Model   ~~Designation~~ Identifier
- Serial Number and Prefix

99.99 lb

Attachment for Agenda Item 1(b)

(DES-78) 58. Time Dependence Test
This test shall be conducted on Class II, III and IIII complete scales and W/LREs in a laboratory. The applied load shall be between 90 % and 100 % of capacity for scales with capacities of 2000 lb or less. For scales with capacities greater than 2000 lb, the load cell or load cells shall be tested individually. The test shall be conducted at 20 °C ± 2 °C (68 °F ± 4 °F) ~~the temperature extremes specified for the device under test (DUT)~~.

For Class III L scales . . .

Technical Advisor's Note: No changes to the Time Dependence Test Form are necessary.

Attachment for Agenda Item 1(c)

(FT 13 – 14) II. Determination of Creep

1. At 20 °C ambient, insert the force transducer (load cell) into the force generating system and load to the minimum dead load. If Procedure I. (which includes increasing and decreasing load tests) has just been completed, wait 1 hr. If a separate creep test is being conducted, exercise the force transducer (load cell) as in Procedure I.5 and then wait 1 hr.

2. If the indicating element for the force transducer (load cell) is provided with a convenient means for checking itself, conduct the self-test at this time.

3. Monitor minimum load output until stable.

4. ~~There are two test methods to determine the creep characteristics of force transducers (load cells). The 1-hr creep test at the maximum load (step 4. (a)) is the preferred form of the creep test; run the return-to-zero creep test (step 4. (b)) only when justified by limitations in the test equipment. The NTEP will conduct step 4. (a) creep tests whenever possible.~~

   ~~Take readings at 1-min time intervals for the first 10 minutes and every 10 min thereafter.~~

   a. **Test for Creep.** Apply a load equal to 90 % to 100 % of the maximum capacity of the force transducer (load cell) and record the indication 20 sec after reaching the load. The time to load test weights and read the indicator shall be as short as possible and shall not exceed the time specified in Table 5. With the load remaining on the load cell, continue to record indications periodically, thereafter, at time intervals over a 30 min period.

   ~~Note: A 30-min test is acceptable if the creep test is performed in accordance to OIML R 60 tolerances.~~

   b. **Test for Creep Recovery.** Remove a load equal to 90 % to 100 % of the maximum capacity of the force transducer (load cell) that has been applied for 1 hr. Record the indication after 20 sec. The time to unload test weights and read the indicator shall be as short as possible and not exceed the time specified in Table 5. Continue to record indications periodically thereafter at time intervals over a 30 min period ~~(or 30 min period if the creep test is conducted according to OIML R 60 requirements)~~.

Table 5 Loading Times		
Load		
Gtth	Tdildi	

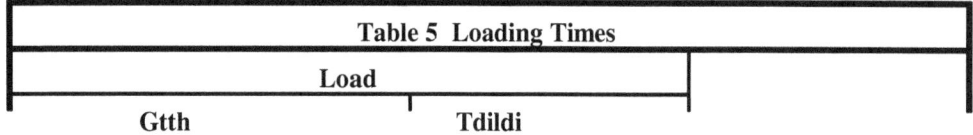

5. Repeat the operations described in steps 2 through 4 at the high and low temperature limits for the accuracy class. If the manufacturer has specified a smaller or a larger range, repeat operations at the limits marked on the cell, provided the temperature range is at least the range required for the accuracy class.

6. With the resulting data, and accounting for the effect of barometric pressure changes, determine the magnitude of the creep and compare it to the tolerance in NIST Handbook 44 Scales Code Table T.N.4.6.

Table T.N.4.6. Time Dependence (Creep) Maximum Permissible Error (mpe) * for Load Cells During Type Evaluation			
mpe in Load Cell Verifications Divisions (v) = p_{LC} x Basic Tolerance in v			
Class	p_{LC} x 0.5 v	p_{LC} x 1.0 v	p_{LC} x 1.5 v
I	0 - 50 000 v	50 001 v - 200 000 v	200 001 v +
II	0 - 5 000 v	5 001 v - 20 000 v	20 001 v +
III	0 - 500 v	501 v - 2 000 v	2 001 v +
IIII	0 - 50 v	51 v - 200 v	201 v +
III L	0 - 500 v	501 v - 1 000 v	(Add 0.5 v to the basic tolerance for each additional 500 v or fraction thereof up to a maximum load of 10 000 v)

v represents the load cell verification interval
p_{LC} represents the apportionment factors applied to the basic tolerance
p_{LC} = 0.7 for load cells marked with S (single load cell applications)
p_{LC} = 1.0 for load cells marked with M (multiple load cell applications)
p_{LC} = 0.5 for Class III L load cells marked with S or M
* mpe = p_{LC} x Basic Tolerance in load cell verifications divisions (v)

Attachment for Agenda Item 4
D. Force Transducers (load cells) to be Submitted for Evaluation

Force transducers (load cells) of essentially the same design may be considered to form a family that can be listed on an NTEP CC. If force transducers (load cells) within a family are made from different materials, such as aluminum, alloy steel, or stainless steel, then all material types must be submitted for evaluation. If the force transducers (load cells) within a family are available in either a 4-wire or 6-wire version, then at least one 4-wire version and one 6-wire version must be evaluated. This policy applies to all applications for new or amended NTEP Certificates of Conformance received after January 31, 2007. This policy is non-retroactive for NTEP Certificates of Conformance issued prior to February 1, 2007.

Under the Mutual Acceptance Arrangement (MAA) for the International Organization of Legal Metrology (OIML), it is possible to obtain either an NTEP CC or an OIML R 60 Certificate or both with a single evaluation. NCWM is a utilizing participant under the MAA and as such will accept test data from issuing participants within the MAA. Evaluations performed by NTEP laboratories can only result in an NTEP CC. These certificates can cover a family of force transducers (load cells) based on the evaluation of representative samples from the family. In order to determine which specific models of force transducers (load cells) are to be used for evaluation, the following selection criterion shall be used:

1. *Evaluation of New Force Transducers (load cells) for NTEP Certificates Only*

Required Information

The following information is required from the manufacturer for review and selection of sample force transducers (load cells):

a. Properly completed request for evaluation

b. Drawing of each capacity force transducer (load cell) within the family to substantiate that they are of the same basic design

c. Quality or accuracy class

d. Maximum number of scale divisions requested (n-max)

e. Minimum verification scale division requested (V-min)

f. Force transducer (load cell) capacities

g. The type(s) of material from which the force transducers (load cells) are made

h. As applicable, outline dimensions and general description illustration of any special equipment (loading fixtures, interconnection boxes, etc.) that are intended to accompany the force transducers (load cells) submitted

i. A complete set of test data on the force transducers (load cells) submitted for evaluation. (Test data is only required for those force transducers (load cells) submitted for type evaluation; test data for each capacity model in the family is not required.)

j. The technology employed by the force transducer (load cell); e.g. strain gage (analog or digital), hydraulic, vibrating wire, piezoelectric, or other. Applicants for analog strain gage force transducers (load cells) must indicate on the application whether 4-wire or 6-wire (or both) design force transducers (load cells) are included in the family.

Note: The manufacturer may market force transducers (load cells) with a smaller number of scale divisions (n-max) and/or with a larger V-min value than those listed on the approval certificate; however, the force transducer (load cell) or accompanying documentation must be marked with the appropriate n-max and V-min for which the force transducer (load cell) may be used.

Selection Criteria

A. Selection of force transducers (load cells) from the family shall be based on the following considerations:

1. The selection of force transducers (load cells) shall be such that the number of force transducers (load cells) to be evaluated is minimized.

2. Where force transducers (load cells) of the same capacity belong to different groups within the family, approval of the force transducer (load cell) with the best metrological characteristics (greatest n-max, smallest V-min) implies approval of the force transducers (load cells) with the lesser metrological characteristics. When a choice exists, the force transducers (load cells) with the best metrological characteristics shall be selected for the evaluation.

3. Force transducers (load cells) with a capacity in between the capacities evaluated, as well as those with a capacity greater than the largest capacity model tested, but not over five times the largest capacity evaluated, are deemed to be approved.

4. For any family of force transducers (load cells), the model with a capacity nearest the center of the range of capacities and with the best metrological characteristics shall be selected for evaluation. When the ratio of the largest capacity force transducer (load cell) within the group or family to the smallest capacity force transducer in the same group or family is 10:1 or less, a cell with a capacity nearest the center of the range shall be selected. The capacity of the selected cell shall not have a ratio greater than 5:1 in regard to the capacity of the force transducers (load cells) at the each extreme of the capacity range. If this is not possible, a second force transducer (load cell) must be selected for evaluation (see Item 5 below). If the selected mid-range capacity cell cannot be evaluated due to laboratory limitations, the NTEP representative should be contacted to select the specific model for evaluation.

5. When the ratio of the largest capacity force transducer (load cell) within the group to the smallest capacity force transducer (load cell) within the same group or family significantly exceeds 10:1, then another force

transducer (load cell) shall be selected for evaluation. The selected force transducer (load cell) shall have a capacity between 5 and 10 times that of the first force transducer (load cell) that was selected for evaluation. When no capacity meets this criteria, the selected force transducer (load cell) shall be that having the smallest capacity that exceeds 10 times that of the nearest smaller capacity force transducer (load cell) that has been selected for evaluation. Should the capacity of the selected cell exceed the capacity of the greatest capacity model in the family or group by a ratio greater than 10:1, an additional model must be selected for evaluation.

6. If both 4-wire and 6-wire designs of force transducers (load cells) are included in the family, then at least one of the selected models for evaluation shall be of the 4-wire design and at least one of the remaining models shall be of the 6-wire design.

7. If the family of force transducers (load cells) includes two or more types of material used for construction of the device, then at least one of the selected models for evaluation shall be of each type of material used for construction.

8. If the family of force transducers (load cells) includes two or more means of environmental sealing (potting, welded cups, etc.) then at least one model using each sealing means shall be selected for evaluation.

9. If the family of force transducers (load cells) includes two or more output levels (2 or 3 mV/V), then at least one model with each output level shall be selected for evaluation.

B. Examples of force transducer (load cell) model selection for evaluation:

a. Force Transducer (load cell) Family A characteristics
   1. Both stainless steel and alloy steel models
   2. 2 mV/V and 3 mV/V outputs
   3. Bending beams in smaller capacities and shear beam in larger
   4. 4-wire and 6-wire designs
   5. n-max is 5000 on all models
   6. Potting or welded metal cup sealing variations
   7. All V-min values equal to 0.015 % of cell capacity
   8. All capacities in pounds:
      500, 1000, 2000, 2500, 4000, 5000, 7500, 10 000, 15 000, 20 000

The following cell models would be selected for evaluation:

- One - 500 lb stainless steel, potted, 3 mV/V, 4-wire bending beam cell
- One - 2500 lb alloy steel, potted, 2 mV/V, 4-wire shear beam cell
- One - 15 000 lb stainless steel, welded, 3 mV/V, 6-wire shear beam cell

Note that Item 2 in Part A above is not applicable in this situation since the metrological characteristics (n-max and V-min) for all of the models are equivalent.

Note that Item 3 in Part A above is met since the 20 000 lb model is less than five times the capacity of the greatest capacity model selected for evaluation (15 000 lb).

Note that Item 4 in Part A above is met since the 2500 lb capacity model of force transducer (load cell) is the closest to the center and is able to meet the requirements in both Item 4 and 5 and therefore was selected for evaluation.

Note that Item 5 in Part A above is met since the ratio between the capacities of the models selected for evaluation does not exceed five.

Note that Item 6 in Part A above is met by having at least one of the models selected of a 4-wire design and at least one of the models selected of a 6-wire design.

Note that Item 7 in Part A above is met by having at least one of the models constructed from each type of materials used.

Note that Item 8 in Part A above is met by having at least one of the selected models with each environmental sealing method employed within the family.

Note that Item 9 in Part A above is met by having at least one of the selected models with a 3 mV/V output and at least one with a 2 mV/V output.

  b. Force Transducer (load cell) Family B characteristics
     1. Compression cells constructed from either alloy steel or stainless steel
     2. All cells are Class III L
     3. Cells from 10 000 lb to 75 000 lb have an n-max of 7500 and cells from 50 000 lb to 200 000 lb have an n-max of 10 000
     4. All cells are 2 mV/V
     5. All cells have the same environmental sealing
     6. All cells have V-min values equal to 0.018 % of their capacity
     7. All cells are of 6-wire design
     8. Cell capacities are:
        10 000; 25 000; 50 000; 75 000; 100 000; 200 000

The following models would be submitted for evaluation:

- One - 50 000 lb with an n-max of 10 000 in stainless steel
- One - 10 000 lb in alloy steel

Note that Item 2 in Part A above is met with the selection of the 50 000 lb model with an n-max of 10 000 since it has the best metrological characteristics.

Note that Item 3 in Part A above is met with the selection of the 10 000 lb model. Selection of the 200 000 lb model could have taken place but the 10 000 lb model was chosen because of the ease of testing.

Note that Item 4 in Part A above is met with the selection of the 10 000 lb model since it is within the 5:1 capacity ratio of the 50 000 lb model initially selected.

Note that Item 5 in Part A above is met with the selection of the 10 000 lb model since the ratio of its capacity to that of the 50 000 lb model does not exceed 5:1.

Note that Item 6 in Part A above does not apply since all models are of 6-wire design.

Note that Item 7 in Part A above is met with the selection of the 10 000 lb model in stainless steel and the 50 000 lb model in alloy steel thus covering both types of material used for construction of the force transducers (load cells) in the family.

Note that Item 8 in Part A above does not apply since all models use the same means of environmental sealing.

Note that Item 9 in Part A above does not apply since all models use the same output level of 2 mV/V.

  2. *Evaluation of New Force Transducers (load cells) for OIML R 60 Certificate or OIML R 60 Certificate and NTEP Certificate of Conformance under the DoMC*

Required Information

The information needed for an OIML R 60 evaluation is listed in OIML Recommendation 60. If the manufacturer is seeking an NTEP Certificate of Conformance for the force transducer (load cell) family or individual model, the information shown in Section 1 above shall also be provided along with a properly completed application for NTEP evaluation. All NTEP requirements are to be met in this type of evaluation. The manufacturer must make certain that the issuing participant selected for the evaluation of the force transducer(s) (load cell(s)) is aware that the submittal is for both NTEP and OIML R 60. A completed application and copies of all submitted data must be sent to NTEP. Once the evaluation has been successfully completed, the issuing authority will provide an OIML Evaluation Report that may then be used to secure an OIML R 60 Certificate. This report is also sent to NTEP. NTEP will evaluate the OIML Evaluation Report and issue an NTEP Certificate of Conformance based on this evaluation. Note that issuance of an NTEP Certificate of Conformance may require the conduct of other tests not performed by the issuing participant. If this happens, the costs of these tests are the responsibility of the applicant.

Note: Should the force transducers (load cells) submitted fail to comply with all OIML R 60 requirements and the manufacturer then seeks to secure an NTEP Certificate of Conformance based on the OIML Evaluation Report, additional testing may be required in order to fully determine compliance of the device(s) with NTEP requirements. The costs for any additional testing deemed necessary for completion of the NTEP review will be the responsibility of the applicant.

Selection Criteria

Selection of the force transducers (load cells) for evaluation shall be based on the OIML R 60 selection criteria as described in OIML Recommendation 60.

3. *Amendment of an Existing NTEP Certificate of Conformance to Add Capacities and/or Change Metrological Characteristics in Conjunction with an OIML R 60 Evaluation Under the DoMC*

Required Information

The information needed for an OIML R 60 evaluation is listed in OIML Recommendation 60. If the manufacturer is seeking to amend an existing NTEP Certificate of Conformance for the force transducer (load cell) family or individual model, the information shown in Section 1 above shall also be provided along with a properly completed application for NTEP evaluation. All NTEP requirements are to be met in this type of evaluation.

Successfully completed, this type of evaluation will result in a test report and test certificate that may be used to secure an amended OIML R 60 Certificate. The test report will be reviewed by the NTEP and if the appropriate criteria are met a NEW NTEP Certificate of Conformance will be issued. Note that the original NTEP Certificate of Conformance will remain active and will not be amended. The new NTEP Certificate of Conformance resulting from this evaluation will list the new capacities added and/or the change in metrological characteristics. Note that the appropriate NTEP Certificate of Conformance number must be marked on the device in compliance with G-S.1. Marking Requirements of NIST Handbook 44.

Note: Should the force transducers (load cells) submitted fail to comply with all OIML R 60 requirements and the manufacturer then seeks to only amend the existing NTEP Certificate of Conformance based on the test report, additional testing may be required in order to fully determine compliance of the device(s) with NTEP requirements. The costs for any additional testing deemed necessary for completion of the NTEP review will be the responsibility of the applicant.

Selection Criteria

The proper models for evaluation will depend upon the nature of the change or addition to be made. Because of this, NTEP personnel shall be contacted and shall determine which model or models of force transducer (load cell) are to be submitted.

4. *Amendment of an Existing NTEP Certificate of Conformance ONLY*

Required Information

The required information will depend upon the nature of the change being made. If additional models of force transducers (load cells) are being added to a family, then the same information and selection criteria as listed in

Section 1 above apply. If the change is to add another version of the force transducer (load cell) listed on the current NTEP Certificate of Conformance the nature of the change or addition must be fully disclosed in the application.

Selection Criteria

The necessity of an evaluation to implement the requested change will depend upon the nature of the change. In general, addition of new models of force transducers (load cells) with capacities outside the 5:1 ratio of those previously evaluated will require additional evaluation. Addition of a 4-wire design with no change in capacity will require an evaluation while the addition of a 6-wire design with no change in capacity will not. The addition of models constructed from a different material will require the evaluation of at least one model constructed of the new material. NTEP personnel will inform you of what models, if any, require evaluation after review of the application.

Attachment for Agenda Item 5
31. Multi-Interval Scales

.
.
.
.

There are several considerations regarding the proper operation of tare on multi-interval scales.

- All tares must be taken in the minimum increment. Therefore, the maximum tare allowed is the maximum capacity of the smallest weighing segment (WS).
- Whenever gross and tare weights fall in different weighing segments, (hence the scale divisions for the gross and tare weights differ), the net weight must be in mathematical agreement with the gross and tare weights that are indicated and recorded, (i.e., net = gross - tare).
- Scales that display or record only net weight values (e.g., most computing scales) may semi-automatically (pushbutton) take tare values to either the internal resolution or the displayed scale division.
- Manually entered keyboard, thumb-wheel, and digital tare values, and programmable tare values stored in memory for multiple transactions must be entered to the displayed scale division.

In applying these principles, it is acceptable to:

- round the indicated and printed tare values (in the ~~upward direction to the nearest)~~ to the nearest appropriate net weight scale division.

- or display net weight values in scale divisions other than the scale division used in the display of gross weight, as when the gross and tare weights are in different ranges of the device. For example, a scale indicating in 2-lb divisions in the lower range and 5-lb divisions in the next higher range may result in net values ending in three or eight in the higher range.

In every case, it is required to maintain the mathematically correct equation:

~~net + tare = gross~~ net = gross - tare

For multi-interval instruments, all tares, except for semi-automatic tare, must be taken in the minimum increment. Therefore, the maximum tare allowed is the maximum capacity of the smallest weighing range.

Semi-automatic tare may be taken to the internal resolution of the scale and any indications or recorded representations of tare shall be rounded to the nearest verification scale division.

31.1. The requirements for the displayed scale division and the mathematical agreement of gross, tare, and net values depend on the information that can be displayed or recorded by the weighing system and may be summarized as follows:

31.1.6.	Keyboard, programmable, and digital, tare entries, and tare stored in memory for multiple transactions must be consistent with the displayed division size. Incorrect entries may be rounded to the nearest displayed scale division or rejected.	Yes	No	N/A
31.1.7.	Devices equipped with a tare capability must, at all times, indicate and record values that satisfy the equation net = gross - tare.	Yes	No	N/A
31.1.8.	Devices equipped with a semi-automatic (push-button) tare must meet the tolerances for net loads for any tare value.	Yes	No	N/A
31.1.9.	Scales that display or record only net weight values (e.g., most computing scales)			
	• may take semi-automatic (push-button) tare and gross values to ~~either~~ the internal resolution of the scale. Printed and displayed net weights shall be rounded to the nearest division, or ~~the displayed scale division.~~	Yes	No	N/A
	• may take all tare values to ~~either the internal resolution or~~ the displayed scale division, and~~,~~	Yes	No	N/A
	• must always begin with the lowest weighing segment on the device regardless of the amount of tare that is taken.	Yes	No	N/A
31.2.	For scales that indicate in only one mode (gross or net) while under load, the scale division for the net weight, whether positive or negative, must be displayed in scale divisions consistent with the weighing range in which the net weight falls.			
31.2.4.	Devices equipped with semi-automatic (push-button) tare must meet the tolerances for net loads for any tare taken up to the tare capacity of the scale.	Yes	No	N/A
31.2.5.	Whenever semi-automatic (push-button) tare is taken and a scale is equipped with only a net display mode, the net weight values must always begin with the lowest weighing range on the device.	Yes	No	N/A
31.2.9.	For all weighing segments ~~ranges,~~ e must equal d.	Yes	No	N/A

32. Multiple Range Scales

A multiple range scale is an instrument having two or more weighing ranges with different maximum capacities and different scale intervals for the same load receptor, each range extending from zero to its maximum capacity. The weighing ranges may be either manually or automatically selected. Each weighing range is considered to be an individual scale and evaluated accordingly.

The capacity and verification scale division for each weighing range must be conspicuously marked near ~~on the~~ reading face of the weight display. The range in use must be clearly indicated. If a scale has a decimal point and a different number of decimal places in each weighing range, the position of the decimal point and the number of digits following is an adequate definition of the weighing range in use. If the weighing ranges do not utilize a decimal point and differing numbers of decimal places, (e.g., scale division are 20 lb, 50 lb, and 100 lb), another method such as an external range indicator must be provided to indicate the weighing range in use.

Whenever gross and tare weights fall in different weighing ranges so that the scale divisions for the gross and tare weights differ, the net weight must agree mathematically with the gross and tare weights that are indicated or recorded (i.e., net = gross - tare)

On a multiple range instrument, a tare value may only be transferred from one weighing range to another one with a larger verification scale interval and ~~but~~ shall then be rounded ~~in the upward direction~~ to the nearest scale division of the latter verification interval.

32.1.	The range in use shall be conspicuously indicated.	**Yes**	**No**	**N/A**
32.3.	Devices with a tare capability must indicate and record values that satisfy the equation net = gross - tare and round the tare value up ~~to~~ the nearest larger ~~division~~ size when entering the larger division. Examples, 2 g changes to 5 ~~0~~ g not 0 ~~5~~ g and 3 g changes to 5 g not 0 g.	**Yes**	**No**	**N/A**
32.4.	Keyboard tare entries must be consistent with the displayed scale division.	**Yes**	**No**	**N/A**

Attachment for Agenda Item 8

37. Grain Test Scales
Code Reference: G-S.2., S.2.1.2., and S.2.3., UR.1.4.

Grain test scales are those used for weighing grain samples to determine moisture content, dockage, weight per unit volume, etc. These scales may compute percentages based upon a stored sample weight and a load placed on the scale platform. The scale may also compute a weight per bushel or hectoliter based upon a specified volume of grain placed on the platform.

If a scale is to be used by the Grain Inspection Packers and Stockyards Administration (GIPSA, ~~formerly the Federal Grain Inspection Service, U.S. Department of Agriculture)~~, for the official grading of grain, the scales must meet more stringent requirements than are necessary for Handbook 44 applications and listed on the NTEP CC. These differences are given in Items ~~7, 8, and 9~~ 37.8. and 37.9.

37.7.	For Handbook 44 only (non-GIPSA) applications, percent calculations may not be displayed unless the value of the scale division is less than or equal to 0.2 g for loads up to 500 g and less than or equal to 1.0 g for loads greater than 500 g. (See NIST Handbook 44 Scales Code paragraph UR.1.4.)	**Yes**	**No**	**N/A**
37.8.	For GIPSA grain test scale applications to be listed on the CC, calculations for test weight must be based on a sample size of one quart only. Calculations are not to be based on a sample size of ~~a 1~~ pint nor shall the capability to compute the test weight per bushel on the basis of 1 pint to ~~be permitted on scales for use by the GIPSA~~.	**Yes**	**No**	**N/A**
37.9.	For GIPSA grain test scale applications to be listed on the CC, the following requirements must be satisfied:			
37.9.1.	The percent values shall be rounded and displayed to at least 0.1 %. ~~To calculate and display percent values, the verification scale division cannot exceed 0.01 g for loads up to 120 g and 0.5 g for loads in excess of 120 g through 1000 g.~~	**Yes**	**No**	**N/A**
37.9.2.	The verification scale division (e) for grain-test scales shall not exceed: - 0.1 g for separations from loads through 500 g, and - 1.0 g for separations from loads above 500 g through 1000 g. For scales used to weigh separations from loads of 100 g and less, d shall be less than or equal to 0.01 g, but may utilize expanded resolution. ~~The percent values shall be rounded and displayed to at least 0.1 percent.~~	**Yes**	**No**	**N/A**

37.9.3.	Selection of a scale with an appropriate division size shall be a user requirement, based on the work portion size, and both the work portion and the separation shall be weighed using a scale with the same (or smaller~~better~~) ~~maximum~~ division size. For example: ~~To calculate and display test weight values, the verification scale division cannot exceed 0.5 g.~~	Yes No N/A

GIPSA Required Division Sizes		
Work Portion	**Division Requirement**	**Accuracy Class**
≤ 100 g	e ≤ 0.1 g; d ≤ 0.01 g	II ~~(expanded resolution*)~~
> 100 g	e ≤ 0.1 g; d ≤ 0.1 g	II, III
> 500 g	e ≤ 1 g ; d ≤ 1 g	II, III

~~37.9.4.~~	~~For official weighing, the GIPSA has three categories of electronic laboratory scales used as grain test scales: precision, moisture, and general. The accuracy classes and scale divisions used for these scale categories shall not exceed those given in the following table.~~	~~Yes No N/A~~

~~Category~~	~~Accuracy Class~~	~~Scale Division~~
~~Precision~~	~~II~~	~~e ≤ 0.01 g d ≤ 0.01 g~~
~~Moisture~~	~~II, III~~	~~e ≤ 0.1 g d ≤ 0.1 g~~
~~General~~	~~II, III~~	~~e ≤ 0.5 g d ≤ 0.5 g~~
~~**NOTE:** For Class III scales e ≤ d. GIPSA requires that e = d for Moisture and General Categories, Class II grain scales used in GIPSA applications.~~		

~~List the models and capacities that satisfy the requirements for each category.~~

Attachment for Agenda Item 9

11. Indicating and Recording Elements – General
Code References: G-S.2., G-S.5.1., G-S.5.2.2., and S.1.2.

There are several general requirements to facilitate the reading and interpretation of displayed weight values. Other requirements address the proper operation of indicating and recording elements.

11.19	As used in this section, a wireless communications device may include weighing elements, load-receiving elements, indicating elements, recording elements (output), etc. that are capable of transmitting and/or receiving metrological information between elements.	
	The following procedures shall be used to evaluate indicating elements that communicate digital weight and other information from separable load-receiving elements or other peripheral equipment (i.e., PC or remote control) by means of a radio transmitter/receiver or other wireless communication devices. At least two (2) complete devices (e.g. crane scales) ~~indicating elements~~ shall be evaluated to ensure:	
11.19.1	There is no interference from one complete device to another of the same type.	Yes No N/A
11.19.2	The signal from a weighing element is sent to the **appropriate** (correct) indicator.	Yes No N/A
11.19.3	The indicator displays an error message or displays meaningless information that could not be mistaken for a valid weight indication, when the signal from the weighing element (or the metrologically significant	Yes No N/A

	peripheral equipment) is interrupted or blocked by all of the following actions:				
11.19.3.1	-turning the power off to the weighing element,	Yes	No	N/A
11.19.3.2	-turning the power off to the metrologically significant peripheral equipment,	Yes	No	N/A
11.19.3.3	-attempting to block the signal with a steel plate, or	Yes	No	N/A
	-moving the indicator away from the weighing element, or			
	-moving the indicator away from the metrologically significant peripheral equipment.			
	Record the actions above (e.g., distance) at which an accurate indication is maintained: _____.			
	This information is for reference purposes and will not be listed or reported on the CC.			
11.19.4	If the indicator can be connected to more than one W/LRE at the same time, by means of a radio link or other wireless means, the indicator will be evaluated with at least two weighing elements (placed side by side) with the wireless communication capability and shall meet all the same requirements as an indicator using physical connection to the weighing elements.	Yes	No	N/A
11.19.5	If more than one wireless communicating device indicator~~can be~~ connected to one single communicating device ~~weighing element~~at the same time using the wireless communication method, the evaluation will be performed with at least two indicators (placed side by side) and connected to the weighing element using the wireless communication method and shall meet all the same requirements as indicators using physical connection to the weighing element.	Yes	No	N/A
11.19.6	If the wireless communication is battery powered, the device continues to perform within applicable tolerance when the DC voltage to the device is lowered to the lowest DC voltage where a weight display is available and raised to the highest voltage recommended by the device manufacturer.

If the manufacturer does not specify the highest DC voltage, the device will be tested with a DC power supply equal to the nominal DC voltage. The device will then be tested with a DC power supply equal to the nominal DC voltage plus 10 %. The low power supply testing will be conducted at the maximum range (distance) determined at the nominal DC voltage which an accurate indication is maintained. | Yes | No | N/A |

Attachment for Agenda Item 10

51. Proportional and Percentage Tare

Code References: G-S.2, G-S.5.1, G-S.5.2.2, G-S.5.6

Proportional tare is a value, automatically calculated by the scale, proportional to the gross weight indicated by the scale. A proportional tare can be a percentage tare or a fixed tare value proportional to a range of gross weights (i.e., a 10 g tare for gross weights between 0 and 2 kg, a 20 g tare for gross weights between 2 kg and 4 kg, etc.). A proportional tare is, therefore, not limited to being a percentage tare.

Percentage tare is a value, expressed as a percentage (i.e., 5.6%), that represents the percentage of tare material compared to the gross or net weight of the commodity. A percentage tare is one form of proportional tare.

The following terms and abbreviations will be used in determining percentage tare:

GW1 = First Gross Weight	%TV = Percentage Tare Value (example: 2 %, 5 %)
FTW = Fixed Tare Weight	%TW = Percentage Tare Weight
GW2 = Final Gross Weight	NW = Net Weight

51.1	The scale does not accept negative values for percentage tare. The tare shall operate only in the backward direction.	Yes No NA
51.2	Percentage tare values may only be entered through the keyboard when the device is at gross load zero and in a "configuration" mode.	Yes No NA

Percentage and/or proportional tares may be preprogrammed into PLU codes. PLU codes may be entered or changed at any time, whether or not a load is on the platter.

Both fixed and percentage tares may be deducted from the gross weight to obtain the final net weight for a transaction. For instance, a PLU code may be preprogrammed with fixed and percentage tares; or a platter or keyboard tare may be manually entered first. Then a percentage tare may be applied, through a PLU code.

51.3	The tare weight shall not be rounded prior to subtracting the tare weight value from the gross weight. The tare value(s) must be deducted first and then the final net weight value rounded off to the nearest scale interval. Rounding of the net weight is not performed until the last mathematical operation.	Yes No NA
51.4	The visual confirmation that a tare has been applied (i.e., "Net" annunciator) must only be enabled if the percentage tare multiplied by the final gross weight represents one or more scale intervals after the appropriate rounding. The turning on of the "Net" annunciator must only occur if tare has actually been applied to the gross weight.	Yes No NA
51.5	Percentage tare shall be manually entered or preprogrammed as part of a PLU in units of percent (or as a decimal fraction, e.g., 1 % = 0.01). Percentage tare shall not exceed 99.9 %.	Yes No NA
51.6	Except for POS systems, the net weight must be displayed when a percentage or proportional tare is entered.	Yes No NA
51.7	If the device deducts both a fixed tare and a percentage tare from the gross weight, the fixed tare shall be deducted first.	Yes No NA

When percentage tare is used, the preferred method* of calculating the net weight is:

Net Weight = (GW1 − FTW) − GW2 (%TV/100)

The net weight of the following example is:

Scale	GW1	FTW	GW2	%TV	%TW = %TV * GW2	NW
15 kg x 5 g	355 g	10 g	345 g	10	34.5 g	310.5 g

Net Weight = (GW1 − FTW) − [GW2 (%TV/100)]
= (355 g − 10 g) − [345 g (10/100)]
= (345 g) − 345 g (0.10)
= 345 g − 34.5 g
= 310.5 g   Rounded to the nearest scale division = 310 g

*Note: Another acceptable method of calculating the net weight is based on the percentage of net weight (%NW).

The percentage of net weight = $[1 - (\%TV/100)]$.

Net Weight = $GW2 [1-(\%TV/100)]$

The net weight of the following example is:

Scale	GW1	FTW	GW2	%TV	%TW − %TV * GW2	NW
15 kg x 5 g	355 g	10 g	345 g	10	34.5 g	310.5 g

Net Weight = $(GW1-FTW) [1-(\%TV/100)]$
= 345 g [1−(10/100)]
= 345 g [1−(.10)]
= 345 g [.90]
= 310.5 g   Rounded to the nearest scale division = 310 g

Attachment for Agenda Item 12

4. Additional Marking Requirements – W/LREs
Code References: S.6., Table S.6.3.a., and Table S.6.3.b.

W/LREs and indicators that are; (1) in the same housing, or (2) permanently hard wired together, or (3) sealed with a physical seal or an electronic link, shall have markings that comply with Section 1, Markings - Applicable to Indicating, W/LREs and Complete Scales. This does not apply to indicating elements that have no input or effect on W/LRE calibrations or configurations.

W/LREs that are not permanently attached to the indicator may be interfaced with many different indicators. Consequently, these W/LREs must be marked with information that clearly identifies the manufacturer, the model, and the capacity of the W/LRE.

Since the United States permits indicating and W/LREs to be evaluated separately with different indicating and W/LREs to be assembled at the time of scale installation, additional marking requirements were adopted in 1987. To facilitate the proper installation of equipment and to permit verification by the enforcement official, a W/LRE not permanently attached to an indicating element must be marked with:

1. its accuracy class,
2. the maximum number of scale divisions, n_{max}, and
3. minimum verification scale division, e_{min}, for which the W/LRE complies with the applicable requirements.

W/LREs not permanently attached to an indicating element shall be clearly and permanently marked with:

4.1.	The nominal capacity of the W/LRE.		Yes	No	N/A
4.2.	Its accuracy class. Indicate class: _____		Yes	No	N/A
4.3.	The maximum number of scale divisions for which it complies with requirements. The preferred abbreviation or symbol is n_{max}.		Yes	No	N/A
4.4.	The minimum verification scale division for which it complies with requirements. The preferred abbreviation or symbol is e_{min}.		Yes	No	N/A

4.4.	The minimum verification scale division for which it complies with requirements. The preferred abbreviation or symbol is e_{min}.	Yes	No	N/A
4.5.	The W/LRE shall be marked with the operating temperature range if the temperature range is other than 14 °F to 104 °F (−10 °C to 40 °C).	Yes	No	N/A

76. List of Acceptable Abbreviations/Symbols

Device Application	Term	Acceptable Not	Acceptable
General:			
Values Defined:			
*Exceptions to Gen'l Tables Of W&M, HB44:			
Weighing and Indicating Elements:	maximum number of scale divisions	n_{max}	N
	Section Capacity	Sec C or Sec Cap	SC
W/LREs	minimum value of verification scale division	e_{min}	E
Load Cells	maximum number of scale divisions	n_{max}	N
	single or multiple cell applications	S = Single; M = Multiple	
	load cell verification interval	v_{min}	V

Attachment for Agenda Item 13

8.2. Additional criteria for vehicle scales, railway track scale, combination vehicle/railway track scale, and other platform scales greater that 200 000 lb.

A CC will apply to all models having:

e. **spans** between sections of not more than 20 % greater than the equipment evaluated; (for vehicle scale no greater than the device evaluated)

Notes for e:

1. On a combination Vehicle /Railway Track Scale, a test of the CLC for the vehicle portion of the scale is not required provided the scale has been evaluated as a Railway Track Scale.

2. The device must be evaluated using the smallest e_{min} value that will be listed on the certificate. This may require the use of a multiple range weight indicator for combination vehicle/railway track scales.

3. The CLC for the vehicle scale portion of the device must not exceed the maximum test weight used for the section test section capacity of the railway track scale. The CLC listed on the CC shall be no greater than what would be permitted in Section 8. d.).

Attachment for Agenda Item 14

E. Modification of Type (DES-12-13)

~~9. Adding a rotary dump feature/option/modification to a railway track scale~~ requires an evaluation to be listed on a new or existing CC.

69a. Additional Tests for Railway Track Scales with a "Rotary Dump" Feature: Repeatability Test

In addition to the tests in Section 69, an additional "return to zero" and "section" test using the available test weight(s) shall be conducted on railway track scales with a rotary dump feature.

69a.1	After the strain-load test(s) have been completed according to Section 69.7:	Yes No NA

1. With the zero-tracking mechanism disabled, zero the indicator.
2. Move a loaded car on to the scale and record the gross weight.
3. Dump the loaded car using all the installed equipment that is used in the dumping process including retarders, vibrators, car ejector, etc., and record the tare weight.
4. Then move the empty car off the scale.

The indications shall return to zero within applicable tolerances.

69a.2	To verify repeatability of the scale accuracy,	Yes No NA

1. Rezero the scale if necessary;
2. Perform a complete section test in both directions using the same maximum test weight(s) used in paragraph 69.5.

The results of the section test after dumping a loaded car shall repeat the indications of the initial test within acceptance tolerances.

Attachment for Agenda Item 16

46.1.1.	A separate continuous display of tare.
46.1.2.	The device has selectable GROSS, TARE, and NET weight display modes with proper descriptors for this information.
46.1.3.	The device has selectable GROSS and NET weight display modes with proper descriptors for this information.
46.1.4.	The display indicates only the net weight and a NET legend or annunciator appears when a tare weight is entered. Gross weight is displayed when the tare weight entry is zero and the NET legend or annunciator is off.
~~46.1.5.~~	~~A lighted legend or annunciator of TARE ENTERED or words that clearly state similar statement is used to indicate that a tare value has been entered and the display indicated net weight.~~
46.2.	An entry of "zero" tare should not acti~~vate the TARE ENTERED annunciator or cause~~ the display to automatically switch the NET display mode. (Scales equipped with a continuous tare display or tare display mode will indicate zero when the tare weight entry is zero; however, the entry of zero tare must not cause the display to automatically switch to the net mode.)

Appendix B

2006 NTETC Weighing Sector Meeting Attendees

First Name	Last Name	Organization E-mail	Address
William	Bates	USDA, GIPSA, FMD, PPB	william.e.bates@usda.gov
Steven	Beitzel	Systems Associates, Inc	sjbeitzel@systemassoc.com
Andrea	Buie	Maryland Department of Agriculture	buieap@mda.state.md.us
Luciano	Burtini	Measurement Canada	burtini.luciano@ic.gc.ca
Steven	Cook	NIST, Weights & Measures Division	steven.cook@nist.gov
Scott	Davidson	Mettler Toledo	scott.davidson@mt.com
Terry	Davis	Kansas Department of Agriculture/W&M Division	tdavis@kda.state.ks.us
Robert K.	Feezor	Norfolk Southern Corporation	rkfeezor@mindspring.com
William	Fishman	New York Bureau of Weights & Measures	Bill.fishman@agmkt.state.ny.us
Darrell	Flocken	Mettler-Toledo, Inc.	darrell.flocken@mt.com
William G.	GeMeiner	Union Pacific Railroad	wgemeiner@up.com
Paul	Hadyka	USDA, GIPSA, FGIS	paul.hadyka@usda.gov
Scott	Henry	NCR Corporation	scott.henry@ncr.com
Richard	Harshman	NIST, Weights and Measures Division	richard.harshman@nist.gov
Ken	Jones	California Division of Measurement Standards	kjones@cdfa.ca.gov
Takashi	Kawazoe	New Brunswick International, Inc.	TKService@nbidigi.com
Stephen	Langford	Cardinal Scale Manufacturing Co.	slangford@cardet.com
Jean	Lemay	Measurement Canada	lemay@ic.gc.ca
Paul	Lewis	Rice Lake Weighing Systems, Inc.	paulew@rlws.com
Todd	Lucas	Ohio Department of Agriculture	lucas@mail.agri.state.oh.us
L. Edward	Luthy	Brechbuhler Scales Inc	eluthy@bscales.com
Nigel	Mills	Hobart Corporation	nigel.mills@hobartcorp.com
Don	Onwiler	Nebraska Division of Weights & Measures	donwiler@agr.ne.gov
Stephen	Patoray	NCWM	spatoray@mgmtsol.com
Kenneth	Ramsburg	Maryland Department of Agriculture	
Byron	School	USDA, GIPSA, FMD, PPB	Byron.C.School@usda.gov
Louis	Straub	Fairbanks Scales, Inc.	strauble@yahoo.com
Otto	Warnlof		warnlof@aol.com
John	Wong	Teraoka Weigh-Systems P/L	john@teraoka.com.sg
Jesus	Zapien	A&D Engineering, Inc.	jzapien@andweighing.com

THIS PAGE INTENTIONALLY LEFT BLANK

Appendix C

Attachments

Attachment for Agenda Item 5

NCWM Form 15
Proposal to a Standing Committee
Committee: Specifications and Tolerances

Date: October 16, 2006	Regional Association: SWMA
Name/Address of Contact Persons: Steven Cook Weighing Sector NIST Technical Advisor NIST Weights and Measures Division Attention: Specifications and Tolerances Committee Phone: (301) 975-4004 Fax: (301) 975-8091 e-mail: steven.cook@nist.gov	Regional Actions: (votes for and against)

Please Attach Additional Pages and Information as Needed

Proposal: Amend Handbook 44 – Appendix D Definitions as follows:

Amend the following definition for tare mechanism:

Tare Mechanism. A mechanism (including a tare bar) designed for determining or balancing out the weight of packaging material, containers, vehicles, or other materials that are not intended to be included in net weight determinations and setting the indication to zero when the tare object is on the load-receiving element:

- by reducing the weighing range for net loads [e.g. subtractive tare (e.g., 15 kg Gross – 5 kg Tare = 10 kg maximum net weight)], or
- without altering the weighing range for net load on mechanical scales [additive tare mechanism (e.g., tare bar on a mechanical scale with a beam indicator)].

The tare mechanism may function as:
- a non-automatic mechanism (load balanced by an operator),
- a semi-automatic mechanism (load balanced automatically following a single manual command),
- an automatic mechanism where the load balanced automatically without the intervention of an operator. An automatic tare mechanism is only suitable for indirect sales to the customer (e.g. prepackaging scales).

Add the following new definitions:

Gross Weight Value. Indication or recorded representation of the weight of a load on a weighing device, with no tare mechanism in operation.

Net Weight. See the current edition of NIST Handbook 130 Uniform Weights and Measures Law Section 1.10.

Net Weight Value. Indication or recorded representation of the weight of a load placed on a weighing device after the operation of a tare mechanism.

Tare. The weight of packaging material, containers, vehicles, or other materials that are not intended to be part of the commodity included in net weight determinations.

Tare Weight Value. The weight value of a load determined by a tare mechanism.

Problem/Justification:
The Scales Code in Handbook 44 has very few requirements for the operation, indications, and recorded representations, specifically for tare. These requirements include paragraphs S.2.1.6. Combined Zero-Tare (0/T) Key, S.2.3. Tare., S.2.3.1. Monorail Scales Equipped with Digital Indications, and T.N.2.1. General (Tolerances). NTEP has further developed type evaluation criteria for tare based on the reference Handbook 44 paragraphs, General Code paragraph G-S.2. Facilitation of Fraud, and other General Code paragraphs for indicating and recording elements and recorded representations. It has increasingly become difficult to support the NTEP evaluation criteria citing paragraph G-S.2. since it is general in nature and subject to multiple interpretations. Additionally, the general nature of G-S.2. makes it difficult for weights and measures officials, device manufacturers, and device owners and operators to be aware of the tare requirements that have been agreed upon by the National Type Evaluation Technical Committee (NTETC) Weighing Sector. (Note: The Weighing Sector is comprised of weight and measures officials, device manufacturers, and NIST, USDA, and Measurement Canada).

Background: In 2006, the NTETC Weighing Sector formed a small Work Group (WG) to review "Tare" operation and requirements, and make recommendations on how tare is applied to single range, multiple range, and multi-interval scale operation. The WG was also asked to develop a recommendation(s) for changes to Publication 14 and Handbook 44 and provide the Weighing Sector guidance on checklist requirements.

The WG, having met on five occasions through conference calls, developed a list of action items including proposed changes to NIST Handbook 44. The Weighing Sector, at its 2006 meeting, reviewed the list of action items and agreed the WG should submit their proposals to amend Handbook 44 Appendix D by amending the term "tare mechanism" and adding new tare definitions to ensure a uniform understating of the terminology used in Handbook 44.

Additionally, the "tare" WG is currently developing proposed recommendations to amend the Handbook 44 tare requirements that will increase the accuracy of net weight determinations, clearly state what is permitted for indication and recorded representations of net and tare weights, and identify tare weights that are determined at the time objects are weighed or tare weights that are determined prior to the time the objects are weighed (e.g., semiautomatic and stored tares). Adoption of the above proposal to amend Appendix D will facilitate developing specific language for Handbook 44 specifications, test notes, and tolerances for different types of tare (e.g., tare, preset tare, percentage tare, etc.).

Other Contacts: (Provide position statements, comments, etc. from names and addresses of individuals, firms, manufacturers, and/or trade associations included in developing the proposal.)

Other Reasons For: (If none, please indicate none have emerged.)
None have emerged

Other Reasons Against:
None have emerged

Additional Considerations: (provide cost estimates and state the anticipated benefits for all parties or indicate how the proposal may affect other requirements, programs, etc.)

| **Attachments:** (list the accompanying documents, data, studies etc.)

A listing and original source material for the proposed changes to Appendix D from the NTETC Weighing Sector Tare WG. | **Suggested Action:** (Be specific on what action the committee should take on the item.)
Recommend NCWM   Adoption   Withdraw
Developing Item
Informational Item
Other (Please describe) |

NCWM Form 15
Proposal to a Standing Committee
Committee: Specifications and Tolerances

Date: October 16, 2006	Regional Association: SWMA
Name/Address of Contact Persons: Steven Cook NIST Weights and Measures Division Attention: Specifications and Tolerances Committee Phone: (301) 975-4004 Fax: (301) 975-8091 e-mail: steven.cook@nist.gov	Regional Actions: (votes for and against)

Please Attach Additional Pages and Information as Needed

Proposal: Amend paragraph S.1.1. (b) as follows:

S.1.1.1. Digital Indicating Elements.

(a) A digital zero indication shall represent a balance condition that is within ± ½ the value of the scale division.

(b) A digital indicating device shall either automatically maintain a "center-of-zero" condition to ± ¼ scale *division or less, or have an auxiliary or supplemental "center-of-zero" indicator that defines a zero balance condition to ± ¼ of a scale division or less. The auxiliary or supplemental "center-of-zero" indicator may be operable with a zero net weight indication.*
[Nonretroactive as of January 1, 1993]
(Amended 1992 and 200X)

Problem/Justification:
The Scales Code in Handbook 44 has very few requirements for the operation, indications, and recorded representations, specifically for the use and performance of tare mechanisms used in weighing devices. These requirements include paragraphs S.2.1.6. Combined Zero-Tare (0/T) Key, S.2.3. Tare., S.2.3.1. Monorail Scales Equipped with Digital Indications, and T.N.2.1. General (Tolerances). NTEP has further developed type evaluation criteria for tare based on the reference Handbook 44 General Code paragraph G-S.2. Facilitation of Fraud and other General Code paragraphs for indicating and recording elements and recorded representations. It has increasingly become difficult to support the NTEP evaluation criteria citing paragraph G-S.2. since it is general in nature and subject to multiple interpretations. Additionally, the general nature of G-S.2. makes it difficult for weights and measures officials, device manufacturers, and device owners and operators to be aware of the tare requirements that have been agreed upon by the National Type Evaluation Technical Committee (NTETC) Weighing Sector that are published in NCWM Publication 14. (Note: The Weighing Sector is comprised of weight and measures officials, device manufacturers, and NIST, USDA, and Measurement Canada).

An example of an NTEP interpretation is that a device may display a "center-of-zero" indication with a load on the scale provided that the load on the scale has been balanced off by the tare mechanism and the resultant zero net indication is within ± ¼ scale division.

Background: In 2006, the NTETC Weighing Sector formed a small Work Group (WG) to review "Tare" operation and requirements and make recommendations on how tare is applied to single range, multiple range, and multi-interval scale operation. The WG was also asked to develop a recommendation(s) for changes to Publication 14 and Handbook 44 and provide the Weighing Sector guidance on checklist requirements.

The WG, having met on five occasions through conference calls, developed a list of action items including proposed changes to NIST Handbook 44. The Weighing Sector, at its 2006 meeting, reviewed the list of action items and agreed with the WG should submit its proposals to amend Handbook 44 Scales Code paragraph S.1.1.1.(b) Digital Indicating Elements to clarify that an auxiliary or supplemental "center-of-zero" indicator is permitted with a load on the scale provided the object used for tare has been balanced off by the tare mechanism and the resultant zero net indication is within ± ¼ scale division.

Additionally, the "tare" WG is currently developing proposed recommendations to amend the Handbook 44 tare requirements that will increase the accuracy of net weight determinations, clearly state what is permitted for indicated and recorded representations of net and tare weights, and identify tare weights that are determined at the time objects are weighed or tare weights that are determined prior to the time the objects are weighed (e.g., semiautomatic and stored tares). Adoption of the above proposal to amend Appendix D will facilitate developing specific language for Handbook 44 specifications, test notes, and tolerances for different types of tare (e.g., tare, preset tare, percentage tare, etc.).

Other Contacts: (Provide position statements, comments, etc. from names and addresses of individuals, firms, manufacturers, and/or trade associations included in developing the proposal.)

Other Reasons For: (If none, please indicate none have emerged.)

Other Reasons Against: None have emerged

Additional Considerations: (provide cost estimates and state the anticipated benefits for all parties or indicate how the proposal may affect other requirements, programs, etc.)

Attachments: (list the accompanying documents, data, studies etc.)	**Suggested Action**: (Be specific on what action the committee should take on the item.) Recommend NCWM Adoption Withdraw Developing Item Informational Item Other (Please describe)

NCWM Form 15
Proposal to a Standing Committee
Committee: Specifications and Tolerances

Date: October 16, 2006	Regional Association: SWMA
Name/Address of Contact Persons: Steven Cook NIST Weights and Measures Division Attention: Specifications and Tolerances Committee Phone: (301) 975-4004 Fax: (301) 975-8091 e-mail: steven.cook@nist.gov	Regional Actions: (votes for and against)

Please Attach Additional Pages and Information as Needed

Proposal: Add a new note to Scales Code paragraph S.1.2.1. as follows:

S.1.2.1. Weight Units. – *Except for postal scales, a digital-indicating scale shall indicate weight values using only a single unit of measure. Weight values shall be presented in a decimal format with the value of the scale division expressed as 1, 2, or 5, or a decimal multiple or submultiples of 1, 2, or 5.*

Note: The requirement that the value of the scale division be expressed as 1, 2, or 5, or a decimal multiple or submultiples of 1, 2, or 5 does not apply to net weights that are calculated from gross and tare weight indications where the scale value of the gross weight is different than the scale value of the tare weight(s) on multi-interval or multiple range scales. For example, a scale indicating in 2 kg divisions in the lower range or segment and 5 kg divisions in the higher range or segment may result in net values ending in three (3) or eight (8) or a scale indicating in 20 lb divisions in the lower range and 50 lb divisions in the higher range or segment may result in net values in 30 or 80.
[Nonretroactive as of January 1, 1989]
(Added 1987) (Amended 200X)

Amend Scales Code paragraph T.N.2.1. as follows:

T.N.2.1. General. – The tolerance values are positive (+) and negative (−) with the weighing device adjusted to zero at no load. When tare is used, the tolerance values are applied from the tare zero reference (zero net indication) ; the tolerance values apply to the net weight indication for every possible tare load using certified test loads only.
(Amended 200X)

Add a new note to the AWS Code paragraph S.1.2.1. as follows:

S.1.2. Value of Division Units. – The value of a division d expressed in a unit of weight shall be equal to:

   (a) 1, 2, or 5; or

   (b) a decimal submultiple of 1, 2, or 5.

Note: The requirement that the value of the scale division be expressed as 1, 2, or 5, or a decimal multiple or submultiples of 1, 2, or 5 does not apply to net weights that are calculated from gross and tare weight indications where the scale value of the gross weight is different than the scale value of the tare weight(s) on multi-interval or multiple range scales. For example, a scale indicating in 2 g divisions in the lower range or segment and 5 g divisions in the higher range or segment may result in net values ending in three (3) or eight (8).
(Amended 200X)

Amend Scales Code paragraph T.N.2.1. as follows:

T.2.1. General. – The tolerance values are positive (+) and negative (−) with the weighing device adjusted to zero at no load. When tare is used, the tolerance values are applied from the tare zero reference (ze<u>ro net indication)</u>; the tolerance values apply to the ne<u>t weight indication for every possible tare load using</u> certified test loads ~~only.~~ (Amended 200X)

Problem/Justification:

In 2006, the NTETC Weighing Sector formed a small WG to review "Tare" operation and requirements in general and make recommendations on how tare is applied to single range, multiple range, and multi-interval scale operation. The WG was asked to develop a recommendation(s) for changes to Publication 14, Handbook 44, and Handbook 130 (if necessary) and provide the Weighing Sector guidance on checklist requirements.

The Tare WG discussed the problems of rounding tare on multi-interval and multiple range scales when the net weight was in a different weighing range than the tare weight. Whenever gross and tare weights fall in different weighing segments on a multi-interval scale or in different weighing ranges on multiple range scales the scale divisions for the gross and tare weights differ. The net weight must be in mathematical agreement with the gross and tare weights that are indicated and recorded, (i.e., gross – tare = net).

This becomes a problem when tare vales are rounded to the net weight scale division that is larger than the scale division of the tare value. For example, a 0.004 lb tare in a weighing range or segment with 0.002 lb intervals in the lower weighing range or segment may round to zero when the net weight falls in the upper weighing range with 0.01 lb intervals (10.05 lb Gross - 0.004 lb Tare = 10.046 lb which rounds to 10.05 lb Net). This results in a transaction where an object being sold or purchased on the basis of gross weight or by taking insufficient tare.

Essentially, the rounding of tare in either direction from a smaller scale division to a larger scale division provides a less accurate net weight.

This proposed note to paragraph S.1.2.1. allows the display and printing of net weight values in divisions other than the scale division used in the display of gross weight.

The proposed amendment to Scales Code paragraph T.N.2.1. and AWS Code paragraph T.2.1. is intended to clarify that Table 6 tolerances also apply to net weight indications regardless of the gross load on the scale. During the Tare WG discussions, OIML R 76 was consulted for possible areas where Handbook 44 could be aligned with international recommendations and noted that Handbook 44 did not specifically state that tolerances also apply to net load indications. The current language in Handbook 44 states the tolerances are applied from the tare zero reference when tare is used. The group believes that the language in Handbook 44 is equivalent to OIML R 76, but that the language in Handbook 44 could easily be restated to clarify that tolerances apply to net weight indications.

Other Contacts: (Provide position statements, comments, etc. from names and addresses of individuals, firms, manufacturers, and/or trade associations included in developing the proposal.)	
Other Reasons For: (If none, please indicate none have emerged.) None have emerged	
Other Reasons Against: None have emerged	
Additional Considerations: (provide cost estimates and state the anticipated benefits for all parties or indicate how the proposal may affect other requirements, programs, etc.)	

Attachments: (list the accompanying documents, data, studies etc.)	**Suggested Action:** (Be specific on what action the committee should take on the item.)
	Recommend NCWM Adoption Withdraw
	    Developing Item
	    Informational Item
	    Other (Please describe)

Attachment for Agenda Item 7

NCWM Form 15 **Proposal to a Standing Committee** **Committee: Specifications and Tolerances**	
Date: October 16, 2006	Regional Association: SWMA
Name/Address of Contact Persons: NTETC Weighing Sector Steven Cook, NIST Technical Advisor NIST Weights and Measures Division NIST Technical Advisor NTETC Weighing Sector Phone: (301) 975-4004 Fax: (301) 975-8091 e-mail: steven.cook@nist.gov	Regional Actions: (votes for and against)
Please Attach Additional Pages and Information as Needed	
Proposal: Amend the AWS Code (AWS) Table S.7. Notes for Table S.7.a. Note 5 as follows: 5. Required only on automatic weighing systems if the temperature range on the NTEP CC is <u>narrower than and within</u> ~~other than~~ −10 °C to 40 °C (14 °F to 104 °F). (Amended 2007)	
Problem/Justification: An NTEP participating laboratory received an application for an automatic weighing system with a marked temperature range larger than the −10 °C to 40 °C temperature range in Handbook 44 AWS Table S.7. Note 5. The participating laboratory performed the tests over the larger temperature range. However, they became concerned that manufacturers would infer that AWSs with the larger temperature ranges would be a higher quality device and subsequently a marketing issue. The laboratory was also concerned that testing at higher and higher temperature ranges would be a health and safety concern for the evaluators and that the larger temperature ranges would exceed the testing capabilities of the NTEP laboratories. It was also noted that the marking requirements in Scales Code Table S.6.3.b. Notes for Table S.6.3.a. Note 5 states that the temperature range only had to be marked if the scale had a temperature range that was narrower than an within −10 °C to 40 °C. This issue was discussed by the NTETC Weighing Sector during their 2005 and 2006 Annual Meetings. The Sector reviewed the 1991 and 1999 S&T Committee discussions regarding temperature range marking requirements and agreed to align the AWS Code with the Scales Code marking requirements for temperature range. The NIST Technical Advisor also recommended that similar amendments be made to other Section 2 (Weighing) Codes; however, the Sector stated that the other codes need additional evaluation and should be submitted to the S&T through the normal process.	
Other Contacts: (Provide position statements, comments, etc. from names and addresses of individuals, firms, manufacturers, and/or trade associations included in developing the proposal.)	
Other Reasons For: (If none, please indicate none have emerged.) None have emerged	
Other Reasons Against: None have emerged	
Additional Considerations: (provide cost estimates and state the anticipated benefits for all parties or indicate how the proposal may affect other requirements, programs, etc.)	
Attachments: (list the accompanying documents, data, studies etc.) Additional background information from the 1991 and 1999 S&T Committee Reports on the markings for temperature ranges in the Scales Code.	**Suggested Action:** (Be specific on what action the committee should take on the item.) Recommend NCWM Adoption Withdraw Developing Item Informational Item Other (Please describe)

THIS PAGE INTENTIONALLY LEFT BLANK

Appendix E

National Type Evaluation Technical Committee
Software Sector Meeting

May 7 - 8, 2007, Sacramento, California
Meeting Summary

Agenda Items   **Page**

Carry-over Items: 3
   1. Review..3
       1.a. NTETC Software Sector Mission...3
       1.b. NCWM/NTEP Policies – Issuing CCs for Software..3
   2. Definitions for Software-Based Devices..4
   3. Software   Identification/Markings...6
   4. Identification of Unapproved/Unauthorized Software..6
   5. Software Protection/Security..9
   6. Software Maintenance and Reconfiguration...9
   7. Verification in the Field, by the Inspector..14
   8. NTEP Application – [mfg documentation to be submitted]...14

New Items:...14
   9. S&T Item 310-1/G-S.2 Facilitation of Fraud..14
   10. Next Meeting...15

THIS PAGE INTENTIONALLY LEFT BLANK

Carry-over Items:

1. Review

1.a. NTETC Software Sector Mission

Source: NCWM Board of Directors

Background: In 2005 the Board of Directors established a National Type Evaluation Technical Committee (NTETC) Software Sector. A mission statement for the sector was developed at that time.

Mission of the Software Sector:

- Develop a clear understanding of the use of software in today's weighing and measuring instruments.
- Develop NIST Handbook 44 specifications and requirements, as needed, for software incorporated into weighing and measuring devices. This may include tools for field verification, security requirements, identification, etc.
- Develop NCWM Publication 14 checklist criteria, as needed, for the evaluation of software incorporated into weighing and measuring devices, including marking, security, metrologically significant functions, etc.
- Assist in the development of training guidelines for Weights and Measures officials in verifying software as compliant to applicable requirements and traceable to an NTEP Certificate. Training aids to educate manufacturers, designers, service technicians, and end users may also be considered.

Discussion: The Chair asked the question: Is the sector comfortable with the Mission Statement?

The Sector discussed the process of other NTETC sectors, the NCWM structure, and how/why the software sector was developed. After lengthy discussion, there was consensus among the Sector members that the Mission Statement was correct. However, the sector noted the broad range of items listed in the Statement but agreed the steps in the Mission Statement were correct. The steps build on each other in an orderly progression. It was further agreed that, whenever possible, items would be addressed in the sequence of the Mission Statement.

The Chair noted that the scope of this sector is somewhat broader than some other sectors. The work of this sector is more closely aligned to that of the Grain Analyzer Sector in that focus is on development of possible language for:

- NIST Handbook 44,
- checklist criteria for NCWM Publication 14, and
- appropriate field guidelines.

1.b. NCWM/NTEP Policies – Issuing CCs for Software

Source: NCWM Reports

Background: Excerpts of reports from the 1995-1998 Executive Committee were provided to NTETC Software Sector members at their April 2006 meeting. The chair asked the sector to review the following NTEP policy decision adopted by the NCWM in 1998 relative to the issuance of a separate Certificate of Conformance (CC) for software:

The NCWM has struggled with software issues for many years. Prior to 1995, NTEP had evaluated stand-alone software (e.g., weigh-in/weigh-out, POS, and batch controller software) and, in some cases, had issued CCs for stand-alone software. The Board established a software WG to study the issues and make recommendations.

Many issues were discussed by the WG, including: first indication of the final quantity, metrologically significant software, definitions, software marking, software checklist evaluation, a software EPO for the field inspector, user-programmable software, and third-party software. According to NCWM Conference reports, in

1997 concerns were raised about the direction of the WG. In 1997, after the NCWM Annual Meeting, a new Software Work Group was appointed by the NCWM chair.

During the 1998 NCWM Annual Meeting, the following recommendation was adopted as NTEP policy:

- "Software, regardless of its form, shall not be subject to evaluation for the purpose of receiving a separate, software Certificate of Conformance from the National Type Evaluation Program."
- "Remove all of the software categories from the index of NCWM Publication 5, NTEP Index of Device Evaluations."
- "Reclassify all existing software CCs according to their applicable device categories."

The policy is still in effect today.

Also noteworthy is a statement in Section C of NCWM Publication 14, "Administrative Policy" which states,

"In general, type evaluations will be conducted on all equipment that affect the measurement process or the validity of the transaction (e.g. electronic cash registers interfaced with scales and service station consoles interfaced with retail fuel dispensers); and all equipment to the point of the first indicated or recorded representation of the final quantity on which the transaction will be based."

Discussion: At this point in time, NTEP evaluates a "software-based device" as a functional device. The performance of the device is evaluated.

There was a suggestion from the floor that the 1998 policy be amended so the sector can move toward the other steps in the process. Discussion from the floor centered on how to or if there needs to be a change to the device type in the "FOR" box of the CC. The consensus of the Sector is that the current NCWM/NTEP policy should be changed.

Recommendation:

Software Requiring a Separate CC: Software which is implemented as an add-on to other NTEP-certified main elements to create a weighing or measuring system and its metrological functions are significant in determining the first indication of the final quantity. Such software is considered to be a main element of the system requiring a separate CC.

NOTE: OEM software **may** be added to an existing CC or have a stand-alone CC with applicable applications (e.g., a manufacturer adding a software upgrade to its ECR or point-of-sale system, vehicle scale weigh-in/weigh-out software added as a feature to an indicating element, automatic bulk weighing, liquid-measuring device loading racks, etc.) and minimum system requirements for "Type P" devices (see proposed software definition below). It may be possible for a manufacturer to submit a single application for both hardware and software contained in the same device. A single CC would be issued.

In this instance, OEM refers to a third party. The request to add software could be made by the original CC holder on behalf of the third party. Alternatively, a new CC could be created that refers to the original CC and simply lists the new portions that were examined.

The sector recommendation will be submitted to the NTEP Committee.

2. Definitions for Software-Based Devices

Source: NTETC Software Sector

Background: The Sector discussed marking and G-S.1.1. requirements. Initially it was suggested that "not-built-for-purpose" be removed from the wording in NIST HB 44 G-S.1.1. However, after further discussion, it was agreed this may not be the correct or final decision. There is no definition for a not-built-for-purpose device in HB 44. The current HB 44 definition for a built-for-purpose device reads:

Built-for-purpose device. Any main device or element which was manufactured with the intent that it be used as, or part of, a weighing or measuring device or system. [1.10] (Added 2003)

There was also the suggestion to use the definitions from the WELMEC document for Type P and Type U instruments. They were modified by the Sector. It was also suggested that a list of examples be provided.

Draft definitions for consideration:

Built-for-purpose weighing or measuring instrument (device) (Type P): A weighing or measuring instrument (device) designed and built specifically for the task in-hand. Accordingly, the embedded software is assumed to be designed for the specific task. It may contain many components also used in PCs, e.g, motherboard, memory card, etc.

A weighing or measuring instrument (device) using a universal Computer (Type U): A weighing or measuring instrument (device) that uses a general-purpose computer, usually a PC-based system, for performing legally relevant functions.

Examples:
Type U
Weigh-in/Weigh-out
Open Architecture

Discussion: The Sector agreed that the NTEP CC should reflect "software" is a separate main element. If this is true, then there needs to be definition.

The Sector agrees this change in policy and appearance on CCs does not have a major impact on our current type evaluation process.

Measurement Canada sites three main areas of software function: sensing physical phenomena (mass or volume), computational, and controlling the system.

After a lengthy discussion related to the terms "built-for-purpose and "not-built-for-purpose," the Sector agreed the terms were not clear and should be replaced with the terminology proposed below. A main reference point that the sector used in this discussion was OIML R 76 *Non-automatic weighing instruments* sub-sections 5.5.1. (Type P) and 5.5.2. (Type U).

(*New Definition*) **Electronic devices, software-based**. Weighing and measuring devices or systems that use metrological software to facilitate compliance with Handbook 44. This includes:

(a) **Embedded software devices (Type P)**. A device or element with software used in a fixed hardware and software environment that cannot be modified or uploaded via any interface without breaking a security seal or other approved means for providing security, will be called a "P", or

(b) **Programmable or loadable metrological software devices (Type U)**. A personal computer or other device and/or element with PC components with programmable or loadable metrological software, and will be called "U". A "U" is assumed if the conditions for embedded software devices are not met.

Conclusion and Recommendation: The Sector agreed to submit the above-proposed definition to the NCWM S&T Committee for consideration. This change would clarify and define what currently is done in NTEP and would represent it properly in NIST HB 44 to assist the inspector.

3. Software Identification/Markings

Source: NTETC Software Sector

Background: At the last meeting, there was discussion on specific sections of the WELMEC document that deal with TYPE P and TYPE U requirements. The comments and recommendations under consideration follow:

Discussion: There was lengthy discussion on the value and merits of markings. This included the possible differences in some types of devices and marking requirements. After hearing several proposals, the sector agreed to the following recommendation.

Technical changes represented below:
1. CC No. must be continuously displayed or marked,
2. Version must be software generated, not hard marked,
3. Version required for embedded (Type P),
4. Print option created
5. Command or operator action option created,
6. Type P must display or hard mark Make, Model, S.N.

Recommendation:

TYPE U shall meet one of the methods:

Method	NTEP CC No.	Make/Model	Software Version/Revision
Hard-Marked	$X^{1,2}$	X Not	Acceptable
Continuously Displayed	X^2	X X	
Via Menu (display) or Print Option	Not Acceptable	X	X
[1] Only if no means of displaying this information is available			
[2] Information on how to obtain the remaining items (Make/Model, Version/Revision) shall be included on the CC.			

TYPE P shall meet one of the methods:

Method	NTEP CC No.	Make/Model/Serial No.	Software Version/Revision
Hard-Marked	X	X	Not Acceptable
Continuously Displayed	X	X	X
By command or operator action	Not Acceptable	Not Acceptable	X
Note: Information on how to obtain the remaining items (Make/Model, Version/Revision) shall be included on the CC.			

The "Via Menu (display) or Print" option may be supplemental for devices that use the hard-marked or continuously displayed identification method for the NTEP CC Make/Model, Serial No. information.

The Sector will forward these items, when completed, to the Regional S&T committees for consideration.

4. Identification of Unapproved/Unauthorized Software

Source: NTETC Software Sector

Background: During the last meeting, much discussion was generated. Many comments were addressed.

Segregation of parameters is currently allowed (see table of sealable parameters).

Presently there are two methods of sealing a device: physical seal and audit trail. The sector debated if some other category was necessary.

Currently, industry reports they protect third-party software, but it is not via audit trail. There is an issue of audit trail capabilities; if the software is not running in a normal mode or there is no a software service, the changes could be made and not tracked by audit trail.

There is no way to tell someone how to do sealing; you can say what needs to be accomplished.

Examples of methods of sealing:
• authentication
  • access   control
  • X509   Certificates
  •   PCATS certifies vendors
  • Version   Number
  • application   (checksum)

There is a "challenge response" with different certifications. Challenge responses validate who the user is, sets limits, or verifies data received.

The Sector was in general agreement that HB 44 does not need to be changed.

The Sector agreed that Weights and Measures needs to know that software is not being manipulated,

X509 is a standard for a public key infrastructure (PKI). This is a system where a third party holds the key to decode an encrypted program to ensure against fraud.

Scale System Controller
The scale system controller has approval certifications for the United States and the European Union. In this case, a commercial off-the-shelf (COTS) PC is used in conjunction with a scale system (terminal and weigh platform). The scale system provides the PC with approved gross weight and accepts commands to zero the weight indication. The PC application program performs the following functions:

- stores and recalls weights;
- computes net weight using a stored weight or manually entered weight;
- provides the user display of net weight;
- may compute price based on the net weight and a selected commodity code; and
- may print a weigh ticket.

Some features of the Scale System Controller are:

1. **Protection of configuration and price parameters:** Metrologically significant parameters are maintained within the scale terminal where they are controlled. Other parameters are stored in a password-protected database. The user controls password protection access and distribution.

2. **Separation of software:** Separation of metrological and application software as described in the WELMEC documents is maintained.

3. **Protection of software:** Metrologically significant software is supplied only as binary code. Each such module is protected by a CRC32 checksum. The expected checksums, revision levels, and dates are kept in an encrypted configuration file. If run-time values differ from expected values, the system will not operate. The configuration information can be recalled by an inspector using the Help/About menu in the application program.

4. **Protection of active data:** Data from the scale terminal is wholly owned by the scale server metrological interface. No other agent can acquire that data when the scale server is running, and the application program will not accept data except from the scale server.

Transactional information is stored in an encrypted Alibi Memory log. No access is permitted to this data except via the supplied application program. Data can be exported via the application program for external use, but no user modifications are permitted to the original transaction data.

5. **Protection of operating system user interface:** There are no special restrictions to the operating system. The application program runs as any other on the PC and can be started, stopped, or minimized.

In Europe, there are things like safety, highest-level security, etc. First modification there would be a limit to the risk classes developed by WELMEC.

6. **P5: Protection against accidental or unintentional changes:** Legally relevant software and measurement data shall be protected against accidental or unintentional changes.

7. **Specifying Notes:** Possible reasons for accidental changes and faults are: unpredictable physical influences, effects caused by user functions and residual defects of the software even though state-of-the-art development techniques have been applied.

    This requirement includes:
    a) Physical influences: Stored measurement data shall be protected against corruption or deletion when a fault occurs or, alternatively, the fault shall be detectable.

    b) User functions: Confirmation shall be demanded before deleting or changing data.

    c) Software defects: Appropriate measures, e.g., plausibility checks, shall be taken to protect data from unintentional changes that could occur through incorrect program design or programming errors.

8. **Required Documentation:** The documentation should show the measures that have been taken to protect the software and data against unintentional changes.

9. **Validation Guidance:** Typical Examples
    Checks based on documentation:
    Check that a checksum of the program code and the relevant parameters is generated and verified automatically.
    Check that overwriting of data cannot occur before the end of the data storage period that is foreseen and documented by the manufacturer.
    Check that a warning is issued to the user if he is about to delete measurement data files.
    Functional checks:
    Check by practical spot checks that a warning is given before deleting measurement data if deleting is possible at all.

10. **Example of an Acceptable Solution:**
    The accidental modification of software and measurement data may be checked by calculating a checksum over the relevant parts, comparing it with the nominal value and stopping if anything has been modified.
    Measurement data are not deleted without prior authorization, e.g. a dialogue statement or window asking for confirmation of deletion.
    For fault detection, see also Extension I.

Discussion: At this point around the room, there was a great deal of discussion. It was pointed out that it would be difficult, if not impossible, for the NTEP-evaluated software to identify if unauthorized software was "added" to the device. It is not possible to identify all unapproved software (e.g., add-on software, pirated software).

There was general agreement this may be a field enforcement issue and that it was not appropriate to continue discussion on this item at this time.

Recommendation: The sector recommended moving this item under agenda item 7, as a sub-item, for discussion at a future meeting.

5. Software Protection/Security

Source: NTETC Software Sector

Background:

Discussion: The discussion from the last meeting on this issue is mingled in item 4. Appropriate sections need to be pulled out by the Sector.

The Sector reviewed the applicable items, line by line in the MID Software Work Package 2 and the OIML TC9/SC1 R 76-1 Draft Recommendation to determine items appropriate for the evaluation checklist.

Recommendation: Jim Pettinato from FMC Technologies, agreed to pull together additional information regarding the checklists that we have just developed for this section.

6. Software Maintenance and Reconfiguration

Source: NTETC Software Sector

Background: After discussion during the October 2006 meeting, it appeared these issues may go beyond the scope of current NTEP procedures, and possibly NTEP resources. The question was asked, does the Sector need to address this issue? There was a split vote, no consensus, so it remains on the agenda.

OIML D-SW 5.2.6. was discussed. Comments included:

Only versions of legally relevant software that conform with the approved type are allowed for use (see OIML D-SW 5.2.5). Applicability of the following requirements depends on the kind of instrument and is to be worked out in the relevant OIML Recommendation.

It may differ also on the kind of instrument under consideration. The following options OIML D-SW 5.2.6.1 and 5.2.6.2 are equivalent alternatives. This issue concerns verification in the field. Refer to OIML D-SW chapter 7 for additional constraints.

Discussion points and questions:

- This appears to be covered by Cat 3 and enforcement.
- This may appear to be covered by other sections or security.
- This section should not include eproms.
- Is there a security key?
- Does it download correctly?
- OIML says that the audit trail needs to be updated.

The following flow chart, developed to assist the manufacturer/designer, was discussed in depth.

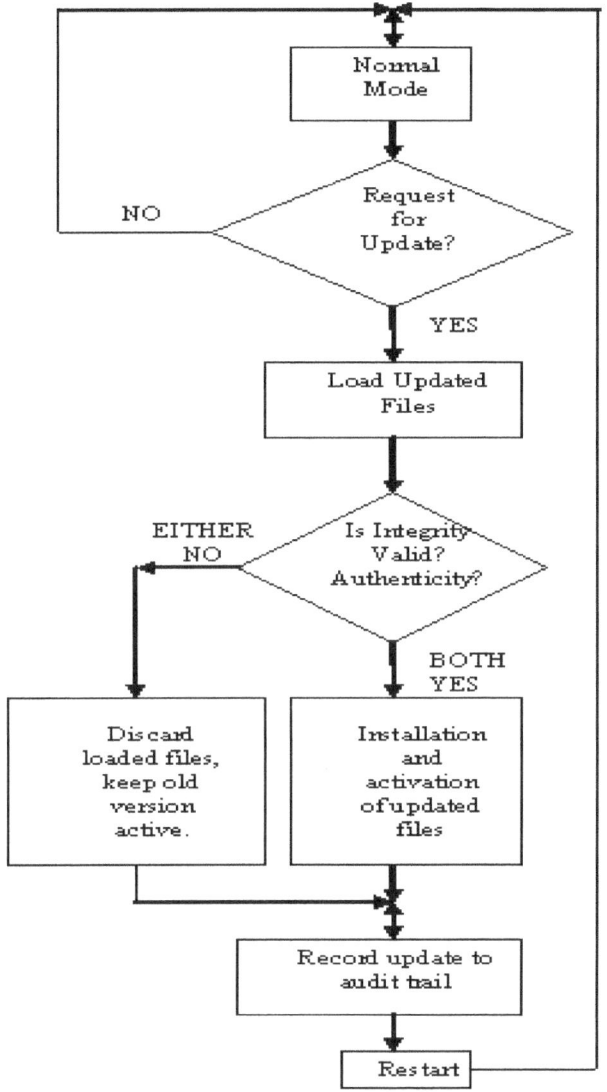
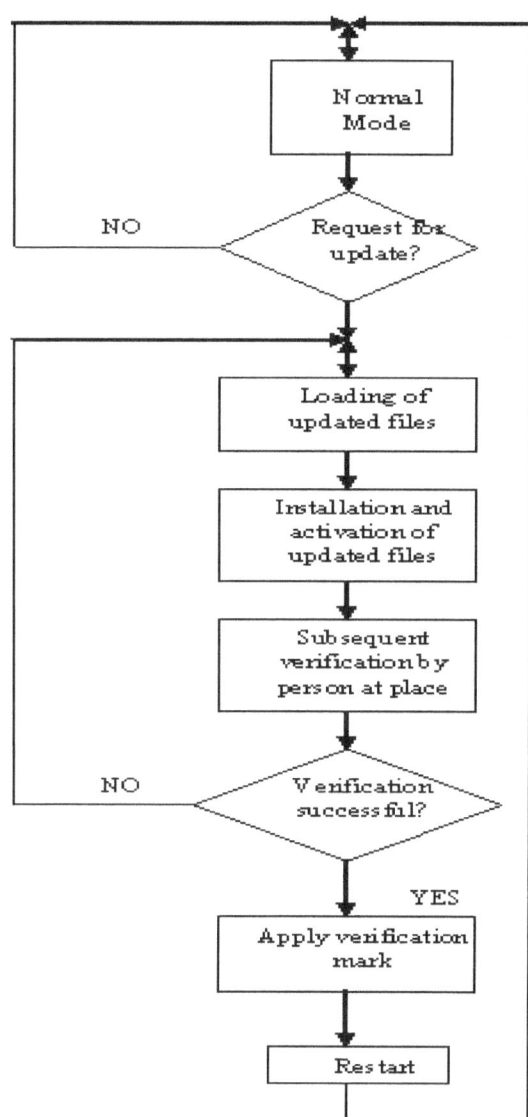

Figure 1.0 Traced Update Requirements Figure 2.0 Verified Update Model

Conclusion: More study and understanding of these complex issues are necessary and more discussion will need to take place during the next meeting. Sector members are encouraged to submit specific proposals for consideration.

Discussion: Traced update provides the ability to update the software either remotely or with equipment that is not part of the device, i.e., Category 3 Method of Sealing; it is in line with current technology. It is a feature that currently is being requested.

Recommendation: After lengthy discussion on this item, the Sector came to general consensus that the information in the recommendation below should be considered for developing type evaluation checklists and field test procedures. It was pointed out that these issues are relevant to agenda item 8, NTEP Application.

Traced means audit trail record - requires Category 3 audit trail.

Verified means evaluator verified - requires breaking a seal and placing back into service by registered agent or Weights and Measures official. D-SW requires an agent to be present to verify the update. It was noted that in some jurisdictions, this role may be performed by a registered service agent.

There was discussion on procedures for verifying the versions of software and it was discussed that these procedures should be part of the NTEP CC.

The sector will continue to develop this area.

This section was taken from Document OIML D-SW 1 WD:

5.2.5 Conformity of production-line devices with the approved type

Requirement:

The manufacturer shall produce devices and the *legally relevant* (is this term correct?? sap) software that conform to the approved type and the documentation submitted. There are different levels of conformity demands:

(a) identity of the *legally relevant functions* described in the documentation (6.1) of each device with those of the type (the executable code may differ),

(b) identity of *parts of the legally relevant source code*, and the rest of the legally relevant software complying with (a),

(c) identity of the *whole legally relevant source code*, and

(d) identity of the *whole executable code*.

The degree of conformity suitable has to be defined for each kind of instrument or area of application by the responsible technical committee. The technical committees could define a subset from these conformity degrees for a particular kind of instrument and let the approving body decide the degree of conformity to be applied.

Except for (d) there may be a software part with no conformity requirements if it is separated from the legally relevant part according to 5.2.1.2.

Means described in 5.1.1 and 5.2.1 shall be provided to make the conformity evident.

5.2.6. Maintenance and re-configuration

Requirement: Only versions of legally relevant software that conform with the approved type are allowed for use (see 5.2.5). Applicability of the following requirements depends on the instrument and is to be worked out in the relevant OIML Recommendation. It may differ also on the kind of instrument under consideration. The following options, 5.2.6.1 and 5.2.6.2, are equivalent alternatives. This issue concerns verification in the field. Refer to chapter 7 for additional constraints.

5.2.6.1 Verified update

The software to be updated can be loaded locally, i.e., directly on the measuring device or remotely via a network. Loading and installation may be two different steps (as shown in Fig. 5-1) or combined into one, depending on the needs of the technical solution. After update of the legally relevant software of a measuring instrument (exchange with another approved version or re-installation), the measuring instrument is not allowed to be used for legal purposes before a (subsequent) verification of the instrument as described in chapter 7 has been performed and the securing means has been renewed (if not otherwise stated in the relevant OIML Recommendation or in the approval certificate). A person responsible for verification must be at place.

5.2.6.2 Traced update

The software is implemented into the instrument according to the requirements for traced update (5.2.6.2.1 to 5.2.6.2.6) if it is in compliance with the relevant OIML Recommendation. Traced update is the procedure of changing software in a verified instrument or device after which the subsequent verification by a responsible person at place is not necessary. The software to be updated can be loaded locally, i.e., directly on the measuring device or remotely via a network. The software update is recorded in an audit trail (see 5.2.6.2.5). The procedure of a traced update comprises several steps: loading, integrity checking, checking of the origin (authentication), installation, logging and activation.

5.2.6.2.1 Traced update of software shall be automatic. On completion of the update procedure the software protection environment shall be at the same level as required by the type approval.

5.2.6.2.2 The target measuring instrument (device, sub-assembly) shall have a fixed legally relevant software that cannot be updated and that contains all of the checking functions necessary for fulfilling traced update requirements.

5.2.6.2.3 Technical means shall be employed to guarantee the authenticity of the loaded software, i.e., that it originates from the owner of the type approval certificate. This can be accomplished, for example, by cryptographic means like signing. The signature is checked during loading. If the loaded software fails this test, the instrument shall discard it and use the previous version of the software ~~or become inoperative~~.

5.2.6.2.4 Technical means shall be employed to guarantee the integrity of the loaded software, i.e., ensuring that it has not been inadmissibly changed before loading. This can be accomplished by adding a checksum or hash code of the loaded software and verifying it during the loading procedure. If the loaded software fails this test, the instrument shall discard it and use the previous version of the software ~~or become inoperative~~.

5.2.6.2.5 The manufacturer shall ensure It ~~shall be guaranteed~~ by appropriate technical means, e.g., an audit trail that traced updates of legally relevant software are adequately traceable within the instrument for subsequent verification and surveillance or inspection. This requirement enables inspection authorities, which are responsible for the metrological surveillance of legally controlled instruments, to back-trace traced updates of legally relevant software over an adequate period of time (that depends on national legislation).

The audit trail shall contain the following information: ~~notification success/miscarriage~~ of the update procedure, software identification of the installed version, time stamp of the event, identification of the downloading party. An entry is generated for each update ~~attempt regardless of the success~~.

The traceability means and records are part of the legally relevant software and should be protected as such. The software used for displaying the audit trail belongs to the fixed legally relevant software. **Note: This needs to be discussed further due to some manufacturer concerns about where the software that displays the audit trail information is located and who has access if this feature is provided.**

5.2.6.2.6 It shall be guaranteed by technical means that software may only be updated with the explicit consent of the user or owner of the measuring instrument. ~~Relevance of this requirement depends on national legislation.~~

5.2.6.2.7 If the requirements 5.2.6.2.1 to 5.2.6.2.6 cannot be fulfilled, it is still possible to update the legally non-relevant software part. In this case the following requirements shall be met:

- There is a distinct separation between the legally relevant and non-relevant software according to 5.2.1.2.
- The whole legally relevant software part of the WELMEC software section cannot be updated without breaking a seal.
- It is stated in the type approval certificate that updating of the legally non-relevant part is acceptable.

Traced Update

```
          ┌──────────────┐
          │ Normal       │
          │ operating    │
          │ mode         │
          └──────┬───────┘
                 ▼
          ╱ Request for ╲
    NO ◄──╲   update?   ╱
          ╲╱
           │ YES
           ▼
      ┌──────────────┐
      │ Loading of   │
      │ updated      │
      │ files (Note 1)│
      └──────┬───────┘
             ▼
         ╱ Is integrity ╲
  NO ◄───╲   valid?     ╱
          │ YES
          ▼
      ╱ Is authenticity ╲
  NO ◄╲    valid?       ╱
       │ YES
```

Branches:
- NO (integrity/authenticity) → **Discard loaded files, keep old version active**
- YES → **Installation and activiation of updated files (Note 1)**

Both merge into:
- **Record information about update to audit**
- **Restart** → back to Normal operating mode

Verified Update

```
          ┌──────────────┐
          │ Normal       │
          │ operating    │
          │ mode         │
          └──────┬───────┘
                 ▼
          ╱ Request for ╲
    NO ◄──╲   update?   ╱
                 │ YES
                 ▼
      ┌──────────────────┐
      │ Loading of       │
      │ updated files    │
      │ (Note 2)         │
      └────────┬─────────┘
               ▼
      ┌──────────────────┐
      │ Installation and │
      │ activiation of   │
      │ updated files    │
      │ (Note 2)         │
      └────────┬─────────┘
               ▼
      ┌──────────────────┐
      │ (Subsequrent)    │
      │ verification by a│
      │ person at place  │
      └────────┬─────────┘
               ▼
          ╱ Verification ╲
  NO  ◄───╲ successful?  ╱
 (Note 3)       │ YES
                ▼
      ┌──────────────────┐
      │ Apply verification│
      │ mark             │
      └────────┬─────────┘
               ▼
          ┌─────────┐
          │ Restart │
          └─────────┘
```

NTEP - E13

Figure 5-1: Software Update Procedures

Notes to Figure 5-1:
1) A *Traced update* is separated into two steps: "loading" and "installing/activating." This implies that the software is temporarily stored after loading without being activated because it must be possible to discard the loaded software and fall back to the old version if the checks fail ~~or become inoperative~~.
2) In case of *Verified update*, the software may also be loaded and temporarily stored before installation but, depending on the technical solution, loading and installation may also be accomplished in one step.
3) Here only failing of the verification because of the software update is considered. Failing because of other reasons doesn't require re-loading and re-installing of the software, symbolised by the NO-branch.

7. Verification in the Field, by the Inspector

Source: NTETC Software Sector

Recommendation: Cover this at a later time.

8. NTEP Application – [mfg documentation to be submitted]

Source: NTETC Software Sector

Recommendation: Cover this at a later time.

New Items:

9. S&T Item 310-1/G-S.2 Facilitation of Fraud

Source: NCWM S&T Committee

The S&T Committee has Item 310-1 on its agenda as a voting item. They have requested a position, pro or con, from the NTETC Software Sector. The following is Item 310-1 as it appears in NCWM Pub 16.

Recommendation: Amend Handbook 44, Section 1.10. General Code paragraph G-S.2. as follows:

> **G-S.2. Facilitation of Fraud** - All equipment, and all mechanisms, and devices ~~attached thereto or used in connection therewith~~, **without limitation**, shall be so **designed**, constructed, assembled, and installed for use such that they do not facilitate the perpetration of fraud. **(Amended 2007)**

Background/Discussion: This proposal modifies the language in paragraph G-S.2. to clarify that the prohibition against facilitating fraud applies to the electronically programmed and coded components of weighing and measuring devices to address electronic manipulation or alteration. Some argue the existing language in Section 1.10. General Code. Paragraph G-S.2. Facilitation of Fraud is intended to address only hardware components of weighing and measuring devices. That is, "equipment, mechanisms, and devices" and the mechanics of how they are "constructed, assembled, and installed" appear to deal with tangible components. Fraud issues in the past ten years involved: (1) altering, manipulating, or interfering with software interfaced or installed in equipment; (2) microprocessor issues such as additional pulser units hidden in gas pumps and taximeters; and (3) software programs permitting manipulation of motor truck scale data used to generate weighmaster certificates.

The CWMA, the SWMA, and the WWMA recommended this item move forward for a vote.

The NEWMA recommended this item be referred to the NTETC Software Sector for review and input.

At the 2007 NCWM Interim Meeting, the Committee considered the WWMA proposal and an alternate proposal developed by the SMA. The Committee acknowledged that neither proposal was reviewed by the NTETC Software Sector. The Committee agreed that updating the requirement could be accomplished by adding general terms to

address the types of electronic and software-based technology being fraudulently used today. The WWMA proposed language naming specific software applications that should not facilitate fraud. Whereas, the SMA alternate proposal included broader language that is intended to prohibit fraudulent use of software, wireless connections, and all future technology "without limitation." The Committee agreed that the SMA proposal encompasses all possible equipment configurations and more appropriately addresses the problem at hand. Therefore, the Committee agreed to present the SMA proposal for a vote at the 2007 NCWM Annual Meeting.

The Sector reviewed Item 310-1 as requested by the NCWM S&T Committee.

Discussion: There was lengthy discussion of this item by the Sector.

Sector Position: The consensus of the Sector was to support the Central (CWMA) recommendation as a voting item and delete words "and all" since it was associated with the "attached thereto and ..." language. The term "design" adds value. "Software" adds clarification.

G-S.2. Facilitation of Fraud - All equipment, ~~and all~~ mechanisms, **software** and devices ~~attached thereto or used in connection therewith, without limitation~~, shall be so **designed**, constructed, assembled, and installed for use such that they do not facilitate the perpetration of fraud.

10. Next Meeting

The NCWM Board agreed to fund a May 2007 meeting of the NTETC Software Sector. This is the third meeting of the sector in a 13-month span. The meeting is being scheduled leading in to a meeting of NTEP laboratory representatives. The scheduling was intentional, as the decision has been made that it is the "best fit," in an attempt to have as much NTEP lab(s) representation as possible. Piggybacking meetings also saves travel costs. Therefore, the next planned meeting of the Software Sector will be for the spring of 2008 adjacent to the NTEP lab meeting.

Discussion: Some members of the sector have expressed concern that waiting a year to meet again may be too long. The possibility of meeting electronically was suggested, allowing for electronic ballots, etc. The other alternative is to ask the BOD to have an additional meeting in the fall.

Conclusion: It was the consensus of the sector to request that another meeting of the Software Sector be held in the fall. This may be in conjunction with one of the Sector Meetings, or as a separate meeting, possibly in Ohio. Shortly after the meeting, a request was submitted to the NCWM Board for consideration of funding this meeting.

THIS PAGE INTENTIONALLY LEFT BLANK.

NCWM 92nd Annual Meeting
July 8 - 12, 2007 • Snowbird Resort • Salt Lake City, UT
Attendee List

Mahesh Albuquerque
Division of Oil and Public Safety
633 17th Street, Suite 500
Denver, CO 80202
Ph: (303) 318-8533
Fax: (303) 318-8488
E-mail:
mahesh.albuquerque@state.co.us

Edmund Baniak
American Petroleum Institute
1220 L Street, NW
Washington, DC 20005
Ph: (202) 682-8135
Fax: (202) 962-4797
E-mail: baniake@api.org

Joe Benavides
Texas Dept. of Agriculture
1700 North Congress Avenue
Stephen F. Austin Building,
11th Floor
Austin, TX 78701
Ph: (512) 463-7401
Fax: (512) 463-8225
E-mail:

Jim Allred
Idaho National Laboratory
P.O. Box 1625 - MS 4137
Idaho Falls, ID 83415-4137
Ph: (208) 526-2017
Fax: (208) 526-5462
E-mail: jim.allred@inl.gov

Dennis Beattie
Measurement Canada
4th Floor 400 St. Mary Avenue
Winnipeg, Manitoba R3C 4K5
Canada
Ph: (204) 983-8910
Fax: (204) 983-5511
E-mail: beattie.dennis@ic.gc.ca

Stephen Benjamin
North Carolina Dept. of Agriculture
1050 Mail Service Center
Raleigh, NC 27699-1050
Ph: (919) 733-3313
Fax: (919) 715-0524
E-mail:
steve.benjamin@ncmail.net

Ross Andersen
New York Bureau of Weights &
Measures
10B Airline Drive
Albany, NY 12235
Ph: (518) 457-3146
Fax: (518) 457-5693
E-mail:
ross.andersen@agmkt.state.ny.us

Steven Beitzel
Systems Associates, Inc.
1932 Industrial Drive
Libertyville, IL 60048
Ph: (847) 367-6650
Fax: (847) 367-6960
E-mail:
sjbeitzel@systemsassoc.com

Daniel Bernaciak
Stanislaus County Dept. of
Agriculture
Weights & Measures
3800 Cornucopia Way, Suite B
Modesto, CA 95358
Ph: (209) 525-4730
Fax: (209) 525-4790
E-mail:
danielb@mail.co.stanislaus.ca.us

Robert Atkins
County of San Diego
Dept. of Agriculture Weights &
Measures
5555 Overland Avenue, Suite 3101
San Diego, CA 92123
Ph: (626) 575-5451
Fax: (626)350-3243
E-mail: bob.atkins@sdcounty.ca.gov

F. Michael Belue
Belue Associates
Court View Towers, Suite 111A
201 North Pine
Florence, AL 35630
Ph: (256) 768-9917
Fax: (256) 768-9912
E-mail: Bassoc@aol.com

Linda Bernetich
National Conference on Weights &
Measures
15245 Shady Grove Road,
Suite 130
Rockville, MD 20850
Ph: (240)632-9454
Fax: (301)990-9771
E-mail: lbernetich@mgmtsol.com

NCWM 92nd Annual Meeting
July 8 - 12, 2007 • Snowbird Resort • Salt Lake City, UT

Attendee List

Robert Bailey
Virginia Product & Industry Standards
P.O. Box 1163
Richmond, VA 23218
Ph: (804) 786-2476
Fax: (804) 786-1571
E-mail:
Robert.Bailey@vdacs.virginia.gov

Lawrence Belusz
Perry Johnson Registrars, Inc.
26555 Evergreen, Suite 1340
Southfield, MI 48076
Ph: (800) 800-7910
Fax: (248) 358-0882
E-mail: lbelusz@pjr.com

Doug Biette
Sartorius North America
6542 Fig Street
Arvada, CO 80004
Ph: (303) 403-4690
Fax: (303) 423-4540
E-mail: doug.biette@sartorius.com

Tom Bloemer
Kentucky Dept. of Agriculture
107 Corporate Drive
Frankfort, KY 40601
Ph: (502) 573-0282
Fax: (502) 573-0303
E-mail: tom.bloemer@ky.gov

Rex Brown
Petroleum Equipment Institution
P.O. Box 2380
Tulsa, OK 74101
Ph: (918) 494-9696
Fax: (918) 491-9895
E-mail: rbrown@pei.org

Jerry Butler
North Carolina Dept. of Agriculture
1050 Mail Service Center
Raleigh, NC 27699-1050
Ph: (919) 733-3313
Fax: (919) 715-0524
E-mail: jerry.butler@ncmail.net

Christopher Bradley
Seraphin Test Measure
P.O. Box 227
30 Indel Avenue
Rancocas, NJ 08073
Ph: (609) 267-0922
Fax: (609) 261-2546
E-mail: cparker@pemfab.com

Norman Brucker
Precision Measurement Standards, Inc.
1665 Bonaire Path
Rosemount, MN 55068
Ph: (651) 423-3241
Fax: (651) 322-7938
E-mail: sharnoma@fontiernet.net

Marc Buttler
Emerson Process Management – Micro Motion
7070 Winchester Circle
Boulder, CO 80301
Ph: (303)530-8562
Fax: (303)530-8459
E-mail:
marc.buttler@emersonprocess.com

Jonelle Brent
Illinois Dept. of Agriculture
P.O. Box 19281
Springfield, IL 62794-9281
Ph: (217) 785-8301,
Fax: (217)524-7801
E-mail: jbrent@agr.state.il.us

Mark Buccelli
State of Minnesota, Dept. of Commerce
Weights & Measures Division
South Cross Commerce Center III, 14035
South Cross Drive, Suite 150
Burnsville, MN 55306
Ph: (651) 215-5840
Fax: (952) 435-4040
E-mail: mark.buccelli@state.mn.us

Joe Buxton
Daniel Measurement & Control, Inc.
1161 Sarahlyn Lane, Suite B
Statesboro, GA 30461
Ph: (912) 489-2383
Fax: (912) 489-2390
E-mail:
joe.buxton@emersonprocess.com

NCWM 92nd Annual Meeting
July 8 - 12, 2007 • Snowbird Resort • Salt Lake City, UT
Attendee List

Michael Bridges
Alabama Weights &Measures
1024 Tram Road
Marbury, AL 36051
Ph: (334) 569-3946
Fax: (334) 240-7175
E-mail:
marlema.surles@hei.alabama.gov

Ken Butcher
NIST, Weights & Measures Division
100 Bureau Drive, MS 2600
Gaithersburg, MD 20899-2600
Ph: (301) 975-4859
Fax: (301) 975-8091
E-mail: kenneth.butcher@nist.gov

Judy Cardin
Wisconsin Dept. of Agriculture & Consumer Protection
P.O. Box 8911
2811 Agriculture Drive
Madison, WI 53708-8911
Ph: (608) 224-4945
Fax: (608) 224 4939
E-mail:
judy.cardin@datcp.state.wi.us

Mark Brown
Sutter Co Weights & Measures
142 Garden Highway
Yuba City, CA 95991
Ph: (530) 822-7500
Fax: (530) 822-7510
E-mail: mbrown@co.sutter.ca.us

Tina Butcher
NIST, Weights & Measures Division
100 Bureau Drive, MS 2600
Gaithersburg, MD 20899-2600
Ph: (301) 975-2196
Fax: (301) 975-8091
E-mail: tina.butcher@nist.gov

Loretta Carey
U.S. Food and Drug Administration
5100 Paint Branch Parkway
College Park, MD 20740
Ph: (301) 436-1799
Fax: (301)436-2639
E-mail: loretta.carey@fda.hhs.gov

Stacy Carlsen
Marin County Weights & Measures
1682 Novato Boulevard, Ste 150-A
Novato, CA 94947-7021
Ph: (415) 499-6700
Fax: (415) 499-7543
E-mail: scarlsen@co.marin.ca.us

Phillip Chase
AssetSmart
2800 28th Street, Suite 109
Santa Monica, CA 90405
Ph: (310) 450-2566
Fax: (310) 450-1311
E-mail: pc@assetsmart.com

Richard Clark
Utah Dept. of Agriculture & Food
P.O. Box 146500
Salt Lake City, UT 84114-6500
Ph: (801) 538-7158
Fax: (801) 538-4949
E-mail: richardwclark@utah.gov

Charles Carroll
Massachusetts Division of Standards
One Ashburton Place, Room 1115
Boston, MA 02108
Ph: (617) 727-3480, ext. 21131
Fax: (617) 727-5705
E-mail: Charles.Carroll@state.ma.us

Tim Chesser
Arkansas Bureau of Standards
4608 West 61st Street
Little Rock, AR 72209
Ph: (501) 570-1159
Fax: (501) 562-7605
E-mail: tim.chesser@aspb.ar.gov

Michael Cleary
California Dept. of Food and Agriculture
1220 N. Street, Room 315
Sacramento, CA 95814
Ph: (916) 651-1183
Fax: (916) 229-3026
E-mail: mcleary@cdfa.ca.gov

Cullen Casey
Walz Scale
656 High Point Lane
East Peoria, IL 61611
Ph: (309) 694-3200
Fax: (309) 694-3285
E-mail: ccasey@walzscale.com

Alan Christian
USDA GIPSA R&SP
1400 Independence Avenue, SW, Stop 3641
Washington, DC 20250-3641
Ph: (202) 720-7051
Fax: (202) 205-9237
E-mail: alan.r.christian@usda.gov

Thomas Coleman
NIST, Weights & Measures Division
100 Bureau Drive, MS 2600
Gaithersburg, MD 20899-2600
Ph: (301) 975-4868
Fax: (301)975-8091
E-mail: t.coleman@nist.gov

NCWM 92nd Annual Meeting
July 8 - 12, 2007 • Snowbird Resort • Salt Lake City, UT
Attendee List

James Cassidy
Cambridge Weights & Measures
831 Massachusetts Avenue
Cambridge, MA 02139
Ph: (617) 349-6133
Fax: (617) 349-6134
E-mail: jcassidy@CambridgeMA.gov

McCrae Christiansen
Utah Dept. of Agriculture & Food
P.O. Box 146500
Salt Lake City, UT 84114-6500
Ph: (801) 538-7158
Fax: (801) 538-4949
E-mail:

Belinda Collins
National Institute of Standards and Technology
100 Bureau Drive, MS 2000
Gaitherburg, MD 20899-2000
Ph: (301) 975-4500
Fax: (301) 975-2183
E-mail: belinda.collins@nist.gov

Yi-Yi Chang
Thelen Reid Brown Raysman & Steiner LLP
101 Second Street, Ste 1800
San Francisco, CA 94105
Ph: (415) 369-7732
Fax: (415) 369-8932
E-mail: ychang@thelen.com

Raymond Cioffi
Vermont Agency of Agriculture, Food & Markets
103 South Main Street
Waterbury, VT 05671-0101
Ph: (802) 244-4510
Fax: (802) 241-3008
E-mail: raycioffi1@yahoo.com

Steven Cook
NIST, Weights & Measures Division
100 Bureau Drive, MS 2600
Gaithersburg, MD 20899-2600
Ph: (301) 975-4003
Fax: (301) 975-8091
E-mail: steven.cook@nist.gov

Clark Cooney
Oregon Dept. of Agriculture
635 Capitol Street, NE
Salem, OR 97301-2532
Ph: (503) 986-4677
Fax: (503) 986-4784
E-mail: ccooney@oda.state.or.us

Phil Crowther
Utah Dept. of Agriculture & Food
P.O. Box 146500
Salt Lake City, UT 84114-6500
Ph: (801) 538-7158
Fax: (801) 538-4949
E-mail:

Jim Delperdang
Ventura County Weights & Measures
800 South Victoria Avenue, Suite 1750
Ventura, CA 93009
Ph: (805) 654-2446
Fax: (805) 654-5177
E-mail:
jim.delperdang@ventura.org

Rodney Cooper
Actaris Neptune
1310 Emerald Road
Greenwood, SC 29646
Ph: (864) 942-2226
Fax: (864) 223-0341
E-mail:
rcooper@greenwood.actaris.com

Richard Davis
Georgia-Pacific
1915 Marathon Avenue
Neenah, WI 54957-0899
Ph: (920) 729-8174
Fax: (920) 729-8089
E-mail: richard.davis@gapac.com

Mark S. Demings
Utah Dept. of Agriculture & Food
P.O. Box 146500
Salt Lake City, UT 84114-6500
Ph: (801) 538-7158
Fax: (801) 538-4949
E-mail: bgurney@utah.gov

NCWM 92ⁿᵈ Annual Meeting
July 8 - 12, 2007 • Snowbird Resort • Salt Lake City, UT
Attendee List

Chuck Corr
Archer Daniels Midland
1251 Beaver Channel Parkway
Clinton, IA 52732
PH: (563) 244-5208
Fax:
E-mail: corr@admworld.com

James Dawson
Shell Oil Products US
P.O. Box 691153
Houston, TX 77269
Ph: (713) 241-0502
Fax:
E-mail: jim.dawson@shell.com

Vicky Dempsey
Montgomery County Weights & Measures
451 West Third Street
P.O. Box 972
Dayton, OH 45422-1027
Ph: (937) 225-6309
Fax: (937) 224-3927
E-mail: dempseyv@mcohio.org

Richard Cote
New Hampshire Dept. of Agriculture Markets & Food
P.O. Box 2042
Concord, NH 03302-2042
Ph: (603) 271-3700
Fax: (603)271-1109
E-mail: rcote@agr.state.nh.us

Doug Deiman
Alaska Div of Measurement Standards/CVE
11900 Industry Way
Bldg. M, Suite 2
Anchorage, AK 99515
Ph: (907) 365-1210
Fax: (907) 365-1220
E-mail:
doug.deiman@dot.state.ak.us

Phillip DePriest
Marathon Petroleum Company LLC
539 South Main Street
Findlay, OH 45840
Ph: (419) 421-4637
Fax: (419) 429-5370
E-mail: phdepriest@marathon.com

Mark Coyne
Brockton Weights & Measures
45 School Street, City Hall
Brockton, MA 02301-9927
Ph: (508) 580-7120
Fax: (508) 580-7173
E-mail: measures@verizon.net

Kenneth Deitzler
Bureau of Ride & Measurement Standards
2301 North Cameron Street
Harrisburg, PA 17110-9408
Ph: (717) 787-9089
Fax: (717) 783-4158
E-mail: kdeitzler@state.pa.us

Sarah Dodge
NATSO, Inc.
1737 King Street, Suite 200
Alexandria, VA 22314
Ph: (703) 739-8566
Fax: (703) 684-4525
E-mail: sdodge@natso.com

Harold Eaton
Boston ISD Weights & Measures
1010 Massachusetts Avenue
Boston, MA 02118-2606
Ph: (617) 635-5328
Fax: (617) 635-5383
E-mail:
robert.mcgrath@cityofboston.gov

Darrell Flocken
Mettler-Toledo, Inc.
1150 Dearborn Drive
Worthington, OH 43085
Ph: (614) 438-4393
Fax: (614) 438-4355
E-mail: darrell.flocken@mt.com

Michael Gaspers
Farmland Foods, Inc.
800 Industrial Drive
P.O. Box 490
Denison, IA 51442
Ph: (712) 263-7384
Fax: (712) 263-7354
E-mail: mpgaspers@farmland.com

NCWM 92nd Annual Meeting
July 8 - 12, 2007 • Snowbird Resort • Salt Lake City, UT
Attendee List

Dennis Ehrhart
Arizona Dept. of Weights
& Measures
4425 West Olive Avenue, Suite 134
Glendale, AZ 85302
Ph: (623) 463-9937
Fax: (602) 255-1950
E-mail: dehrhart@azdwm.gov

Kurt Floren
Los Angeles County Weights &
Measures
12300 Lower Azusa Road
Arcadia, CA 91006
Ph: (626) 575-5451
Fax: (626) 575-5451
E-mail: kurtf@acwm.co.la.ca.us

Regine Gaucher
OIML-BIML
11 Rue Turgot
Paris, 75009
France
Ph: 33 1 48 78 12 82
Fax: 33 1 42 82 27
E-mail: regine.gaucher@oiml.org

Chuck Ehrlich
NIST, Weights & Measures Division
100 Bureau Drive, MS 2600
Gaithersburg, MD 20899-2600
Ph: (301) 975-4834
Fax: (301) 975-8091
E-mail: charles.ehrlich@nist.gov

Michelle Foncannon
NIST, Weights &Measures Division
100 Bureau Drive, MS 2600
Gaithersburg, MD 20899
Ph: (301) 975-3289
Fax:
E-mail:
michelle.foncannon@nist.gov

Thomas Geiler
Town of Barnstable
200 Main Street
Hyannis, MA 02601
Ph: (508) 862-4670
Fax: (508) 778-2412
E-mail:
Tom.Geiler@town.barnstable.ma.us

Lewis Ekstrom
Utah Dept. of Agriculture & Food
P.O. Box 146500
Salt Lake City, UT 84114-6500
Ph: (801) 538-7158
Fax: (801) 538-4949
E-mail: bgurney@utah.gov

Maurice Forkert
Tuthill Transfer Systems
8825 Aviation Drive
Fort Wayne, IN 46809
Ph: (260) 747-7529
Fax: (260) 747-7064
E-mail: Mforkert@tuthill.com

Victor Gerber
Wyoming Dept. of Agriculture
2219 Carey Avenue
Cheyenne, WY 82002-0100
Ph: (307) 777-6586
Fax: (307) 777-6593
E-mail: vgerbe@state.wy.us

Steve Everly
Kansas City Star
Kansas City, MO 64108
Ph: (816) 868-5275
Fax:
E-mail: severly@kcstar.com

Carol Fulmer
South Carolina Dept. of Agriculture
P.O. Box 11280
Columbia, SC 29211
Ph: (803) 737-9690
Fax: (803) 737-9703
E-mail: cfulmer@scda.sc.gov

Steve Giguere
Maine Quality Assurance &
Regulations
28 State House Station
Augusta, ME 04333
Ph: (207) 287-4456
Fax: (207) 287-5576
E-mail: steve.giguere@maine.gov

Greg Gittins
Utah Dept. of Agriculture & Food
P.O. Box 146500
Salt Lake City, UT 84114-6500
Ph: (801) 538-7154
Fax: (801) 538-4949
E-mail: bgurney@utah.gov

Christopher Guay
Procter & Gamble Co.
8579 Charleston Woods Drive
Mason, OH 45040
Ph: (513) 983-0530
Fax: (513) 983-8984
E-mail: guay.cb@pg.com

Jonathan Handy
Colorado Dept. of Agriculture
3125 Wyandot Street
Denver, CO 80211
Ph: (303) 477-4220
Fax: (303) 477-4248
E-mail:
Jonathan.Handy@ag.state.co.us

NCWM 92nd Annual Meeting
July 8 - 12, 2007 • Snowbird Resort • Salt Lake City, UT
Attendee List

Jason Glass
Kentucky Dept. of Agriculture
107 Corporate Drive
Frankfort, KY 40601
Ph: (502) 573-0282
Fax: (502) 573-0303
E-mail: jason.glass@ky.gov

Paul Glowacki
Murray Equipment, Inc.
2515 Charleston Place
Fort Wayne, IN 46808
Ph: (260) 484-0382
Fax: (260) 484-9230
E-mail: pglowacki@murrayequipment.com

Joe Gomez
New Mexico Dept. of Agriculture
MSC 3170, P.O. Box 30005
Las Cruces, NM 88003-8005
Ph: (505) 646-1616
Fax: (505) 646-2361
E-mail: jgomez@nmda.nmsu.edu

Steven Grabski
Division of Measurement Standards
2150 Frazer Avenue
Sparks, NV 89431
Ph: (775) 688-1166
Fax: (775) 688-2533
E-mail: sgrabski@agri.state.nv.us

Gary Hartt
Utah Dept. of Agriculture & Food
P.O. Box 146500
Salt Lake City, UT 84114-6500
Ph: (801) 538-7158
Fax: (801) 538-4949
E-mail: ghartt@utah.gov

Brett Gurney
Utah Dept. of Agriculture & Food
P.O. Box 146500
Salt Lake City, UT 84114-6500
Ph: (801) 538-7158
Fax: (801) 538-4949
E-mail: bgurney@utah.gov

Terry Gurrister
Utah Dept. of Agriculture & Food
P.O. Box 146500
Salt Lake City, UT 84114-6500
Ph (801) 538-7158
Fax: (801) 538-4949
E-mail: tgurrister@utah.gov

James Hale
Southern Company Services, Inc.
366 Three Oaks Subdivision Road
Langley, KY 41645
Ph: (606) 285-3635
Fax: (606) 285-3635
E-mail: jahale@southernco.com

Monica Hammon
DHL Express, Inc
116 Hawthorne Drive
Washington Court House, OH 43160
Ph:
Fax:
E-mail: monica.hammond@dhl.com

Thomas Herrington
Nestle USA - Prepared Foods Division
5750 Harper Road
Solon, OH 44139-1880
Ph: (440) 264-6467
Fax: (440) 248-1709
E-mail: Thomas.Herrington@us.nestle.com

Mitzi J. Hansen
Utah Dept. of Agriculture & Food
P.O. Box 146500
Salt Lake City, UT 84114-6500
Ph: (801) 538-7158
Fax: (801) 538-4949
E-mail: mhansen@utah.gov

Dennis Harrison
West Virginia Weights & Measures,
Division of Labor
570 McCorkle Avenue West
St. Albans, WV 25177
Ph: (304) 722-0602
Fax: (304) 722-0605
E-mail: dharrison@labor.state.wv.us

John Hart
Great Lakes Cheese
780 West 1400 South
Fillmore, UT 84631
Ph: (435) 743-5000
Fax:
E-mail: hart@greatlakescheese.com

Ryanne Hartman
Michigan Dept. of Agriculture
940 Venture Lane
Williamston, MI 48895
Ph: (517) 655-8202
Fax: (517) 655-8303
E-mail: hartmanry@michigan.gov

Brad Hoffman
Tanknology
8501 N. MOPAC
Suite 400
Austin, TX 78759
Ph: (512) 380-7154
Fax:
E-mail: bhoffman@tanknology

NCWM 92nd Annual Meeting
July 8 - 12, 2007 • Snowbird Resort • Salt Lake City, UT
Attendee List

Ronald Hasemeyer
Alameda County Dept. of Agriculture
Weights & Measures
333 5th Street
Oakland, CA 94607
Ph: (510) 268-7343
Fax: (501) 444-3879
E-mail: ron.hasemeyer@acgov.org

Ronald Hayes
Missouri Dept. of Agriculture
P.O. Box 630
Jefferson City, MO 65102-0630
Ph: (573) 751-2922
Fax: (573) 751-8307
E-mail: Ron.Hayes@mda.mo.gov

Scott Henry
NCR Corporation
2651 Satellite Boulevard
Duluth, GA 30096
Ph: (770) 623-7543
Fax: (404) 479-1170
E-mail: scott.henry@ncr.com

Marilyn Herman
Herman and Associates
3730 Military Road NW
Washington, DC 20015
Ph: (202) 362-9520
Fax: (202) 362-9523
E-mail: mherman697@aol.com

Gene Inglesby
Western Petroleum Marketers
Association of America (PMAA)
P.O. Box 571500
Salt Lake City, UT 84157
Ph: (703) 351-8000
Fax: (703) 351-9160
E-mail: genei@wpma.com

James Hewston
Scale Source
1621 South 35 Street
Council Bluff's, IA 51501
Ph: (402) 455-2143
Fax: (402) 455-2146
E-mail: jhewston@scalessource.com

Tyler Hicks
Oklahoma Dept. of Agriculture,
Food & Forestry
2800 N. Lincoln Boulevard
Oklahoma City, OK 73152
Ph: (405) 522-1897
Fax: (405) 522-4584
E-mail: thicks@oda.state.ok.us

Paul Hoar
AgriFuels LLC
73 Dayton Road
South Glastonbury, CT 06073
Ph: (860) 633-9811
Fax: (866) 466-2764
E-mail: paulhoar@agrifuels.com

Carol Hockert
NIST, Weights & Measures
Division
100 Bureau Drive, MS 2600
Gaithersburg, MD 20899-2600
Ph: (301) 975-5507
Fax: (301) 975-8091
E-mail: carol.hockert@nist.gov

Raymond Johnson
New Mexico Dept. of Agriculture
MSC 3170, PO Box 30005
Las Cruces, NM 88003-8005
Ph: (505) 646-1616
Fax: (505) 646-2361
E-mail: rjohnson@nmda.nmsu.edu

Kristen Hossler
National Conference on Weights &
Measures
15245 Shady Grove Road,
Suite 130
Rockville, MD 20850
Ph: (240) 632-9454
Fax: (301) 990-9771
E-mail: khossler@mgmtsol.com

Wes Huibregtse
Great Lakes Cheese
2602 County Road PP
Plymouth, WI 53073
Ph: (920) 892-6643
Fax: (920) 893-1151
E-mail: huibregt@greatlakescheese.com

Jeff Humphreys
Los Angeles County Weights &
Measures
11012 Garfield Avenue
South Gate, CA 90280
Ph: (562) 940-8922
Fax: (562) 861-0278
E-mail: jeffh@acwm.co.la.ca.us

Doug Hutchinson
Measurement Canada
232 Yorktech Drive
Markham, Ontario L6G 1A6
Canada
Ph: (905) 943-8732
Fax: (905) 943-8738
E-mail: hutchinson.doug@ic.gc.ca

Dmitri Karimov
Liquid Controls
105 Albrecht Drive
Lake Bluff, IL 60044
Ph: (847) 283-8317
Fax:
E-mail: dkarimov@idexcorp.com

NCWM 92nd Annual Meeting
July 8 - 12, 2007 • Snowbird Resort • Salt Lake City, UT
Attendee List

Grace L. Jan, CMP
National Conference on Weights & Measures
15245 Shady Grove Road, Suite 130
Rockville, MD 20850
Ph: (240) 632-9454
Fax: (301) 990-9771
E-mail: gjan@mgmtsol.com

Randy Jennings
Tennessee Dept. of Agriculture
P.O. Box 40627 Melrose Station
Nashville, TN 37204
Ph: (615) 837-5147
Fax: (615) 837-5335
E-mail: randy.jennings@state.tn.us

Dennis Johannes
California Division of Measurement Standards
6790 Florin Perkins Road,
Suite 100
Sacramento, CA 95828
Ph: (916) 229-3000
Fax: (916) 229-3026
E-mail: DJohannes@cdfa.ca.gov

Gordon Johnson
Gilbarco, Inc.
7300 West Friendly Avenue
Greensboro, NC 27420
Ph: (336) 547-5375
Fax: (336) 547-5079
E-mail: Gordon.Johnson@gilbarco.com

Alan Johnston
Measurement Canada
151Tunney's Pasture Driveway
Ottawa, Ontario K1A 0C9
Canada
Ph: (613) 952-0655
Fax: (613) 957-1265
E-mail: johnston.alan@ic.gc.ca

Zina Juroch
Pier 1 Imports
100 Pier 1 Place
Fort Worth, TX 76102
Ph: (817) 252-8348
Fax: (817)252-6220
E-mail: zmjuroch@pier1.com

Robert Kaehler
AssetSmart
2800 28th Street
Santa Monica, CA 90405
Ph: (310) 450-2566
Fax: (310) 450-1311
E-mail: robert.kaehler@assetsmart.com

Jack Kane
Montana Bureau of Building & Measurement Standards
P.O. Box 200516
Helena, MT 59620-0516
Ph: (406) 841-2240
Fax: (406) 841-2060
E-mail: jkane@mt.gov

Yefim Katselnik
Dresser Wayne
3814 Jarrett Way
Austin, TX 78728
Ph: (512) 388-8763
Fax: (512) 388-8456
E-mail: phil.katselnik@wayne.com

Kerry Kaullen
Missouri Dept. of Agriculture
P.O. Box 630
Jefferson City, MO 65102-0630
Ph: (573) 751-4278
Fax: (573) 751-0281
E-mail: kerry.brettschneider@mda.mo.gov

Michael Keilty
Endress & Hauser Flowtec AG
2350 Endress Place
Greenwood, IN 46143
Ph: (317) 535-2745
Fax: (317) 535-1341
E-mail: michael.keilty@us.endress.com

Jaclyn Kerper
National Conference on Weights & Measures
15245 Shady Grove Road,
Suite 130
Rockville, MD 20850
Ph: (240) 632-9454
Fax: (301) 990-9771
E-mail: jkerper@mgmtsol.com

NCWM 92nd Annual Meeting
July 8 - 12, 2007 • Snowbird Resort • Salt Lake City, UT
Attendee List

Grant Kimura
Chevron Corporation
6001 Bollinger Canyon Road
Room A-2116
San Ramon, CA 94582
Ph: (925) 842-3436
Fax:
E-mail: grant.kimura@chevron.com

Leon Lammers
Avery Weigh-Tronix
1000 Armstrong Drive
Fairmont, MN 56031-1439
Ph: (800) 533-0456
Fax: (507) 238-8255
E-mail: llammers@awtxglobal.com

Harvey Lloyd
Measurement Technology International Ltd.
311 - 33 St. N.
Lethbridge, Alberta T1H 3Z6
Canada
Ph: (403) 320-1830
Fax: (403) 320-1678
E-mail: harvey@mid-westgroup.com

Ted Kingsbury
Measurement Canada
151 Tunney's Pasture Driveway
Ottawa, Ontario K1A 0C9
Canada
Ph: (613) 941-8919
Fax: (613) 952-1736
E-mail: kingsbury.ted@ic.gc.ca

Stephen Langford
Cardinal Scale Manufacturing Co.
203 East Daugherty, P.O. Box 151
Webb City, MO 64870
Ph: (417) 673-4631
Fax: (417) 673-5001
E-mail: slangford@cardet.com

Todd Lucas
Ohio Dept. of Agriculture
8995 East Main Street, Building 5
Reynoldsburg, OH 43068
Ph: (614) 728-6290
Fax: (614) 728-6424
E-mail: lucas@mail.agri.state.oh.us

Russel Knight
Utah Dept. of Agriculture & Food
P.O. Box 146500
Salt Lake City, UT 84114-6500
Ph: (801) 538-7158
Fax: (801) 538-4949
E-mail:

Paul Lewis
Rice Lake Weighing Systems, Inc.
230 West Coleman Street
P.O. Box 272
Rice Lake, WI 54868-2404
Ph: (715) 234-3494 x5322
Fax: (715) 234-6967
E-mail: plewis@ricelake.com

Girard Lukowiak
City of East Orange
143 New Street
East Orange, NJ 07017
Ph: (973) 677-8923
Fax: (973) 266-5402
E-mail: girardluke@yahoo.com

Dennis Kolsun
H J Heinz Co
357 6th Avenue
Pittsburgh, PA 15222
Ph: (724) 778-4503
Fax: (412) 658-1158
E-mail: dennis.kolsun@hjheinz.com

Richard Lewis
Georgia Dept. of Agriculture
Agriculture Bldg.
19 MLK Drive, Rm 321
Atlanta, GA 30334
Ph: (404) 656-3605
Fax: (404) 656-9648
E-mail: rlewis@agr.state.ga.us

L. Edward Luthy
B-Tek Scales, LLC
1510 Metric Avenue, SW
Canton, OH 44706
Ph: (330) 471-8900
Fax: (330) 471-8909
E-mail: eluthy@bscales.com

NCWM 92nd Annual Meeting
July 8 - 12, 2007 • Snowbird Resort • Salt Lake City, UT
Attendee List

Dale Kunze
Utah Dept. of Agriculture & Food
P.O. Box 146500
Salt Lake City, UT 84114-6500
Ph: (801) 538-7158
Fax: (801) 538-4949
E-mail: bgurney@utah.gov

Robert Lilley
San Luis Obispo County
Weights & Measures
2156 Sierra Way, Suite A
San Luis Obispo, CA 93401
Ph: (805) 781-5924
Fax: (805) 781-1035
E-mail: rlilley@co.slo.ca.us

Kristin Macey
Colorado Dept. of Agriculture
3125 Wyandot Street
Denver, CO 80211
Ph: (303) 477-4220
Fax: (303) 477-4248
E-mail:
kristin.macey@ag.state.co.us

Roger Macey
California Division of Measurement Standards
6790 Florin Perkins Road, Suite 100
Sacramento, CA 95828
Ph: (916) 229-3043
Fax: (916) 229-3026
E-mail: RMacey@cdfa.ca.gov

Daniel Maslowski
LTS Sales
421 W. 12th Street
Erie, PA 16501
Ph: (814) 454-1818
Fax: (814) 454-6363
E-mail: dmaslowski@ltssales.com

Richard Miller
FMC Measurement Solutions
1602 Wagner Avenue
P.O. Box 10428
Erie, PA 16514
Ph: (814) 898-5286
Fax: (814) 899-3414
E-mail: rich.miller@fmcti.com

Keith L. Mahan
Merced County Weights &Measures
2139 Wardrobe Avenue
Merced, CA 95340-6495
Ph: (209) 385-7431
Fax: (209) 725-3961
Ph: E-mail: kmahan@co.merced.ca.us

John Maynes
Petroleum Marketers & Convenience
Store of Iowa
1303 50th Street
West Des Moines, IA 50266
Ph: (515) 224-7545
Fax: (515) 224-0502
E-mail: john@pmcofiowa.com

Charlie Mitchell
Total Petrochemicals, Inc.
P.O. Box 849
Port Arthur, TX 77641-0849
Ph: (409) 963-6885
Fax: (409) 962-3458
E-mail: charlie.mitchell@total.com

Steven Malone
Nebraska Division of Weights Measures
301 Centennial Mall South
Box 94757
Lincoln, NE 68509-4757
Ph: (402) 471-4292
Fax: (402) 471-2759
E-mail: smalone@agr.ne.gov

Thomas McGee
PMP Corporation
P.O. Box 422
25 Security Drive
Avon, CT 06001-0422
Ph: (860) 677-9656
Fax: (860) 674-0196
E-mail: tmcgee@pmp-corp.com

Kristin Moore
Renewable Fuels Association
One Massachusetts Avenue
Washington, DC 20001
Ph: (309) 830-6154
Fax:
E-mail: kmoore@ethanolrfa.org

Andrea M. Martincic
Arizona Petroleum Marketers Association
P.O. Box 93426
Phoenix, AZ 85070
Ph: (480) 460-9016,
Fax:
E-mail: apma@cox.net

James McGetrick
BP Products
Mail Code J-8, 150 W. Warrenville Road
Naperville, IL 60563
Ph: (630) 420-4579
Fax: (630) 420-4832
E-mail: james.mcgetrick@bp.com

Lynn Morrissette
American Meat Institute
1150 Connecticut Avenue, NW #12
Washington, DC 20036
Ph: (202) 587-4200
Fax: (202) 587-4300
E-mail: lmorrissette@meatami.com

NCWM 92nd Annual Meeting
July 8 - 12, 2007 • Snowbird Resort • Salt Lake City, UT
Attendee List

Monte Martinson
Norac, Inc.
1290 Osborne Road NE
Fridley, MN 55432
Ph: (763) 786-3080
Fax: (763) 786-3101
E-mail: steve@norac.ca

Virgil Musil
Kroger Co.
10251 East 51st Avenue, Suite A
Denver, CO 80239
Ph: (303) 715-5915
Fax: (301) 715-5905
E-mail: virgil.musil@kroger.com

Scott Negley
Dresser Wayne
3814 Jarrett Way
Austin TX 78750
Ph: (512) 970-6274
Fax:
E-mail: scott.negley@wayne.com

Don Nerdin
Utah Dept. of Agriculture & Food
P.O. Box 146500
Salt Lake City, UT 84114-6500
Ph: (801) 538-7158
Fax: (801) 538-4949
E-mail: bgurney@utah.gov

Robert McGrath
Boston ISD Weights & Measures
1010 Massachusetts Avenue
Boston, MA 02118-2606
Ph: (617) 961-3376
Fax: (617) 635-5383
E-mail: Robert.Mcgrath@CityofBoston.gov

Charlene Numrych
Liquid Controls LLC
105 Albrecht Drive
Lake Bluff, IL 60044
Ph: (847) 283-8330
Fax: (847) 295-1170
E-mail: cnumrych@idexcorp.com

O.R. "Pete" O'Bryan
Foster Farms
P.O. Box 457
Livingston, CA 95334-9900
Ph: (209) 765-4978
Fax: (209) 398-6742
E-mail: obryanp@fosterfarms.com

Daniel Okon
United Parcel Service
55 Glenlake Parkway, NE B1F7
Atlanta, GA 30328
Ph: (404) 828.6246
Fax: (404) 828-7857
E-mail: dokon@ups.com

Bob Murnane
Seraphin Test Measure/Pemberton
P.O. Box 227
30 Indel Avenue
Rancocas, NJ 08073-0227
Ph: (609) 267-0922
Fax: (609) 261-2546
E-mail: rmurnane@pemfab.com

Stephen Pahl
Texas Dept. of Agriculture
1700 North Congress Avenue,
Stephen F.
Austin Building, 11th Floor
Austin, TX 78701
Ph: (512) 463-7483
Fax: (512) 463-8225
E-mail: stephen.pahl@agr.state.tx.us

Beth W. Palys, CAE
National Conference on Weights & Measures
15245 Shady Grove Road,
Suite 130
Rockville, MD 20850
Ph: (240) 632-9454
Fax: (301) 990-9771
E-mail: bpalys@mgmtsol.com

Steve Patoray, CAE
National Conference on Weights & Measures
15245 Shady Grove Road,
Suite 130
Rockville, MD 20850
Ph: (240) 632-9454
Fax: (301) 990-9771
E-mail: spatoray@mgmtsol.com

NCWM 92nd Annual Meeting
July 8 - 12, 2007 • Snowbird Resort • Salt Lake City, UT
Attendee List

Neal Nover
Nover Engelstein & Assoc., Inc./
WinWam Software
AtriumExec. Sts, 3000 Atrium Way,
Ste 2203
Mt. Laurel, NJ 08054-3910
Ph: (856) 273-6988
Fax: (856) 271-0559
E-mail: NealNov@wimwam.com

Jennifer Nuckolls
Siemens Energy & Automation, Inc.
One Internet Plaza
Johnson City, TN 37602
Ph: (423) 262-2909
Fax: (423) 262-2231
E-mail:
jennifer.nuckolls@siemens.com

William Pierpont
Hawaii Measurement Standards
1851 Auiki Street
Honolulu, HI 96819-3100
Ph: (808) 832-0694
Fax: (808) 832-0683
E-mail: william.e.pierpont@hawaii.gov

Michael Pinagel
Michigan Dept. of Agriculture
940 Venture Lane
Williamston, MI 48895-2451
Ph: (517) 655-8202 ext. 301
Fax: (517) 655-8303
E-mail: PinagelM@michigan.gov

Marvin Pound
Georgia Dept. of Agriculture
815 Milledeville Highway
Devereux, GA 31087
Ph: (404) 656-3605
Fax: (404) 656-9648
E-mail: mpound@agr.state.ga.us

Don Onwiler
Nebraska Division of Weights &
Measures
301 Centennial Mall South
Box 94757
Lincoln, NE 68509
Ph: (402) 471-4292
Fax: (402) 471-2759
E-mail: donwiler@agr.ne.gov

Henry Oppermann
Weights & Measures Consulting,
LLC
3313 Prytania Street
New Orleans, LA 70115
Ph: (504) 218-5422
Fax: (504) 218-5422
E-mail: wmconsulting@cox.net

David Rajala
Veeder-Root Company
P.O. Box 1673
Altoona, PA 16603-1673
Ph: (814) 696-8125
Fax: (814) 695-7605
E-mail: drajala@veeder.com

Kenneth R. Ramsburg
Maryland Dept. of Agriculture
50 Harry S. Truman Parkway
Annapolis, MD 21401
Ph: (410) 841-5790
Fax: (410) 841-2765
E-mail:
RamsbuKR@mda.state.md.us

Robert Reinfried
Scale Manufacturers Association
6724 Lone Oak Boulevard
Naples, FL 34109
Ph: (239) 514-3441
Fax: (239) 514-3470
E-mail:
bob@scalemanufacturers.org

Robert Penn
State of Alabama Dept. of
Agriculture and Industries
236 County Road 6616
Troy, AL 36081
Ph: (334) 566-0298
Fax:
E-mail:

David Pfahler
South Dakota Weights & Measures
118 West Capitol Avenue
Pierre, SD 57501-2080
Ph: (605) 773-4091
Fax: (605) 773-6631
E-mail: david.pfahler@state.sd.us

Bill Rigby
Utah Dept. of Agriculture & Food
P.O. Box 146500
Salt Lake City, UT 84114-6500
Ph: (801) 538-7153
Fax: (801) 538-4949
E-mail: brigby@utah.gov

Bill Ripka
Thermo Electron
501 90th Avenue NW
Minneapolis, MN 55433
Ph: (763) 783-2664
Fax: (763) 780-1537
E-mail: bill.ripka@thermo.com

Kirk Robinson
Washington Dept. of Agriculture
P.O. Box 42560
Olympia, WA 98504-2560
Ph: (360) 902-1856
Fax: (360) 902-2086
E-mail: KRobinson@agr.wa.gov

NCWM 92nd Annual Meeting
July 8 - 12, 2007 • Snowbird Resort • Salt Lake City, UT
Attendee List

Harold Prince
Maine Dept. of Agriculture
28 State House Station
Augusta, ME 04333
Ph: (207) 287-3841
Fax: (207) 287-5576
E-mail: hal.prince@maine.gov

Julie Quinn
State of Minnesota, Dept. of Commerce
Weights & Measures Division
South Cross Commerce Center III,
14035 South Cross Drive, Suite 150
Burnsville, MN 55306
Ph: (651) 215-5823
Fax: (952) 435-4040
E-mail: julie.quinn@state.mn.us

Brett Saum
San Luis Obispo County Weights & Measures
2156 Sierra Way, Suite A
San Luis Obispo, CA 93401-4556
Ph: (805) 781-5922
Fax: (805) 781-1035
E-mail: BSaum@co.slo.ca.us

Dale Saunders
Virginia Product & Industry Standards
P.O. Box 1163, Rm 135
Richmond, VA 23218
Ph: (804) 786-2476
Fax: (804) 786-1571
E-mail:
Dale.Saunders@vdacs.virginia.gov

Robert E. Reynolds
Downstream Alternatives Inc.
1657 Commerce Drive, Suite 20B
South Bend, IN 46628
Ph: (574) 233-7344
Fax:
E-mail: rreynolds-dai@earthlink.net

Ralph Richter
NIST, Weights & Measures Division
100 Bureau Drive, MS 2600
Gaithersburg, MD 20899-2600
Ph: (301) 975-4025
Fax: (301) 975-8091
E-mail: ralph.richter@nist.gov

Donald Scott
National Biodiesel Board
P.O. Box 104898
Jefferson, MO 65110
Ph: 800-841-5849
Fax: 573-635-7913
E-mail: dscott@biodiesel.com

Prentiss E. Searles
American Petroleum Institution
1220 L Street, NW
Washington, DC 20005
Ph: (202) 682-8227
Fax: (202) 682-8051
E-mail: searlesp@api.org

Mike Rude
Norac, Inc
1290 Osborne Road NE
Fridley, MN 55432
Ph: (763) 786-3080
Fax: (763) 786-3101
E-mail: steve@norac.ca

Hiroe Sakai
Advanced Industrial Science and Technology (AIST)
Tsukuba Central 3-9, 1-1-1
Umezono
Tsukuba, 305-8563
Japan
Ph: 81-29-861-4149
Fax: 81-29-861-4202
E-mail: h.sakai@aist.go.jp

Terrance Shook
Lake County Weights & Measures
105 Main Street
P.O. Box 490
Painesville, OH 44077-0490
Ph: (440) 350-2535
Fax: (440) 350-2667
E-mail:
ezupancic@lakecountyohio.org

John Siebert
Owner Operator Independent Driver Assoc., Inc
PO Box 1000
Grain Valley, MO 64029
Ph: (816) 229-5791
Fax: (816) 427-4468
E-mail:

NCWM 92nd Annual Meeting
July 8 - 12, 2007 • Snowbird Resort • Salt Lake City, UT
Attendee List

Alex Schuettenberg
ConocoPhillips Petroleum
148 AL, Phillips Research Center
Bartlesville, OK 74004
Ph: (918) 661-3563
Fax: (918) 661-8060
E-mail:
alex.schuettenberg@conocophillips.com

Mark Schwartz
Accu-Sort Systems, Inc.
511 School House Road
Telford, PA 18969
Ph: (215) 721-5053
Fax: (215) 799-1600
E-mail: mark.schwartz@accusort.com

Rebecca Schwartz
Shook, Hardy & Bacon, L.L.P.
2555 Grand Boulevard
Kansas City, MO 64108
Ph: (816) 474-6550
Fax: (816) 421-2708
E-mail: rschwartz@shb.com

Lawrence Stump
Indiana Weights & Measures
2525 N. Shadeland Avenue, #03
Indianapolis, IN 46219-1791
Ph: (317) 356-7078
Fax: (317) 351-2877
E-mail: lstump@isdh.state.in.us

Ellen Shapiro
Alliance of Automobile
Manufacturers
1401 Eye St., NW Suite 900
Washington, DC 20005
Ph: (202) 326-5533
Fax: (202) 326-5568

Janet Sheiner
PETCO
9125 Rehco Road
San Diego, CA 92121
Ph: (858) 453-7845
Fax: (858) 638-2247
E-mail: janets@petco.com

Agatha Shields
Franklin County Weights &
Measures
373 South High Street, 21st Floor
Columbus, OH 43215-6310
Ph: (614) 462-7380
Fax: (614) 462-3111
E-mail:
aashield@franklincountyohio.gov

Mark Thompson
Measurement Technology
International Ltd.
311 - 33 St. N.
Lethbridge, Alberta T1H 3Z6
Canada
Ph: (403) 394-0111
Fax: (403) 394-0112
E-mail:
sales@measurementTech.com

Michael Sikula
New York Bureau of Weights &
Measures
Building 7A State Campus
Albany, NY 12235
Ph: (518) 457-3452
Fax: (518) 457-2552
E-mail:
mike.sikula@agmkt.state.ny.us

Steven B. Steinborn
Hogan & Hartson
555 13th Street, NW
Washington, DC 20004
Ph: (202) 637-5969
Fax: (202) 637-5910
E-mail: sbsteinborn@hhlaw.com

Louis Straub
Fairbanks Scales Inc
3056 Irwin Drive SE
Southport, NC 28461
Ph: (910) 253-3250
Fax: (910) 253-3250
E-mail: strauble@yahoo.com

Manuel Villicana
Kern County Dept. of Agriculture
and Measurement Standards
3708 Rainier Court
Bakersfield, CA 93312
Ph: (661) 868-6300
Fax:
E-mail: villicam@co.kern.ca.us

NCWM 92nd Annual Meeting
July 8 - 12, 2007 • Snowbird Resort • Salt Lake City, UT
Attendee List

Richard Suiter
NIST, Weights & Measures Division
100 Bureau Drive, MS 2600
Gaithersburg, MD 20899-2600
Ph: (301) 975-4406
Fax: (301) 975-8091
E-mail: richard.suiter@nist.gov

Michael Timmons
City of Medford
85 George P. Hassett Drive
Medford, MA 02155
Ph: (781) 393-2493
Fax: (781) 393-2415
E-mail: mwtimmons@medford.org

Gilles Vinet
Measurement Canada
151Tunney's Pasture Driveway
Ottawa, Ontario K1A 0C9
Canada
Ph: (613) 952-0657
Fax: (613) 952-1736
E-mail: vinet.gilles@ic.gc.ca

John Sullivan
Mississippi Dept. of Agriculture
12575 River Road
Natchez, MS 39120
Ph: (601) 877-3802
Fax: (601) 877-3872
E-mail: johns1@mdac.state.ms.us

James Truex
Ohio Dept. of Agriculture
8995 East Main Street
Reynoldsburg, OH 43068-3399
Ph: (614) 728-6290
Fax: (614) 728-6424
E-mail: truex@mail.agri.state.oh.us

Ketan Vithlani
Comptroller of Maryland Motor
Fuel Testing Lab
7275B Waterloo Road
Jessup, MD 20794
Ph: (410) 799-7777
Fax:
E-mail:
kvithlani@comp.state.md.us

Michael Thomas
Hamilton County Weights & Measures
Hamilton County Judicial Center
One Hamilton County Square, Suite 181
Noblesville, IN 46060
Ph: (317) 403-0639
Fax: (317) 776-8525
E-mail:

Pete Turner
Anniston Pump Shop, Inc.
d/b/a APS Petroleum Equipment
2800 Highway 431 N
P.O. Box 1198
Anniston, AL 36202
Ph: (256) 820-2980
Fax: (256) 820-2981
E-mail: pete@apspetro.com

Shelley Walker
Utah Dept. of Agriculture & Food
P.O. Box 146500
Salt Lake City, UT 84114-6500
Ph: (801) 538-7158
Fax: (801) 538-4949
E-mail: bgurney@utah.gov

Dave Thompson
Measurement Technology International Ltd.
311 - 33 St. N.
Lethbridge, Alberta T1H 3Z6
Canada
Ph: (403) 320-1830
Fax: (403) 320-1678
E-mail: dave@measurementtech.com

Tim Tyson
Kansas Dept. of Agriculture/
Weights & Measures Division
P.O. Box 19282/Forbes Field
Building 282
Topeka, KS 66619-0282
Ph: (785) 862-2415
Fax: (785) 862-2460
E-mail: ttyson@kda.state.ks.us

John Walsh
Framingham Weights & Measures
150 Concord Street
Framingham, MA 01702
Ph: (508) 532-5480
Fax: (508) 626-8991

E-mail: jbw@framinghamma.org

NCWM 92nd Annual Meeting
July 8 - 12, 2007 • Snowbird Resort • Salt Lake City, UT
Attendee List

Dave Wankowski
Kraft Foods, Inc.
801 Waukegan Road
Glenview, IL 60025
Ph: (847) 646-0098
Fax: (847) 646-4820
E-mail: dwankowski@kraft.com

Lisa Warfield
NIST, Weights & Measures Division
100 Bureau Drive, MS 2600
Gaithersburg, MD 20899
Ph: (301) 975-3308
Fax: (301) 975-8091
E-mail: lisa.warfield@nist.gov

Gord Wedel
Kraus Global, Inc.
311 - 33 Street. N.
Winnipeg, Manitoba T1H 3Z6
Canada
Ph: (204) 663-3601
Fax: (204) 663-7112
E-mail: gwedel@krausglobal.com

Nathaniel Wieselquist
Sick, Inc.
800 Technology Drive, Suite 6
Stoughton, MA 02072
Ph: (781) 302-2553
Fax:
E-mail: nate.wieselquist@sick.com

Bryice Wilkes
US Dept. of Agriculture
Packers & Stockyard Program
210 Walnut Street, Suite 317
Des Moines, IA 50309
Ph: (515) 323-2548
Fax: (515) 323-2590
E-mail: bryice.a.wilke@usda.gov

Dylan Wilks
Wilks Enterprise, Inc.
345 Riverview Drive
Boulder Creek, CA 95006
Ph: (831) 338-7459
Fax: (831) 338-3393
E-mail: srintoul@wilksir.com

Juana Williams
NIST, Weights & Measures Division
100 Bureau Drive, MS 2600
Gaithersburg, MD 20899-2600
Ph: (301) 975-3989
Fax: (301) 975-8091
E-mail: juana.williams@nist.gov

Robert Williams
Tennessee Dept. of Agriculture
P.O. Box 40627 Melrose Station
Nashville, TN 37204-0627
Ph: (615) 837-5109
Fax: (615) 837-5015
E-mail: robert.g.williams@state.tn.us

Cary Woodward
Hamilton County Weights & Measures
Hamilton County Judical Center
One Hamilton County Square, Suite 181
Noblesville, IN 46060
Ph: (317) 403-0639
Fax: (317) 776-8525
E-mail: caw@co.hamilton.in.us

Richard Wotthlie
Maryland Dept. of Agriculture
50 Harry S. Truman Parkway
Annapolis, MD 21401
Ph: (410) 841-5790
Fax: (410) 841-2765
E-mail: wotthlrw@mda.state.md.us

Russ Wyckof
Oregon Dept. of Agriculture
635 Capitol Street, NE
Salem, OR 97301-2532
Ph: (503) 986-4767
Fax: (503) 986-4784
E-mail: rwyckoff@oda.state.or.us

Walter Young
Emery Winslow Scale Company
73 Cogwheel Lane
Denver, CO 06483-3919
Ph: (203) 881-9333
Fax: (203) 881-9477
E-mail: wmyoung@emerywinslow.com

George Zelcs
Korein Tillery
205 North Michigan Avenue, Suite 1950
Chicago, IL 60601
Ph: (312) 641-9750
Fax: (312) 641-9751
E-mail: gzelcs@koreintillery.com

NCWM 92nd Annual Meeting
July 8 - 12, 2007 • Snowbird Resort • Salt Lake City, UT

Guest Attendees

Shelly Allred

Marlene Belue

Jackie Bernaciak

Corinna Brown

Sharon Brucker

Wendy Bukowski

Judith Davis

Mary Dawson

Cindy Deitzler

Marianne Delperdang

Linda Forkert

Carolyn Hicks

Beverly Johnson

Deana Johnson

Ruby Johnson

Carol Johnston

Klara Katselnik

Judy Kingsbury

Rose Marie Lammers

Susie Lilley

Bev Luthy

Marcia Malone

Stehanie McArdle

Geraldine Mitchell

Sue Okon

Peggy Onwiler

Frances Shook

Robin Smith

Deborah Straub

Carol Suiter

Margaret Turner

Ellen Walsh

Lauren Young

THIS PAGE INTENTIONALLY LEFT BLANK.